PHILOSOPHY OF THE LAW

PHILOSOPHY OF THE LAW

The Political in the Torah

❧

Shmuel Trigano

With a Foreword by David Novak

Translated by Gila Walker

SHALEM PRESS

JERUSALEM AND NEW YORK

PHILOSOPHIE DE LA LOI
L'origine de la politique dans la Tora

Shalem Press, 13 Yehoshua Bin-Nun Street, Jerusalem
Copyright © 2011 The Shalem Center

Copyright © Les éditions du cerf 1991

Ouvrage publié avec le soutien du Centre National du Livre—Ministère français chargé de la culture.

Published with the support of the National Book Center—French Ministry of Culture.

Cover design: Erica Halivni
Cover picture: "The Tribes of Israel Reunited around the Ark of the Covenant in the Sinai Desert, after the Exodus from Egypt," c.1630 (coloured engraving) / Private Collection / Archives Charmet / The Bridgeman Art Library/ASAP Creative

ISBN 978-965-7052-71-6

Printed in Israel

∞ The paper used in this publication meets the minimum requirements of the American National Standard for Information Sciences—Permanence of Paper for Printed Library Materials, ANSI Z39.48-1992

CONTENTS

Foreword

SHMUEL TRIGANO's *Philosophy of the Law: The Political in the Torah* is a powerful and original Jewish *philosophy*. It is especially welcome at the beginning of the twenty-first century, when Jewish philosophy itself desperately needs both definition and direction.

Jewish philosophy seems to designate two distinct types of inquiry conducted by two distinct types of Jewish thinkers. On the one hand, Jewish philosophy is the inquiry into Judaism or the Torah using the philosophical method with which the Jewish philosopher is most at home. One could say that this is bringing worldly wisdom to the Torah. After all, the Torah speaks in human language and, therefore, it admits of human inquiry, of which philosophy regards itself to be the epitome. One could call this type of philosopher a philosopher *of Judaism*. On the other hand, philosophy is the inquiry into the most basic questions humans ask concerning their existence in the world. Here Jewish philosophy is the existential questioning employed by a philosopher who asks the same kind of questions others rooted in Judaism have asked in the past. One could call this type of philosopher a philosopher *from Judaism*.

Looking to the very recent past, one could say that Franz Rosenzweig and Abraham Joshua Heschel were mostly Jewish philosophers of the first type. Philosophy, as it were, modified their Judaism in the way an adjective modifies a noun and thereby enables more of the noun's meaning to be known than would be the case were the noun not so modified. Martin Buber and Emmanuel Levinas, however, were mostly Jewish philosophers of the second type. Judaism, as it were, modified their philosophy in a way that would not have been the case if these philosophers had come from another tradition (or pretended to come from no tradition).

Shmuel Trigano is a Jewish philosopher in both senses of the term. He is a philosopher *of Judaism*, insofar as his inquiry is sustained philosophical inquiry into the meaning of the Torah. That is, what is the Torah's essential teaching? He thus asks of the Torah the sort of questions philosophers have always asked. Yet he always allows the biblical texts to be spoken through him, never merely using them to illustrate ideas whose origin one could find elsewhere. But he is also a philosopher *from Judaism*, insofar as his inquiry is not just for the Torah's adherents. Instead, he is convinced that the Torah has something of vital importance to say to the world at large, a message his method of inquiry brings to the world that is, if and when those in the outside world think the Torah is also addressed to them.

These two types of Jewish philosophy come together in that Trigano is offering here (and in his earlier works, too) a covenantal (*berit*) philosophy of Judaism and a covenantal philosophy from Judaism. This coming together is made possible by the fact that Trigano and we, his readers, are quite self-consciously living at a historical moment when the Jewish people has returned to the land of Israel and is now in the process of building a new Jewish *polity* there. To truly understand the covenantal needs of the hour, and to learn how these covenantal needs have ever been the Torah's concern, that is the greatest challenge facing Jewish thought now. Only thinkers who are presently situated within the Jewish people—which means they are convinced Zionists—are able to offer those building this new order any guidance on how to make it both authentically Jewish and authentically covenantal. And to do this with both Jewish learning and philosophical insight, the thinker needs to be both a philosopher of Judaism and a philosopher from Judaism.

First, that thinker must be able to find within the Torah a covenantal message. This Trigano does by showing how the biblical idea of covenant (*berit*) bespeaks a covenantal reality essentially different from the major leitmotif of modern covenantal philosophy: the social contract. Trigano does this with philosophical insight by uncovering the ontological presupposition of the uniquely Jewish idea of covenant in the equally unique Jewish idea of creation *ex nihilo* (in Hebrew, *yesh me'ayin*). Second, that thinker must be able to show how and why that covenantal message addressed to the Jews is, nonetheless, something the nations of the world can overhear and appropriate for their own covenantal needs in the world. Trigano does this, too, with philosophical insight by arguing that the nations of the world need to find for themselves, as we Jews need to find for ourselves, a politics of nation-hood that enables them to survive in the world through covenant without becoming assimilated into some nameless *totality,* and without attempting to dominate the whole world, both of which involve the loss of the nation's own singularity in the process.

The rabbis say reward is commensurate with effort (*lefum tsa'ara agra*). This book is not easy reading. It is a sustained meditation that carries its readers along with its trajectory, never stopping to step out of that trajectory to argue or acknowledge who has influenced it. Optimally, this book should be read in one sitting, but few readers will have the mental stamina to do that. Nevertheless, its meaning will emerge only for the reader who is willing to read all of it, and not just selectively. For those readers who can and will do that, Trigano's powerful and original voice, one that bespeaks the Torah in a way it does not need to use the first person *I* to do, will resonate long after they have put this book on the shelf. And when one needs to overcome the banality of most covenantal discourse today (most of which is little more than propaganda), especially concerning the covenantal meaning of Jewish existence now, he or she will go back to Trigano's *Philosophy of the Law* again to hear a different and better voice.

David Novak
Toronto, Canada
I Adar 5771/February 2011

BOOK I

✢

CROWN

On the Origin in the Political

UNLIKE THE social contract, the covenant binds human beings to one another only indirectly. The covenant established between Israel and God initiated the process by which the people of Israel is instituted. It is through the covenant with God that a covenant between Jews is forged. Does the foundation of the *polis* by the agency of the divine amount to theocracy? Does the birth of the Hebraic body politic under the auspices of the Master of the Universe imply clericalism? Beyond such polemical categories, one of the defining characteristics of power and of the political may very well be found in this hidden origin in the apparent origin: the covenant with God hidden in the covenant between the children of Israel.

Contemplating the beginning is impossible, and yet, it is equally impossible to turn one's attention away from the absoluteness of the origins. The "foundation" of the political is both impossible and desirable! And this truth resists refutation where least expected—namely, in the case of the social contract, which mythically founded modern society upon a *tabula rasa*, cleaning the slate of heritage and filiation, and leaving only the transparency of individual will and freedom.

In Jean-Jacques Rousseau's conception, the very origin of the social contract remains unthought and unthinkable. The theoretical act by which "each of us puts his person and all his power in common under the supreme direction of the general will, and, in our corporate capacity... receive[s] each member as an indivisible part of the whole,"[1] this supposedly real act was quickly dropped, in act as in theory, in favor of a "before" lost in the mists of time or an "after" with no basis in reality.

According to this seminal text in modern political theory, the social contract is supposed to have always existed, although its clauses were never formally stated and it is known only when it is violated. The philosopher brought all his skill to bear on finding a procedure in the social contract that,

---

1. Jean-Jacques Rousseau, *The Social Contract*, book i, ch. 6, "The Social Compact."

despite the union of each person with all, allows the individual to be as free as *before*. This "before"—this state existing prior to the rational, voluntary act of consent to the social contract—is the cardinal principle underpinning the assembly of human beings, but one that remains in the realm of the unconscious and the innate and that precedes by far the rational denouement that the philosophy of the social contract sees in itself.

The whole, impressive dialectical system developed by Rousseau in *The Social Contract* aims at establishing the basis of a situation where "each man, in giving himself to all, gives himself to nobody,"[2] where the sovereign, although formed by the association of individuals, does not know them, and where everything changes but nothing moves. Indeed, the social contract has great difficulty grounding itself in the tacit, pristine contract that it is purported to formalize. It was as if the whole had to exist before its parts when it is, declaratively, supposed to have been forged out of their union, as if a governmental act were required to form the government!

But Rousseau does not turn his thought to this original contract and consequently, on this point, he remains on the same level of irrationality as the conservative, antirevolutionary Edmund Burke, with his theory of a polity founded on a "pact," which has a transcendental nature. This (mythical) unthought dimension in the doctrine of the social contract became the wellspring of unknown demons in political modernity.[3] The whole and the part, the origin and its offspring, the collective and the individual repelled each other in an impossible association that sought to compensate for its failure with the totality of totalitarianism or with the dissociation of nihilism. A void occupied by none subsists in the modern social contract. It is the consequence of the contract's aspiration to constitute the "foundation," to set itself up as the primal origin, while apprehending itself on the basis of what preceded it, and doing so unwittingly, since this does not coincide with the rational clarity that is its conscious law.

In truth, this situation does not derive merely from the nature of the contract; it proceeds from the very essence of power. And modernity constituted the limit experience of this, because it was the avowed experience of a *tabula rasa* of traditional power, of power linked to a tradition, to anteriority. The nature of power is a secondary nature. Experience itself illustrates this. Whereas the idea of power conjures up notions of dominating, controlling,

---

2. Ibid.

3. The great political religions of the masses. Cf. Shmuel Trigano, *The Democratic Ideal and the Shoah: The Unthought in Political Modernity,* trans. Gila Walker (New York: SUNY Press, 2009).

and taking possession of the world, its primary arena, namely, the political, is a place of emptiness and absence, a place of affluence in which the individual man is absent—be it because he is absorbed by the mass, or because he has lost all subjective singularity to the political role and the supreme power that is his, or because he has been effaced by the totality that he is supposed to represent, or, more prosaically, because all temporal activity necessitated by the function leaves him no time for "himself."

The experience of the political is the paradoxical experience of disappearance. The rise of an individual to supreme power and the concentration of the power, which occurs in a crowd, are actually experiences on the threshold of evanescence. One sinks into power as into a yawning abyss. Power, like quicksilver, is never at rest; it is always passing on. It passes from hand to hand at a dizzying speed, the object of frenetic dispossession and of ongoing controversy and rivalry. Having power is basically a matter of transmitting it. "Bela reigned... and Bela died, and Jobab reigned in his place... and Jobab died, and Husham reigned in his place..." (Gen. 36:32 ff.) and so goes the litany of succession in the biblical story of the first kingdom in history. For a long time, historical narratives understood the history of peoples through a litany of dispossessions (rather than accessions to the throne). The political is the experience of the void. An absence is hidden at the core of all power, which can be perceived through the secrecy with which the powers that be seem to surround themselves, a secrecy that is not so much a stratagem as a painful sigh.

The king is the death of the king, but there is no power that is not an attempt to bring him back to life. The secondarity of power is manifested not only in its exercise; it is expressed in its source of legitimation! Power can be created only in the attempt to establish its own foundations, to find a principle, an origin (the Ancestor, the Contract, and so on) whose place it holds, standing in as a faithful "place holder" for the long disappeared and forgotten principle. The political cannot be examined, founded, or contested without evoking its origins. *Deus sive Natura* has always been the dual path of political thought. Power does not carry its own meaning inside it. While power aspires to assert its presence fully and immediately, to manifest itself in all its glory, it always refers, despite itself and beyond its awareness, to something outside itself.

Thus, a power cannot authorize itself of its own accord (and this is true even of the most powerful dictatorships); its authority is always grounded in the other, in a reputedly superior power (father, god, idea, people, or law). This need to refer to something greater than itself in order to have its supremacy recognized as legitimate and effective is even the sine qua non for power in society. Those who aspire to power never do so in their own name. This is what ironically drives the cruelest of tyrannies to speak in the name of a superior morality and a sovereign good. Psychological or strategic explanations are far from exhausting the significance of this fact.

All powers are maintained solely by virtue of an absence, even as the entire political apparatus strives to define its contours, be it in the form of the people, the nation, the divine, or the constitution. All these definitions are as frail and fleeting as words engraved on emptiness and absence. Power is the power to formulate and elucidate absence. This is why there is no "founda-tion" for the political. The political moment is one of flight, withdrawal, and departure. Wholly impregnated with the immanence of the world, the political arena raises the question of transcendence in the social existence of human beings much more poignantly than the field of education or the economy. Perhaps this is because the political prism is that of gathering and unifying all worldly experience. One could even say that it is the movement of this transcendence that makes the weighty immanence of the political possible.

Consequently, it is the connection between these two dimensions that is the key question in the analysis of the political. Discussing the political in terms of immanence alone (which would be the method, for example, of a strict sociology of power) necessarily misses the point, even though it is clear that to arrive at its transcendence, this immanence cannot be disregarded. It is rather this "before"—this anteriority to power, which is already present in actual power—that determines our comprehension. To posit the political, both democracy and theocracy confront the same experience—namely, the necessity, prior to any effort at clarification (be it rational or traditional), to forge the myth of an origin, which always remained outside the realm of investigation. In this way, against all expectations, the "myth" has remained omnipresent in rational democracy, as exemplified by the social contract.

Wholly preoccupied with "founding," modern thinking persistently disregarded the question of absence, and, by refusing to take it up as an object of reflection, it consigned it to the depths of the repressed or the mythological.[4] In classical thought, the question of absence (via the concept of transcendence)[5] constituted the very basis of political theory, whether the

4. Isn't this inevitable "myth" of origins present at the heart of all the main currents of modern thought (Freud and the original murder, Marx and primitive communism, Lévy-Strauss and mythology)? Here we are touching on the very core of modernity.

5. The experience of transcendence is the experience of that which escapes our grasp, the experience of absence.

answer to it was found in natural law (following Aristotle's idea of man as a "political animal") or in the theocratic conception of medieval religion (the political sphere organized in accordance with God's perfectly clear, positive will). The origin in politics was seen in Nature as a hypostasis, or in God, and with modernity, in human beings (the social contract). But only modernity thought in terms of "foundation," for it is senseless to speak of foundation if the source is God or Nature, since both pertain to the positive, full order of things and of the being in which the political is embedded (natural law or God's will); hence an approach to the political as a dependency or outgrowth of natural law or God's will.

In contradistinction to modern thinking, such an approach recognizes transcendency, the vacuum that exists in power, even though it fails to grasp it. Classical recourse to the divine or to Nature had the merit of underscoring the decisive importance of bringing a judgment to bear on the world in the attempt to arrrive at an explanation of the political. At the other end of the spectrum from Rousseau, this is what Hobbes illustrates in *The Leviathan*. It is paradoxically the modern experience of the political—where this absence has been manifested in the most tragic way[6]—that demonstrates the pertinence of classical thinking, not insofar as the latter provides answers (the positivity of nature or the self-evidence of the divine), but because it helps unravel the way in which these concepts have been recreated under the surface of modernity, in the founding myths of democracy.

The social contract—the prism through which modernity sees the political—has to be reinvested with the instruments of traditional comprehension (God or Nature) turned upside down and inside out. Indeed, the social contract draws on the consequences of the failure of traditional thought to the extent that it strives to break free from the *given* positivism that implicitly discounts the political by overlooking the absence that inhabits it. In seeking its origin in disregard to its past, modern thought addresses the question of the political with greater veracity. This is why the political in modernity has been instituted as a universal (the autonomy of the political), detached from its traditional dependency. But by replacing the latter with an inherently rational positivism (everything begins in the clarity of the contract) and by evading (but nevertheless relying upon) an anteriority (upon which traditional positivist thought insisted), the social contract theory and modern political thinking in general failed to answer the question they raised. Ultimately,

---

6. Precisely because, in the name of immanence, transcendence was denied, yet all the while unconsciously revived in the myth of the social contract.

they turned a blind eye to absence even as they were violently and painfully haunted by it, in their attempt to find their own finality within themselves. For this reason, the perspective that we will be developing here can be said to be beyond modernity: from a position midway between the two political eras, it questions the categories of tradition with the instruments of the social contract and examines the contract by the yardstick of the "before" and the origin, while testing them both in the fleeing light of absence and the void.

The key question of the political in this period after modernity that we have entered is the question of absence and of the void at the heart of the crown. What are we seizing from the world when we take hold of power? What is real? "What profit does man have for his labor beneath the sun?" (Eccles. 1:3) is the question that Kohelet, "king over Israel in Jerusalem" (1:12), insistently asks. In this regard, the historical and textual experience of Israel as a people brings the seeds of a novel perspective, of a modernity greater than modernity.

It is the world of positivism that conceived of nature as the antithesis of the divine and imagined that it could take it over as you can take hold of an object with your hands. This was a far cry from traditional society's conception of the ungraspable immensity of the divine, which could be approached only through hearsay and transmission. The entire modern era is in this opposition. Something of the two opposing figures has to be retained to understand the Hebraic vision of worldliness, as simple and trivial as physical nature and as secret and abstract as the divine.

The centerpiece of this vision is the Hebraic covenant, the *berit*. In addition to everything found in the social contract (procedure, negotiation, clarification of terms, presence of partners, and so forth), it has a dimension of the origin of creation structurally embedded in it. "Behold, I seal a covenant before your entire people. I will make wonders that have not been *created* in any country or nation" (Exod. 34:10). "Keep... the covenant of YHWH that he has sealed with you" (Deut. 4:23). "I appoint *day, heaven, and earth* to bear witness against you" (4:26). The *berit* revives and reactivates the world's creation (*beria*). Indeed, both terms derive from the same verb root, *bara*, meaning "to choose, to eat, to cut." We can begin to unpack the meaning of this convergence of terms in the expression used to describe the act of the covenant. Unlike most verbs that are formed from the radical of the noun (e.g., "to give a gift," "to sing a song"), there is no "accusative of the internal object" in the covenant. The verbal action of the covenant is not involved in the covenant, and hence the covenant is an act whose origin is not internal, an act that refers to something else. One does not "covenant" a covenant;

one "cuts" it (*kerot berit*) or "sets it apart," since the same verb denotes the excommunication or ostracism (*karet*) of someone who has committed a depraved act and is therefore cut out of the community of Israel.

How can the act of breaking, or, more precisely, of cutting off or setting apart, lay the foundation for the act of bringing together and uniting?

The problematics of the *berit* run counter to that of the social contract, whose quest for universality and totality (the "general will") leads it to negate the particular and act as if it did not exist when it is supposedly the very reason for the contract ("the total alienation of each associate, together with all his rights, to the whole community").[7] In the covenant, to the contrary, everything is aimed at producing a particular and a particularization: a single being in particular is set apart from the massive, unreal totality of the world, and a covenant is sealed with this individual who becomes a *ben berit*, a son-partner of the covenant. And, indeed, the verb root of *berit* signifies not only selection and choice but also clarification (*barer*): the appearance of the face of a single interlocutor out of the undifferentiated chaos of the world. Before the covenant, unlike the social contract, there are no names and no particular beings. After the social contract, there are none anymore.

But how are we to account for this setting apart? Could it be that the appearance of a particular facing me carries with it a setting apart, as if the birth of a community would carry with it the exile (*karet*) of the other? The simultaneous nature of this particularization and setting apart plots the field of inquiry into the question of the universal that is at the very heart of our discussion. It is tempting to see the principle of the excluded middle, or *tertium non datur* ("there is no third"), at work here: it is because the "third" (God, the world, the other) is excluded that the I–You relationship is possible.

Is there exclusion in the covenant? Does the particularization that it induces turn its back on the universal? The fact that one does not "covenant a covenant," that one "cuts" it, can lead us in the direction of a response to these questions. The covenant is not its own end purpose. The cutting out is to be understood not in relation to a "third" but rather in the framework of the covenant itself. *Karet* also means cessation, exhaustion, and end. To make a covenant is to disappear, to be gone. This is indeed a paradoxical conception of the commonality of community.

This disappearance is not to be interpreted as a death or as death in general, but as something greater, as the very principle and nature of being and existence, of which death is but one of the expressions or modalities among

7. Rousseau, *Social Contract*, book. i, ch. 6.

others. That which speaks of extinction, setting apart, or cutting off in the *berit* is that which pertains to the world. The radical of *berit*, which does not give us a verb to designate the act of making a covenant, is also the radical of the term *beria*: creation ex nihilo. It is as if, in the covenant, the creation of the world was implicated more than the two partners to the agreement.

Is this the absent one in question? And does this mean that there is, in fact, an excluded middle, a "third"? The etymological proximity of the terms for creation and covenant prompts us to turn the question around: Isn't the creation of the world directly and in its very structures a covenant? The repeated calls on the heaven and the earth for testimony every time a covenant is concluded (Deut. 4:26) suggest as much. And this is what we can see in the narrative at the end of the flood, where the covenant with Noah (Gen. 9:9) is described in cosmic terms (the rainbow); it is a covenant that includes not only all humankind but also all the natural elements (the waters, the earth, the animals, the plants, and so on). When God creates the world, he enters into a covenant, a *berit*, and all ulterior covenants derive from this foundational world-covenant (*berit-olam*), in which what is absent refers neither to God the creator nor to the world in relation to us, but to the very nature of the covenant and of existence. The absence is not outside us as makers of the covenant; it is within us. The covenant creates absence in us. And this is precisely what needs to be grasped. What is it in existence itself, in presence itself, in God-for-us, in the very act of the world, that is absence? It is to this dimension of being that the absence, the cutting off, the setting apart in the *berit* refers. In sum, the *berit* directly raises the question of the nature of reality and of the world in which we seal a covenant. This covenant generates power and norms, to be sure, but power over what, and what kind of power? What does power take hold of? The world, precisely.

But, as the Hebrew root *olam* indicates, the world is disappearance. Creating, for the Divinity who then occupied the whole dwelling place of being, amounts to making a *berit* (with the world), that is to say, breaking, cutting off, absenting himself from his being, withdrawing from himself, like a womb opening and creating an empty space within to make room for the embryo.[8] It amounts to suspending himself in the very covenant that is the world.

8. See "Le Retrait," in Shmuel Trigano, *Le Récit de la disparue, essai sur l'identité juive* (Paris: Gallimard, 1977), p. 31 (hereafter *Story of Disappeared Presence*).

God's withdrawal, which is the schema of creation itself, can be read in its immediacy as a disappearance. "In the mercy (*hesed*) of disappearance-world (*olam*), I wombed you (*rahamtich*)" (Isa. 54:8). In the words of the Midrash, "God is the place of his world (*olam*), and the world is not his place."[9] This we read in the light of the root *olam*: "God is the place of his disappearance, and disappearance is not his place." Absence is not an absence in relation to the other, but an absence within oneself. It precedes the other. And from the standpoint of our inquiry into the fundaments of power and the political, the disappearance is more significant than the withdrawal, because the former is the outcome of the latter, and we are addressing the question here on this very level, the level of man (of the political) and not of the creator. Man's experience is firstly one of absence and disappearance.

The absence within oneself is by no means absence or obliviousness to the other, as one might think. The absence lodged in the *berit* that makes the world is precisely what makes the world possible. It is what underlies its very manifestation; it is the place of the world. The absence and disappearance borne from the "cutting" of the covenant must be understood by considering them not in opposition to presence but at its core. Admittedly, disappearance is close to death,[10] but the *olam* does not biblically bear the mark of such a connotation. "The maiden/*alma* bore a son..." (Isa. 7:14): *alma* is from the same root as *olam*. The *olam* indicates not entropy and dereliction, but germination, advent, and birth. The moderns thought they saw in it the trace of a "primal murder." But, in fact, the absence at the origin expresses a displacement, a movement, and a process that enable the appearance of creation and thus of the other vis-à-vis God. Disappearance is the very substance of the temporality that consists in "making room" for the other, for the gestation of the other. This disappearance, which is pure temporality because the other is impending, is what the world (*olam*) is. That it is possible, seen from the perspective of the world, to view disappearance as a death has to do with the experience of the world and with its fundamental pitfall, but not with the nature of *olam*. The book of Ecclesiastes is wholly devoted to recounting (and overcoming) the ordeal ("Vanity of vanities...")

---

9. Midrash Rabba on Gen. 68.

10. In the same way, the absence at the origin led to theories about "God's death," which harbor an element of real experience but from a distorted perspective. They are, in fact, but the modern translation of medieval negative theologies (see Shmuel Trigano, *La Demeure oubliée, Genèse religieuse du politique* [Paris: Lieu Commun, 1984], hereafter *Forgotten Dwelling*). The latter were maintained in the knowledge of God by faith, not intellect.

of existence. Indeed, if we dismiss the *berit* in an explanation of the world and the real, all that is left is nothingness, the nihilistic acknowledgment of the void that is the world: "they went after *hevel* ('vanity' or 'transience'), and they dragged us with them" (Jer. 2:5).

The world-covenant (*berit-olam*) is not in the disappearance and the absence that it generates. Rather than neglect and obliviousness, it is birth-giving mercy (*rahamim*),[11] the withholding of the self in anticipation of the other. Thus, every time God renews the covenant with Abraham, he is promised many descendants, so that faces will at last arise from the absence. The attribute that governs the covenant and binds the partners in it is not the equanimity of the social contract but mercy, the gratuitous gift, *hesed*. *Hesed* is the only virtue capable of "governing" absence and disappearance, a world in which all objects slip away.

"The *hesed* of YHWH [goes] from *olam* and to *olam* for... those who keep his covenant and remember his commands" (Ps. 103:17–18). "He keeps the covenant and *hesed* for those who love him" (Deut. 7:9). The strict rigor that governs the equality and justice of the social contract can deal only with the being-there, not with the heralded being-to-come. If this were the viaticum for the passage across the disappearance-world that is human life, the result would be destruction and desolation. Something else is needed. *Hesed* is the sole attribute that can govern the *berit* and its contracting parties. It withholds being, judgment, and apportioning, thereby leaving human beings the time to do and to become. The gift brought into the world by *hesed* is not purely gratuitous; it withholds the bounty and fullness of being, as in a hidden wellspring from which all the waters of creation and of the world's continuity are drawn. *Hesed* is the vehicle of the covenantal relationship, without which the disappearance (of God) that is the world would condemn us to an irreversible absence that would banish all communication and cause God's reappearance in the place of his withdrawal and hence the destruction of the world. Presence is kept hidden in absence, and it is through absence that we communicate with it. The world is held together by the withhold-ing that characterizes *hesed*. We can thus see in a new light the words so often pronounced in liturgy, *Leʾolam hesdo*: his *hesed* is for the *olam*; it is everlasting, it is for the world, or, in other words, it is for the disappearance that is the world.

The covenant, the act by which power is instituted, by which the collec-tive takes possession of the world, is commensurate with the world. It is a

---

11. For more on the concept of *rahamim*, see pp. 35, 99–100.

relinquishment, a forgoing. "To bear witness against you I appoint the day, heaven, and earth" (Deut. 4:26) expresses the testimony in terms of fading light, since the Hebrew day starts at nightfall.[12] Only such a metaphor can evince an *olam-berit*, which is not, as most translations would have it, an "eternal covenant" but rather a "covenant of disappearance," which is another way of designating the world-covenant.

12. See Shmuel Trigano, *La Nouvelle Question juive, L'avenir d'un espoir* (Paris: Gallimard, 1979), p. 86 (hereafter *New Jewish Question*).

CHAPTER 1

World-Covenant

THE COVENANT IS a voiding process.[13] To seal a covenant is to expand the vortex of the void throughout the realms of weightiness and fullness; it is to recall in the course of time the pristine moment of origin. The covenant reactualizes the world's very "substance" (i.e., emptiness) in the unfolding of the world, which is where forgetting lurks. The operation would be impossible if the origin were one of fullness; but because in the beginning was the withdrawal out of which the world emerged, making the moment of origin (by way of the covenant) surge forth into the world that followed, it leads not to destroying the world but to restoring the vital impetus of its pristine moments. The moment of the covenant is (and hence always recalls) the moment of origin, of the beginning, the *reshit*, the start of creation. It is remembering. To make a covenant is to "remember" the covenant. It is "with emptiness" (*bereshit*) (Gen. 1:1) that God created—that is to say, created by way of covenant, and any covenant is a recollection and a reviviscence of the *reshit*, of a beginning that is paradoxical, since it is one of withdrawal and absence.

The void is the first moment of the world, but also the moment that accompanies all moments. It is the absence that inhabits every instant, that makes it an instant in its constitutive evanescence, by constantly undermining its illusion of being there. And because it is continually deconstructing the instant, it enables the passage and course of time. The beginning haunts all of reality. The void ceaselessly absorbs and engulfs the fullness it produces—the creatures and creation—as if to compel us to remember what has disappeared. It is at once the first principle and that which is hidden in the innermost

---

13. There is an echo of this void in the Greek conception of the pact. The two contracting parties break a piece of pottery in two, and each takes a half of the "symbol" or token of identity. The exact fit of the two pieces along the line of the break will testify later to the pact. In this case, however, the pact produces its effect when the break is nullified. How could it be otherwise, when it is an object that bears witness to the pact and not man in his ability to remember? (See below, "The Covenant between the Pieces," pp. 79–100)

recesses of the existent, ever ready to leap out; it is that which enables but also annihilates the existent. This is why such a common question as the relationship between the self and the world is absolutely impossible from the perspective of the *olam*. The world is a relinquishment; it is where the self forgoes itself. The world is a process of slipping away. Everything in the world escapes us. Taking "power" in the world—and one cannot do otherwise—represents therefore the apotheosis of our experience of the "world." And it is ineluctably an attempt to grasp what escapes our hold.

What is the nature of this void? Several currents of thought have had a presentiment or vision of it, in regard both to the experience of power and to the experience of existence. The interpretation of this emptiness, which is the essential human experience, and its place in the economy of being are the decisive criteria of these currents. Marx's conception of alienation is close to the "void." And there is some truth to his strictly political interpretation. The political (or rather, the economic) is aptly designated as the place where the gap between oneself and one's acts in the world develops and becomes manifest. But even though he evaluated this alienation in relation to "nature" via the mode of production ("the extraction of nature's wealth"), he conflated it with the political, in the sense that the "void" was seen as characterizing political reality but not material reality. And this misses the very gist of the concept of emptiness. Marx rightly saw that the theater in which the drama of alienation is played out is the theater of power, but he did not have an inkling of the scale of the void that directs it and that would enable us to gain a better understanding of its implications.

The Freudian unconscious represents another approach to the void, inasmuch as it designates, at the very peak of our dreams of self-control, the part of reality that escapes our grasp and is continually haunting us. Freud's definition of the unconscious in its relationship to the family and to the generations evinces a much deeper understanding of the nature of the void than Marx's concept of alienation: whereas the former includes the dimension of power in general (although the social aspect is seen as secondary), the latter ignores the psychological subject. But Freud loses the positive dimension of the void and cuts off its potentiality by naturalizing it (as a matter of impulses and untrammeled natural instincts) and developing an economy of scarcity[14] (i.e., castration). *Totem and Taboo* shows the extent to which the Freudian perspective interprets the void in terms of death, murder, and the unavowable, and not as a chance for life, testimony, and giving birth.

14. For more on the concept of an economy of scarcity, see pp. 290–294.

Lastly, the ethnological interpretation, which Freud picks up in *Totem and Taboo*, depicts the void in power as the "execution of the king." This approach concentrates exclusively on the outer appearance without attempting to grasp its inner meaning. Admittedly, seen from the outside, the beginning is marked by death. The creational retreat (of God) and the absence that bears witness to it may look like a death, but only if one disregards the movement of the Being we are striving to understand.

The question of the void comprises all these perspectives at once, but it harbors other possibilities of meaning and interpretation. One should avoid theorizing the void too quickly. Doing so is a way of "filling" or negating it by putting it back into an initial totality. We must strive, on the contrary, to understand it as it is, to perceive it not as the adverse of fullness, as a being in itself, in its intrinsic positivity. The lack, the absence, the alienation, the unconscious, and death are but secondary consequences or modalities of its being. To speak of the "being" of the void is to use two antithetical terms, because the nature of this being is to give way[15] in a movement of never-ending passage to other than oneself. Man cannot be a founder, because the foundation escapes his hold. Indeed, there is no foundation save in motionless death, in Being conceived and experienced outside its void. Isn't this what is exemplified by Cain the murderer, who, in his flight, founded the first city and named it after his son Hanoch, whose name means "inauguration"? (Gen. 4:17). Is the very "foundation" of the world anything other than the emergence of the void in God? There is no foundation save in the breath of the cloud!

But the void is the very condition of freedom. It is through the void that God makes room for the created in the pure potentiality of being, in the upsurge of a being to become. Through absence, God's total concern for man, and hence God's presence, amounts to total freedom for man. God's creational sovereignty elevates man's freedom to its heights. In this sense, there is complete uncertainty in the void, which is a chasm over which freedom hovers, like the spirit of God hovering over the primal abyss: the choice of life or death ("You shall choose life," Deut. 30:19). Yet this pure freedom does not imply the rule of randomness, for if there is a chasm of nothingness opening up in the void, the narrow path of life runs through it as well. Beyond the undifferentiated and indifferent appearance, a paradoxical geography stands out in relief. The void is bustling with surprisingly regular flows, movements, and currents.

---

15. See "L'épreuve de l'être qui se dérobe," in Trigano, *Story of Disappeared Presence*, p. 213.

To put it paradoxically, the void is a "reality" in its own right. It is not an absence of being but being absent to itself. The work[16] of man, and notably his political work, consists in delving into it, drawing from it, even requiring it[17] to yield its hidden power, and thereby "redeeming" it. This is why there is nothing more than an *alef*, the only unpronounceable letter in the Hebrew alphabet (hidden in the first word of the creation, which begins with the second letter, the *bet*), to distinguish *gola*, the exile of being, from *geula*, redemption.

To draw out the memory of this *alef*, to make its silence resound, this is what redeems the world from its disappearance. Such an operation is also necessary to understand the political, for the void is not the nonexistence of the political, as those who see the void as a lack to be filled and the political as a foundation (the "founding fathers" of modern states or the mythical "founding father" of ancient traditions) are wont to believe.

What if the absence that the void engenders is to be interpreted not as a lack in relation to a fullness, but as an elsewhere of the being-there, an addition, an overplus, a more (*od*) to the totality of the being? The void is absent because it comes as an addition over and above the totality of the being, an addition to the Being of God the creator, in such a way that the world that wells up in it, that arises in the midst of God's retreat, tends to forget it. What to man is God's withdrawal is to God an overplus to his being. The work of man is to reverse the state of the world, to draw being out of the void. The Hebraic totality, *kol*, contains the notion of destruction and annihilation, *kelaya*. "You shall eat of all (*kol*) the garden trees, and of the tree of knowledge of good and bad, you shall not (*lo*) eat" (Gen. 2:16–17). This is not an arbitrary prohibition, a pure imperative; it indicates to the Adam that the ambition of totality amounts to his own destruction, that to subsist he must leave a not (*lo*) somewhere, an area "set apart" from the totality. After all, his very being as a human is constitutionally the product of this area, of this overplus to the totality of the divine, of this compelling force of the Being to conceive more than himself, but not less than himself. If the latter were the case, the being of man would be formed from a subtraction from God in relation to himself; we would be divine minus his totality, and it would be our vocation to reconquer this totality in our ultimate divinization. There would be, from this standpoint, a negation of totality and perfect

16. The famous *amal* from Ecclesiastes.

17. This is precisely the meaning of *derash*, which comes from *darash*, meaning "to draw out, to require, to inquire," and from which the word *midrash* is derived.

unity of the divine being (one does not remove from God) and, at the same time, a negation of the freeedom of man (existence would be synonymous with the anguish of the lack).

Such a conception of an overplus to the being points to the inadequacy of determining the void by the "being" (a concept specific to Greek philosophy). The biblical verse clearly states that this tree of which one must not eat is outside the "all," in addition to the whole (while standing in the whole, since nothing can be outside the whole). The concept is paradoxical. How can we comprehend the prohibition (*lo*) in the Garden of Eden not as a negation, as a limit, but, to the contrary, as a liberation from all limits and all lack? What seems to man to be a prohibition, a setting aside (the forbidden fruit), is, from the divine perspective, an overplus, an addition, a blessed profusion. There is a difference in perspective of the totality inherent to creation. That which, for the creator, goes beyond the totality of being—the emergence of a universe that is something other than being, the void, the emptied place where man can take his place (this *lo* beyond the "all" of Eden)—represents, for the created, a withdrawal, an absence, a lack of being and a dismemberment of the totality. Idolatry (personified by the Edenic snake) stops at this immediate perspective in its attempt to remember the totality (by eating the only forbidden fruit) or to erase its dismemberment (the "murder" of God or of the founding father, the memory of which must be obliterated). Idolatry is, in fact, the attempt to eliminate the overplus, to annul the creation of man and the status of the created—that is to say, to annul freedom. It is animated by a fundamental misconception, which consists in mistaking the void for nothingness and trying to fill it.

Everything is held in this paradox of a subtraction ("the retreat") that is an addition, as we will gradually come to see. What man sees as a lack is not a gap that can be filled, despite the human aspiration to plenitude and totality, a tragic aspiration since human beings are already, without knowing it—through their immediate experience of lack—in a state of unending excess and overplus. Thus, the experience of a lack that will grow the more it is satisfied is a misconception of reality—that is to say, of the experience of an overplus that drinks at the source of the infinite profusion of being. The difference in this experience of the void between what the void constitutes and what it seems to be, the discrepancy between the overplus and the lack, stems not only from the bifocal nature of the viewpoints of man and God, but also from the reality of the experience of the world that all creatures must traverse, moving from lack to overplus, across a place and time of inversion and reversion.[18]

This seeming paradox is possible because the overplus is hidden. Beyond the whole, it leaves the confines of visibility. The leeway is admittedly small between this leaving the confines of visibility and invisibility per se, between the overplus and the lack. But it is paradoxically the world that is in invisibility, in disappearance, because the bounty inherent in the overplus, the original place of the world, is not quantifiable, whereas totality is marked by unity. Multiplicity is never totally visible and graspable. No one can know *all* of humanity; it is an impossible project. Yet, in the reality of overplus, where we dwell without knowing it, we aspire to the destructive totality that preceded it. This is what we mistakenly call "the one," this desire to still the burgeoning of the world and totalize it in a single sum. Such a desire for oneness is a deceptive, morbid form of nostalgia, a mockery of the divine Unity forged in the process of setting the world apart as an overplus to the being. The overplus is hidden in the disappearing and veiling; it is hidden from the orderly transparency and exposure that is the all.[19] In this it is, at first glance, a matter of "not" (Gen. 3:17), a negative command: it is forbidden from visibility, and this is what founds the world, the possibility of *olam* that would be absorbed otherwise, involuted in the crystal of totality. This dimming of light is the very condition of possibility for man.

The world sustains and bears more than itself. In this sense, it is "disappearance." The veiling that is the *alma*,[20] the maiden who has yet to reach maturity and fulfillment, is the world—a mantle of emptiness that cloaks the divine, a screen, curtain, veil, or cloud of "fog" (Deut. 4:11), a swirl of smoke in which God the creator hides so that the totality of his splendid being does not overwhelm the embryonic world in an unequal confrontation. The whole substance and thickness of the world is held in this whirl of smoke. There is no divine distance and disdain for humankind; there is,

18. See "Le mouvement du retour," in Trigano, *New Jewish Question*, p. 87.

19. As we will see (with regard to the concealment of the sacrificial bird in "The Covenant between the Pieces," pp. 79–100), what the Adamic couple is forbidden to grasp, what is kept secret, is the one that opens the all to the passage but is impossible in the passage and must be hidden. An a posteriori proof: once Adam has transgressed this prohibition, he discovers he is "naked," exposed to the world, and he hides (Gen. 3:7–8) to repair his trangression and redeem the one in the world.

20. *Alma*, as mentioned above, has the same root as the word *olam*.

to the contrary, grace and nearness, giving birth and nursing, the continuity of the self in a being that comes out of the self and that one nurses on the outside, outside oneself, besides oneself, in secrecy. "Remember us in your birth-giving mercy (*rahamim*), YHWH, for there is nothing more/no overplus (*od*) apart from [what comes] from you"; this ritual daily prayer is usually translated as "there is no other [God] beside you."

The world is a coming out of the totality. The concealment makes the world (*olam*), but it has a reverse side. The disappearance that constitutes the world frees a place. The world is "inside," but it has irreversibly an outside, an exteriority. We have here another perspective on the lack and the overplus. There are two moments in the void: that of interiorization and that of its residue, its remnant (*she'ar*), the inside and the outside. All relationships to the world are relationships between these two moments, an effort to come out of the place where one is, out of exile and forgetting, out of the absence to the world, the exteriority in which we are initially projected, and an effort to come in the secret place where Presence is, in the inside where the world originates, in a rebirth that repeats the gesture of creation: "the remnant will return" (Isa. 10:21). Israel begins to exist when it comes out of Egypt, just as Abraham came out of Ur. But it is not, in fact, coming out. One cannot come out of the exterior. Once outside, it has already come out, but it does not immediately know it. And so it comes in. For this reason, any gathering or assembly is called *knesset* in Hebrew, which means "entry" (*knesset Yisrael*, the assembly, or entry, of Israel).

Any assembly is inside, in the world-disappearance.[21] And so you have to step outside the world to really be inside it. The inside is a departure, a departure from the self, from sovereign totality. It is only logical that God dwells inside—"I shall dwell within them" (Exod. 25:8)—inside the cloud. Similarly, the interior is all love. "Its interior is fitted with love" (Song 3:10), because the interior is a movement outside the self, outside disappearance, a turning toward the other, a movement of love.

This movement of love and this step outside the totality indicate to us the privileged place of the particular. Love chooses one person out of many. The entry is always to a singular dwelling, to a name, to the knowledge of

21. The Roman *comices* met in a place called *mundus*, a world that stands out in opposition to the Hebraic *olam*. Like the Greek *cosmos*, *mundus* also referred to the orderly arrangement of a woman's dress and ornaments, the visible and splendid manifestation of an aesthetic order, whereas *olam* is akin to *alma*, the veiled, retiring maiden, the Shulammite from the Song of Songs who hides "in the cranny of the rocks" (2:14), the *alma* who will give birth (Isa.7:14), the *alma*, the sister of Moses, who "went and called the child's mother" to nurse him, at the bidding of Pharaoh's daughter (Exod. 2:8).

one name in particular, taken out of the multitude and the interchangeable "universal" of the outside: the choice of the beloved, who is hidden away, separated from the vulgarity of the exterior.

The *olam* envelops a being in particular in its unity, a unique, chosen being. Presence is always a matter of the particular, inside, of the discovery of a name. This is why when the divine Name is revealed during the episode of the burning bush, it is said, "This is my Name *le'olam*" (Exod. 3:15), meaning "forever," for the world, for disappearance; similarly, God accompanies Moses' passage through the water during the exodus from Egypt "to make himself an *olam* Name" (Isa. 63:12). The Name is the other name for the primal void, the Name in particular, the particular Name of divine presence, of a God who has a name. It is in this sense that it is said, "His glory fills the *olam*" (prayer). In the *olam* of excess ("full" of his glory) resides his Name. In the lightness of the void, in the winds of disappearance, resides the *weight* of his *glory* (for *kavod* means both). The pristine void is the procession of the Name, in the disappearance.

From this standpoint, we can see how Israel is defined as an interior, an interiority that houses the divine presence—"I will dwell in the interior of the children of Israel" (Exod. 29:45)—and contains the Name in the world of exteriority—"I will give them an *olam* name that will not be taken away" (Isa. 56:5). Israel is the place of a name in particular, removed and hidden from the totality of nations: the lack on the obverse side, the overplus on the reverse side. It is in this sense that it is not "taken away." And in the lack, which is an illusory, passive, and fleeting version of the overplus, stand the nations that, riveted to the being-there of the world, to the dream of its fixity and its naturality, regard the hidden as nothingness and crown totality in all its aspects. Nature is the void of the divine Name, the imprint left in clay of the Name that hid in the cloud of *olam*.[22]

There is no clash between what is hidden and what seems to be absent or missing, between the wilderness (*midbar*) and the desolation (*shemama*)[23] that ignores its own existence. But the very experience of the world (*olam*) is in this hiatus. The *olam* institutes two human states, which are two states of consciousness itself: an inside and an outside that traverse the consciousness of every individual from outside in (Abraham comes from Ur, and Moses from Egypt). Is the world of exteriority, of cold nature, absent to itself and to man,

22. As the experience of nature demonstrates, the void is a "structure." There is also a specified number of seventy nations in the world.

23. See Shmuel Trigano, "*Midbar-shemama*," *Traverses* 19 (June 1980), pp. 98, 104. The *midbar* engenders words (*devarim*); *shemama* is barren desolation.

irreducible? All individuals are projected into the appallingly disinterested, ice-cold world of objects, which are implacably exterior and indifferent to the individual. This is the experience of every human consciousness, and it is the experience of Israel. "A people, in solitude, it will remain" (Num. 23:9), and this solitude is that of the dweller,[24] the one who lives amongst those who have no home and live scattered throughout the world in spite of the splendor of their citadels (Cain's cities). Cain's wanderings are the fate of men of the *world* in the land of Nod (Gen. 4:16), a destiny of erring and emptiness, in which what is done is continually being undone. Such is the experience of humankind, huddled around a campfire, confronting the adversity of the empire of "nature" that shatters the proximity of the desire and its fulfillment. When Israel experiences exile, this is the adversity of exteriority that it endures, in a way that is at once more painful and less serious. Because it comes from the interior, its journey through the exterior is an "exile" (in view of a "return"), not a sinking into desolation. But if it carries the hope of the interior with it, it suffers more from the experience of exteriority, because it is less hardened to it, more sensitive to its bite.

In the midst of this pristine landscape of uncertainty and anguish, *knesset Yisrael*, the assembly of Israel or the "entry" of Israel, arises out of this journey from the exterior to the interior that describes a path in creation, which turns the experience of the void as lack into an experience of the void as overplus. This is, at first, a silent, solitary journey in the person of the patriarchs, but their arduous march swells gradually into a collectivity and eventually into a people. This is the place of all collectivities, where creation is still incomplete, where the world of disappearance has yet to be built by man. This is where people gather together, because it is the interior that is at stake, the interior where all is proximity and alterity.

The project of any collectivity is the completion of creation. It is by gathering together that human beings can nearly instinctually ward off the suffering from lack and absence, and it is also in the depths of this gathering that they experience the overplus, in the innermost recesses of which is nestled the principle of the world. All gatherings are an experience of the origin, of the creation of the world. Indeed, when God created the universe, he created humanity as a whole, the whole of humanity at the same time, for that very moment but also for the future. All of humanity forever and ever is present in the first man. Any gathering of human beings is a recollection of

24. See below, ch .2, "The House of Israel: Sovereignty."

the first Adam. This is why the experience of the void is the unique, powerful experience of the collectivity. There is a repetition of the origin in the
collectivity, as if its being had escaped its control and were sliding forward.
The void on earth, the essential trial of existence, inhabits the assembly of
human beings. In the gathering of men, it is always the divine that is in
"question" and omnipresent. We have already had a glimpse of this in the
secondarity of all power. The collectivity does not have its being in itself;
it is the threshold of transcendence, not only of the divine but also of the
universe of nature. What makes this trying is that it is an experience of self-
relinquishment, one in which our whole being can escape our grasp in the
enclosed, adverse exteriority: the figure of death emerges on the horizon of
this road. When I gather together with others, the substance of my being
nestled in the interiority of my consciousness is relativized and reduced to
nothing more than an undifferentiated element in a crowd of others of my
kind. I am brought down to the zero state of my story and my person. But
it is also the collectivity itself that carries death with it, because it seems not
to have a soul. It is in a state of perpetual ruin, made and unmade by the
random movements of the massive, formless crowd. The collective is always
in a state of "crisis"; it is always breaking down and collapsing. This is because it is, at first, the most powerful experience of the awe and terror of
the void, of the primal darkness that hides the chaos, the *tohu va'vohu* of the
elements, the experience of an absolute, implacable exteriority that does not
seem to be animated by any soul, any birth-giving mercy, or any interiority
for a human being whose sole origin it is! This terrifying void is no doubt
the first moment of the *olam*, of disappearance: the poignant (and harder to
gain) hidden side of absence, the internal side woven from love and light.

The experience of collectivity can follow the two modalities of *olam*.
If we start from the idea that, for man, who comes from the interior, the
experience of the void is unbearable, it is easy to understand why human
beings are relentlessly trying to fill it, in one way or another. There is an illusion of fullness, a mirage of plenitude in the void, which derives from the
refusal to endure the trial and assume its stakes. As everything constantly
slips through the grasp of human beings, the collectivity, in a supreme effort, tries to arrest movement. Finding the confrontation with the origin
unbearable and mortifying, its first reaction is to block or evade it. This is
the time of idols, of totems, and of the golden calf, when the humanized
object stands in the way of the terrifying void and fills its yawning abyss.
The scattered collective recognizes itself as a collective by converging upon

a unique object[25] and organizing itself around this object. The origin and memory of the creator are occulted in this process, which is the outcome of the collectivity's impatience with waiting for an interiority that seems to take a long time manifesting itself, when, in fact, it is the very condition of interiority to be in suspense in the world of exteriority.

The experience of temporality is wholly bound up with waiting for a presence that takes time to come, sheltered as it is in the recesses of interiority. "The smallest will increase a thousandfold, and the youngest into a mighty nation. I am YHWH; in its time, I will hasten it" (Isa. 60:22).

The collectivity that is crystallized around an idol "denatures," in a manner of speaking, the world of *olam* that is disappearance, inasmuch as it tries to bring it to completion. Hebrew has another term to designate the world that clearly expresses the fall of the *olam*, and that is *tevel*. *Tevel* refers to the Earth as a terrestrial globe, but also to incest and sodomy, and, strangely enough, to the harmony of voices.[26] It is the world of coalescing and filling in where the void is driven behind an artificial concert of individualities. *Tevel* does not hold otherness or the secret of the *olam*. It negates the locus of the origin, the principle of disappearance by which the creator adds to himself a being beyond himself and separates and differentiates himself from this being. There is neither separation nor sanctification—*keddusha* means both—in *tevel*, only fusion and incest.[27] Murder hovers over the origin, because murder is the cutting off of the other.

The collectivity of *tevel* is tragic. It chooses exteriority but desires interiority. It chooses *tevel* only because of its irrepressible impatience for interiority. This is why, even though the very fabric of its society is woven with incest, everything in its external discourse prohibits incest and murder. The prohibition of incest, which stands at the core of all civilizations on earth, is there only in response to the universality of incest in the principle of every civilization. The *tevel*, which would be a world of unaccomplished manifestation, is truly the world of incest, in Hebrew the *uncovering* of the

25. Certain biblical covenants stand in the way of this unique object: when Jacob made a covenant with Laban, he "took a stone and raised it up as a monument" (Gen. 31:45). This later became an altar for sacrifices (Josh. 8:30).

26. See below, "The Face in the Voice," pp 500–515.

27. The consciousness that characterizes the *tevel* misunderstands the meaning of the suspension of totality that creation represents. The *tevel* knows only natural determinism and ignores the fact that creation happens through the suspension of the rigor and law of Being. This suspension is mercy (*hesed*), the chance given to human beings to redeem themselves through their acts. But the *tevel* mistakes this for incest, because *hesed* means this, too!

nudities, or *giluy arayot*. What is incest if not the opposite of birth, of the separation of the child from parental bonds? Thus, guilt governs the humanity of *tevel*, but it is more a pretense than actual remorse. The end purpose of *tevel* is to simulate the completion of creation, even though the world is still disappearing!

Abraham's peregrinations offer a different experience of the *olam*, an experience of the void that comes out of the *tevel* (Ur in Chaldea) and turns the *tevel* into the *olam* of its truth. This is why the collectivity that Abraham founds, the *eda*, the "community of Israel," "*adat Yisrael*" (Exod. 12:3), goes through the ordeal of the void and endures it in its journey inward, without immediately substituting a sham fullness for it. The journey through the void is constitutive of its being. In this sense it is defined as a community of the covenant, of the *berit*, of the "cut" and the separation. In the experience of Israel, there are times of failure, of course. The golden calf,[28] around which a community of desolation (*shemama*) was forged, will always remain the archetype of the fall of Israel into the world of *tevel*, of the diminution of its being, of regression on the path that was taking it out of exteriority. Exile is Israel's experience of exteriority in the alienation of its interiority. It thus falls back into exteriority but with greater provisions for return, because it now bears the memory of the interior. Yet this exile, which all the nations can see, is a challenge to them; it bears witness in the *tevel* to the installation and realization of the *olam*, of disappearance. The exile of Israel in the midst of the nations serves as a powerful critique of the establishment of nations in the *tevel*, in its globality and its principle. As they bask in the narcissistic contemplation of their excellence, it hints that they are, in fact, wandering in desolation. That Israel is scattered over the whole face of the *tevel* and not in only a few regions is a sign of the universality of exile. This is why the ingathering of the exiles that heralds messianic times awakens the people scattered over the face of the *tevel* and heralds the movement toward interiority by all humankind. "Who is like your people, like Israel, nation One on earth?" (II Sam. 7:23).

The community of Israel exemplifies, in human experience, the strategy of interiority that manages to bridge the divide between the void, the primordial given in the world, and the promise of completion. It is a strategy of secrecy and not of display, one that, despite the tearing that marks the first moment of the covenant, resists the temptation of idolatry. This is the strategy of circumcision, which is described as the "sign (*ot*) of the covenant."

28. See "Le mouvement du retour," in Trigano, *New Jewish Question*, p. 87.

It is the "sign" that helps diminish the pain of the gap that the promise and the waiting introduce into the world. Circumcision is thus the very criterion of adherence to the *berit*.

Signs can exist only in instances of incompletion and absence. The sign testifies to the past; it is the trace thereof. It is at once a trace of the primal cut (circumcision as the cut of the foreskin) but also the herald of what is impending and calls for action. We can see why it is the male sex organ that bears the sign of the covenant: it is the organ of union and procreation engendering the generation that will continue the covenant, the organ that manifests the relationship with the other. "Who is the hero? He who dominates his instinct" (Pirkei Avot 4:1). It is at the very locus of possession and eventual oblivion, immersion in the void ("the little death"), that the memory of the covenant assumes the full thrust of its meaning. Sexual relations of familial proximity are forbidden (incest) because the first moment of the *olam* is removal and distance. Nearness (*kirva*) is a promise, an effort, an act that is conquered and earned. In short, in the *olam*, what is near is far. And this distance is a form of self-domination, the process that makes room for the other, at precisely the place where the greatest danger exists of denying or reifying the other.

The community of the covenant is, hence, this relentlessly renewed effort to "hide" the *olam* and prevent it from congealing in the exteriority of *tevel*. At every instant man can be sucked back into the unfurling void, swallowed by the abyss that "carries" this frail craft tossed on a stormy ocean, the ocean of the deluge that threatens to engulf him if he does not look for the "sign" of Noah's covenant: the rainbow. But one can also disappear in the flow of postdiluvian humanity, without Abraham's sign, for Abraham is the Noah of a humanity after God (because of his covenant with Noah), promised that there would be no other deluge. Thus, the interior is always in the process of being lost, swallowed by the undifferentiation that is lodged in the void (just like the Name). We are born and we die. A generation comes and a generation goes. We form an identity and we lose it. We build and everything is destroyed. We love and we separate. We conceive and we give birth. Nothing can hold on for long over the void; at every instant everything is being put into question and slipping through our grasp. We are in the *olam*, in the passage of being. All is perpetual passage.

CHAPTER 2

Passage

THE ABSENCE THAT inhabits the world and in which the abode of the world is established is not a static absence, experienced solely as overwhelming lack. That is only one of its aspects (the choice of *tevel*). In fact, the cardinal nature of this absence is passage. And even more, we would say that passage precedes absence. Absence is the immediate perception of passage, but it is incomplete, truncated, and ultimately misleading if it is not superseded. The notion of passage may very well be the "positive" notion that we are seeking to define the void. The *olam* is a passage of the Being.

Ecclesiastes is a masterpiece of wisdom on passage. The fact that it is misinterpreted as evincing the skepticism, unhappiness, and pessimism of old age is due to a lack of understanding of Hebrew terms and knowledge of the Hebraic vision of the "world." Ecclesiastes is a book of physics and natural sciences at their highest level.

In its literary form as in its content, it describes the incessant passage of Being and its paradoxical implication: the fading into death as much as the persistent stream of the living. The term *hevel*, which, according to different translations, means "vanity" or "mist," radically signifies a passage, in the sense of disappearance and extinction (*kala*, with the connotation of *kol*, "all"), but also in the sense of exchange and substitution. *Hevel* is what passes by, what passes on, what is replaced and passes away. "The fall has passed on, the rain has passed/replaced it" (Song 2:11).[29] Ecclesiastes presents the principle of substitution,[30] or rather, of passage, as follows: "Passage of passages, all is passage," which can also be read as "Change of changes, the

29. "Passes on and away" (*holef vekaleh*); see *Daat Mikra* (Jerusalem: Mosad Harav Kook, 1973), "Kohelet," p. 1, n 2.

30. The verbal root *halaf* also means "substitution." This substitution has to be specified: *halaf* also has the sense of entering, passing through, passing by, as well as sprouting. This substitution is not as massive and self-contained as one might imagine. It is open-ended. Transubstantiation would probably be a more appropriate term if it did not have such strong connotations.

all is changed" (Eccles.1:1). The totality (*kol*) is a passage that does not know it is, and that is why in the totality (*kol*), as in the *hevel*, there is loss and destruction. This is the world that Ecclesiastes speaks about when it describes the unending movement of generations, of the wind, of water, and of all things. "All things are in motion" (1:8). Every being in the world moves toward a point that seems to have been set for it: the rivers flow into the sea, the wind spins round and round, the sun goes west and returns from the east. It is as if each being were filled with the desire to go elsewhere, with an irresistible craving, an absolute yearning that tears it away from the place where it could stand still, from its place of fixedness: "[the sun] yearns for its place" (1:5). And this incessant motion, which the Hebraic literary text expresses to perfection, is hard to define. It cannot be said, and neither the eye nor the ear can grasp all of what it carries: "the eye is never sated with seeing, nor the ear filled with hearing" (1:8). The totality is ungraspable. A human being, a discourse, a life cannot suffice: "a man cannot speak" of the all; the all cannot be "told" or "counted" (*saper* denotes both). The truth of the whole evades us. Even if all the streams flow into the sea, "the sea is never full" (1:7), and the waters return whence they came. Who can say what is before and what is after? "There is no recollection for the first ones nor for those who will come after them" (1:11).

The world is a creation beyond the totality, an exodus beyond the all. In this sense, totality, the totality of the divine Being prior to creation, is passage. Creation is the movement by which the totality forgoes itself to open to freedom and the advent of humankind. For the world, however, the totality will always be incomplete: "the sea is never full" even though all streams flow into it. And this is because the human being who perceives this totality is precisely the being who comes as an overplus to it. The totality could very well turn into a self-contained and self-sufficient entity: this is its immanent nature, its incipient tendency prior to creation. And human beings could very well perceive this aspect alone. Indeed, this is the initial movement of the human intellect and the ambition of the sciences of the nations. Humans can get caught up in nostalgia for the whole that has been dismembered and try to recreate it. This impossible enterprise has sustained empires and the quest for knowledge!

Ecclesiastes opens onto another type of wisdom when it asks the question "What is the *yitron* (the overplus, the "more," the profit) for man in all his work?" (1:3). If "all has been heard" (12:13), if the totality is self-contained, if all is driven by perpetual motion, in what way is man an overplus to the totality, and what is the usefulness of his labor? In what way does his toil "add" (*yitron*) to the world that revolves in seeming independence from and indifference to the deeds of human beings? It is not by accident that Ecclesiastes is the only book in the Bible that contains the Hebrew word *kevar*, meaning "already [done]" (1:10ff.). If everything "flows" and ceaselessly returns, where is the place of human beings, and what is the value of their deeds?

From the outset, Ecclesiastes raises the question of the "more than," of the additional (*yeter*). Passage is what makes this question possible; it is because the totality is passing that we can raise the question of the additional (*yeter*) and hence the question of man, of the very principle of man. Passage is the process of creation itself, embedded in the structure of all creatures. The problem at the origin and the problem of the origin is to make something in particular appear outside the skein of the all, to dissociate the threads from the skein of all. How to make something appear where there is the all (that is, nothing in particular)? How is the other possible? At the very beginning, the divine totality corresponded to the nonexistence of the world. The creation of the world came as an upsurge, an eclipse, and a twinkling. A being came to be that was neither expected nor even possible. This sudden appearance of the being-other, when *all* has always been there forever, because the totality precedes the origin, is possible only in the passing, in the continual slipping away of the all, in the spinning around itself of the being, out of which a particularized being (in relation to the all) emerges: the being of man (in relation to God). Creation is the movement of passing from the all to the one, from wholeness to oneness, from the universal to the particular. That is why the vocation of man's being is to become particularized and specified (*yihud*, or unification-specification), for the human arena is that of the one. It is a matter of leading the one, the unique, to appear outside the all, but also outside the many, which is the main challenge of the passage. The one must be set apart from the all, but it must also resist the multiple.

The multiple characterizes the experience of passage from wholeness to oneness. It is the moment of infinity, of the uncountable in Ecclesiastes: the abyss into which the all can sink and where the one (*yahid*) can recede, never to emerge again. Infinity is this intermediary moment on the way of the all to the one.[31] The all opens onto infinity only because it gives itself as an overplus and because it is open to particularization. There is infinity only for the one. Infinity manifests itself like an aureole around the magnificent all, like a faded, ethereal fringe through which the all forgoes itself to allow the one to appear. It is like a halo that creates a distance from the sun so

31. See Trigano, *Story of Disappeared Presence*, p. 31.

that, no longer blinded by it, we can see the real all the better. But infinity, if it is cut off from the door of the one (of the particular), is involuting, and in its abyss sinks the all. The one is the doorway to infinity, its interiority. The many is its exteriority. It is in infinity that the all is set into motion. Infinity is its reversal (the multiple). In this sense, the one is the reversal of a reversal.[32] In the one there is an echo of the primeval totality, but it has gone through the fragmentation of the all in the many.

This is why creation is the passage of God, and the divine is characterized by passage and not by the immobility of the sacred, contained within its boundaries and limits.[33] The passage of God is, therefore, a process of particularization traversing the experience of the many. Indeed, God's passage goes from the all to the one. It is the emergence of the particular, the participation, the partaking, the discernment of the "part" instead of the undifferentiation of the primeval whole. But the election of the unique that is creation is possible only by traversing the multiplicity that is the dissolution of the all and bears the mark of the all, whereas the passage bears the mark of the one. The nostalgia for the multiple is the all. And such is the basis of the natural consciousness of man. The hope for the multiple is the one, the *yihud*/unification through particularization, the effort of Israel.

I. ATTRIBUTES

The question of "attributes" arises here,[34] because it is in the passage of his attributes that God reveals himself to Israel. "YHWH passed/will pass over his face and named/will name: YHWH, YHWH, merciful (*rahum*) and compassionate God, slow to anger, abounding in/multiple of grace (*hesed*) and truth…" (Exod. 34:6).

Creation is God's departure from totality into exteriority via the multiple (which is thereby constituted). This is how his Names become many: reflections of the created world that seem to be "added on top" of his perfect, universal being like instances or particularizations of this world that philosophers

---

32. See "La Brisure des Tables," in Trigano, *New Jewish Question*, p. 167.

33. The sacred, as manifested in religion, is passage arrested and congealed. The object produced in this way is but an inert shadow of the divine, even still animated by a "spirit" (the famous "mana" of early sociological theorists).

34. This is the fundamental question of theology—that is, of religion as philosophy. See Trigano, *Forgotten Dwelling*.

regarded as erroneous and deceptive, all that the feeble intelligence of man could hope to perceive. The hermeneutics that the philosophers devised to get around the question and eliminate it had one sole purpose, and that was to recreate the whole (in the name of unity) and ward off what looked like its dismemberment.[35] Now, it is said, "this is My Name for the *olam*" (Exod. 3:15), the world of exteriority, the world of disappearance, the world of God's Names. In this world of exteriority that we qualify as the world of nature, it is as if we were moving through the land of God's Names. To refuse this journey, as philosophers have sought to do, is to negate the world and reject the challenge of the one that is lodged in it, for the procession of divine Names and their attributes is a sign of the unfolding of the being toward the one. It bears the mark of infinity, of a breaking loose from totality, to be understood in the framework of the one, not the all, for the multiplicity of attributes is the way to unity and to the particular. The divine Names can only be anthropomorphic, for they are the shape of the created world, shapes of the *olam*, of that which slips away from us and is always in motion. For this reason, they are pronounced as in a single breath. In the murmuring of the great Being, the divine Names are chanted one by one to the sound of trumpets and songs in a sky where many stars rise. The world, the very essence of the human, is this royal chariot[36] that moves in a procession toward the dwelling place of the one.

Knowing the Names has always been the privilege of men of power. Doesn't Moses ask God to see his "glory," to know his "way" (Exod. 33:13), so he will find favor in his eyes in view of his own relationship with God's "people, this nation"? These Names reveal categories of divine government of the world, the principle of control over the elements, the archetypes of power in all of the world's manifestations. The passage traverses infinity and reconciles the fragment and the one: this is the very project of power and the collectivity. It is also historically true that kings have drawn the reason for and principle of their powers from the passage of the divine attributes, placing themselves under the banner of divine authority. In fact, in its very essence, passage is the origin and nature of power.

Admittedly, from the point of view of the whole, the passage appears to reflect dissolution, absence, and lack. From this standpoint, the "divine attributes" are merely traces, hollow imprints of God in the world, and human power merely occupies the vacancy of the divine power of totality. On the

35. See "Maïmonide," in Trigano, *Forgotten Dwelling*, p. 115.
36. The *merkava* in the vision of Ezekiel.

other hand, from the point of view of the one, the passage is subtle and light, to be sure, but it is also the powerful procession of majesty into the one. That power is born out of the passage is what gives it, of course, its specificity, its uncertainty and mobility, like quicksilver, always hovering between ruin and splendor, the object of perpetual relinquishment.

Moreover, the concrete privilege of power is that of passage, the possibility of passing everywhere without meeting obstacles. All the doors suddenly open in an impression of fluidity and lightness before the man of power, who bears its legitimate signs; all distancing ceases. Everything is near and present. In spite of the recurrent precariousness and adversity, this is one of the basic attractions of power. Among human beings, the power seeks to draw presence outside the confines of absence. This is why it is accompanied by gold and pomp proclaiming glory. Power seeks to simulate the splendors of the abode of the one here and now. But this appearance cannot last, because it runs against the law of passage in which it is maintained and where all beings can ever only surge up and surprise, like creation ex nihilo, the upsurge of a "there is (*yesh*)" out of "there isn't (*me'ayin*)," without any durable, logical connection explaining the contiguity of the two.

It is in the passage that the face, the flight of presence, is maintained. It is solely in the twinkling of a star that power can be maintained. The veiling and darkening are other names for the passage, because appearance as full presence would annul the passage by placing it in the context of that which has come to be, of the primal whole. After all, isn't the one a whole that has endured the trial of passage, that has traversed it and come out?

Despite the splendor of the procession, the trial is real because, from the standpoint of the all—and as long as the one has not yet come to be—the infinity of passage is a failure and an upheaval. It is the relinquishment of the divine all that makes room for human power, which thereby harbors bits of infinity and can be exercised in the moment—a very long moment, since it is all of temporality—of passage toward the one that is the creation of the *olam*.

For this reason, the time of passage also engenders the time of the empires of history—during which the power of man is established as a substitute for divinity! It is the attribute as trace (and not as path to the one) that manifests itself in this case. The mechanisms of passage are there but misused. The trace is all humility and self-erasure, and yet it is the site where citadels are built, where the Tower of Babel is elevated as an expression of man's aspiration "to make themselves a name lest they be dispersed" (Gen. 11:4), a forgetful, substitute name in place of God's Name. Such is the first society and the first power *founded* by humanity after the deluge.

The divine veiling, the secret of the world that is a merciful hovering of benefaction, becomes the basis of strategies of a worldly power that surrounds itself in secrecy and wraps itself in mystery in order to govern by way of this distancing, which is one of its primordial devices. The surprising voiding that is the world in the divine becomes the arena of political combat, where surprise is one of the main means of attack. The light that heralds the one and contains presence becomes the absolute weapon of domination that requires that all things be perfectly visible and transparent, the better to possess them. Throughout history, this has been the ultimate dream of sun kings and police states. The privilege of passage is used to deny entry and passage in certain places that become the sole prerogative of those in power and a mechanism of control over those who are excluded.

Falling under the domination of exteriority is the risk of passage. The divine in passage can "forget" the world of the *olam* on its way to the one, but man can also "forget" the divine passage in the *olam*. In other words, the world of exteriority that surges up in infinity risks breaking free from the power that draws it to the one, to the abode of interiority. It risks "losing its soul." The world of exteriority then turns into a boundless prison. What proceeded from grace and its drama involutes in an implacable system of iron where man is consumed. The movement of passage breaks down.

Exteriority is a stage on the way to interiority. It is because it is expecting interiority that exteriority settles down for a while; it is because it is pregnant with the one that infinity leaves the all. God's attributes, also described as "measurements" (*middot*), are meaningful. They are the moment when interiority is measured by exteriority and the one by infinity.[37]

This measurement is the moment of space and place. In this sense, the attribute of attributes, the very archetype of attributes for God, is *Hamakom*, the Place. But all places and spaces are instances of passage; that is to say, contrary to appearances,[38] their very principle is one of mobility and movement. The place is the upsurge (*kom*) that stretches and swells in the distension provoked by the creational retreat and the extension of the all toward the one. Space thus bears a form of testimony to its extremities: the all and the one.

---

37. This explains, for instance, the strange undertakings of such kabbalistic tracts as *Shiur Koma* (not "the measurement of size" but the "measurement of the upsurging"), in which the author sets out, outrageously, to measure God.

38. See below.

This testimony is infinity. The places and landscapes that we *pass through* thus bear an echo of infinity.[39] All horizons are laden with the infinite, which is our primeval milieu, even if we are touching the finite, which is the limit of infinity for us. Things on earth, the realities of nature, have a finiteness on the verge of implosion, for they are but points of departure toward what infinitely exceeds them: road markers indicating the passage and the way.

From this standpoint, the land of Israel, its geographical and physical horizon, to which Abraham is summoned and which is a key element in the covenant,[40] is an essential crossroad in the passage of the being. The place that swells in infinity is the locus of all things on earth and in life; it is their organizing principle. The place and space dimension in power is therefore fundamental, but probably not (in terms of principles, as Max Weber thought) in the sense of "territory" and exclusion, because space in this case is a perpetual passage.

The history of Israel illustrates this: Here is a people in passage over its land without this land's ever ceasing to be its over the centuries, a land that has been, moreover, the *passage obligé* of all the empires in history, the place where the empire knows that it is but a passenger with a short life, where it strives to prove its everlasting nature and regularly fails in this enterprise. Once again, space can be misused, as when human powers congeal the spatiality of infinity for their own purposes. Space then becomes boundary and exclusion, obstacle and conflict, the (misdirected) principle of the organization of power.

The attributes serve only to testify to the passage that is the being—that is, to act as the link between the all and the one, and not leave human beings in the abyss of expanding infinity. To put it otherwise, the attributes bespeak man, creation, creatures, and places. They are therefore necessarily "anthropomorphic," and this anthropomorphism is not, as we have seen with philosophy, a concession to the limits of human understanding, because "the Torah speaks the language of men."[41] This is the standpoint not of the one but of the all (and ultimately of "science"), in which infinity is perverted. The attributes can only be anthropomorphic and God can only be measured against the world, since this is the moment that is in question. Man is born and is at one[42] with the passage of God. This is even the locus of the *guf* that

39. This explains the uncanny impressions of déjà vu, of recollecting a place that one has never seen before.

40. See below, "The Openness of Levitical Space: The Land," pp. 304–324.

41. See "Maïmonide," in Trigano, *Forgotten Dwelling*, p. 115.

42. *Faire corps*, the expression used in French, literally means "to make (one) body."

designates physical existence, not the "body"[43] but the "volume" created by the distension of the all.

Contemplating the attributes is tantamount to studying the world. And this contemplation reaches its limit in the experience of power, which confronts the essential trial of passage, the place where the passage narrows, where the passenger loses mobility. This is the ultimate human experience, because it is that of divine creation, the main mode of which is passage. Hence, power is the mooring point of the fluidity of passage—that is to say, the point at which everything can be overturned and infinity can be left stranded in the finite. It is the highest and lowest point of infinity. Everything is always in passage, but there is a point of balance or imbalance in this movement, and this is the experience of power.

All of the misguided ways in which human power can misuse creational power basically boil down to one and the same thing: arresting the mobility of the being in order to invest oneself with the extraordinary energy that it harbors and take it away from other human beings, and arresting it at a restricted point in the universe that acts as a screen and container for this energy. This is not possible on the scale of the universe, but it is possible in the framework of kingdoms or states that apportion infinite space (the notion of *portion* is important here).[44] Hovering is turned into an iron grip, birth-giving mercy (*rahamim*) into millstones (*rehayim*, from the same root as *rehem*), the generosity of the place into the parsimonious scarcity of territory, the gift into hierarchical power, transparency of light into a method of domination, and the creational veiling into the ruse of an empire. The passing is congealed. The movement is petrified. And pyramids are built. The divine is turned into Molech (akin to *melech*, or king), who devours the children sacrificed to him as burnt offerings (Jer. 32:35). The saint shuts himself up in sacredness. A flagrant mockery of passage!

43. The Hebraic "body" is thus "transactional" and "passing."

44. In this sense, the experience of the empire takes this approach to its extreme. The empire aspires to measure up to God. The project is explicit in the story of the Tower of Babel, where the people's ambition to make a name for themselves bespoke their ambition to raise themselves to the level of the divine Name.

II. THE TEMPTATION OF FIXITY

Such is the essential trial of passage, the trial of idolatry. It is to be understood from the perspective of the all and not of the one. Idolatry is the product of the suffering (of man) of the all. For the all, the experience of passage involves the positing of the One, as if a portion of the all had been *cut off*, removed from the total count, so that it remains a promise, the promise of an *addition*, of something over and above what has already been brought together in the totality. The subtraction would secretly carry with it an addition. And the passage is this hiding of a portion of being that is already there, a portion whose concealment opens to the world and to creation a space of arising. It is this concealment, which makes and subtends infinity, that enables the world to arise (*kom*). It is in this flight of the all to the one, in this escape from the all of the one, which is one only when it escapes (because the one is not part of the all, even if it can constitute a portion thereof); it is here that the face (*panim*) appears.

Before anything else, the face is the instance of the flight of the all, laden with the promise of the one, of the presence that is not yet there but whose light shines intermittently in its traits. *Panim* is in the plural, an echo of the flight and of the promise. The face bears the power of its own dissolution, of its fall, of its unfinished flight: "his face fell" is the description given of Cain, who after Abel's murder, freezes the passage and the radiant power of the one and thinks he can run away from God (Gen. 4:5, 16). It is the beam of the scales, the sign of passage. This is why it is said, "You will not be able to see my face, for no human can see my face and live" (Exod. 33:20). Sight presupposes an object exposed to view, an exposure where all is said and revealed in exteriority. When Moses consults God, he "presents himself to the fog" (Exod. 20:18). On Sinai, "you were not seeing an image, only my voice" (Deut. 4:12).

It is a matter not so much of God's being (which would be invisible in its essence) but of the gaze of man upon God. If a human being, whose very being is passage, were to see God (who is passage), he would set himself outside the passage; by his very gaze, which implies an arrest and a stable position, he'd become an obstacle that the passage would inevitably break. If God's face is invisible, it is due not to God but to man: it is to safeguard human beings in their contact with the divine. Isn't it also written that Moses "gazed at the image of Yнwн" (Num. 12:8)? So Moses saw "something," beyond the prohibition "you shall not make an image" (Deut. 5:8), and no doubt because this gaze was initially prohibited. A time comes in the passage when the sight of the divine, of the divine face, is possible. It had always been possible in the framework of the one, but in the uncompleted infinite, still so powerfully laden with the all, this sight was impossible and would no doubt have been deadly. It is in the assumption of infinity, under the one, inside, that the face is revealed, but then it is something other than exposure. The chariot of attributes that passes before Moses, composed of the many but moving toward the one, is thus the "image" of God-for-the-world, the *tzelem* (Gen. 1:26) in the image of which Adam was created. It is the divine face of the passage that is the world and man in the time of the *olam*.

We can see, then, why idolatry crystallized around the representation of the face in general and the divine face in particular. There is in it, admittedly, an attempt to bring out the light of the one, of the elective particular, but in stone and paint, which are forever bereft of awe and surprise! Pagan statuary and the art of icons reached summits of perfection, but such perfection is mortuary and deadly. The work of art is meant to be an instrument (*keli*) of passage, but it risks becoming a tragic simulation thereof, mired in the illusion of reality and immediacy even when it strives to subvert it. This is why art for art's sake, art as a vehicle of the sacred, derives from the practice of idolatry. Idolatry is a deviation from the path, which means that it is also an expression thereof. It aspires to passage and yet negates it by refusing to abide the trial of infinity, the long wait for the one. It obstructs the call of the Being, even as it attempts to respond to it in the quagmire of exteriority. And it lets itself be trapped in exteriority because of its haste to reach interiority. Idolatry is a fundamentally tragic thing: the more it reaches for interiority, the more mired it becomes in exteriority. Ultimately, its desire for interiority contrasts sharply with the "obscenity" of its vehicles, as does its aspiration to elevated heights with its technical stratagems. Idolatry is the experience of the tragedy of the all, dilated by infinity and fragmented in the multiple, prey to the nostalgia of origin. It is, of course, man's primal experience, the alchemical trial of his being, that generates this spontaneous reaction, that drives him to ignore the passage, to ignore the temporality of the world and the being and to try in a supreme effort to recreate this dismembered, original totality.

This temptation is inherent in the intellect (*sechel*) ("that [which is] all," *shehu hakol*). The intellect aspires to totality and to the universal. It cannot

understand the one[45] and the particular. It cannot withstand the pressure of
infinity. In it, all is calm, order, and silence. Awe is eliminated by the weight
of reason. Intellect is, of course, one facet of the divine, but this is not where
human beings dwell. It is incapable of comprehending passage and creation.
For the intellect, the attributes are all-too-human artifices created by man.
The God of the intellect is the God prior to creation, the God of the terrifying, abyssal depths over which the "breath of God" (Gen. 1:2) will come to
awaken the inanimate. The primal thinking of humankind is related to this
wisdom of the all and the universal, one where human beings and their pain,
their birth, and their freedom have no place; where the passing, the basic
movement of life, is experienced as a dereliction and not a consummation;
where the one is a travesty of its promise; and the inside is the reverse side
(the repressed, concealed side) of the outside and not its transcendence, its
milieu of election.[46] Unlike the wisdom of passage, which sees the world as a
milieu governed by depth, interiority, and volume, primal wisdom apprehends

45. It can conceive of it only as a concept, which means that it cannot comprehend it.

46. Isn't philosophy the tragic (and heroic) agent of such an approach, insofar as it
covers up the passage by the representation, the mask of the all placed over the many of
infinity? The world is held to be no more than a pale, finite representation of a different
truth, of an irremediably distant presence (the eternal Ideas) and not the movement of
emergence of the one. From its standpoint, the aim is to maintain, save, and recreate the
all, whose oneness is theoretical and immediate. For the wisdom of passage, the aim, to
the contrary, is to enable the emergence of the one, whose oneness is concrete and felt
by the multiple. It is, of course, the status of multiplicity and infinity that is in question
in these two ways of posing the issue: seen as accursed and harmful from one side, and
as blessed and productive from the other. To philosophy the world is but a shadow of
reality. It is so hollow on the inside that its only field of existence is on the outside; it is
residue and not upsurging. To the wisdom of the one, it is, on the contrary, a harbinger
of the truth, a seed-containing void, arousing awe and surprise. This is why an antitheory
of Ideas is to be seen in the passage of attributes: an antiscene to Plato's cave. Moses does
not run away from the scene before his eyes; he hides his face. The scene is not silent; it
speaks, and it is the words that pass by. The screen is not an opaque wall but an act in
itself with all the depth and relief of existence. An entire society witnesses it. The divine
attributes are anti-ideas: through them the world is a measurement of God with the *olam*,
the vehicle of divine creation, the ways and paths in/of infinity, the modality of passage.
Whereas Ideas were immobile, theoretical paradigms of which the world was but a pale
reflection, the attribute is in touch with the world. It is the flesh of life and history, the
multiple (whence the structural anthropomorphism and multiplicity). The attribute is thus
the driving force and the swirling of reality (see below, Book III, ch. 2, "God's Concealment:
The Passage of the One in His Attributes"). It is the form of the world itself, the power that
stirs its multiplicity and subtends it in the germination of the one. Similarly, the episode
where Bezalel envisions the plans of the Tabernacle (Exod. 31:1) before building it is not
to be understood in Platonic terms. It pertains to a different grasp of temporality as the
locus of the world and of human beings, immersed in the sphere of the one. From the
point of view of the one, all times coexist (see "Le temps retrouvé," in Trigano, *Story of
Disappeared Presence*, p. 244).

the world as a flat arrangement of exterior sets, like theater décor with clearly defined, cut-out contours and bodies—in other words, as a representation.

Now what's at issue in the passage is the mobility of the world. The passing pulls all beings out of fixity, and the concealment is what makes room for the movement, for the upsurging that makes the living world possible. Presence, while we are still in infinity, cannot abide exposure. This is the basic threat weighing on the passage; this is its "trial." Prey to the trying experience (from the standpoint of the all) that paradoxically constitutes it, human beings could refuse to go to the end of the road. Caught between the dissolution of the all that is the multiple and the one of which there is as yet no sign, they could be tempted to mask the passage. They could cover it with a representation that would calm the waiting and take the place not so much of the one as of the recreated whole, dressed in the colors of the one, as if the latter had already come—an all that would do without infinity and passage, and that would therefore bask in the finite, in an exteriority whose fragmented multiplicity would be subsumed in the construction of the representation of the all. This representation is the image of a God who is no more because, from this point of view, since we are already in the *olam*, in the infinity of passage, he has been dismembered! It is a mask put on the face of the deceased deity who has been abandoned by life! Creation fails when human beings seek life and their way below the threshold of the passage, disregarding it when it is the very being and structure of man and of God-for-man.

III. THE ABODE OF THE WORLD: THE FINITE
AND THE INFINITE

This world of fragmentation, loss, and multiplicity is the world of nature, which provides the most rending experience of the trial of passage. Here, in effect, is where death appears. How could it be otherwise, since space is the quintessential attribute that is manifested in the *olam*?[47] Nature actualizes the divine attributes and arises in the infinite. It is not a finite, autonomous, everlasting "thing," self-contained and complete, outside of us and offered to

---

47. Space is to be understood as that which rises up and is continually in danger of falling into the abyss, where death is lodged; space requires an ongoing effort.

exposure; it is at one with passage.[48] The procession of attributes on Mount Sinai could very well constitute a description of nature. It is in this sense that it is said, "this is my Name for the disappearance (*olam*)"; the divine Name would be the very essence of the physical reality of the world. And only human interpretation (*derash*) could raise it to existence and manifestation. There is, thus, a parallelism between the study of the divine word and the study of nature.[49] To interpret is to draw out the riches of nature, "to produce." In the passage, nature is therefore fundamentally mobile. Because it is inhabited by the void and by the Voice of the Name that is announced, all "objects" in nature are ceaselessly verging on the abyss. The entire universe stands on the brink of collapse: it is swallowed up and reborn so quickly that we do not even perceive it. It is because the attributes continue to pass on that the natural world exists. The creational will—that is to say, the will to passage—is what founds it in every instant.

The Cycle of Nature

But, more prosaically, nature also presents a mobility that reenacts the whole drama of creation. The cycle of the seasons, which contains all the cycles of nature (meteorology, hydrology, and so forth), epitomizes the mobility of nature. Why must spring follow winter, and dawn come in the wake of the night? Herein lies the greatest mystery of Being. What is usually retained in this phenomenon is a deterministic version of nature: the cycle of seasons and the recurrence of natural phenomena ad infinitum. But it ought to be seen as a sign that the world, though it collapses, arises again (*kom*), that it surges up again in the void, through this passage where the fixed loses its solidity, and yet we keep on walking. This is why nature is a field of perpetual destruction where beings wither and fade, and yet spring bursts into bloom. The partial mobility of nature across the seasons heralds a greater mobility,

48. Midrash Rabba on Ecclesiastes interprets the seven occurrences of the term *hevel* ("vanity") as indicating the elements of the seven days of creation: the heavens and the earth, the firmament, gathering the waters, the luminaries, filling the waters with life, man, and the possibility of repentance and *kappara* which redeem a transgression on the seventh day, Sabbath.

49. Science is one modality thereof, no doubt the poorest in terms of explanatory power, because it addresses only the immediacy of nature. It has an idea of the all but not of the one. However, in comparison with philosophy, which represents a movement of the all in infinity, science progresses more deeply into infinity, even if it does not attain the wisdom of the one.

that of the passage that is the natural world in infinity and that testifies to its ultimate transcendence: the "end" of nature, the end of the world, the end of disappearance in the time of the one. The cycle of seasons testifies to the fleeting character of the world as a "phenomenon," a character whose very figures are embedded in the world as an overplus. The bud bursting through the ice-hardened outer skin is a faint echo of the fact that something can "come to be" in the mute world of physical nature, that surprise is not to be discounted, as scientific determinism may suppose. Determinism is, in fact, a highly restrictive interpretation of a much vaster phenomenon. The recurrence that it selectively isolates in the mobility of nature has more to do with the logic of infinity and passage. The endless repetition of the same phenomena is like a setting afloat of the world in the fluidity of the disappearance that consumes it, thus maintaining it in its precarious existence until the time comes for boarding the era of the one. In this sense, the fact that there is a reproduction of the same phenomenon is a sign that the world is the product not of chance but of an ongoing will, the creational will that is ceaselessly renewing the world as the natural cycles go by. In a way, nature sinks and rises in every instant, because the one inhabits it and summons it to the effort of testifying. Making the effort to last so as to reach the one—this is the testimony. The being declines in the passage, but this is the condition of the being's existence, that is to say, of the passage until it has reached completion.

Hence, the cycles of nature are to be understood in the infinity of passage and not in the eternity of totality. This repetition, which is the organizing principle of the cycle of nature, is the sign of the infinite. Infinity (which is the passage, the "novelty" of passage in relation to the pristine all) is formed only from its incessant failure, from its recurring fall into the finite. In experience, it is because the finite is finite, because it ends, and the world continues anyway that we have a notion of infinity. Infinity is the universe of the negative in relation to the absolute positivity of the all. This is why the finite is the key moment in it. Why the finite? Because the departure from the all, which is the universal, carries with it a potential breakdown of the cosmos, a potential of death. The cycle of nature picks up from the fall and the decomposition in the direction of life.

The incessant return of (apparent) sameness thus evidences the being's powerful effort not to give way (in the waiting) on the verge of the other, the effort of the infinite on the verge of the one. The everlasting "return" is a breach in the everlasting oblivion that characterizes the all. It gives a taste of infinity to the all, but it is not yet the advent of the one: it is the cosmic effort (of unhinging the self) that the all makes to get closer to the one. The natural cycle is the being's effort to hold together, despite and through the passage, in view of going beyond it, in view of its potential consummation beyond its cyclical being. It is the sign in the passage of this potential consummation, of the one in its particularity. The determinist scientific interpretation of the natural cycle contains only a small element of truth, because it proceeds from the logic of the all. The cycle is read as but a repetition of sameness, whereas, in the light of the one, it figures as the drama of a departure from sameness, not the sign of the mutism and self-absence of nature but rather something like the jerking movements of a cripple trying to stand up, to show that he is alive, and to participate in the passage and in the wait for its accomplishment. The cyclical character of natural phenomena carries the gasping breath of passage at the heart of exteriority to the most impenetrable recesses of the movement of life: at the bottom of the void, it testifies to the quivering that grips the being in its movement from the all to the one. This is why the natural cycle heralds the one, the living world, a structure of astonishment, and not the petrified corpse of the all, of the "all has already been said." This is how we can explain the existence in the world of the possibility of something random and unpredictable coming to pass that would overturn the natural order.

The whole project of passage is to perpetuate and repeat itself, to lift itself up and keep going until the time of the one. This is because there is a risk at every moment of being swallowed up. Creation is an exclusively transitory, incomplete world, and it is because the being aspires to the one that there is incompletion and transience. The project of creation, then, is to prevent the perishable from engulfing the passing being; this is a project of duration and time. Time exists only as a waiting for the one, as its germination. Time is the measurement of passage. It is the chronicle of the struggle between the finite and the infinite, between passage and the all in the horizon of the one. It is the dehiscence of the all that engenders time, that spawns the *olam*/ world, and space is nothing but the punctuation of passing time. Space is the instant of infinity, the bursting forth of the unfinished in the all, the displacement of the all toward the one, the vehicle of the one, the link between the infinite and the finite. Space transcribes time passing (invisibly) by through its cycles and movements or the movement to which it gives rise. Death and birth are there, along with all the key experiences of time. Temporal rhythm is but a succession of ends of time, the fall and the recoveries. We can feel the whole drama of the world in each passing instant, and the instants pass one by one, for time is pregnant with the one.

The cadences of passage that we have noted in the succession of attributes,[50] of periods in the natural cycle, or of generations stem from the effort of the all to raise itself to the level of the one (this explains the reason for the attributes), in the same way as a man making a physical effort will alternate between tensing his muscles and relaxing them to regain strength and oxygen. Efforts always involve fits and starts. This is the principle of passage. From the perspective of *hevel*, of passage, Ecclesiastes centrally insists on *amal*, or labor: "What profit does man have from all his labor beneath the sun?" (Eccles. 1:3). What is the meaning of man's life on earth, marked by the succession of time ("For everything, a time and a period, for each thing under the heaven, a time to be born, a time to die" [3:1–2]) and the experience of having to resume the work again and again, so that one wonders what's the use? Here is a moment of wisdom, enthralled by the dissolution of infinity and the ineluctable death in the passage, and possible precisely because there is a project of life! Time is synonymous with the effort to keep up to the level of the one in this dehiscence of the all (the life facet), the effort of the all in infinity to reach the one (an experience of death for the all), but it can also engender morbid regression for the being who turns away from the one and aspires to the all that is dying in the passage.

The Cycle of Generation

The fitfulness of the passage is the structure of passing time: the revelation of the attributes, nature's cycle, the generation of human beings. It is no doubt laughter that best represents this experience of time: it reaches deep down into man and comes bursting out of his inner depths. Laughter touches man's innermost depths in a movement that goes down to the bottom and gushes back up to its heights. This accounts for the fitful tone and shaking of laughter, which is an ecstatic experience in which the being shines forth.

---

50. Succession is an important term here, because it points to erasures and substitutions following from and giving way to one another. Time exists not because there is a substitution of being (of man to God), but because there is an opening of the being to another being. And time lasts as long as this other being has not appeared. At every instant, it breaks down and rises again from its ashes.

In the moment of this outburst, there is not one iota of death in man, not one area of numbness. The being is radiant incandescence. Situations of laughter are those in which the stable world of everyday life, the confidence that the world stands on solid ground, is shaken. It is the experience of the void, of the *olam* in the fullness. This is why the biblical text uses the verb "laugh" to refer to sexual relations, especially in speaking of the patriarchs and matriarchs (Abimelech saw "Isaac making Rebecca, his wife, laugh," Gen. 26:8); it is also why one son was named for laughter—"Isaac," meaning "he will laugh," for "Sarah laughed in her bosom" (18:12). Here, generating and engendering are of the same nature as the action of passage. It is the very process of the world and of creation that is repeated between a man and a woman, the process going from the all to the one, through the spasmodic and ultimately odd, comical game of sexual relations. The sexual act (the "laughter") is the time of the secret of the world: "the way of man through the young woman (*alma*)" (Prov. 30:19), both of whom are the unique Adam. It is the passage in man that created woman, but in the biblical narration of Eve's creation, the woman is the passage, the echo of the passage in which man was created. In the proximity of the "little death" of pleasure and the insemination with new life, sexual relations repeat the gesture of creation (and, in this sense, the Talmud can say that God is always present with a man and woman in procreation).

This is why the passage harbors more meaning as it is played out in human life than in nature and its cycle or even in the attributes. It is the phenomenon of generation that gives shape to the passage in (of) the human. Every forty years, "a generation goes, a generation comes, and the earth exists for disappearance" (Eccles. 1:4). Such is the abode of humanity in the world! The Hebraic term for generation, *dor*, also means dwelling place (*dur, dar*). A generation is all the lodgers (*dayarim*) of the earth who live in the same period. This suggests, no doubt, the idea that humankind abides in the interiority of an abode, but also that this abode is essentially and structurally passing. In the world of the *olam*, we have no "dwelling place" as such; it is the *olam*, or rather, the disappearance that is this dwelling place, because this disappearance, the passage of generations, is what leads us into the dwelling of the one, and only the one is a dwelling. Such is our dwelling in the world! Its walls lack the fixity of stone, and its paneling is woven from the breath of passage. The layout of the rooms changes with every step, and no plumb line can determine an imperturbable vertical direction therein. What we build there collapses, and with the ruins we construct new houses.

The circle of generations is one of the most powerful and violent experiences in human life, an astonishing process that cyclically depopulates the world, making it a wasteland where life goes on nonetheless. A generation comes, strains to build its abode, reaches a high level of balance, struggles up to the summit, and passes away. And everything has to start all over again. This is even more patent in the collective experience, with the need to once again, with each new generation, achieve the unity, cohesion, and consensus conquered by the preceding generation. How can a collectivity maintain its identity when it is cyclically dying? Isn't this the essential problem of the collective and of the political? How does a society persist, in practical terms, in this perpetual, disorderly flux? How does it withstand its incessant disappearance into the abyss of time? The problem resembles that of the passage of attributes: how does the being of God subsist in his creational retreat and passage? How is the one not lost in it?

The basic experience of the generations is that of the absence inhabiting presence, and one could say that the passage of generations is the effort of humanity, which is ceaselessly drawn into the void of the abyss, to maintain itself on the level of the one, in its wait for presence. Humanity is this very effort, because humanity is the absolute name of passage; it is at one with the passage of the attributes, or the extension of created physical "nature." It is in the dehiscence of the all and inhabits the space left by the all—that is to say, the void. In sum, it is in infinity.

The fact that humankind cannot be truly and precisely counted and inventoried is a sign of this. Ceaselessly swallowed up by the finitude of death, by nothingness, it is incessantly pulling itself together. Is this why there is "nothing new beneath the sun"? (Eccles. 1:9). Through generations, isn't one occupying the same place with the same presence, beyond the recurring death?

The succession of generations, unlike the succession of attributes (each different but all bound up with the divine being) and unlike nature's cycles (all of which adhere to the regularity of natural laws), raises the question of the specificity and unique value of each generation in relation to all of humanity, past and future. Is a generation to be regarded as the interchangeable figure of the same humanity that is always there, always the same since the beginning? This question, which is inherent in human self-consciousness, shows the extraordinary specificity of humanity in the passage. The question mainly concerns the individual. Am I here, in this generation, only as a *replacement* for my father, or am I here because there had to be a time when I and no one else would come to be? Does a generation have an intrinsic value, or does it have only the standard value of humanity in its endeavor to maintain itself at the level of the one during the time of its passage?

This question is important because in it we can hear the echo of the one, of the particular in the infinite that designates the human being as the bearer of the vocation of the one in infinity. Indeed, in the problematics of the infinite, the return of generations may very well be never ending. In this case, the void of infinity would be a bottomless pit opened in the side of the all. There would be no "repetition," the effort that transcends dereliction and the end. The return of repetition and the "natural order" indicate, to the contrary, that the universe has a purpose and creation a direction (the one).

Finiteness in Passage

What is it, then, that comes back gradually over generations? Is it the same humanity from the origin, transcending its disappearance across the unfurling wave of generations, the forward surging of the crest and the receding motion of the deep that make a wave? We take the place of our lost ancestors, and we represent them until the time when the one will be possible. In this case, we would each be but the envelope of the first man. Is this what tradition is telling us when it says that all Jews throughout time were present at the revelation at Sinai,[51] when we know that six hundred thousand Hebrews were gathered there? Tradition draws from this the necessity for this number to gather together for there to be a Jewish "community," which is a dwelling for the divine presence on earth. Knowing that the demography of Israel has changed since Sinai, the classical interpretation sees a decline in Israel's spiritual strength and maintains that it now takes fourteen million people to find six hundred thousand genuine Jewish souls. According to this outlook, there would be a specified number of souls, a collective number, regardless of the individuals or the actual number at any time. But there could be another approach, one in which the vocation of the time of infinity would be to drain the primal void, to exhaust it through the souls of individuals. This, then, would be the role of humanity: to transform the void into souls (*nefesh*), to bring absence to presence, because humanity inhabits the space left by the all, that is, by the infinite void, and to bring out the one, this void must be exhausted. The souls of individuals exhaust it one by one; it is the one that has to appear and in the multiplicity (since it is in the infinite) until all of

51. This is restated every year in the Passover Haggada when each reader is deemed to have personally left Egypt.

the void is humanized and internalized, until absence is returned to presence, until the cosmos becomes the man it promises to be and the embryo that is the world is born to the child it has the potential to be in the passage.

The birth of souls on earth would be this jolting movement of time that we have seen at work elsewhere. The most urgent task of humanity would thus be to give birth to children so as to bring the moment of the one closer and leave nothing concealed in the *olam*. In other words, in the succession of generations and the flow of time, a progression would be accomplished: the exhaustion of infinity, the fulfillment of passage. And death (the finitude that passes souls one by one from the infinite reservoir through the narrow eye of its needle) would be its paradoxical architect. The more generations that succeeded one another in the world, the closer we would be to the one. This supposes that humanity, which is the being of passage, corresponds to a set, finite number from the origin, which is up to us to bring into existence. The souls that must be given access to their multiplicity in infinity, to their birth in the *olam*, come from the closed, fixed world of the all. Whereas in the all, they are tallied as a closed whole, they multiply in infinity, but this condition is transient. So as not to lose themselves in the *olam* of infinity, they must tear themselves from the retrograde nostalgia for the all and desire the one. It is because there is a set tally that there is finitude in the midst of infinity. This is what makes it possible to subdue infinity and prevent it from spreading endlessly.

Logically, this is the way infinity can be suspended before the one. In this sense also, death is the architect of infinity. In a certain sense, the finite that subsists in the infinite is a perpetuation of the all, so that it would be the work of the all in infinity (or of infinity in the all) to produce the one. What would make for the regularity and structure of infinity (basically, its narrowing prism) would be the residue of the logic of the all in infinity. Two interpretations are possible: either this residual logic prepares the one, or infinity actively struggles to break away from this logic to render the one possible.

The issues that this question raises are as follows: Why, in the passage and the infinity that implement the destructuring of the all, would there be a set number of attributes, a determined number of natural laws, and a lim-ited number of generations?[52] Why is there finiteness in infinity? And what does this mean with regard to the one, and to the relations of the all and

---

52. This may not be as clear-cut as in the first two cases, but it is a hypothesis that could be posited by analogy.

the one? We see here once again what we have already found—namely, that the one is not the opposite of the all but the result of the work of infinity in the all, in the universal. The one is the universality of the all traversed by the infinite and the multiple; God the creator passes from the all to the one: the announcement of the unity of God is the announcement of the advent of humanity, and it comes to be through the multiplicity of attributes.

Nevertheless, the question of a set number of generations of human-ity—or, to put it otherwise, the possibility that the advent of the one will bring an end to time—poses a manifest problem. Out of the three vortexes of passage that we have numbered—God, nature, and humanity—the latter is the only one that remains "incomplete" and uncertain in the passage itself. For nature, it is self-evident. For God, it is understood, since the attributes concern only God-in-passage, God the creator. But what about the reckon-ing for man? Is there a set number for humankind, an end of time, where the human would come to an end in a certain way, by reaching the one, the other side of the *olam*?

Doesn't the time of the human last no longer than the time of the pas-sage in which it rises? This question evidences the power of infinity in the human, which manifests itself in the apparent absence of laws as regular as nature's. The milieu of the human seems to be marked by the absence of implacable norms and rules. The finite in the infinity of the human is formless and malleable, vague and disputable, yet it is very real. It has to be shaped by man in order to appear and yet, even then, men disagree on it. This is what makes man the being of infinity, the being who experiences most deeply the drama of infinity in the passage. Unlike nature or the creator, man can lose himself and be destroyed in the passage. This is because the all is not as strong in his being, which is basically governed by the one. The experience of the passage is for him, firstly and immediately, an experience of undifferentiation. "What has been is what will be"; "No memory remains of the earlier ones and none of the later ones" (Eccles. 1:9, 11).

IV. THE UNDIFFERENTIATED AND THE
SUFFERING FROM INFINITY

These generations follow one another to the rhythm of the fleeting, fragile experience of life. They erase the remnants and memory of preceding gen-erations, and empty themselves out to make room for those who will follow them and about whom they know nothing. This never-ending flood of waves rising, falling, and returning causes each human being to lose a sense of his own being, of his own individual uniqueness. The particular appears like a wisp of straw in the turbulence of infinity, in the spinning whirlpool of the passage. To what extent do we lose ourselves in our lives? Birth and death, the very frame of the generation, are limit experiences in vanity, in the transience of the particular self, of individuality. And this experience is found at the acme of generation (the generational being)—that is to say, in sexuality.

The sexual act brings together all of these traits. The act itself brings individuals to a state of impersonality, in which they lose control over their consciousness and their selves. Indeed, sex is a powerful experience in passing: the passing from one sex to another of the generative seed, the passing from one's original family to a new one, and from the nothingness of the child to his birth. All of the world's passage coalesces in the act of sex, for the sexual relationship is the narrow path of the cycle of generations—that is to say, of the passage for the order of the human, which is not the case for nature or for God. There is, then, in sexuality something that is in unison with the laws of nature and the procession of divine attributes. No doubt, this is why, just as Moses covers his face before the triumphant, grandiose passage of the divine attributes, the sexual act must be "hidden." Sexuality constitutes a limit experience for the human species, in which the individual paroxysmally pushes himself to the limit and then disappears in the march of the species. On its shore individuality runs aground and dies, the individuality of men and women driven by an irrepressible desire, the expression of the impetuosity of passage that leads to the one but can also get caught in a whirlpool that brings it back to the all.

The three key moments of generation (birth, sexuality, and death) bear the imprint of the undifferentiated: they are times when the passing itself is omnipresent and predominates more than what passes. Are we to see in these moments, as we've seen in nature, the echo of the all in infinity—that is to say, the dimension of finitude and of natural "laws" that exist in humanity? This would be paradoxical inasmuch as these are precisely the moments when human beings open to the other! What appears more clearly here is that the finite helps to mark out the path to the one that opens to the dehiscence of the all through infinity. To these moments must be added the activities without which man cannot maintain himself in the passage, because of the consuming and eroding dynamics that inform it at bottom—namely, the activities involved in feeding oneself and in toil (*amal*) in general. Without these, the passage would no longer be possible, and humans could not withstand the disappearance that would engulf them. In the short run, feeding oneself is the main ongoing human activity: eating the world to maintain oneself in the world, swallowing to withstand the swallowing that characterizes the world of disappearance, in unison with its basic dynamics. Eating is what enables the being to stay on the level of the *olam*. It is an essentially "metaphysical" and not directly biological function; it is the structure of the *olam* that induces eating as a cosmic act. At the summit of Sinai, during the time of presence that expands and disappears (while ordinary time continues at its foot, and the people grow impatient), Moses does not eat, and yet he does not die. The light of revelation feeds him for forty days and forty nights! He is the guest at the messianic banquet of the one. In a similar vein, the manna that the Hebrews eat in the desert produces no waste and no residue in the organism.

But effort is the absolute category of self-nurturing and being in this world. This is because effort alone is what allows human beings to stand in the fluence of the passage in order to draw (*derash*) out of the void and out of nature the means of subsistence that they need to sustain them, to engender, to be born and to die, to raise children, and to act in the world. All is work, experience of the void of passage, of the gap between the particular consciousness of the self and the "presence" and the world/*olam* of emptiness, depersonalization, and alienation. Work is a pure experience in passage, a time of absence from the self, of the eclipse of the individual, of disappearance; and its end purpose—namely, the construction of a place in the world—is continually being called into question. "What is the 'more' of labor?" In this sense, work is the act of withstanding in the world of passage; it is the incessant effort that the irresistible fluidity of the world renders necessary, the effort to draw exteriority out of disappearance, in pursuit of the one. But it is also the place where the human experience of the *olam* is revealed, which is fundamentally the experience of the undifferentiated. Confronted with infinity, with the perpetual task of starting over with each new coming generation, human consciousness loses itself in the world, and memory fades; the uniqueness of each event tends to wear away, drowned in the rhythm of passage, in the apparent Sisyphean circularity of time. Everything in our being reflects this anxiety, the anxiety in the face of the undifferentiated, at being lost in the abyss of the world. Isn't the very thought that grasps this situation an experience of the undifferentiated? When we call things to mind, when we represent them, aren't we effecting a passage by substituting concepts and words for things and reality? Thinking enacts a process of transfer, a shift that brings the world back into the circuit of fluidity. It is, in sum, a *lieu-tenance*, a "place-holding" of the *olam*—what holds the place of *olam*, but also what replaces it. It is not a human failing to know the real world only through words, representations, ideas, and metaphors. To the contrary, it is the only possible way of knowing the world, which is in total harmony with the nature of the world. Thought and the world are of one and the same nature. In God, the world/*olam* is like a thought. These representations have a spontaneous social, collective, and even historical dimension, and even though they are forged in the mind of the individual, their particularization is an illusion. When individuals think, they join the infinity of disappearance that is the world of passage. They no longer belong to themselves; and their names as individuals, their particularities, lose all meaning and substance. This experience in meditation, which is a self-effacement in infinity, can take two directions. First, the direction of the concept, of conceptual thought in its attempt to grasp the multiple as a category of the all and the universal, but which, by its very nature, lasts only a short time,[53] like everything that aspires to fixity and lastingness in the passage as long as the passage has not been consummated. The second direction is that of the metaphor, of a different type of thought that accompanies the passage with an eye not to the all but to the one. The prototype of this path is prophecy. One of the characteristics of human thought is its inability to grasp the multiple in infinity, just as we can never grasp the world totally, because nothing is ever the same: "Three are miraculous, and four I do not know: the way of an eagle in the sky, the way of a snake upon a rock, the way of a ship at sea, and the way of a man in the maiden (*alma*)" (Prov. 30:18). And so we cannot really grasp human-ity, peoplehood, the collectivity, or the divine. It is always by the agency of the all, that is, of the negation of infinity and hence of *olam*, the locus of the human, that people have catastrophically tried to apprehend them. From the perspective of the all, every being of passage vanishes.

It is something of this that is manifested by the face, which always escapes our grasp. This is the limit site of exteriority, the place where exteriority should cease and offer us respite in the universe but where presence continues to escape our grasp. The face bears the memory of the flight of presence. In it, there is a poignant element of absence. Even the eyes that gaze seem to "see" nothing at all. One of the great mysteries of human life is that for the eye that tries to seize the universe, there is a front and a back: I cannot see

53. There has been such a depressing succession of philosophical systems that today it is the very possibility of such a system that has collapsed.

behind me, and it is as if the nape of my neck presents no interest from the standpoint of presence. That there is a front and a back for human beings evidences the extent to which the face harbors the flight from the all to the one, a backward-moving flight because the face that is born in infinity gazes in the direction of the all. Through this gaze, the face spontaneously and naturally bears a passion and nostalgia for the all, whereas the unexposed nape of the neck, hidden in the rear under the hair, bears a proximity to the one. Thus it is said of Israel that it is "stiff-necked" (Exod. 32:9), and this is a compliment, because the gaze is turned forward, but the presence gathers behind. This is why Moses hides his face to see God pass, and all he can see of God is his "back" (33:23)—that is, the attributes that carry the one. It is as if his face had turned into a head of hair in the contemplation of the one God. Turned toward the one, the face "hides" and becomes hair; this is the experience of the nape. Thus, the one is revealed not in the aesthetic majesty of the horizon but in the bushiness of the hair or the shrub (3:2), which is, nonetheless, bright and incandescent.

It is on the threshold of the face that we feel the absence, strangeness, and exteriority of the world most powerfully. Here lies the most intensely poignant experience of the human being lost in the infinity of passage and seeking, at the cost of his life, a spark of presence where he can feel at home. Confronted with the gigantic passage that is being, does my face—what makes me more than anything else—exist only in the world of exteriority? Doesn't my face disappear in death? At the start, representation was an attempt to counter this difficult truth, in the form of a death mask, a cast of the dead person's face used to cover it for public display. Death is the dissolution of the face, the point when it returns to the passage and is put back into the game. In this respect, the actor probably has a greater experience of death than most people. In sum, the face, the only thing in nature that breathes from a vibration of presence, appears only because the passage of the being traverses the world of exteriority. Will I disappear one day altogether, in accordance with the law of passage, engulfed by the fathomless abyss of infinity? Will the multiplicity of faces of humanity in the passage experience the same fate as the stars that shine for a while and then vanish into the infinity of the sky, whose death is their only presence? So, in addition to the creational problematic, the *olam* involves a consumptive dimension that accounts for most of human suffering and everyday life, and against which human beings struggle with all their might or yield. One of the most powerful experiences of passage is that of loss: loss of personality, of the specific uniqueness of the subject; loss of the individual's name, which seems to return to the abstract, undifferentiated logic of the species where, in the multiplicity of individuals, the particularity of each person is submerged, annihilated, annulled, or where, in the worst of cases, it returns to the logic of nature and the world, in which the particularity of the self has no greater meaning, substance, or value than the smallest stone. What prevails in this powerful experience of passage is the sense of the impersonal, the neutral, the absence of differentiation, and of the elective problematic of individuals.

Human beings can indeed get lost in the "sea" of infinity. A fundamental question arises: Is death an absolute disappearance of the person? But that is not, in fact, the real question, for death is a phenomenon of passage of generations; it is the reemergence of the void in the unfinished tally of humankind. In this symbolical sense of death, we can say that there are dead people in life, people who are still alive and whose physical death is but an epiphenomenon. The real question is as follows: Can the paths of human beings, of individualities, be totally lost? Can the experience of the undifferentiated be totally accomplished and the undifferentiated be more than an immediate trial to endure? Can human beings really be annihilated? Can parts of humanity be lost in the passage? The question is even more far-reaching: If the archetype of passage is the passage of attributes, can attributes or parts of nature-in-passage be lost in passing? Or, to put it still otherwise, can the passage not lead to the one?

The infinite's power of being is such that our answer can only be that this is indeed possible. The passage cannot be dissociated from the trial of passage. Infinity is a moment in the suspension of the all, the boundless interspace that opens the all to creation. Only true infinity can open the all to creation; only infinity can counter the all. So there is a moment when there is really a void in the all with an unfathomable bottom, a void as cosmic and universal as the all. This is the milieu that creates the passage and that the passage creates, and in which the passage can therefore lose itself: nature can die entropically, the attributes cannot unite,[54] and humanity can vanish.

Total death? Even though one never dies totally in infinity (since the finite is suspended), the infinite is so immense that the disappearance in its midst is tantamount to death, all the more so insofar as infinity ceases when the one is revealed. Infinity is an absolute hiatus in the all; it is the condition of possibility for passage. And the culmination of the passage, the access to the one, is a departure from infinity, the fruit of infinity but also

54. This is why the liturgy celebrates the people of Israel, who "unify his Name, evening and morning."

the separation from it. The passage is passage to the one, but the one is a leap (*pasah*) out of infinity. Leaving infinity is comparable not so much to climbing a mountain step by step until one reaches the summit as to docking a boat on the riverbank. The same type of relationship exists between the one and the infinite as between infinity and the all. It is important to understand that infinity is a moment of absolute suspension, and whatever cannot (with)stand this suspension can, in fact, disappear in it. The infinite is thus necessarily, in the immediate, a moment of indetermination and undifferentiation. In infinity there is nothing but movements, of species and of the void, and there is very little if any individuation and particularization. What prevails there are entities (humanity and so forth). The particular is the promise of the one. It is the fate of all humankind that is fundamentally in question there.

The elective adventure of the one comes to crown a trial that not everyone successfully completes. The elements of the all in their journey through infinity face the danger of losing everything. A happy ending is by no means guaranteed in this passage where absolutely everything is at risk. The "reality" here and now of souls, a reality that can be counted, is in the all. Infinity is but a fleeting passage for souls, which they must leave one by one, and where they can get lost on the way.

The moment of passage, then, is necessarily a moment of indetermination and undifferentiation. This is readily understandable, because the vocation of infinity is to circumvent the all, to surround it everywhere from within itself. Yet despite the adversity of the experience, indetermination plays a "positive" role on the road to the one, because it breaks the absolute fullness of the all, its absolute control, its narcissistic and solipsistic contemplation, and it opens onto the process of the world's creation.

Suffering is what characterizes the infinite that does not yet fully realize that the one is impending in it, and which, for this reason, stands in the framework of the all, from the standpoint of which it constitutes a dismemberment and dissolution of identity. The suffering from infinity expresses this experience, like a sinking into the abyss, because the all is not aware that the one is in gestation in it: indetermination is even the ploy, the veil that hides the finality of its dismemberment, of its half-openness, without which the one would not be born. Such is the finality of the concealment of God.

In fact, in the framework of totality, which is the other name for identity, for the ebbing of the undifferentiated, there is no possible overplus: "What overplus is there for man in all his work?" (Eccles. 1:3). But if the question of the indeterminate comes up in infinity, it is possible only from the perspective of the one. Only through a particular individual's suffering can the one be sensed; only the individual catches a glimpse of the horizon of the one while knowing the impossibility of attaining it here and now. It is here that the mind experiences the reality of passage and infinity: it is not given to the individual to reach the time of the one by himself, independently of the whole of humanity. Individuals can, to be sure, conceive of it; they can know it, but they cannot attain it, because the rest of their generation (the generational *"esprit de corps" oblige!*)[55] is completely unaware of it and still far from it. This gap between the individual's time (the time of the one) and collective time (the time of the all to move toward the one) designates the necessary temporality of passage and infinity.

The passage moves forward step by step. There is no way of bypassing the time needed for germination, even if the dry, buried seed knows in all its wisdom that it bears the flower that will emerge, to the open air and the sun. The one is not possible as long as the passage has not matured enough in infinity, which confirms the collective character of the passage. The passage is there only for the species as a whole. In the experience of the indeterminate that we have, we can detect the project of the one only from the perspective of the one, not from that of the declining all. This is the very experience of the generational being. Each generation accumulates achievements that will serve the generations that follow, so that the more we progress through time, the greater the knowledge and power of human beings. But each one is duty bound to accomplish its task, at the point in time where it is situated, the task that the evolution of humanity imposes upon it even if it has the ability to envisage the landscape of a consummation.

This vision of consummation can only be prophetic, since even the prophet cannot reach it from where he is and can do no more than he does. Similarly, before being able to draw maps based on satellite photos, the very possibility of plotting a map had to be envisioned in the Middle Ages. Even if a medieval scientist had grasped the notion of the earth's roundness, he would not have been able to produce a cartographic reproduction thereof. There is, then, an insurmountable period of time that it takes for the passage to make the one possible, a period during which the world becomes more fluid and abstract in its movement toward the one. This is what is at stake in the generation.

The vision of the one is what makes life worthwhile, and all individuals who glimpse it seek to reduce the distance and alienation within. But from

---

55. It is the entire generation, the *dor*, that "dwells" in the abode of the world.

searching too much, they can die and lose the one, because they ineluctably forget to engender. Procreation will seem like an obstacle to such people when, in fact, it brings them to the one, not through self-contemplation but through self-relinquishment, selflessness, passage, giving, and infinitization. They will end up cutting themselves off from the effort of humankind to rise to the level of the one, through *amal*, begetting children, productive work, and everything that draws us structurally and genetically closer to the one but individually puts us at a distance from it, alienates us, deprives us of the contemplation of presence. The experience of absence is the experience of the tension between the end of time and now, between the one and the infinite, between the collective and the individual. It is the experience of the conflict that arises between them while waiting for presence to come. Absence raises the question of the future, and this is where suffering from indetermination takes hold from the perspective of the one.

V. THE PATHS OF THE WORLD

The suffering in the passage and the anxiety of the being in infinity are signs of a movement and structure that is heading to the one. The echo of the finite can be heard in this structure, which is not solid but labile, a structure that resembles deep-sea carrier currents animated by a strict regularity in the swirling of an infinite ocean. This anxiety compels the *nefesh* to leave the undifferentiation of infinity and seek out the paths of the one. "From the straits did I call Yhwh, and he answered me in the expansiveness of Yhwh" (Ps. 118:5). The narrowness in the infinite is the principle underlying the laws of infinity that, by their very (finite) nature, bear the mark of lack and scarcity (the cycle of seasons, of natural aging, of the presence and eclipse of God, and so on).

What is there to say about the laws that govern access to the one in the passage? The moderns have pointed to a principle of lack that is systematically at work in human beings, and they have built a system of laws around it (in terms of alienation, the unconscious, and so on), but unlike natural laws, there is, significantly, no consensus about these laws. If we take into account humanity as a whole, notably in terms of the generational problematic, we cannot help but observe an overriding principle of differentiation and particularization at work: the principle of peoples, or, if you prefer, the national principle. Indeed, the human species organizes itself unit by unit,

and in the context of these units the generational experience takes place.
What is human is not experienced in immediacy, just as it does not gain
access to the world spontaneously; it does so through the prism of belonging
to a people, and this is a cultural prism but also a practical, economic, and
technical one. The world of nature can be grasped only through the filter of
an affiliation with a people, a collectivity that belongs to the human species
but is distinct from it. In the national principle, then, there is a principle of
essential differentiation at work that structures the human according to a law
of scarcity. There would be a set number of collectivities and no more, with
each people forging its unity by excluding that which doesn't belong to it.
There is, of course, no agreement on how many peoples there could be on
earth, but apparently the number cannot increase ad infinitum. There is even
reason to believe that the overwhelming majority of peoples were formed
by the end of the twentieth century, even if some "artificial" peoples have
states and some "real" peoples are scattered over several states. The national
principle does not necessarily coincide with the state prism, although the latter constitutes a decisive moment in its organization. When Jewish tradition
speaks of seventy nations on earth, plus Israel (and organizes the Sanhedrin,
its key political expression, on the basis of this number),[56] it seems to be
expressing this idea of human "laws," following the example of the laws of
nature or of the expansion of the *sefirot*; that there are seventy nations, plus
Israel, and no more.

The organization of the human must pass through this matrix or disappear. This is the narrow strait in the universality of humankind. Just as a
certain number of attributes run through infinity, so a certain number of
laws govern nature, and a certain number of peoples "structure" humanity.
The people, the attribute, and natural law can be read as a dimension of the
divine in the passage, a figure of the infinite. Similarly, the same tradition
tells us that the seventy nations have seventy patron angels who crystallize
their essence in infinity.[57] The Hebrew term designating these nations, *umot
ha'olam*, becomes clear to us in this regard: the "nations (or rather the 'mothers') of the *olam* of disappearance." The nations are in disappearance; they are
wombs of disappearance (in relation to the whole of humanity). But also (by
their wombing side), they are the fixed point, a vector, that remains in the

---

56. Each member of the Sanhedrin was to know the language and culture of one of
the seventy nations and represent it in this arena, the expression of Israel's particularity.

57. Infinity as an "angelic" sphere, the sphere of angels born of God's passage to the one.

labile and fleeting disappearance: generations die and are reborn; humanity is remote and evanescent, but nations remain.

There is, then, an elective principle of particularization already at work in the seventy nations of the *olam*. What is interesting in the principle of nationality in peoples is that everything in life and every generation develops unit by unit, society by society. We are born within a people, not within humanity. In this concert of nations, special mention should be made of Israel. That the tradition designates Israel as coming in addition to the seventy nations incites us to do so. In fact, Israel's place in humanity is problematic from the standpoint of the nations as from Israel's own intrinsic standpoint. Israel is at once apart, differentiated, and distinguished, as are the nations, but also very close, by its exile amongst the nations, to the indeterminate and the undifferentiated, so that it effectively joins singularity and universality. Israel is at once what it is electively and also what the others are separately. In the differentiation of the human, in the narrowing of the finite, Israel represents the infinite, the incomplete portion that throws the nations back into their incompleteness in the passage. Its being is the locus of a fascinating perpetual movement in which the nebula of exiles ceaselessly gravitates and revolves around centers that rise and fall, that brighten and disappear, as if its settlements were in perpetual passing. Whole parts vanish into nothingness, then reemerge to twinkle elsewhere, and finally shine brightly in the distance.

The scope of Israel's experience of exile is an extraordinary phenomenon in humanity. This passage of twenty-five centuries from one frontier to another, from one civilization to another, across the vicissitudes of history with the permanence of its singular existence raises a question that almost pertains to the realm of natural physics. There is a cosmic scope to Israel's exile, one of universal passage, on a par with the procession of attributes, the laws of nature, or the existence of the nations of the world. It is in this sense that Israel's existence pertains to the cosmic order, as Jeremiah suggests: "Thus spoke YHWH, who created the sun as a light by day and gave the moon and the stars the mission to light by night, who agitates the sea and makes the waves roar, he whose Name is YHWH-*Tzevaot*; if these laws ceased to be immutable before me, said YHWH, only then could the posterity of Israel cease to form a nation before me all the days of time" (Jer. 31:35–36). Empires rise and fall, communities of Israel take shape and dissolve, but Israel lives on, bound to its original tradition, beyond the vicissitudes of its own consciousness.

The very term used to designate the Hebrew, *ivri*, denotes passage.[58] For the universe, Israel embodies passage, bears witness to it, and accompanies it. It clears the path from allness to oneness. It evinces both the frightening void in the human—the unbearable image of the cycle of death and birth, of the disintegration of the all, and of the intrinsic instability of the being in the passage—and the way to the one. Its specificity and "chosenness" draw the humanity of the nations to the one, out of infinity and the undifferentiated. In a way, Israel's election is the principle of chosenness of the seventy nations, which is why Israel is not counted among the "nations of the disappearance/ world/*olam*." It is the very principle of their "disappearance," the locus of their worldliness, but also, insofar as history is redeemed, the project of escaping disappearance, of leaving the exile of perdition in infinity. Its exile is not a random nomadism dictated by circumstance; it is the advance of the one at work in the cosmos. Thus, the ingathering of the exiles always has a messianic, salvational significance. God "assembles the castaways of Israel" (Isa. 11:12). The God who gathers the exiled of Israel leaves the passage and appears in the interior of his dwelling, the dwelling of the one. The collective dimension of the assembly of Israel has implications for all of humanity: it gathers the perdition of the infinite into the one. In effect, the seventy nations have the potential of becoming humanity as a universal assembly. It is the gathering of Israel beyond the infinity of exile that makes this universal assembly appear. This is why the assembly of nations in Jerusalem accompanies the return of Israel to Zion in the prophetic discourse.

How are we to understand the institution of Israel on the same cosmic level as nature, the attributes, or the existence of nations?

What matters most in the passage is mobility. We have seen that there is undifferentiation in the passage but also laws and fixed pathways. The main thing is that all these laws and narrowing prisms have to be passageways (to the one) in the midst of the neutrality of the undifferentiated, not monuments of achievement or regressive traces of the now-forever-gone all that human beings are supposed to spend their lives contemplating. The great danger for life is that the *olam* carried by the passage loses its mobility, and, by ceasing to move, it loses itself and dissolves into infinity. This danger is more tangible for humanity than for nature or God (although one of Israel's

58. See "La judéité," in Trigano, *Story of Disappeared Presence*, pp. 102–103.

tasks is to sanctify nature and unify God's Name), because it is humanity
that is summoned to the one. In the undifferentiation of the passage, human
beings could see the particularization with which they live, the laws of nature that govern their lives, and the God of many attributes that they know
as the ultimate purpose of the world. They could even totalize these in the
problematics of the all but not see that they are parapets along the passage
leading to the one. The nation is thus deemed the supreme value when it
merely heralds the particularization of the one who chooses individuals.[59] The
attributes of God are held to be the absolute revelation of the divine when
they merely herald the unity of God, and the deterministic laws of nature are
regarded as the ultimate truth of terrestrial life when they merely herald the
transfiguration and humanization of nature in the one, the end of its exposure
in exteriority.[60] In sum, the fixedness in the universe, which is an element in
the strategy of passage, runs the risk of becoming autonomous and departing
from the project of passage, which is the redemption and reparation (*tikkun*)
of the *olam* and its foundational disappearance.

The passage not only harbors the undifferentiated and death; it also carries with it a way that allows the passage, provided that human beings use
it and do not close it off. The absence of the *olam*, when people can find no
way to the one, leads to the experience of lack and to strategies of substitution, among them the strategy of idolatry, which substitutes the icon for the
one in this world of disappearance. Making an icon of the one[61] is making
it into an object, an obstacle that interrupts the flow of passage. Idolatry
perpetuates this world by falling for the illusion of its advent and of its true
birth. The *olam* is the world where things are produced by the toil (*amal*)
of man.[62] The danger is to see these things losing their value as instruments
(*kelim*) of passage in such a way that human beings are reduced to the level
of objects and overtaken by alienation and absence, the processes by which
they produce objects and exert an effort to reach the one. Toil would, in this
case, lose its vocation. It is from this standpoint that the species prevails over
the particular in the passage, so that the fluidity of the passage opens onto
the particular in the one and the particular does not have the illusion of be-

59. This is the case of nationalism when what could be a vehicle of the one (the nations) reverts to a recreation of the all in infinity. This experience necessarily attracts an
enormous amount of perverse energy in the world.

60. Let us not forget that the earth was cursed, reduced to exposure for having "swallowed" Abel's blood (Gen. 4:10), and thus corrupted its interiority.

61. The nation's self-image is a case in point.

62. *Amal* is composed of the same letters as *olam*, world or disappearance.

ing the manifestation of the one. But if it does not open onto the particular, then the species becomes established in its infinity in the deceptive form of the one and the particular. This is the monstrous image of the god Molech, the devourer of newborn babies.

Yet even the icon set up on the passageway will one day be smashed by the energy of passing that cannot be forced to stand still for long. Such is the tragedy of strategies of establishment in the passage: the passage will submerge all such attempts and continue on its way, or else it will get lost. Such is the ordeal of the *olam*. If the world stops, if it stands still for but a moment, it will break down and disintegrate into infinity which is why one cannot "find" God. "I've seen all that God has done, for man cannot find what is being done under the sun" (Eccles. 8:17), because this would signify finding God *in* the world when he is, in fact, passing and can only be heard in the abode of the one.

God departs and it's the *olam*, but he leaves his Name in the *olam*: "This is my Name for the *olam*," disappearance on the one hand and hidden presence in this disappearance that is the world, as if God were saying, "Where there is loss and erasure, here is my chosen Name, which transcends them and acts as a viaticum for the passage." Human beings, provided that they open themselves sufficiently (through repentance), can have recourse to the Tetragrammaton, which is the very structure and process of disappearance and of the *olam* and the very principle of mastering the currents of passage. Ultimately, the supreme law of passage, its narrowing prism from which all the laws of the world derive, is the law of the Tetragrammaton, which alone governs access to the one or— if the one is not the end purpose—the deterministic involution into the petrifying all. There is no ineluctable necessity in the world, impermeable to birth-giving mercy (*rahamim*). Everything is in suspension. Anything is possible, even insofar as the laws of nature are concerned, as long as human beings aspire to the one. This is why God's secret Name is entrusted to Israel for all of humanity and more especially to the high priest, the master of natural flows, who alone can pronounce it in the Holy of Holies on Yom Kippur. This is why the main task of all Israel is unifying the Tetragrammaton (*yihud*).

The narrowing of the passageways in the world at the core of the infinite is the locus of torment and violence. This is the violence that the pressure of passing exerts on the narrowness of the pathway and on the instrument through which the passage can reach the one. Such is the conflict that arises from the contiguity of the finite and the infinite. This is why the areas bordering the paths of the *olam* (revelation of attributes, laws of nature, relations between nations, the existence of Israel) are marked by violence, and this violence can intensify when the force of its energy comes up against an obstacle on its path: idolatry, insofar as God is concerned; a cataclysm, for nature; and totalitarianism, for the nations.

This violence is the expression of a misguided search for the one that tries to keep God and the human inside, when it is outside that it is happening, as if one could do without the exterior and without passage. Basically, it is a regression to allness that surfaces in this caricature of the one. The elements that chaotically run through the passage draw together, attract, and repel one another around these pathways. Their seemingly disorderly trajectories could be structured around the universal poles of the processes that govern the passage through differentiation, assembly, individuation, and germination.

In this context, the function of Israel's passage becomes clear in the light of the Torah. Indeed, there is a way other than violence to approach the one from the passage in infinity, and that is the practice of the *mitzva*, which involves assuming and controlling the violence. The pathways left in the world of the *olam* protect human beings from sinking into nothingness and carve out a shelter for them in infinity, a protective shelter in the passage. Through the *mitzvot*, the Torah prevents the passage from sinking into nothingness and channels it in the direction of the one.

The *mitzva* renders every act of our absence in the world unique, even the most insignificant, the most commonplace (and covers it with appropriate words of benediction). Every object or act provides a reason to search for the sanctification—that is to say, for the separation—that will keep it from getting lost in time. By giving priority to details and choosing one form of action over another, the *mitzva* removes us from the undifferentiation of infinity. Measured against the "universal" and the infinity of passage, the *mitzva* seems extremely small and petty, particularizing and insignificant. It constitutes, to be sure, a narrowing of the passage, because one has to pass there and nowhere else, but this is the way to the one.

The Torah, through its detailed *mitzvot*, is another pathway of the *olam*, a way in the infinite that is commensurate with the laws of nature and that escapes the usual violence provoked by the pursuit of the one. The *mitzva* awakens the power of the *olam* and of passage in that which has become congealed and causes it to pass on to the one. *Mitzvot* are all temporal procedures for extricating human beings and the world from neutrality and indetermination, like scansions of the passage to the one. Holiness (*kodesh*) is meaningful only in terms of this "separation" from the undifferentiated, and this is because there is nothing immediate, since the origin is veiled. In the sacredness that characterizes idolatry, on the contrary, there is no point of passage, but rather a prohibition (the taboo), an arrest of movement. What is a separation becomes a boundary and a break—a "temple," from the Greek root "to cut." This is why Ecclesiastes, which seems a priori to offer a justification for despair, ends with an appeal in favor of *mitzvot*: "The end of the discourse. All is heard. Fear God and keep his *mitzvot*, for this is all of man; for all God's deeds will come in judgment on all that is *ne'elam* (gone, absent, or made worldly), be it good or bad" (Eccles. 12:13–14). This in no way contradicts the thrust of what is mistakenly regarded as a philosophy of disenchantment and skepticism. It is, to the contrary, coherently connected to the thoughts on *hevel* and *amal*, the thoughts on the natural physics of humankind. "For all things, there is a time (*et*) and a rule (*mishpat*)" (Eccles. 8:6). The Torah takes all deeds out of the world, one by one. It takes them out of the vacuum of everyday life, out of the workings of absence, and makes them unique and memorable, detaching them from their neutrality, rousing them from their sleep, and dissociating them from the world as a total system. Otherwise they would be meaningless, interchangeable, and anonymous, merely cogs in a monstrous machine. By instilling the sense of the one in our acts in the *olam*, the Torah releases us from the pursuit of the all and keeps us from sinking totally into infinity. The Torah awakens Israel to the one as Israel awakens the nations to the one by detaching them from their hypnotic enthrallment with the all and with the oblivion of the world.

The Torah follows the movement of the *olam*, this movement that is the void at the core of inhabited lands and divine plenitude, and also the pathway through the infinite wilderness to the one.

CHAPTER 3

The Milieu of Freedom

THE VERY VIVACITY of the passage carries with it the possibility of forget-ting and erasure. The danger for the being gathered in the Name is to find itself engulfed by the oblivion that overwhelms it as it is pronounced. This disappearance can be heard in the words "This is my Name for the *olam/* disappearance." For this reason, life is an essential struggle between forgetting and the ever-repeated proclamation of names and of the Name. Everything dies and passes away in each and every instant. Every instant is a welling forth similar to the creation of the world, a critical moment giving rise to uncertainty and drama. Some spiritual traditions—in India and elsewhere in Asia, for instance—refuse the struggle and choose to surrender to oblivion. From that point on, their destiny is but an involution into the pristine all through the passage—in this case, a passing back. This amounts to a denial of creation in the sense that existence and history no longer strive to reach the one. The forgetting of individual names and of the Name is elevated to a spiritual ideal. Such wisdom does not go beyond the passing.

Forgetting and Redemption

Another approach chooses neither to forget nor to remember but to enjoy each passing moment and the momentary flickering of being, of the unac-complished being that exists in each moment. The perdition in this case is even deeper, because the all is totally absent from a context in which individuals are but particles forever attracting and repelling each other. But there is another approach that struggles against oblivion. If the forgetting of names exists, it is made possible by the forgetting inherent in being on a much deeper level: the forgetting of the being-for-himself that is the vehicle of being-for-the-world, with God giving way to the world by suspending his being. This struggle is one of mending the world, of "repairing" (*tikkun*) the passage. What characterizes human beings as creatures is that they are called upon to become the architects of the reparation, safekeeping, and "redemption" (*geula*) of creation. This is the vocation of Ruth, who refuses to rest until she fulfills the levirate commandment: a widow redeems the name of a husband who died without a male heir by marrying her brother-in law; thereafter, the child he gives her is considered the son of the dead brother. What can be regarded as an intrinsic flaw in creation (the creational oblivion) can also be regarded from another standpoint in a positive light, because this is where the kingdom of man unfolds, a wild kingdom that needs to be tamed, a dark chaos where light does not yet shine, but a kingdom in which man is king.

The suspension of God, the eclipse of presence that is creation, is actually awaiting man, who is called upon to stand up, come forward, act, and constitute himself. Creation is divine altruism, which is why it institutes the sphere of human freedom, just as, in a relationship, the first words are followed by the time of waiting for a response that may or may not come and may or may not be welcome. This means, however (because there is this waiting for a response), that at bottom freedom is not utter nothingness, that it is summoned and convoked to respond. Such freedom is intrinsically caught in a relationship with the other and does not stand all on its own, since the other is implicated in it. But hearing this voice in the absolute freedom into which we are born is not evident. It requires an effort, indeed a method, which is why freedom starts in the arena of action. It is a practical disposition of the world.

Human freedom must recall its origin and that in response to which it exists, namely, the freedom of the creator, for the world is founded on his self-forgetting and his appeal to the other. Freedom without alterity is an illusion or an act of consuming the self and the world. The realm of freedom is that of repairing (*tikkun*) the oblivion to the creator's Name. To actuate their freedom, humans are basically called upon to redeem and repair the absence of the world.

The purpose of freedom is to turn absence back into presence, "to repair the *olam*/disappearance in the Kingship of *Shaddai*/the God of satisfaction" (prayer), so as to save the world from the disappearance that threatens it. Thus, the arena of human freedom is in God's creational forgetting, a forgetting that calls upon humans to remember, and the exercise of freedom consists in mending this oblivion (through recollection). Human freedom is thereby nurtured by the relationship in which it is caught, by the (creational) freedom of a human-liberating (self-forgetting) God. It is not an immediate, passive benefit, even if it comes from God. But it is practically absolute, since humans are born from the suspension of God, from the limitation of divine power that puts them in a position of autonomy when they would otherwise have remained creatures in a relationship of dependence. This, then, is a nearly absolute freedom that does not contradict the Other!

Yet such freedom requires a method and a course of action to be effective, which is further proof that it is real freedom. It is through remembrance (*zecher*) that freedom comes for man (and there is no remembrance that is not of a name). Indeed, in remembrance lies the only possible form of relationship in the world of passing and disappearance, the type of relationship in which what binds me to the other is not a "concrete" bond but rather a relationship in which the absence of the other is integrated, a relationship that is not destroyed by the other's absence, a destruction that is ineluctable since the other inevitably escapes my hold. Remembrance is the very foundation of the relationship in absence. This is why remembrance is the basis of all communities and all relationships—in practical terms, of course, since there are times when the other is not there; but also fundamentally speaking, because the other can come to us only through remembrance.

The others whom we meet are but the remembrance of the original other. It is because there was this original moment of otherness, of God the creator's estrangement-absenting in relation to himself, that we can even conceive of the possibility of the other. Every time the other appears, the remembrance of the origin is rekindled in us, because in the world of passing, in the world of my consciousness, where I am totally present, others do not exist, not yet. Their being is yet to be; it is forthcoming in the one. One cannot think of a relationship with others or with the collectivity or with God in terms of total conformity, imagining that others could be totally present, exposed, and revealed in the concrete experience of the relationship, that they could suffice unto themselves in the economy of remembrance. In the world of passing, we are always meeting one another somewhere other than where we are, that is to say, our meeting always brings back the place of origin, bears witness to the remembrance of the origin, repeats the original creation. "He remembered for the *olam* his *berit*, the word he commanded for a thousand generations" (Ps. 105:8).

Memory as the Mode of Relationships to Absence

God who created the *olam*, God disappearing from disappearance, is present in all our encounters. To sustain the possibility and even the idea of a relationship, one must lend reality to that which seemingly has none and bear witness to a presence when all is absence. This is true in day-to-day life, where, most of the time, I am not totally present, neither to myself nor to the other. The same is true for the other, and yet our relationship survives, and thrives on the remembrance of the exceptional moments when we were present to ourselves and to each other, those exceptional moments of earnestness and openness. This remembrance of a unique moment of presence forms the framework of our relationship, which can then go through ups and downs and through crises without danger, without being engulfed by passing time.

We can see the extent to which remembrance is bound up with giving, with generosity, with the faith and the power of the soul, with *rahamim*. Only *rahamim*, birth-giving mercy, can lend existence to what is absent. It alone adds to what seems to be and lends reality to more than appearance. It alone makes it possible to conceive real humanity, to bring to life a collectivity, the totality of which can never be grasped by an individual, for I as an individual can never know all those who are present and whose presence I am forced to recognize through my perception of their absence. "Remember us, YHWH, for there is no more other than (by) you." The structure of the relationship for which remembrance is the very paradigm can also be found in other forms: in the oath, in the obligation or the debt, in the promise when it is an established relationship between two partners, or in gift giving and expectation when the relationship is less formal because its weight stands on a single partner. No doubt we could say that giving and waiting are the basis of the oath, the debt, the promise, and remembrance. They are the basis of any relationship in which one of the partners is not there. In the case of giving, I am the one who steps aside and yields to the other, giving all without knowing how my partner will react, and without waiting for something in return in the moment of giving. In the case of waiting, it is the other who steps back and yields to me, and I muster all my presence and project my whole being toward the other who is far away.

In the case of an oath, I commit myself to doing certain things, even if circumstances stand in my way. In the case of a debt, I commit to returning what I owe, under specific conditions. In the case of a promise, I commit to giving something no matter what. Finally, in the case of remembrance, I hold as certain the presence of something, even though circumstances have changed. These four types of relationships stand up to the wearing effects of time and to the law of passage. In them, the passage is assumed, but the commitment to the relationship is maintained nonetheless. They hold to a presence that seems to be contradicted by the facts. They are capable of keeping the memory of the other alive even though the other is gone.

It would be a mistake to see these relationships to the world as a negation of temporality, as one may be readily tempted to do. In point of fact, they totally assume temporality while struggling to transcend it. Indeed, these relationships are mechanisms of temporality. If this were not the case, it would be impossible to even imagine them. And it is by virtue of temporality that they harbor the certainty of the coming, beyond the passage, of the one. In the flow of passage, they have the strength to cling to the announcement of the one as something certain. Thus, in the dissolution of the passage, the testimony to the origin and the anticipation of presence despite absence clearly point to the realm of oneness and transparency.

Such practices of remembrance have played a central role throughout the history of Israel; they have been invested with much greater importance than any more imposing institution. Oath and remembrance are the two pillars of the covenant: "YHWH, your God, is a merciful God; he will not fail you, and he will not destroy you, and he will not forget the covenant of your fathers, which he made on oath with them" (Deut. 4:31). "He remembers his covenant... for a thousand generations, which he made with Abraham, and his oath to Isaac" (Ps. 105:8–9). The promise governs the destiny of Israel and its relationship to its land. Is "reparation" (*tikkun*) to be understood in terms of a search for fullness (*shlemut*)? The point is not to strive to recreate the mirror (in which the being is absorbed in his reflection) prior to creation, for it is the one and not the all that is at issue in the experience of true freedom.

The paradigmatic model of *tikkun* is the sacrifice (*korban*), a procedure of giving a part of one's property, which brings one closer (*karev*, from the same root as *korban*) to the other (God or man), whose presence is assumed even though he is absent. The sacrifice picks up and redeems a deed that has already been accomplished and consigns a being in the world (an animal or a plant) to disappearance, to its "*olami*zation." Processes of remembrance always involve loss and passing. In the "presentification" of the absent other, which remembrance brings about, those who remember suspend their fleeting present and put themselves in a state of passing and awaiting. For this reason, the wholeness to which freedom aspires is always evaluated in relation to a retreat and a suspension, and it is not realized, no doubt, in its total embodiment. It is a withdrawal, a cutting off from the whole that makes the one appear, in addition, over and beyond the passing. This dream of wholeness that is at issue in freedom is a dream of the pristine totality. This is why the experience of freedom often encounters totalitarianism, which is the result of a misguided struggle against forgetting that aspires to the absolute embodiment of presence at the cost of denying the one, creation, and the vivifying passage. Mending the world means fighting against the void but also resisting the temptation to fill it, the temptation of the all. A way must be found between alienation (not enough passage) and dissolution (too much passage).

The Temptation of Representation

The temptation to fill the void lends itself to representation, which is an attempt to achieve presence in the passage without giving the passage its power and its germinative time, the time to give birth to the one. Representation resorts to the past coherence of the all to create the illusion of the one in the unfinished passage. Re-presentation is a "copy," a semblance of presence insofar as it evidences impatience before the one. If being is passage, and hence the slipping away of the original being (and the decline of the all), then presence—the appearance of the one, the dynamic unification and essential irrigation of all the planes of the universe—is in the waiting.

The passing flows and spreads. In the trough of its whirlpool, we may not see its intention and direction. But if there is passage, it is because the being pours out and flows to the one, outside the all. The one is its child and its promise, but from the perspective of origin (whose self-relinquishment makes the passing and hence the one possible), the one advances on its own. At the end of the passage, it advances, emerging on the other bank from the interior of this continent where it has always dwelt, hidden from the world, and making the passage possible by opening the all to a pole outside itself.

It is in this sense that the relationship to the one is one of patience, because this suffering of time, the telltale sign of temporality, echoes the unfurling of the passage and the maturation of the place left to human beings to be born and to give birth to the one, which is the project of their history. Representation is the abolition of time and passing, a refusal of historicity, gestation, and germination. Too eager to reach the one, it embodies the refusal of time and is prey to a regressive involution into the all. For this reason, representation produces a formidable increase in power; it stands

under the banner of the all when we are in fact in the passage, which is
its diametrical opposite. It braces against the flow of passage, and its fight
against such a powerful current generates enormous power, the power of a
dike against a raging torrent. Representation designates the instance when
the all moves into the passage and obstructs it, thereby suspending, containing, and holding back life.

To be sure, there is presence in representation, but it is bypassed and
misled. For this reason, representation is a semblance of being. It cannot
endure the absence in the passage, so it tries to cover it up and silence its
uproar. Whatever pertains to the order of disappearance (of *olam*), a beneficial
but trying order of creation, is understood as pertaining to a logic of lack.
The experience is the same, but it is interpreted from the standpoint of the
all, which conceives of self-relinquishment as tantamount to dissolution. It
sees the passage as unbearably naked and tries to cover it up. This is why
representation, which is meant to exhibit presence in total exteriority, actually
drives presence away and offers nothing but a mockery of presence, because
the sole presence possible for our world resides in the process of passage.
Presence can be manifested not in the eye but in memory, in an abstract
inner sight that is directed at what was once outside, and that contemplates
and seeks presence without arresting the passage of the world.

Presence and alterity appear only as a memory or a promise, but a
memory of what? There is necessarily a memory of the origin, but is this a
memory of the all? And if so, is representation also a memory of the all? In
remembrance, there is surely the memory of the pristine all, but inasmuch as
memory can arise only in the passage, that is to say, as an effort in a milieu
that generates forgetting, it is also the memory of the project of the one, for
whose sake the all was shattered and the passage opened up. The project of
the one underpins the possibility of memory because in the unique order of
the all there is neither forgetting nor remembering.

Memory is therefore drawn to two aspirations. There is the "nostalgia"
that is its immediate inclination, the eternal return to the origin, to the lost
integrity of the all. But there is also the hope. This is when memory aspires
to the one in such a way that it breaks away from the all and engenders
passing. In so doing, it paradoxically becomes a generator of the future.
Remembrance as hope is what governs the covenant (*berit*). "He remembered
his covenant" (Ps. 105:8), and it is in the light of the covenant as a cut and a
break that we can understand this, for what is remembered is not the unique
integrity of the all but the break and the project of the one. Remembrance as

a relationship to the being is the sole relationship in which the being does not run the risk of exhibition, of the illusion of total manifestation that its manifestation in the world of passage would be. There is sight in memory, but it is a hazy, totally internalized view of objects. Remembrance is the first moment of interiorization in which the one can appear, the moment when exteriority is submerged by interiority, concealed in the intimate depths of the being. It is a critical moment in the history of the being, so it is understandable that, at this moment, when everything hangs in the balance, representation (the memory of the recreated whole) surfaces on the road to the one. Memory wavers between the immediate materialization of its desire (the icon, the reproduction of the all) and the preservation of the enduring subtlety of being, a relationship with the one that can only be one of waiting and hoping. With remembrance as hope, what arises at last in the passage is the waiting and its promise.

I. THE POLITICAL MOMENT

This crucial crossroads where representation (the obstruction of passage), dissolution (the triumph of forgetting), and *tikkun* (the effort) meet is the critical moment for the being. This is where the confrontation between idolatry and the Torah takes place, because idolatry emerges from the same experience of the being but in a radically different economy. "Be mindful not to forget the covenant of YHWH, your God, that he concluded with you and not to make a statue, an image of all, that YHWH, your God, commanded you" (Deut. 4:23). The triumph of forgetting could be considered the path of hedonism and skepticism. To this one might add an additional avenue, that of modernity, which combines representation and forgetting to yield a new abstract, nonfigurative form of representation that seems like an approach to the one. Indeed, modernity probably moves representation in the direction of the one, but the representation remains embedded in nostalgic remembrance, in a myth of origins that is generated paradoxically by the desire for progress and the future.[63] In modernity, forgetting goes hand in hand with recourse

---

63. Take the example of political Zionism. Decidedly modern, it nonetheless needs to elaborate a myth, like all modern ideologies, in this case, that of the Maccabean state.

to the totality, since the one is actually eclipsed, even though abstract forms of representation look much closer to the one.

Representation, despite its own discourse of presentification, is immediately forgetting, because it is still in the passage. And because its discourse is contradictory, it produces idolatry, the full exposure in exteriority of the divine whose secret is given away. The icon of the one, representation's supreme ambition, be it of God or of the state, is a mockery of the one, a simulacrum. There is no higher representation than that of God (or of the state, which took over from it),[64] insofar as it is the supreme figure of all. By the icon or the idol of God, both of which are supposed to truly represent or facilitate the presence of God, it is the world and the world of man that are negated, and the wait for the one that is defused. The passage is denied even though the one has not yet come to be. And so we fall back under the spell of the all. Idolatry goes hand in hand with the pursuit and experience of inordinate power. It is marked by an inherent violence and exerts a destructive power of fundamental alienation upon human beings. It is from this standpoint that the Jewish conception of presence and invisibility is to be understood.

The Struggle for 'Tikkun'

This moment of the struggle and effort of *tikkun* is the epitome of the political moment. It is the place where the political is lodged in the being even if it is also the privileged moment of divine experience. It is fundamentally political for two reasons: power and number. This struggle, torn between the all and the one—because it musters the energy needed for the confrontation with an absent interlocutor and garners all the forces of the being in an intense outburst of energy—gives rise to power, which thus appears as a consequence, perhaps the most synthetic, of the pursuit of presence. But also to the extent that it brings the faltering, scattered universe together into a whole, it is out of this struggle against forgetting and against the eventual dereliction of passage that the gathering of human beings is born.

There are several reasons for this. Firstly, in the void of passing, humankind assumes the form of a whole from which individuals do not stand out (even though it is bustling with the movement of the many), a whole that,

---

64. Essentially, since any place of power is the place of God, but also historically, with the advent of modernity, when the political occupies the sphere of religions (see "L'idée moderne," in Trigano, *Forgotten Dwelling*).

without this moment of the political, would remain negative, nothing but a shapeless, chaotic, brutally massive whole. Secondly, the struggle pits the human being against God, the creator of the universe. An interlocutor on this level of abstraction and generality calls for a similar level on the part of human consciousness, which approaches God only on the level of the collectivity, the whole of humanity, and human destiny. This is what makes it a consciousness even if one can hear the sighs of the self in it. The confrontation of human beings with the divine creates humanity as a globality, and this is the relationship that underpins the political.

One may add a third reason that makes this a political moment, and it is that the reparation (*tikkun*) implies the ambition to (re)construct the world, and to encompass all of society at once. The *tikkun* aspires to take in the totality and bring together the scattered elements of the world. Now isn't this precisely the fundamental experience of the political through which social unity is attained? A group cannot be constituted as such without this capacity to grasp itself as a single whole. This means that the human being who performs *tikkun* elevates himself to the level of the divine creator, who mustered his unity to create. It is when one takes hold of the many and brings them together in a sheaf that the dilemma of the all and the one arises. The first experience of this political moment was the building of the Tower of Babel, when all of humankind, braced by the insolent power of the tower, endowed itself with the image of unity. Thus it is written that the people of Babel loved each other so much that they spoke only the same "united words (*dvarim ahadim*)" (Gen. 11:1).

The Emergence of the One

The experience of the origin passes through this moment of memory, and hence through the political experience. But this passage of the origin, this passing origin, differs from the origin itself by the fact that it is a recommencement: "Carve for yourself two tablets of stone like the first" (Exod. 34:1), and "Write these words for yourself, for *on the mouth* of these words, I have sealed a covenant with you and with Israel" (34:27). On the mouth, according to the commentary, refers to the oral Torah, which was added the second time to the written Torah. This difference, this meta-phor,[65] this

---

65. See "Langue du passage et principe métaphorique," in Trigano, *Story of Disappeared Presence*, p. 318.

"transfer" of the origin, is the deep-seated nature of the political. It draws
the being toward the manifestation of the one (when it does not fall into the
regressive trap of totality). The political process is a process of emergence
for the one, the particular, the detail, pulled out of the faceless, nameless
anonymity of passage and its infinite multiplicity. It is a process of differentiation. Consequently, it entails a secondary process of classification and
hierarchization of human beings.

It can be seen at work on several levels. The political struggle is entirely
bent on the emergence of a power (a leader or a ruling group) that stands
out from the pristine mass. From this point of view, it resembles the process
of sanctification (*kiddush*), which means "separation." To sanctify a person
is to make the person appear out of an original mass and to make his name
heard. In this light, we can better understand marriage (*kiddushin*), for
example, as the emergence for an individual of a privileged person from a
formless mass: "Here you are separated/sanctified for me" (prayer). And in
this light, we can also understand the *kiddush*, which is the separation of
God's Name: his appearance and manifestation. Holiness is the appearance
of the one, and the act of sanctifying consists of helping it appear, taking
it out of the passage. This appearance is, of course, a privileged moment of
manifestation, a moment of splendor, of royal magnificence.

It is on this level that the law is instituted, in a moment of recommencement of the origin and as a dissociation from the totality, to be sure, but
also as the emergence and institutionalization of the particular and of the
detail. The law applies to particular circumstances, cases, and events. In the
Torah, it is the oral Torah (the Talmud) that embodies this law. In sum, law
is directly a matter of jurisprudence. Thus, the first tablets were destined to
be broken, for they belonged still to the serenity of the all and could not
be received in the arena of struggle with the being and in the being that is
the political arena. The breaking of the tablets is the foundational act of the
people of Israel in history. This breaking brings out the specificity of the
people, its departure from the Egypt of undifferentiation. The law does not
belong to the realm of the "universal"; it is a vehicle of particularization
that brings out and sanctifies details from the stream of passage and makes
faces emerge out of a whole.[66] If "nature" is seen as the world of passage in
its tragic determinism, then the law is greater than nature, insofar as it is
removed from the passage. In this sense, too, the political is superior to the

---

66. The existence of positive and negative commandments participates in this differentiation. This distinction breaks with the anonymous equivalency of all things in the passage.

natural order. The political experience carries the experience of an "overplus" with it.[67] And this is what determines the nature of the state as an institution that brings together the stakes of the all and the one.

The Temptation of the State

Indeed, as we have systematically observed, the moment of the emergence of the one runs through the seduction of the all. The passage moves the being toward the one but, during the passing, the all can look like the only way out of the dereliction of the being and the weakening of the presence inherent in it. At the end of the passage, the powerful image of allness interferes, obstructing the path to the one and turning unity into totality.

The historically dated time of the modern state represents this detour. On the way to the one and in the history of politics as the emergence of the one, humanity has basically gone through two types of experiences until now. Firstly, prior to modernity, the one manifested itself in kingship, in the solemn appearance of an imperial or royal figure. This aristocratic model assumed a republican form when, instead of a single figure, there were several clothed in the same royal splendor and endowed with the same exceptional power. This is the model of the one and "the ones." With the advent of modernity and the invention of the state, the one was invested with the all. Whereas the model of "the one and the ones" strives to get out of the passage and the vacuum through personalized particularization (consigning the rest of society to an undifferentiated mass), the modern state tries, while it is still in the realm of the one, to get out of the passage through totalization—that is to say, by recreating in a way the original all over and above the passage, thereby theoretically nullifying passage, even though in practice it continues its work of disintegration (magnified all the more insofar as the totality of the state forcefully opposes it). This is what accounts for the catastrophic consequences of the instability of the state as a form: in the instability inherent in the political, the entities at stake are enormous. It is no longer a single human being or several, but the all that is at stake every time.

Naturally, the structural problem of the state is the contradiction between the universal and the particular, the multiple and the unique. To be sure, the state aspires to surpass particularities and particular interests. The discourse of the all is what annuls the unending dismemberment of the passage. But

---

67. But not of a Hegelian *aufhebung* although Hegel's concept is a reading of the overplus (see below, Book III, ch. 1, "The Theory of the Safeguarded Portion").

the problem is that the reality of the passage remains irrevocable. There is therefore something tragic about the state as a form, for it tries to do without the world and its multiplicity (which is why it assumes a timeless, universal, and eternal aspect). Another problem is that this representation of the all is set up on the ground of the one; it is established on the riverbank, the only suitable place for such a representation, since it constitutes a departure from the passage. The state thereby conflates the bank of a brand-new continent with the continent of origin, as if the crossing were but a senseless, pointless drifting, an illusion of accomplishment. The moment of the state is a moment of negation of history, generation, and germination, a moment of departure from history, because history is the emergence of faces, names, and the one.

Ultimately, the state puts itself in the position of a creator god who would annul his creation and revert to his narcissistic mirroring. This is the moment of the possibility of representation in the being, which explains why the *representative* system developed at the same time as the modern state. It is a structural and essential necessity thereof, its very soul. This modern moment of the state is at once different from and close to the ancient time of idolatry, which was the main target of the prophets and which saw the birth of a radical conflictuality within Israel, and between Israel and the nations.[68] The state may distort the one, but, unlike idolatry, it is closer to the one than to the all. That this is the case is due, no doubt, to its abstraction.

The Bearer of God's Image

The moment of resumption of the world of disappearance is the moment of the human. What is at stake at this point is its innermost being, prey to total perversion, in the inversion of creation and the infinite fall of the light. To put it otherwise, what is at stake is the successful conveyance of light in the passage to its radiance in the one. In sum, the risk of creation is wholly bound up with what becomes of "God's image," the *tzelem Elohim* in which man was created and which is his viaticum for the passage. The cast shadow (*tzel*), the secret, of this image constitutes the place of the human,[69] an image that arises from projection, from setting into motion the passage of the all to the one, and this passage, which makes all the being of the human being, is the locus of the movement of the all to the one. The *tzelem* is essentially mobility and passage. It is through the *tzelem* that God created his world,

---

68. See "Alterité contre normalité," in Trigano, *New Jewish Question*, p. 57.
69. See "Les Visages," in Trigano, *Story of Disappeared Presence*, p. 72.

his disappearance, in a paradoxical image that portrays only absence and disappearance. But it portrays them nonetheless; otherwise, it would not be an image.

In this sense, the attributes can be described as the successive strokes in this portrayal of disappearance. All of the attributes together compose the projected image that is the paradigm of the world, or rather of God-for-the-world, since we are dealing with disappearance. Representation can be understood as human beings' way of interposing a wooden plate on the pathway of this sublime procession, in front of this impetuous retinue of riders pulling the image-bearing chariot, thereby capturing all the power of the light, the last glimmers of which fall lifeless onto this inert surface. Representation acts as a mirror: it receives the projected image, the living project that has become a flat image, and casts back onto the all its own echo, throwing the passage back onto the all, repeating the all in the passage, and forever masking, in the dazzle of such a powerful condensation of light, the project and the process of the one in whose place it aspires to stand. Man alone can be the architect of this, because he is the one who arranges the elements of light to form a comprehensible pattern. He paints the icon and carries it. Thus, the man who carries God's *tzelem*/image (in other words, the attributes) holds the power and the key to the passage, for the attributes are the rays of light that capture the energy of creation, the structure of creational divine power.[70]

The narration of the attributes stands in God's place, so to speak; it alone bears witness to his presence in the world of passage. The biblical text, when it speaks of the attributes, says that God "passed over his face" (Exod. 34:6), which can also be read as "he veiled himself," or as "he put himself into his face." The attributes are all of God's being for the passage. This is God in passing. They are the counterpart of representation of the idol, a purely nominal anti-icon. That the power they induce differs from that to which representation gives rise results from the "material" of which they are made: oral and written words, the very sites of that which passes. The passage itself

70. The considerable import of the question of divine "attributes" can be seen in the sizable Jewish philosophical debate on the subject. Instead of interpreting them negatively (*shelilat hahe'ader*, or the negation of absence), removing from God the attributes we have added, as Maimonides does, they are to be seen as part of the inner logic of disappearance. God's Name and attributes are there only for disappearance; they are there only for the world and humankind. This is God in passage. They cannot be an object of negation, nor can they be deemed criticizable and even idolatrous as an (anthropomorphic) addition to original divine unity, for such a judgment proceeds solely from the perspective of the all. The attributes are to be regarded instead as an overplus of God, as creation is, the sense of which is in this retreat with regard to reality. The attributes do not contradict the one; they are the metaphor, the transfer that moves the all toward the one.

is the creational word of God that opens onto the totality of the vacuum of appearance, the *olam*.

The conveyance of the *tzelem* by the man of power and the type of power it causes are marked by the nature of *tzelem* and passage, to be read as a process of the one and not as a reflection of the all. The power arising from the passage is not a projection of the all but the work of the one in infinity and multiplicity. It is a prophetic power, not an imperial one. It endeavors to release the present world from exteriority and restore the *olam*'s mobility, whereas the type of power that representation produces arrests the world in its exteriority, freezes the multiple and the mobile to reduce them to the one, and replaces the world by a model of the all. To define the world as a representation is to directly posit the being as a political field. How can we occupy the place of passage and of infinite freedom into which we are projected? Since Greece saw itself in the context of the all, the only solution it could imagine was that of substitution, the representation that reproduces the all in infinity. For this reason, freedom in the Athenian city-state had more to do with representation and its perfection than with an (always particular) existential condition (as is indicated by the status of foreigners, who did not benefit from freedom). On the other hand, the wisdom of the one strives to accompany the void, to follow the movement of the *olam* so as to make the one come to be. It follows the voiding of the *olam*; instead of trying to fill it, it seeks to bring it out, to cultivate its absence. The Hebraic power takes the form of a person who makes the *olam* audible and visible in this world, someone like David the psalmist or Solomon—Kohelet—"king of Israel in Jerusalem."

The image forged by representation originates in the religious spirit of the icon but reaches its inordinate apogee in the modern state, which incorporates not merely attributes and traits of light but also, first and directly, human beings, the multitudes, to the point of producing a purely abstract, verbal representation in discourse and the law. There is no dearth of effigies, emblems, flags, and portraits of leaders in the state, but they are merely leftovers of the cult of icons of the religious age. The heart of the matter lies elsewhere, as is wonderfully evinced by Hobbes' comparison of the state with the Leviathan, as a gigantic artificial assembly of people. The state manifests itself like in the vision of Nebuchadnezzar, a "statue, which was huge and its brightness surpassing, stood before you, and its appearance was fearsome" (Dan. 2:31). This does not mean that the age of iconic representation ignores the political. Quite the opposite. The icon synthesized (as would subsequently the state) the crux of the political and the political relationship. Both the state and the icon are modalities of representation in the passage; the state constitutes the apotheosis thereof. Whereas the icon portrayed the attributes of God in an object relationship and by way of mediation, the state embodies them in an abstract, negative way and internalizes the mediation.[71]

II. THE COVENANT BETWEEN THE PIECES

There is, then, a procession of attributes that stands opposite representation (of the iconic or state type) and speaks of another type of relationship to passage and another mode of conveyance of light—namely, the covenant (*berit*).

The covenant, by definition an act of union, reunion, and synthesis—which can thereby produce representation—has a cutting thrust in Hebrew. The ceremonial aspect of the covenant[72] is structured around two poles. First of all, there is the cutting involved in the sacrifice (*korban*) that accompanies it, a break in the system of the living organism, and the food that it provides will make possible a second break, that of the bread-breaking ceremony that unites the partners in a solemn communion over a shared meal. The fact that the covenant establishes the basis of a human relationship on the modality of a break shows that the relationship arises not out of natural necessity or a pre-established order but from the kind of grace or mercy (*hesed*) that suspends nature. "Keep the covenant and the *hesed*" (Deut. 7:12); "in the grace (*hesed*) of the disappearance (*olam*), I wombed you (*rihamtich*)" (Isa. 54:8). The cutting expresses the break in the natural totality and in the immediacy, which makes the *berit* possible. It introduces movement into the illusion of stillness that we experience in this world of passage and returns the being to passage (especially when it opens onto the other in the collectivity). It is only logical, then, that the ceremony of the covenant comprises a rite of passage between the cut pieces of the sacrifice.[73]

The *berit* is consequently a way of animating the world that shatters the original all (or the nostalgic illusion thereof) in the passage. It acts like a

71. See annex 2 in Trigano, *Forgotten Dwelling*, p. 427.

72. Witness the covenant between Laban and Jacob, "Let us make a covenant you and I... Jacob took a stone and set it up as a monument... and they ate there on the mound" (Gen. 31:44).

73. The Covenant between the Pieces in Gen. 15:18 or the covenant described in Jer. 34:19, where the partners to a covenant pass between the parts of a sacrificed cow.

memory of creation, a reviviscence of the original shattering of creation,[74] putting the momentarily arrested world back into the movement of the origin. It is a way of making a single, privileged one, a unique partner and ally, step outside the world and stand out from all others. The *berit* thus permits a relationship with the other, which maintains a hiatus and a difference in level. A void subsists in it, one that is not and cannot be filled, and that the *berit* preserves from fatal objectivation, from the reproduction of representation. The possibility of a nonplenishing relationship safeguards the image (*tzelem*) against representation, and this is why the *berit* is the very mode of the human being's relationship to God: the hollowing and voiding of the being as a totality that generates the one, the divine unity despite and in the relationship of human beings with God. Thus, lodged at the core of the covenant between human beings is the covenant with God, which is the covenant of God with the world, the world as covenant (relationship to oneself), but also God as covenant in itself (relationship of the all and of the one in God). The *berit* creates the prospect of a covenant in which the relationship to oneself would not be solely a relationship of constitution, as is the case with the state, but rather a relationship in which the void is maintained. This is a structure of existence in which the coming has not yet come to pass, one in which it is impending. This unstable structure *obliges* the being to make continual efforts to rise to the level of the other, which amounts to striving to maintain the level of the self. The self is not a given from the start; it is an effort of passage and that which authenticates the pursuit of the one.

The covenant is also structured around a second pole. If its first stage is the memory and repetition of the original break, the setting into motion of passage, the passing cannot be left to itself and the breaking abandoned to its chasm. The break is consummated in an oath that transcends and redeems the memory of the origin. The oath *obliges* us to the other—that is to say, it enjoins us to situate ourselves in relation to the other's presence, even and especially in his absence. In the oath, the other is ceaselessly present, even when eclipsed, so that the being strains toward the appearance of the one. The oath thus completes the *tikkun* of the world that the *berit* undertook. The repetition of the *tikkun* is more than a repetition. It engenders an overplus, an addition of being, and in so doing, it rediscovers the meaning and secret of existence. The world of disappearance sinking into oblivion prepares the way for the covenant, which is redeemed from oblivion, but oathless remembrance is like a barren woman. The oath is a *keddusha*, a sanctification-separation;

---

74. See above Book I, ch. 1, "World-Covenant."

it is a procedure of birth and coming to be that draws the one out of the depths of a past revived by remembrance and leads it to the present and on to the future. The *keddusha* is an act of separating from the separation, from the break, from the cut, and so it is a reparation of the origin. The break is inherent in the passage. If remembrance is related to the origin, the moment of the all prior to the break, the oath is related to the one; and the covenant forms the structure of time, for it is posited in exteriority yet assumes this exteriority in the interior.

This dimension of sanctification is what accounts for the singular nature of the *berit*; it is what makes it radically different from the contract and any other binding procedures. Instead of establishing a static balance between partners, each of whom maintains his apartness, his *quant-à-soi*, the covenant impels enormous creative mobility. Whereas contracts provide a safeguard against forgetting, the covenant is a commitment to remembering and a move in the direction of the one. The "symbol," whose institutional function in Greece was very close to the *berit*, further underscores the uniqueness of the latter. The aim of the symbolic procedure was to bring together separated partners through a mutual recognition based on an object. Before separating, the partners cut an object in two, usually a clay fragment. Each one kept half, eventually passing it on to their offspring. The two parts brought together served to identify the holders and prove their previously contracted relations of hospitality. All of this is diametrically opposed to the oath. In the case of the symbol, the memory and the commitment are confined to an object. No effort is required, no necessity to stay on the lookout, nothing but the passive insouciance of chance to reunite the divided pieces. No remembrance here. The relationship is abandoned to total exteriority, and the aim of bringing the "symbol" back together again is bound up with the objective reconstitution of the original unity, of the original whole broken in the passage of the meeting and of time passing. Nothing has come to pass in the meantime. The other has not been an exigency, someone to whom one is *obliged*. The separation of the two partners has never been an experience of emptiness; it has never shaken their reciprocal integrity. In the symbolic relationship, memory requires no effort, and the present need not strive to overcome forgetting so as to join up with the missing, absent other; it is rather the passive consequence of chance. We can already see the state and the obsession with the all emerging in the "symbol."

The Covenant between the Pieces, which binds Abraham to God (Gen. 15) provides us with an archetype for the *berit*. The central question that brings about this covenant is the question of heritage, of the substitution

of one for the other in the ownership of property in this world, a property
that is, as we will see, presumed and putative, since the land that Isaac's
son inherits is as yet but a promise. "You have not given me an offspring,
and here the son of my household[75] inherits me" (15:3), Abraham says. The
succession (the substitution of presence) to the world of the father, who is
summoned to die, hesitates here between filiation (offspring; literally, "seed")
and objective habitation (the emphasis on the house).

Which one of the two will govern the filling of the vacuum? The personalized, individualized relationship, the birth-giving, dynamic relationship of
filiation, or the static and passive relationship, even if it is characterized by
affectivity, of geographic space? Which principle will structure presence in the
world, beyond the passing of generations and of a world that is continually
coming undone? Will it be the principle of the son who emerged from his
father's bosom, from his interiority, out of the undifferentiation of past generations, he who will be called by his one and only name ("Your son, your one
and only," Gen. 22:2) and who, beyond the silence and absence of his youth
(the young man, *elem*, is the "absent" one), will succeed his father and finally
really appear in a second appearance (adulthood), which is the *tikkun* of his
first appearance (birth)? Or will it be the principle of the one whom chance
has placed there, in spatial proximity, who has not come out of the interior
of his father, out of his father's longings and hopes, and whose presence (in
the succession) will only cover up the absence of the father by "representing" him? Choosing Eliezer, "son of the household," would be choosing the
state, in a manner of speaking, because it would turn the *household* into the
criterion of continuity for Abraham's presence in the world, a criterion of
exteriority. On the other hand, choosing Isaac, or rather the possibility of
Isaac, is choosing the one, a criterion of interiority and testimony. It is also
worthy of note that choosing Eliezer would amount to opting for what is
immediate and obvious. Eliezer is all in this world, in the illusion that the
world of *olam* is that of appearance, manifestation, and phenomena, whereas
Isaac takes time to come. He is the object of a hope, a promise, and an effort.
The children of the patriarchs always take a long time being born. And it is
those who are born second who are the true heirs, at the end of a period of
waiting and an effort to bring out the one.

---

75. Household in the sense of *oikos*: the reference is to Eliezer, Abraham's adopted son,
who is designated first as *ben meshek beiti* (Gen. 15:2), the son of my economic household,
and then as *ben beiti* (15:3), the son of my household.

Indeed, in the demanding dialogue that Abraham enters into with God, the divine word recurrently echoes the call to "go out." God "takes him outside," out of the house precisely, out of the spatial enclosure of the dwelling where God could only have been "represented," and outside himself, so as to announce to him the promise of a descendance. This barely discernible and materializable descendance can be perceived only by looking skyward, as one would look to see the countless stars. "Look at the sky and count (*sfor*) the stars, if you are able to count them" (Gen. 15:5).

The son who is thus announced is so as a gift ("What will you give me?... You have not given me seed," "I took you out... to give you this land..." 15:2–8), a gift endowed to a man who has left his native land ("I took you out of Ur to give you..."), has gone through the ordeal of emptiness, and has been able to "recall" the presence of the absent other in the passage, to "give" without an immediate return, without even the certainty that there will be one. And it is out of this ordeal that the son is born, a son who already appeared in the waiting and the promise when he was not yet there, a son whose real presence was nurtured by his feverish absence. So Abraham's gift (here "*tzedaka*")—that is, his readiness to wait, the fact that he "believed in" or "accredited God" (*leha'amin, aminut*—credibility)—was "*yahsheveha* (meaning reckoned or counted or deemed) in his favor" (15:6). The son comes as a recompense for the gift of Abraham, who withstood the torture of the son's absence, accredited the promise of an announced son when there was none, made room for a son who was not yet there, and worked toward his appearance. In answer to the ability to count the countless (15:5) comes the reckoning (*yahsheveha*) of the gift. This ordeal ties together two completely different orders: the infinite and the finite, passage and permanence, dereliction and hope. Which is why "Abraham's faith" (15:6), his trust in the promise, is already a partial fulfillment of the promise. And it speaks of much more than a "Pascalian" wager, for it involves the commitment of the entire being who is summoned. The waiting is a form of asceticism, not a nonchalant expectation.

How does Abraham respond to this critical moment? "He brought for him all these (sacrificial animals: the heifer, the she-goat, the ram, and the turtledove), severed (*yevater*) them in the middle (*tavech/toch*),[76] and gave to each (*ish*) its half (*bitro*) in front of (*likrat*) its counterpart (*re'ehu*), but the bird he did not sever (*batar*)" (Gen. 15:10). And "there appeared a smoking oven and a flaming torch which passed (*avar*) between these pieces (*gezarim*).

76. *Tavech*, the middle, *toch*, inside: the word is the same; only the vocalization differs.

On that day God cut a *berit* with Abraham" (15:17–18). What is being established in this critical scene is a complete economy of the one and the all,
a viaticum of passage, and a dynamics of presence. The covenant appears
here as the outcome of a break, of the act of severing, and even linguistically,
there is a proximity between *berit* and *batar*.[77] The multiple, diverse totality
of animals—with its notable threefold (*meshuleshet*) character: "a threefold
[three-year-old?] heifer, a threefold she-goat, a threefold ram, a turtledove,
and a dove"—is taken together and cut in the middle and consequently in
two. What emerges from this cutting of the all is the one (*ish*). Each one in its
serial quality is defined here in relation to the other part from which it is cut
off. It is the cutting that creates its very being, described firstly as "its piece
(*bitro*)" and thereafter as "its counterpart (*re'ehu*)." Abraham accomplishes this
passage from the "piece" to the "counterpart" by an act of rapprochement: he
places the cut and separated piece "in front of" or "toward" (*likrat*) its other
part, and it is this act of associating, of moving the cut piece forward, that
makes it exist as a counterpart. Individual ones (*ish*) appear therefore in the
cutting of the whole, but it starts in a state of anonymous undifferentiation
as a substitutive one identical to any other in the infinite multiplicity that
arises in the passage. It is Abraham's act that turns the scattered ones into
"counterparts" held in a relationship.

We are now in a better position to understand the meaning of the Hebrew
term for sacrifice, the *korban*, which brings closer (*karev*) by way of loss and
absence (of the sacrifice itself). Abraham's act of rapprochement is like a
sacrifice within the original sacrifice; it is, no doubt, its *tikkun*, as it mends
the anonymity and perdition of the "ones" that have arisen in the world.
The procedure of bringing "to the front of" is an act of bringing together
and reuniting. This is the arena of the political. It can lead to the state, for
representation (the recreation of the pristine whole) is a powerful temptation.

As described by Hobbes, the state is an assemblage of individual pieces,
united into a mosaic of multiplicity that has something so monstrous and
terrifying about it that he likens it to a Leviathan.[78] This finite, irrepressible multiplicity carries with it the (demonic) spirit of the collectivity: the
Leviathan, a monstrous phantom of totality in a world where the latter has
disintegrated. The rapprochement sought by the separate entities in the

77. The radical is made up of the same letters, one of which—the *resh*—is not in the
same place. This is a common procedure in the formation of Hebrew words.

78   Leviathan can be read as *Levi eytan*, powerful Levi, and the Levite is, etymologically, a companion (see below, Book II, ch. 4, "The Public of Israel: The Levitical Principle
in the Fabric of the State").

passage can spawn the Leviathan, which is the reverse side of the original sacrifice. There is, to be sure, a sacrifice in this, too, but one that retains only the bloodiness, because the rapprochement that it elicits is an illusion, a mockery of closeness. The Leviathan wraps a society of violence and murder in its shadow; it covers the uproar around the golden calf.[79]

Abraham stops short of uniting the pieces and creating a Leviathan. What he does is summed up in the subtle nuance of the term *likrat*, "to the front of" or "to meet," which speaks of an approach based on recognition of an interlocutor. Moreover, the kind of rapprochement that the dust particles and atoms gravitating in the passage mechanically seek is redeemed by Abraham's act of giving. That "he gave (*vayiten*)" (Gen. 15:10) bespeaks a fundamental posture of sacrifice that sustains the presence of the other by standing back in modesty and restraint rather than trying to create an assemblage, to produce an immediate, artificial unity. The point at issue here is well illustrated by the fact that this verse lends itself to two readings: "he gave each one to its part, to meet its counterpart," or "he placed each one with its part, opposite its counterpart" (meaning that "he set each half facing the other"). The term *gezar* used to designate the pieces a few verses later (15:17) brings home their intrinsic nature as cut parts. The recreation of the totality in the passage is a grave illusion, the illusion of idolatry that leaves no room for the other to pass through.

The Concealed Bird

But the act of bringing together the pieces is ultimately held in suspense also by the fact that all the animals were cut but one ("but the winged species,[80] he did not sever [*batar*]"). In the dividing of the all that initiates the passage, one of the elements of multiplicity, the bird, is set aside; in the division of the passage, a unity is safeguarded, its internal oneness kept intact. But already it seemed to stand out by its very nature from the three other animals, all of which were three years old (or were there three of each?). The bird was probably younger than the other animals. At any rate, the term by which it is designated, *gozal*, gives us an idea of the nature of the act and procedure used in setting it aside.

---

79. Representation resembles a sacrifice without the gift giving.

80. The *tzippor*, from a term that does not designate the two bird offerings: the *tor* and the *gozal*.

The root of *gozal* means to wrench, to rob, to plunder. In the overall destiny of the division and separation that await the being in the passage, the concealment of the one, the safeguarding of a witness to the one, can almost be said to come under the heading of a "theft." Something is abducted, removed, forcibly wrenched out the multiplicity of the world, for there is no way to remove from the count, save by force. If it were simply taken away, this would mean that it had been counted in the total (a term that takes on new meaning for us). But it is wrenched out of the total before the count, with absolutely no apparent logical reason in relation to the remaining sum in the world. Furthermore, it is set aside and hidden; we do not know what becomes of it. This is incomprehensible from the rational perspective of the sum total, of the whole that is now, theoretically, a remainder and, in any case, a mockery of genuine totality, henceforth impossible in the passage, since one of its parts has been snatched from it, and its oneness preserved, even before being counted. The original zero, without which we cannot reach ten, serves as a reminder of this wrenching of the origin, the wrenching of the one, the vacuum that makes it impossible for any tallying and totaling to be complete. This concealment is also suggested by another possible root of the term *gozal*, and that is *goz*, which denotes passage, disappearance, transport, flight, and eclipse. Similarly, the root of the term for turtledove, *tor*, signifies passing through, strolling, and touring.

Wrenching (or theft) on the one hand and disappearance (or passage) on the other refer to the same movement of setting apart the bird. Is it even sacrificed? We do not know, because the text tells us only that "Abraham took all these animals, divided each in the middle... but he did not divide the bird." Likewise, we do not know which bird is set aside and not cut. Does *tzippor*, meaning "bird," refer to the turtledove (*tor*) or the fledgling (*gozal*)? Or was it the generic bird? Unlike the other animals, the two birds are presented without mention of their age. Both belong to the same winged species, which suffices to distinguish them from the other animals, but it is from within this single species, in this alternative between the two birds, that the one is chosen to be safeguarded and concealed, and the other to be sacrificed. In the apparent sacrifice of the one subsists the wrenched and hidden one.

There are many illustrations throughout the Bible of this process in which the eventual coming of the one is accomplished by means of a trick or "theft," which is the most spectacular form of wrenching.

The 'Toch' and the Public Arena

Fundamentally, it may very well be because the one was concealed and kept out of the separation that the bringing together was held in suspense and the trap of the all avoided. This may have been what made it possible to maintain the disjunction between the parts and not let it disappear in an apparent assemblage. It is thanks to this safeguarded and concealed one that Abraham was able to maintain the space for passage, this "middle (*tavech*)" that he exposed in each consecrated animal and through which the divine passed,[81] a "middle" that did not exist before the sacrifice-rapprochement, before the gift giving. But this whole procedure of sacrifice is possible only because the one was removed from the start, wrenched out before the origin, so that it was not cut into when the all was dismembered in creation.

The polysemy of *tavech* can be understood in this light. *Tavech* means "middle" or "midst," but vocalized differently, as *toch*, it denotes the inside. For it is by placing the concealed one within that the interiority of the inside is constituted, leaving the world in the (relative) exteriority of *tavech*, an exteriority that is not an end in itself, since it is spontaneously the middle and the place of the passage through the parts, through the individual, separated pieces. For this reason, the place where Abraham will accomplish the rapprochement (the *kerev*) of the sacrifice (*korban*) is the place of the collectivity, of the gathering of human beings, and it raises the question of the state as a form of assembly and of the one. We can understand this directly, since there is here a place of passage and hence one that can accommodate everyone, where all can meet and that all can freely traverse—the place of "passing over" particularities that the state pretends to be, according to its highest aspirations. But we also know that there is here a milieu that, according to Abraham's intention, is inside, in interiority, so that the place of the political is posited as being within and not without.[82]

It is, of course, this possibility of a different economy of *toch* that determines the nature of the political relationship. Is the *toch* the place for going beyond individualities? Is it the common space outside the closed citadels of each individual where all can circulate when they leave their own places? As a rule, it is in these terms that the democratic state and the *res publica* have been conceived. The law and the rules of conduct in this public arena

81. "There appeared a smoking oven and a flaming torch that passed (*avar*) between these pieces" (Gen. 15:17).

82. See below, Book II, ch. 5, "Abode of Testimony: The Political Arena."

of circulation have always been the criteria defining the nature of this space: Who has the right to pass in between the encapsulated individualities? One? Some? Several? All? This is the key that locks or unlocks the households.

But the question is altogether different from the prophetic perspective. It is to know if the *toch*, the place reserved for the passage, is meant for use by the public or for the coming of the one, for its gestation. In the latter case, it would retain a dimension of potentiality and creative effervescence that could not exist in a public arena conceived as a place where individualities cross each other's paths. Finished and complete, such a public space is a nondescript place of passage where each person carries around his or her individuality in perfect anonymity and is not even seen anymore. The public arena is uninhabited. The place where mass presence is greatest is the place where presence is as absent as can be! The "public thing" (*res publica*) is that which is neglected and abandoned. But if the place of *toch* is what is left when the one is wrenched from the all, it can be something other than the place of the hiatus of the all that allows the individualities and the elements of the world to be constituted and to romp and frolic about (all of the movement is on this level). It can be the place that, in the *olam*, bears the imprint of the one, the vestige of the one, not as a tombstone but as a portent of the one to come: a remembrance that lives up to the promise.

The *toch* thus becomes the place in the passage that bears the germination of the one and heralds its return, its *tikkun*. When the *toch* is made public, the one is renounced as living presence; the place it deserted, where individuals are manifested as feeble, distant echoes of the archetypical one, is held to be forever a desert. To be sure, the one haunts this place in a vague way, but the only effect of its virtual memory is to feed the desire to recreate it in the form of a representation, an artifact, using the pieces that are held to be forever shattered. It is the state that responds to this fascination with the one by falling into the trap of the all. The state institutes the desert like impersonality of the place. It reifies and turns its back on it, considering it dead and inert, and, if it feels the need to misrepresent it as the all, it is because it has totally lost faith in the life and future of the one.

A totally disoriented and misguided use of the passage is established in this way. The passage that is the procession of the being from the all to the one becomes the setting for all possible paths, an infinite passage with no beginning, no end, and no purpose, nothing but an inert universe of rock and dust: a monumental city, not the abode of human beings. The passage elevated to an absolutized being henceforth lacks the purpose of the passage. The state, which is supposed to crystallize absolute passage, becomes an obstacle to it. The "public thing" masks the one, covers it up, and consecrates its burial beneath the anonymity of paving stones.

The same mechanism is at work in the state as in the passage of attributes and in representation in general. Whereas exteriority is immediately accessible, in interiority, because the reality of the *toch* is a vehicle of emergence, the other is manifested slowly, takes time to emerge, flounders in time. The state is impatient with time. This is why it misses the birth of the sons. It tries to bypass the path of the being by pouring cement over the openings of the disjunction and hiatus that is the world, and trampling the frail flower growing in the loose earth. But the being and the attributes pass through the passage, through the disjunction of the world, and they do not stop there. And when they pass by, man covers his face the way Moses did, for they cannot be the object of representation, since they are being called to the one; or perhaps he covers his face to show that what is passing is inside, not outside. Thus, "there appeared a smoking oven and a flaming torch which passed between the pieces [placed around the *toch* by Abraham]. On that day God 'cut' [concluded] a *berit* with Abraham" (Gen. 15:17–18).

The sacrifice of cut pieces offered by Abraham (notably in the relationship of the all and the one, of the cut pieces and the inside) is what makes it possible for the divine attributes to pass through the *olam*, for the being to pass without falling into the trap of reification. It is, no doubt, also the inner logic that is at work in the sacrifice of Abraham that can best evince the nature and function of the attributes and answer the question of how, in the world of *olam* and of the particularization that dismembers the all, God can "pass" and manifest himself in the horizon of unity. We can now understand on a higher level how the attributes could conceptually found the bases of power and the political sphere throughout Jewish history.

The Land of the Covenant

The narrative of Abraham's sacrifice also shows us how the passage has a direct bearing on the political. "The covenant [is concluded] to say" (Gen. 15:18) political matters. Its main focus is on the land intended for Israel, on Israel's collective destiny, its status, its relationship to the nations, and so on.[83] The covenant here establishes the basis for Israel's collective existence and does so in a way that already suggests the main outlines of a political

83. Midrash Rabba sees this verse as prefiguring the four empires that would dominate the Earth and oppress Israel. Cf. Genesis Rabba, *Lech Lecha* 44:15.

paradigm that is not the state. More generally, it is the mode of Israel's collective presence and residence in the world that is at issue in this text, which is connected to a vision, and not the terms of the covenant.

The vision came when, after Abraham had driven away birds of prey that had descended upon the carcasses of the sacrifice, the sun began to set, and he fell into a deep, dreadful slumber.[84] What is announced to him is what escapes him. The first time the land is mentioned, when it is in relation not to Abraham alone but to the collectivity of Israel as well, it is in negative terms: "a land not theirs" (Gen. 15:13), where Abraham's children will be *gerim*, or guest-residents,[85] where they will be in exile and even serve as slaves to the "nation (*goy*)," and, after the fourth generation, "they will *come out* with a great acquisition" (15:16). That is when they "will return" to a land that they never in fact left, a land that is described in the covenant in detail, complete with its boundaries and the names of the peoples living there (15:18–21).

We go here from the most poignant absence, the "land that is not" (a moment of "darkness"), to light passing through the night ("a flaming torch" [15:17]). The act that governs Israel's relationship with the land is one of giving: "To your offspring, I gave this land" (15:18). As we have seen, the relationship of giving involves setting the self aside, retreating to leave room for the other. Such a relationship cannot be complete from the start or established on a basis of "equality"—that is to say, of exteriority of one to the other, of absence, of turning one's back on the other precisely when the relationship is being initiated.

Equality is a relationship of mutual externalization of two beings, who create a bond only by the agency of an objectified external referent. The relationship we are speaking about here has an interior dimension: In it, the other lives in my home. I give and he receives. But because the beneficiary of the gift is filled with gratitude toward me, and because my presence pervades him too greatly, the giving relationship is an incomplete and unfulfilled relationship. This is suggested in the text through the notion of completion or wholeness (*shalem, shalom*), which comes up twice in reference to the enslavement of the Jews and their return. After "they are enslaved" and they "come out with a great acquisition" (Gen. 15:12), "you [Abraham] will go to your fathers in peace (*shalom*), you will be buried at a good old age." As for

84. See "La somnolence d'Adam," in Trigano, *Story of Disappeared Presence*, p. 225.

85. This condition as foreigners on the land does not contradict the concept of "pariah people" developed by Max Weber and picked up by Hannah Arendt to define the Jews, but it actually designates something altogether different (see below, Book II, ch. 4, "The Public of Israel: The Levitical Principle in the State").

them, "the fourth generation will return here, for the sin of the Amorites is not yet complete (*shalem*)" (15:16).

The second completion (*shalem*) is employed in reference to the time of Israel's exile and its ultimate salvation, and it is assigned a negative factor. It concerns the Amorites, one of the nations from the land of Canaan, whereas the first completion concerns Abraham. Abraham's completion is the counterpart of the incompletion that is the exile. The second occurrence signifies that completion is defined via a negative criterion, even if it indicates its ultimate surpassment. In other words, incompletion is not a (dialectical) stage in completion; the completion is never whole and knows no consummate fullness. The exile and enslavement of the collectivity do not stand in the way of the individual's (Abraham's) completion, but what kind of wholeness can there be if the children are enslaved? Furthermore, the *shalom* here is contiguous with the burial. There is a very harsh, ironic side to this situation. The completion is associated with death, at a time when the children are in darkness. But the return is not possible as long as the sin of the Amorites has not been completed. The Promised Land has at last been given, but it remains defined solely in terms of this negative relationship to the accomplishment of a sin: it hangs in the balance of the Amorite's sin. In other words, as long as the sin is not accomplished, the land will not be Israel's, and Israel will not return to the land.

In what way does the sin of nations living on the land that has been promised to Israel govern its relation to it? How do relationships of fullness and absence, of plenitude and incompletion, define the nature of the land of Israel? "A stranger (*ger*) will be your seed in a land not theirs" seems to describe the exile in Egypt, but it could also describe the relationship with the land of Israel, a relationship of passage and nonfixity to that which would seem to epitomize what is objective, external, inert, arrested, and finished: namely, the land and rootedness in a land. Israel can be outside this land, and nations can occupy it; it can be given the land when it does not know it, and a moral criterion can determine its occupation! It is in this regard that the passage is most palpable and most powerfully trying, because a people's land is the cast shadow of a collectivity in the world, the strongest sign of its existence.

Conditioned by the iniquity of the Amorites, the land of Israel resembles a forfeit, a deduction from the *olam* of disappearance and incompletion. Severed from the existence of Israel, it attests to the nature of Israel's manifestation: absence. Isn't the land of Israel inhabited by the Amorites, whose iniquity spreads and who inhabit the land only until their iniquity is complete?

We have here an asymmetrical relationship of *giving*, in which one member is absent but held to be present by the other member, who acts as if the missing one were present. The absent other is consequently structurally and essentially lodged in the being of the one who is thinking of and waiting for him, but his absence puts him at a distance, out of the control of the one who is present, and in a position of freedom. This is why the other takes time coming and is the fruit of patience in (of) the being. This is an attitude of total openness to the other's absolute freedom, because the room that is made for the other holds a secret that cannot be mastered. It is as if the other were "posited" in a way that anything could come of him. This suspension of being in the face of the other, which makes the other possible, is the mechanism that wards off idolatrous representation. It takes the other out of my control and creates the arena of his exteriority to me, establishing the basis of the exteriority in the being where the other can be manifested. In this way, it avoids the temptation of fusion, of recapturing and reincorporating the other as soon as he has come out of me. This is the function of the sacrifice (*korban*). It is also the principle of the world's creation: God's waiting vis-à-vis man.

Patience in the 'Olam'

The waiting, or patience, in the world of *olam* (which is what makes for the permanence of Israel) constitutes the absolute category of Israel's existence. Whatever variations it undergoes, all are expressions of the same principle. Remembrance, giving, the oath, the promise, and the intention are all strategies of the patience and waiting that underpin the abode of the other on earth and constitute the very spirit of the covenant and the sacrifice. For this reason, the being of Israel that is lodged in the middle/interior (*toch*) of the covenant and of Abraham's sacrifice of pieces takes the form of a "promise"; a relationship (to the land and to the son) is posited as certain and called upon to take place; and even though it is not here yet, we are living, here and now, under its jurisdiction and according to the principle of its reality.

Thus defined, otherness emerges in the *olam* only through gestation in temporality. And there must be duration in time, since human history is the history of the *tikkun* of man, of his completion through the *olam*. The secret in the being, which makes the other possible, also defines man, who appears in the shadow of God, a being of emergence from the being coiled up in the foundational secrecy. What makes this depth possible, this echo in which the other is nestled, is the concealment in secrecy of the one wrenched from the all. In the question of the other, it is the question of the one that is at issue, for it is only in the withdrawal, distancing of, and distension of the one that the other is possible in the passage. And it is because the one is hidden away and given as a promise to its absence (which creates the passage) that the passage is not absorbed by the disappearance inherent in it and that human beings have the time to take form in their passage through the world.

This is why it is primordial—such is the law of being—to preserve the one even though we are in the passage, to protect it by concealing it in a secret place. This is the meaning of God's concealment in the heart of the *polis*; it is the meaning of the unification (*yihud*) of God's Name within the multiplicity of passage, a unification that is like a veiling or darkening[86] in the world and for the world. The very possibility of the world is based on the concealment of the one, as is its continued existence and its movement inward to interiority and consummation.

If the middle/interior (*toch*) in between the pieces, which is the site of the political, is formed from the wrenching of the one (and its concealment), this means that the one is the deep-seated principle underpinning the *polis* and the political. The political usually seeks the one, trying to make it emerge and come to be in the immediacy of the state. When human beings give in to impatience in their quest for the one, they obtain only a representation of the all, as if the pursuit of the one involved recomposing the all prior to its decomposition, when, if this were so, the one would be a particular element and a detail of the all, whence the idea of wrenching the one from the whole. This is not a "logical" operation; it is more akin to a theft or an abduction.

There is, on the other hand, a "logic" in trying to set up a representation of the one, which could only ever be a recreation of the all, an illusion, a mock speech, and a mock presence. This is why the promise opens onto the category of a totally different political form, one that seeks not to manifest and crystallize the one in the place of the *toch*, the place of its wrenching (the solution of the state and of representation), but to safeguard it and preserve it in secrecy. The *toch* is, in any case, the original place of the political, that is, of the effort to get out of the passage and move toward the one. The modality of the state develops an economy from the *toch* that subverts and reverses it, turning it inside out like a piece of clothing. At the very site of the interior, it opts for the path of exteriority, whereas the modality of patience develops

86. The *Shema Yisrael* is recited with eyes closed.

an economy based on secrecy and not display. The one dwells in the Hebraic
toch, in secrecy, veiled, stolen, and hidden from sight.

This concealment, or "theft," manifests love, not disdain: "Its midst (*tocho*)
is woven with love" (Song 3:10). The interior of *toch* is a whole that conceives
love, a relationship of intimacy that is constantly inhabited, even in absence,
by the remembrance of and waiting for the beloved's presence. The greatest
danger that could befall the one is to find itself exposed in exteriority, that
is, in the passage, when in fact it must be kept secret in the shadow of the
interior, because we are still in the passage. There is a tension at the heart
of the political experienced in the *toch*, a tension between veiling and unveiling, darkness and light, the short term and the long term, patience and
immediacy. This tension is constitutive of the *toch*, and one must certainly
not try to find a solution for it, for that would mean defusing the very gist
of the *toch* and the interplay of presence and absence.

It is exactly the same thing for God's attributes. In them is hidden the
divine unity that must be safeguarded; it is, in fact, at the very site of the
wrenching of divine unity that the attributes are constructed. Their ambivalence is essential and dynamic; they must not be congealed and leveled in
a philosophical construct that cannot grasp the moving, dynamic metaphor
they represent.

'Polis' Versus 'Mishkan'

These two possible approaches to the milieu-of-the-pieces of the sacrifice
correspond to two very different theaters of the political. The theater of
the state is the *polis*, the city-state embodied by Athens, while the secret of
patience constructs the *mishkan*, which has been mistranslated as "temple"
but actually refers to much more than a building: the *mishkan* is the dwelling place, it is dwelling itself.[87] Naturally, it is in the place of dwelling, in
the place where the presence or its simulacra appear, that the political body
convenes and authorities meet. In Rome, the Senate could meet only in a
place consecrated by the oracles, a division of space, sky, and earth within
which, from the *interior* of which, it examined and interpreted omens. In
Athens, the *polis* designates the Acro*polis*, the sacred enclosure of the gods. It
was in the shadow of the Temple of Jerusalem that the Sanhedrin assembled,
too, at the precise place of the *toch*, which is between the cut pieces of the

---

87. See below, "The 'Polis' at the Gate," pp. 231–243.

animals of Abraham's sacrifice, and which establishes the foundation of both the Temple and the Sanhedrin.[88]

Whereas the temple is a division of space that differentiates an interior and an exterior in a way that is purely spatial, thereby recreating a simulacrum of interiority where presence is exercised, a *mishkan* is a relationship, a dynamic, a posture, a way of behaving. The *mishkan* is the Hebraic counterpart of the *polis*. To designate, on the other hand, the "Temple" as monument and separation, the appropriate term is *Beit Hamikdash*, or House of Separation-Holiness. Even when the *polis* is deployed in a delimited, separate space, it is structured on the principle of exteriority. First of all, the interiority that is created relies on the prior division of space and the boundary between the sacred and the profane. One could say that there is a need for the monumental temple to secure presence. In the case of the *mishkan*, the relationship of presence precedes the monument and the Temple, and, effectively, the *mishkan* is the essence of the Temple of Jerusalem: the itinerant, dismountable desert Tabernacle precedes the building of the Temple; this means that there is a place prepared for the presence, independent of the walls of stone that will constitute its ulterior abode. The presence can be veiled and hidden without the protection of a walled enclosure.

Light and Power

There is in this institution of secrecy a whole relationship to light that differentiates the *mishkan* and the *polis*. The passage is animated by the movement of light; its milieu is light. And light, like remembrance and giving, refers to the other. Its source is always elsewhere, even as it is at one with each and every object that it brings to light and takes out of the chaos of darkness by giving shape to it. But it remains ungraspable, and it is always already leaping on to other, more distant places, awakening everything it approaches, and spreading darkness when it departs.

One of the greatest experiences of passage is in the path taken by the day (*yom*),[89] by passing time, by the coming and going of light. Darkness is embedded in the story of light, and darkness raises the same question as passage. Is its love for light so immense that it pursues it in its displacement

---

88. Midrash Rabba sees in the sacrifice of the pieces a prefiguration of the Temple, where the Sanhedrin would assemble.

89. See "Altrité contre normalité," in Trigano, *New Jewish Question*, p. 86.

and exile at dusk?[90] Or is darkness, in the passage of light, a compassionate turning toward daybreak that advances beyond the spreading night? In
darkness, as in the original covenant, the presence is there, veiled and kept
secret but not inexistent. The critical issue is what human beings will do with
it. There is a drama inherent in darkness. The awareness of darkness arises
from the excessive love for light, which runs the risk of seeing darkness as
the enemy of light.

In the passage, darkness is waiting and patience, not despair. Impatience
builds its empire in darkness, in the manner of Egypt and Greece, whose
yearning for light paradoxically spread darkness over the earth. What is
the beauty that the Bible sees as the archetype of Greece (Noah's son Yefet,
meaning beauty, is considered its ancestor) if not impatience with darkness?
Indeed, when art aims at representation,[91] it seeks to transcend darkness,
to ward off absence, by employing shadow as an instrument to make light
useful. All art forms—painting and sculpture, to be sure, but also, if more
subtly, music—are, to a great extent, grounded in contrast, in the contrast
between darkness and light or between short and long intervals. The principle of art is chiaroscuro, light and dark, the rhythmic and tense interplay
between shadow and light, the position of an object whose forms consist of
a relationship between near and far, presence and absence. Art is this erotic
relationship in an unbridled search for light, a search that places the obstacle
of darkness on its path, that is exalted and sublimated thanks to darkness,
and refuses to give itself totally to the object of its pursuit, repudiating it
so as to love it from a distance: light seen from the standpoint of darkness.
Art thus sets up something that it never attains, which is why it is tragic.
There is a relentless harshness running through its works, even though they
dream of reflecting a bit of grace and creating intimacy. It is there in the
icy perfection of a Greek statue, in the eternal remoteness of an icon, in the
ungraspability of music barred from space. Light shimmers there, but it is
veiled. In this case, the veiling is not the creational retreat of the original
light; rather, it participates in an "economy" of light that the artist aspires
to master. It becomes a utilitarian tool,[92] and it is used not in the sense of

90. The excessive pursuit of goodness and unity can give rise to evil. Out of love of
light, we may be tempted to see night as darkness only, in which case all hope of "repairing" the world is lost.

91. Schools of art developed in modernity that sought to overcome the ineluctability
of representation.

92. The significance of the prohibition of using Hanukka lights for utilitarian purposes
becomes clear from this point of view, especially insofar as Hanukka commemorates a

bounty, of concealing the other and its "overplus," but in the sense of sameness and scarcity. Hence, the light is used[93] on the plane of shadow, night goes on forever, and dawn is not brought forth.

The same sort of reversal of the project of being is found when Esau sells his rights as the firstborn son in exchange for a lentil stew, turning what belongs to the realm of grace into a product in the world of *din*, or rigor, the world of power struggles. This is light used in the economy of the night instead of the other way around.[94] The memory and the origin of light are eclipsed as a result, and henceforth, the source of light is in the night.

It is in this sense that we can understand the prophet Zechariah's vision of the golden *menora*, interpreted in the text itself as a vision of the relationship between two economies of being, founded on the principle of light or night, Israel or Greece: "not by an army and not by violence but by my spirit" (Zech. 4:6). In this perspective, light is united with "lifebreath (*ruach*)," and their course through darkness can be traced from dusk to dawn. The statue that sets light up in the dark at the cost of using the night is violence for the being: it is the antithesis of a problematic of lifebreath, of *ruach*.

Light is the natural medium of power. The sun and the moon were created to "govern" day and night (Gen. 1:16). It is in reference to this and not to the land and its division into territories that the first occurrence of a term designating domination (*memshala*)[95] appears in the Torah. We know from historical experience that all ruling powers conceive of themselves in terms of light and try to recreate the brightness in their pomp. The very notion of order and reason is an offshoot of the notion of light. The Sun-King ruling over his perfectly straight, geometrical parks is the archetype of this association between light, power, and order; order produces a stream of luminescence in things that contributes to the transparency of the world. The ruling power

victory over Greece, at a time when a statue of Zeus had been set up in the Temple of Jerusalem, in the light of the great golden *menora*.

93. This "use" of light can be heard in the well-known phrase from Ecclesiastes, "there is nothing new under the sun," as the word for sun, *shemesh*, derives from the same root as *shamash*, which designates utility.

94. The ruse that Rebecca suggests to Jacob that will enable him to inherit the birthright has to do more with concealment than with deception. The biblical ruse is the stratagem of prophetic clairvoyance that aims at confronting each person with the responsibility and role the person would assume if he or she were clear-sighted. It situates the absence in a situation of overplus and is to be read in terms of an overplus rather than a retreat or a lack.

95. And even conflict, for, as the Midrash tells us, the moon and the sun fought for the same crown, necessarily conceived as unique ("How can there be two kings for a single crown?"), even though the light is so immense that it cannot be measured (all the more since it is concealed).

sees all, passes through all. It encounters neither obstacles nor opacity. Its passage is absolute. Is power, then, the cardinal attribute of light?

Light harbors infinite might, but its being-for-the-world is passage and comprises a moment of veiling, of dimming, in the manner of the night that follows the dusk in the unity of the same "day" (the Hebraic *yom*). The greatest creational power of light is deployed in its being-for-the-world, its passage, its darkening, its fading into night, its being hidden away and kept secret, its power as an overplus to spawn the dawn. Human power derives from this infinite power, but it surfaces as an attempt to block the passage, to create mechanisms to capture and imprison the light (the state is one such mechanism). However, there is nothing malefic about the veiling as such, for it is contained in the creational intention. The nonvisibility of the pristine light is, in fact, a dimension of birth-giving mercy and compassion: ceaselessly light keeps returning in its absence. Such is the role of the luminaries: "Their splendor is beautiful in all the *olam*... Beauty and glory they bestow upon his name, jubilation and glad song upon the memory of his reign" (prayer). They are there in the sky as reminders of a light of such absolute brightness that it could cast the world back into nothingness. Here the splendor is clearly the relationship of light and disappearance. Isn't this also what defines remembrance? (And all memories are memories of the kingdom, of absolute presence.)

But, as we have seen, this place of the coming of the world that is the moment of creation harbors the possibility of its inversion, of holding passage back. Human beings can draw power from the light of the original grace. They can form an accumulation from that which is volatile, subverting it to their own ends, usurping it for their own advantage, not gratuitously (like the sun) for the purposes of growth and germination or (like the moon) to make the waters swell, but for organizing scarcity, measurement, distribution, ownership: the opposite of bounty (*shefa*). As in the case of aesthetics, light here is used on the plane of darkness and congealed in calculated relationships of measurement. This is why tradition tells us that the pristine light is reserved for the righteous (*tzaddikim*), whose righteousness (*tzedaka*) is informed by the primal gratuitousness (witness the Covenant between the Pieces, where Abraham is said to have *tzedaka*), by the compassionate light whose splendor is so great that it is not visible in the world (hence the tradition of the "hidden righteous").[96] In this creational veiling, the power of

---

96. This is why it is a matter of "righteousness" in the sense of justness and correctness, in the sense of compliance with *din*, with rigor, a rigor that, were it not concealed,

human beings can stand as a mockery to the power of God. The scope of human freedom is such that it can be used to set up a false construction, and to do so in God's Name. The veil over the face is then contorted in the rictus of the mask and the representational icon.

There is darkness in power firstly because it participates in the project of light. Power that aspires to master light is already, from the outset, in the shadow in which the world was created and thanks to which it stands. But the exercise of power makes it doubly dark, because, in trying to imprison light, power brings the passage to a standstill and obtains the opposite of what it seeks. It perpetuates the night and prevents it from passing on. Aspiring to absolute passage, the potentate destroys the passage that makes him be.

The darkness that characterizes Egypt (Exod. 10:21) or Greece (which the Midrash tells us "dimmed the eyes of Israel" by prohibiting the study of the Torah in the period before the revolt of the Maccabees) is more precisely the darkness in which is buried the face of the other, the face of God, and in which one cannot see the other, when, in the confusion of languages, all communication is miscomprehension, where meaning goes from one darkness (that of human beings) to another (that of the being-*olam*) without ever glimpsing the light that subtends it. It is this "great darkness" (Gen. 15:12) that overwhelms Abraham after his having accomplished the sacrifice of the Covenant between the Pieces, because what he saw then was the succession of the empires of the world that would cast his children into exile over the course of history. This is why it is imperative to come to understand the face in the political,[97] because this is the way to make the face radiate what is lost in the shadow of the absence of knowledge.

What underpins power, what underpins its own overstepping, its own subversion? It belongs, in effect, to the principle of light, even if its modality is faulty. The paradoxical fundament of human power is the creational light. Rigor (*din*) inhabits mercy (*rahamim*) and is not possible without it. Without light, power is nothing. There is therefore no power or evil that is absolute and radical: nestled in the depths of evil is good, which is why evil is destined to be subverted through and through. Even if it casts light out into exile in the very remotest part of the world, darkness will ultimately be overcome by it and cannot subsist without it, not even for a moment, for no sooner does light appear than darkness disappears. "Like the dawn,

---

would be so powerful it would destroy everything in its passage, since the world could not measure up to its standards.

97. See below, "The Face in the Voice," pp. 500–515.

God's emergence is prepared" (Hos. 6:3). The same is true of Israel among the nations. The same is true of the righteous of the earth, who sustain it but cannot be seen. This is why only "the blind seers, full of light (*sagi nahor*)" are capable of seeing in the dark, for they are blind to the darkness, but their inner eye sees beyond it. Thus, man is summoned to be transparent and bright in the world and in the darkness. The saying in *Pirkei Avot* that is usually translated as "be cautious with power" (2:3) can also be interpreted as "be transparent or bright (*zahir*) in power." Only light is more powerful than power, because it is its (betrayed) secret.

This problematic is etched in the text preceding the *Shema* (prayer) on the Sabbath. At the outset, there is an ambivalence: "Yhwh/our Elohim, king of the *olam*, forms light/creates darkness, makes peace/creates all." Then comes the turning around of faith: All will know you, and all will praise you, and all will say, 'There is no holiness/apartness like Yhwh.'" And then one side joins the other: 'All will exalt you, o you who forms all." And then it's the bounty of benediction that spreads: "The El who opens daily the doors of the gateways of the east... and who illuminates the *olam* in its totality and its inhabitants, whom he created in his birth-giving mercy (*rahamim*). He who illuminates the earth and its inhabitants in *rahamim* and in his good-ness renews daily, always, the act of *bereshit*... The supreme king, he alone since then, who rises above the days of *olam*, Elohim of *olam*, in your great *rahamim*, birth us, master of our strength."

BOOK II

⚬

KINGDOM

CHAPTER 1

The Assembly of Israel: Sociality

GOD WITHDRAWS TO make room for creation, and the place of creation is in this withdrawal of the divine. But this place remains inhabited by a divine presence, without which it would be doomed to dereliction and entropy, with death as a potential, since the living God would have retreated from it. God withdraws but leaves his Name in the void left by his retreat. This retreat corresponds, in other words, to the appearance of the four-letter Name of God, which is something of the structure or "skeleton" of the pristine void. The Name is the place of a withdrawal of presence, what makes it a place.

This absence of presence could potentially involute into radical absence, but it also harbors the power of real presence, the only possible modality of presence in the world of human beings and of creation. Consequently, right from the beginning, human beings are confronted with a choice from which they cannot escape, since the world, by its very origins, is caught in the weight of inertia that is inherent in withdrawal and finds its consummation in death.

The whole task of humankind will consist of spinning the thread of life. This enterprise is summed up in the concept of *tikkun*, the mending of the world, a mending necessary from the origin, a mending *of* the origin. By the very fact that the world comes from God, it is from the outset incomplete, for what is the world if not the upsurge of an alterity to God and hence a withdrawal of the presence of God that makes room for the presence of the other? In a way, the divine Name is only maintained in the void for man. It is the name for this void whence man emerges, the root of the name(s) of man whose filiation, across the generations of names, does nothing other than transmit the Name of God. If man has a name, if he exists, it is because God has a proper Name that man can call, that he can invoke, that can be heard in the very depths of darkness and suffering, a Name that is the last, tenuous thread of his being, but which is in the realm of the "further," the superfluous, the overplus, as the Name does not appear immediately. And in fact he is in disappearance: "I will be who I will be... Elohim says *further* to Moses: this is my Name for always/for disappearance (*le'olam*), and it is my memory (*zecher*) from generation to generation" (Exod. 3:15). "YHWH is your God, and there is no *od* beside him," which means that there is no "further" or no "more" beside him, but which is usually mistranslated as "there is nothing outside him."

I. KINSHIP OF THE NAME

The Name appears in the retreat, with, as a result, a relationship of interiority and exteriority that is instituted, for if God's presence disappears, it is in this world here, the *olam*, the place of his disappearance, the disappearance that wombs the place. Divine presence draws entirely into its interiority,[98] hiding in relationship to the world that has thereby appeared.

It keeps itself in secrecy. And it is with respect to this interiorization of God's presence that the world's exteriority comes pouring out. The *olam* is the kingdom of exteriority in relationship to God (all interiority) but also no doubt to itself. The *olam*, left to itself, is the realm of boundless despair, of exteriority, where there is no hope of creating intimate bonds. But the *olam*, if it knows what its origin is, if it is aware that it springs from disappearance, can overcome its apparent inertia and move toward interiority through *tikkun*. It can redeem its lost interiority. Knowledge of the *olam*, of disappearance, is of course knowledge of God.

Is such knowledge possible? If the *olam* spawns exteriority, and the Name is the very structure of the disappearance that is the world, is this to say that the Name belongs to a sphere of absolute, radical exteriority? Indeed, it is impossible to grasp the Name fully, because it rests on the withdrawal of presence; it waits to be called and spelled, to be taken out of its inertness. Exteriority awaits its redeemer, who will know how to call it by its name and immerse it in interiority, like Moses' staff turning the rock into a spring and the waters of the Red Sea into a passageway.

The Tetragrammaton is given to us without its vocalization—that is to say, in its absence to itself. It is unpronounceable. The *tikkun* of the world is therefore the mending of the Name, since the Name that God leaves in the world needs redemption; left to itself to lie in exteriority, it breaks down

---

98. It could not hide in exteriority, because the latter emerges from its disappearance. Yet it is not out of reach of exteriority. The relationship between the two is more dynamic and essential than spatial.

and sinks into perdition. And so it is man's task to "unify God's Name" daily at times when the light is passing,[99] to reestablish it in the oneness of its interiority.

This unification of God's Name establishes the basis once again of the experience of interiority (*toch*) on Earth; it produces a disappearance in the world of disappearance that gives us indirect access to presence. The first thing human beings have to do after creation is to block the path of return to the origin so as not to surrender to nostalgia for the pristine oneness, not to give in to the irresistible attraction that the all exerts upon the created world, an attraction that leaves no room for the other to be manifested.[100] This is why man must separate/sanctify (*kadesh*) the Name, removing it from the exteriority where it lies lifeless and giving it shelter: "You shall not profane the Name of my separation/holiness; I shall be separated/sanctified in the interior (*toch*) of the children of Israel; I am YHWH, who separates/sanctifies you" (Lev. 22:32). It is in this interiority, this concealment of the Name, that the *tikkun* of the world of disappearance takes place and the separation/sanctification of the Name is accomplished. The Name is hidden from sight, whether it is veiled or pronounced in its vowels: it becomes voice and listening. Its concealment redeems exteriority.

This manner of proceeding may seem odd.[101] Why should man redeem the exteriority of the world by an interiority whose constitution was necessary for this very exteriority to be manifested? Isn't there a nullification of creation in this? Herein lies the narrowness of the scope of the world. It is from the distancing of God's being (that is to say, from the interiorization of God) that the world is born, but the world could die from too much distance; it could not survive if the remoteness were irremediable. For man, gaining access to the presence that vivifies him in the exile of the exterior rhymes with recreating interiority in the barren desolation of the world. But whence could interiority derive if not from another interior, from the pristine interiority of God? Interiority is always embedded in the interiority of God. Indeed, if the exterior leans against the interior and arises from the contemplation of the latter, the opposite is impossible. To dwell "in the midst of the children of Israel," God came to "take a people (*goy*) from the midst (*kerev*) of another people" (Deut. 4:34).

99. Through the "reading of the *Shema*" in daily prayers.
100. Thus, incest is the most spontaneous gesture.
101. And our purpose here is to try to penetrate its meaning.

Yet this recreation of interiority is not a repetition of the interiority that presided over creation. The people of Israel does not reiterate Egypt, out of which it came. When the all draws into its interiority to give birth to the exterior, it is the one of the all that is interiorized and given as a promise to the being. The interiority is never in the past; it is not a model that can be repeated. The "repetition" here is a movement toward the one that does not yet exist. The emergence of interiority in the space of exteriority is a form of imitation of God, of cleaving to his disappearance, of "sticking"[102] to him.

Placed in the exterior, man immediately follows the divine, who has receded (to enable him to exist), and this is what prevents man from vanishing into nothingness. This is the crux of the ambivalence of the being. And it is why the anticipation of the being, the being in the future of "I will be who I will be," is embedded in memory ("it is my memory," Exod. 3:15); but the being whom we remember is already waiting for us beyond the future. As compared to the one who is shining presence, we are always already in the past.[103]

Forgetting is the foremost threat to man in the void through which generations are continually passing ("from generation to generation"). This is why "memory" forms the basis of the constitution of interiority, "memory of the exodus from Egypt" (daily liturgy). The paradigm of this approach is to be found in the leviratic law that enjoins the brother of a deceased man, married without children, to redeem (*goel*) his sister-in-law and perpetuate the name of the deceased by giving her children. The created world is like the sister-in-law, like Ruth, looking for her redeemer, seeking the person who will perpetuate the name of the one who is gone.

The Place

It is thanks to this recreation of an interior in the world of exteriority that the human being has a place on Earth, a frail shelter in the labile, irresistible torrent of passage that, if he were totally delivered to it, would engulf him once and for all. There is a place (*makom*) only for man, because it is in this place alone that he is manifested, that he rises (*kom*) and stands out from the anonymous passage of the flow of being in the creational current. Since,

102. In line with the powerful image of *devekut*, "and you who are glued to YHWH your God" (Deut. 4:4).

103. See "The Recaptured Time of the *Vav* of Reversal," in Trigano, *Story of Disappeared Presence*, pp. 278–304.

as we have said, the Name founds the passage, this means that to be "effective," the Name must be sheltered[104] and concealed. That is what its *tikkun* is about. Indeed, the passage is not "anonymous," it is not nameless, since it is founded upon the Name. But for man—a creature of physical and emotional frailty, and the most sensitive being of creation—the spatial exteriority that arises in the passage remains an implacably rocky wilderness if he can find no place to take shelter.[105]

What precisely is the hand of the murderer seeking when he kills a man? Killing is taking the being out of his interiority, out of his shelter, casting him out of his dwelling place, and reducing him to a corpse, to a purely external, reified object.[106] Exteriority is potentially the arena of murder and death; human beings cannot resist too great a flow of being. But it is also, nonetheless, the place of man. Thus, for man, God is the supreme *makom*: the *makom* arises in divine interiority and maintains itself in interiority, as the divine presence in the Tabernacle shows us. To Moses on Sinai, "God *added*, there is a place (*makom*) with me (*iti*), you will stand on the rock when my glory will *pass by*, I will hide you in a cleft of the rock, I will cover you with my hand, until I have passed by, and I will take my hand away, and you will see my back, and my face you will not see" (Exod. 33:20–23): a place with me, a place of interiority hidden in the midst of nature (the rock), where a relationship of otherness can be preserved (indeed, the particle "*iti*," with me, in this verse points to the relationship of objectivity).

It is only in "my place" in particular that I can recognize the other. It is only in my particularized relationship with God (who sees me and speaks to me)[107] that I can know God. And it is this relationship of particularity and particularizing that makes the universal, whose key is interiority—interiority in the form of an "addition" ("God added")—a surplus. The exterior is effectively the universe of scarcity, the place of passage where things are always slipping away and lacking, where everything is counted (and there can be counting only because there is negativity). The interior, on the other hand,

104. Therefore King David wanted to build a "House" for the Name: "I, with my heart, wanted to build a house of rest for the Ark of the Covenant of Yhwh and for the place of our God's feet" (I Chron. 28:2), defined later by God as a "House to my Name."

105. Thus, human beings must build a shelter, a house in space, in order to live in the world (see below, "Stranger in the Abode," pp. 190–209).

106. The *guf*, the body, or rather the "volume," is the *nefesh*'s shelter. Killing one person destroys a world (in the words of the Talmud). In sum, it is to destroy his disappearance and expose him irremediably to the world's exteriority. Killing Israel profanes the Name sheltered in Israel in the world of disappearance.

107. Through the attributes.

seems to be "added" to the accomplished world of exteriority. In this sense, the place of man is a supplementary place; it is the place of God because in it the attributes of God are revealed, the place of extreme bounty and not of scarcity,[108] the frail place of human carnality.

The place is the realm where the being voids itself and the creature arises. It is therefore that which sustains the other and carries the one who is beyond me, who comes in addition to me.[109] In a way, the interior is a place of gratuitousness, of *rahamim*, and not of will to power. "From his place, he turns his face in his *rahamim* to his people, who unify his Name evening and morning" (Sabbath liturgy). Since he makes room for the other, he stays hidden and does not continually remind him of his existence. Hence the ease with which we can forget that we are in the place, that we can forget the place itself.

It is in the nature of the world of exteriority to believe in its own fullness, to disregard the voiding of its forgotten interior, and to ignore that it itself occupies a place in a greater interior. It thinks of itself as the place of all things when it is in the place of the other. This is why any attempt to "uncover," to expose in the place amounts to its ruin, to the exile of the presence that dwells in it. This is what happens with incest, *giluy arayot*, literally, the uncovering of nakedness, which is an uncovering of *hesed*, the pristine grace. Interestingly, from this perspective, *hesed* has a secondary meaning of incest. The place is a sort of rest for the being, a resurgence for the being in the destructive depletion of passage, the place where the being regains momentum in its movement toward the one: "All the streams flow to the sea, and the sea is not full. To the place (*makom*) to which they flow, there they return to go" (Eccles. 1:7).

In relation to the flow of passage and to exteriority, the place constitutes in a very concrete way a separation (*kiddush*) and distanciation. To make a place[110] is to sanctify God. In this world, this means "repairing" his Name, redeeming it from its perdition. In relation to the creational will, this signifies repeating the original act of creation, that is, the distanciation in the being that makes the world. In separating himself from himself, God promised himself to unity and to the future, and the world came pouring out of this

108. Unlike apophatic theology that describes the divine attributes by way of negation (see *shelilat hahe'ader*, the negation of absence, in "Maimonides," p. 124).

109. This place appears for the first time at the time of Eve's creation: "he took one of his sides and closed up the flesh underneath" (Gen. 2:21). The "underneath" is a reference to this place.

110. [*Faire place* also means "to make room." Trans. note.]

hiatus. It is this hiatus that enables consciousness. This hiatus between me and myself is where the other emerges; without it I would be totally self-involved. This is why we can know God only in our conscience, by drawing into an interiority, and not in the barren desolation of exteriority. The place is then the experience of a void, of the place where I step out of myself so that the other can emerge, the place of ex-planation, of inter-pretation, of a displacement.[111]

How would the distanciation of the place and the absence give rise to the bounty of interiority? By enabling the overplus that was not "planned" at the start, a place set apart from the world of lack. The *makom* is empty only for the exterior; it is suspended and withheld only for the passage, because, in itself, it harbors bounty; there, like the sea, are gathered all the waters of all the streams that are ceaselessly flowing and passing by. The *makom* gives rise to two conceptions of the world: a critical approach based on a conception that visualizes being in the world in terms of negativity and absence, but also a conception of the positivity of the world, not the classical figure of the positivity of the being-there, but rather the positivity of beyond the negative-of-the-positive of exteriority. These two conceptions of the *makom* are modalities of *point of view*: the negativity is the point of view onto the world from exteriority and passage, while the positivity beyond the negative is the point of view of the one that grasps the temporary negation of interiority in the movement progressing toward the one.[112]

This suggests that the *makom* is the very fundament of the being insofar as it is the milieu/interior (*toch*) of absence and presence, of the world and the one, of God and man. It corresponds to the philosophical *logos* but is diametrically opposed to it. The distanciation that it introduces into the world of passage establishes the basis for the one by differentiating the universe of passage and by taking it out of the absence of the Name. One could say that God's interiorization engenders the passage and the world, and man's interiorization draws passage out of itself and God out of his absence. This is why the *makom* is the basis of all thought, what makes the very act of thinking possible. And in the thought that the *makom* produces we find all of God's passage (unlike the abstraction of *logos*). It is in the *makom* that the divine being draws inward, leaving his absence in the *olam*. This interiority is the form of his presence in the world. And this is why the *makom* is the

111. The interpretation of the Torah is what makes the place of the collectivity of Israel (see "Le processus idéologique," in Trigano, *Forgotten Dwelling*, p. 364).

112. In the case of the attributes, it is a matter of finding what their positive interpretation could be without lapsing into positivism.

entranceway on whose threshold an echo of divine government can be heard: "the veil [is] at the entrance to the tent" of the Tabernacle (Exod. 39:38). Whereas the *logos* fills the world completely in an attempt to cement all the openings, the *makom* unseals the totality of the world.

Consequently, the place is the principle of all places and even of exteriority. Its shelter in concealment maintains a perpetual reservoir of potentiality for man. Whoever enters it is immediately reborn. It bestows beneficial bounty, for the future is announced in it to those who are paralyzed by the past. In the place, the distanciation of time is annulled in the imperturbable time of the one; in it the remoteness decreases, the peace of the one is mended, and the separated are reconciled (thus, Aaron, who is in charge of the *mishkan*, Tabernacle, the dwelling of the one, is known for promoting peace in human relations).

We can see why, in the world of passage, this is the place of remembrance where the distanciation of time and space is annulled. All seeing is the seeing of this place. The *makom* comes to redeem the forgetting inherent in passage: it traverses this forgetting and transcends it. But because the place is endowed with all these virtues, it comprises a point to which we can never gain access, which is always out of reach, a point that accounts for all its strength, and without which there would be no memory. Of this place, it is said, "Do not come close to here (literally, do not come into the *kerev*, the proximity or kinship, of here)" (Exod. 3:5). This is the place in the midst of the place, like the Holy of Holies in the Temple, where only the high priest can enter. Without this place hidden within the hidden, there would be no Temple. The *makom* houses the one, transports it through the passage of plurality to its transcendence. It is the place where all cannot be reckoned, where all of the finite space cannot be spanned. Something will always remain that is ungraspable, something divinely volatile. No doubt, this is because it is the place of God and the place of man, "a place with me" (*makom iti*)—that is to say, a place that comes before and after me, while accompanying me. Isn't this the place of the family with its passing generations? The place that makes for the fact that I am not totally my own person, that there is that which oversteps me from all sides, behind me, in front of me, and beside me? My ancestors, my descendants, and my collaterals draw me out of myself. I am embedded in the genealogy of a Name.

Therefore, the *makom* is never an abstract place, carved from nothingness, but rather a place "given in heritage." As a heritage, the *makom* escapes its own grasp, and if it does not belong to itself, how can it belong to man? Thus, the land of Israel, the place of Israel's ingathering in interiority from out of the exteriority of its exile, is, first and foremost, a land of promise and heritage, a place that can come to be only in the context of heritage, overstepping the self, and memory. In this sense, the land of Israel, as thoroughly geographical as it is, stands in interiority. If it leaves this interiority, if only for a moment, it is as if the Jewish people had been thrown out of it. The geographical land does not easily abide a noninteriorized Israel, an Israel that does not stand in its interior/midst (*toch*), in its *makom*. This interiorization of the land happened progressively. The patriarchs cleared the field for the *makom*,[113] that is, for interiority in the world, and we benefit from their merit because they made a clearing[114] in the darkness of the world. They transmitted a name to those who had none and a place to those living in the anonymity of space. It is therefore filiation that makes for the fact that the *makom* is an infinite place that cannot be "possessed": the filiation of God, the filiation of men, the lineage of the one and of the Name.

Inhabiting the Place

The *makom* is a place that must be inhabited and populated. It is this populating and the tangle of interconnections of these genealogies that makes it. It is in this Name that becomes the place (*makom*) that the assembly of human beings is held. And this gathering together is logically related to the creation of the world, wherein man is confronted with the dilemma of exteriority and interiority, of "*tohu*" and of "settling," that is to say, with the dilemma of assembly. "For thus said YHWH, the creator (*borei*) of heaven, he who is Elohim, the shaper (*yotzer*) of the land and its maker, he established it, non-*tohu* he created it, to be inhabited/populated/settled, (*shevet*) he created it: I am YHWH, and there is no more/and the void is a 'more'" (Isa. 45:18).

The *tohu* is missing the *alef* of the origin,[115] which is "inside," in the *bohu*,[116] and it is from the inside (*penim*) that the face (*panim*) appears: "the name of the place (*makom*) [is] *Peniel*/face of God, because I saw God, *panim el panim*, face-to-face, and my *nefesh* came out alive" (Gen. 32:30). And "there

---

113. Of Abraham it is said, "to the place where he stood" (Gen. 19:27), of Isaac, "he went out in the field to meditate as evening approached" (24:63), and of Jacob, "he touched the place" (28:11).

114. *Zach*, meaning clear, yields *zechut*, meaning merit and transparency.

115. *Tohu* can be vocalized as *tav-hu*: with a final *alef*, the *hu* would yield the third person singular, so *tav-hu* could be read as saying, "this is a sign."

116. Literally (with the added *alef*), *bohu* signifies "in it, he is."

(sham)" is where the angel asks Jacob, "What is your name (shem)?" and where Jacob receives the name Israel.

In the text from Isaiah, the two verbs that govern the *tohu* and the *shevet*, the "seat" (in this case, the populating), stand in a revealing contradistinctive relationship to one another: the *tohu* is negatively related to creation ex nihilo (*bara*), but the "seat" (or the "sitting") is directly related to shaping (*yotzer*)—that is to say, to an existing creation, all of which is part of the intention of creation. Yet the end of the verse connects the populating of the world, which is the divine intention, with the Name of God and with the declaration that "there is no other (*ein od*)," which should be read as saying, "and the *ein*, the void, is a 'more,'" meaning that this populating is in the *ein*, in a way that resembles the creational disappearance, and this pertains not to the negative but to the positive of interiority. The void of the assembly and of creation is related to an overplus, not to a lack; to bounty, not to scarcity.

The void is therefore paradoxically at the heart of this populating that is continually bringing additional (*od*) generations to humanity but whose destiny is to pass away (*ein*). The biblical text tells us, "these three were the sons of Noah, and from these, the whole world was peopled" (Gen. 9:19). According to biblical tradition, all the nations descend from them, so this is the common trunk of all the human genealogies that make up the universal human *makom*. The root, *nafotz*, used to denote this "populating" that makes the *makom* evinces a sense of separation, dispersion, and shattering.

In sum, the engendering amounts to an explosion of the pristine totality, and the addition of a generation amounts to an effacement and a cutting away of sorts. Another text from Genesis confirms this more explicitly: "Let us make a name for ourselves, lest we be dispersed over the face of the whole world" (Gen. 11:4). The word used here for dispersion is *nafotz*. The children of Noah tried to retain the integrity of the all and resist the experience of passage, emptiness, and separation. Rashi in his commentary even tells us that in this generation, there was total peace and an idyllic love and willingness to help one another. Humankind was, in the words of God, "as one people with one language for all" (11:6). But it was a peace from which no faces stood out; no voice stood out against the dull rumble of the many thousand footsteps, in which the other, in spite and because of this love, was not recognized.

Men stricken by the all hesitated to "separate," to allow for emptiness and hence to "populate" the earth, or, in other words, to engender. They saw fragmentation and loss as a danger and mistakenly believed that the Name is a matter of retention and self-contained fullness, not emptiness and passage,[117] and that the one comes prior to the multiple, when in fact the divine Name arises and becomes unified only by passing through the multiple. In trying to keep the all intact and not to give, out of fear of loss, they end up losing all. This is why the society of Babel is a rebellion against the Name that is Name only because God is God the creator. So they aspired to substitute their name for God's, saying, "Let us make a name for ourselves," as if human beings could name themselves, as if their name were not passed down to them by those who preceded them, to be passed on to those who will come thereafter.

Babel's approach negated creation: in refusing the separation, the society of Babel refused to build the interior where humanity could be constituted from child to child. It sought to enjoy the world as if there had never been birth or passage.[118] It doomed man to exteriority, to the breakup of the ineluctable passage that it attempted to cast as immutable eternity. In Babel, procreation, heritage, and transmission across generations had become impossible. There were no more families, no principles of particularization at work in the magmatic totality of the human. The summit of the Tower of Babel attained nothing but its destruction. Babel is the experience of a misguided gathering of man in the *makom*.

But once the ineluctable fall of Babel had occurred (because the all cannot help but give way in the passage of the being), human beings, like scattered particles in the spiral of passage, looking for a way out of the dereliction inherent in the necessity of the passage, sought to reassemble; and for this purpose, they had two paths from which to choose. For out of this trial two types of people come (if we leave aside those so overwhelmed and lost in the passage that they can do nothing but drift aimlessly): the fugitives and the exiles. Wandering and exile are close but radically different experiences resulting from the foundational ordeal of passage in the being. The citadel of the original all was shattered, and the "survivors" left in droves. For some, this experience is the epitome of the tragic, because the original unity is broken, and they see themselves as doomed to wander endlessly, like eternal fugitives,

117. The Name emerges from the void, from unsealing the being from the all. Structurally it carries the mark of creation and the memory of God.

118. Which is why the divine punishment is to disperse them over the face of the earth and differentiate their language, thereby forcing them to face the distance, the unsealing, and the trial of passage that is the void. And what greater experience of the void can one have than in the dissimilarity of languages, when the proximity of the other is broken by the difference of language, by the void with which his language confronts us? In this light, the act of translation is an ordeal of passage, the supreme ordeal of the world.

in the stream of passage. The sole project that sustains them is recreating the pristine all and blocking the pulverization of birth and filiation, in an attempt to hold onto the Babelian identity.

Fugitives are overwhelmed by the frightening immensity of the world. Seeing neither an end to it nor any rhyme or reason, they are tempted to create a strategy (which is what makes them fugitives, not drifters) with a twofold aim. On the one hand, they isolate in a void an objective, spatial world devoid of reason (the "sensible" world) so as to dissociate it from a truth that would be abstract and absolute, independent from the reality of the world (the "intelligible" world). This is how they make sense out of the senselessness of the world and the dispersion outside the all, which they see as tragedy, destruction, and death. At the same time (and because, notwithstanding their aims, they continue to "suffer" from their existence in the world), they carve out an area of intimacy in the *olam*, in an abstract and geometric way, and artificially ascribe to it the intimacy and interiority that they actually deny themselves, because they deny the reality of the *olam* and the passage. This "sacred" area that they abstractly set apart (the Greek word "temple" means cut) is like a clearing in the jungle or an oasis drawn out of the desert, a place in which they can gather around the crackling flames of a sacred furnace that lights their faces, a place where they can believe in light, turning their backs on the passage and holding onto the prospect of the serenity of the all.

But the exiles have an altogether different vocation. They perceive the meaning of the world in the passage and the movement. This is why their strategy is that of mobility, or "nomadism," if you prefer. Space is there to be traversed, not used as a pretext to barricade and brace ourselves against a world that slips away from us. The crux of everything is there in the passage, not the tragic antithesis of the sensible and the intelligible, but the agile relationship of metaphor to follow meaning. The sense is in the passage that is thus perceived to be no longer dereliction and death, but rather a gestation, a germination, a power rising within the being.

The exiles accompany the movement because they know where they come from (the citadel's destruction is not occulted) and where they are going; there is a geographical sense in the world. Despite and throughout all the peregrinations and traveling in circles in the desert, the destination is Jerusalem, the Moriah, abode of the one, where the Covenant between the Pieces and the binding of Isaac took place. This is why interiority dwells inside them as they proceed, an interiority that has nothing to do with a division of space (sacred-profane) and everything to do with a movement of ingathering and assembling: their interiority camps there, ready to move tomorrow.

There is no "temple," then, in exile, but rather a *mishkan*, a dwelling, an abode, or, more precisely, a "making present," a residing, in the manner of the movable, dismountable Tabernacle (*mishkan*) in the desert and in the early days in the Promised Land. The ingathering makes the place of existence and light paradoxically appear within this dark intimacy. This is the meaning of Balaam's prophecy "this people alone will dwell," which we may read alternately as "this people (being-with) in its uniqueness, in the solitude of its ingathering, will dwell" or "will make the presence shine forth."

The presence shines on the inside, so that the interiority is not the enemy of the world (the profane), it shines on it. It does not repel it, it attracts it. It makes individual "ones" appear out of the desert of anonymity rather than casting them back into it. Thus, in hospitably opening his tent, Abraham gave rise to many a "soul (*nefesh*)" (Gen. 12:5). The desert is the place of the *mishkan* and not the "clearing" in the forest or in the jungle, for the light shines in it, not in the manner of a refuge that turns its back on the world, but in an intimacy that lights up the outside, like the "shut-transparent (I Kings 6:4)" windows of the Temple, which throw light onto the outside world from within the interiority.

THE SECRET OF THE FAMILY

Thus, it is in this *makom*, this place of the world, that human beings come together either to forget the Name that is lodged in it or to shelter and hide it. This is why any gathering creates a name, the name of a collectivity, of a people. For this purpose, human beings will either endeavor to "make a name for themselves" or strive to undertake the *tikkun* of the Name, to redeem the passage and herald the one in the many. And thus the assembly of Israel is naturally called *knesset Yisrael*, or the "entry of Israel," for it is the constitution by Abraham's family of an interior in the midst of the passage of the world. It is in the gathering place that the four-letter Name abides, and the Name is what makes this very place, so that any assembly is the memory of this place in the passage of the *olam*. "I will be who I will be…. And God said *in addition* to Moses… this is my Name for the *olam* (for the world, forever, for disappearance). This is my memory from generation to generation. Go and *asafta* (assemble or collect) the senators of Israel... I have remembered you" (Exod. 3:14–16). The assembly has meaning only in the *olam*, in the disappearance and in the void of passage.

"And I am sending a messenger... to bring you to the place (*makom*) that I have made ready; safeguard yourself from his face, and listen to his voice; do not rebel against him... for my Name is in his bosom/his proximity (*kirbo*)" (Exod. 23:21). God's being harbors in a way the being of society, and the secret of the Name YHWH harbors the secret of Israel. Thus, any rebellion against God results in the banishment of society in very concrete physical terms. When Korah revolted, *he* and his followers were swallowed up into the bowels of the earth.[119] Similarly, "anyone who blasphemes his God will bear his sin, and anyone who 'pierces' (*nokev*) YHWH's Name will die. The whole community (*eda*) will stone him; the resident (*ger*) as the citizen who 'pierces' the Name will die" (Lev. 24:15–16). Anyone who removes himself from the divine Name automatically detaches himself from the society of Israel. The collectivity, which is his shelter in the world, slips away from him, so he immediately finds himself in the passage, and this passage, deprived of interiority, returns to nothingness and dereliction, to the death that is embedded in it. Cast into exteriority, he is swallowed up by the void of passage.

Now we can see why idolatry is forbidden and why those who worship idols are cut off from the collectivity. The Hebrew expression used in this regard is enlightening (Sanhedrin 63b). The prohibition of idolatry for the sons of Noah is a prohibition of "associating the divine Name with something else." Associating the Name with something other than him amounts to breaking the unity of *knesset Yisrael*.[120] It is as if we could understand the assembly of Israel through the meaning of the Tetragrammaton: to ascend all of its letters is to climb up through the whole of the social realm. When all of Israel is assembled, the Tetragrammaton is unified. The Name designates Israel in its unity. Thus, the Torah is the very fabric of Israel's peoplehood-being, as suggested in the reading of the Torah by the king before all Israel (*klal Yisrael*) gathered together at the end of the Sukkot festival (Deut. 31:10–13).

That the Name is unpronounceable also tells us much about the nature of the collectivity of Israel and its concealment. The people of Israel as a totality is mostly hidden, for if it were reunited, God would appear in it. The appearance of "all the people" (*klal Yisrael*) is a divine appearance, an

119. See below, "All Israel and the Prohibition of Census Taking," pp. 367–390.

120. Because the Name is already what emerges from the being who withdraws from the exterior and places himself as an overplus in the interior.

unveiling of the *Shechina*, and this is a highly rare occurrence indeed. The invisibility of the totality of the Jewish people is akin to divine invisibility: this is the condition of its existence and permanence. Total exposure would destroy the world by throwing it into the weightiness of the passage. This is why the totality of the existence of Israel is collected at the innermost, most secretive point in its midst: the Holy of Holies.

We are now in a better position to understand why the entry of the high priest into the Holy of Holies once a year on Yom Kippur accomplishes the collective redemption (*kappara*) of Israel (Lev. 16:2). Indeed, this divine presence in the midst of the collectivity of Israel is subject to a "limitation." After all, isn't the place firstly the mark of a limitation, of the withdrawal of God, who retreats to make room for the world? In the interiority of Israel, God is not spontaneously in a state of rest. His dwelling is movable; it is in passage in the midst of the quiescent repose in the passage. God may very well be in the midst (*kirva*) of the people, but this does not mean the people can approach him at will: "You shall set bounds (*gvul*) for the people all around" (Exod. 19:12), because they must not draw too close. This is why they say to Moses, "Speak to us, and we will be able to hear, but let not God speak to us, lest we die" (20:16). When the people are physically gathered together, they never appear totally exposed. Even in their manifestation and revelation, a part of the people remains hidden in secrecy. Only the manifestation at Sinai comprised the totality of the people, entirely present to itself in this unique moment. "You are convoked/present today, all of you" (Deut. 29:9).

Maybe this secrecy serves to protect the collectivity of Israel, for if its assembled totality is not perfect (and how could it be?), its appearance before God of all perfections could be dangerous for it. But maybe this hard core of secrecy has another purpose, and that is to preserve the passage in the Name, because if the interior shelters the one, the one has not yet come to be. That the interior is the temporary shelter of the one in the passage of the multiple is true of the Name of God and of Israel for itself. It is true of humanity, too, but it does not know it. What is the end purpose of the passage if not to increase and gather together in the sanctifying separation of the interior, the shattered being that it produces—in other words, its own redemption? Thus, the passage of God over Egypt redeems Israel from amongst the Egyptians, and the rescue of the firstborn sons of the Hebrews redeems the destruction that this passage causes in Egypt (the death of the Egyptian firstborn).

This paradigm of passage evidences the way in which the being of Israel is the departure of Israel from the "interiority" of Egypt. Because the ends of the world are good, the finality of the passage is its own *tikkun*, its redemption, its reparation, which is accomplished in the weaving[121] of an interior, or, to put it otherwise, in the "mending"[122] of the passage. The secret that subsists even in the disclosure of the whole of Israel, and even in the revelation of God, serves to enable this "mending" of the world, for we know that the existence of Israel in and through this world is not yet the advent of the one, and therefore we know that to be itself, Israel has something to do. This means that hidden in the interior is an even more secret interiority.

The Story of a Family

Now we can understand why the story of the people of Israel begins with the story of a family, the patriarchal family. Knowledge of the Name is firstly due to the family of Israel. Isn't the family the first stage in this enterprise of dwelling in the interior? The *nefesh*, or "soul," that is projected at birth into the harsh exteriority of the world finds its first shelter in the family. Similarly, as people are confronted by the exteriority of the passage and are scorched by it, they find their first shelter in their families, who provide them with protection and enable them to survive. The family is the fundamental place for concealing the Name in secrecy. How could it be otherwise, since the *makom* is the place through which generations pass, through which the family passes, and the *makom* is under the seal of secrecy?

To found a family is to cover up a portion of the world of exteriority, to remove a piece of the totality of the world and hide it. This is why the family is underpinned by the prohibition of incest, by an obligation of concealment and secrecy. The Hebrew term for incest is telling in this respect: incest is *giluy arayot*, which means the "uncovering" of skin, flesh, or nakedness. When a man and a woman come together, it is to hide something from the world, to remove it from sight, to weave their *nefashot* into a fabric that covers a portion of the world. The sexual act, "the way of the man in the maiden/ in disappearance (*alma*)" (Prov. 30:19), is the paradigm of the soul-weaving loom, and it works exactly like a weaving loom. This is why tradition describes

121. The "making" of the interior can be compared only to weaving, to the process of interweaving threads to form a single piece of fabric, even as the threads remain what they are. The weaving of the curtain for the Holy of Holies or the high priest's clothing resembles such an enterprise. This is why the Song of Songs says that "its interior is woven (*ratzuf*) with love" (3:10).

122. [*Reprise*, literally, "taking back," denotes resumption, repetition, revival, but also mending (clothing) or darning (socks). Trans. note.]

the cherubim, who hide the Ark of the Covenant, as "embracing like a man and a woman" (Exod. 25:20). But the couple is merely the framework of this interiority. In and of itself, it does not constitute this interiority. Indeed, the prohibition of incest would not play out fully if the implications concerned the couple alone, even if each member of the couple were the product of the prohibition in his or her respective family. The uniting of a couple, like the sexual act, only produces a passing in the world of exteriority, which sees itself as stationary when in fact it resides in the passage. In their embrace, the couple rediscovers the deep-seated nature of the world: the passing in its formless infinity. This means that, like the world, it, too, is waiting for its *tikkun*. When two lovers unite, they breathe life back into the *olam*/world/ disappearance. They do so by bringing a child into the world, an overplus to their union/disappearance, because that is when a portion of the world is removed from the exterior and truly hidden away in secrecy, through the prohibition for children to go back, toward their parents, to uncover their nakedness, through the violation by the two lovers of the prohibition of incest.

The family is, consequently, characterized by a lack of equilibrium. When it is founded, the prohibition of incest applies to its future only, in relation to its as-yet-unborn progeny. The family is founded on the union of two individuals from two different filiations, but it does not exist until children are born. Children alone make the family and are indissociably of one "piece" (*faire corps*) with it, because the man and woman who have become parents may be united by love, but they will always remain merely individuals in this world and in the world to come, even though they are united by a covenant of separation from the world. They are the hitches of the tent of interiority, but not the interior. They are the ever-distinct threads that weave a single fabric.

This is why the family owes everything to its children. The individuals in the couple unite and come out of their solitude only in the child who is born to them, and yet this child will soon turn away from them. In the ultimate solitude of the human being (evidenced in birth and death), the soul nonetheless paradoxically conceives the family and multiplicity without ever being able to totally dissipate the solitude. Solitude subsists in the covenant of love and presence. That is why this fabric bears witness to the community of marriage, an unstable, fragile community that can be "forgotten" and can be built only by children.[123] This community is the model for all communities and, of course, for the community of the "*children* of Israel." And the

---

123. According to the etymological parallel between *ben*, son, and *boneh*, builder.

prohibion of incest, the cardinal principal of the *halacha*, serves as a procedure for hiding Israel in secrecy.

Consequently, the family is a temporary shelter, a fragile tent pitched in the passage. It is not destined to be permanent, neither for the spouses nor for the children who are called upon to leave their family in order to found another. In sum, for the soul to be born in the world, it must pass through a family, it must traverse an interiority, a dimming. It is as if the soul were caught in the midst of bushes like Abraham's ram in the branches, as if the family could be compared to a bush and the birth of the soul to the "sacrifice" of the soul. And indeed, the closeness (*kirva*) generated by the kinship (*kirva*) has something to do with the "sacrifice" (*korban*).[124] This is why the birth of sons imposes the necessity of a *tikkun*, in the form of the circumcision and "the redeeming of the firstborn" to take the soul out of the fatality of the sacrifice that is its birth, to give it back the light it lost in the temporary dimming of the family, this sacrifice that is its birth when it falls in the passage, when the "passage" (*maavar*) that is the embryo (*ubar*) passes via its mother into a family to come out into the light of day.

The 'Korban' of Kinship

But why is there a need to "hide" a portion of the world, in the prohibition of incest, in circumcision, and in the act of redeeming the firstborn son? Once the Name has come into the passage via the couple, it must come out of its exteriority, and its presence must dwell in the world. The one must be able to twinkle in the world of multiplicity and never-ending passage. Achievement must become a tangible promise. Only then is God present in the founding of families, only then do his Name and his unity dwell in the House. The act of founding a family is the decisive procedure of concealment in the world of passage, but it is ultimately accomplished only through the "redeeming" made possible by the child's birth. The harsh, solitary destiny of the *nefesh*, at this precise moment of the family, of the covenant between the parents' *nefashot*, is "redeemed" in this way; the temporary frailty of the family, of the comforting heat of the union, and of the community is then compensated by the permanence that the family kinship (*kirva*) acquires. By this redemption, the Name is bestowed, the patronymic is passed on that from generation to generation will carry the *nefesh* to the bank of the one.

---

124. See above, "The Covenant between the Pieces," pp. 79–100. Now we can see why it was at the moment of the sacrifice of the pieces that Abraham founded the "family" of Israel.

The "eternity" of the family and of the *nefesh* resides in this Name, in the continuation of this Name. In other words, its fundament is "memory." And this, as we have seen, is the charter of creation.

We are now in a better position to understand why naming in Genesis always takes place on the occasion of a sacrifice (*korban*) and of a manifestation of place. Family is the unique structure that enables the human being to fight against death (in this world already), because it establishes the basis of the primordial interior in the world. Thus, it is something of the primal scene of all things in human society. It is paradoxical indeed to found the collectivity of human beings and companionship with God by drawing inward outside the world while being in it, of course. With the family, something is hidden from the *olam*, firstly in a theoretical sense, since the family creates a shelter against the world of passage, but also in practice, because founding a family immediately involves a separation from the world and from others, building the walls of a house, closing the door, withdrawing, and gathering around a fire in the hearth. Founding a family and a kinship involves separating from the world and from the collectivity, but for the purpose of establishing a new community. The kinship and proximity (*kirva*) is acquired through distanciation and withdrawal. And, once again, this seems to mirror the creation of the world when God became present to us and even created our presence by moving away from us and withdrawing from his royal universe. To found a family is to imitate God, to create a world. And so, lodged in every family name, passed down from generation to generation, is the Name of God, the frailty and strength of eternity; and the Name of God is frequented by the names of the family members bearing the same name.

The purpose of the secrecy imposed at that point is to block the return to the origin and to the pristine all that would be consummated in incest, to obstruct the return to the undivided, to the indivision, to the individual before the couple. This secrecy enables the heralding of the one, its separation/sanctification, its gradual emergence in the multiplicity of passage, and the gradual surfacing of memory in and through oblivion. When we speak of *erva*, of nakedness or incest, we are speaking of passage and of the exteriority that it manifests, the exterior in which it is exposed. "To hide one's nakedness" is to hide the exterior in a place, to weave an interiority where man and the Name can take shelter, to repair the world, to remove a world that is actually as mobile as quicksilver from its inherent weightiness, and to re-embed it in its foundational project.

This is why *erva* can be said of many things. Of course, it is a matter above all of the *erva* of sex, since "uncovering the *erva*" is committing incest, in other words, having a *sexual* relationship with a relative (*karov*), taken in a parental proximity (*kirva*). "You shall make them linen breeches to cover their flesh of *erva* from the hips to the thigh" (Exod. 28:42). Any covering, any secret hides the sexual organ, which epitomizes in man the movement of passage, and notably the passage of generation. Noah's son Ham, who saw his father's *erva* and publicized it (Gen. 9:22), was cursed and practically driven out of the line of descent of the Name. But the term *erva* can also be used to speak of land, especially the land of Israel, the place where Israel's interiority is actuated in the world of nations. When Israel betrays this interiority, the land becomes an indecent exteriority; it sinks back into the passage and slips away because the whole being of the land of Israel is in interiority. Therefore, a place where the interiority of Israel is valid is a place where there is no *erva*, where *erva* is hidden: "Your camp will be separated/holy and no *erva* whatsoever will be seen in you" (Deut. 23:15). We can see why the prohibition of *erva* is a sanctification, a separation from the world of the outside, an interiority. Thus, the union of a couple is dissolved when *erva* appears in it, and a man can divorce his wife only if he finds some kind of *erva* in her (Deut. 24:1). Likewise, a collectivity breaks down when *erva* develops within it, because, from that point on, there is no more responsibility; one can no longer be rescued and redeemed by the other. "There is no support for nudities (*arayot*)" (Ketubot 13). An interiority in which *erva* reemerges is doomed to disappearance and dislocation. Bared and exposed, it returns to the passage, where it is consigned to being consumed by the void. In this way, when Joseph's brothers go down to Egypt, the still incognito Joseph accuses them of coming to see Egypt's *erva* (Gen. 42:23), in other words, its weakness, so as to attack.

Abraham set himself apart from the nations (*goyim*) by way of circumcision; in fact, they became "nations"—that is, exteriority to Israel—precisely because he set himself apart from them. The cutting and setting apart involved in circumcision serve to cover the *erva* of the nations. The cut-off foreskin acts as the hidden portion, because the foreskin is the exposed *erva* that masks interiority. It was as if the foreskin were hidden from view, and, paradoxically, this concealment was a revealment, because it enabled the glans of the sex organ to appear and interiority to become manifest. That which is cut off and set apart is also an overplus, a surplus.

There is a very clear parallel in Hebrew between the male organ and the character of the "nations." The sex organ is called *rosh hagvia*, literally, "corpse head," from the same root that designates the *goy*, or nation, the outside of Israel. The *gvia*, corpse, or *gayut*, foreignness or outsideness (of the nations), designates the exteriority that exists in a collectivity, which must be "hidden" or cut off. This is the purpose of circumcision, which seals the entry into the Abrahamic household and interiority. Israel becomes thereby a "holy/separate nation (*goy*)" (Exod. 19:6). It is this exteriority of the collective body (whose nature it is to be "exposed," to be wholly surface and exteriority) that turns it into a lifeless body, a corpse, in which each member ignores in the inmost depths of his own body who and what any other member is.

We are now in a better position to understand why circumcision is at the heart of the covenant. It institutes a oneness, an implication of the being and of the body, a "responsibilization" of the whole body that weaves the weft of the relationship of interiority.[125] This is why what creates a secret for the exterior paradoxically corresponds to the revealment of a secret inside, to the carnal uncovering of the glans, the fundament of the one in interiority, removed from the dispersion of passage. The glans that the removal of the foreskin discloses, which comes as an addition over and above the removal, is therefore termed *rosh hatzaddik*, meaning "the head of the righteous."

The importance of the family experience explains why the patriarchal migration founded and preceded the history of the people that actually began only with the twelve tribes— that is, with Jacob's twelve sons. There are two histories of Israel: the lineage of individuals and the development of the collectivity. The history of Israel begins unfolding even before Israel exists. That is what we are given to understand in the vision that Abraham has after he concludes the Covenant between the Pieces. The torpor and great darkness that overwhelm him come to "eclipse" his individuality and herald a lineage of many offspring and even their temporary exile. The "disappearance" of Abraham's individuality is, to a certain extent, the "price" to be paid for a child to be born, who will accomplish his *tikkun* and enable the emergence of the people.

There are two levels of the same story here. And the criterion that can help us distinguish between the two is that of divine presence. Whereas in the patriarchal story, divine presence manifests itself from time to time to individuals, in the story of Israel, it manifests itself to the whole collectivity. It takes the coming of the twelve tribes for the divine presence to dwell on Earth in the Tent of Meeting, the Tabernacle of the wilderness, and then in the Temple. This puts the accent on the strength of the genealogical prin-ciple at the very basis of Israel in relation to the political principle of the

125. The commentary compares circumcision to an *akeda*, on the model of *akedat Yitzhak*, the binding of Isaac, also known as the "sacrifice of Isaac."

collective. The "family of Abraham" is stronger and more fundamental than the "people of Israel," the "children of Israel." The people may break down, but everywhere they are surrounded and permeated by the family. When the Jewish people "disappear," the families of Israel remain. And when the people rise, the family of Abraham does not yield to them, because the family is the irreducible core of the secret of the world. Genealogy, the family, and the transmission of the Name and of memory are more powerful than the collective and escape its control. Jewishness is greater than a ruling power, and belonging to the family of Abraham does not depend on such a power.

THE SOCIAL: THE 'KEREV' OF THE CHILDREN OF ISRAEL

The family is situated mainly in interiority. To be constituted, it comes from outside what it will become; ultimately, its future precedes its present. It is because it harbors the promise of the child in the future that the couple founds a family and exists in the "present." It remains in its own past as long as the child does not come to it. Its past, in this case, comprises the solitary singularities of the future mother and father. Their filiation is the exterior of the family. As long as the child is an adolescent, in Hebrew an *elem* (the masculine of *alma*), meaning "disappeared,"[126] the family is entirely inside, in disappearance. But the family is a passing state, because once the children come out of their disappearance, out of their youth, they leave their families. The exteriority to the family where children go plots the field of the social and plays a decisive role.

This exteriority must be distinguished from the original exteriority, the natural exterior where creatures, having found themselves abandoned to the elements, to the exteriority of the world of passage,[127] had to recreate a shelter of interiority in order to survive. Yet once this interiority had been recreated, an interiority that sheltered humankind and came from the Noahide salvation, the milieu of interiority became the human milieu. It was from this milieu, which had become that of the nations (*goyim*), that Abraham

---

126. This idea is found in the Latin *infans,* which gives us "infant" and means "incapable of speech," so the infant is in a state of absence; his education is his *tikkun.*

127. Note that this exteriority and passage are manifested in the interiority and internalization of God. Therefore children leave the complete interiority of their family and find themselves outside, an outside impossible without the interiority of the family.

separated to establish the interiority of Israel. And then, once the interiority of Israel had become a collectivity, it became the natural exteriority to the families descended from Abraham.

How is this exteriority that is the collectivity of Israel constituted in relation to families? Once they have left the interiority of their families in the past, children find themselves in the poignant exteriority of sociality, where they go through the ordeal of the *nefesh* in the world. This world is not, however, totally uninhabited; it is composed of the aggregate of families, each one of which is turned inward onto its own interiority, although it stands in proximity to the others. This foreign proximity indicates the place, the in-between space, where the children who have left their families meet and look for a partner, a companion, in their search to found a family and recreate an interiority. This place between all other places is replete with a multitude of individual trajectories passing, ignoring, or bumping into each other; they pass endlessly through the densest of exteriorities, which are not without recalling the pristine exteriority of the universe of nature. But the danger of sinking into nothingness is not as great, since the family (of Abraham) has already been constituted and stands in the way of the terrible harshness of the passage. The individuals who pass through this place have come from a family, from an interiority, and thus they have already benefited from a sign of presence.

So, paradoxically, the place of the collective, where families dwell along-side one another, is a place inhabited by individualities, by emptiness and solitude, by the hushed footfalls of those passing through it. In the collective, at this stage, one is close to the absolute adversity of death, nature, and the dereliction of passage. Indeed, it is as if the interiority of the family—in which the being is a passenger—had been annihilated. It is difficult in this collective place to create and preserve the closeness (*kirva*) that makes the family. The social is born at that point from the fall of families into death. Therein lies its basic problem: in the collectivity, in the assembly, there are no more families and no more interiority.

Now we can more fully grasp why the family is a temporary being, a passing shelter, albeit of crucial importance, and why its interiority is funda-mental yet insufficient. The real question of interiority is raised on the level of the collectivity; the family cannot put an end to exteriority, since the col-lective state revives the terrible absence and disappearance of the origin. To be sure, wandering individuals, exiles from their families, eventually find a solution by founding a family, but what happens in the meantime? The crux of the social is in this intervening period of time and in the question of the interface between the families who tend to ignore one another, for each is gathered inward around its own hearth, safeguarding their child inside, for the child is the secret hearth of the one.

What could be the hearth of hearths? Is the soulless public space that individuals traverse en route to their own homes, "each at the entrance of his tent" (Exod. 33:8), anything more than a corridor provided with traffic rules (a "constitution") to make sure passersby do not bump into one another? And on what basis are such rules instituted? More than ever, in this moment of the social, individuals find themselves separated, atomized, and prey to the anonymous dereliction of an unending passage. Even when there are rules, the exteriority is undiminished, because rules are impersonal and external. It is at this stage that the illusion of individuality can take hold, because the light of the one shines in the interiority of the family gathered inside, so one may have the impression that, having gone outside, the child is the consummation of this interiority when, in fact, it merely twinkles inside the ingathered family, since the very being of the family is pending.

This is why the term for "individual" in Hebrew bears the imprint of the unfinished, of a lack of consummation—*prat*, meaning detailed or detached, and *yahid*, unified or solitary—in contradistinction to the Latin word, which denotes a negation of division, the indivisible, the consummate, ultimate being. The *yahid* harbors the memory and strength not of a past or impending whole as the sum of its parts (recomposition of the ideal all) but of the unification (*yihud*) and promise of the one. Therefore, the individual is not the anticipation of the one, as is generally thought, but rather the very being upon whom the act of uniting (*yihud*) is enjoined, a twinkling of the one surfacing from the interior of the family, who needs a *tikkun* to shine forth fully. The individual represents a stage beyond the separation/sanctification that the family constitutes, but he is not yet the one, because the one is not the opposite of the assembly.

Society as Obscurity

The family twinkles like an *erev*, a twilight or mingling, of a greater light to come, which is followed by the darkness of the night, when individuals, still warmed by the light of the family hearth, find themselves in a crowd, beset by the anxiety of anonymity and passage. The individual is a moment of being absent to the self but also one of the pure passage of withdrawal that is not yet forthcoming. It is the same experience as divine creation. The moment of the collective is physically a time of darkening and opacity. The crowding mass of individuals darkens a place that was empty by filling it and covering it, as it were, with the shadow of a cloud. The collective is disappearance, reviviscence of the founding disappearance of the *olam* in human interiority (in the family). And so the collectivity is not transparent in the least; something disappears, and everything is projected into exteriority. Thus, the *am*, people/being-with, is *omem*, hidden/darkened (from the same root); it is absent to itself, outside itself. The collective is an eclipse, a moment of vanished light. Its being is continually escaping its grasp, precisely when it thinks it has truly grasped it, in the presence-generating assembly.

The society, the exterior of the family, which is itself between two exteriors (nature and society), embodies the resurfacing of the original exteriority of nature, and it is in need of a *tikkun*, of safeguarding an interior in a secret place. Those who leave their families come together in a place that is close to the *olam*, a place of absence through which each individual is merely passing. They are all there together, but each ignores the other. Interpersonal and personalized relations explode due to numbers; no individual, cherished and encouraged in his individualization in the midst of his own family, can safeguard his individuality. Overwhelmed by the anonymity and the reduction of his being to an element, he becomes interchangeable, just one more element among others. For this reason, the collectivity is the place of crowds where no one can hold still! It is significant in this regard that the Latin term for community comes from *meo*, "to go" or "to pass" (as does the German *gemein*). The community is where we habitually come and go, the place of exchanges (*mu*), of change, and, for this reason, it is the place where the common (*mein*, *gemein*, *meen*) and the mutual (*mutuus*) are established, but in a movement of reciprocity, not of essence and interiority. This is why the place of the collective is the place of migration (*migrare*) and mutation (*mutare*), of a *mutuum*, a loan that will be paid in kind without interest or increase.

Abraham's family was thus born of Abraham's migration. The Latin world sets up the human camp in this absolute void of passage, since it conceives of it as epitomizing the political place. The *mu* is the place of *munus* (official function), of *municeps* (the one who participates in municipal matters), and of *communis*, the common that shares things, the place of communication between beings whose only truth is exchange: pure passage without interiority, exchange without a "message"—such is the scope of the void.

In a similar way, public figures step into the void as soon as they acquire publicity. They become absent to themselves because they represent others, because they take care of others. From this derives their power and the fact that others listen to them; they crystallize the passage through the void that the collectivity is. Kohelet, man of the public (*kahal*), who was "king in Jerusalem," clearly evinces the extent to which the collective being is directly bound up with the void, "evanescence of evanescences" (Eccles. 1:2). The experience of the collective is like a couple whose relationship is purely sexual and lacking in intimate depth. *Coitus* is a "coming together," a passing of one into the other, of one to the other, which is nothing but a formal void, a passage leading nowhere. From this perspective, Solomon, Kohelet, does not understand "the way of the man in the young woman (*alma*)."

The passage through the collectivity is inescapable: it is the state of the world right after creation and, in this respect, it harbors the potential of the world's freedom, an unaccomplished potential in need of *tikkun*. Left to itself, as an end in its own right, it involutes to destruction and dereliction. Society may have more freedom than the state, but neither is an instance of freedom. For the one, freedom is incomplete, while for the other, its completeness is a semblance. Society, like human beings, is always on the brink of sinking into death and nothingness. That, in fact, is the very foundation of the possibility of the social (and the foundation is always ahead, to be done, and not behind; founding means safeguarding in a secret place, suspending action in readiness for the future). It is therefore in this dimming of the light, which is the collectivity at its outset, that the *tikkun* must be effected; it is from this dark night that spreads over the family that the "gazelle of the dawn" (Song 22), *knesset Yisrael*, will rise. This is where memory must triumph.

Twilight (*erev*, or the mingling of the crowd) and dawn (the *shahar* of liberation/*shihrur*) are the two modalities and the two successive moments of the assembly. Dusk is an ineluctable moment in any collectivity. Thus it is written, "there was a dusk, there was a dawn" (Gen. 1:5). It is for this reason that Jacob is *obliged*, against his will, to marry Leah before marrying Rachel. Laban made a feast (29:22) and then in the darkness, when "evening came" (29:23), he gave him Leah instead of Rachel: *Leah*, meaning "without God," and *Rachel*, meaning "breath of God."

In the hollowing of the crown (*keter*), a supreme point of emergence, the kingdom (*malchut*), must appear. In the void of divestment, an *inyan*, something, must appear that is intended. The intention cannot appear before the divestment, neither can the kingdom before the crown. The mistake of the generations of Noah was precisely to seek wholeness without separation. Dawn represents a narrowing of the void. This is why *knesset Yisrael*, the assembly of Israel, is compared to Esther, whose "narrow womb" gave her husband pleasure like on the first day. Dawn: the narrowing of dusk.

And so it is Israel's vocation, in its community, to unite dusk and dawn, to "unify his Name, evening and morning" (daily liturgy), to shine the light of interiority in the inescapable void of the collectivity, to conduct its *tikkun*. The unification of the Name is paradigmatic here, since after the individual's leaving the family, the question that arises is how the Tetragrammaton can find shelter again, how it can dwell in the collectivity—the Tetragrammaton that was present between (alongside) the spouses (no doubt through the sign of circumcision) at the moment the child was conceived.

The Simulacrum of 'Tikkun'

The collectivity is therefore the privileged place of *tikkun*, and, consequently, it is the place where the dilemma of existence, the trial of the world is played out: life or death, redemption or the way of the world. This is the first moment of the political in society, and it lends itself to pretense and lies. The *clair-obscure* of twilight dissociates the two poles of the partially open being, light and darkness, and the temptation is strong to take hold of them in a bipolar dichotomy when they are to be taken in their co-mingling (*erev*), which is the very name of twilight. In this failure of the collective, the state can emerge as the model of the lost whole, the simulacrum of the *tikkun* that is needed at this time. With the state, it is as if the collectivity could not resign itself to light's disappearing into the night and sought tragically to stop its motion by lighting a furnace to prevent the nocturnal eclipse and illuminate the night. The hope of the dawn vanishes; the night, the time of the social, is disregarded, artificially covered by a model of perfection.

The state thus represents the way of abstraction by which the passage is "covered up." The unity that is built in it brings together individual elements but merely to repeat the whole of the origin. The state is a simulacrum of interiority. In fact, it is all exteriority, and its unification masks the ordeal of the void, which it negates and fills. It is the fetish of the vanished community. This is not the case for the "assembly of Israel," which takes a different path from the state, one in which the *tikkun* is accomplished by assuming the void instead of covering it up, by a separation/sanctification that opens onto a beyond-the-void, to the realm of the one, where genuine freedom rules. For although there is real freedom in the collective prior to the *tikkun*, it is vain and hollow, bereft of inner light. In the state, the other does not have the time to come to be, the time to appear. The other is merely represented and set up as a fetish. State peace is an abstract peace, like in Babel. It fails to understand those who inhabit it, individuals so thoroughly identified with the Babelian project that they are of a piece (*font corps*) with the rock of the tower. In this case, the rapprochement between them is impossible, because there is no differentiation.

The assembly of men does not start from nothingness; it does not stand on abstraction. The being must be drawn by particular threads, by individuals who leave their families. They can be disregarded, out of impatience, only at the cost of a grave misunderstanding. Such is the mock universal of the state: it does not draw individuals out through the collective; it represses them and covers them up. The assembly of Israel, to the contrary, endeavors to draw together passage and separation, which means not ignoring the trial of passage and the void. Greece is stuck with the state in the middle of the night. If it steps out of the twilight, it does not leave the night; the owl is its symbol. Israel leads the way to the dawn: the gazelle of the dawn is its symbol.

How, then, is interiority woven into the collectivity so that the one and the Name can dwell in it, an interiority that is neither a state nor simply a "big family"? How, in other words, can the interior of the family be recreated in the empty space of the collectivity? The prohibition of incest was the constituent principle of this family interiority by virtue of which something was "hidden" (in this case, the sexual character of the origin), from which the family would be born. This prohibition is the archetypal principle of all forms of interiority and separation/sanctification, and it serves not to enable women to be exchanged between families but to enable human beings to adjust to one another, to enable families to be constituted. Removing the share of the origin from the visible world allowed a secret to be spun that would weave the weft of a filiation and an alliance in the midst of a kinship (*kirva*).

The Sacrifice of the Assembly of Israel

It is the *korban*, or sacrifice, which is an act of *hakrava*, of "rapprochement," that enables not the reproduction of kinship (*kirva*) on a collective scale but rather a *kerev*, a milieu or an interior, a proximity amid the destruction of the multiple. This is what Abraham's Covenant between the Pieces tells us, for it is during the act of sacrificing animals that the promise of descendants is announced: "God cut [with] Abram a covenant, to say,[128] to your seed, I gave…" (Gen. 15:18). It is a promise that encompasses more than a family,

128. According to the commentary, *lemor*, to say, always contains a reference to incest.

a promise of a collectivity of people, for the narrative announces the destiny of Israel in history. This sacrifice is the very framework of Israel's collective being over and above the families of Israel, over and above the patriarchal migrations.

Why would a collectivity, an assembly, of people, be founded on sacrifice? In the sacrifice, individuals give up part of their property (livestock or crops), which is thereby diverted from their personal consumption; this act, which belongs to each individual, founds a community, which thereby consists of the "sum total" of the private belongings that remain from each individual and each household[129] after the totality of their gifts has been removed. This process corresponds to the cardinal act of creation: the withdrawal and concealment of God beyond his potentiality of being. This remoteness is, paradoxically, the sole closeness possible for the divine with human beings. In this sense, the sacrifice (korban) is a passage between the universal and the particular, the holy and the profane. There is a breakup of the whole in the sacrifice, a passage of "pieces." The sacrifice puts the nefesh back into "circulation"; it "olamizes" and hides the nefesh in the passage, for "the nefesh of the flesh is in the blood" (Lev. 17:11). Likewise, in society, it is the process from the particular to the universal. It breaks into pieces and moves from there to unifying consecration. The sacrifice that aims at "hiding" an animal or other food product from human beings is the underlying principle of a whole ethical approach to life, because the consumption of food, like the consummation of a sexual union or the act of gathering, raises the question of sacrifice, confronts the test of its challenge.

Can an act of union acknowledge that some part is inaccessible? Can it recognize the withdrawn portion of God? Such recognition leads the world right back to its principle of existence: the principle of the gift. Hence, the removal of part of my vital strength founds my proximity to the other, limits the unbounded extension of my sovereignty, and "narrows" the sphere of my power. This is also why an assembly is always a narrowing.

The sacrifice perpetuates memory by countering the oblivion of the void that characterizes the generations. It is the vehicle of passage to the other in the stationary world of families that have withdrawn into themselves. It breaks their self-closure and self-sufficiency by introducing a rift into their circuits (of consumption). In this respect, the sacrifice resembles the act of generation, since it manifests something buried, toward the One. In

---

129. Note the polysemy of the Latin mu with munus/gift and communis/common.

these terms, the collectivity of Israel is "sacrificial."[130] By this I mean that
any assembly, any *kirva*, any society (*kerev*) of the children of Israel is of a
sacrificial type. It has sacrifice lodged in its midst, and it is accompanied by
a sacrifice. The sacrifice on Mount Ebal, where, under Joshua's leadership,
the covenant of all Israel was reaffirmed (Josh. 8:30ff.), is paradigmatic of
sacrifice as a process of making the Name dwell in the community of Israel.
"My Name is in its midst (*kerev*)" (Exod. 23:21): My Name is in its society,
and it is so because the *korban* weaves the interiority of the collectivity by
enacting the universalization of the prohibition of incest, which can concern
only individuals within the family.

The sacrifice of the red cow (Num. 19) illustrates how sacrifice is embedded in the core of the collectivity of Israel, insofar as this sacrifice, made in
the name of all of Israel, is presented as founding the very possibility of the
people's survival. The ashes of the red cow deposited outside the camp serve
as the basis for the water of lustration that will be used for the purification
of the children of Israel who have become unclean through contact with a
corpse (the unique principle of all impurities)[131] and thereby permit them to
stay in the community of Israel. With Abraham, the *korban* appears as the
very structure of the covenant, the *berit* that seals the promise of the land
that is made to him, as to the whole collectivity that will come from him.
Abraham's passage between the cut pieces of the sacrifice plots the arena of
the political and of power. This is the locus of the "Temple polity" of Israel.[132]
The sacrifice, then, is a figure that rivals the state: secrecy versus display,
particularization versus abstract universalism, prohibition of incest versus
revealment (the covering of the state is a pretense, since the state discloses
and displays in exteriority). Where the reciprocal giving of the *korban* doesn't

130. In the very special sense of the Hebraic sacrifice, whose economy is governed not
by the principle of "sacrification," that is to say, of sacralization, but by sanctification. The
removed or hidden portion that makes the sacrifice (*korban*) is not "sacred," in the sense
of being prohibited by a taboo; to the contrary, it opens up a place for passage and for
the collectivity. It is inhabited; in fact, it is the very act of inhabiting. The "sacrifice" as
sanctification/separation founds the other who is facing me, even if his face is hidden.
This can give rise to all sorts of misconceptions, notably the one that depicts the hidden
portion as a scapegoat, when in fact, the hiding is not an outlet for conflict. The Hebraic
"sacrifice" is memory, not flight or semblance.

131. This is because impurity and the dead body are figures of loss in the passage, of
the lack of the separation/sanctification that generates concealment.

132. See below, Book II, ch. 2, "The House of Israel: Sovereignty"; Book II, ch. 5, "Abode
of Testimony: The Political Arena."

exist, what we have is a spreading arena of battle (*krav*),[133] and hostile proximity rather than loving or fraternal closeness.

The Ornament of the 'Eda'

When the community is present to itself, when there is no intermediary between it and the divine, it wears "ornaments" (Exod. 33:4). According to the commentary, this ornament (*adi*) comes from the drops of blood of the covenant (*dam haberit*) splattered over the clothing of the children of Israel as they were offering the sacrifice that accompanied the covenant. And *Midrash Tehillim* (2:103) tells us that the blood of the covenant is the separated Name (*shem hameforash*), the Tetragrammaton, the Name worn like an ornament, which is the trace of the divine withdrawal to make the world. In the world of darkness and forgetting, the sacrifice makes the Name resurface in the place of the world; it recreates *kirva*, the parental closeness with God upon which social closeness is patterned, both of which are in interiority. And so it is from this ornament, the *adi*, of the sacrifice of the covenant, that the community, the *eda* (from the same root) of the children of Israel, comes.

It may appear odd that such a seemingly crude and bloody act as a sacrifice can be the agent of interiorization. Wouldn't the union of souls and hearts be enough? The bloody nature of sacrifices should not be overestimated. It is commonplace for human beings to slaughter animals for food, and the sacrifice is precisely an act that redeems this situation. In this act, all that man does is remove a portion from his food and consecrate it to God,[134] thereby decreasing the benefit he derives from slaughtering animals for sustenance. But above all, the dimension of exteriority that exists in the sacrifice serves its ultimate purpose, because the proximity that the sacrifice produces must not be total and fusional; an exteriority must subsist—in this case, the exteriority of the sacrificed animal.

In all relationships of closeness, there is a danger of fusion. That the rapprochement comes by way of sacrifice simply serves to prevent fusion. Indeed, the interiorization counters the fusion, for whereas the latter is bound up with the all, the purpose of the former is the detachment of the one, the birth of children. We have already seen that the essence of interiority escapes us, that it comprises a passage. "Do not approach (*tikrav*) here" (Exod. 3:5) can be read as meaning "Do not sacrifice here." Lodged in the innermost

133. From the same root as *kerev*: the "closeness" that fails deteriorates into "fighting."
134. To be precise, it goes to the tribe of the Levites and the priestly family.

depths of the sacrifice is its surpassing, made possible by the irreducible and necessary crudeness that it carries, too. To renounce such exteriority is to renounce the exteriority of the other, which is the foundational moment of interiority, not so much its "surpassing" as its *tikkun*. With all its spectacular dimension, the sacrifice safeguards the other while departing from exteriority in such a way that the interiority, where faces meet, is not the negation of the outside but the manifestation of the one, a step toward the one.

This is echoed in the famous "We will do and we will hear" (Exod. 19:8). The dimension of doing (with all the crudeness of its objectivity and exteriority) precedes the much subtler and refined dimension of hearing, but this preeminence underpins the safeguard of the other, which is the universal aim of creation. If God withdraws from his world, it is for man to exist in himself. For this purpose, God's infinite being grows heavy with the crude weight of a physical world, the very continuity of which evinces the generosity of creation. If this objectivity did not exist, there would be no need for "drawing near." One approaches what is outside, seeking to bring it inside.

Hence, the objective and instrumental materiality of the sacrifice, the archetype of the materiality of all *mitzvot*, takes up such a great amount of space in the biblical text. The *korban* is an act of sacrifice; but it also involves a whole protocol, ritual, and ceremonial, that is to say, a spatial and temporal distribution of acts and human beings—what can be described, in sum, as a distanciation. The sacrifice in its materiality is the tense agency of distancing and remoteness in rapprochement and closeness. There is an antithesis between the end purpose (interiority) here and the means (preserving the exteriority), because the interiority aims at enabling exteriority to reach the one. Such is the paradoxical stake of creation. This is why the sacrifice, like the ceremonial, runs two risks: being purely and simply apprehended as such, in which case the social loses all its depth and becomes nothing more than a set of signs for the masses;[135] or being a misleading décor whose purpose is to cover up the void instead of separating/sanctifying it, instead of bringing out the one. It is worth noting that as societies have become modernized, they have abandoned sacrifices but kept a ceremonial that continues to play a role in bringing people together. There is an ambivalence, then, in the moment of the social, which is transcended when the interiority of the sacrifice is genuine.

135. This is the interpretation given by Maimonides and Mendelssohn, for instance (see Trigano, *Forgotten Dwelling*).

The Social

Because the sacrifice is a dynamic relationship, it is hard to consider the *kerev*, or the social, as a separate entity. In the *kerev*, the exteriority to the self that is the ceremonial or the sacrifice serves to ward off the danger of fusion and to posit otherness, to preserve the other, but its end purpose is in the rapprochement inside. In the *kerev*, the exteriority still seems irreducible, which implies that, even in the sacrifice, the *kerev* must undergo a *tikkun* that is superior to it and hence superior to the sacrifice.[136] However, the exteriority that exists in the *kerev* is an already redeemed exteriority. It is the interiorized, softened exteriority of the world and of nature, which is still difficult, to be sure, since it unfolds after the family phase, but which has already been "separated/sanctified." The social is the sphere of an interiorized exteriority, translated into human terms. Whatever pertains to the ceremonial and to protocol is meaningful only to preserve the principle of the exteriority of the other in the interiority and to avoid the destructive fusion that is the pull of the interior (the pull of the exterior is depletion). The sacrifice brings closer, creates interiority, but by its very nature it also perpetuates the objectivity and otherness of the outside. It is at the crossroads of the family and the social; it founds the *kerev*. This is why the social is the sphere of "clothing" and "appearances."[137] And this is what accounts for its "thickness" and ambivalence, for clothing (*levush*) can be merely a disguise and a mask. But clothing saves the exteriority of each individual within humanity. It makes use of exteriority, but its function is to preserve the individual's sphere of interiority[138] in his contact with others. The "form" and distinctiveness of clothing peculiar to each person in the *kerev* also indicate that the *kerev*'s purpose is to enable the particularization and specification of human beings. First the family rescues human beings from the anonymity of the *olam* (which, left to itself, is depletion, even though it harbors the Name) via interiority and concealment (of the Name). But then it has to give birth to people and names, to individuals who will be projected into the *kerev*. There are two challenges involved in this: forging the *kerev*, the collectivity,

---

136. See the analysis of *toch*, or interior, below, "The Interior of the Children of Israel," pp. 350–367.

137. Aaron the high priest's clothing is deemed to have an intrinsic power of *kappara*, meaning redemption but also covering.

138. "Habit," or clothing, is close to habitation. In kabbalistic language, the body is "the clothing of souls (*levush haneshamot*)."

by imparting to it the interiority dissipated in the family, but also enabling children to gain access to the one, to their uniqueness. We find here, once again, the ambivalence of the sacrifice: the interiority (in the making of the *kerev*) and the exteriority (in preventing fusion by reviving exteriority in interiority) that make up the whole reality of the social.

Thus, the finality of society (the *kerev*) is the particularization of individuals and their specification (classes, states, corporations), but this individualization emerges concomitantly with the practical universality of the *kerev* that the sacrifice produces, practical because it sticks to the "rapprochement" (*korban/kerev*) between people, an intermediary step toward weaving an interior, which is the superior degree of the collective destined to become the arena of the political. It is in this sense that the sphere of the *kerev* and the *korban* requires a *tikkun*, when it is itself the *tikkun* of the family, which is, in turn, the *tikkun* of nature and the world. The social has the political in its womb. It could dispense with its birth, but then it would remain unfulfilled. This is the case of the family in relation to the social. The family ceases when the children go off alone in the *kerev*. Each of these three levels of *tikkun*—the family, the social (*kerev*), and the political (the *toch*)—is autonomous and self-sufficient, but it is their superposition and their interlocking that make the *tikkun* complete and enable them to reach the one.

The symbolic representation of the patriarchs can be examined from this perspective: Abraham as the family, Isaac as the social (he is the being of sacrifice, the being rescued from sacrifice), and Jacob as the political. Jacob represents the redemption of the social and of the particularization that carries the seeds of division[139] and dispersion. With Jacob (the political), man reaches the oneness of being, a particularization based on unity that is manifested to him when he becomes Israel, in an accession to specificity that is not in contradiction with the community. This is why the political itself opens onto the one, albeit without understanding it.

The Femininity of Society

The act of concealment, of safeguarding something in the secrecy of the family or the social sphere, is bound up with the destiny of femininity. The prohibition of incest concerns women first and foremost—even if it is

---

139. Isaac is born from a conflict (Isaac versus Ishmael) and engenders a conflict (Jacob versus Esau), a conflict that concerns the particularization of each person and the heritage of the Name.

addressed to men—since its purpose is to prohibit the return to the mother and the origin.

The figure of Esther may be seen as symbolizing the femininity of the collectivity of Israel.[140] She is the "hidden" one (from *astir*, "I will hide"), who hides her face and does not reveal her identity to King Ahasuerus to secure the ultimate safety of her people. This interiorization of the feminine does not deepen the darkness of the night. That is what Lilith (from *laila*, or night), the first, unsuccessful Eve, represents for the Midrash: refusing separation and differentiation, Lilith slipped into the darkness of the night to become an enemy of children and procreation. Esther's concealment, to the contrary, heralds the dawn, and in fact, one of the names used for Esther is "gazelle of the dawn," after the title of Psalm 22, *ayelet hashahar*, which she is said to have recited when crying out to God for help.

It is in this sense that we understand the sentence "the honor (*kavod*) of the king's daughter is inside" (Ps. 45:14). This honor, which is to be understood in the Hebrew sense of the term *koved*, meaning heaviness or weightiness,[141] refers not to the pomp of glory but to the weight of assuming the destiny of the other, the destiny of the collectivity. Such is the "honor" of God and the "honor" of the collectivity: an increase in weight in the form of childbirth, a growing heavy with the weight of the embryo like God the creator with the weight of the *olam*. "Look, the *alma*/the disappeared has conceived and given birth" (Isa. 7:14). Esther thus appears as the *tikkun* of the female figure personified by Lilith, for Esther does not tear herself away from her weightiness.

From this perspective, and more generally, the male is a being of exteriority, who seeks to redeem himself in the interiority of the woman. The sexual act is the *tikkun* of the masculine *nefesh* that takes the man out of the exterior. Masculine and feminine are two figures of sacrifice (*korban*), one in interiority and the other in exteriority; indeed, one could see the sacrifice as the coming together of masculine and feminine, the structural act of birth giving, of the conception of the embryo across the void.

In comparison with the man, who essentially dwells in exteriority, the woman draws away in the collectivity. During the period of menstruation, the woman keeps to herself. She is entirely given over to her interiority and sexually forbidden to her husband, who is reduced, as a result, to his strict

140. "If you keep silent at this point in time, relief and deliverance will come to the Jews from somewhere else, while you and your father's house will perish" (Esther 4:14).

141. See "La Volonté créatrice," in Trigano, *Story of Disappeared Presence*, p. 54.

exteriority. This is a period of radical differentiation, introducing a suspension of the course of life and evidencing one of the key laws of the social.

The laws of *nidda* (the period of menstruation) are a reflection of the structures of the social. By her withdrawal, the woman in *nidda* remakes the interiority of the couple and hence of the family, because if she gave herself over entirely to the day-to-day relationship, she would lapse into total exteriority. *Nidda* "saves" the couple and effects its *tikkun*. Likewise, the social needs to arrange for periods of retreat and interiorization.[142] During *nidda*, the woman goes into "exile," into a state of wandering (*nidda* from *nod*, meaning "wander"), and this wandering of the social in itself evinces the nonfulfillment of society. The feminine is echo, sign, and evidence of this; she comes to remind the exteriority that reemerges in the social that it is in need of a *tikkun*.

The feminine is the time and place by which the social escapes from itself. This is the reason women have been most closely associated with clothing and why they have been the objects of domination.[143] In this case, clothing no longer serves a function of intimacy; it becomes a mask that contributes to staging the illusion of an advent and accomplishment precisely where they are most out of place. It plays a role in covering up the void of nonfulfillment and interiority. Actually, the withdrawal of the female in the social, the remnant of interiority in an exteriority that has come to be, bespeaks the temporality of the social. *Nidda* testifies to the fact that there is duration in the social, that everything is not already here in the present. There are times when everything escapes us; there are ups and downs in time. From this standpoint, *nidda* is one of the pillars of the genealogical principle and of the purity of the *kerev*. This withdrawal reminds us that generations follow one another in the void of the world and that we are not the world's consummation.

This temporality finds expression in the festival cycle (the ceremonial and the protocolar in this case), the sign that time flows by like sand in an hourglass, one grain at a time, and differently every instant. Passover is not Yom Kippur, and from Yom Kippur to Passover, we pass through all the phases of being, from withdrawal to revelation. Sacrifice, the manifest rite of the cycle of festivals, is inseparable from this passage. The social is organized

142. *Ed*, the piece of cloth used by menstruants to absorb the blood, is the same term that designates the community, or the *eda* (see below, "The 'Eda' of the Children of Israel," pp. 167–176).

143. The same holds true of the Jews in exile, whose exile attests to the nonfulfillment of the world.

around the essential temporality of the sacrifice and is built up throughout the different stages of the sacrifice over the course of the yearly festivals. The collectivity (*eda*) never exists fully and completely at the same time, like the stellar vault where each star shines one by one until dawn lights up the entire sky. The female figure is cardinal in this temporal perspective. It is the withdrawal of femininity at the time of *nidda* that introduces the principle of separation in the social. We have seen that the prohibition of incest, of returning to the mother, introduces separation/sanctification into nature and founds the family. This separation of the female in society acts as a relay and founds the search for interiority in the redeemed exteriority that is the social. It is a call for the political,[144] an element in the struggle against massification and anonymity, against forgetful exteriority; it echoes passing and emptiness in fullness. For this reason, femininity is one of the essential wellsprings of the potentiality of the political and of *tikkun* in general.

Masculinity and Femininity of the Social

By vocation, the feminine remembers; the feminine recalls the founding sacrifice and the revelation made within. "Can a virgin forget her ornaments?" (Jer. 2:32). The ornaments refer to clothing but also, as we have seen, to the community (*eda*), arrayed in splatterings of blood from the sacrifice of the covenant. Femininity has to do with blood, and "the *nefesh* of the flesh is in the blood" (Lev. 17:11). The driving principle of the universal movement of *tikkun*, it is through the feminine that the being is attached in companionship, in *hibbur*,[145] to the divine (who is separated); it is the principle of companionship inherent in society. We are told that Ruth "cleaved (*davka*)" to Naomi (Ruth 1:14). It is through the masculine that the being is divided (Eve is Adam divided from himself). And so the woman separates/sanctifies,[146] and the man seeks to reunite.

A reversal of the principles of separation/union occurs as a function of whether one is in the state of creation or in the state of the creature. The path of *tikkun* is the enterprise of man searching for the one, but the surfacing of

144. If, for Freud, the man separates (the child from his mother), and the woman unites (with her child), the Hebraic femininity sets the social into motion by figuring separation.

145. This is, however, a paradoxical form of companionship, since it is structured on separation.

146. "Behold, you are sanctified/separated for me" are the words of the betrothal benediction.

the one in the *olam* is feminine in character. Thus, Isaiah proclaims that the "young girl" will give birth, and the author of Proverbs does not understand "the way of the male in the *alma*/young girl" (30:19). This is why the *mitzvot* are addressed first to the masculine, the exteriority, the universe of "we will do," but make sense only insofar as they unveil what preceded it (the feminine, the interiority), the hidden place of the first appearance, which, because it is veiled, is announced to man in the future. The masculine always comes from the feminine, the "we will do" always comes from "listening" ("Listen to my voice," says Rebecca to Jacob, Gen. 27:8) and goes to "we will listen." The act of doing is immersed in the act of listening, the exterior in the interior, but the interior and the ability to hear are within the reach of the conjugal unity born of dialog.

A movement of the masculine and feminine unfolds in the process of *tikkun*, the aim of which is to found the assembly of human beings in the *olam*. "It is not good for the human being to be alone into itself" (Gen. 2:18). This is the supreme question of creation. Is it good for the divine being to be alone unto itself? The dualization of the being who founds the birth of the other, the separation from the other (and the other exists, since there is separation within and without), is the cardinal intention of creation. But how is it possible for the being to "become two," which is a form of giving birth? The thing is unheard of. How can being be born of being, and man of God? How can two heads wear the same crown and two beings stand in the same place?

The sequences of the two genders are clearly set down in the first story of the creation of the masculine and feminine in Adam (Gen. 1:27):

—He created *Adam*.

—He created *him* in his image... he created him male and female (*bara oto zachar u'nekeva*).

—He created *them* (*bara otam*).

What is essential here is the order of the successive acts and the placement of the direct object of the divine act: that is, the Adam in "his" two genders. If the Adam's duality is at the heart of the intention of creation, the human is created first as a single, undifferentiated being (the Adam), then differentiated in unification (the singular direct object *oto*, meaning "him," comprises *zachar u'nekeva*, male and female), and finally separated (the plural direct object *otam*, or "them").

Unity is the path to the multiple in the sense that the being comprises the potentiality of the male and the female, summoned to unite in a third being through childbirth, the *tikkun* of a world that would otherwise be in danger of breaking into a polarity. Then, finally, the divine creates them separated, as male and female. It is as if the position of the one prior to differentiation was meant to obstruct polarity, division, multiplicity, and the dereliction of passage.

The interior is posited as the principle prior to the exterior; it underpins the exterior. And the one that is posited in the intention of the dualization is by no means a totality; it accommodates multiplicity and fructification because only the two can shatter the all. The one that comes after is a transcendence of the all that provides access to the particularization of the face. That the one precedes the differentiated two points to the fact that there is reciprocal gift giving and birth giving from one to the other, from the male to the female, just as at creation. Without this, the world could not exist. This is why the woman is described as a "helper" (Gen. 2:18), because she takes man out of his exteriority and redeems him from within.

But the manifestation of the feminine runs two risks. The first is that of appearing to man as "against himself (*ezer kenegdo*)," which can happen if the interior deconstructs and drains the exterior. The second is that of appearing to man "as himself,"[147] as if man saw only himself in the feminine, as if he dressed up the feminine in clothing that disguises it and covers it up as one would obstruct the void, thereby exteriorizing it and reifying the interior in incestuous disclosure. But the *kenegdo* can also mean "facing himself," and in this sense creation is on its way to *tikkun*. Because femininity is the being of the interior, for man, it is the voice calling[148] and the testimony in the world of exteriority. It is the vehicle of hearing in the world of doing that it will ultimately submerge.

This is why the foundational act of the assembly of Israel is contained in the declaration "We will do and we will hear," harbinger of the ultimate unity of the exterior in the interior. And this is why Israel "unifies the Name of God evening and morning" (liturgy), in the manner of the union of masculine and feminine in a being that is never totally night (since he is the being of the evening) but never totally day (because she is the being of the dawn). The fullness of the light can shine only out of their union, unless the project of creation reverts to its antithesis, the night. Thus, Israel unites two modalities of collective being: the collectivity as pure exteriority (which heralds the dawn but is initially threatened by the weight of the night and anonymous

147. *Ezer kenegdo* lends itself to all these readings.

148. In Hebrew *zachar*, male, and *nekeva*, female, can be read as meaning "remember" and "call."

passage) and the community reconciled in interiority (which is the *tikkun* of the original collectivity that was potentially in its accomplishment). Woman was potential in man at the origin, then it was man who was potential in woman. And it is this movement that makes for the accomplishment of the being. The social thus runs through the being from sunset to sunrise, but the broad light of day does not belong to it.

Femininity is the vehicle of a "narrowness" in the social, since this is the way inside, the entrance, the way to form the community, *knesset Yisrael*, meaning the assembly of Israel but also the "entry" of Israel. The principle of the community is kept hidden and secret; its nudity is hidden even though its clothing is manifested outside. This manifestation of the community that shelters the light-radiating nudity of inferiority could be regarded as an illusion. But it would be more to the point to see it as a limited truth in terms of the being. This principle of interiority, which generates a certain opacity in society, is actually the very characteristic of the social, its working principle and the wellspring of being for its development.

The secret of Esther helps us understand the very condition of Israel's salvation. But this interiority, which makes for the fact that the essential facet of Israel does not pertain to the visible world, is called upon to manifest itself one day, a little more during the *tikkun* of the social in the political, and fully in the *tikkun* of the political, which is the quintessential messianic moment, the moment of licit, nonincestuous exposure (it is in this sense that it is said that the prohibition of incest will be lifted in messianic times).

The Figure of Aaron

Hence, the time of the social is also the apparent time of man and his preeminence, but all its potential is in the feminine, a potential that will be revealed even more in the "weaving" of the political.[149] Consequently, even as we must keep in mind the profound ambivalence of each phase of being when we think of the social, we must first focus on the exteriority and its implications, on what characterizes the masculinity and the relative autonomy of the exterior.

This autonomy is embodied to perfection in the identity and role of Moses' brother, Aaron, the high priest and founder of the priestly class. He crystallizes, in all his characteristics and functions, the being in society. His

---

149. "Its interior is wholly woven (or inlaid or contiguous) with love" (Song 3:10). See below, "The Interior of the Children of Israel," pp. 350–367.

power does not extend beyond the confines of the Temple; he is, in fact, prohibited from political power, which remains an exclusively royal prerogative. His children die for overstepping the boundaries of their functions (Lev. 10:1–2), for the covenant with Aaron (Num. 25:13) is not identified with the covenant with David (Ezek. 37:25), and the Aaronic power does not extend to the political. According to the commentary, "Do not come close to here" (Exod. 3:5) forbids Moses, a Levite, to approach the power of royalty. Similarly, King Saul seriously transgresses the limits of his prerogatives by claiming for himself the right to sacrifice (I Sam. 13:9–10) when kings have no such right.[150] And, as a result, Samuel takes away Saul's royal authority. Aaron's power derives from a twofold source—his attire, a key propitiatory element of the ritual, and the practice of the sacrifice; both redeem the *nefesh*. It is, of course, God's covenant with the sacerdotal family, with the Aaronites, that confers his sanctifying authority upon him. He sanctifies/separates impurity, just as he was sanctified/separated from his brothers. But one gets the sense that an essential part of Aaron's identity, including his power of purification, derives from his clothing, described as "clothing of holiness/separation," to be made by "the wise of heart" that God fills with the "lifebreath of wisdom" (Exod. 28:1–4). Without his vestments, Aaron cannot fulfill his office, which is not the case for the king or for Moses.

To be sure, the main function of the high priest is the sacrifice that he alone, with the whole Aaronite family, can carry out, and this makes him the great architect of *kerev*, the great marrier of the social, the maker of interiority in the collectivity. By means of the sacrifice, we can see how Aaron and the whole priesthood constitute the authority that characterizes the social sphere. It is the priesthood that oversees the economy of the social, not only because the sacrifice brings together the collectivity, but also because the priestly family sanctifies/separates the family from its own deadly weight. This it does by the priestly benediction (*birkat kohanim*), the redemption of the son (*pidiyon haben*) (Num. 18:19), and protocolar and procedural rules of purity in all areas (*nidda*, and so on.) The priesthood also sanctifies the *nefesh*, it sanctifies individuals, because it oversees procedures of redemption of wrongs committed by individuals due to their deeds and not due only to the very nature of family.

150. The reason Saul gave for the sacrifice is very significant. The prophet Samuel failed to come at the appointed time, and "the people began to disperse" (I Sam. 13:11), or more precisely, "the people dispersed from above me (*am nafotz*—the same term is used to refer to the generation of Babel's fear of 'dispersion,' but also to the 'populating' of the Earth by Noah's children)." Whereupon Saul felt compelled to sacrifice.

Thus, the priesthood is the main girder of the social, all the more so insofar as its separation from the rest of the people and its exceptional (land-less) status[151] structurally and institutionally introduce an incurvature into the people, a hiatus that is one of the surest wellsprings for the safeguard and development of interiority in the movement of *tikkun*. By its sole presence (prior to its function), the priesthood is the adequate structure of the social, the privileged agency of its *tikkun*. By its sole presence, the priesthood makes the *tikkun* of the social necessary in the political.

Beyond the external vestments of the high priest, priesthood shadows forth interiority at the heart of the social.[152] In fact, it oversees the Name's abode in the heart of the polity, which liberates the polity from its incompleteness. The Temple is the necessary place and condition for the accomplishment of the sacrifice. It is interesting to note that there is one altar only in Jerusalem, because the sacrifice, even the sacrifice made by individuals, concerns the whole of the people and has validity for it alone. But its presence in the heart of the *polis*—affected by the prohibition of representation—also bespeaks a void in space and the failure of the signifiers that weave the fabric of social space. The Temple is the place where the polity is absent to itself, where God is absent to the world, the incurvature into which everything pours.

II. WHAT DOES IT MEAN TO ASSEMBLE?
CONCEALMENT AND AUGMENT[153]

If assembling involves concealing something and keeping it secret, the im-plications of this concealment should be observable in the way people are added, combined, and interrelated with one another once they have left

---

151. See below, Book II, ch. 4, "The Public of Israel: The Levitical Principle in the Fabric in the State."

152. There is a danger for the priest in the exteriority of the social, the danger of letting himself be drawn into it and forgetting he is but the vehicle, the passage that leads to interiority. In this case, the sacrifice is corrupted. Exteriority is diverted from its purpose, and the social becomes an end in its own right when it has not yet been accomplished, has not yet been separated/sanctified in the political. This is the time of the prophets, who speak to the priest and society from the interior (the *toch* and not the *kerev*) that is their place, bearing witness to the truth.

153. [The term augment could not be translated otherwise, since it is fundamental, as the reader will see, to the author's development of the concept of retreat being coextensive with augment, and to the neologism he coins to describe this process: augret. Trans. note.]

their families. The "weaving" of this social fabric[154] confronts sociality with its greatest challenge. How can interiority be recreated outside the family? How can atomized individuals find themselves together in a single unity, in an interior? How is the unity of the multiple created?

The rational and especially the modern answer to this question is to see the assembly as the product of an accumulation, a mathematical addition of already existing units (the individuals). The collective is conceived of as a "response" to an original situation, a situation of lack, of an absence to which units are added that appear from elsewhere to cover and repress what is missing. The addition of the collective would come to compensate for this pristine lack, to fill in the gap. This "lack" refers, of course, to the many figures of passing, and foremost among them, the experience of natural cycles and death.[155] This form of concealment is not yet the concealment that characterizes the prohibition of incest. It may even be a perversion thereof, insofar as the real concealment is a sanctification, a separation that brings out objectivity and generates no obliteration or repression. However, what is being posited here is not so much objectivity as fusion, the fusion of the crowd filling the agora, as if the other were covered up by the discourse of the same and by the autochthony of the collectivity—in sum, by oblivion. From that point on, what is covered up and hidden away loses its germinating potential for the one and becomes the figure of death. We have here the root of all the theories of the social as repression of an original murder that has to be expiated. All these views of the social are based on obliterating otherness, posited as if "by default."

The Crystallizing Object

This lack of otherness founds the intrinsic exteriority, disguised as interiority, of such a society. It is because the other is absent and there is no interiority that the relations in such a society are purely external. This misguided exteriority is not the exteriority of a relational differentiation from the other that arises out of genuine interiority. Put otherwise, although incest is forbidden—its prohibition is what underpins society—it is being committed all

154. In the manner of the curtains of the Tabernacle, which are joined, each one (*isha*) to its sister (*ahota*) (Exod. 26:3).

155. Rousseau, for instance, saw the accidents of nature (seasons, etc.) as the cause of the passage from a state of solitude to one of association. But there is no reason to believe solitude is absent in association.

the time. Bringing human beings together in this case is basically a matter of organizing relations of exteriority between them (hierarchy, bureaucracy, collective representations, and so on), organizing the absence of community,[156] with no solace for the loss of true interiority; and the fact is that no one is actually taken in by the simulation of interiority, by representation attesting to the continual presence of the collective for each person.

The collectivity, from this standpoint, is at once exterior to itself and prey to the longing for an interiority that it gave itself as its fundament, to an unquenchable, nostalgic yearning that spawns demons because it is a lie. There is no interior in such a collectivity, which is why the social is sought in the disposition, attachment, and addition of individualities, the addition of exteriorities whose connection is purely external. After all, how could individual units unite if they did not know each other beyond themselves, if they had no place where they could depart from their singularity?

The exteriority inherent in the social is, in this case, perverted. The ceremoniality of the social no longer functions to ensure the objectivity of the other or to protect the interior, becoming instead an end to itself, from which each person is absent. All of the social is gathered together here in an object exterior to each person and exterior to itself, in relation to which all position themselves, and in which all recognize themselves externally to themselves and to the collectivity.

This is what creates an "interiority" in such a society. This object could be a ceremonial, collective symbol whose circulation forges the collectivity. In a word, it is by the relationship that everyone forms with the representation (the "object") that the collective is asserted. The collectivity becomes absent to itself and concentrated in the object. Such is the society of idolatry. The idol is supposed to shine light on the assembled collective, when in fact it casts the latter into the dark abyss of violence, where unity is achieved by blurring distinctions. The harmony of such a society is attained by negating the interiority of the social, so the prospect of the one collapses, and there is no more movement in the being.

This is an assembly of the *erev*, the twilight mix of light and dark that will never give way to the dawn. The crystallizing object is in fact the sum obtained by the addition of individual elements, which has taken on a life of its own. The sum is independent of the individual added elements, so

---

156. From this perspective, the community would have to be an empty, anonymous place to be able to accommodate everyone, one by one.

that ultimately all individuals can feel like outsiders to the society they contributed to making.

The modern period saw the emergence of a form of representation unlike the idol—namely, the social contract, seen as the foundation of a totality and a collectivity henceforth forged not through the agency of an external object but by a reciprocal agreement between its constituent elements. To be sure, the contract remains an object exterior to each individual and to the whole (since it is a theoretical moment that precedes the whole),[157] but it is an abstract, interiorized object, a pure representation of the collectivity engendering itself the function of representation. The contract is therefore closer than the idol to the interior, but it is still a form of representation. In the mathematical equality yielded by the contract, the added elements are more important than the plus sign or the total sum. The object is interiorized by it but remains an object and hence a mediation nonetheless. The contract provides more shelter than the idol for individuals, but it loses something of the totality and collectivity that the idol crystallizes. In both modalities, the multiple remains unthought and unrecognized, be it subsumed by the individual in the contract or by the collectivity as a whole in idolatry. In neither case is the collectivity recognized for what it really is, and consequently it remains exterior to itself.

And so the assembly, whose being has no real interiority, is imbued with the desire for the one, which, precisely because of its lack of interiority, becomes a desire for fusion and undifferentiated wholeness, for a depraved unity. This desire produces such phenomena as massification (fusion) and the cult of the leader, as the "one." The collective as an addition means adding one to one, which can be achieved only through the contract or the idol, and the product of the addition, the sum of its parts, remains in the realm of representation. Neither the contract nor the idol forges an interior. The "shadowy" areas each creates are not hidden areas; they are shadows covered by violence and fusion.

Concealment may not exactly be a "rational" operation, but it is a formal, discursive, and procedural act carried out deliberately. This is why it is the moment of the law, a formal moment not only objectively, but also in the sense that it is formulated in language and in the text. Its very milieu is linguistic, whereas the act of covering up is deaf and dumb, and it remains in the realm of the unconscious or lapses into abstraction.

---

157. After all, the agreement between individuals is supposed to establish the foundation of the whole.

Because addition is governed by the law of accumulation, exteriority is inescapable. In the realm of accumulation, there is no *korban*, of course; what there is is a mockery of *kirva* (society and kinship), since everything there is full. Nothing passes. Indeed, the totality yielded by accumulation remains in a radical immanence. The addition one by one imposes absolute transparency, an irreducible objectivity whose sum is actually impossible.[158] Consequently, the insatiable desire for objectivity, confronted with the tension of the sum, culminates in representation: an artificial, ideological overlaying of the one onto the multiple.

The totality thereby obtained eliminates the multiple; the sum total of the addition cancels the components of the addition. Hence, from the standpoint of the sum through addition, the consideration of the multiple in the collectivity is impossible. The collectivity immediately vanishes, divided as it is and fragmented ad infinitum. Representation serves to cover up and spatialize the perpetual turmoil agitating this gaping hole. And by covering, it clouds what was set up at the outset as absolute transparency.

Unity Without Totality

So the unity of the multiple can be only in the interior. To find a way out of this aporia necessitates finding an "accumulation" (since multiplicity exists in any case) that is also passage. But where there is passage, there is an unclinching and a "failure" of sorts; the passage speaks of remainder and remnant, of vacant space and surplus. The unity of the assembly cannot be achieved on the basis of a totality through addition. Without a reserve, without a remainder, this unity does not meet the major challenge of the being—and that is the passage or, to put it otherwise, the phenomenon of generation or, yet again, in a word, time.

How can the being survive the course of generations, endlessly returning to inhabit the absence (or rather, the secret) that is the world? How can the all be perpetuated? This would imply the paradox of a collective that consists of increasing and multiplying while passing—that is to say, while subtracting.[159] "I passed through the land of Egypt"—the purpose of this passage is to collect and strengthen sanctity over uncleanliness.[160] The collectivity of Israel

158. The all is a concrete impossibility, and modern society an impossible dream.

159. This is the aim of our analysis.

160. Rabbi Abraham Isaac Kook, *Olat Re'aya*, commentary on the Haggada (Jerusalem, 1963), p. 43.

is born from the passage of God through the heart of Egypt, from a setting apart, a removal that leads to an accretion—the birth of the Jewish people as an overplus to the nations; and to an assembly—the gathering of the community of Israel. This is the fundament of the idea of chosenness. This setting apart is translated, of course, into the death of the firstborn Egyptians. And because the flip side of this loss to Egypt is the accretion that is the birth of Israel, Israel is forever "indebted," which is why the sacrifice (*korban*) is often explained as redeeming the death of the firstborn Egyptians, when the firstborn Hebrews were saved.[161] Until the sin of the golden calf, it was the task of the firstborn of Israel (who had been saved in Egypt) to sacrifice for all the people. Thereafter, the priests conducted the sacrifices, but they did so on behalf of the firstborn.

This emphasis on the firstborn (redeemed by *pidiyon haben*, Num. 18:15), on the "first" (*reshit*) of the harvest (redeemed by the offering of the first fruits at the Temple on Shavuot, Exod. 23:19), draws our attention to the *reshit*, the first, the one of the origin that constitutes the major obstacle to the gathering of a collectivity and that must be "sacrificed," "brought close" (*kerev*). Maybe the Egyptian firstborn died from the passage of God because Egyptian society could not detach itself from the cult of the origin (*reshit*), from the illusion that the origin is immanent in humankind or in the world. Egypt is the society of stone and oppression where Israel suffers—Israel, which is potentially an overplus. It is the society in which the sacrifice of the *korban* is not possible, where the Pharaoh is worshipped, as the first of men and the only perfect man, a cosmic incarnation. But when Israel assembles, it gives something, a remainder, an augmentation inassimilable into the addition and the sum of components, without which the collectivity would be impossible. This "remnant" is the result of the concealment, the site of unspent and unconsumed giving to which one can continually return,[162] no matter how far away one has gone from it in the *olam*, to rediscover one's name, the place that the generations come to occupy.

Consequently, the collectivity that arises from this concealment is not obtained by addition. There is always something missing from the addition for it to yield a sum of the total. This collectivity can simply not be reduced to a sum total, not because it "lacks" something to form a collectivity, but because it is always additional to itself. That which, from one side, appears to be a lack in the total (the impossibility of a totality) is, from the other

---

161. Exod. 13:13–15.

162. Notably through rituals and other consecrated occasions.

side, an overplus that comes in addition to the sum and makes it possible for the unity of the collective to be achieved. The community is forged not as the product of an arithmetical addition but as an overplus, an augment, which is not "usable" and is not part of the addition circuit. It is "concealed," and it is in this respect that it is not an object. Isn't this the meaning of the concealment? What is added as a overplus does not figure in the total sum; it is removed from the reckoning. This concealment (concealment of the one—the firstborn?) founds the collective as a multiplicity, thereby removing it from its tragic position. Otherwise put, the concealment opens the place of *rahamim*, of birth-giving grace. It founds a universality that is essential, not mathematical, whereas the overplus makes it possible to transcend sameness and founds the freedom of the other by weaving an interior and setting it aside for safekeeping.[163]

Society as Overplus

We have thus gone from an approach to the collective through addition to one based on an overplus. This overplus develops on two levels: it manifests itself first as a lack and a subtraction (from the standpoint of addition),[164] but ultimately it turns out to be an augment. "This lack cannot be numbered... and I have added wisdom onto myself... for with much wisdom comes much anger; he who increases knowledge increases pain" (Eccles. 1:15-18). "To the sinner, He has given reason to gather and amass... but this too is evanescence and pursuit of wind" (2:26). "Whatever God will do will be for *olam* (forever/ for disappearance/for the world); to this, nothing can be added, and from this, nothing subtracted" (3:14). The world is in a state of disappearance: there is, therefore, nothing to be removed from it and nothing to be added to it.[165]

We see in all these examples from Ecclesiastes how "the more," that is to say, what remains in surplus (addition and excess) and hence as an advantage and a profit, corresponds to absence, to the beyond-reckoning, to emptiness; how the surplus is a painful ordeal in this world; how, in the void, subtraction and addition are equivalent. Kohelet never ceases to question the overplus: "What is the overplus (*yitron*) for man in all his work?"

163. According to tradition, the survival of humanity depends on thirty-six hidden righteous people.

164. But why even say it? Herein resides the whole relationship of Kohelet to language and writing.

165. One may seek to reckon it, but it cannot be found.

(Eccles. 1:3). These words are pronounced by the person who assembles a public (*kahal*) and is king of Jerusalem: "Solomon gathered together the senators of Israel" (I Kings 8:1).

In what way do the acts of assembling and accumulating carry the void with them? The assembly (*asefa*, or accumulation) was summoned from the moment God revealed his Name in the *olam*/disappearance, in the form of a memory, from generation to generation, from passage to passage, but also and especially as something said in addition, as an overplus, an increase, an augment. "God said in addition (*od*) to Moses... this is my Name for *olam*, my memory from generation to generation. Go and gather/accumulate (*asefa*) the senators... to say, I have remembered you" (Exod. 3:15–16). It is on the basis of the *od*, of the more, of one plus one plus one, that the assembly is constituted. Which raises the burning question of lack *or* augment, the question of the origin, the question of the divine and of the Name.

We can now see why there is always something missing in the *asefa*. This absent-for-us that is in fact in addition to us is God, whose retreat founds the place of generations: retreat/subtraction founding the addition, the augment of the divine that is the world, the giving birth to man. Retreat for us, but actually increase for God. But, from this perspective, the retreat is summoned to become augment. This is the wisdom (wisdom as augment/addition [*hosafa*], in the manner of Kohelet 1:16) that manages to pass through the immediacy of appearances and turn retreat into increase, the absence of *olam* into a secret of interiority. Therein resides the model of the *tikkun* of the world, because the reversal of the origin in which only the retreat is manifest is the very process by which the world was formed and without which it would not exist.

The gap between the retreat and the augment in the same being underpins the possibility of the world. In Babel this gap was erased, and history could not take place. Such is the process of the messianic, wherein we go from exile to return, from lack not to fullness but to augment. We can see why exile plays such a decisive role in the ingathering of Israel, for it corresponds to a total concealment of the people (the exile is not limited to one country or even several; it encompasses the world as a whole) and to a total retreat with respect to itself. The priest (more than the king, who disappears almost completely), then plays a key role in redeeming the missing collectivity, the families whose interface has come to be dislocated. But this concealment, this lack in exteriority, harbors an increase, whose advent reverses the exile (with which it is coextensive, since the augment was always hidden in the retreat); the retreat becomes reversed into augment. This explains why the messianic figure has the traits of kingship, for it is the realm of the king that opens in the being, the king who is the flip side of the priest as augment is of retreat. The redemption effected by the priesthood opens onto kingship. The priest deals with the lack, the king with the retreat.

Society as Concealment

Founded in the surplus, the community is woven together in concealment, not revealment. "Moses gathered/convoked (*kahal*) the whole *eda* of the children of Israel and said to them... Six days you shall work and the seventh day will be separate/holy, Sabbath/inactive for YHWH; whoever does work shall be put to death" (Exod. 35:1–2). So the whole assembly of Israel is gathered together to announce the "cessation" of doing, the departure from the world of *olam*: Sabbath, which is a separation/sanctification. And in the concealment thus created resides the Name of God, expressly designated here as the place of suspension. Never is the community of Israel "fuller" than in the time of Sabbath, a time of cessation.

In the sacrifice of the red cow (Num. 19:9), the community (*eda*) is posited alongside the act of setting aside and safeguarding the ashes of the cow, sacrificed for the whole of Israel "outside the camp" for the purpose of cleansing human beings of the impurities caused by death, so they won't be "cut off from Israel" (19:13). The suspension that the institution of the red cow brings about for the whole *eda* has a beneficial function of redemption. This is why assembling is a matter not of appearing but of "entering" (*knesset*), of hiding outside the *olam*, stepping outside the visible, giving, removing from oneself, and hence, perforce, remembering. The assembly is memory, which is to say it is not immanence. It is surely not its own origin. An assembly cannot be created ex nihilo, but it is the echo of the original *nihil*, the memory of what is concealed, of the place (of the) one (*makom ehad*, Eccles. 3:20) where all the waters in the world gather, regardless of the lay of the land and the direction of the flow. In this sense, the secret place of the community is a place of bounty and gathering of individuals. The assembling of the collectivity is often accompanied by a flow of water: "Gather the *eda*, you and Aaron... and you will speak to the rock before them, and it will give its waters, and you will bring forth for them water from the rock and give the *eda* to drink." "Assemble the people, and I shall give them water" (Num. 20:8; 21:16).

It is because the collectivity is hidden that a census cannot be taken of it, for when something is concealed, it is removed from the total sum, or, if you prefer, it is added over and above the total. And if it must be counted, it is at the cost of another concealment, of a *korban*, which serves to avoid petrifying the vivacity of the community's coming. This is why the people of Israel always create the effect of a surprise and an event in history. This idea of a hidden community is also found in the figure of the innumerable: "Look at the sky and count the stars, if you are able. So shall your offspring be," Abraham is told (Gen. 15:5) during the Covenant between the Pieces.

Innumerable they may be, even if their size is small in terms of numbers, because what innumerable designates is that which cannot be numbered because of its very quality. The prohibition of the census[166] indicates to us the very nature of the collectivity and that it is hidden in secrecy. It isn't until the community collapses, in the sense that it loses its secrecy, that it creates objects externally materializing its collective being. Thereafter, it exists only by virtue of this object deposited outside it, in the exterior. So when Moses, who had gathered all the people of Israel at the foot of Sinai, stayed away too long, the community that was waiting for him—a wait that forged its Israel-being—collapsed and built the golden calf, divesting itself of all interiority.

The golden calf episode shows *a contrario* one facet of concealment: concealment as covenant (*berit*). The act by which a people becomes a people is this act of concealment, which is termed a *berit*. Why, then, is the people "in the wrong" (Exod. 32:17), if not because it broke the principle of the covenant, which is concealment in secrecy? The covenant is the "we shall do" before the "we shall hear." This is why it is the object of "memory," of passage, the revival of an origin and not the origin itself, so much so that it is to be seen not as the founding act of a collectivity but as a process coextensive with the very existence of the assembly. Thus, the blood from the sacrifice of the covenant is the ornament (*adi*) and the assembly (*eda*). The covenant is a procedure of augment; its "breaking"[167] is tantamount to a retreat, and yet it adds to reality. In the light it projects, there is darkness (Israel's exile announced in the Covenant between the Pieces); in the presence it creates, there is absence. In a way, the *berit*, thus defined, is also the

---

166. *Mifkad*, or census, is related to *pakad*, or memory, especially when it concerns God. It would be a misuse of memory to disregard the secret, to count only the "heads" in a community, as if they existed in exteriority alone, and thereby, in effect, expose the community to death and the "evil eye" (see below, "All Israel and the Prohibition of Census Taking," pp. 380–403).

167. On the idea of "breaking" a covenant, see above, Book I, ch. 1, "World-Covenant."

model of God's relationship to the world and to himself. The collectivity follows the eclipse of God.

The Solitude of the Collectivity

There is absence, passage, and hence, solitude in the collectivity in echo to the absence and solitude of God the creator. When the collectivity gathers together, doesn't it retreat from the outside and find itself paradoxically alone in its withdrawal? Within the affluent multiplicity, the being is seized by its individuality. Herein lies the most powerful and immediate experience of the multiple. Why does solitude arise from the multiple? Because the multiple that inhabits the void of the world of passage is drawn to its origin, to the one. The solitude that arises in the concealment designates not individual self-enclosure but the generating nearness of the one. It is because the one is hidden, because God has hidden his unity in his withdrawal, that the world was created in the passage and gave rise to multiplicity. Consequently, this solitude is loving; it is the solitude of lovers,[168] of the uniting couple, solitude not with regard to the collective but with regard to oneself, not the solitude of individuals but the solitude of the one that is hidden in the meeting of two people and in the multiple, and that makes their union possible. The solitude in the *olam* is a revival of the one and of the community. It is as if the loner (*yahid*) of love carried the heart of the collectivity, separated to such a great extent from others that it passes for the enemy of the human species; but, in fact, those who are gathered by way of addition and who are convinced that they are together are but a chaotic hodgepodge, because adding one to another does not make a community. The solitary is hidden, because it carries the one in a world that is the fruit of the one yet does not recognize it. It hides because it bears witness to that which preceded it and is to come: namely, the one. "A being-with/a people (*am*),[169] in solitude, will be present" (Num. 23:9), it is said of Israel. Similarly, the beloved in the Song of Songs who personifies the community of Israel is in solitude herself, searching for her husband. The unions in this world are not complete; they merely foreshadow the unity to come. Thus, marriage is a concealment, an eclipse, a placing in solitude, since it produces the prohibition of incest. But it is a lack to outward appearance only; it is also an overplus brought to the world, because marriage conceals a portion of the world in the two who are

168. *Ehad*, one, and *ahava*, love, have the same numerical value.
169. *Am*, or people, can be read *im*, or being-with.

united, adding it to the *olam* (hence, marriage is a covenant). This overplus will be manifested in the birth of a third—that is, the child. This is why companionship (*hibbur*) through concealment—that is to say, marriage according to the law—is an *ibbur*, which can mean conception of the child, being-to-pass, or passing. "According to the law" is an important condition, because only the law (*halacha*) prohibits incest and makes the marriage something more than the temporary conjunction of two individuals. Without the law, there would be neither concealment nor augment. The solitude is the result of the separation/sanctification that produces the concealment that is the very principle of communion. Solitude in the being is qualitative, not quantitative.[170]

The Individual: Echo of the One

The individual is therefore an echo of the one but a misguided echo if he holds himself to be a consummate unity, because, in this case, the passage would be arrested and the individual (etymologically, the "undivided") would lapse into division, into a corrupted form of particularity. It is because the one is posited and hidden in secrecy that the multiple comes to be. This perspective affords a wholly different conception of the particular and the universal. Admittedly, the concealment of the one can give rise to misunderstandings, because it looks like the removal of a singular portion from a universal whole, like a particularization of the universal.[171] But the removal of a portion of the whole is not a dismemberment of the all, a lack in or failure of the whole. This setting apart is a concealment. The portion is placed in hiding and announced for the future, and it is under the shadow cast by this future that the collectivity grows. Could the one have been otherwise? Hidden, it runs the risk of being regarded as one in relation to two, three, four, and so on, a portion of an infinite all when in fact it is the one of all the twos, threes, fours, and so on.

This is why the particularity cannot be an individual share taking, breaking the whole down into components, as in suffrage, where each voice is a fraction of the whole, and the will of the all is composed of an addition of its parts (which gives each part the illusion that, as a part, it possesses the

170. Sabbath, the place mapped by the community, is the privileged moment of *reshut hayahid*, the sphere of the one, as opposed to *reshut harabbim*, the sphere of the many (the public arena), but this is the place where the solitary *yahid* must accomplish *yihud/* unification.

171. This is what is said of God the creator, designated by the particularization of his attributes.

whole and that the whole belongs to it, when it possesses it only because it is the memory of the one).

This individualist form of particularity is the misguided particularity that develops at the time of the golden calf. Aaron calls the people and says, "detach/separate into parts (*parku*) the gold rings from the ears of your wives, your sons, and your daughters, and bring them to me," and the people "detached/separated into parts/broke down (*hitparku*)" (Exod. 32:2–3). The rings, given one by one, represent the democratic count of the people. The golden calf, the representation of the people, is made by dividing the total-ity into parts and totaling the sum of these parts. So many rings equal so many voices. This is a mockery of the community of Israel! And these rings (*nezamim*) are a mockery of the ornament (*adi*) that forges the community (*eda*) of Israel during the covenant with God. The *nezem* here is a representa-tion, an idol, a surrogate fetish for the *adi* that the people had lost. What is a representation if not the one of the multiple, a simulation of the one that, unlike the real one, leads to arresting passage in the being and presence? And, paradoxically, this representation, which is supposed to create unity, actually creates a division (into parts). Representation always particularizes and divides into parts. Consequently, it is driven willy-nilly to fight against the multiple so as to impose itself. For this reason, it establishes the basis of a power and a center. And those who escape its control are seen as an individuality apart and an enemy of the whole.[172] This is the fate that the one, the loner out of love, can incur in the empire of representation. This has been the fate of Israel, "enemy of the human species," which was actually born out of love by its concealment. Thus, the universality of the collective is founded on the particularity, on the removal of a part from the original whole and its concealment. "On that day, Joshua sealed a covenant with the people and imposed a law and rules upon them in Shechem. Then Joshua recorded these things in the book of divine law.... And Joshua dismissed the people, with each returning to his territory" (Josh. 24:25–28). Likewise, God's revelation takes place with "each standing at the threshold to his tent" (Exod. 33:8).

The individual, echo of the one, is not a lack in the all, but an overabun-dant surplus, an addition in/to the all that enables it to be an inhabitable dwelling for each person. The rooms of the house are not divided between the inhabitants; each person finds a place in the house because a room is

172. In the case of the golden calf, the Levites, who remained faithful to the divine one, were accused of particularism, because they dissociated themselves from the democracy of the calf and thus became the target of hatred. One commentator recounts the murder of Moses and Aaron's brother-in-law Hur in this context.

added, and the state of scarcity and conflictuality is abolished. This addition of a room is a concealment in the dwelling, because the room does not figure in the tally. Therefore it immediately appears as a lack and an absence, when in fact it is an overplus. The flip side of "scarcity" is bounty. It is the totality, the universal that harbors the lack (precisely by trying to cover it up with a representation). The one harbors accomplishment. But, dialectically speaking, if the all is a lack, this is because it is already inhabited (without knowing it) by the one of the overplus. The mistake that needs to be avoided, then, is that of making a representation to cover up the lack instead of weaving a place of concealment that shelters the one that is overadded.

It is on this mode of the one that the multiplicity of Israel is described to us. Israel is likened to sprouting (*tzemach*): "Numerous (*revava*) as the sprouting in the field" (Ezek. 16:7). Sprouts do not appear one by one; sprouting bursts forth, the many appearing as one at the same time.[173] The unity of Israel comes from each one brightening and darkening in turn.[174] The fleeting concealment of passing light in unceasing motion is what gives the impression of a constant light that does not pass, that neither brightens nor darkens. This would be a black light. There is light only for this world—that is to say, for the passage, the eclipse, and the absence. This is why light's greatest moment is at dawn, after the night. The multiple therefore resembles a luminescence.

Indeed, the passage of light gives us insight into the relationship between the one and the multiple, for the one flashes endlessly in the multiplicity of the world, and the quantifiable multiplicity is forged from these sparks of the one. "And I saw that there is a surplus (*yitaron*) of wisdom over stupidity, as the surplus of light over darkness" (Eccles. 2:13). This surplus is the dawn. The dawn is hidden in the night, is born from the night, and gives rise to the night. Because the one is hidden in the seed (the being), the stems and flowers that will form the whole plant come out, one by one. Despite the apparent infinity of the multiple, it is the one that gives rise to it, the one that is secretly nestled in the recesses of the multiple. Exteriority is structured on the interior: all individuals exist only in relation to the other and to the all because the one is absent; to "mend" this beneficial birth, we must seek the one, which can be "found" only once it has been concealed, and repeat this concealment again and again, as if it could not be found. "He put the

173. See Maharal's commentary in the Haggada on the growing number of children of Israel in Egypt. The efflorescence is at once unique and multiple. This is what generates its brightness.

174. Similarly, it is because Israel is in exile, hidden in the totality of the world and spread over the whole earth, that a single land appears for it in its particularity: Eretz Yisrael.

olam in their hearts, without man's ever finding the deed that God did from beginning to end" (Eccles. 3:11). "Man will not be able to find the deed that is done under the sun" (8:17).

Thus, it is when the collectivity effects concealment that the individual is not a lack in the all or lacking in relation to the all, but rather the overplus of the all, the one made possible and summoned to existence (in the call) through concealment. It is the concealment in the collective that enables the individual to truly arise, because it prevents the collectivity from closing up into a totality. The concealment is like a reference point, a marker embedded in the multiple where individuals can go, from time to time, to take shelter and disappear for a while,[175] to be able to reemerge thereafter in the multiple. And this marker testifying to the one in the multiple comes to shatter the totalitarian totality, for this is how man's *nefesh* escapes the anonymity and interchangeability to which it is condemned in the all. Concealment is the secret treasure of the being which, hidden in the collective, allows each individual to emerge and to make a name for himself.

It is not a contract, concluded in exteriority and leaving individuals walled into their divisions, that forges the collectivity, but the act of concealment—that is to say, the prohibition of incest that is the principle of the whole law.[176] The law is a procedure of concealment, and it establishes the basis of the collectivity and safeguards the individual. But it is not contractual; it is passed on from generation to generation, proceeding from divine concealment in the origin and the Sinaitic revelation. In this sense, the principle of Hebraic law is passage[177] and concealment, whose finality is to ensure the *tikkun* of the human world through unification (*yihud*) with the one in the midst of the multiple. This concealment is what makes unification possible in each and every moment, without, however, negating the nebulae of the multiple.

From this perspective, we can see the fascinating movement of particles in the nebulae of the multiple, with elements rising, uniting, separating, overtaking each other, continuing on their course, disappearing, flashing, producing other elements. All this makes up the infinite nebula of particles that is the social, which is why it is incomprehensible if we stick to the infinite dimension of its multiplicity. The ideas of the one and of concealment give

175. The place of the Temple, with its procedures of access (sacrifices and rituals), is the preeminent symbol of this.

176. See Book II, ch. 5, "The House of Israel: Sovereignty"; and Book II, ch. 2, "Abode of Testimony: The Political Arena."

177. Whence its name, *halacha*, the going or the way.

us insight into the law of this fascinating movement: the one is its only law, and concealment its dynamic principle. If we trace the course of particles, starting from the all and traveling through the family, the social, and so on, we can grasp the luminescence of a light, the foaming of a wave, the steady streaming of water. It's a law of light, and this law is the law of human society, a "natural" law, one could say, but vastly superior to that of the physical world for which it is the secret law—which clearly evinces that it is the one, the augment, much more than the all that is the object of knowledge. Real knowledge (Kohelet's wisdom) focuses not on the breakdown of the all, following the Cartesian method, but on the process of the one, whose concealment underpins the all and its illusion.

A Vision of the Divine

The reader will have understood that this vision of the social contains, at bottom, a vision of the divine, with its movements of expansion and dispersion, of the rise of the particular and the withdrawal of the all in the one, of concealment and appearance, of twinkling. In it should be seen the law that governs the relationship of God to the world, a relationship of "particularization" and universality. How could it be otherwise, knowing that the social revives the origin and arises from the eclipse of God, whose presence it finds through concealment? "They will exalt Him in a public (*kahal*) of being-with/people (*im/am*), and in the session of senators they will praise Him" (Ps. 107:32). The assembly is always in divine presence (or in its idolatrous reversal). Society always brings God into play. "Moses went out and spoke the words of YHWH to the people, and he gathered seventy men from among the senators" (Num. 11:24). The manifestation of the community is bound up with the manifestation of God. This is why the whole of the community, the *klal* of the people, is righteous: "All your people are righteous" (Isa. 6:21). *Klal Yisrael*, all Israel, is without sin, since it stands before God and does not die, even if particular individuals or groups of people in Israel are sinful. This is because there is a concealment in the *klal*. Hence, the *klal*, the all of Israel, seeks to unite in the one, in the interior, inside the Temple, which, as the social institution of concealment, functions to redeem it.

When God created the world, he absented and concealed himself: he hid his unity and announced it in the future. This is what makes the multiple and the particulars possible. In sum, God is particularized without the one, while the natural world left in the passage is "universalized." This particularization of God is what founds the natural universal that will, however, tend thereafter toward fragmentation and particularization. In this it is manifesting its hidden principle (the particularization of God). It would be a mistake to think of this fragment, this particularity, as a structural degeneration of the all of natural universal, tragically embedded in the all and in nature, when, in fact, this manifestation of particularity is the work of the one in the natural all, the work of the passage and the evolution of the being toward the one. This particularity in the whole announces the one from the very instant the all comes into being, and what it announces is no longer the creational particularization of the origin, but the return to (of) the universal of the one, a universal that has established in the meantime the place of an other than itself—to wit, man.

In other words, the one hides and makes room for the multiple, but, because it is in hiding, the multiple can only be passing, which means that it is haunted by the return of the one that will gather it into itself in separation/sanctification. In sum, if there is passage, it is because the one is hidden in the multiple, and the particular, in the universal. Herein lies the principle of movement and passage.

In the particularization, God sets himself as an addition to the world and the being, even if his concealment has every appearance of being a subtraction, for there is no subtracting from God. But is there adding to him? "Everything God will do will be for the *olam*; nothing can be added to it and nothing can be subtracted from it" (Eccles. 3:14). It is the problematic of augment that is raised once again in this question. This subtraction is an addition because it is a concealment; it is therefore (simply) out of this concealment that the world is born. The world and time are other names for this gap between retreat and augment. It is forbidden to "associate the divine Name with something else" (Sanhedrin 63a), but isn't man "YHWH's associate (*shutaf*)" (Kiddushin 30b)?

It is from the standpoint of this "addition" that the question of attributes arises, the cardinal question of the arena of the social and of power but one that is unanswerable if considered only in terms of addition. We have to rethink this question in the context of the system of retreat and augment. The attribute is to be seen not as an addition but as a gratuitous overplus, over and above the void and absence, which calls therefore to be interpreted (because the attributes are the object of high wisdom and do not lend themselves to immediate legibility), not in terms of the logic of scarcity (with all the impasses to which subtraction leads) but in terms of the bounty that governs the production of augment—that is, concealment.

The attributes thus appear to pertain to the dimension of the hidden one, whose chosen place is man because, in all the universe, the one is hidden for man alone. Naturally, therefore, the attribute is anthropomorphic. Seen in the context of retreat, it is an offense to God, but this is not so in the context of augment, in which case it refers to the creation of man, made possible by the augment superadded to God that is God announcing himself in his retreat, in his absence, through the one hidden in secrecy. It is then no longer a matter of interpreting the augment/attribute in terms of the "negation of absence (shelilat hahe'ader)," as Maimonides does, and as a negation of the initial stage.[178] It is a matter no longer of negating or denying but of hiding something in the passage of attributes in the world and in the text of the revelation. It is a matter no longer of designating (divine) positivity via a negation of absence—which, in any case, is a secondary sense of the attribute, the philosophical translation of positive attributes—but, to the contrary, of assuming the trial of absence (he'ader), that is, the world, by enabling it to pass rather than denying it, arresting it in an abstract representation of unity that covers up multiplicity and reality. It is a matter of seeking the one in the anthropomorphic multiple, through an act of concealment.

The attributes manifest in the world in the passage of the being that is hidden in the one. In a way, they are already a tikkun of the void and the retreat, but human beings still have to accomplish a tikkun of them, a tikkun through passage, through passing from particularization to the one. The one of the divine is not primordial in a way that would make the attributes a degeneration thereof, and if it is primordial, it is so in the same way as its announcement in the future, as a frail, twinkling presage, a glimmering hope in the spreading darkness of the retreat, which was the source of all things.

In Search of the Hidden Love

The vocation of human beings and society is to seek the hidden love that created the world, without falling prey to the more tragic misconceptions of mistaking the solitude of love for abandonment or nothingness, or seeing the augment as an addition. In this case, man would cover up the abyss with

178. The term actually designates a hidden meaning, because Maimonides, assuming the positivity of reality and the principle of particularization underpinning it, endeavors to deflect the positive categories of reality from God and focus on negating his purported absence (which remains entirely theoretical); this is a way of theoretically reconciling the divine and the positivity of reality. See "La lettre en creux: les attributs négatifs," in Trigano, Forgotten Dwelling, p. 124.

a representation or equate addition with a sum (God being nothing more than the sum of his powers and attributes). Instead of running away from the trial of retreat, he must hide a portion of his life in order to understand the one whose concealment enabled him to exist. Out of this trial of retreat comes the augment, the one, the union of love within. Through the act of concealment, man "particularizes" himself in the manner of God, thereby reviving the creational gesture that redeems the lifeless world; without this act he would remain in the illusion of individuality, of a particularity that sees itself as simple and complete in itself, a fraction of the all, posited in its relationship to the all and not to the one. This is why the social cannot, without betraying itself, be a straightforward, positive affirmation, although neither is it a negative one. These were the terms of the alternative in which the lost Hebrews were locked after their departure from Egypt, when they asked: "Is the Name among us or not?" (Exod. 17:7), or more precisely, "Is YHWH in the mode of there is (yesh) in our midst/kinship/society (kerev), or is he in the mode of there isn't (ayin)?" This is a false aporia, because it is informed by an ignorance of the passage and an avoidance of the concealment that makes the kerev. Admittedly, at the time, the Hebrews did not have a priest to deal with the structural failure of the social and help them bring about the passage and concealment.[179] Indeed, they will later spontaneously turn to Aaron the high priest to make the golden calf, the representation covering up the passage, intended to mask the absence (he'ader)—that of Moses to begin with—that is the immediate experience of the social as of the world and of being. Indeed, Hebraic society is founded before receiving the procedures of its tikkun, which goes to show that society is instituted secondarily, or, to put it otherwise, that it is posited prior to its tikkun and exists solely by its tikkun. The augment is not a positive assertion, but neither is it in negativity, due to the combination of retreat and augment. This is the way out of the aporia of the social left to itself.

III. FIGURES OF ASSEMBLY: 'AM' AND 'EDA'

The principle of the community is in its secret. It is in this interior that it maintains and constitutes itself, but doing so is an act of man, a tikkun, a way of proceeding and a process that make up the elective arena of human

179. This is actually an ideal condition, if only one can be equal to it.

beings, that elevates them to the level of divine creation. If there is "process" in sociality, it is because sociality is a category of time. How could it be otherwise, since it manifests itself and develops only in the passage, which is the journey of time through the being? The *tikkun* that enables and redeems sociality and proceeds by way of a concealment is the reactuation of the passage of the world manifested in the divine passage. The only way to accomplish the *tikkun* of the world and of passage, the only way out of the passage, is through passage. This is the only way out of the illusion of the eternal infinity of passage, the illusion of the absolute and inanimate objectivity of the being-there of the world. Indeed, the passage opens onto the abyss of nothingness only if it escapes the divine project (and it can indeed escape, because it belongs to the realm of human beings, who are called upon to create in the manner of God, meaning to effect the *tikkun* of creation). The end purpose of the passage is to reach the interiority of the one. Reactuating the passage of the world means effecting concealment. Now, if sociality, which culminates in the political, is the arena where this happens, it is because it experiences the different moments and phases in the process. Different steps can be discerned in the act of gathering, all of which are facets in the process of sociality and informed by a logic of temporality. We find the very precise terminology of this development of the collectivity in the many Hebraic words that designate the gathering: *knesset, am, eda, kahal, tzibbur, klal Yisrael*, and so forth.

This evolutive logic points to the evolutive character of the one. Human society, a microcosm of creation, accomplishes the whole process of its destiny and experiences its perversions and accomplishments. But there is nothing irreversible in this process; attaining the one does not amount to definitively leaving the outside far behind, as if the issue were simply to "get beyond" the multiple. On the contrary, the concealment is a challenge at every moment and in every era. It is a matter not of reducing or superseding the multiple but of making it possible through the fulfillment of the one. It is not a matter of moving into the interior once and for all and eradicating the exterior; this would be a mockery of *tikkun*, divesting it of all meaning.

The interior, and the concealment that allows us to dwell in it, is a source of renewal for the exterior. The one must dwell in the midst (*kerev*) of the multiple, and this is what makes the social. All categories and facets of the assembly coexist; it is their intersection that makes the *community*. In other words, each facet exists apart and for itself, but they are all in the light of the one and the interior, and all have the one for a horizon. In a way, they coexist almost simultaneously. "You stand/are summoned, all of you, today"

(Deut. 29:9). The collectivity is continually called upon to be present to itself, in all its members, as a united body. No one can escape this summons,
and the collectivity must always be equal to this exacting requisite for unity.
And the summons calls for effort and action. We are told that this requisite
of presence is made *hayom*, "today," or "according to the day."[180] "There is
evening, there is morning," both times of collective presence. After all, isn't
the social experience to bring the light of dawn forth from the darkness of
the twilight (*erev*) of assembling, turning the mixture (*erev*) of the undifferentiated multiple into a dawn (*shahar*) of liberation (*shirur*)? It is easy
to confuse the two at first. How many times has an immediate dawn been
announced, only to end in totalitarian darkness? There is a misunderstanding
inherent in sociality that has to do with the coexistence in principle of different moments in time, all of which are in presence, when they are manifested
successively and chronologically in phenomena for man in exteriority. The
desire for immediacy is a very understandable temptation, which is why
tikkun is a necessity that is natural and inherent in sociality. Even perverted
societies carry out a semblance of *tikkun*.

'Tzibbur': The Crowd

The dusk and dawn that form the "day" are cardinal modalities of the collective, and the assembly swings back and forth between these two poles.
Erev, the evening, is associated with night and war, with the *erev rav*, the
mixed multitude (of non-Hebrew slaves from Egypt) who joined Israel (Exod.
12:38). According to this principle, the assembling involves an addition, an
adjoining.[181] The time of the *erev rav* refers to the moment when the community is packed together in a place darkened by the swarm of people—the
continuation of the night in the twilight. It is the mixed multiplicity without
self-awareness, the utterly external being-there of the gathering. Herein lies
the origin of the gathering of humans, the origin of humanity lost in a dark,
remote, mythical past. The adjoining can take place through confrontation

---

180. See "Alterité contre normalité," in Trigano, *New Jewish Question*, p. 86.

181. I thank Nicole Loraux for drawing my attention to the Greek root *ar*, which is very
suggestive in this respect. It designates a close fitting together of the parts of a whole, the
adjoining of men in the fray of war, locked together in battle. Thus "harmony" is a joining
of differences; it is equivalent to the night, when differences fade. Likewise Ares is the god
of war, and Areopagus oversees the city as a well-joined totality.

and combat (*krav*), which is also a way of drawing close (*karov*) together. The memory of this combat lingers in sociality (*kerev*). This first community was informed by strength and power. This notion is found in the *tzibbur*, which can be translated as "crowd" and designates a heap, a pack, an accumulation, and the constitution of a force and a power (*tzvirat koach*).

The *tzibbur* is the coexistence in a state of indifference of individuals and classes of individuals. "Man goes off in the shadow, but evanescence (*hevel*) they conceive; he accumulates (*yitzbor*) and knows not who will assemble (*osef*)" (Ps. 39:7). This idea reappears in the Hasidic interpretation of *tzibbur* as an acronym for *tzaddikim*, the righteous, *beinoniyim*, the mediocre, and *ra'im*, the bad, "united" in a single place with no prospects. The *tzibbur* category describes this first community, this primal horde, more aptly than *erev rav*, which basically refers to the same thing. The *erev rav* is posited in the Bible in a relationship of exteriority to Israel and appears only once. It is significant that Jewish experience of the social (*bnei Yisrael*, the children of Israel, versus the *erev rav*, the mixed multitude) is distinguished from this *tzibbur*, even if it assumes it fully. But the *tzibbur* remains exterior to the community, and, in fact, the term is very rare in the Bible and never used to refer to the collectivity.

All of these notions shed light on the liturgical passage "Your people (*am*), Israel, who unify [in the plural] your Name evening (*erev*) and morning (*boker*)," because the community of Israel, described like Esther, the hidden one, as "the gazelle of the dawn," is forged from the union of two modalities, evening and morning, the dusk of combat (*krav*) and the dawn of sociality (*kerev*), and it points to the dawn within the dusk. This process of unification, which is the very process of sociality and concealment, works on the basis of the system of retreat and augment. Night falls because light is hidden, kept secret, as a promise of dawn beyond the night. And, indeed, twilight contains the memory and promise of a light (which is already being overwhelmed by the night). Dusk and dawn are the basic structures of the overall system of the day (*yom*), the system of the process of sociality. The *kahal* is formed thanks to the overall operation of concealment, to which the category of *knesset Yisrael*, the assembly of Israel, corresponds. But this concealment conforms to the system of retreat and augment. The *am*/people/being-with is constituted from the concealment of the community-of-witness, the *eda*. The whole problematic is in the interplay of *am* and *eda*, in the field opened by the concealment that is *knesset Yisrael* carried out in the *tzibbur*, the primal gathering that heralds the *kahal*, the community-of-voice (*kol*), where the voice circulates and hearing takes place; the *knesset* culminates in its accomplishment.[182] Thus, we speak of the "*kahal* of YHWH" (Deut. 23:2–4).

Rachel and Leah

The *am* is the category of retreat, exteriority, and the void; the *eda*, that of the concealment of interiority and augment. Externally, the community of Israel is *am*, internally, it is *eda*, and it is from the union and the agreement of the *eda* in the *am* that the *kahal* will be formed, "your people, Israel, who unify your Name evening (*am*) and morning (*eda*)."[183] This process designates the eternity of Israel, for the expression *le'olam vaed* can be read as "forever" and also "for disappearance and testimony"—that is to say, for the *am* and the *eda*.

We can see something of the interplay of these notions in the story of Jacob's marriage (Gen. 29). Seeking to wed Rachel, Jacob was tricked into a union with Leah, her sister, whom he mistook for Rachel, when, after a "drinking feast" to celebrate the marriage, Laban substituted one for the other under the cover of the night (*erev*). Jacob was thereby forced to marry Leah before he could eventually marry Rachel after a further seven years of work for Laban. Leah and Rachel are two figures of the community of Israel, made with Jacob, father of the twelve tribes.

Jacob's mistake at nightfall[184] became the source of the majority of his offspring, since Leah and her servant, Jacob's concubine, gave birth to most of his sons. Rachel, when he finally married her, had trouble conceiving and finally gave birth to Joseph (literally, "the added one") and Benjamin. Hence, the retreat/*am*/Leah spawns the multiple, whereas the hidden augment/*eda*/Rachel, concealed in the distance, harbors only the one and is hard to recognize. Nonetheless, the augment is the flip side of the retreat, and Rachel is the principle of Leah. If not for his love for Rachel, there would have been no union with Leah; without *eda*, there would be no *am*. It is Rachel who is announced, but it is Leah who comes, and Jacob has to marry Leah first

182. The two terms are very close: *kahal* is the Aramaic translation of *knesset*. We might run the risk of suggesting the following neologisms: "testate" for *eda*, from *ed*, meaning testimony, and "vocie" for *kahal*, from *kol*, meaning voice.

183. This union characterizes the institutions of the priest (*kohen*) and the king: the *kohen*, who deals with exteriority, is the echo of the *eda* in the *am*, and the king, who deals with the interior, echos the *am* in the *eda*. Therein resides a fundamental inversion of terms.

184. When Jacob unites with his wife, he is thinking only of his end purpose, which drives him: the dawn, Rachel, who, although he does not know it, cannot come immediately.

when it is Rachel whom he desires. This obligation came about as a result of trickery; but it could not have been otherwise, for the misunderstanding inherent in sociality requires a *tikkun*. Jacob aspires to the *eda*, but he must first build the *am*. To marry Rachel, Jacob must undertake the *tikkun* of Leah, about whom it is said that she is *Lo-H'/*not God—the very illustration of retreat. Jacob must first pass by way of Leah and allow her to pass, too. It is "just" that she has more children than Rachel, the loved one, because it is the multiple that has to be redeemed. The one, Rachel, the place of augment/secrecy, has in a way already come to be.[185] Dawn has been hidden in secrecy at nightfall. It is already in the light; what needs to be redeemed is dusk, which must be taken out of the night that overwhelms it. Otherwise put, the collectivity, like light, has something blinding. Its first impression is that of twilight, the flickering of an intense light (*erev*) followed by the blinding (night). Then the eye grows accustomed to the dark, and a little light wells up (the dawn) before the broad light of day is possible. Blindness is one of the moments of the social.

THE 'EDA' OF THE CHILDREN OF ISRAEL

The *knesset* designates the whole process of concealment by which the collectivity of Israel is woven against the backdrop of the throng that is the *tzibbur*. Israel is thereby founded by *departing* from the *olam*/disappearance, so its appearance as a collectivity is paradoxically a hiding in secrecy in the interior.

The Agora and the 'Knesset'

Knesset Yisrael is established on the basis of a retreat (the *am*), which means that it positions itself as an overplus to itself (the *eda*). In this sense, it stands in opposition to the *tzibbur*, which works on the basis of a purely mechanical addition of one to the other. Concealment contrasts sharply with this addition, but also, and especially, with all conventional ways of conceiving the group and the collectivity. In ancient Greece,[186] people assembled outside. After leaving their personal homes, individuals met in the agora, a huge, empty

185. Rachel gives birth to Joseph, the added one, who will count as two tribes and become the head of Israel over all the other tribes.

186. See Jean-Pierre Vernant, *Mythe et pensée chez les Grecs* (Paris: Maspero, 1974).

space exposed to light. The process of assembling involves passing over the threshold from inside to outside. This exterior is regarded as the center of the city, a center reputed to be located at an equal distance from all private homes, from individualities, and hence "universal" in relation to the interior particularities of each house, where the fire burns on the family hearth.

But how can such an utterly punctual collectivity survive, since it is impossible to stay outside all the time? The Greeks' abstract solution was to transpose the "private" hearth to the agora and light a fire on a public hearth. This situation, diametrically opposed to the *knesset*, explains why the Greek hearth, the very figure of interiority that is presided over by the goddess Hestia, has something artificial about it, even when it is private, for Hestia must remain a virgin. In exchange for the privilege of watching over the fire, Hestia must renounce marriage. The hearth is thus a place forbidden to each individual in particular, and this is what is supposed to make it universal. The one that is supposed to glow from the hearth inside is not a principle of passage; in Philolaus' words, "the one in the middle of the sphere is called Hestia."[187] It is, moreover, another god who presides over the threshold, Hermes the herald, who opposes Hestia as passage opposes the occupation of space. The collectivity of the agora typifies the *tzibbur* and *krav*/combat. Doesn't the term that designates the people in Greek, *laos*, also refer to the army? To make an agora, that is, a collectivity, is thus "to assemble the army (*laon agorein*)." Consequently, the assembly of men can be no more than a place of "passage," an endless passage in the anonymous, interchangeable sinking of the world.[188]

So we see what makes for the rare uniqueness of the *knesset*, whose place is made by an act of entry and hence a gathering together in the one. The agora is a residual place, the residue of the particularities of each individual; it exists outside the private place of the individual, in the exterior. To assemble, one must go out to the exterior (and the abstract hearth of the city-state will not remedy this) and hence turn one's back to the interiority of each person. For the Hebrews, assembling is entering; it is finding the interiority and intimacy of each person. There is no agora in the Jewish city, only interior courtyards. The being of Israel is referred to as the "house of Israel,"[189] and the divine presence as *Shechina*, the inhabitant. Whereas the Greek goes outside to meet the other, the Hebrew goes into his home, and,

---

187. Cited by Vernant, ibid., p. 126.

188. The Latin *community*, from *comeo*, speaks of this endless passage.

189. See below, Book II, ch. 2, "The House of Israel: Sovereignity."

not surprisingly, the foreigner (*ger*) is the one who resides (*gar*). The house of Israel is open to the other, to the point that Israel itself is regarded, like Abraham, as being a *ger vetoshav*, resident-foreigner (Gen. 23:4). How is Israel a house? Mainly because the *korban*—the part set aside as an offering to God, "God's portion" (Deut. 32:9), a portion removed from its own body politic by the consecration of the Levite tribe—founds its being. The portion, kept hidden in secret in the people, is the *eda*.

This concealment is what enables the existence outside of the *am*, or people. *Knesset Yisrael* is structured on the principle of retreat and augment and gathers together the two dimensions of *eda* and *am*. This establishes the basis of Israel's existence in the world. Hidden "in the secret of the upright and the *eda*" (Ps. 111:1), this portion, set apart from the being of Israel, is termed *eda*, which is close to the root *od*, to testify,[190] only in relation to the *am*, never in itself. The "retreat" of the *eda* has meaning only for what remains, which is why it is qualified (from the standpoint of what remains) as "testimony." What is the testimony if not the discourse of the presence of him who (or that which) has disappeared and is gone? This is the discourse of faithfulness.

The Hidden 'Eda'

In the gathering, the *eda* bears witness to the original void of the universe—that is to say, to the mode of God's presence in creation. It is the memory of passage, the memory of time in the being. It is a direct reminder in the gathering of men that their assembly does not originate in itself, that it is not "contractual," for if it were, it would be entirely reduced to exteriority. The *eda* introduces a suspension, a secret, the echo of the incompleteness of the being-in-itself, the echo of the gift. In this way, the *eda* is the very fundament of the collectivity, for it revives in the gathering of human beings the principle of creation, namely, concealment. "Your camp will be holy/separate, and no nudity (*erva*) of anything will be seen in you" (Deut. 23:15). *Ervat davar*, nudity of something? Nudity of anything whatever?

It is, of course, exteriority that the *eda* hides so as to make the meeting possible inside. One might think that, because we are dealing with a collectivity, the reference would be to the "nudity of the land." And indeed the land must not be "disclosed," because when the concealment is not

190. And etymologically to *adoh*, meaning to pass by, and to the causative, cause to pass by, to depart, or to remove.

accomplished naturally (habitation in the world) and morally (transgression of the prohibition of incest), there is a breakdown of society, a dissolution of the responsibility that arises from consciousness. Thus, the Canaanites and later the Hebrews were chased out of the land of Israel because of their depravity. The *eda* does not, in this case, keep the *am* together. This hiding place in the camp underpins its existence. The public shamelessness of total exposure that is at the heart of the Greek city, with the agora, irremediably drives the *eda* away. From this point of view, the *eda* is the antipode of modern society, which is basically founded on appearance and nudity.[191] Now we can understand why Esther, the hidden one, embodied the destiny of the community of Israel, the hidden *eda*. The whole of the book of Esther and all of the Five Scrolls[192] are structured on the system of the *eda*, on retreat and augment.

The *eda* testifies to that which has "disappeared" out of *hesed* for the creature, and the act that forges the *eda* is the sacrifice (*korban*). During the golden calf episode, when Israel broke this testimony that links retreat and augment, it lost the ornament (*adi*) that made it *adat Yisrael*, and God departed, sending a messenger in its midst to represent him. "I will send before you a messenger, and I will drive out the Canaanites... for I will not go in your *kerev*... lest I consume you on the way. The people heard this bad news and went into mourning, and none put on his ornaments (*adi*)." In the *eda*, there is neither mediation nor absolute exteriority. When divine presence ceases to dwell in the house of Israel's breath, spirit, and heart, Israel is naked; it loses the vestments of the covenant, the secret of the Name (because the Name is sheltered in the *eda*), and finds itself given over totally to exteriority. The *eda* is woven in the "blood of the covenant."

The Sacrifice of the Red Cow

The story of the sacrifice of the red cow (Num. 19), which is a public sacrifice, shows the relationship between sacrifice and gathering, and how the *korban* is the principle of the *eda*. The remains of the consumed sacrifice are "gathered (*asaf*)" by a man who is pure and they are deposited "outside the camp," hidden, removed to a "holy place"; and this hidden portion will be for the *eda* of the children of Israel a testimony for Israel, permanently safeguarded (*mishmeret*)—this is what safeguards the *eda*—for the waters of *nidda*.

191. See "L'idée moderne," in Trigano, *Forgotten Dwelling*, p. 341.
192. Song of Songs, Ruth, Lamentations, Ecclesiastes, and Esther.

Nidda is a strange term in this context, since it refers to the period of a woman's menses. It can be interpreted in its etymological sense as "sprinkling." But it can also be understood in the sense of our problematic of *nidda*. The woman's *nidda* is the kept portion that structures her: loss/retreat of blood that makes the augment, the ovulation, possible, a time of concealment in the very being that enables and sanctifies her union with man. This is why the woman is concealment in the human, and especially in the masculine. She is the figure of the *eda*,[193] the place of testimony, of memory (*zecher*) in the very being of the human being, which the male (*zachar*) (and hence the *am*) must recall so as not to be scattered in the emptiness of the world. Femininity is the principle of sanctification/separation of the masculine, the principle of its passage inside. There is a swing between the gathering (*osef*)[194] of the ashes of the sacrifice and the *eda*. The ashes are set aside, which is what enables the *eda* to be maintained in cleanliness and to maintain a relationship to what is hidden, suspended but not prohibited, the vehicle of its redemption and its overplus. The *eda* gathers the ashes of this sacrifice, which is foundational to the separation/sanctification of the public. "It will be for the children of Israel and for the *ger* who dwells in their interior (*toch*) a law of *olam*/disappearance" (Deut. 19:10). The law emerges not from the *am* but from the *eda*, from testimony to the origin, from the *olam*, from the memory that gives form to the prohibition of incest and to the concealment. Legislative power resides in the *eda* and not in the people, because the law helps the people externalize itself in the world. Only a principle outside exteriority could do so adequately. The *eda* prevents the *am* from sinking into the nothingness of the *olam*. "Descend, testify (*ha'ed*) in the *am*[195] lest they be destroyed facing YHWH, to see, and many of it[196] die" (Exod. 19:21). The *eda* carries out the *tikkun* of the collectivity: "The people cannot go up on Mount Sinai, because you have testified in/against us, saying, 'Limit the mount, and separate/sanctify it'" (19:23).

Whereas the *eda* knows God in an imperturbable way, the people is "limited" within the bounds of exteriority. The *eda* is a perpetual source of sanctification and life for the people. As we can see in the procedures of sacrifice of the red cow, the *eda* removes death from the people; it is an

193. *Eda* refers to the menses and the cloth that absorbs the blood and attests to menstruation.

194. The same term as *asefa*, assembly.

195. This is what *knesset Yisrael* is, the union of *am* and *eda*.

196. It is therefore the unified, interiorized *eda* that enables the multiple that is the people.

ongoing principle of resurgence for the *am* that is constantly on the threshold of death. To avoid being *cut off* from the *kahal*, from the perfect concert of the souls of Israel, man reimmerses in the *eda* (aquatic sign of the *nidda/* lustral water). The *eda* is a principle of life, and, indeed, it is the concealment and hence the passage for a world that, if it surrenders to the illusion of its reality and positivity, cuts itself off from the passage and is doomed to die. The separation of sanctification is basically a separation from death, from the weightiness of the passage that characterizes the exteriority and must be repaired. As Rashi writes in this regard, death is the underlying principle of all impurity. It stops the passage. The sanctification/separation puts the world back into passage.

The *eda* is therefore perpetually in life and is a source of revival for the *am*, which is on the brink of death and exteriority. Thus, the *eda* is the original milieu of the collectivity of Israel, its chosen place, and the *am* continually strives to measure up to the *eda* and draw on it fully. The golden calf episode shattered this original harmony because it broke the testimony. From that point on, the Levites rather than the elders conducted the sacrifices on behalf of the people, because they alone were faithful to the memory. The sprinkling of the blood of sacrifice, testimony to the covenant with Aaron, was thereafter the task of Aaron and his sons and not of the people. "You shall sprinkle [with blood] Aaron and his clothes and his sons and his sons' clothes" (Exod. 29:21); so the Levites would wear the *adi*, the ornament of the *eda*.

The Levites

Was this a catastrophe, or did the golden calf represent an inescapable stage in the development of the collectivity of Israel,[197] the moment when the *eda* is interiorized and the *am* is forged in its reversion outside? This is what is implied in the story of the sacrifice of the covenant (Exod. 24:6–8). After Moses "told the *am* all the words of YHWH," he wrote them down, built an altar at the foot of Mount Sinai, set up twelve stones standing for the twelve tribes, and sacrificed *olot* and *shelamim* to YHWH. "Moses took half the blood and placed it in basins, and half the blood he threw upon the altar," then he read the words of YHWH and the *am* said, "We will do and we will listen." Half of the sacrifice was an *ola*, an ascent or holocaust, and the other half a

197. See "Le Mouvement du retour," in Trigano, *New Jewish Question*.

shelamim, a sacrifice of wholeness. The *ola* stands for the *am*, the *shelamim* for the *eda*. The Levite stands precisely at the pivotal point in the relationship between the *am* and the *eda*. He is the instrument and the sign of their differentiation, of their separation/sanctification, the principle of sanctification and renewal. In this light we can understand why God tells the Levites to deposit the book of the law "as a testimony in/against you" (Deut. 31:26). The testimony is positive before God, who has withdrawn. It positively recollects the presence of God. But it is also negative, inasmuch as it opposes the people's forgetting ("against" the people). And it is the Levites, bearers of the ark, who carry this testimony in relation to the *am* and to the rest of the tribes. The logic of memory carries inside it a force that can be accusative and destructive. When the giving and mercy summoned by the effort to remember are exhausted, the failing memory exposes itself to judgment and rigor, which are as great as giving and mercy. In sum, memory oversteps absence; its failure causes it to sink into the absence entirely.

This is why the Levites are, to a certain extent, exterior to and outside the count of the *am*. They are in the *eda*, and, through them, so is the *am*. The *am* cannot be counted, because its secret is in the *eda*, in a concealment that cannot be reified. The *eda* is the vocation and the end purpose of the *am*. On the other hand, a census of the *am* can be taken in exchange for a sacrifice. Performed by the sacerdotal tribe, this sacrifice rejuvenates the *eda*, by recreating the concealment and the covenant broken by the census-taking that takes the *am* into a reifying exteriority. This is why the Levites are described as an *asefa*, an assembly, during the golden calf episode, when the *am* cut itself off from the *eda* and lapsed into exteriority. "The children of Levi gathered (*asefa*) to him (Moses)" (Exod. 32:26). The Levites constitute the principle of the assembly, and when the people move away from the *eda* and the testimony, they fall from an *asefa* to an *asafsuf* (a compound of *asefa* and *sof*, end or extinction) (Num. 11:4), an undifferentiated mass, the dregs of the universe. Without the *eda*, the *asefa*, as a mere addition of individuals, lapses into an *asafsuf*.

This is why the *eda*, governed by the Levitical principle, shelters the *kerev*, the families and lineage of generations, the thread of transmission of the Name. It is always called *adat bnei Yisrael*, the community of the children of Israel. This is also why, when the Name is profaned, the whole *eda* is concerned. "If someone blasphemes his God, he will bear his sin, and he who pierces (*nokev*) the Name of YHWH will die; the whole *eda* will stone him" (Lev. 24:15). Like the Levite, who signifies withdrawal from the *am*, or rather for the *am*, but who is actually hidden, since he is the overplus, the *eda* represents withdrawal and cessation for the *am*.[198] It is in fact its concealment, which is why it is most fully manifested on the day set aside from the other days, in the suspended time that characterizes the day of sanctification, the Sabbath. For this reason, the announcement of Sabbath as *kodesh*/separation in the Bible is addressed to the entire *eda*: "and Moses assembled (*kahal*) the entire *eda* of the children of Israel" (Exod. 35:1). The entire *eda* is in Sabbath. Sabbath, cessation and retirement from the *olam*, is like the *tikkun* of the community acting in the everyday world, its sanctifying separation and its rejuvenation by immersion in interiority. In the light of the Sabbath, we can see that the *eda* is the future of the *am*, just as Sabbath foreshadows the world to come; but it does no more, because, in the world of passing, Sabbath is a mere twinkling of the one, the messianic future of the eighth day.

'Moadim'

Thus, the *eda* has more to do with temporality than with relational spatiality. This is borne out by the fact that the *eda* is the responsibility of the Levites, who have no tribal land and intervene only in questions that concern the *nefesh*, time, and passage. The *moed*, which can be translated as "appointed time" or "meeting" and which refers to the festivals in the Jewish calendar, is the unit that measures the life of the *eda* (and *moed* contains the same letters as the radical of *eda*) when it assembles as a united whole for a significant temporal passage.

The *eda* is sporadically regenerated from within through these celebrations, before stepping back out into exteriority. The religious festivals for which the people as a whole assemble belong to the category of Sabbath, that is to say, they effect a concealment, a cessation in the everyday activity in the *olam*. This sporadic resurgence of the *moed* over the course of time carries with it the testimony (*edut*) in time and passage in a diffuse way. It differentializes time and takes passage out of its inherent weightiness, its anonymity, and its calling to nothingness. In this respect, the *moed* is a sanctification/separation.[199] The rhythm of the *moed* is highly significant; it reproduces the

198. It is interesting to see how, when *am Yisrael* became an impossibility in modernity, and its existence was denied (see Shmuel Trigano, *La République et les Juifs* [Paris: Les Presses d'aujourd'hui, 1982]), the Jewish collectivity gathered and huddled in the *eda* (the absence in the *am*), that is to say, in the synagogal religious community, temporally structured around Sabbath and the festivals.

199. *Moed* also refers to the "sacrificial victim."

course of light's disappearance and return acted out in every day (*yom*). The year of *moadim* is structured accordingly: from the new year and Yom Kippur, twilight burning with the last, most intense light of day, with Sukkot, which ends the cycle of fall festivals, to Passover, the dawn (*shahar*) of freedom (*shihrur*), to culminate in the broad Sinaitic light of the festival of Shavuot, the giving of the Torah, and on to pursue its course with a new dusk marking the beginning of a new year. The fall festivals see the *am* judged according to rigor (*din*) and recreated on Sukkot,[200] when the *eda* already shoots out a beam of its presence before drawing entirely inside. Finally, at Passover, the *eda* reappears in the *am* that has been desolated by winter, and on Shavuot the *kahal* awakens in the union of the *eda* and the *am*.

The procession of *moadim* points to the progression of the *eda*, made of successive fleeting appearances, surfacings that go through periods of near extinction before surfacing again. Because it is hidden, the *eda* has "knowledge" of disappearance and therefore the ability to withstand the passage of being and time. In a manner of speaking, it is "nomadic," like the Ark of the Covenant, which originally traveled from city to city, but it calls for a place—and particularly its chosen place, the land of Israel[201]—for the reunion of the *eda* in the *moed*. For this reason, over the course of time and passage, Israel withstands exile and the dislocation of the *am*. It is the *eda*, the original union of testimony, in the assembly of the people of life-breath and heart, that establishes the basis of the place and the land, and not the opposite.

When the *eda* is ready, the land (re)appears in the history of Israel. The reappearance of the land indicates the imminence of the sovereign manifestation of the *eda*. This is, in a way, a cataclysm in the life of the *am*, a sudden irruption that is ultimately difficult for the people, because the *eda* puts the *am* to the test by the absolute yardstick of its being. Whole parts of the people can disappear as a result. Whereas the *eda* knows, for instance, that its chosen place is the land of Israel and is unfailing in this knowledge, the *am*, which is transient, can forget and lapse into error. The *eda* knows the land of Israel is central to the promise made to Abraham in the Covenant between the Pieces (Gen. 15:17) and at Sinai (Exod. 3:17). In a manner of speaking, even though the term is incorrect, through the *eda*, Israel is "eternal." It carries within an absolute power of passage, because its establishment on the land vibrates with the rhythm of time and being. We

200. The new year induces "the entry of Israel," the *knesset*; it's on Sukkot that the *am* finds itself alone.

201. Because the land of Israel, "God's portion," is set apart from the world. See below, "The Openness of Levitical Space: The Land," pp. 304–324.

can understand from this perspective why the Talmud says that a Jew who converts is a Jew nonetheless from the standpoint of his responsibility. He remains in the *eda*, because the testimony, the memory of the presence, is absolutely indelible. There is no "individual" choice in the *eda*. But such an individual cuts himself off from the *am*; he disappears from the people. This lack of individual choice is not the absolute constraint of agreement between God and man. Firstly, it is due to the fact that the world and humans were created. Without going back that far, I exist as my parents genetically, mentally, and culturally made me. It is an inherent fact of my existence that I cannot deny. The same is true of the creator. Only illusion or insufficient knowledge can allow an individual to deny the divine reality, which is infinitely more real than ephemeral physical nature. Having said this, the meeting between God and man in the (hidden) presence of the *eda* is a covenantal relationship, a *berit*, but a nearly existential *berit*. It comprises consent to the contract, to be sure, but also much more: the experience of disappearance and presence, the viaticum of the journey through the passage that is the world.

Thus, the *eda* escapes the problematics of the majority. Its existence and life do not depend on a majority of opinions or actions, or on the consent of individuals. It is the sphere of the *klal*, of the whole of Israel, independent of the individual therein. It stands on the level of history and not of circumstantial events in history; it harbors the permanence of Israel. The *eda* in itself does not pertain to "the more" or "the less." It cannot be apportioned. It is not a "public thing" in which each individual would have his share. It is indivisible.

This is why it transcends exile and the vicissitudes of passage. It is the infallible rudder of the ark of the people.

THE 'AM' OF ISRAEL

This set of characteristics emerges when we consider the *eda* as something apart, but we must never forget that the *eda* is, in fact, conceivable only in relation to the *am*, that it has no reason for being outside this relationship, just as the inside exists only in relation to the outside. The being of the *eda* needs to be grasped as part of this dynamic structural relationship whose underlying principle is concealment.

The *eda* merely "twinkles." It is the instant of presence. This means that it cannot manage the *am* on a day-to-day basis, even though the law is founded on the *eda*. The principle of sovereignty is in the *eda,* and from it comes the law, but the effectiveness of this absolute, transtemporal sovereignty pertains to the *am*, which is engaged in the *olam* and in circumstance.

This is clearly evidenced in the narrative of the renewal of the covenant, when, in this moment of *eda* (Josh. 8:30–35 and 24) that follows the oath, the people disperse, "each to his heritage." This "dispersion" is the true place of the *am*, since the *am* is the locus of the multiple, but a locus that needs a *tikkun* to survive; and it finds this *tikkun* in the *eda*. The *eda* is in a state of accomplishment, but this accomplishment is the vocation of the *am* and has no meaning without it. Here again we find the hiatus between augment and retreat.

So what has been said so far about the *eda* should be read in this light— that is, according to the permanent, twofold picture of augment and retreat. For example, if the *berit* defines the *eda*, its destiny is also played out in the *am*; after all, the *am* can break the *berit*. But even if it breaks it, the tie woven by the *berit* subsists, preserved intact in the *eda* if only the *am* repents and finds its *tikkun*. The *berit* thus presents two aspects (as we have seen with the sacrifice): the retreat, which is the lot of the *am* (with all the connotations of consensus, yoke, and exteriority connected to the *berit*), and the augment (with all its connotations of permanence, generosity, transmission, and interiority). It is the *am* that is committing itself with the words "we will do and we will hear." At a point in time when it hasn't yet the necessary perfection to "hear" on the level of the *eda*, it is the *am* that rises to a level that it does not yet comprehend. It thereby etches the testimony and the promise in its very being. A problematic of temporality is played out in the *eda* and of spatiality in the *am*. And there is, of course, no contradiction, since time is the principle of the successive spatial states of the world. Spaces are but signs of the flow of time. One could say that whereas the *am* stands on the agora, the *eda* stands in the forecourt to the Temple or to the *ohel moed*, the tent of the *moed*. ("Whenever Moses went out to the tent, the entire people rose, each standing at the threshold to his tent," Exod. 33:8), to the place where the *korban* is brought. One is on the verge of prayer, the other on the verge of speech, on the brink of the empty and exposed square. But speech is a modality of prayer that is prayer to God, whose presence is hidden: words with no reply (at least not immediate or apparent).

The 'Tikkun' of Language

One speaks and communicates to oneself as "the voice speaks to itself" when it communicates with Moses (Num. 7:89). One speaks and writes only inwardly, within oneself, despite the illusion in the moment of an I-you dialogue, the illusion of exteriority, of discourse. Our human being is essentially inside, and hence, language, too, is essentially inside. Whenever it goes outside, it goes into exile; it disappears and becomes discourse or an instituted scientific discipline, which are forms of exile for language and truth, even though they are also the crux of existence in the world.

This is how one speaks (by withdrawing, stepping back, veiling one's face, turning one's back to the other, keeping silent...).[202] This is how we understand one another, how we have to understand one another, by means of a *tikkun* of language, which is a *tikkun* of the *am* by the *eda*, because if words speak, if the inner *eda* speaks inwardly, it does so only for human beings, for the *am*, for the other. The *am*/other is impossible at first. The spoken words are inaudible; the written words, illegible; the other is incomprehensible. This is the starting point of "dialogue" and "communication," as a return to the words both spoken and written, with the *am* picking up the echo of the *eda*, interpreting the texts in an act of *tikkun*.

This is why the interpretation of oral and written words forms the hinge of the relationship between the *am* and the *eda*. We have already seen how the law governs the passage from *eda* to *am*, insofar as it provides the *am* with procedures for performing the concealment. The *am* itself exists only inasmuch as the law precedes it (let us not forget, though, that *am* and *eda* coexist and have an integrated being). This relationship is predictably also found in the categories of the oral and written word. The Levites keep the tablets of the written word for the *am*, but the Torah is originally oral; its orality (augment) is the flip side of its scripturality (retreat). The *eda* holds its orality, while the *am* sees only its scripturality. For this reason the *eda* holds its legislative power, the power to interpret the law, the *halacha*, which is basically an oral "customary" law that adapts the permanence of legal precepts and concealment procedures to the *am*'s circumstantial nature.

The oral and the written, the narrative and the legal, the *aggada* and the *halacha* are, in a way, categories of the collective, figures and modalities of gathering. The *eda* is by vocation in the *aggada*, the overplus, and the *am*

---

202. See below, Book IV, ch. 3, "The Vision of Israel's Voices."

is by vocation in the *halacha*, the retreat, although this distinction is purely theoretical. The relationship is a dynamic one, since the *halacha* that governs the people emanates from the *eda*, and the *aggada* that attracts and unites the *am* (*aggada* from *iggud*, "assemblage") resides in the *eda*. The material of the vocation of one entity is the vehicle of communication of the other. In other words, *knesset Yisrael* is forged from the synthesis of *halacha* and *aggada*.

The Phenomenology of 'Am' and 'Eda'

What is important to retain from this dialectical sequence is the categorical unity of the collective being and its differentiation. Nonetheless, an inner logic emerges from the relationships between the *am* and the *eda*. Augment and retreat are its paradigm, but the very fact of concealment induces a specific relationship of a phenomenal nature. It is in the nature of concealment to manifest itself in the immediate as a retreat when it is in secrecy, an overplus that is foundational to the retreat. In a way, the secondary state of being is manifested as being first, and what founds it appears as an overplus. But it is really overplus, overplus of God. This is the misunderstanding inherent in creation. This is what we learn from the idea of creation that revives the principle of an origin of a rather special type, since it derives from its self-effacement.

In the phenomenal world, we see only the *am*. The *eda* is seldom visible when it is not purely and simply relegated to the realm of myth, faith, or the imaginary. Consequently, the experience of *eda* in the *am*, and hence of testimony, is often construed as an ordeal of solitude. In the *am*, the *eda* is not seen, and, from a phenomenological standpoint, one steps outside the *am* when one bonds with the *eda*. One withdraws into isolation, one is alone, and the *am* does not realize that it is the bonding of this apparent aloneness that founds their intimacy. Indeed, the aloneness of the *eda* is an optical illusion that characterizes the perspective of the *am*. In fact, the *am*, if reduced to itself as it imagines it is (unaware of what exceeds it), would be the one to live in the solitude of the multiple devoid of interiority, the great solitude of passage that affords no shelter to the individual and to sociality (*kerev*). The *am* is unaware of its flip side, the *eda*. So for the *am*, the *eda* seems withdrawn into solitude, but it is in fact the *am* that would be alone if not for the *eda*.

In the *eda*, even if one is by oneself, one is never alone, because there is always the presence inherent in the testimony, a form of presence that withstands absence. In the *am*, even if one is in the company of millions of others, one can be alone, because the presence is hidden in the *eda*. The *tikkun* of the *am* has to be undertaken, and this requires rising to the level of the *eda*. This is what is being said in the famous verse "a people in solitude will live," which can be read as "the *am*, in solitude, will enjoy presence (*Shechina*)" (Num. 23:9).

To speak of *am* is already to imply the concealment and the *eda*, just as when we speak of "retreat," we are already speaking from the standpoint of consummation and completeness (and, hence, of augment). Trapped in the phenomenal world, the *am* sees itself as being in the fullness of fulfillment and does not realize it is in a state of retreat.

Is this phenomenological reversal of the chronological process[203] due solely to the misunderstanding inherent in the world with which sociality is confronted? This reversal actually has its own intrinsic purpose. Indeed, this disjunction comprises the place of the *olam* and of passage; it is the locus of *tikkun* and ultimately the place of the human. But when the *am* sees itself as an absolute positivity, it misreads the disjunction and negates it. Instead of departing from the passage, it short-circuits it and simulates the *eda* by making it impossible. In any leader of the *am*, there is a semblance of the high priest, but without the redemption. Only when the collective conceives of itself in a state of retreat (through the act of sacrifice or giving, which removes a portion of its vital strength) is it truly an *am*, the flip side of the *eda*.

Levites and Kings

We find another expression of this reversal of terms (from the standpoint of the phenomenal world) in the reversal of functions representing the *eda* and the *am*, which we have discussed above. The Levite officiates within the *eda* but for the *am*. The king reigns over the *am* but by virtue of the *eda*. The Levite who dwells in the *eda* exists only for the *am*, and vice versa for the king (one of whose main tasks was to read the Torah to the *kahal* at the

---

203. This reversal is somewhat reminiscent of Maimonides' notion of the twofold object of the law: "the well-being of the soul and the well-being of the body" (*Guide of the Perplexed* 3:27). The latter is "anterior in nature and time" to the former, which is "first in rank." The second object, which is always second, even if it alone makes the first possible, is "established by a proper management" of society, and this is required before the second can be obtained. According to Maimonides, this is why the Torah is elaborated in such great detail. So for Maimonides, the hiatus of the reversal, which would be the site of the political, is isolated in a meaningless vacuum (see Trigano, *Forgotten Dwelling*, p. 137), in a perspective that is decidedly different from that of augment and retreat.

end of *shemita*, the sabbatical year when the land lies fallow). The sociality (*kerev*) of the *am* is incomplete. It needs the sphere of the Levitical *eda* for its *tikkun*; this is an ongoing need if it is to subsist in the exterior. The *am*'s need creates the Levite, but the Levite belongs to the *eda*. The *am*'s need makes the Levite emerge in the *eda*. But the king himself is instituted as a result in the *am*. He constitutes the gift from the *eda* to govern the collectivity. The *eda*'s gift creates the king, but the king belongs to the *am*.

Functionally speaking, and insofar as the principle of power is concerned, this implies a reversal of terms, a reversal that characterizes the political arena[204] and the nature of sovereignty itself. This reversal merely translates the system of retreat and augment: either augment is conceived on the basis of retreat, and we have the Levite, or retreat is conceived on the basis of augment, and we have the king. Levite and king are processes that link the *eda* and the *am*. From the *am*'s standpoint, the *eda* is in retreat, and hence the *eda* can be overadded only by *tikkun*: for the *am* to open to the *eda*, it has to conceive of augment. From the *eda*'s standpoint, the *am* is overplus. This is the standpoint of the divine creator. The whole point of the world is for the *am* to extricate itself from the illusion of its own immediacy and positivity, to depart from deceptive mediations (representation), to rediscover its principle, the overplus and the augment that it is, to find in its innermost depths the *eda*, and to elevate itself to its level and standpoint.

And so, reduced to itself, the *am* is in obscurity, gradually dimming like the embers of a dying flame. The *am* was constituted from the glow of the *eda*, from the hidden flame smoldering powerfully beneath the black coals. Once the *eda* has withdrawn, the *am* is doomed to rampant extinction, unless it can rejuvenate itself from time to time in the *eda*. This is one meaning of *am/im*, the being-with,[205] the accompaniment of someone. The *am* is the being-with with the *eda*, with the Levites, who are themselves accompanists.[206] The *am* is thus defined just as much by what it is as by what it isn't: "in order to establish you today as an *am*... and not with you alone do I seal this covenant and this pact but with whoever is standing with us (*imanu*) today before YHWH, our God, and with whoever is not with us today" (Deut. 29:12–13). And if the *am* is being-with, companionship in itself, *kerev*, it is so only because the *eda* is hidden in its midst, because the principle of accompaniment, the Levite, dwells inside it. The superposition of the *am* and

204. See below, Book II, ch. 5, "Abode of Testimony: The Political Arena."
205. See above, note 73.
206. Which is one meaning of *levi*.

the *kerev* is a telling sign of the *am*'s incompleteness, its need for its own *tikkun*, and of the Levites who are found in the *eda*. To be more precise, the *kerev* denotes the act and process of sociality in the making, whereas the *am* is the legal category that designates the *kerev*, just as the *eda* is the category that designates the process of the repairing *korban*. Let us not forget that the king, who falls within the province of the *am*, does not sacrifice; this substantiates our analysis.

The Destiny of the 'Am'

The proximity between *am* and *kerev* can also be seen in another sense of the word *am*, used to refer to a close relative (*karov*) such as an uncle. In a way, the *am* is the experience of the withdrawal that is in the *berit*, and the two eventualities to which this retreat leads: either the search for the *eda* and the consummation of the passage, or the dereliction and perdition of the passage. There is, then, a power of destruction and decomposition in the *am*. The *am*, an effect of augment, requires a *tikkun* when it is left to itself. And what enables this *tikkun* is the concealment of/in the *eda*. When this concealment takes place, the *am* is truly reconstituted. This is why the *am* is the locus of all sorts of crises. The *am* can die or disappear, as has been the case often throughout Jewish history.[207] When the *am* disappeared, the Jews were dispersed, and their only means of existence and persistence was through the *eda*, which keeps watch in secrecy in its dazzling light. The king, the senate, and the prophets were all gone, but not the very foundation of the concealment: the judge (the *halachic* court) and the priest, the *halacha* and divine service. The eternity of this sphere and its safekeeping by Israel guaranteed its permanence beyond the destruction of the *am*. The disappearance of *am Yisrael* does not mean the disappearance of Israel, because the *eda* is in the presence, and it continues to harbor the potential of the *am*'s revival.[208]

We must consider that the *am*, the being-with that makes human beings feel close to one another, is in exteriority. "Moses went out [of the Tent of Meeting] and spoke to the *am*, then he gathered seventy men from among the elders of the people and stationed them around the tent" (Num. 11:24).

---

207. This has notably been the case in the context of Jewish modernity. See my *La République et les Juifs*, *La Demeure oubliée*, and "Le Peuple juif à l'épreuve de la Shoa," in *Penser Auschwitz*, special issue of *Pardès* (Paris: Éditions du Cerf, 1989).

208. The *am* suddenly resurfaced in the modern State of Israel. The relations of being-with have been established once again, and with astonishing speed, but the *eda*, which is necessarily present, has not yet manifested itself.

The closeness that the *am* affords is surprising insofar as it is in exteriority. This runs counter to everything the philosophers of dialogue have told us, and it would mean that there is no real dialogue or communication in the *am*. When we meet in the *am*—and that is where we meet—we do not see one another; no presence unites us. In the exteriority that is the *am*, we do not meet or hear one another. The voice speaks but does not reach the other, and it is not heard. The voice must speak to itself, that is to say, it must surface in the interior ("speak" in the *eda*) for the other to hear it.

To put it otherwise, a concealment must occur in the exterior for the voice to be heard, and this concealment is accomplished by all the methods discussed above. It is in the shade of this concealment (the *eda*, in sum) that one can "be-with," that there can be conviviality. This concealment is not the position of the *tertium non datur*, the excluded middle or "third," which many theories see as the underlying principle of all relationships. Quite the opposite. What we have here is an addition, not an exclusion, the addition of an overplus of presence, of an augment, not a "middle" or a "third" but the withdrawal of a portion from each member of the relationship, whose beam is hidden in secrecy in the relationship.

There are different procedures for undertaking this concealment, one being the *mitzvot*, which produce the unification of the one: *yihud*. But there are also perverted paths of concealment from which the *mitzvot* protect us: theft, adultery, murder, and all the acts forbidden by the Ten Commandments. These are misguided paths for constituting an intimacy for oneself and one's associates; they are a mockery of concealment.[209] Its name and appearances notwithstanding, the *am* is in total exteriority—"see your people (*am*), this *goy*" (Exod. 33:13)—which is why it needs a *tikkun*, a concealment of the *eda*.[210] The *eda* accomplishes the *kappara*, the expiation of the *am*. So the divine word is heard only atop the *kapporet*, the expiatory cover over the

209. Theft, for example, enables the individual to create a secret in the world of exteriority. Indeed, people do not steal openly and publicly but rather in hiding, and only the thief is supposed to know about the theft. This is a (perverse) form of "taking cover" in the exteriority of passage. To steal, commit adultery, or kill is an act that removes something in/from the being, a mockery of the *korban*, because what is taken is taken from the other (the other's possessions, spouse, or life) and not from oneself. Idolatry can be understood in the same light: to make a statue or an icon in order to create an intimacy with the divine is to remove from God and not from oneself.

210. It is the failure of this *tikkun* that accounts for the breakdown of the *am* in the golden calf episode. In the narrative, it is the *am* that is at issue (Joshua hears the "voice of the people in evil" [Exod. 32:17] but perceives it from where he stands withdrawn on Mount Sinai from the standpoint of the *eda*). The people, reduced to its exteriority, can no longer form an *eda*, and the Levites, upholders of the *eda*, have to separate from it

Ark of the Covenant (25:22). That is where God says to Moses, "*Noadti*, I will set a meeting with you" (*noadti* from the same root as *eda*). This is the place of the *moed*.

The Sphere of the Political

This necessity is that of the political and of the political arena. The political sphere is in the movement of the *am* toward the *eda*, but it is the *eda* that is the constitutive principle thereof—its principle, not its consequence. The *eda* is woven only in the weft of the *am*'s movement. The Levites keep the law and instruct it, but they do not apply it by force. The priest is at the behest of the *am* when the latter wants to offer a sacrifice, but he cannot force it to do so. The *eda* is woven from the movement of the *am* even though its principle is embedded in the innermost depths of the *am*'s existence, without the latter's awareness. The *eda* exists in a certain state of passivity; it is the community of the Sabbath, as we have seen. Activity is inherent in the *am*, which is why executive power is in the hands of the *am*, and the *eda*, instituted and represented by the Levitical tribe, has no control over this. Conversely, if the *am* extended its control over the *eda*, it would lose the very foundations of its power. It cannot do so without structurally destroying itself in the short or long run. Such control would be the opposite of the concealment that works to make the sphere of the *eda*, the law, and the *korban* emerge in the sphere of the *am*.[211] The *eda* is not identified with the *am*. A whole system of differentiation, separation, and institutionalization of these figures of collectivity aims at keeping the *eda* from falling prey to the perversion of its vocation in temporality, and the *am* from falling prey to the illusion of absolutism. This dual system ensures that both *eda* and *am* continually escape their own solitary control. The Levites without the people are a mockery. The people without the Levites rhymes with obscurity. "A kingdom of priests, a holy/separate *goy*" (Exod. 19:6). The kingdom is in the priesthood and the holiness in the *goy*, the people of appearances; each term

and do not partake in the worship of the calf. The *am* is nonetheless in need of the *eda*, even if only a semblance thereof, so it turns to Aaron to make the calf.

211. This problematic could also be analyzed in terms of the categories of femininity (*eda*) and masculinity (*am*), with the concealment being an act of union.

in the relationship has its echo in the other.[212] One could not find a better definition of the relationship between the *am* and the *eda*.

This is why the self-presence of each of these spheres in the evolution and constitution of society is always mobile, pending for itself and for the other. In this way, the *eda* is forged through *edut*, bearing witness, a procedure that makes what is absent present, ensuring this presence through the *moadim* of the calendar. In this way, the *am* needs exterior signs (*otot*) that signal and signify its existence, as, for instance, the circumcision as a sign of the covenant, the tablets in the Ark of the Covenant, the Tabernacle, and the Temple. The *ot* is to the *am* what the *moed* is to the *eda*: both show us the exteriority of sociality that is the condition of otherness but whose underlying principle is interiority and interiorization. Even in the *eda*, the testimony bears witness to an other outside myself who is not an object, outside myself but still a being. That is the peculiarity of exteriority as it exists in the *eda*. The *ot*, on the other hand, tends to testify to objective exteriority, as is the case regarding the tablets of stone. Every time there is an agreement to a *berit* in the story of the patriarchs and thereafter, a stone is raised as a monument to bear witness to the *berit*, to testify to it to the world outside (for example, Josh. 24:25).

The specificity that makes the collective an uncontrolled being, structurally in passage, is crystallized in the image of the high priest's vestments (and prior to that in the image of the ornaments splattered with the "blood of the covenant" from the sacrifice). These vestments bear witness for the *eda* (after all, it is the high priest himself who wears them!) and for the *am* (since he wears them when performing sacrifices for the people). That is why the priestly clothing includes the breastplate, representing the twelve tribes, which reminds God, during the service, of his covenant with all of Israel and which reminds the people of its commitment to God. Here, the exteriority of the sign guarantees separation and sanctification. The sign (*ot*) translates in the people and in space, the *moed* of the *eda*. But they are two sides of a single being.

212. See Trigano, *La République et les Juifs*, p. 252. In the people (*goy*), the priests (*kohen*) are present through holiness (*kadosh*), and in priesthood, there is the kingdom (*mamlacha*). "Holiness" in the people refers to the "priests." Because the people is more than a *goy*, because it is holy, it is at the heart of priesthood. The "kingdom" in the "priests" refers to the "people." Because the priests are more than a priesthood (since there is kingship in them), they are at the heart of the people.

The 'Kahal'

This lack of "rest" in the *am* and the *eda*, this perpetual mobility and instability, indicates the extent to which neither *eda* nor *am* suffices unto itself,
as such or as a structural relationship. *Eda* and *am* have different roles in
the great operation of concealment and entry that is implemented in the
olam by *knesset Yisrael*, which unites both without being confined to them.

The *knesset* encompasses all the movements of Israel's collective being, *eda*
and *am*, its levels and modalities, and the inner organization of this operation (and since it involves subtraction and addition, the term "operation" is
appropriate). But these two or three levels (depending on whether *eda* and
am are counted separately), which are different levels of approaching the
same being, the collectivity of Israel, hide a fourth level, the higher level of
this collectivity, and that is *kahal Yisrael*, from a term related to *kol*, "voice."
Assembling people involves spreading the voice: "they made the voice pass
through the camp" (Exod. 36:6); this designates the *kahal* gathered around
the *mishkan*, the Tabernacle at Mount Sinai, so the place of gathering is none
other than the voice, not the city. "The entire *kahal* sealed a covenant in the
House of God with the king" (II Chron. 23:3). "And David called in *kahal*
(*vayikhal*) all Israel" (I Chron. 13:5).

The *kahal* is not the synthesis, the integration, or the supersession of
the system of *eda* and *am* that the *knesset* establishes. The process is not
dialectical in the traditional sense of the term. We are not dealing with
three or four temporal or genetic stages of development. Each of the four
figures discussed is a particular designation of the whole, a modal figure, all
of whose components coexist, in every generation and every Jewish society.
At no time would the pristine state of the *knesset* be actual and the *eda* and
the *am* not be posited. If there is *knesset*, there is systematically *eda*, *am*, and
kahal.[213] And still, each of these modalities has its own arena of evolution, a
specific type of power and authority, its own time in the social problematic.
A modality can disappear, like the *am* in times of exile; in this case, the *eda*
becomes the recipient of its totality, but the *kahal* is on standby, because it
is missing the *am*. In this case, the operation of *knesset* is incomplete, and
there is a lack of balance in the being of Israel. But from a theoretical standpoint, for the purposes of a logical analysis, one can break down the four
instances of the collective (four letters of the Tetragrammaton) into separate

213. Even if one of these figures or another remains a potentiality.

entities. First the *knesset* makes Israel "enter" by taking it out of the *olam*. This is done by way of concealment; this is the *eda*. The concealment makes the *am* possible as a community in exteriority, which thus runs the risk of losing itself again in the passage. Then the work of interiority resurfaces in the exteriority of the *am*, and with it the *kahal*, the return of a consummate interiority in a harmonized exterior.

The *kahal*, consequently, is not the unifying reconciliation of the *eda-am* pair but rather their adequation, the consummation of the system of retreat and augment. Then, presence truly inhabits the people, present to itself and to the world. But even in this case, *eda* and *am* subsist in the *kahal*; they are the *kahal*'s organizational structure set into motion in a germinal way. The *kahal* must absolutely not eliminate the *eda* and the *am*. In the system of the collectivity of Israel there is no false, pseudomessianic instance of this type, which would spell the end of separation/sanctification, whereupon access to the one would dissolve into an undifferentiated, fusional multiplicity. "The entire *kahal* sealed a covenant in the House of God with the king" (II Chron. 23:3). We have here the perfect example of the union of the *kahal*, of the *am*/king under the auspices of the "House of God," that is to say, the *eda*. The *kahal* is therefore the consummation of the operation of concealment begun in the *knesset*.[214] Then the voice (*kol*), the voice of YHWH, resounds in the *knesset*. Then the voice of man carries to his fellow man! This is why the group always *kahalizes* around a voice, the voice of a man who emerges from the *eda*: "Moses gathers (*vayakhel*) the whole *eda* of the children of Israel" (Exod. 35:1). This is why the *ohel moed* is the privileged place of the *kahal*; in it, the temporality of *moed* overlaps the spatiality of the *ohel*: *eda* and *am*.

This *kahal*, where all resonates, is the very heart of the political; its interior (*toch*),[215] and the various centers of power and authorities are linked to its agencies. If the king represents the *am* and the high priest, the *eda*, the *kahal*, is prefigured by the Sanhedrin, the senators (or elders) of the assembly of Israel who assisted Moses at Mount Sinai (Num. 11:25). These are the men of the "great *knesset*" who received the oral traditions and laws that Moses had received at Mount Sinai and passed them on to the generations that followed.

The voice circulates in this great concert. But left to itself, the voice can be lost in the surrounding uproar. If the assembly of senators embodies the

---

214. In Aramaic and in Hebrew, the terms *kahal* and *kenes* (from which *knesset* is derived) are equivalent.

215. See below, Book II, ch. 5, "Abode of Testimony: The Political Arena."

kahal, we must not forget the overplus itself that is conveyed in and by the *kahal*, the overplus that is the voice: the prophet and his authority. If *eda* and *am* are characterized by high priest and king, *kahal* is characterized by the prophet. But the prophet lacks the institutional "authority" of the high priest and king, for the simple reason that he personifies the voice's frailty itself. So it is the assembly of senators that is the institutional agency of the *kahal*, the concert of all the voices of Israel that call and hear one another, counterbalanced by the voice of the prophet, whose call awakens the *kahal*. In any case, the authority of the Elders derives from absolute prophetic authority: "Moses received the law at Sinai. He transmitted it to Joshua, Joshua to the Elders, the Elders to the prophets, and the prophets to the members of the Great Assembly."[216] The prophet testifies and restores the *eda* of testimony when the *am* has forgotten it or the Levites have failed to serve it. He continually rewrites the consummate *knesset Yisrael* to which society, which lives in a permanent state of crisis, can aspire. The prophet is therefore something of a "writer," carrying the destiny of the people from the midst of its interiority, the *eda*, when political authorities, the king's entourage, stay on the level of the *am* and lack the power of the *eda*: "they gathered together (*ne'esfu*) around Ezra, the writer" (Neh. 8:13). The prophet in the *kahal* responds to a certain extent to the authority that governs the *knesset*, the procedure of concealment of Israel. We have already seen that the *kahal* echoes the *knesset*, that it is to the culmination what the *knesset* is to the origin. Now, the *knesset*'s characteristic authority is the judge (*shofet*). He is the one who pronounces the law, the prohibition of incest, and assists in implementing the concealment of the collectivity of Israel. The *shofet* is Israel's founding, minimal authority. In fact, historically, government by judges was Israel's first political system. The prophet is thus the judge's counterpart and even his apotheosis. This is personified in the emblematic figure of the prophet Samuel, who was also a judge.[217] He was the one who logically founded the royalty when he anointed Saul, although he did so with regret (which expressed the difficulty involved in differentiation). Samuel thus embodied the totality of agencies of *knesset Yisrael*.

However, there is no prophet—as a man of the *kahal*—without an assembly of senators. This we know from history. The prophets disappeared when the Sanhedrin stopped meeting. For the *kahal* exists only on the level

216. Pirkei Avot 1:1.

217. The fact that Samuel was from the tribe of Ephraim would turn out to be of some significance. See below, Book II, ch. 3, "The 'Children of Israel,' or the Josephic Principle at Work in the Fabric of the Nation."

of this senate. The voice of the prophet as the conscience of the *eda* or the *am* can manifest itself on this condition alone. What's more, the prophet hasn't the authority of the king or the high priest to be in charge of the *kahal*. The prophet's institutional basis is too weak, and prophetic manifestations too unruly and circumstantial. That is the contradiction of prophecy and the voice. The senate oversees the *kahal*. It is the steady string of Israel's voice. The prophet is its subtle vibration. The *kahal* is thus dualized in a way that may perhaps translate the voice's intimate dualization, when it is said, using the reflexive pronoun, that "the voice speaks to itself" (Num. 7:89). The voice speaking to itself is the voice of dialogue between the prophet and the senators. Likewise, in the book of Joshua (8:30–35), we see *kahal Yisrael* during a covenant renewal ceremony, geographically divided between two different mountains on each side of the Ark of the Covenant and the Levites.

In addition, both "foreigner and citizen" gather together in the *kahal*. This means that whereas the *am* and the *eda* include only the "children of Israel," the *kahal* is concerned with the "foreigner within your gates" (Exod. 20:10) who is part of Israel and lodges (*ger* means foreigner and resident) in the house of Israel. This foreignness is transmitted by the prophet in the *eda*, and it is the concern of the senate in its politics. It is the sign that the voice carries the other, while at the same time speaking to itself alone. This is why the prophet is not in charge of political affairs. Here, there is a fully developed conception of sovereignty in the form of dwelling.

CHAPTER 2

The House of Israel: Sovereignty

THE WITHDRAWAL of a part (the *eda*) that gives rise to the collective being that is the people (*am*) introduces a relationship of estrangement into collective life. Indeed, the collective being knows itself to be structurally lacking in immediate, intrinsic fullness when it tries to grasp itself. The collectivity of Israel is more a project and a course of action than a fact of nature. Collective being is first and foremost a vacuum. The relationship of the collective being to itself is an experience of estrangement, as if there were an other in the innermost recesses of the self. This apperception of collective existence as identity and autochthony is highly rare. Israel does not occupy all of its being from the start. There are empty, vacant spots in it. This is what makes its collective being a dwelling, a place where one receives and is received, an *ohel moed*, Tent of Meeting (where the *eda* keeps the fire on the welcoming hearth lit). Such a place is at odds with the places where nations usually abide, which are generally enclosed spaces of plenitude marked by boundaries and off-limits to outsiders. The collective being of Israel, precisely because it has within it something exterior to itself (the *eda* in relation to the *am*), is an abode,[218] the "house of Israel" (Exod. 40:38), a dwelling and interiority that houses someone else, a guest-resident, the stranger in the abode. There is otherness in the being.

I. STRANGER IN THE ABODE

This estrangement, lodged at the core of Israel's being, constitutes the main avenue by which Jewishness apprehends itself (knowing that this "self" is

---

218. A place is a dwelling where I abide, enveloped in my interiority, only because it is exterior to me; I cannot be conflated with it. It is the place in the (infinite and anonymous) exterior where I hide and take shelter in the world, and the place from which I take leave of myself.

already more than itself, that it already comprises the other). Doesn't the collectivity of Israel, that is to say *knesset Yisrael*, the "entry" into Israel, come from a "departure," the "exodus from Egypt"? It is the departure, the move out of the interior of another people (Exod. 3:12, 12:31), that founds the interior (*toch*) of Israel, as an aftereffect. This makes for a strange scene of foundation in motion. "Going out" is lodged in the constitution of the collectivity of Israel, in the "entry" (*knesset*) of Israel. The memory of the other is posited before identity, which, consequently, does not provide its own grounds, as if it could suddenly appear on the blank slate of an original void. But this entry inside that proceeds from a departure emerges not from the interiority of Egypt (for Egypt's interiority is found only in death, and its concealment in the grave that is the pyramid) but from its exteriority, from the "(incestuous) nudity of the land" (Gen. 42:9) that characterizes Egypt. The concealment of Israel in the world, its abode, its dwelling in presence, is constituted from this departure; and it is, in a way—because its "entry" is a departure, because of this reversal in the usual sense of inside and outside— that some of the strangeness that always exists in what is exterior to oneself subsists in it. The departure is at the heart of dwelling and of presence itself: "I will dwell/be present (*eshkon*) in the inside (*toch*) of the children of Israel, and I will be a God for them, and they will know that I *am* YHWH, their God, who took them out of the land of Egypt to rest my presence in their midst (*tocham*). I am YHWH, their God" (Exod. 29:45–46).

Hebrew uses the same root to speak of dwelling and strangeness. The *ger*, which in the Bible designates the foreigner (but also the guest and the convert to Judaism), is also the *gar*, the sojourner. In the one who dwells, something is not there, something absent. And this experience of strangeness has continually haunted Israel's conscience despite the natural temptation to forget it from the depths of its abode: "you have known the stranger's *nefesh*, since you were strangers/sojourners in the land of Egypt" (Exod. 23:9). According to Rashi, when Jacob says, "with Laban, I sojourned," he was implying, "I was not made a prince or a resident. I have remained a *ger*." David, too, presents himself along with Israel as a *ger*, "because I am a *ger* with you, a sojourner like all my fathers" (Ps. 39:13). True, the announcement of the otherness of Israel is already at the heart of the promise made to Abraham in the Covenant between the Pieces (Gen. 15), and it goes together with the promise of the land, "*gerim* will be your seed in a land not theirs," thereby shedding new light on the fixing of geographical limits to the Promised Land. The narrative of this covenant is telling. Abraham asks insistently for a concrete, objective sign ("By *what* will I know...?") of the inheritance, since "to me you have given no offspring," as if the divine promise did not suffice. Some commentators see the announcement that his offspring will be strangers in Egypt as a punishment for this, but it should be regarded rather as a reminder of the nature of the covenant, a reminder of divine presence in the place of men, generations, and collectivities.

Abraham, who questions the inheritance and the children to come, has forgotten that he is a *ger* and that what he has to pass down is not subject to property rights, since what is at issue is the testimony (*edut*), the announcement of the other (the son), of this interiority that he will then found. It is not in the "what," in the world of appropriable exteriority, that the object of transmission and testimony is found, but rather in the passing, in the birth of the son. Abraham did not understand this, even though God "took him outside" several times to show him the nature of his descendants, "he who will *come out* from within you," uncountable, unidentifiable (Gen. 15:5); "I took you out of Ur" (15:7). "They will leave with great wealth" (15:14) and yet the main act in the covenantal rite is not to stand still but to "cross," to "pass" between the pieces of the sacrifice.

Testimony generates a relationship to the land, to the apprehension of the world in general, that is different from appropriation. Thus, the promise of the land of Israel is announced to Abraham at the same time as his exile. The two opposite propositions are to be taken together, simultaneously and not chronologically. What is at stake is a relationship to being, an original mode of presence that supports at once the disappearance of exile and the presence in the land, that manifests exile in autochthony and autochthony in exile. The exile of Israel will always be "inhabited" by the land of Israel, and the land of Israel will always be on the brink of exile and evanescence. It is because the constitutive act of the collectivity of Israel is a concealment, like the unfolding of a curtain (the *ohel moed* was made out of curtains, Exod. 26:1–2). Doesn't it say that "the Ark of God *dwells in the 'toch' of the curtain*"? There is a space in the place of the collective that is hidden, a space in the midst of the crowd that is removed from sight, a haven of strangeness amidst what is known, what is too well known. There is a hidden portion in the sacrifice of the pieces about which the Bible tells us very little: what happens to the "bird" that "he did not cut up" (Gen. 15:10)? The undivided bird disturbs the symmetrical arrangement of the animals, "each piece opposite its counterpart." The hidden bird in Abraham's sacrifice testifies to the strangeness within the sacrifice, its incompletion, its necessary structural imperfectibility.

The relationship of strangeness induces transcendence to the world. A principle of "resistance" to man's control is manifested in the world (*olam*). The world escapes our grasp. But, at the same time, we escape its weighty pull; by our mobility, we tear ourselves away from the disappearance that is the world. The sole certainty and reality in the world are summed up in man, the man of concealment. The strangeness (*gerut*) of man is what underpins his power of being in a world that is continually sinking into the abyss of nothingness and perdition. Man separates himself from the world as disappearance, and this is why objects that were formerly illusions of objects appear within him, in his specificity as a subject. In this way the land of Israel appears in its objectness. In the concealment of the people of Israel, the land of Israel emerges from the world of disappearance to appear in the interiority of Israel, surfacing, in truth, in the passage of the being, along the way. In sum, there is history in relation only to man, not to nature or to lands. Strangeness is a principle of being that maintains and strengthens the principle of life and rescues the *nefesh* from its reification. Thus, the human escapes measure, which is always the measure of the world according to criteria of the world and not of man, the dissolution of man in the world, his mineralization and naturalization. Therefore, Abraham's offspring cannot be counted.

Hebraic citizenship has nothing "bourgeois" about it, since it does not reduce the estrangement of man in the world. In this, it frees him. In the strangeness, hiding in the depths of myself and in the fullness of my identity, an other exists who is silent and whose reserve puts me in a state of suspense, the other *par excellence*, God the creator, whose "mark" I bear and who will always cause a name other than my own to resonate in me, the echo of another in the innermost depths of myself and whose very concealment makes my existence possible (despite the sense of uncanniness that it gives me). "The land shall not be sold forever, for the land is mine, for you are *gerim* and residents with me" (Lev. 25:23). By creation itself, man is in essence a stranger in God's dwelling, accommodated in the being of God, who no longer lives in the totality, his original dwelling. In fact, this is what makes him an abode.

In sum, by creating man, God estranges himself. He accommodates another within himself, but he also withdraws into himself, giving rise to the multiplicity of the world. He hides his Name and conceals his unity. The stranger in the being, in God, is the one whose very concealment makes the world possible and who causes every being to feel like a stranger in the world, exiled from the one. "Hope of Israel, its redeemer in time of trouble, why should you be like a *ger* in the land, like a guest sleeping over for the night?" (Jer. 14:8). And because Israel accompanies God, it is a stranger in the land but also "one people": "who is like you, Israel, one *goy* on earth?"

From this standpoint, idolatry is an attempt to diminish the strangeness of the divine, to manifest divine concealment and hence, because we are in the world of *olam*, to dismember the one in the objects in the world. It naturalizes man in the world by casting the stranger out of it. But the stranger (*ger*) is in no way the opposite of the citizen; the stranger dwells (*gar/dar*).

There is a distinction in Hebrew between the *ger* and the *nechar*; the latter is the alien in the absolute and tragic sense of the term. To be sure, the strangeness of the *ger* can lead to such alienation, but so can the well-established citizenship of the bourgeois. However, whereas the *ger* has a tradition, the *nechar* is in the jungle. He is the negative side of the citizen, secure in his convictions and in the demands for and use of his rights. *Nechar* is close to the root *machar*, sell. The *ger* is set apart from the world and hidden in secrecy; the *nechar* is caught in a relationship of exchange based on measurement and value assessment. The *ger* is not a pariah.[219] He embodies a different type of relationship to the world, not the opposite of the sovereignty that citizenship founds but an altogether different sovereignty. The term is telling in its own right: the *ger* is the one who resides (*gar*), who dwells, who stays on the ground and in a full, integral city. The term that accompanies it in the verse from Leviticus (25:23) cited above clearly expresses this: "for you are *gerim* and *toshavim* (residents, settlers)" at the same time.

A Mode of Dwelling

It is this seemingly contradictory two-dimensionality that must be understood if we are to truly grasp *gerut* and not yield to the specious caricatural mystique of exile and rootlessness. The *ger* represents a mode of residing that is embedded in the passage and not in the rootedness of autochthony (land of sameness). He is passing through, but he is here at the same time. The foreign status in Egypt, announced to Abraham in the Covenant between the Pieces, is to be read together with the land, which, in this case, is a Promised Land, and hence a land that involves waiting, effort, and testimony: a land whose being is in suspense. He is a *ger* in the land reserved for him,

219. This is what Weber failed to come to terms with in *Ancient Judaism*, notwithstanding his strong intuition in this regard.

but he is nonetheless in this land. The strangeness in Egypt can give rise to slavery, to alienation in the sense of *nechar*, but then the *ger* that is Israel is awaiting its departure from Egypt. It is not completely in Egypt's power. It has a positive and foundational ground on the basis of which it will break free. The prerevolutionary period, when Moses asserted himself through a series of symbolic acts, aims at disclosing this foundational ground, whose manifestation alone liberates Israel, for Israel is not a marginal, persecuted minority in Egypt but rather an independent avenue in history that stands up to the totality of the Egyptian figure. Then, the alien (*nechar*), the slave, is transfigured by the *ger*. When the Haggada tells us that the children of Israel were outstanding (*metzuyanim*) in Egypt, it is because they did not renounce their names. This strangeness lodged in the depths of Israel's being is evinced by the special status of the *gerim* of Israel, "one law for you and for the *ger* who sojourns" (Num. 15:15), because persistence of the *ger* is provided for in Hebraic citizenship.

In sum, the process of disappearing outside the world that is the assembly of Israel is the experience of this estrangement. In the world of exteriority, only memory reveals the stranger that all have forgotten. The prohibition of representation must also be understood in this light, because the stranger is absent, and the hidden, absent part of the being, the estrangement within the being, makes its grasp and representation impossible. This is the sole modality of the being, at once manifested by the many and hidden in secrecy inside. Estrangement is, consequently, the very process of being, because it rescues presence from dissipation in the world. Fullness is what characterizes presence, but how can it be manifested in the world of disappearance that is the *olam*? Presence, perpetual effervescence, if wholly manifested, necessarily breaks down in the world of the outside and the object. Through representation, man seeks the illusion of the permanence of presence. The *ger* keeps the being "in reserve," maintaining a tension between absence and presence, which is the only possible vehicle of presence in the world. This means that the *ger* removes from the being, so the being always harbors the bounty that the *olam* wastes by nature. He stands out against the totality that leaves no space "empty," where everything stands in absolute coherence, where nothing loses its grip on itself. The *ger* stands apart from the whole as singular, unique, individual, separate, and particular.[220] One could say that in this sense he epitomizes the one in relation to the organic, multiple whole. He detaches

---

220. Whereas the status of the *ger* is always individual, one by one, it is Sodom as a whole that is doomed to destruction.

himself from the whole by following the perfect one, not subtracted from the many but founding the multitude by unhinging it from the whole in which it was embedded and giving it depth, time, and a future where it can abide. The one is in secrecy, and it is the secret of time that passes.

In the estrangement we are analyzing here, the stranger is not an end unto himself, and rootlessness is not an absolute or an exaltation. Strangeness is rather the strategy of presence made possible by the nature of the *olam*. The stranger bears witness to the extent of lack of presence in the *olam* and denounces the illusions of presence in this world when it is restricted to itself alone, when it is instituted in and of itself. The stranger in the *olam* testifies to the strangeness of the *olam* to man: to be a stranger in such a world bespeaks not a lack in relationship to this world but a different world in which presence is full. This is why the stranger is the active and enterprising herald of a world that has finally come to be. The *ger* is only a stranger to a world weak enough to believe that it already resides and that this world here is all there is. He testifies that the world, if left to itself, is not inhabited. Thus, when Abraham leaves Ur for an unknown destination, he does not get lost in the emptiness of the wilderness. He is summoned to reach the land where milk and honey flow.

Estrangement is not the enemy of land as such. It simply introduces a hiatus between man and the land, and it testifies to the fact that man is not born from his land, that he is a stranger in precisely the place where he ought to feel most in tune with the world (in connection with the earth, with "his" land), that he is greater than the world that sustains him. This is why the land of Israel is a Promised Land: there is a gap between the land where one is and the land that is heralded and that is, moreover, heralded to itself, too, for there is a promise of fertility beyond its aridity. The hiatus between man and his land also testifies to the world's incompletion and, conversely, to the created nature of the world, to the creational void between God and man. The *ger* is not the only one to experience this distance from the land; men of rootedness and idolatry feel it in a twisted way in war. Indeed, for a collectivity, a land in the world of *olam* is always there to be either conquered or defended. The effort needed for the concealment of estrangement (and all lands aim to "hide" a collectivity) is twisted into violence. War becomes a form of relationship to the world in an overly full world that does not know how to give of and remove from itself (through the *korban*) and will destroy itself in war. The stranger becomes an incitement to war and not the occasion for birth-giving mercy (*rahamim*); war or *gerut* is the choice that the being of man faces in his relationship to the *olam*. It is in this sense that the God of concealment, Yhwh, the secret Tetragrammaton, is called "Yhwh of armies," God of combat, of the struggle involved in concealment, which is the perfect antithesis of war. It is hence no accident that the *ger* is the preeminent victim of war, the principle of a mode of being governed by war. The *ger* is the one who manifests an empty space amidst all the occupied spaces of civilization, which is intolerable to the powers that be, because it cannot be integrated into their empire, and therefore it gives the lie to the idolatrous simulacrum of the plenitude of presence. The persistence of alterity contests this mockery of fullness, and no one knows what to do with the *ger* in a world marked by nudity instead of concealment. The experience of estrangement is the experience of the place and space that manifests the gap in God that is the creation of the *olam*, a long, empty interval that man is invited to leap into again and again as if for the very first time, an emptiness at the heart of civilization, a land from elsewhere that testifies to the possibility of transcending the world, in and starting with the world.

Understanding the *ger* always involves knowing and dwelling in this place, the *makom*, whose strangeness stands out as distinctly different amid the lands of civilization. This place maintains an irreducible strangeness within the known, explored, and dominated world, and is nonetheless a positive land, even though we cannot see it, one that is hard to divide and to cut off from the lands of the world, a place where the stranger already lives. Every sensation of strangeness that we experience in the world, every uncanny impression of déjà vu is a memory of this land, itself a kind of memory of the origin of the world. Every departure (exodus from Egypt), every appearance of Israel reactualizes the beginning of creation, the *reshit*. Thus, when Moses is blessed in God's revelation, "he saw a *reshit* for him" (Deut. 33:21), precisely when presence is being manifested: Moses saw something greater than the real land of Israel. Estrangement therefore attests irremediably to the beginning, to *reshit*, to the principle of things and of being.

The Phenomenon of Generations

For this reason, the *ger* is the very figure of incompletion but at the same time of perpetual renewal and of the difficulty of maintaining oneself constantly in presence. In its relationship to dwelling, the phenomenon of the stranger (*ger*) is similar to that of the generation (*dor*). The quality of both is to dwell (*gar* and *dar* both mean "dwell"). The same type of presence exists for the generation phenomenon as for the *ger*;[221] always in motion,

---

221. See above, "The Abode of the World: The Finite and the Infinite," pp. 39–48.

disappearing and giving way to another generation that feels as much a stranger in the world it inherits, each generation testifies to the generation that is passing away and the one to come. For humanity, the experience of generations' succeeding one another is the experience of estrangement in its very bosom, the experience of passage and the flow of time. Through this unending cycle the perpetually shifting land of the *reshit* emerges, the Place (*Hamakom*), the principle of being where every being is always in the place of something else, in the *makom* of the other, the *makom* of God, so much so that it is in this place through which we are only passing that we dwell.[222] Generation is humanity's collective mode of dwelling in the *olam*. The *ger* is its individual mode. The generations are the abode of humankind in the *olam*, its shelter, its concealment, its passage. The *ger* is the abode of the people of Israel, the shelter of peoples.

It is through the phenomenon of generations that man comes to know that he is only sojourning in the world, that he is a stranger to and different from it, that his finality does not reside within him. Generation is the category of strangeness in humanity; generation marks the place where humankind passes and escapes from itself. Humans try to counter this trial by means of inheritance, in the hopes of using the principle of property to fill the void that is continually emptying out in the midst of lands, even when they are owned. The most powerful king knows he will die and leave his place to his successor! The system of inheritance endeavors to thwart this by enchaining the following generation.

What Abraham wants to know in the episode of the Covenant between the Pieces is who will inherit him. And the answer he receives speaks both of estrangement and of the Promised Land: the promised son, Isaac's begettal. Isaac's place will be born with difficulty, since Abraham will not conceive it until much later, at the tip of the knife he raises over Isaac, bound on the altar (Gen. 22). It takes Abraham time to understand that if there is transmission, it concerns not the land ("By what will I know...?") but the Name, eventually the name of the land, its promise (through which the land is hidden) the surest foundation possible for the acquisition of the real land. Thus, the collectivity of Israel undergoes the quintessential experience of the estrangement of *gerut*. Balaam defines it as "a people (*am*), in solitude, it will remain/be present, and among the peoples (*goyim*) it will not be counted/conceived/held to be something" (Num. 23:9). This solitude, which is paradoxical insofar as it designates the being-with that is the people, reflects the

222. *Dar* means to sojourn, dwell, circulate.

strangeness in Israel's being more than its strangeness amidst the nations. Indeed, this verse needs to be read more carefully: "a being-with/people, in solitude, it will remain/dwell (*yishkon*)" (from the root *shechina*, "presence"). What a strange solitude this is, since it benefits from the presence that is the dwelling, where one is not outside! Could it be the solitude of love, the solitude of the one that presence is? Or could it be the solitude of presence in the collective being?

We have already seen how the one, love's end purpose, was alone in the world of the many even as it found the many. But the strangeness in the collective being of Israel, echoed in this paradoxical solitude, must be understood in a more systematic fashion. The fact that the collective being of Israel comes to feel a stranger to itself in the very place where it would ordinarily feel in total control of itself and in perfect accord with its intimacy demonstrates that the people of Israel does not belong to itself, that it is in a state of estrangement within and vis-à-vis itself.[223] This is an expression of the principle of the *ger* in collective existence.

How is this estrangement structured? If the people (*am*) is alone, it is because it is confronted with a relationship of dwelling (*yishkon*), with the presence of the *Shechina*, with the *eda* and the concealment that is in it and gives rise to it. Once the *eda*, community of testimony, withdraws, the rest of Israel, the being-with (*am*), is in solitude. It is *omem*, opaque, and has removed itself from itself. Something in the assembly is hidden that makes for the persistence of solitude. But when the people forget the *eda* hidden within it and assume the appearance of unity through idolatrous representations, it is the *eda* that feels utter solitude, the solitude of the Levites, who alone remained faithful when the rest of Israel was making the golden calf.

It is in this coessential relationship to the *eda* (and the memory of concealment) that the *am* knows itself and benefits from presence, from the dwelling that is also its own presence to itself. The *eda* founds the place of testimony, it detaches identity from the identical to make room for receiving the other, but it is the *am* that must testify, that must try to always rise to the level of presence, to fulfill the exacting requirement with which the memory of a withdrawn presence, if not memory itself, charges it. The people/*am* is called upon to clarify the opaqueness that its constitution conferred upon it, to purify and cleanse it in order to blossom in the *eda*, to welcome the

---

223. And isn't this how the nations define Israel? Balaam, prophet of the nations, prophesies about the being of Israel, seeing its vocation from afar, and Haman himself describes Israel as "a people-one, scattered and divided among the nations" (Esther 3:8).

flame of testimony and the warmth of presence into its numb, dumb heart. This is the only deed that the people as such can accomplish. That is why it is said, "we will do (*am*) and we will hear (*eda*)." The movement that goes from *am* to *eda* (because prior to this, the differential position of the *eda* made the existence of the *am* possible) is the very movement of sovereignty in Israel's collective being, through which presence grasps the multiple being of the gathering. This movement founds the source of legitimacy and power in Israel, born of the conjunction of *am* and *eda*, the people and the community, through a complex structure of procedures and institutions within each of the two entities but also going from one to the other.[224] In sum, for the people there is no form of sovereignty other than in testimony—that is to say, in the total presence of the other and not in narcissistic self-contemplation.

An Unaccountable People

Sovereignty, understood in this way, is not structured on a principle of mediation and representation that crystallizes the total being of the collectivity in a way that could only be reifying, alienating, and, when all is said and done, fundamentally idolatrous. Two institutions evidence this: the high priest and the civic power (king, judges, assembly) share sovereignty, and the latter can be effective only in the movement that joins the two. We find here again the effect of the dwelling, of the presence (*Shechina*) that is stated in Balaam's prophecy, "among the *goyim*, it will not be counted/deemed important." The mode of being that exists in dwelling cannot be measured; it cannot be divided into so many equal portions, into individual electoral "voices" the sum of which would yield sovereignty, for in this case equality would amount to an equality with oneself, a composite self, the artificial being whom Hobbes describes as a Leviathan. The national home, conceived in terms of exclusion of the other, is a dark, drafty place where people sometimes manage to create the illusion of dwelling by lighting great, votive fires. Likewise, the people of Israel as announced to Abraham in the Covenant between the Pieces is presented as uncountable, because as a collective being it cannot be reduced to the sum of individuals who compose it, and hence it cannot be mediated, represented, or idolized. It is in this sense that it does not "exist" among the *goyim*, the nations of exteriority, as a totally exposed exteriority. Moreover, isn't Israel a *goy* (a *gvia*, phallus) from which something has been removed

---

224. We will return to this below, in "King and Levite," pp. 219–225.

and hidden: the circumcised foreskin? What makes the Jewish people or Jewishness is what remains of the nations after their circumcision. In sum, Israel is not counted among the nations because it is the excision practiced on them, the removed portion set apart, their shelter and concealment, and hence the very principle of their existence, of their dwelling in the world. But to dwell in the house of Israel, the Jewish people also practiced a setting apart.

We have intimations of this in what happens right before Jacob and his family enter the land of Israel (Gen. 32:9). The being of Israel, as it is about to pass across to the other side (*ever*) of the Jordan River to enter the place of its institution, the land of Israel, is divided into two. Frightened by his imminent encounter with Esau, Jacob divides Israel into the "camp of the one" and the "camp of the rest." Jacob divides the collectivity of Israel into two to "do the *kappara* of his face," which means to "appease him," but it connotes so much more, since *kappara* signifies a covering up. And whose face is it? Esau's? Or could it be God's, as we may suppose from what follows, when Jacob wrestles with an angel and names the place Peniel, meaning the Face of God? Jacob thus "sacrifices" to God in connection with the collectivity of Israel; he brings Israel closer (*mekarev*) to God (through the *korban*); he redeems the people of Israel. In light of the discussion so far, we know he "makes *eda*," he effects a concealment. The text supports this analysis, because what Jacob shelters and hides, what he keeps away from Esau's eventual animosity, is the "camp of the one."[225] So having removed the *eda* from the collectivity, Jacob sends the *am*, the multiple people, which is thereby exposed to the exterior, to the world of Esau, to its eventual dangers; but the *am* draws all its power from the fact that behind it stands the camp of the one.

Haman's "oracle" evokes a similar figure, a "people (*am*)-one, scattered and divided among the *goyim*" (Esther 3:8), where oneness goes together with multiplicity. This unity that resides in the dispersion of the multiple is the fundament of the sovereignty of Israel, which involves a process that is neither mediated nor represented and that does not eliminate the structural movement of the one and the multiple, that does not try to reduce either or supersede them in a third term. Thus, what is at stake in both Balaam's and Haman's "oracle" is sovereignty (in the classical sense of the term this time,

---

225. As we will see, this "camp of the one" is Joseph's, because Leah and her children cross first, before Rachel and Joseph, Jacob's favorites. Joseph, the one, comes after, over and above, the last ones. This reading, which goes against the grain of the literal one, is paradoxical only in appearance, for Jacob's procedure does not identify each camp, although they may be identified in Esau's gaze, since he is said to be able to attack the "camp of the one." But Esau's gaze is hardly a reference.

as absolute power in relation to the other). Balaam compares Israel to the nations (basically from the standpoint of the nations of the world of power, Israel is not sovereign), and Haman continues his malicious talk, with the words "their conceptions are different/dual... and there is no value in them for the king" (ibid.). Essentially, the existence of the Jews, thus defined, is a threat to the sovereignty of Ahasuerus.[226] But there is wisdom in Haman's malicious speech, as there is in Balaam's, whose curses turn into blessings. Just as a true judgment about the being of Israel can be read in the first words of this verse, so the second can be interpreted as meaning "and their understandings/conceptions are dual/differentiated, and the vacuum (*ain*) in them equals a king." Beyond the one hidden in the multiple, we see here as much the bipolarity of the sovereign as the estrangement implicated in sovereignty and royalty. For Haman as for Balaam, this is how the collective being of Israel differs from the nations.

This procedure of setting apart and overadding power is the characteristic feature of sovereignty in Israel. It immediately points to a structural absence and emptiness in the assembly of Israel. "For you to pass through the covenant of YHWH and his pact... in order to establish you today as an *am* to him... and not with you alone do I seal this covenant and this pact but with that which is with us and is standing today before YHWH, our God, and with that which is not with us today" (Deut. 29:11–14). God enters into a covenant (*berit*) and a pact (*ala*)—here, too, the bond is twofold[227]—that makes of this people (*am*), which sprang up (*hakim*) in a place (*makom*), an *am* to God ("to him"). And this bond concerns not only "the *am* that is with us today before God but also that which is not with us today." Beyond the reference to the succession of generations that is implicit in that which is not here, there is also the *eda*, as absence in Israel's immediate and actual being-there, and this absence is a matter of principle and structure, not circumstance. In any case, it is through the *eda* that the people of passing generations endures over time in the same unity of Israel, a unity achieved once and for all and hidden in secrecy, a unity that is not forged from the accidental, circumstantial addition of the being-there of the people. The people/*am* is thus defined as what is here today, but it also adheres to that which, in the being-with that it brings together, is here today an *ayin*, a void

226. Or maybe what Haman means to say is that Israel has no sovereignty because there is too much multiplicity in it.

227. Covenant for the *eda* and pact for the *am*.

or lack, and which is the *eda*, that which in fact founds the very appearance of the *am* here and now.

This is why forgetting is the greatest temptation of the people. Because the people that knows it is in a state of incompletion is tempted to "mend" its being (*tikkun*), believing it possible to rise to the level of being in the *eda*, to the level of the one that it knows it is lacking, and to do so without recourse to the *eda*, to do so not through testimony (a form of presence that faces absence) but through representation (which is a mockery of presence, since it refuses the trial of absence). The people that "is here" is by definition missing something, so it is illusory to believe it can be counted. A census will never be taken of the *eda*. God (who is present in its midst) will never be counted. It is in the one, and hence it is hidden! In the system of democratic representation, where every individual's voice is counted again and again, the unstoppable phenomenon of abstention echoes the fact that no elected representative can ever claim to really represent the whole political collectivity. Abstentionism echoes in representation the vacuum of the *eda* in the *am* that thinks it can undertake to grasp itself by itself without the *eda*.

Presence in Strangeness

The full light of presence can be heard only through a singular voice in the world, the voice of the *ger*. The migration of the *ger*, which breaks down the whole and endures the particularization in the *olam*, heralds the one, the time when light's luminescence finally reaches its goal while returning to its source. Thus, the particularization of Israel departing from Egypt speaks also for Egypt, insofar as the passage of Israel aims not restrictively at a differentiation from Egypt but rather at the one, and the ultimate redemption of Egypt. We must grow accustomed to seeing presence as the sky in the changing light of day and night, from dusk to dawn. What is covered by the darkness of the night is thereafter overcome by the light of day. Light is greater than the particular variations of light in each passing hour, but nonetheless, each hour is the vehicle of its progression through the narrow straits of each passing instant.

The formulation in the Song of Songs, "a garden locked, my sister, my bride, a wave locked, a fountain sealed" (4:12), wonderfully expresses this concept of presence: extreme yet contained, abundant yet withheld, suspended flight and generous outpouring. "Who is this who ascends from the wilderness, clinging to her beloved?" (8:5): the embrace but also the wilderness. "Turn your eyes away from me" (6:5): I'm here, but do not look at me. As soon as I'm in your presence, "flee, my beloved, and be like a gazelle or a young hart on the mountains of fragrance" (8:14). "I opened for my beloved, and he slipped away, he passed on; my *nefesh* departed at his word; I asked for him and did not find him; I called him, and he did not answer" (5:6). The entire text describes this search for a presence that is continually slipping away.

There is an opposition in this search between, on the one hand, the city and the rooted vineyard that the beloved woman must watch over and, on the other, the pasture where the beloved shepherd moves from one place to another. "Go to yourself in the tracks of the sheep, and graze your kids by the dwellings (*mishkan*) of the shepherds" (1:8). "The absent maidens (*alamot*) will love you" (1:2); "you will be recalled" (1:4), for it is not in the walled cities that your presence is found: "the walls of our houses are cedars, our furnishings are cypress" (1:17). Presence is an invitation to strangeness (*gerut*), to the movement of passing. Fragrance and the sense of smell best express the subtle, diffuse, and "absent" reality of a presence that is nonetheless persistent and all-pervasive: "like a gazelle... on the mountains of fragrance."

This presence that we can feel, that we seek but that cannot be "found" (5:6), echoes Ecclesiastes (3:11) and the act of God that cannot be "found" in the world. Only the shepherds know how to follow its tracks. The "watchmen" think they have found it—"They found me, the watchmen patrolling the city" (5:7)—but what they catch is merely a shadow thereof. The search is difficult and close to a sickness, lovesickness, the longing for the one in the world of multiplicity. Presence can be given only in the form of the announcement, of the promise. And so the beloved gives an oath; four times she evokes her oath (Song 2:7, 3:5, 5:8, 8:4), because the oath naturally involves warding off the impatience that characterizes the search for presence. "Do not rouse the love until it pleases"; in other words, do not take presence out of its im-mediate, temporary absence, lest you lose it! But this oath does not give up hope of presence. Indeed, the love in question is the one! The one cannot be awoken while we are still in the *olam*. It is passing toward itself, toward its own disclosure, which only its will governs. And it is this very passing that makes it possible. This presence, which one can only sense, which makes one "run" (1:4), "leap," and "skip" (2:8), which one embraces without grasping and which invites the reader to depart in strangeness, adds to the being despite its loss. "I sleep but my heart is awake" (5:2): despite my absence to myself in sleep, my heart is awake; I am added to my departing self....

The whole of the Song of Songs, in its problematical, seemingly chaotic, linear development, describes this process of presence and accompanies its movement. Its very structure is twofold, caught in the dialogue and the reciprocal search of the beloved man and woman. But it is the unfolding of the chase that illustrates this best. At the start, the two lovers can't find each other, though they sense each other's presence. The "shepherd in the roses" (2:16) is heralded by the fragrance of flowers spread by his passage through them. "In his shade, I sat" (2:3). He is like a "cluster of myrrh" (1:13), many gathered together in a single group. Each calls out to the other at first (2:13–17), but they do not meet. It is after the second oath that the beloved appears in a subtle way, "ascending from the wilderness, in the pillars of smoke and smells of perfume, in the fragrant powders of the wilderness" (3:6). This is when the beloved appears on his throne, his palanquin lined with love/with the one of the daughters of Jerusalem, frail manifestations of wholeness: "the scents of your garments/fullness/completeness" (4:11) in a world that cannot sustain its sight.

The attributes of these appearances (air, liquid, fragrance) are highly significant insofar as they all bespeak at once mobility, passage, and total permeation. But as soon as this brief, radiant sight appears, the text tells us that the presence must "slip away": "I opened for my beloved, and he slipped away and is gone" (5:6); "My beloved has descended to his garden" (6:2), "my soul departed" (5:6). It is in this descent—"I went down to the garden of nuts" (6:11)—in this absence, that one must look for it, see if "the pomegranates and grapes have budded" (6:11), in "my mother's house, in the interior of the one who conceived me" (3:4), in the secrecy of the "nut," inside time, on "the chariot of my generous people" (6:12). It is when we despair of the flight and passage of presence barely glimpsed, that we can and must behold the beloved who is presented here as Shulammite, the complete, which is related to *Shlomo*, Solomon the complete, king of the complete city/ *Yeru-shalem*/Jerusalem.

At the time of despair and wandering, a return, a recalling takes place: "return, return, O Shulammite/the complete one. Return, return, and we will look upon you" (Song 7:1). This sight, which underpins the continuity of the splendid and fleeing revelation that comes before, occurs under the seal of the third oath (5:8). This time, however, we know the subtle nature of this presence, "like the dances of the dual camp" (7:1), like the two parts of a loom weaving the fabric, weaving the interiority of the union. Once the lover has understood this, he goes away and keeps on walking. Therefore, the fourth oath is different: "I adjure you... what love will you rouse?" Here the oath concerns the "what" and not the "if" (as in the three preceding oaths). Indeed, we have finally realized that we cannot awaken the one and that whenever we approach presence in the *olam*, there is absence at its heart: wilderness and intertwining, the solitude of lovers, the solitude of the community. "Who is this who ascends from the wilderness, clinging to her beloved?" (8:5). And only the *berit* can sustain and shelter this poignant absence at the pulsing heart of presence. Only the covenant can safeguard it from evil, death, and Sheol: "place me like a seal on your heart" (8:6), a covenant binding one and the other, under the banner of the one but where the two live together, because, in its midst, there is an emptiness, a *gerut*, that enables them to stand individually and face one another: "its interior is full of love" (3.10). This is indeed an inflexible, exclusive covenant, because it binds two partners, apart from the rest of the world, in a *hityahud*[228] arousing "jealousy" and "inflamed" demands (8:6). But this is when one is in the fragrant gardens, "like one who has found completeness (*shalem*)" (8:10).

The Written Torah in the Passage

The being is in passage but is not doomed to perdition, because even though the one is absence in this paradoxical conception of being, it is nonetheless heralded in this absence through a whole series of signs and markers that bespeak its existence, like the "tracks of the flock" that the shepherd in the Song of Songs follows to find his sheep (1:8). "Walk in the tracks of the flock," could be the essential injunction addressed to Israel. The track is the difference in level that we encounter in a world that is otherwise full and flat, evidence that someone has passed, that someone has come before me. Thus, the track is evidence of truth surfacing from the ground, the truth of creation. Fullness is not where we thought it was, and this missing piece, this gash in the solidity of the ground, heralds the surplus of the other.

In the emptiness of the *olam*, the words of the Torah are the tracks left by the one in the disappearance that is the world, the only possible track sustaining the ordeal of its passage. Voiding by its letters the emptiness that is the world, the Torah becomes an addition, an augment right where it slips away: "Yhwh will add you (*yeter*) in every act of your hand, in the fruit of your belly... if you listen to the voice of Yhwh, your God, to keep his *mitzvot*, his written laws in the book of the Torah.... The word is very close (*karov*) to you, in your mouth and in your heart to do it" (Deut. 30:9–15). The Torah thus etches the letter at the heart of the being, an infinite echo to

---

228. A term that denotes the process of rendering particular, unified, solitary (cf. *Forgotten Dwelling*, pp. 384–385).

the hiatus in which the world stands, a bond spanning the emptiness of the world, the only possible being that can measure up to the void, the vehicle of reversing the void into overplus.

A closeness and a sociality can be founded upon this overplus for the world that is the Torah, and this is man's only possible true "doing," insofar as this is where the interiority of man is situated, in this path of the one etched in the anonymity of the *olam*. It is in the written word (in the Torah) that such a presence can be reached while we are still in the *olam*. The collectivity of Israel draws from the wellspring of presence in this Scripture, the only possible framework for its reunion in the world of *olam*: "You are all convoked today before YHWH... to pass by the covenant of YHWH... in order for him to establish you as an *am*... as he spoke to you and as he swore..." (Deut. 29:9–12). The public reading by the king from the Torah that he has copied with his own hand (17:18), a reading to the people gathered together for this purpose—and this is one of his cardinal commandments at the end of the sabbatical year—is to be understood from this standpoint. As shepherd of the flock and of their spirit, he truly gathers Israel together. He covers and conceals it in its foundational place. He reactivates Israel in the place of origins. And it's a blessing....

In the absence in the vacuum of the *olam*, the only presence that exists is the Torah, the written Torah, filled with words and prospects for human beings cast into the emptiness, augment of blessing of the void. The written Torah (and here the writing is important as a trace) is like the fault line of the *olam*, the mirror of the strangeness that structures being, the track in the void for the migration of the *ger*. The written word is the stranger in the being, the vehicle of the spirit of strangeness, and the whole being comes down to the written word in the void, to this "more" in what appears like a "less" in the illusion of more that the world can be: "even if I wrote to him all of my Torah, as a stranger (*zar*) it would be deemed/counted" (Hos. 8:12).

All of presence is gathered together in the written word. In fact, the world—inasmuch as it is reflected in and attains consciousness, and inasmuch as it is concealment, too—is consubstantial with writing and with the biblical narrative. The "House" of God (Gen. 28:17) that Jacob discovers, the "dwelling (*mishkan*) of the shepherds" (Song 1:8), is writing, the principle of concealment that is itself the very foundation of the world, because, in the withdrawal, the written word is the track of human reality. Writing is not anterior to the world; it is coexistent with it. We move around not in the "world," in space, but in writing and in words, the very archetypes of the rockiest and most fluid places in the world. To read the text is to experience the world. Writing is at the bottom of all things. Manifested in its concrete signs, it is the strangeness at our innermost core, the bottomless bottom of our being. Text and language are not agencies or instruments, as most people think; they are the very milieu where we are, the being that we are, given, of course, that we are in the passage. That is to say, there is a strangeness in us that transcends our identity, so that language "belongs" to us and at the same time it doesn't, so that the text is ours and at the same time it escapes our hold. It pertains to the realm of the Name.

We can now understand why presence cannot come to be in the "fantasy" of the "body," power, and possessions, and according to a principle of exposure, that it requires the veiled light of the Song of Songs. The written word is this strangeness in being that has to be redeemed and "repaired" (*tikkun*), taken out of the exteriority into which it has been cast from the origin, because it is itself exteriority surfacing from within the withdrawal. The stranger ends up arriving somewhere. This redemption is accomplished through the oral word, through the concealment that is reading. "Carve for yourself two stone tablets like the first ones, and I will write on the tablets..." (Exod. 34:1), "for according to/*on the mouth* of (*al pi*) these words, I have sealed a covenant with you and with Israel" (34:27).

At the outset, the Torah lies lifeless in exteriority. Its reading (*mikra*), the royal reading during which the text files past and passes through the people, and its interpretation in the Levitical commentary effect its *tikkun*, the concealment of its "exteriority," so that its meaning can shine forth. The concealment of the Torah occurs when the assembly of Israel unravels the text and transposes it into laws that are inscribed in text's midst. There is a strangeness at the heart of its very being, as if the Torah, a written text, came prior to the existence of this people. The presence of the text in the Ark of the Covenant is therefore of structural more than "symbolic" import.

The interplay between the written and the oral echoes the system of augment and retreat. The written is mainly in the immediacy of creational retreat, since it is the very locus of the world. But from the standpoint of the world, it is absence; it comes in addition to the world. It takes the oral word, the oral interpretation of the written, to bring out the augment that it is. We can now understand why the interpretation is done by the Levite tribe, embodiment of the *ger* among the tribes. The *eda* harbors the orality of the text that is the people. In its public reading, the king consequently brings together in unity the two figures of Israel.

Thus, at bottom, the place where power is exercised, the sovereignty that characterizes Israel, harbors the written Torah, the self-domination of God in his own creation (as it is ordered by words), the itinerant strangeness, and the dwelling, rather than a tautological assertion. This is why power in Israel contains a withholding, a suspension of sorts, a hovering of propitiatory and redemptive clemency.

II. SOVEREIGNTY

The institution of Hebraic royalty and the history of the Davidic dynasty evidence the strangeness at the bottom of sovereignty. The kingship emerges first outside Israel and, more precisely, in the figure that is antithetical to it—namely, in the family of Esau, Jacob's twin brother, whose royalty is specifically stated to have preceded the establishment of a kingship in Jacob's family: "these are the kings who reigned in the land of Edom before a king reigned over the children of Israel" (Gen. 36:31). Could royalty be exterior to Israel's essence, or could it be that Esau, out of envy of Jacob's primogeniture, precipitated the imitation of Israel? Be that as it may, royalty is defined here according to the cycle of determinism of generations, modeled more on death than on life: so-and-so "died," and so-and-so "reigned in his place." Interestingly, the reign of each monarch is essentially summed up by the name of the capital city he established. Are we to see this as an intimation of the Babel enterprise, the human folly of establishing a kingship over the world, substituting the name of man for the Name of God, so that the latter no longer provides shelter to the collectivity and is no longer sheltered in its midst? This interpretation is borne out by Obadiah, who sees the kingship of Edom aspiring to replace divine kingship, when he tells us that after Edom is judged, "the kingdom will be Yʜwʜ's" (Obad. 1:21).

Royalty involves an experience of substitution and absence, a manifestation that blots out the other, be it God or the "represented" community, but also the assertion of a power that is sorely tested by the passage (of time and generations), a substitution for the other but also for oneself, for we are told that from king to king on the same throne, each king "reigned under him/in his place."

Knowing that the kingship of Edom is governed by death and consuming passage alone, how does the kingship of Israel work to accomplish its *tikkun*? The Davidic royal house is presented as descending from one of the Hebrew midwives who saved Israel when Pharaoh set out to have all the firstborn sons killed.[229] It is Ruth, the stranger from Moab, the poor widow, archetype of the outsider, who is the key heroine of the story. In a way, the book of Ruth constitutes the biblical charter of the foundation of royalty and contains the most complete model thereof.[230] Ruth, a descendant of Moabite kings, asks to be admitted to the Jewish people, and for this purpose, she seeks out Boaz, a descendant of her childless dead husband's family, the family of Judah, and gets him to marry her in application of the levirate commandment. We have here in a nutshell all the constituent elements of kingship in Israel.

The Incestuous Origins of Kingship

The foreign origin of the "mother of kingship"[231] governs this figure of sovereignty. And there is a specific nature to her foreignness. In undertaking to enter into the bosom of Israel, Ruth is reproducing something of the journey of Abraham, whom she greatly resembles and who is himself an example of the *ger*. She, too, leaves her country, and both are seen as personifying the same cardinal value: grace (*hesed*) and solace.[232] In both cases, God is invoked as Shaddai. According to tradition, in becoming Jewish, the *ger* is merely recalling a distant memory, remembering his remote and incomplete belonging to Israel. After all, the Moabite kings descend from the daughters of Lot, Abraham's alter ego, endowed with the virtue of hospitality (witness the story of Sodom) but without all its qualities. Moab was the offspring of an incestuous relationship. After the destruction of Sodom, Lot's two daughters, thinking that all humankind had been destroyed, got their father drunk and conceived a future for the human species (Gen. 19:37). Moab (*mei-av*, from the father's waters) represents a humanity that is oddly founded on an anticoncealment (incest) of a man whose name is a summons to concealment (the radical of Lot means "secrecy"). An incest, not by concupiscence

229. According to the Talmud (Sota 11b), commenting on Exodus 1:21, "the midwives feared God; he [God] made them houses." One of the midwives, Shifrah, founded the Levitical house, through Jochebed, Moses and Aaron's mother; the other, Puah, founded the royal house through Miriam (whose complex genealogy is traced by the Talmud).

230. According to tradition, Samuel is its author. This is particularly significant in light of his role as a priest and judge and his purported antimonarchist stance.

231. The daughter of the Moabite king who had Israel cursed by Balaam, Ruth belongs to a people that is never allowed into the *kahal* of YHWH (Deut. 23:4–7).

232. In both stories (Ruth 2:20 and Gen. 24:27), gratitude is expressed to God, "who has not abandoned his *hesed*."

but by altruism. By moving to Israel, Ruth redeems an Abrahamic spark lost and gone astray.

This incestuous origin of kingship is confirmed on Boaz's side as well. Boaz descends from Judah, who married the "daughter of an alien god,"[233] Shua, whose sons, Er and Onan, died one after another. When Shua died, Er's widow, Tamar, seeing that she had not been given to Judah's last son, Shelah, as a wife, disguised herself as a prostitute and tempted Judah to conceive a child from him and perpetuate Er's name. Peretz was born from this union. Interestingly, the people of Bethlehem express the wish that Naomi be blessed like Tamar, who bore Peretz to Judah. So the two families that unite to give birth to David (Ruth and Boaz) and to kingship in Israel are both incestuous. The direction of each incest is different, though: Ruth goes from idolatry to the God of Israel; Judah goes from the God of Israel to idolatry, as did Elimelech and Naomi in leaving the land of Israel for Moab, in a movement of deadly entropy (the death of Judah's children and Elimelech and his children). These two movements intersect, and Ruth is the negentropy thereof. Each time, it is a woman who reverses the deadly descent: Ruth in Elimelech's case, Tamar in Judah's.

The woman's role in these acts of incest is decisive. Both Lot's daughter and Tamar take the initiative and trick Lot and Judah respectively. Both are united by the same aim: to give a child to a lineage in Israel that is about to die out, because there is no heir. The two women are protagonists in the levirate commandment whose purpose is "to raise the name of the dead over his property" (Ruth 4:5), so that it not be obliterated. They seek to substitute a son for the departed and recreate the missing link. This, incidentally, is Ruth's only aim, and she succeeds better than Lot's daughters and Tamar, because she achieves her purpose without incest by getting Boaz to "redeem" her. The progressive steps in this redemption of incest are worthy of note: with Lot's daughter, the incest is between father and daughter; with Tamar, between father and daughter-in-law; and with Ruth, the incest is redeemed.

In this genealogy of kingship, it seems that it is the women[234] who bear a greater role in the vocation of remembering God the creator's retreating to leave room for his world, the vocation of Israel. Isn't it the vocation of the midwife to bear witness to the birth of so-and-so from so-and-so? Trickery

233. Genesis Rabba 85:2 on Gen. 38:2, "Judah went down."

234. Without forgetting that the royal dynasty descends from the midwife Puah. Moreover, the "house (*bayit*)," also denotes the vulva.

and subterfuge also play an important role[235] in compelling the men to do what they would not otherwise do. This is reminiscent of the trickery used by the matriarchs to secure the appropriate attribution of the right of inheritance (particularly when Rebecca tricks the blind Isaac). Need we recall Jacob's ploys?

What is the meaning of the (tactical) centrality of incest in a kingship saved by it twice? Perhaps the royal incest should be grasped on the basis of its redemption by Ruth, who accomplishes the end purpose of the two prior acts of incest without resorting to it herself. Maybe the kingship is the heroic gesture of redeeming incest, incest being the temptation for a collectivity or a nation to retreat into the narcissistic reproduction of self, into the rejection of strangeness. Isn't the levirate commandment itself close to incest? Ruth (royalty) in this way manages to effect the concealment that helps a collectivity to be constituted in truth. She comes to "seek refuge under the wings of Yнwн" (Ruth 2:12) and asks Boaz to spread his "wings/robes/ protection over his servant" (3:9). One could also see in this verse a sign of the strangeness of the kingship in relation to the laws, not only because of the incest but because Ruth is a Moabite, whose lineage, even in the tenth generation, cannot be part of Israel. The establishment of royalty would, in this case, run counter to the very laws that govern it (Deut. 17:15) and that prohibit its access to non-Jews.[236] If the principle of royalty in Israel is the concealment that makes the collectivity of Israel, it must be itself "redeemed." Its strangeness, the savage royalty that Esau inaugurates, that gives nothing of itself, hides nothing of itself, and seeks total, integral control of itself must be redeemed. The deeds of the heroines shed light on this end, for they undertake to fulfill the levirate duty, to give a name and descendants to one who is dead, to perpetuate his name on earth, to add to that which is nothing anymore.

From Scarcity to Bounty: Ruth's Deed

Doesn't royalty, and the ruling power in general, use a strategy similar to the levirate? It endeavors to extricate itself from the absence of man in the

---

235. Tamar makes use of the very emblems of royalty (Judah's staff, signet, and purple cord) as security and evidence. Ruth has recourse to "uncovering" Boaz's legs.

236. "One of your brothers must be your king; you shall not submit to an outsider who is not your brother. A brother is defined as someone who comes from a mother in Israel" (*Shulhan Aruch, Hoshen Mishpat* 1:7).

presocial crowd, and to manifest presence. But this absence is the effect of the divine royalty that supports its presence. The essential question facing power and the collectivity is how to posit a human kingship that is deployed only in God's self-effacement but without masking divine kingship. It is a matter of "repairing the *olam* in the sovereignty of Shaddai/who [said,] "enough" (liturgy). It is in the universe of the creational retreat that the kingship is established, in the void of the *olam*, in the grandeur of the disappearance. As we have seen, the danger that threatens it is the illusion of its consummate presence in this world of passage. This is an illusion, because the kingship is a kind of mask to God who withdraws, the clouding of his Name and not his triumphant appearance. Royalty is the space and time manifested between God and his creation. David's "seed will endure for the *olam*; his throne is before Me like the sun. Like the moon, it is ready for the *olam*; and the witness (*ed*) in the sky is faithful" (Ps. 89:37–38). The remoteness of the creator constitutes a foundational moment that the whole logic of being calls on us to overcome. In fact, God's withdrawal adds to the being, and it is in kinship that the interplay before retreat and augment becomes manifest.

This original absence over which divine kingship reigns has to be redeemed lest the world be depleted and engulfed. This is the experience that Lot's and Tamar's daughters have, the extinction of a species and a name. This is the type of experience that Ruth and Naomi have in famine and poverty.

The whole story of Ruth is structured on a movement that goes from scarcity via asceticism to bounty and satiation. At the outset, we are told that the land of Israel was afflicted by famine in the days of the Judges (Ruth 1:1). The judge represents the antithesis of the king, insofar as the power of judges is extremely decentralized. The Hebrew people come to Samuel, himself a judge, to put an end to this regime of judges and request a king (which he understandably opposes). The "rule of judges" is thus presented to us as a failure for Israel in comparison to which the kingship appears to be a benediction. But Boaz, from the royal offspring of Judah, is also a judge, so the book of Ruth shows in fact a continuity between "judgeship" and kingship, and this serves to legitimate the latter.

Thus, there is an unaccomplished kingship in Elimelech, from the family of Boaz. *Eli-melech*, "My God is king," in his tragic destiny, leads us to an understanding of the beneficial kingship established by Ruth, who redeems Elimelech's unfulfilled family. Elimelech was, in fact, very rich, and it was not so much to escape famine that he left the land of Israel as to avoid helping the poor. He thus represents the failure of a type of kingship as a principle of narcissistic power and not of gift giving, for this can only lead to destruction (his children, Kilion, meaning destruction, and Mahlon, meaning sickness, die childless, and Naomi is left alone and without possessions). In the passage that is the world, this proud confidence is destined to fall apart, leaving only the remains of what was, the remains that Elimelech would not relinquish: "the woman remained of her two children and her husband" (Ruth 1:5); "full I left, and empty Yʜwʜ made me return" (1:21). In sum, Elimelech's family has to learn *hesed*, grace. And this is precisely what Ruth embodies, asserting from the outset not power but withdrawal and grace. She goes even further than what justice, strictly speaking, requires of her, first by staying with her mother-in-law and then by seeking the levirate when she does not really have a close relative from whom she can demand it.

Ruth personifies the giving that transcends rigor. As a stranger, a widow, and a poor person, she is naturally akin to the Levite, who "has no portion or inheritance as you do, and the stranger, the orphan, and the widow who are at your door" (Deut. 14:29). Ruth gives but she also solicits, pushing the other to step out of the confines of *din* (rigorous justice). Boaz is not *obliged* by law to marry her, and he asks his workers to deliberately let sheaves fall for her, which the law also does not require him to do. David's kingship is not derived from power and violence; it proceeds from the gentle steps of a stranger treading on the wheat of Bethlehem and begging for sustenance. The king in Israel stands "at the corner of the field" alongside the Levite, the widow, and the orphan, who live off "forgotten" leftovers from the harvest ("When you harvest your land, do not destroy/finish the corner of the field,"[237] Lev. 23:22). And of course this grace and this gift bring a benediction in return. The "house of food" that is Bethlehem at last opens to give its resources, and Ruth benefits from this bounty. "Come hither (*halom*) and eat"; "she ate to her fill and had some left over" (Ruth 2:14), and "what she had left over after eating her fill, she gave to Naomi" (2:18). Ruth has reached a place (hither) where there is bounty and leftover. For the commentary, the place designated by "hither (*halom*)" always refers to kingship.[238] When God says to Moses, "Do not come closer to here (*halom*)" (Exod. 3:5), he is ruling out kingship for him, since Moses is a Levite. This place of bounty is at once terrifying

237. This corner of the field is like the unfinished corner of the world that is left for man to build.

238. Rabbi *Elazar* sees an indication that the house of David will spring from Ruth, because this house is called *halom*, here, as it is written: "Then King David came in and sat down before God and said, Who am I, my Lord, Yʜwʜ? And what is my house, that you brought me here (*halom*)?" (II Sam. 7:18)—a place where bounty relieves poverty, a place no doubt frightening to behold.

(the burning bush) and gentle (a voice speaks from it, and the fire does not consume it), but one can reach it only by self-concealment, self-limitation, and giving. It is the place of the between-sacrifice of the Covenant between the Pieces, when the promise of possessing the land of milk and honey assumes its full significance.

To Naomi, who asks, "Have I more (*od*) sons for me?" (Ruth 1:11), the answer is "thus God will add (*yosif*)" (1:17), "God will pay/accomplish (*yeshalem*) your action, and your payment will be accomplished (*shlema*)" (2:12). Naomi has come to understand the lesson of Elimelech. "She then arose... to repent for/return from the fields of Moab, for she had heard (*shama*) that God had remembered his people to give them food" (1:6). It is from this memory of God, the memory of the bounty beyond famine, that kingship springs, as if the king called God back to earth, recalling not his power but the withdrawal, the gift giving, and the concealment from which the world is born. This testimony has a public thrust, as we can see when Boaz, to accomplish the levirate commandment, calls upon the people to bear witness, for in kingship it is effectively the people who are concerned. Kingship enables the people to redeem themselves, to enact their concealment. The son whom "God gave" (4:13) to Ruth and who heralds the figure of the Messiah, through David, is like the shimmering of the one inside the dwelling, the augment produced by the retreat.

The king is therefore a figure of bounty for the collectivity. Its genesis plots the path that society takes in seeking the bounty that will deliver it from scarcity. Naturally, for Boaz, the "woman who is coming into your house" is blessed with the qualities of Rachel and Leah, "both of whom built the house of Israel" (Ruth 4:11), and hence with the entity of Israel whence sovereignty emanates. If Leah precedes Rachel chronologically and narratively, here, in the blessing, it is Jacob's beloved Rachel who comes first; Rachel, whose long-awaited child is Joseph, meaning "he will add"; Rachel, who is the heart of the house where the increase is manifested and who is, moreover, buried in Bethlehem, where the story of Ruth takes place (Gen. 48:7).

And so Ruth, the mother of kingship, is given equal weight to the entire house of Israel, with its twelve tribes. Isn't her name mentioned twelve times in the book of Ruth?

The sovereignty to which Ruth gives rise is marked as much by the absence and void of strangeness as by the astonishment of overplus and augment. A similar problematic is at work in the choice of Jerusalem as the seat of the kingship and of divine presence. Since Jerusalem belongs to no tribe in particular, it comes in addition to the total count. Absent from the tribes and superadded to them all, it is chosen in relation to David, born from Ruth: "From the day I took my people out of the land of Egypt, I did not choose a city from among all the tribes of Israel in which to build a Temple where my Name would be, nor did I choose a man to be a ruler over my people, Israel. I chose Jerusalem for my Name to be there, and I chose David to rule over my people, Israel" (II Chron. 6:5–6).

The Royal Function

Hence, the royal function is paradoxical. It is at once exterior to the collectivity of Israel by the recurrence of the strangeness in its origins and that by which the strange collectivity of Israel accomplishes its interiority, its concealment in the world. At bottom, it is a technique of concealment by way of which the status of people is established, not through a hierarchic procedure but through a process of voiding. It's the king (or, in other words, the civic power) who, by the absence to which he testifies at the heart of the collectivity and by his strangeness, assembles the people (the citizens). The king is the locus of resonance, the empty space where each individual can find a place without taking it from another, where all can gather without limitation to the number of places, and in which all can see themselves. The image of Ruth gleaning in Boaz's field is symptomatic of the royal function: she "gathers" the ears and unites them into a "bundle," like the king who gathers the children of Israel one by one and unites them to form a single "bundle." The king gathers the "ears of grain" like a gleaner, like a poor person who feeds himself from "leftovers," from the surplus graciously left behind, and not like an owner who appropriates the harvest.

There are two ways of gathering: accumulation on the one hand, a "florilegium" on the other, where what is gathered is not accumulated but is tied together one by one, in the gift. Bent over the ears of grain, the gleaner king goes looking for the children of Israel in the void of the *olam*, one by one, like the shepherd from the Song of Songs who follows "the tracks of the flock." The figure of the gleaner[239] is echoed in an exact parallel by the figure of the shepherd. The latter walks behind his flock, and his sheep do not see him; they can even walk far ahead of him in all directions. What makes him the shepherd is precisely that he knows how to walk behind his flock, to find it by following its hollow tracks in the earth. And he knows

239. The verb *kanes*, enter, which yields *knesset*, also means glean.

not only how to follow its trail but also how to identify it and especially, when it comes to gathering it all together, to have an idea as much of the whole flock (*eder*, from the root *he'ader*, which designates absence) as of each animal. Such is royal knowledge, a knowledge of absence, an ability to read the people's absence, one by one, and not as a mass.

David, the shepherd and son of a foreign gleaner, is the perfect embodiment of such royalty. Humility, reserve, waiting, and a giving life are shared by both figures of royalty, the gleaner and the shepherd, the one characterized by the relationship to the land and to the inanimate, the other by the relationship to *nefashot*, the animate, animality, and transhumance in the world. We are dealing here with two parallel problematics: the leftover (for the land) and the track (for the animate). In the established world of the polity, where all the illusions of positivity and of accomplishment in the *olam* can be played out, the king provides an echo of sorts to the void, the wilderness, passage. He puts the world and the collectivity back into movement in the passage, to the one. Isn't he himself a herald, the "one" in relation to all, to each and every individual?

By his knowledge, the king, like sovereignty, is equal to the task of "handling" the Torah. Isn't the Torah what was left when God, "proprietor" of the world, withdrew at the end of the harvest, what Israel receives in grace in the posture of Ruth? And what remains if not letters, signs, the tracks of divine passage in the *olam*? The king closely follows the tracks left by this passage and gathers the traces to arrive at an idea not of the all but of the one. In its voiding, the track, whose sign is the letter, is as much the memory of the disappearance of the king of the universe as the memory of the collectivity continually dismembered by the passage of generations (doesn't the king hold the thread of a genealogy[240] that unites them all?). Thus we understand why the book of Ruth ends with "Now these are the generations of Peretz…" (4:18). This is why one of the most important functions of the king, the one that makes his sovereignty, is the obligation, on the one hand, to duplicate for himself a copy of the Torah kept by the priests, a *mishneh Torah* (duplicate of the Torah) from which he is to read "all the days of his life, so that he will learn to fear Yнwн, his God, to keep the words of this Torah and perform its decrees" (Deut. 17:18), and, on the other hand, to read it to all the people assembled together at the end of the sabbatical year. The king reads, and does not comment, from a copy, and not from the original, because the original (31:26) and the commentary (31:9–10) are the responsibility of the Levitical

---

240. Genealogy is the greatest contribution of kingship to the collectivity.

tribe. Royal power thus partakes in the secondarity of the human condition in its relationship to God (remainder and trace), in the void where human beings stand in relation to divine plenitude.

Indeed, the reading of the Torah before the assembled people is the best vehicle for this experience. In this relationship, one person alone reads and is listened to by each individual in particular in a listening that makes the unity of the assembly, internally and externally, an immaterial unity forged not from physical bonds but from a passage, the text passing by eyes and ears, the passage of the world carried by the voice, "the voice of YHWH on the waters..., the voice of YHWH in power, the voice of YHWH in majesty" (Ps. 29:3). And this reading comes at a very special moment, during the festival of Sukkot when, after the harvest, the people of Israel are obliged to leave their dwellings, come to Jerusalem on a pilgrimage, live in temporary shelters, and offer a sacrifice. So this is a moment when, amid possessions, one experiences the frailty of the world and the passing of the being. In such circumstances, the public reading becomes a political institution of utmost significance, whose social importance comes just behind the sacrifice, an experience in the gratuitous and the void of the world whose only hope resides in the one.

Royalty is the dimension of memory in the assembly of Israel (memory of the one), straining in the passage between the all and the one. What makes for its frailty also makes for its permanence. It may happen that it is forgotten, that it is blotted out. In the parable of the trees that give themselves a king (Judg. 9:6–15), one after another, the richest trees (the olive tree, the fig tree, and the grapevine) refuse the royal privilege, because none of them wants to give up the source of their interior richness, which, in their case, is the sap of their fruit. None will agree to exteriorize itself, to giving. And, in essence, this is the figure of Elimelech. Ultimately, they turn to the poorest of trees, the buckthorn, which bears no fruit and offers no shade. And it accepts. If the choice is made in good faith, it will shelter them, transported by the gift of its poverty to shade-providing luxuriance. But if it is made in bad faith, fire, not shade, will emanate from it and consume the other trees. In sum, it is solely in truth that royal poverty effects grace and benediction and is reversed into bounty.

The king is in a state of overplus. The original state of kingship (of power in general) is that of the regime of Judges, in which there is no king, where strangeness has no place, and the assembly of the people of Israel has difficulty staying together. Everyone is off in his own corner reading. There is no sovereignty. The Hebrews ask Samuel for a king in order to be "like all the *goyim*" (I Sam. 8:20). What does this expression mean from our perspective? Simply that the Hebrews want strangeness in themselves in order to come together, that they want to institute *gerut* in themselves, that is to say, the Hebraic principle of sovereignty. Far from seeking to abandon divine kingship, as a straightforward reading would lead us to believe, they are looking to establish it in their very bosom. And after Saul's failure,[241] Samuel turns to David, a descendant of Ruth. The judgeship and kingship models are to be seen in a developing, chronological, and not antithetical relationship. The regime of Judges is followed by kingship, which is a more accomplished model of collective being, the return of the one in the initial dispersion of *olam*, the first step toward the one.

KING AND LEVITE

The royal figure has a classic Levitical thrust. The Levite points to an echo of passage and transhumance in the world of rootedness and property that is associated with the king. However, it is even in its very institution that royalty echoes the Levitical principle, when the king recopies his duplicate of the Torah from its Levite holders. When he gathers ("harvests") the people around his reading, isn't the reading itself an offering taken away from his harvest, an offering to God as the first fruits of souls? Isn't the aim of gathering these people, this *am*, to "make *eda*," to withdraw into testimony a portion of the collective being so that, from that point on, the external gathering becomes an interiorized community? In this respect, we are at the very gates of Leviticism.

The legitimacy of kingship is based on a deeper, greater, and subtler legitimacy than that of the Levitical authority. The king draws on the Levitical source to establish his power, which emanates from the people. Sovereignty in Israel resides in a procedure that moves from *am* to *eda* in which the king is the key actor. Indeed, if the king issues from the people,[242] he is consecrated by Levitical unction, drinking as he does from the spring of the

241. Saul, a Benjamite, is a descendant of Rachel and from the same family as Joseph. Why was this trial with Saul necessary before coming to David? Samuel tries to institute the throne first in Joseph's house, because Joseph embodies the principle of royalty, as we will see below, but this principle cannot be put into effect. It is Judah who is the effectuation of kingship.

242. The people asked for a king, but they did so from Samuel.

Torah, of course, but also and especially from the removal, from the real absence-in-the-people represented by the Levite tribe (deprived of land) to produce presence throughout the people. We have seen that the *am* cannot survive if it does not "make *eda*." Leviticism is a "detour" by which the *am* can do so, so that in the background behind the king, who seems at first glance to make the *eda* possible, stands the Levite who withdraws. The Levite is the supreme *ger* in Israel, but a passive form of *ger* in a way that is not put into effect, because the effectuation is not the Levite's responsibility. It is the people who awaken the Levite by soliciting a king. This explains why the Hebrews did not immediately ask for a king. The Levitical authority is the first to be established, but a time comes when it does not suffice to govern; a higher stage in the development of the collectivity comes when it must help produce what is expected of it—namely, royal power, whose vocation is this effectuation.

In the Hebraic sovereignty, there are two functions, or rather, two modalities of being or, better yet, a movement that swings from one pole to the other or, yet again, a movement of effectuation. What does this movement consist of? The *am* formed in exteriority effects concealment to establish a bond. This concealment, as we have seen, is accomplished by means of a setting apart from and within itself: a gift, an offering. The Levite tribe is this portion set apart and consecrated to God, "Yнwн's portion" (Deut. 32:9). In the secrecy of this concealment resides the essence and principle of the collectivity. But it has to be put into effect; the *am* has to move toward the *eda* to "breathe" and come to life. Every so often, due to the passing of time and generations in the *olam* and accidents of individuals (sins!), it has to replenish itself from the life pouring out of the removed portion, and to regularly renew its concealment. Otherwise, the *am* withers and disintegrates like a living organism that is no longer irrigated.

The king is the vehicle of this rapprochement, this interiorization, which is possible only because the Levite is already secretly there, waiting. The king is king only after he has gone out of the people, entered into the Levitical portion, and come out again to and for the people; this is the function of the unction of separated oil.[243] Only then is he a king, which means that from that point on he puts the sovereignty of Israel into effect, making it actual. Levite and king serve as vectors in the relationship of the *am* to the one, a relationship to the strangeness at the bottom of being. We already know why

243. The king is anointed using the essential oil of the olive, whose internal strength is extracted in the process of transforming the olive from solid into liquid.

there is such a need for the being that is in the *olam* to be "rejuvenated" and interiorized. Sovereignty in Israel is effectual from the perspective of the *tikkun* of exteriority, its ransom, its redemption. Now we can better grasp the "Levitical" dimension of this *tikkun*, but Leviticism is ineffective without the vector of kingship.

This dual system was already manifested when Jacob was about to go back into the land of Israel and, before doing so, as we have seen above, he divided his family into two camps; "he divided the *am* that was with him," into "the one camp," and "the camp of the rest" (Gen. 32:7–8). The "one camp" passes and may be attacked by Esau, and the remaining camp is described in a reiteration as being "for remaining," the term employed this time, *pleta*, connoting flight and refuge. This foreshadows the system of *eda* and *am*, all the more so in that the separation occurs in the crossing of the Jordan (32:11), in the access to the Promised Land, and in the perspective of *tikkun* ("I will redeem [*kappara*] his face with this gift that is deployed before me [the herds], and afterward I will see his face, maybe I will find favor in his eyes," 32:21). Insofar as we are dealing here with the land of the one, the expected order has been reversed, and the camp of the one passes before the camp of the rest, yet it is clear that the camp of the one represents the *eda*, divided off from the assembly, and that this makes the *am* appear as remaining; all the more so in that, paradoxically, the "camp of the rest," the *am*, seemingly presented as an expedient, figures in the context of "flight," disarray, and decomposition, which are intrinsic to the *am*. The camp of the one is the Levitical camp, and the camp of the rest embodies the royal sphere. Thus the portion set apart is revealed first (offered as a gift), when usually in the *olam* it is the remainder that comes first. The concealment is accomplished here, but its order is reversed, because Jacob is crossing over to the other bank of separation. What does this tell us about Jacob and his relationship to Esau? Does it reveal a failure on his part? And through Esau is Jacob addressing God?[244]

The duality in the figures of sovereignty is not to be seen as a dualism or an opposition. It is a system of completion, two interconnected aspects of the same being. The Song of Songs speaks of the male, *shlomo*, Solomon, and the female, Shulammite, and the entire relationship aims at generating *shlemut*, completion or wholeness: "what will you see in the *shulammit* (the complete one)?" (Song 7:1).

244. Many elements in the text support this idea.

Is not the Aramaic word for the succession to the throne "*mashlama-nuta*"? The preeminent king was called Solomon, meaning "the successor," the substitute for the king. The "complete" one is the one who comes afterward. This we already know: the Levite seems to come after the king, in the immediacy of the world, but he actually precedes him, inasmuch as the *olam* is what he is (hidden). The two terms are not interchangeable, but they stand in a systematic relationship with one another through the problematic of augment and retreat.

The Levites are set apart from Israel: this is what builds Israel's dwelling, and it is through them that Israel gathers together. They are like the house where God receives men—whence the Levites' "cosmic" role in the Temple—but this house is also where Israel receives God. In other words, it is through the Levite that there is presence in Israel, that there is *eda*. From the point of view of the *am*, the Levite is absent and gone, but, as we have seen, the Levite constitutes an increase in being for the *am*. Set apart from the *am*, the Levite is in augment in and like the *eda*. The king dwells in the retreat of the *eda* in the *am*. He emerges from this withdrawal to "repair" it, by symbolically carrying the *am* toward the withdrawn *eda*. The king enables Israel to dwell and be present in the abode that has been built in this way.

From the standpoint of the *am*, the king "adds" to the people, but only insofar as he presents himself at the gates of the Temple and walks toward the Levite, where he receives the unction. The king is the effectiveness of the Levitical withdrawal or, if you prefer, the benediction in return harbored by the offering, by the portion consecrated to God, by strangeness, the effectuation of the augment secretly harbored in Leviticism. The Levite is inside sovereignty, the king outside; but they differ and stand apart from one another. Each is the other's *ger*, and both are *gerim* in the people: the Levite because he is inside, cut off from the exteriority where the people are, and the king because he came out of the *goy*, came in from outside. The king's finality-for-the-inside is more apparent than the Levite's finality-for-the-outside; this is due to the fact that the Levitical power is "passive" and the royal power is essentially active, abrupt, and nimble; King David dances (I Kings 15:29) "like the dances of the double camp" (Song 7:1).

The Function of the Two Powers

In sum, the *am* is in the retreat, in the situation following the withdrawal; it is a remnant of the withdrawal. The *eda* is the retreat, which from the viewpoint of the retreat where the *am* is found, is in augment. And each of these figures of sovereignty "handles" this situation that mainly defines its function. In this regard, it is important to specify the inherent twofoldness of each function. The Levitical function is split into two secondary functions: the *kohen*, in charge of priestly tasks, and the Levite, properly speaking, who does not make sacrifices.

The royal function is split between the Sanhedrin (the assembly of the heads of the people and the tribes), which acts as senate and tribunal,[245] and the royal figure himself, the king. This twofoldness is highly significant. If the complex of royal and Levitical functions is undergirded by the principle of the *eda*, the system of their institutionalization and practical effectuation is based on the principle of the *am*, of exteriority. The king and the Levite as people symbolize in the assembly the people's unity in concealment (the interiority in exteriority). They come close to the one because they are in the one. The priest and the Sanhedrin are in the lack, in the wake left by the retreat. They oversee retreat and lack; the king and the Levite oversee augment and presence. When it comes to effectuating the two principles, there is a kind of reversal of terms. The priest (*kohen*), who comes from the Levite tribe, oversees the *am*'s lack: through rituals and sacrifices he helps redeem the people in lack and at fault. Thus, the Sanhedrin, lodged in the lack, undertakes the *tikkun*, the concealment of the society and the people left in the lack. For this purpose, it endeavors to lodge itself in the trail left by the *eda*'s retreat, given, of course, that both are architects of the unity, presence, and sovereignty in Israel that already appear in the king and the Levite. The king brings together the people (for peace or war) and reads the Torah; the Levite sings in the Temple, comments on the Torah, and pronounces decisions about laws and judgments (Ezek. 44:24).

As we see, the Levite is entirely in retreat and interiority; he does not read the Torah in public. When it comes to pronouncements on the law, the Levite is in a passive position, making them only when the *am* manifests a need for them on the occasion of a problem or disagreement. The law as a principle is already set down in the Torah. All further pronouncements are a matter of jurisprudence, depending on the event and accident. The *am* must elicit it for the legislative power of the Levite to be exercised. In fact, the Levite, like the *kohen*, is in the passive modality of sovereignty, but the *kohen* is more directly involved with effectuation; he is the one who sanctifies

---

245. "There was in Jeshurun a king in the meeting of the heads of the people together with the tribes of Israel" (Deut. 33:5).

society.[246] Nonetheless, there is passiveness in the *kohen* too. Besides the perpetual sacrifices that he regularly accomplishes, he offers expiation (*kappara*) sacrifices upon the sinner's behest, sacrifices generated incidentally by the existence of the Temple. The same is true for the active power in the *am*, the Sanhedrin, which is also more directly involved in effectuation, insofar as it organizes society. But there is passiveness in it, too. The laws come to it from the *eda*. There is also a series of intersecting relationships. The *kohen* (the active force in Leviticism) performs sacrifices, but the king (the "passive" force of the *am*) is prohibited from doing so. Consequently, the *kohen* is the one who, in the sacrifice, "dominates" the *am* when it seeks to approach the one; the king, in this area, takes a backseat.

If, on the essential level, it is the king who brings the *am* closer to the *eda*,[247] on the practical level (in an appropriate swing of the pendulum), the *kohen* is the one who implements this rapprochement (through ritual and the *korban*). In parallel, if the Levite comments on the law and makes legal decisions when asked, the Sanhedrin is the body responsible for applying the law and judging. So, on the essential level, the Levite brings the *am* closer to the *eda*, but the Sanhedrin implements this rapprochement on a practical level (by overseeing the material aspects of daily life in society and by its judgments).

Why this division that leads to a power that stands on a quadruple foundation: the four legs of the throne, the "four camps" of Israel, the four camps of the divine presence corresponding to the four letters of the Name? Is it simply based on a division between a practical pole and an essential one, with the Levite and the king on the essential side, and the priest and Sanhedrin on the other? The pivot is actually situated between secrecy and the manifestation of presence or, more deeply, as illustrating that the inner logic at work in the overall system of retreat and augment is also at work in each of its parts.[248]

The *kohen*-king and Levite-Sanhedrin relationships are to be comprehended in terms of retreat and augment, as the secondary expression of the great system: Leviticism-kingship. This system is synthesized in the figure

246. The *kohen* is *gevura*, the heroism that characterizes the world of *din*, rigor, since he performs the sacrifice (although he does so only for *hesed*, grace). The Levite is *hesed*, but he is so only by the overplus of *gevura*, just as music (which belongs to the Levite's world) is grace, made possible only by hard, rigorous work with instruments.

247. Thus it makes sense that the Temple was designed and built by the king.

248. This means that the system of augment and retreat is at work in both the augment and the retreat.

of the prophet, who opposes both the priest and the king and combines the two extremes of the system, the Levite and the Sanhedrin. The prophet gives voice to the Levite's criticism of the *kohen* and the people's criticism of the king. He is the episodic agency of unity. The priest-king relationship is at once the most tangible and the most symbolic, the most visible and the most antithetical. Through his acts, the king brings about the effectiveness of the priest. In them, opposite movements intersect; what's more, their functions are highly personalized.

LAW IN SOVEREIGNTY

This institutional formalization makes Hebraic sovereignty appear profoundly differentiated. In a sense, it cannot be adequate to itself, because it cannot be reduced to a totality. When unity is manifested in it (notably through the prophet, who is, logically, exterior to its four-power structure), it is the result of a process with multiple interconnections and not of the transparency of a smooth, straightforward entity. Such a sovereignty cannot be "represented," since this would presuppose a totality. It gives rise not to an abstract universal but to manifold particular relationships (the four figures); and it is constituted entirely by these interconnections and relationships, in multiple sequences that settle into layers and moments. If an articulation is missing or fails (for whatever reason, including misconduct), sovereignty in its fullness fails. The diversification within it compels the all-presence to go through periodic *clair-obscure* moments of absence and passage.

The principle that governs sovereignty is secrecy and concealment, not exposure. The purpose of all the analyzed mechanisms is to maintain the secrecy in development and hold back the exposure in manifestation as much as possible. The appearance of any figure of sovereignty is always accompanied by the disappearance of one of the other figures. Any plus is the product of a minus. This ultimate dimension of secrecy resides, of course, in the figure of the Levite, hidden behind that of the *kohen*. The Levite ultimately harbors within him the essence of sovereignty and is its inexhaustible source. This is not to be read as a dynastic privilege, but what is especially important to retain is that the Levite is the guardian of the Torah and the laws. He is so at the same time as the Sanhedrin, and thus the two extremes in the system of sovereignty are entrusted with responsibility for the laws. God gave the Torah "to the *kohanim*, the sons of Levi, the bearers of the Ark of the

Covenant of YHWH, and to all the elders [senators][249] of Israel" (Deut. 31:9). The king himself writes his copy of the Torah from the copy given to him by the "*kohanim* Levites." Note that the *kohen* takes precedence over the Levite, for it is the *kohen* who is more manifest. Coming like the king from the *am*, the *kohen* is the prerequisite for reaching the Levite.

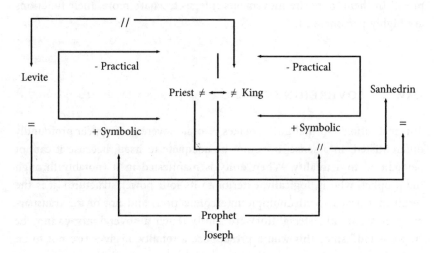

There is a void at the core of Israel's sovereignty, a self-absence, a foreignness to which the Levite's strangeness within the people bears witness and that makes it impossible for the people to ever be completely self-possessed. There are laws in its bosom that come from the Sinaitic revelation. And isn't the law precisely what enjoins me to come out of myself as sameness and to take into account the other (God or my fellow man) in my own conduct? Foreignness is lodged at the core of identity. Not only are the people not responsible for writing the laws (although they can be said to be responsible for the jurisprudence), but they are not even guardians thereof, and neither is the king. At the core of the polity, the laws embody strangeness. They come from elsewhere. And they are the very locus of presence: "In the place that YHWH, your God, will choose to have his Name dwell, there you shall remember that you were a slave in Egypt, and you shall observe and do these laws" (Deut. 16:11–12). And the commentary tells us that when it is said

---

249. The members of the Sanhedrin.

that "the master of the house will present himself before God" (Exod. 22:7), God is referring to the laws and the judges.

The laws precede Israel's sovereignty; they precede the very existence of the people and are greater than it. They precede, therefore, the state and the ruling power. Indeed, they are given in the wilderness, hardly the most propitious place for a people to live. This void at the heart of sovereignty demonstrates that the collectivity of Israel is not founded on a tautology. It does not exist in itself, or rather its existence is not adequate to itself. Between it and itself stand the laws. And power is forged on the basis of these laws as sovereignty ultimately emanates from them. It is from them that the augment, *yosef*/Joseph, emanates in Israel's being, and this is the overriding principle of sovereignty. After all, doesn't the kidnapped Joseph vanish for so many years in Egypt that he is thought to be dead? The fact that all the brothers are in league against him shows that he embodies sovereignty over all of Israel (and perhaps his journey in Egypt is the journey of the one in the multiple that is sovereignty, a loss accomplished in overplus).

It is from this force that the prophet draws the unity of the system, which he echoes within it. In comparison with the dynasties of Levi and Judah, the "dynasty" of Joseph embodies the overhang of sovereignty embodied in the law. Isn't Joseph known as "the righteous" for this reason? He is at the foundation of global sovereignty. This is why in the wilderness the Hebrews transported an ark containing Joseph's bones alongside the Ark of the Covenant containing the Torah. They carried with them in this way the principle of sovereignty and collectivity, without which Moses could not have governed. We can now see why Ruth is blessed first in the name of Rachel, Joseph's mother, before Leah, whom Jacob married first.

Nevertheless, this principle of sovereignty can be effective only under the dynasty of Judah. Joseph cannot put sovereignty into effect, just as the prophet cannot govern. Both participate in the augment—the guarantee and fountainhead of the whole system. Moreover, unlike the Levites and kings, Joseph did not give birth to a dynasty. He is the paragon of the political but outside it. When Samuel wanted to name a king, he turned first to Saul, from the tribe of Joseph's brother Benjamin, but the kingship was a failure until he turned to David. When the kingdom of Israel was established as a separate kingdom opposed to Judah, it too was doomed. This is always the danger threatening Joseph, that he gives in to embodying sovereignty when he is but its principle and fountainhead.

The strangeness at the heart of Israel's being is not a pure, debilitating, and consumptive vacuity. It is inhabited by laws, which are like the abode of God or the other, the abode of the one among men. Israel is Israel by virtue of its laws. In the end, the *gerut* in Israel testifies to the existence of a text at the core of the nation, a text that is the foundation of its institution in the passage.

We can understand why such sovereignty (under the auspices of the one) lends itself to the emergence of only particular figures, not abstract, anonymous entities, as absolute as they are nonexistent. Sovereignty can be contemplated only tied to the Levite's lips, to begin with, but also to the *kohen*'s hands (sacrificing and blessing), the king's arms, the Sanhedrin's legs, or the prophet's heart, as an individual, a particular person, having become the vehicle of the collective and the universal without losing the particularization, the diversified instance of the sovereign that constitutes each one in a vaster relationship.

In this whole system, the Levite represents an important aspect. First of all, let us note the most significant trait of the Levite, that he is outside the confines of the state, which, as we have seen, has no power over the law. The king, like the Sanhedrin, is under the law. No majority can modify the law, although it can decide on questions of jurisprudence in specific cases.

We can see why the law is called *halacha*, meaning "the way" or "the jurisprudence." And what makes these laws special is that, as the Torah shows, they reckon with particular cases and not absolute, general situations that the judge would draw upon and particularize. We go from the particular, the original void of strangeness, to the general before coming back to the particular of the event or accident. Sovereignty's entire path is summed up in the path of the law. At the very heart of the polity and the universal, there is a particularization that opens onto the other, onto the one, and by this very fact escapes man's control, and that is the law.

The Levite is naturally the one who proclaims the law to Israel; this is, in fact, one of Moses' benedictions to Levi's descendants, that "they teach your laws (*mishpatim*)[250] to Jacob and your Torah to Israel" (Deut. 33:10). The effects of this can be seen right away in the Sinaitic episode. Moses has difficulty speaking to the people, particularly because this involves stepping down from the superior stage of prophecy to a lower stage in the diffraction of sovereignty. Since this is the responsibility of the Levites, for Moses it means putting himself in the position of the *kohen*. Note that he never takes the place of the senators in the Sanhedrin. To the contrary, his power is delegated to them. "Gather to me seventy men from the elders of Israel....

---

250. See Maimonides' distinction between *hukkim*, irrational (and hence nonhuman) laws upon which the *mishpatim*, or rational laws, are founded.

I will take some of the spirit (*ruah*) that is upon you to place it upon them. Then they will bear with you the burden of the people, and you will not bear it alone" (Num. 11:16–17). Moses, however, is tempted to take over the function of kingship, which is parallel to that of the Levite in the typical relationship to the secondary principle of effectuation, but God forbids him to add to the priesthood that he already exercises de facto: "Do not come close here" (Exod. 3:5), "Aaron, your brother the Levite... will speak for you to the people" (4:14–16).

From our standpoint, what is significant is the emphasis on the Levite in relationship to Moses the prophet and to Aaron the *kohen*, because Moses and Aaron are from the Levite tribe at any rate. "I will be with your mouth and show you what you will say.... Is there not Aaron your brother, the Levite, whom I designate to speak...? You will speak to him and put the words in his mouth, and I will be with your mouth and with his mouth. He will speak for you to the *am*. He will be your mouth, and you will be God for him" (Exod. 4:12–16). "And Moses went and Aaron, and they gathered the elders of the children of Israel. And Aaron said all that YHWH had said to Moses, and he performed the signs before the *am*" (4:29). If the law (in its concealment) precedes in importance the people that it founds, this very fact makes the people free, because the sovereignty whose core is emptied in this way is less imposing. None of the individual organs that bear and implement sovereignty represents it by itself.

The state is only one of the vehicles of sovereignty for the people, and there is no abysmal face to face between the individual and an impersonal state. In addition, in this system, the people can have its voices heard and participate by the Sanhedrin (or initially the *am ha'aretz*, a Sanhedrin-like parliament) assembling its delegates ("heads of the *am*") and through the royal person, by the multiple and the unique by way of which it is constituted as an *am*.

Insofar as the king is in *gerut*, his kingship houses a certain vacuity, wholly occupied by the people. But doesn't the royal vacuity also express the vacuity of the people,[251] of all peoples? The people, to be forged, conceals within itself a part that forms an *eda*, a portion hidden from sight, which is why the people are always hidden, latent. And the will to "see," to disclose all Israel, as Balaam strove to do, is the will to place it on view and thereby make the *eda*, and hence Israel itself, vanish (Num. 23:9): the will to destroy Israel. Indeed, exposed, without the *eda*, the *am* comes undone. This is why its Levitical strangeness and the strangeness of the king are decisive to the

251. "He who sees populations of Israel should recite the blessing 'Blessed be the Master of secrets, because neither their opinions nor their faces are alike'" (Berachot 58a), yet they constitute a single people. That is the secret.

flowering of its sovereignty, which comes into being as a potential only with the *eda* and comes into effect with the king.

Without the *eda*, the *am* is missing something. It has no law, and it is prey to the erosion of time and space, which tears it limb from limb. The *eda* makes unity dwell in its midst. This is done not by the ideological addition of its limbs but by the (Levitical) setting apart of a portion of its members: in the "body" of the people. There is always a gap, that of its *nefesh*,[252] its concealment, its "absence." The people conceives of its presence to itself only by stepping out of itself in the figure of the Levite, only by the laws and hence by God. The only other way to apprehend itself is through idolatry, which masks absence.

The Levitical function, if it is effective by, for, and in the people, is, however, limited to safeguarding the laws and accomplishing rituals, but the initiative and enactment pertain to the people. The people can always dissociate itself from the *eda* and the laws and choose the path of idolatry. It can disregard the Levitical power: this would be the people's own affair and concern its own condition but would be in no way detrimental to Levitical power as such. Hidden, it would withdraw further and deeper still. It could even sink into oblivion; it would always be there, and the people could always come back to stand before it again. It is the elusive, shifting shoreline offered to the irregular backwash of the waves. The people enjoy the use of a specific arena that could be described as "secular," an arena that could almost suffice unto itself without in any way negating the Levitical arena, which can subsist independently as a pure potentiality never solicited by the *am* that turns its back on it. The golden calf episode exemplifies this situation, but it shows us that such a situation cannot last long, because Israel is a people made by laws. The *eda* always remains too close and the attractive power of the void too great. Thus, the *am* asks Aaron to make the golden calf. We have already encountered such a structure in the *berit*, which contains at once place and void, presence and absence, the one and the multiple. The structure of sovereignty, as we have described it—binding particulars, made neither by mediation nor by representation inasmuch as it fragments totality, founded on concealment and the offering—is the structure of the covenant, binding each figure with God and also with each other (the covenant of the priesthood, Num. 25:13; the covenant of kingship, Ezek. 37:25; the covenant

---

252. The vital "soul," the dynamic, actuated unity of the person. "The *nefesh* of the flesh is in the blood" (Lev. 17:11).

of the people at Sinai, Josh. 24:25; and the covenant of the people with the king, II Chron. 23:3 and II Sam. 5:3).

III. THE 'POLIS' AT THE GATE

Sovereignty structured as an abode maps out a real dwelling place for the community of the covenant, complete with institutions and stages in the passage of the one in the *olam*. Can this dramatic place of meeting and of the exercise of Hebraic sovereignty, this place of assembly for the collectivity, be described as a city-state in the sense of the Athenian *polis*? In this precise sense, the answer is no, which does not mean that the Hebraic *polis* (meaning the spatial, architectural, and territorial forms of the assembly of Israel) has no authentic reality that opens another horizon for human beings.

The whole problem comes from disappearance and passage. Can there be a *polis* type of settlement in the passage? What characterizes the being who is passing is that he cannot be "found" fixed to a place: "...I asked what my *nefesh* loves; I asked but did not find it. I will rise now and roam about the city, the marketplaces, and the streets... I asked but did not find it" (Song 3:1–2). Likewise, Ruth, the stranger, cannot be found in the city, and her arrival with Naomi causes a tumult (*tehom*) (Ruth 1:19), the *tehom* of Genesis (1:2), which submerges the city—a prosaic sign that in the world of *olam*, God cannot be "found." "I saw the whole deed of God, for a man cannot find the deed that was done under the sun" (Eccles. 8:17), regardless of the "efforts" he makes. One cannot "find" presence the way one might stumble across an inert object visible to one and all.

The Hebraic *polis* stands not so much in a cosmic order that determines the human order as in the void of the passage that is the *olam*, where concealment must be woven. This *polis* is built to be a shelter from the world, not to arrest passage but to sanctify/separate it and make it flourish. The *polis* built up in the *olam* is more in interiors than in exteriors; it is gathered into the gesture of Hebraic sovereignty. Already, the *korban* as a foundational act posits a rapprochement (*kerev*) between human beings, their "proximization." One cannot avoid seeing in the sacrifice that opens the way to the seed of Israel—Abraham's Covenant between the Pieces—a kind of charter for a *polis* founded on giving and separating, a paradigm for a city divided into quarters through which one passes to forge an alliance. The multiplication of the passage is nonetheless accompanied by the dwelling of the one, the uncut, undivided but hidden one, like the uncut bird in the story, which is the image of the Temple in the *polis*. Finally, there is a spatial relationship in the separation/sanctification, and hence in strangeness. But this separation—and this is the problem of the Hebraic *polis*—does not display; it hides, for holiness needs a place of concealment and dwelling.

The Limits of the Political

Thus, the sanctification generates the Temple, and the strangeness generates sacrifice. The Hebraic *polis* is the point in time when space flickers and then draws back into the house. This *polis* is on the threshold of the wilderness, not the cool, bright oasis where one can turn one's back on the devouring desert, but the wilderness in the heart of the dwellings. Indeed, in Hebrew there are two types of wilderness: the *shemama*, the devouring desert, and the *midbar*, the wilderness of replenishing passage, inhabited by the spoken word, where the object (*davar*) is fluidified in the word (*davar*) and maintained in passage. There is no opposition between city and wilderness (or country) in the Hebraic *polis*, as there was when Cain founded a city, after his crime, and named it after his son, Hanoch (meaning education or inauguration, Gen. 4:17). To Cain it was as if all of man could be contained in the city wrenched away from the wilderness, which he saw as nothing but desolation (*shemama*) to be fled, a void to be masked. And an entire civilization was established on that basis, since Hanoch's son was named Irat, meaning city. On the contrary, the city in Israel is a way of letting the wilderness dwell in the midst of human beings, letting emptiness and passage be heard in their gathering. This is why, in contrast to the Greek tradition, the Hebraic *polis* does not encompass the totality of existence. The *polis* is not everything. It is but one avenue of the one in the world, one moment, one instant of a much greater gesture that exceeds it in every respect. And consequently the void, the absence, the secret concealment in it constitutes something of a vanishing point of its being.

The *polis* raises a testimonial marker for memory, a sign, a voice passed from one to another: "they made a voice pass in the camp" (Exod. 36:6). This transmission of the voice can take place only in the passage, because the passage is at once the passing of the one in the multiple and the emergence of the multiple. From me to the other, there is passage, and it is in this passage that existence is possible.

This movement is what makes the place (*makom*) that the *polis* merely organizes. After all, what is a city, if not the organization of people circulating, passing smoothly through streets and squares? The *polis* is the higher legal and symbolic organization of the city. At the center of the city stands the Temple, and at the center of the *polis* stands the altar of sacrifices that repay and repair: the *korban*, or rapprochement. As in the biblical narrative, the sacrifice and the altar (of Moriah) come prior to the city. The *polis*, the order of relationships between human beings, or, if you prefer, the *kahal*, comes prior to the monumental city as a relationship of objects in space. After all, doesn't the *kahal* begin in the wilderness of Sinai? And the Hebraic *polis* has gone through historical times when it had no city, when the city of Jerusalem was destroyed.

The *polis* is greater than the city in Israel. This can be read in the very terminology for city, the *ir*, which connotes opacity (the term is close to blindness, *ivur*, and skin, *or*, which hides reality and must be circumcised). In this sense, Jerusalem is a city of the separate/holy, without nakedness (*irum*), given not to "the uncovering of skins (*giluy arayot*)"—that is, to incest—but to concealment; it is a meandering city with shade, plants, and inner courtyards where interiority and entry (*kenes*) are possible because we have freed ourselves from that which masks them. It's a city where one can "see God": "after my skin of blindness has fallen, I will see God from within my flesh" (Job 19:26). This fallen skin is the circumcision. The possibility of seeing God is included, in embryonic form, in the city in general. In *ir*, city, there is *er*, awakening, and if one knows to turn away his gaze and hide his face (just as "Moses hid his face, for he was afraid to gaze at Yʜwʜ," Exod. 3:6, during the revelation at the burning bush), then, through this awakening, one can see God and know the light (*or*), which is a skin (*or*) where light appears, when the eye (*ayin*) is closed.[253]

This is why the Hebraic *polis* is ravished in inward contemplation, gathered together in the forecourt to the Temple around the *tzelem Elohim*, the image of God's shadow (*tzel*), the oneness of God in secret. The term that would be more apt than *polis* to qualify it would be "abode" or "dwelling." The Hebraic *polis* is the *mishkan*, which usually refers to the Temple and presence but more broadly corresponds to the concept of the *polis*. And it would be more suitable to speak of the desert institution, the *mahane*, or camp, rather than *ir*, for city. The *mahane*, the encampment on the road, in the passage,

253. Written with an *ayin*, *or* means skin; with an *alef*, *or* means light.

is the term used for Israel's abode in the wilderness (Exod. 14:19) or during the crossing of the Jordan (Gen. 32:3) when Jacob divides his people in two.

Two Cities

This latter designation in dual form (*mahanaim*) draws our attention to something essential. What are we to understand from this doubling of the *polis*, a doubling that is also found in the name Jerusalem?[254] We can see in it the process of completion (*shlemut*) that is the very project of *jru-shalem*, the complete city, through the reduplication of sovereignty: Levitical and royal-civil. A space of emptiness and passage opens in a city that is pending, a forthcoming, still-incomplete project, called upon to transcend itself through history but also to maintain an ongoing structural relationship with the one, with withdrawal, with gift giving. In it, there are two stages. The multiple is played out on one stage; the one, on the other. Here unfolds an embryonic story, one that is not yet accomplished, that is in limbo. "Blessed is YHWH out of/from Zion" (Ps. 135:21). "From his place, he turns his face in birth-giving mercy (*rahamim*) to the people who *unify* his Name evening and morning" (liturgy).

The doubling of Jerusalem is a procedure against the temptation of cities to institute and perpetuate themselves in stone and monuments. There is no monument in Jerusalem, only streets and voices running through them. Perhaps this dual dimension in the name of Jerusalem and in its identity is a sign of the text that dwells in its midst and unhinges it from identity as sameness, so that the "city" holds to what is "cited," in a relationship that brings to life a new text, which emerges from itself.[255] It is this "remnant" and retreat that make the being of Israel throughout history.

The Hebraic *polis* thus stands at the crossroads of two cities. It is essentially and paradoxically in the passage; it is centered on passage. The cardinal place where this passage is accomplished and that makes for the fact that the *polis* is passage is *Beit Hamikdash*, the House of Separation—in other words, the Temple, the true heart of the *polis*.

254. And which is found again in the designation of the beloved woman in the Song of Songs, who stands for the community of Israel: "Come back, come back, Shulammite, complete one, and we will have a vision of you. What vision will we see in the Shulammite? Like a dance of the double camp" (7:1).

255. It is precisely in this perpetual readjustment of Jerusalem to the text, of the oral to the written, that the arena of the Hebraic political is to be found, born of reimbuing the *polis* with the wilderness experience again and again (see Trigano, *Forgotten Dwelling*).

In this respect, the Hebraic *polis* is the counterpole of the Greek *polis*, which is entirely centered on the agora,[256] its geometric heart. To be sure, the space in the agora is empty, yet it is exposed. The Temple, for its part, may harbor emptiness, the absence that is the halo of presence, but it is a space of covering and concealment; furthermore, it occupies the symbolic middle of the *polis* but not its geographic, geometric center, where equidistant relationships are established between all. Whereas the Greeks meet on the agora, a place of economic exchange and competition but also of political combat (*polis* and *polemos*), the Hebrews meet for the same purposes in the forecourt to the Temple where they listen to the royal reading or enter one by one to have the priest consecrate their *korban*.

The etymologies of "temple" and "*Beit Hamikdash*" are significant in this regard. The *templum* refers to a cutting off, a section or intersection,[257] a static break in space, whereas the "house of separation" designates a process, a procedure of detachment of the one, which brings everyone, one by one, into the house of sovereignty. The "Greek" temple knows sovereignty only through rupture, through the consecration of a space of sovereignty (full, and with statues!), set apart from the totality of human beings, hovering abstractly above them. The *Beit Hamikdash*, on the other hand, diffuses sovereignty[258] in the one, and the one in the accession of each and every one to sovereignty. Furthermore, the *templum* is a procedure of exclusion (and estrangement), while the *Beit Hamikdash* is a procedure for the rapprochement of the *ger*. Such is the real center of the Hebraic *polis*, not the abstract space of the agora, where only (physical or vocal) force makes it possible to speak out and step out of the anonymous mass and partake in sovereignty. The Greek center (*meson*) represents the collectivity and is where power is deposited. The one who enters it takes hold of the scepter, assumes sovereignty, and speaks: the middle of the city is therefore the site of conflict. The circle in the emptiness of which the Greek *polis* sees itself organizes equal relations (*isoi*) between each and every one, which guarantee the equality and like-ness (*omoioi*) of individuals, based on a reversible identity. This uniform geometric setup is impossible in the Hebraic environment, where individual

---

256. See above, "The Covenant between the Pieces," pp. 79–100.

257. In construction, the *templum* is the rafter or crossbeam; in weaving, it's the wooden crossbar in the loom that keeps the cloth stretched crosswise. In sum, any weaving of concealment constitutes a temple.

258. The traditional way of referring to Jewish states by Temple number is significant in this regard, because it is a way of designating the gist of the Hebraic form of power and sovereignty.

entities are not counted (census taking is prohibited) and where the principle of manifestation is based not on exposure and total light but on the secrecy that produces light and shade.

The Temple and the Agora

The unbearable light in which the agora is exposed creates distance rather than closeness. This is evidenced by the status of the alien, who is allowed in the agora but cannot participate in the collectivity and cannot be part of the circle of power, whereas *gerut* is embedded in the very principle of sovereignty in Israel, and there is "one law for you and for the *ger*" (Num. 15:15). The *kirva* is more powerful in the shade of the dwelling, where the relationship is not one of exteriority and exposure, as it can be in the agora. What one hears on the steps of the Temple is not "rhetorics" as an instrument of political victory, but rather the song of the Levites, the reading of the king, and the commentary on the text. For there to be commentary, there must first be a text, and in it darkness and obscurity that the commentary aims to lift. Conversely, the relationship in the agora is spectacular. The word is staged; it is represented. It has an author. This is why Greek theater is the quintessence of the *polis*, the Holy of Holies. On the steps of the Temple, the word is heard from somewhere else; there is no visible face attached to it. The voice does not "communicate"; it comes from behind the veil and can be heard only when the voice but "speaks to itself" (7:89), that is to say, when it turns its back on the audience, which is the only way to testify to presence, to make presence felt in the interlocutor, to make him blush with presence.[259]

The fact that God is hidden in his communication with man is the very basis of the relationship. This is illustrated by the geographic and solar orientation of the Temple: the Jews bow to the west, toward the setting sun, when they come to the Temple to offer sacrifices, since the Holy of Holies is to the west and the halls of the Temple face east. One enters the Temple from the east and heads west, to the place where God is hidden (behind the veil), toward the setting sun and fading light, toward twilight. This is unusual, as, by and large, members of other religions bow to the east, in the direction of the rising sun, as did the Jews who returned to idolatry and were found "bowing eastward to the sun" (Ezek. 8:16). The "orientation" is

259. See, below, Book II, ch. 6, "The Voice of the Prophetic Sign and Political Ethics"; "The Face in the Voice," pp. 500–515.

thereby reversed: we need shade to behold God, who reveals himself to us in darkness and speaks to us when he speaks in himself.

In fact, God is concealed in the Temple, not absent. In a way, stretching a veil across the Temple puts an end to absence. The veil tempers it. Its very existence testifies to the presence on the other side of a being that is hidden. We veil only what is not exposed to sight. The veil is therefore the strongest testimony in the Temple to the divine presence that the high priest "sees" when he stands before God. That which may seem to separate actually brings together and tempers absence.

A whole relationship to light and being is contained in this reversal of orientation (the "occidentation"). Idolatry cannot bear the eclipse of light and sees nightfall as a tragedy. Israel, on the other hand, turns to this setting sun, the sign of a cosmic, political, and psychological gesture, to look at emptiness and absence in the wake of the divine withdrawal in creation. "Occidentation" follows the being in its passage and does not remain riveted to an Orient that gradually turns to night. It looks instead to the Occident as it gradually turns light until the evening comes to embrace it and it sinks into the night. Night is a moment of the day and of light, and Israel's strength comes from its readiness to accept this and live with it, to follow this disappearance until the return of the sun. In its despair, idolatry uses light in an economy of darkness; it uses darkness (an idol) to prolong the withdrawing light (divine presence).

God is present within the Temple in the manner of the veil that hides the western end of it. "There is no more if not him alone" (Deut. 4:35), which means that all is inside him, in the hidden augment. Everything assumes its place in the perspective of this interiority and from the interiorization stands like an island of strangeness at the heart of the *polis* and is the source of its significance and its principle of direction; it's the center of the compass rose. In other words, it is the one that lives inside and opens up at the heart of a *polis* of exteriority and multiplicity, and the arena of the one is governed by strangeness. This is where I free myself from the weight of objects, from exteriority to myself, from the multiple, the place where the multiple, the reflection of passage, does not stand in the way of my own unification, the place where, one, I appear before and in unity.

As we have seen, this inner unity is not solitary; it is in tandem, in an essential relationship, in a dialogue, and this means it is speech. We saw this in the couple in the Song of Songs and in Ruth. Presence is speech and hence dual, at the very least. The figure of two cherubim on the Ark of the Covenant, from above which the voice speaks, testifies to this. In a paradoxical use of aesthetics at the precise place where all aesthetics ends, this representative figure (the cherubim) diverts attention from the One on the ark, so that man does not reify it. The inner unity is not the solitude of virginal iciness. It is the kiss of love, the conjugal union, and the giving birth to the child. For this reason the loved woman in the Song of Songs brings her beloved into "the house of my mother, the chamber of the one who gave birth to me" (Song 3:4).

Now we can understand better why it is at the bedside of the one, in the forecourt to the Temple, that the Hebraic *polis* stands and the people of Israel gather, at the fundamental place of passage and strangeness. Isn't it called "the gates of heaven"? (Gen. 28:17). And according to the Talmud, this place is big enough to accommodate all the people of Israel, extensible enough to hold them all when they gather on the occasion of the three pilgrimage festivals (Deut. 31:10–13). Such gathering means standing before God, and this is a place not of limitation but of bounty. This is why the Tent of Testimony is the tent of the senatorial assembly, the seat of the government of the tribal federation: "Moses went out [of the Tent] and spoke to the people (*am*), then he gathered seventy men from among the elders [senators] of the *am* and stood with them around the tent" (Num. 11:24).

The Temple is the arena of the political, and not for "theocratic" reasons. It is a decisive trait that characterizes Israel. In every civilization, the political tends to be associated with a place whose nature induces its nature: the seraglio, the agora, and so on. The Hebraic *polis* draws from the wellspring of the Temple, and the people who gather together are a "people of priests" (Exod. 19:6) more than a people of warriors, as in Athens, where, as we have seen above, the term for people (*laos*) originally refers to the army of warriors, and assembling the people (*laon agorein*) firstly means assembling the army on the agora.[260] We can now better grasp the purpose of the Temple and Hebraic society: *korban*, the redeeming sacrifice and not *krav* combat, to organize relationships of closeness (*kirva*) that are not murderous and warring. The "centrality" of the Temple at the heart of the *polis* is the antithetical counterpart to the centrality of the agora in the Athenian *polis*.

We know that at the outset in the Hebraic *polis*, the people (*am*) is obscure and hidden (*om*), that the agora is not the light that seems to flood it, that the *am* needs a *tikkun* of its *nefesh* and must come to the Temple to make an *eda*. In the agora, people are continually passing by, moving in all

260. The circle formed by the gathered warriors delineates a space where public debates are held (see Vernant, *Mythe et pensée*.)

directions, going any which way. It is merely a "junction" scattering people to the four winds. But when you enter the Temple, you enter a place with one name, and you stay in the forecourt, at a distance from the place that you do not approach; you hide your face to keep from seeing and to preserve the strangeness that would be laid bare and totally exposed in the rhetoric on the agora. "There is a place with me... When my Glory passes by I will hide you..." (Exod. 33:21–22). "Do not come close here... because this place is separate ground... Moses hid his face" (3:5–6). In exposure, where the multitude throngs, everything can be counted and divided into smaller units (in the Covenant between the Pieces, Abraham does not cut the bird). The *mishkan* is the process of the one; the Greek *polis* is the process of the all.

In a way, the whole Hebraic *polis* is found assembled in the Temple, in the dwelling place of the Tetragrammaton, where it gives itself as a remembrance. And, conversely, we could read in the four letters, the figure and model of the Hebraic *polis*, the place (God is called *Hamakom*, meaning "the place") of gathering. The unpronounceability of the Tetragrammaton already tells us something of a society whose basis is antithetical to exposure. There is also an interplay between masculine (*yod*) and feminine (*heh*) in it. The Name is what is left of God once he has withdrawn. We can see in the conception of the Name as it has developed in Israel the entire landscape of Hebraic society, its institutional edifice, and its spatial structure. The quadripartite layout, for instance, of the camp in the desert, termed the "camp of the *Shechina*," is based on the quadriliterality of the Name.

The City Gate

"Where is the place of his glory to celebrate him?" (liturgy) designates the Temple, whose *makom* is a bigger place than the locality or a locality inhabited by strangeness: "Blessed is YHWH out of Zion" (Ps. 135:21), a placeless place, which it is no doubt because it is the place of a withdrawal, hence, necessarily an emptied place, opened, not fenced in.

The Hebraic *polis* is not a closed place.[261] It is the opposite of Athens (to which the *ger* is a "barbarian" held in disdain), wholly focused on the agora at its center, its back turned to the exterior. Jerusalem, on the contrary, is

261. When Ruth, personification of the principle of *gerut* and kingship, enters the city of Bethlehem, it is said that "the whole city is plunged into an abyss" (Ruth 1:19), meaning that it is the "all" of the city that sinks into the abyss, a city that was closed until then but opened within itself by the strangeness.

gathered at its outer edges: there is the back of the Temple, where the divine presence dwells, which marks the gates of heaven (but it is behind this back wall that the city geographically begins), and there are the "gates" of the *polis*, where its institutions stand (between the gates of heaven and the gates of men). The entire *polis* hovers "in the air" over this pit, which is none other than the orifice where the blood of sacrifices is spilled, situated under the altar of the Temple—that is to say, the very institution for ransoming and redeeming souls, for the *tikkun* of creation.

This "pit" is not a pit of evanescence and depletion. Nothing is "heavier" than air. "Where is the place of his glory?" Glory (*kavod*) is to be read from its radical *kaved*, meaning "heavy." The place of the *olam*/disappearance is the place of his glory, of the weightiness that the world is for him.

Thus, this glory is naturally a place (*makom*); this weightiness is what makes a place for another aside from God, what gives a place to the other, the upsurge of the birth-giving conception of the other in me. I am a place for the other, and I make a place for myself, too.[262] We have here the whole Hebraic conception of reality: there is the *olam* as disappearance, to be sure, but also the weightiness of place and of the other. It is not so much the opposite of worldliness that characterizes the framework of the Hebraic *polis* as its antithesis: a "light," mobile worldliness, in passing.

This placeless place—which is like an "opening" in the gate, at the threshold of which men gather together, and for which the Temple (the gates of heaven)[263] is the vehicle of efficacy—is instituted within the same framework as the city and the *polis*. We have here the very biblical concept of the "gate of the city," which refers, of course, to the physical doorway that opens the city to the outside, but also to an institutional place where the senators of the city assemble, judicial sessions are held, and public affairs are debated. This gate of men echoes the gates of heaven that are the Temple, and it bears witness to the role of the Temple.

The "gate" in the only city where the Temple stood was located in the Temple courtyard (in the same place as the Sanhedrin, etc.). But how could the *polis* be organized in other cities where there was no Temple, if not upon the threshold and in the passage of the gate, the real gate leading to the exterior but also to the road going to the Temple in Jerusalem? In all the

262. At the beginning of the Amida prayer, one takes three steps back, which signifies that the proclamation of God is accomplished not in an interior time but in the exterior world, by keeping a certain distance in space.

263. Jacob's vision of the ladder, the "gates of heaven," is situated at the center of his vision of the twelve tribes.

cities of Israel, the gate testifies to the Temple in its absence, and the public institutions are situated around the city gates, where the *ger* appears, where the stranger stands, as testimony to the strangeness embedded in a place, which draws its sovereignty from this strangeness.[264]

The gate (*shaar*) is the countermodel of the agora, the model of an open *polis*, gathering around the doorway that opens onto emptiness, onto what lies outside the city, unlike the Greek *polis*, all huddled over itself and its accumulation and turning its back to the exterior. There is emptiness in the agora, but it is an abstract, purely rhetorical emptiness, an emptiness in "spirit," from which the stranger is expelled.

In a way, there are no full-fledged cities in Israel; the only veritable city is Jerusalem, which houses the Temple. The others are cities by delegation from Jerusalem and the Temple. This delegation stands in the *shaar*. In fact, at first, as the tribes settled throughout the country to take possession of their land, the cities seemed to be left in the hands of the Levites,[265] who had no land: "the children of Israel must give towns to the Levites out of their holdings for them to dwell in, and a suburb around the towns" (Num. 35:2). The only instituted cities in the Torah are "Levite cities."[266]

Thus, a structural relationship was forged between the city and the Temple (the gate), at the place where the *ger* comes to enter the city, to be "added" to the citizens already there. There has to be an overplus in the city, a "gate" where the *polis* concretely gathers, but also where the emptiness that empties the city testifies to the possibility that something can be added, that the count is not complete, "counted, weighed, measured." This overplus, which comes from the portion set apart to be given to God and the Levites, "you will set it down in your gates, and the Levite, for he has no portion or inheritance, and the *ger*, the widow, and the orphan who dwell with you will come and eat" (Deut. 14:18).

Overplus, strangeness, and marginality (the widow and the orphan), what partakes in the relationship of giving and receiving—this is the fabric of the city, of citizenship, because herein resides the very spirit of the abode. A city wholly given over to light, where there is no shade to accommodate the other, is a city of hate. There is no place for those who receive, since no one

264. See, for instance, Neh. 8:1–4: "they gathered all the people together as one man on the plaza before the water gate."

265. See, below, Book II, ch. 4, "The Public of Israel: The Levitical Principle in the Fabric of the State."

266. This is implied in II Chron. 6:5: "From the day I took my people out of the land of Egypt, I did not choose a city from among all the tribes of Israel in which to build a Temple where my Name would be."

gives in such a city whose fortified walls have no gates and no openings. The gates in cities outside Jerusalem where giving and welcoming are practiced, and where strangeness has its place, play something of the role of the altar, as "the gates of heaven" (Gen. 28:17), the vehicle of rapprochement between human beings. This is why the collectivity takes shape in this place, but it does so in a very special way, because while the doorway is a passage and an opening, it is also a constriction and a narrowing. Indeed, it is a gate on this condition only.

This narrowing, represented for the assembly of men by the covered passage that is the doorway, seems to contradict the purpose of the passage. But, in fact, all the senses of passage are involved. People enter through this doorway one at a time, or nearly, for the gate leads to the one and to completion. Thus Israel enters alone and one in *knesset Yisrael* and the Temple. This entry as one is what is called "chosenness." Seen from the standpoint of a massive totality in which all is anonymous and there is no "gate" and no giving, such chosenness may seem unjust. But the doorway can let people through only one by one. The only way inside from the outside is one by one, because the one inhabits the interior.

There on the threshold, a reversal of direction takes place. Any doorway is the site of such a reversal (as are cities and, more broadly speaking, societies). The *mezuza*[267] bears witness to this. It is affixed to the doorjamb and kissed with a gesture of the hand that differs depending on whether you are entering or leaving the room (the hand reaches across the body on the way out). We can now see why Korah mocks the *mezuza* when he rebels against Moses and Aaron.[268] He is opposing the Levitical principle of sovereignty, the status of the particular and the one, and hence the very structure of election. Entering presence always involves a process of reversal of interior and exterior. Presence itself is such a process. In the Temple in Jerusalem, the windows were built as if the bright light were inside and were to shine from there onto the outside, as if the inside of the Temple were outside and vice versa (I Kings 6:4). This moment of reversal of direction echoes the reversal of function of the Levite and the *kohen*.

It is in such a place that Israel assembles in an assembly in which it can be present in the one, one by one. It is the "*makom ehad*," the one place or

267. The *mezuza*, which contains biblical verses (the *Shema*—Deut. 6:9), is placed on the doorjamb to the right as you enter a room, positioned at an angle with the upper part leaning to the inside of the room.

268. See the traditional commentary and below, "All Israel and the Prohibition of Census Taking," pp. 367–390.

the "place of the one" (Eccles. 3:20) where all flows together, all the waters of the "rivers" of the world (1:7), and this place is like the sea, which is never "full" and can fill no receptacle. There was room for all Israel in the forecourt to the Temple, even though it was spatially delimited, and no matter the size of the gathered crowd. It is in this way that the assembly of Israel occupies the place: in it, there are many vanishing points, unexpected spaces that enable a people that cannot be counted to spread out over the face of the earth.

Such a people conceives a place appropriate to its nature and is born of it. The place of narrowing that is the gate constitutes, therefore, a procedure of nomination, while the agora is a procedure of anonymization. The assembly of Israel, the people of Israel, emerges from this election of the one. The one is not separation from the other. Just the opposite; it is the vehicle of recognition of the other insofar as it crosses the passage. The one passes through the doorway, which is the path of life and the destiny of man, conceived in the passage and in the framework of which everything is played out, since man is called upon to detach himself from the all and move to the one in the passage. This is why it is said that "your doorway is laid with sin" (Gen. 4:7), for this is where everything takes shape.

It is at the gate that the place of trial for human destiny and for the political is situated, at the place of opening to the one, to the other, to passage. The gate is thereby the most significant and critical place in the power topology of the Hebraic *polis*. Whereas Athens identified the *polis* with humanity, and citizenship with humankind, Israel identifies strangeness with humanity and sees citizenship as but a detour, a decisive detour, to be sure, but neither foundational nor sufficient. The sovereignty of Israel is the fruit of a liberation, the liberation of foreign slaves in Egypt. From this departure, the citizenship in Israel was forged.

CHAPTER 3

The 'Children of Israel':
The Josephic Principle in the Fabric
of the Nation

HOW CAN we inhabit a dwelling where strangeness lives? The twelve-tribe system is Israel's way of inhabiting it. This system is the expression of the Hebraic economy of sovereignty embodied by the house of Israel. A problematic of nationality is established via this model, comprising an organized set of characteristics and modalities of assembly in the house of Israel for all those who see themselves as belonging to the Jewish people. The originality of Hebraic sovereignty is matched by the originality of the benefits and enjoyments of rights that go with it.

The key characteristic of such a system is its indetermination and mobility, because there are twelve tribes but the count is not set once and for all. Indeed, it is not always the same tribes that are counted among the twelve. The Bible gives us several configurations of twelve tribes. The story of Jacob's blessing (Gen. 9) and the long register in Numbers (ch. 26) constitute the two key lists. One includes the tribe of Levi and counts Joseph's tribe as one; the other leaves Levi out and counts two tribes for Joseph's two sons, Menasseh and Ephraim. Then there are other lists, offering slight variations. The song of Deborah (Judges 5) mentions ten tribes, leaving out Simeon, Levi, and Judah, while Joseph's is split in two. Moses' blessing (Deut. 33) omits Simeon and counts Joseph as two. Twelve are mentioned in the story of the birth of the tribes (Gen. 29 and 30), but not the same twelve: Benjamin is not included, since he was born much later in the land of Israel, but Dinah, Leah's daughter, is counted; she will never appear in any other list, and her descendants will not form a tribe, but here, thanks to her, the full specified number of twelve is reached again.

We could interpret these different counts as showing the successive systems of tribal organization during the period of settlement in the land of

Israel.[269] But plausible as such a reading may be, it fails to come to grips with the meaning of the system. If there is a problem, it is mostly because the duodecimal structure seems to constitute a fixed point in the biblical counts, regardless of the modalities of counting. "All these are the twelve tribes of Israel" (Gen. 49:28). It is not that twelve is a magical or mythical number.

To be sure, the number twelve is not devoid of symbolic import,[270] but the significance lies elsewhere. At work here is a whole strategy in the positioning of the components of the nation, which requires elucidation. If we disregard for the moment Jacob's only daughter, the place of Levi and Joseph is the main element of indetermination and fluctuation. Neither figure in the final count: Levi, because he becomes the sacerdotal tribe with no land, and Joseph, because he is replaced by his two sons. Usually, the mobility of the constituent tribes comes from an excess number, an overbounty of sons and blessings that makes the set number of twelve too narrow. The critical element in this situation is the destiny of Joseph's tribe that will count as two, with Joseph surrendering his place to his two sons. The phenomenon is odd: Jacob treats Joseph's sons as his own, and, consequently, Joseph is excluded from the tribes and placed in the position of Jacob—that is, as the father of the tribes.[271] "Your two sons who were born in the land of Egypt before my coming to you in Egypt will be mine; Ephraim and Menasseh will be mine like Reuben and Simeon" (Gen. 48:5).

In fact, in view of this overplus in Jacob's blessing that increases the number of children, if Joseph hadn't stood back and Levi hadn't been removed, there would have been fourteen tribes.[272] If we reckon that Joseph's portion is perpetuated in one of his two sons, then the second son alone[273] is in excess.

269. See Martin Noth, *Das System der zwölf Stämme Israels* (*The scheme of the Twelve*) (Stuttgart: W. Kohlhammer, 1930).

270. The number twelve seems to be imbued with conventional symbolism. Ishmael, too (Gen. 25:13–16), had twelve sons. And in Greece, during the same period, twelve tribes formed an amphictyony, a political and religious association of autonomous tribes around a single place of worship. Then there are, of course, the months of the year, the constellations, etc. Jacob's twelve sons are foreshadowed in Rebecca's cry when the twins, Esau and Jacob, "agitated within her, and she said, 'If so, why am I this (*zeh*)?' And she went..." (Gen. 25:22): the numerical value of *ze* is twelve.

271. And, to take it a step further, Joseph is positioned as his mother's husband, which has the effect of removing Jacob from his position this time.

272. Fifteen, counting Dinah.

273. Following a paradoxical pattern regularly found in Genesis, it is the younger of the two, Ephraim, who obtains the primogeniture from Jacob, much to Joseph's annoyance (Gen. 48:17).

He is the one who makes it necessary to rearrange the count, and it is in his shadow that the tribe of Levi is removed from the final tally, though it will still be regarded as a tribe. Consequently, what we need to understand is the rationality for the mobility of Levi and Joseph (via Ephraim)—in fact, Levi alone moves; Ephraim is added—and their significance for the system as a whole, in which they are key components.

I. THE SUBSTITUTED ELEMENT, OR THE
FAMILY SAGA

A look at the "saga" of Jacob's family can help us see why Levi and Joseph are the protagonists in a perpetual inadequation in counting the tribes and all their names. The system is not purely mechanical and does not anonymously give priority to one tribe over another. The genealogy of this singularization of Joseph and Levi sheds light on the overall meaning of a construction in which equilibrium fluctuates.

The first thing to do in examining the dynamics of the protagonists and the tribes is to look at the matriarchs. Their story is decisive in many respects. The tribes come from the union of Jacob with Laban's two daughters, Leah and Rachel, and their servants Zilpah and Bilhah (Gen. 29). Jacob receives the daughters as wives upon completion of two seven (*sheva*)-year periods of service (upon completion of an oath/*shvua*) that Laban demands from him in exchange. This quadruple union is the outcome of Jacob's thwarted love. From the outset, Jacob wants to marry Rachel, but Rachel is the younger of the two, and, upon completion of the seven-year contract, her father substitutes her older sister, Leah, for her on the wedding night. To marry Rachel, Jacob has to commit himself to an additional seven years of service. With each daughter, Laban also gives a servant, who becomes Jacob's concubine. Having been married under these conditions (substituted for Rachel to an unwitting Jacob), Leah feels less loved and is depicted throughout the story as an unhappy, unsatisfied figure.[274] Whereas the beloved Rachel remains barren and laments her fruitless union, the unloved Leah gives birth many times.[275] The servants intervene in this conflictual rivalry between the two

274. "Yнwн saw that Leah was hated; he opened her womb, and Rachel was barren" (Gen. 29:31).

275. It is interesting to read the names of the two matriarchs in terms of the divine Name. Leah is "without God," *lo*-(Y)H(VH) but her name contains the divine *heh*. Rachel's

sisters, one out of love for Jacob, the other for the sake of bearing a child. Whenever the matriarchs stop bearing children, lest the rival sister gain the upper hand, they give their servants to Jacob so he will have children through them. After the birth of Leah's four sons (Reuben, Simeon, Levi, and Judah), Bilhah gives Rachel Dan and Naphtali. Then Zilpah gives Leah Gad and Asher. Finally, Leah gives birth again (Issachar, Zebulun, and Dinah, the only daughter). Only with the birth of Joseph to Rachel after a long period of barrenness (shared by all the loved matriarchs) is fertility at last joined with love in the union with Jacob. All told, Leah has seven children, six sons and one daughter, and Rachel two, while the servants give birth to two children each. The family saga is one of unfulfilled love; of difficulty in bringing love to consummation; of the long wait until Joseph, the first fruit of love, finally comes, Joseph, who himself heralds the coming of another child ("YHWH adds/*yosif* another son for me," Gen. 30:24), and Benjamin, who will be the cause of the death of the tragic figure of Rachel the beloved.

As if suspended and unable to reach its full potentiality, this love gave birth to two flashes of presence (Joseph and Benjamin) before it died, leaving Jacob, who had seen it shine so little in his lifetime, in a poignant state of inner solitude. The tribes of Israel, embodiment of the fulfillment of Israel's being,[276] are born from unfulfillment: the majority from a woman who was unhappy and hurt (which may not have been Jacob's fault but nonetheless resulted from his excessive love for Rachel coupled with the latter's jealousy and bitter disappointment), and the others from a dissatisfied woman whose happiness was incomplete. In the story of this union, an element is always slipping away, continually being put off until later. They hurry in pursuit of it, fight each other over it, and when finally it comes, the end is already nigh. Benjamin, who is born in the land of Israel, is thus the final culminating point of this pursuit.

We can see why the book of Genesis often divides the tribes with reference to their mothers: "Leah's tribes" (comprising her six sons) and "Rachel's

name has no letters of the Tetragrammaton, but Bilhah's has two. Leah bears God even though she is "Godless." She despairs of his absence materialized in the absence of her "man" ("my man will join me," Gen. 29:34). Thus, all her sons' names evoke a call to the other. All her sons are a call to God: to "see" (Reuben), to "hear" (Simeon), to "join" (Levi), to "praise" (Judah). Rachel demonstrates no such tension. She has difficulty giving birth because God did not remember her. Perhaps this was because she took her father's idols (*terafim*) when she left his home (31:19), although we do not know whether she did so to stop him from worshipping them or to worship them herself.

276. Divine presence (*Shechina*) does not hover over Israel. It does not reside in its midst (*kerev*) until Jacob has twelve sons.

tribes" (Joseph and Benjamin). Jacob divides his camp along these lines before
entering the land of Israel and setting off to confront Esau. First he puts the
servants and their children, then Leah and her children, and then Rachel
and Joseph last, in order of preference. Fearing Esau, Jacob keeps those who
are dearest to him "behind" (Gen. 33:2).

The main imbalance in Jacob's two marriages (Leah's primogeniture in
relation to Rachel) inevitably finds expression in the family saga: the position of the firstborn among all of Jacob's children forms the main plot in
the story. Primogeniture is a key issue throughout Genesis. The social and
symbolic implications of biological primogeniture are systematically annulled,
and the younger siblings inherit the father. Primacy is a matter of effort and
patience, a promise more than a right, an obligation more than a privilege
and a passive pleasure. Only the second knows how much it costs to be first.
It could hardly have been otherwise in the family of the promise, born from
departure and peregrination. Between Leah the firstborn and Rachel the
younger sibling, who will have firstborn status? Reuben, the biological and
numerical elder, should have it over Joseph, the firstborn son of Rachel the
cadet, who is himself the cadet (in patriarchal terms). But what happens is
the opposite, and the whole story of Genesis narrates the accession of Joseph
to firstborn status through a whole series of contrasted adventures, which
are recounted in the many chapters (37–50) constituting one of the major
narratives in Genesis.

Reuben dishonors his firstborn position when, after Rachel's death,
he has sexual relations, legally regarded as incestuous, with her handmaid
Bilhah (Gen. 35:22).[277] In doing so, he exposes his father's "nakedness," as
the expression goes (*giluy arayot*). This incest participates in the conflict over
birthrights in Jacob's family, because in disgracing Bilhah, he makes sure that
Jacob can no longer give Rachel progeny through her maidservant. And, in
fact, Jacob has no more children. Reuben is always seen as the good elder
taking his mother's side and striving to attain the victory of the neglected
Leah's clan (the victory of the firstborn, he and his mother) over Rachel's. It
is through his intervention that indirectly Leah gives birth to her last three
children (Issachar, Zebulun, and Dinah), after Zilpah has borne two sons.
He brings mandrakes, an aphrodisiac fruit with reproductive powers,[278] back
from the fields for his mother, no doubt so she will attract Jacob and conceive

277. According to some commentators (Shabbat 55:2), Reuben did not actually commit
adultery; he laid down on his father's bed, in a symbolic expression of incest.

278. According to the commentators the fruit has a human form.

again (Gen. 30:14). And Rachel, for the same reasons, buys them from Leah in exchange for her granting that night with Jacob (30:15), which probably means that he has been neglecting Leah. Jacob sleeps with her, and "YHWH heeded Leah and she conceived" (30:17).

Simeon and Levi, the two brothers next in line to the biological elder, also show that they are unfit for inheriting Jacob by their wrongdoing, which shames him (Gen. 34). Dinah is abducted and dishonored by Shechem, the Canaanite prince of the city of the same name (future capital of the land of Joseph's children), who is drawn to her beauty. In the hopes of righting the wrong and marrying her, he proposes an alliance with Jacob. Jacob's sons set a condition: that the Canaanites be circumcised and join the covenant of Abraham. They comply, unaware that it is a trick, instigated notably by Simeon and Levi, who take advantage of the indisposition after the circumcision to slay all the males in revenge for their sister's lost honor: "Should our sister be treated like a whore?" (34:31). Simeon has a reputation for violence. According to the Midrash, it is he who contrives the circumcision plot, he who, in his implacable hostility to Joseph, instigates his martyrdom, who proposes to kill him and throw him into the well,[279] and who, together with Levi, sells him. Levi has the reputation of a zealot.[280] This is why Joseph separates Levi and Simeon in Egypt, for zeal joined to violence produces catastrophes.[281] Simeon is the brother Joseph chooses to put in prison and keep there until Jacob's arrival. This is why Jacob's view of Simeon's posterity is fundamentally negative: "Simeon and Levi are a pair; their weapons are instruments of violence. Let not my soul join in their scheme and my honor be a party to their union.... Cursed be their anger, for it was violent, and their wrath, for it was hard; I will separate them in Jacob and scatter them in Israel" (49:5-7). With Leah's first three children rejected, only Judah remains.[282] But here we find a recurrent characteristic in Hebraic sovereignty:

279. Zimri, who defies Moses in the Baal-peor idolatry episode (Num. 25), is said to be a descendant of Simeon.

280. The Levite tribe reacts with equal zeal in punishing the guilty in the golden calf episode.

281. Joseph does so, according to Midrash Rabba (on Exod. 22:26-28), to prevent a massacre.

282. It is striking thereafter to note the extent to which Judah will remain separate from the tribes of Israel grouped together as the "house of Joseph" (see Judg. 1:22; I Kings 11:28; II Sam. 19:21, etc.). David is anointed as king separately "by the senators of Judah over the house of Judah" and "by the senators of Israel over the house of Israel" (II Sam. 5:3). Likewise, when David names Solomon as his successor, he makes him king "over Israel and Judah" (I Kings 1:35). The kingdom of Israel is a united kingdom.

the separation between its principle and its effectiveness. Jacob bestows the
firstborn's blessing upon Joseph, but its effectiveness, the kingship, is received
by Judah. Reuben "was the firstborn, but since he defiled his father's bed,
his birthright was given to the sons of Joseph, son of Israel, though Joseph
did not bear the firstborn title in the genealogy. Though Judah became more
powerful than his brothers and a prince came from him, yet the birthright
belonged to Joseph" (I Chron. 5:1–2). Judah would later commit the crime
of incest, which seems to be the lot of Leah's elder sons. Reuben's wrongdoing is foundational; because of it, the birthright is bestowed on Joseph, the
kingdom on Judah, and the priesthood on Levi. In sum, the house of Joseph
effects the concealment in Israel (and in exile, the ten tribes of Joseph will
disappear, because they betrayed their vocation of interiority; the scission
into two kingdoms was a telltale sign thereof), while the house of Judah
effects its exteriorization and is the vehicle of the *am*. We can see why the
king resides in Judah.

Dinah's Story

Read in light of the saga of Jacob's family, the positioning of the tribes follows a significant process that gives us a better grasp of the fluctuation of
the tribal count and the rule of mobility of Levi and Joseph. If we compare
the tribes of Leah and Rachel from this standpoint, Leah loses an entire portion (that of Dinah, her daughter) in the total count; whereas Rachel gains
one that was unexpected at the start, through the splitting of Joseph's (in
this case, the addition of Ephraim). What occurs in this way is a reversal of
the principle of distribution. This is the inner logic of the movement of the
constellation of tribes.

The loss of Dinah is, however, entirely theoretical and principial. Dinah
was never counted as a tribe. The loss for Leah is materialized mainly by
Levi's removal from the total count, since Levi was counted as a tribe. But it
is the loss of Dinah that makes the removal of Levi possible. It is her eviction that creates the empty space, which lends itself to the movement in the
tribal count. Subtracted from the outset from the tally, she is one too many, a
daughter amidst sons. It is this overplus that enlarges the set number of Leah's
children. Dinah is, in fact, Leah's last child. And it is this "over and above"
(inevitably excessive and which therefore immediately disappears because it
comes as a surplus) that, by widening the count through profusion, enables
one of its elements (Levi) to be removed.

We have to examine Dinah's story to gain a better understanding of this configuration. The *aggada* tells us that Leah was supposed to have another son but that, out of compassion for Rachel her sister, she prayed for the child to be a girl, for she knew that of the twelve sons Jacob was destined to have (again a set number), two were supposed to be her sister's. Consequently, if Leah had had a boy instead of Dinah, her son would have taken Joseph's place. It's because of Leah's altruism toward her sister, her intimate sacrifice, that Joseph comes in Dinah's place, a place already arranged and mapped out by the latter. Leah had to reach the end of her count to be able to overstep herself and withhold her power so as to make Joseph possible.

And so Leah's daughter is called Dinah, because of the judgment (*din*) that she pronounced on her (Berachot 60a), but unlike the other children, Dinah's name is not explained in the biblical narrative. It is left unsaid. Dinah appears like a second figure of Leah. She, too, lives outside: "Dinah went out" (Gen. 34:1) to be with the daughters of the land, just as Leah "went out to meet him" (30:16). She was beautiful and wanted to be admired. This was fatal to her in the story of her abduction. Jacob was also partially responsible, because he refused to give her to his brother, Esau, even though he was circumcised. Certain sources (Midrash Rabba on Lev. 37:1) tell us Jacob was punished for staying in Shechem and delaying his departure for Beth El. Desired by Esau, abducted by the prince of Shechem: is this to say that Dinah—whose name sets her in the arena of strict justice, *din*—has something to do with violence? Is this why Levi, whose violence is manifested in the Shechem affair, will materialize Dinah's retreat and the fluctuation in Leah's count? Because it is in the place made by Dinah in addition (outside the count), and in subtraction (removed from the count) and actuated by Levi, that Joseph can rise up.

There are parallels between Joseph and Dinah. To begin with, both are beautiful (Gen. 34:1, 39:6), even if they do not use their beauty for the same purpose. Dinah should have been a boy, and Joseph is born instead of a girl. According to the *aggada*, Jacob abandoned Dinah and Shechem's daughter in order to rescue Dinah from the grips of his sons, who wanted to kill her. This daughter was found and adopted by Potiphar in Egypt under the name Asenath, and Joseph recognized her thanks to an amulet given to her by Jacob and married her. This would mean that Asenath was rejected by her grandfather because of Joseph's brothers, who would later reject him.

We can see why Dinah's defense was so important to Leah's sons: it was part of their fight to oppose Jacob's preference for Rachel's clan, an attempt to prevent Dinah from stepping back and Joseph from taking her place. But

Joseph is called upon to get around this conflict and redeem Dinah. By marrying Asenath (a pagan in appearance)—just as Dinah had been taken for
a pagan—Joseph reincorporates Dinah into the system of tribes, just as he
himself is reincorporated into the tribal count after having been taken for dead.

This may be the reason Joseph takes up two places at the same time a
place is left in Leah (Levi): his own (through Menasseh) but also Dinah's
(through Ephraim). Neither is it an accident that this additional place, occupied by Joseph, is Levi's (one of those responsible for the violent affair in
Shechem, when Dinah took center stage). It is in the place liberated factually
by Levi's withdrawal[283] (but enabled by Dinah's feminine addition) that Joseph
is split in two and becomes the "house of Joseph," an uncommon name for
a tribe but one that encompasses two, and which comes under the heading
of sovereignty in Israel.

In sum, through the prism (of the overplus) of Dinah, Leah loses Levi
in the count but sees Judah's kingship confirmed. Rachel, through the prism
(of the overplus) of Joseph, gains Ephraim (in addition) in the count and
sees the birth of Benjamin confirmed, and it is on Benjamin's land that the
Shechina will abide and the Temple will occupy a place.

Joseph (through Ephraim) and Levi are counterparts of the kingship
(Judah) and the site of the Temple (Benjamin), and thus the two houses
in Israel unite in mutual reversal. To Judah from Leah and Benjamin from
Rachel on one side are joined Joseph from Rachel and Levi from Leah, one
(the kingship) to establish the royal power of Judah, the other (the priesthood) to occupy and oversee the site of the Temple conceded by Benjamin.
And this whole relationship is made possible by the substitution of Joseph
for Dinah and the reincorporation of Dinah in Joseph.

It is this crisscross relationship of Ephraim and Judah, and of Benjamin
and Levi, that brings Dinah back into the tribal count and unites the house
of Israel, and there is this crisscross relationship because the separation is
two by two:

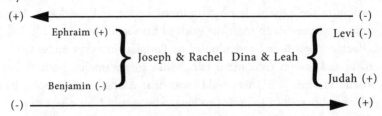

283. This withdrawal was not registered on the symbolic level in the list of tribes, but
it was materialized in reality during the distribution of land between the tribes, when the
tribe of Levi received no territory (Josh. 13:33).

II. THE JOSEPHIC ORDEAL

Everything points to the cardinal importance of Joseph's strange tribe in the nation's formation. It is in its shadow and its promise of impending multiplication that Levi was removed from the tally of tribes. Joseph was the principle and cause of this fantastic architecture, uselessly extravagant only in appearance. Indeed, it is on the occasion of selling Joseph instead of killing him that the clan of brothers unites for the first time to form a nation. This is the classic version of a social bond forged through the murder or expulsion of the "one too many," who has no place anymore in the count, and whose appearance or disappearance nonetheless suffices for the entire nation to be of one mind!

Joseph's story is rich in meaning. It harbors the very spirit of the Hebraic system of nationality, as if crystallizing the story of the tribal entity. Joseph plays the part of the supernumerary element, always left out of the count. "The total number of persons who were of Jacob's issue came to seventy, and Joseph was in Egypt" (Exod. 1:5). His absence is continually implied by the presence of Rachel's second son, Benjamin, who bears witness to his missing brother in a family so intent on being absolutely full that it got rid of the "overfullness."

Benjamin plays a key role in Joseph's absence. According to the *aggada*, Benjamin has no part in the plot against Joseph. And Benjamin is at the center of the ruse that Joseph employs against his brothers when they come down to Egypt ("bring me your youngest brother," Gen. 42:20). At different points in the story, the brothers will offer to both Jacob and Joseph to give themselves[284] as security (for Benjamin's coming to Egypt or his return to Jacob) or as a substitute.

Benjamin, very symbolically, is born well after Joseph; his birth stands apart from the very rapid sequence of births of all the brothers and the only daughter when Jacob is still with Laban. He is born after the family has arrived in the Promised Land, in Canaan, but his birth—like an extra here, too—is "paid" for with the life of his mother, who thereby surrenders her place to him.

---

284. Notably Judah, and this is highly significant, because if Judah vouches so fervently for Benjamin, it is because, as father of the kingship, he is guarantor of the sovereignty that dwells in the house of Joseph.

Benjamin is important. Indeed, he is like one of Joseph's "limbs," "his mother's son" (Gen. 43:29), since he is announced at the time of the birth of Joseph, who carries him in his name ("YHWH will add me another son," 30:24). Benjamin is a Joseph who will be counted among the tribes and therefore given a territory. In fact, the divine presence is called upon to dwell in the Benjaminic portion, where the Temple is to be built (Sifre on Deuteronomy 3:5, §352) and where the Tent of Meeting was set up before the Temple in Shiloh (Josh. 18:1–8) and then in Beth El (Judg. 20:26), on the place that simultaneously houses the fullness of presence, its magnificence beyond fullness, and its strangeness, its absence, its ungraspable nature, a place of both presence and absence, with the Josephic (Benjaminic) augment transcending its absence in the set tally of the being-there of the tribes.

When the incognito Joseph invites his brothers to a banquet in Egypt, he gives Benjamin a portion five times greater than that of the others (Gen. 43:34), like a reward crowning the patience, the giving, the suspension of absence. Those who in appearance are in absence and lack are in truth already in fullness and bounty. The time comes when truth meets up with appearance, when the augment, the overplus of being, the supernumerary will reemerge in the lack and the retreat, where Joseph will reappear in the place left empty among the tribes, which was foreshadowed forth by Benjamin's feeble existence among the tribes.[285]

Construction of the Collective Identity

Joseph's story is a way of constructing "ethnic" belonging to the collectivity of Israel—that is to say, nationality. It concerns, therefore, the area in which the reciprocal overlapping of the cultural and the biological is generally produced; this is the concrete basis that gives substance to the empty forms of citizenship. Usually participation in citizenship overlaps with ethnical belonging. This is the most prosaic of foundations: the people of a place are automatically citizens of the state; they spread out and occupy the whole space contained within boundaries that protect the fullness of the interior and drive all strangers back outside the borders. Belonging to the collectivity is founded at once on total self-adequation based on territory (all those born there are immediately nationals) and on the rejection of the other beyond

285. Whence the dual and contradictory interpretation of Benjamin's name: ben oni, son of my hardship, or ben yamin, son of my right, depending on whether he is named by his mother or father.

the border. Such a "natural" nationality is based on the principle of identity. Everything is full. There are no gaps, no vacuity. The emptiness is outside. This is the classic structure of sovereignty.

The essential articulations in Joseph's story point to something altogether different. Joseph—as his very name, "that which is added," attests—bespeaks the experience and problematics of Israel when it comes to assembling, form- ing a people, constructing its multiplicity, and giving it meaning. The main pivot of his story is the interplay of more and less, of positive and negative. "One too many" for Leah and her children, he is doomed to disappear and reappear again and again. Destined to have all the blessings and the birth- right bestowed upon him, he suffers all the humiliations of fate. Summoned to be reincorporated into the people of Israel, in the end he reappears not personally but through his sons, doubling his portion and his name, and this is the consummation of his trial. The bounty and overplus that exist in Joseph are announced from the start, but they merely twinkle throughout the story. They are manifested in his dreams of sovereignty (Gen. 37), the dream of sheaves (the agricultural referent), and the dream of stars (the celestial referent) that provoke his brother's rejection of him, for Joseph's overplus triggers a surplus of hatred: "they added even more hate" (37:5–8). This rejection of the Josephic principle of sovereignty leads to his being cast out of the brotherhood of tribes. But the latter's survival, in the most concrete terms, when faced with famine, will depend on his reincorporation.

Equal to Joseph's original dreams, the tribes will dream up and simulate his elimination. Was this a failed murder attempt or the elimination of the overplus? With Joseph sold abroad and cast out of the tribal land, the clan of brothers can possess the original land better and more. But he will always be missing, and the land will starve them until, without realizing it, they naturally set out in search of him and end up gathered around Joseph in a royal position in a foreign land, totally dependent on him and his coveted bounty. Simulation of a murder, or rather the concealment of Joseph? The murder may be a warped concealment.

Objectively, Joseph is cast into a pit and disappears, giving his brothers the opportunity to sit down and have a meal together as if concluding a cov- enant (Gen. 37:25). He is hidden and not assassinated, "for he is our brother, our flesh" (37:27). The concealment of Joseph forges the collectivity of Israel.

But there is, as in all concealments, an unaccomplished aspect, an antici- pated future into which the desire of this collectivity is projected. This is a concealment of the one in the multiple. The multiple will relentlessly rejoin it, just as Joseph's brothers were irresistibly drawn to him. By going to the inmost interior (Joseph hidden in Egypt), one ends up reaching the outermost exterior, the Jewish people (the brothers). Like the divine, Joseph is the one preserved in the multiple. This unity comes beyond the multiple, as the absolute one on the basis of which the multiple is conceived and established, the (hidden) one that subtends the very possibility of the (manifested) multiple. The one is greater than the multiple. Joseph's migration is therefore like the journey of the one in the *olam*, the very pivot of the world process.[286] Joseph will always confront this experience of unclenching, of the being's slipping away, which is the primal experience of the *olam*.

The story of Joseph tells of this journey through negativity. Already before his birth, Rachel asks Jacob for children, saying, "Bring me children, and if there are none (*ayin*), I am dead" (Gen. 30:1). When Jacob's sons, bound by their conspiracy, show their father the famous tunic that has aroused envy, they say, "Identify if it is your son's tunic or not (*lo*)" (37:32). Joseph's dilemma is always between presence and absence; he continually faces this choice. Isn't this the destiny of that which is added, of augment? From the perspective of the multiple and of immediacy, he is perceived as poor and absent. From that of bounty, he is as present as can be. In the people of Israel, Joseph is the journey of the "no" of absence, the finality of which is nonetheless felicitous (the return of presence and blessings). He is the vehicle of a constitutive ordeal for the entity of Israel.

Tamar's Story

We can now see why a totally unexpected passage is inserted right into the heart of the biblical story of Joseph—namely, the story of the incestuous relationship between Judah and Tamar. Our discussion sheds light on the rationality of the episode's placement. As the principle and support of kingship, Judah can be inserted only in the foundational framework of sovereignty: the emergence among the people of the "house of Joseph." The power and legitimacy of the kingship proceed from it (and hence from the experience of absence), which clearly demonstrates that Joseph precedes Judah.

Why, then, the incest? Tamar is Judah's daughter-in-law. As the widow of Er, firstborn child of Judah and Shua the Canaanite, Tamar tries to perpetuate

286. This is why when leaving Egypt, Moses took Joseph's bones in the ark that would join the Ark of the Covenant at Sinai. Joseph is compared to the Torah in terms of the destiny of the one, always migrating and returning to the place of departure. But the one (Joseph) who goes to the exterior (Egypt) comes back as bones, whereas the one (the Torah) that goes to the interior (Israel) is forever alive.

her dead husband's name by fulfilling the levirate law with Er's brother, Onan. Onan refuses to comply and give his brother an heir who will not be counted among his own children. Having displeased God, he, too, dies. Seeing that Shelah, Judah's third son, is not ready to take her as his wife, she uses a ruse. Disguised as a harlot, she waits at a crossroad and offers herself to Judah. Judah accepts, and before separating, she asks him for a gage as security for his pledged payment: "your signet, your cord, and your staff that is in your hand" (Gen. 38:18). Then she disappears. Judah sends what he owes her, but no one knows of a prostitute at that place. When Tamar's pregnancy becomes apparent, much to the dismay of Judah, who sentences her to death, she exposes the three gages and reveals the ruse. Judah will father the royal dynasty through Tamar, for Peretz, one of the twins, is a distant ancestor of Boaz, who will marry Ruth.

This story is highly symbolic. The gages given by Judah are emblems of royalty, and they are given to a prostitute! There is ambivalence at work here again. Nowhere is it explicitly said that Tamar sought to prostitute herself. We are simply told that she covered herself with a veil and sat at *petah enayim* (38:14), which can be read as the "gateway of the sources" or the "opening of the eyes." Judah is the one who mistakes her for a prostitute (*zona*) (38:15), which means that he takes the veiling and concealment as an occasion for prostitution (and for incest, although he does not know it). All Tamar did was cover herself with a veil. The rest is a matter of interpretation.[287] She wanted to manifest absence in presence, to bring home the oblivion swallowing Er's name in Judah's family. But this Judah cannot understand, and he mistakes this manifestation for an invitation. Absence, in his mind, is something to be filled and occupied rather than a space for letting the other emerge.

---

287. It is interesting to note that Tamar is "taken/reckoned/thought" to be a whore in a way that is reminiscent of Dinah, whose brothers exclaim, "Should our sister be treated as a whore?" (Gen. 34:41). Dinah is absent from the tally of tribes. Is her absence (which resembles Tamar's veiling) to be taken for nonexistence? Is the vacant place she opens in the tribes (which allows for the possibility of Joseph) to be occupied? Do the absence and passivity that is femininity in the world found its appropriation by the masculine? Is reserve to be interpreted as nonexistence, and the absence of God the creator as nothingness? In this sense, there is some justification for Simeon and Levi's violent reaction, as there will be later for Levi, who defends the memory of divine absence, and whose only portion is God. But their reaction can also be understood on another level. Simeon and Levi think they are fighting to safeguard Dinah's place as Dinah's and prevent Joseph from appearing and taking possession of it. In so doing, they take a stand against Joseph, Levi by pulling in the direction of Joseph's appearance, and Simeon by pulling in the direction of his negation.

He goes inside, literally and figuratively, and this occupation of the place of the absent other is tantamount to incest insofar as sameness (Judah) mingles with his self (his close family) instead of letting the other appear. The father has forgotten his son (dead and gone), whose name is supposed to be perpetuated. Tamar is the one who takes the initiative, for the fulfillment of the levirate commandment is dear to her heart, and she, like Ruth later, seeks to give an heir to a family that is dying out.[288]

The story can be read on two levels, however, because Judah takes Tamar for a prostitute, but when he sends her the kid as payment for her services, "the people of the place" say, "There was no prostitute (*kedesha*) in this (*zeh*)" (Gen. 38:21), using a term for prostitute that is very close to *kedosha*, holy and *keddusha*, holiness.[289] The allusion is clear: Tamar's destiny is one of *keddusha* and *Shechina*.[290] It is Tamar who is given the emblems of royalty as security,[291] as a pledge from Judah for his promise to give her a "kid from his flock," a promise that parallels a sacrificial offering on the altar of the Temple! The emblems of royalty are pledged by this offering, and the vocation of royalty

288. Shua's offspring are decimated. Both Judah and Joseph (the very principles of sovereignty and its effectiveness) marry pagan women. Only Asenath, Dinah's daughter, will have offspring. Through her marriage to Joseph, Dinah recovers her share in the tribal portions, and Leah receives posthumous retribution, as she is recognized and reincorporated into Joseph's blessings. But Dinah receives even more, because, if Joseph's sons are regarded as Jacob's, their mother, Asenath, is elevated to the position of Jacob's wives, the matriarchs.

289. The "in this (*zeh*)" can be interpreted, like Rebecca's words (Gen. 25:22), in reference to the numerical value of twelve. In other words, there is *Shechina* in the twelve but no prostitution.

290. The same is true of Simeon and Levi's presumption of prostitution concerning Dinah. It is the status of overplus that is at stake. And we can see the extent to which Joseph occupies, perfects, and accomplishes Dinah's place. Absent from the tribal count (and by the patriarchal principle that Simeon and Levi represent), she finds no place to invest herself or be invested, and she falls into the trap of narcissistic self-contemplation. Beautiful, as overplus and bounty are, she leaves the tent of interiority, where the one is hidden, to be admired amidst the Canaanite daughters. At that point she is abducted and raped by Shechem, even though he ultimately wants to marry her. This crisis is decisive in the birth of Joseph, because Leah's clan of sons rejects the very idea of Rachel's progeny, of an overplus to themselves. They sense that with Dinah (the first daughter born during Leah's second period of birth giving), the end of Leah's generations are at hand, and the birthright is slipping away. If Joseph does not come, if the overplus does not have children, it will decompose and fade away. If Dinah and the *Shechina* do not produce generations, they are ruined (the rape of Dinah). The augment that finds no way of being recognized and investing itself becomes an erring, mad sign. It's man's role to make a place for the *Shechina*: to practice its service and to build a house for it in order to provide shelter for the augment.

291. The absent *Shechina* receives them, as does the absent Joseph in Egypt.

is to preserve in the collective memory of God, who has absented himself, and to bear witness to the continuation of his action in the world.

Joseph's Absence

The subsequent story of Ruth, mother of royalty, powerfully illustrates this vocation. This story of the genesis of royalty is inserted into the narrative of the sold, absent Joseph, meaning into the phase of absence and eclipse that is part of the people and part of existence. Later in the story of Joseph, before he shows himself, he demands his double, Benjamin, and Judah makes amends for his sin by offering himself as security for him (Gen. 43:9). This is when he becomes worthy, in the bounty and the unveiling, of becoming father of royalty and joining up with Joseph, the nonincestuous, who went through the experience of lack, absence, and sexual rigor (witness the Potiphar affair); who knew how to wait, to withhold; and who received the deposit of emblems of royalty. At this point, royalty actually receives the legitimation of sovereignty. Throughout the genealogy of this sovereignty, what is experienced is the suspension that concerns immediacy in the augment and that explains its absence, the passage that exists in presence: Reuben, the natural elder, forfeits his place due to incest. Simon and Levi are eliminated due to murderous violence. Judah is held in suspense because of incest and disrespect for the levirate law. Joseph is chosen and granted the birthright but in the end does not really benefit from it. It is his sons, and especially his second son, the cadet, Ephraim, who do so. And when Judah and Tamar have twins, Peretz and Zerah, it is the second born who will continue the dynasty.[292]

Thus, the experience of Joseph's absence weaves the weft of peoplehood and notably the arena of civil power (through the foundation of the kingship by Judah and Tamar), which is the arena of memory of the absent people, the arena of the principle of absence that lies at the heart of the nation and that makes the nation. And this movement leads to two possibilities: filling in the absence (the idolatry of the golden calf) or passage (the passing of God's Names before Moses on Mount Sinai). Power is the absence of Joseph, so when Reuben the elder returns to take him out of the pit, he does not find him (Gen. 37:29). Absence founds its power inside the people and outside in Egypt, where, once again thrown into a pit (that is, into prison), Joseph recovers his power from his absence.

---

292. Zerah put out his hand first and had a crimson thread tied to it to mark the first-born, but Peretz pushed harder and came out first.

The nation is matricially forged in the clan of the brothers that is forged in the conspiracy against Joseph, whose absence will gradually become so overwhelming that the whole nation will end up gathered around him, outside of itself, in Egypt. Joseph's power of assembly is evidenced in the text even before he is sold. Joseph is the one Jacob sends to look after the welfare of his brothers (37:14), the one who is concerned with the whole nation and asks on his way about his brothers' welfare (37:15–16).

If Joseph stands for the paradoxical principle of absence in the people (for he is bound up with overplus), it is Judah, the principle of royalty, who is the architect of his return. He is the one who suggests to his brothers not to kill Joseph or let him die in the pit, but rather to sell him and hence to turn the surplus into an element of mobility and exchange. Similarly, he is the one who offers himself to his father as security for Benjamin; and so, by accomplishing the exchange and passage of the people within himself, he moves them all to return to Joseph. Joseph is the principle of the nation (based on the interplay of overplus and absence); Judah is the principle of power whose purpose is the *tikkun* of the nation. The one, Joseph, is the native principle of the nation; the other, Judah, is its completive, effective principle.

This system informs the sacrifice (*korban*) of the portion set aside and consecrated to God that founds all covenantal communities. In this respect, it is not without significance that Joseph was sold to a caravan transporting aromatics, a reminder of the *korban* of incense offered on the golden altar inside the Temple, the subtlest and most accomplished of sacrifices, whose curls of perfumed smoke spiral up to the sky.

This principle of giving is lodged at the very core of the nation right from the outset, from the moment Jacob envisions it in his dream of the ladder right before leaving the land of Israel to go to Laban, where he will take a wife. In the covenant that Jacob establishes with God, Jacob makes a promise that already contains the Levitical principle: "A tenth I will tithe for you" (Gen. 28:22). Of all that Jacob has, he will give a tenth (the basis of the Levitical tithe), including of his children, meaning Levi in this case.[293]

293. In what way is Levi the tenth? Jacob had twelve children, but Joseph's two sons, Ephraim and Menasseh, are said to be his, "like Reuben and Simeon" (Gen. 48:5), so counting them makes a total of fourteen. If we subtract the four elder sons of the four mothers, since they are dispensed from the tithe (according to the principle that holiness/separation need not be sanctified/separated), there are ten remaining tribes, and the Levites are the tenth, which "Yhwh set apart... to serve him and bless in his Name" (Deut. 10:8). How is Levi the tenth tribe? In *Pirkei d'Rabbi Eliezer* (§37) we are told that eight children remained (after removing the firstborn excluded from the tithe); the count begins from Simeon, finishes with Benjamin, the eighth son (still in his mother's womb),

In sum, the Josephic principle (the overplus, the augment of sons announced to Jacob), "everything you will give me" (Gen. 28:22), is subtended by a Levitical principle, "I will tithe for you a tenth," which will later be instituted in the status of the Levite tribe, foreshadowed in Joseph's temporary absence. In its very principle, by this gift from among the sons, Levi—whose portion is God (Josh. 13:33), because he is already God's portion—it is as if the nation were withheld from itself: unfulfilled, unfilled, containing gaps, holes, and empty spaces. No doubt this is why counting the nation is impossible, and even baleful.[294] The existence of an absolute totality of the collectivity is impossible, because it would be complete and self-contained. The uncertainty introduced by Joseph's journey, Dinah, Levi, Joseph's mobility, and Judah's path counts as so many strategies of getting around and breaking with totality.

Joseph's journey, in the nation and in geographical space, structures the nature of nationality through a series of mechanisms informed by the Josephic principle. This paradoxical principle is immediately perceptible; it underpins the overplus and permits multiplicity (the tribes) to be established, but it is itself subtended by an emptiness and absence (the absent Joseph establishing the basis of the nation), destined in the future to be blessed and increased twofold (witness Joseph's two final portions and the reunion of brothers with the absent one and his reintegration into their midst). From this point of view, Benjamin remains Joseph's surrogate and shadow, testifying to the promised bounty that departs at the start of Joseph's journey. The story will not come to an end until Benjamin has rejoined Joseph and the shadow has returned to the body that casts it: Joseph's return to Israel but also the reemergence of Joseph the Hebrew in his Egyptian identity of Zaphnath-paaneah (Gen. 41:45), a different Joseph who reappears as a double.

Judah's decisive role at this moment of disclosure is noteworthy. His intransigence is what moves Joseph to reveal himself (44:18–34); this confirms

and then starts again from Simeon, to get to Levi as the tenth. What is interesting about this count in itself is that it is not straightforward and linear. It is not the biological order that counts; it involves a series of removals and deductions (the four firstborn sons and Dinah); and it is circular. It starts from Simeon, the next in line after Reuben, and comes back to him before reaching Levi. Simeon and Levi are thereby counted twice, but only Simeon counts as two, since Levi is taken out of the count as "God's portion." Maybe the tenth Levi redeems Simeon's wrongdoing, for it is interesting that Jacob links Simeon and Levi in his blessings. The *aggada* tells us that Simeon spawned an enemy of God, Zimri, but from Levi came Phinehas, who punished Zimri and contributed to warding off the destruction of Israel by God (Num. 25:7). It is also interesting that Joseph imprisons Simeon and separates him from Levi, out of fear that together they could destroy Egypt.

294. See below, "All Israel and the Prohibition of Census Taking," pp. 367–390.

the idea of kingship (or the instance of emergence of the collective in the nation) as that which hounds absence and makes it yield to its reversal into presence. When Benjamin stops being Joseph's substitute, his double, Judah really rises to kingship. Joseph and Judah are the two facets of the strategy of emptiness and, in emptiness, of the passage that is Israel, so although Benjamin is a positive, passive witness, representative of Joseph, Joseph is absent from the constitutive process of the nation. It is a temporary absence in the immediacy of augment at the paradoxical foundation of power. Everywhere the cadet, everywhere second (to Pharaoh, for example, 41:40), Joseph is always wielding power, whereas those who are officially entitled to it (Reuben, for example) are continually losing it. Joseph is the portion removed from the people, who embed gift giving in him. And this portion will never be restored to itself; even when Joseph returns to the nation, he does not return to the place he left. What comes back from him, twofold, are his sons, who double his place in the tribes, as equals to their uncles, the eleven tribes.

The Two Thrusts

To sum up, the Josephic principle at work in the constitution of the nation takes place in two dynamic thrusts and two approaches, or logics, whose mutual relationship and code we will have to strive to understand. Joseph, after a brief, fragile, but promising flickering basically makes himself known through absence. How is this absence in presence to be understood, this lack (which quickly assumes the form of famine) in the bounty? To comprehend this is to comprehend the meaning of concealment (illustrated by Joseph, who is continually being hidden—in the pit, in prison, in exile in Egypt—by those who are relentlessly appearing and exhausting themselves in doing so). Effectively, augment can be seen in the problematics of the hidden and the apparent. What is "in addition" is "hidden," because it is out of the apparent count, but this over-the-count does not exist any less fully. Augment can be seen as a sign of the not, of the less, when in fact it is a matter of absolute positivity.

This negative thrust in the Josephic principle introduces a temporal dimension, insofar as it postpones the revelation of the more, the return of Joseph, to later and farther away. Joseph was present among us from the start, here in the pit or in prison, although we did not see him.[295] What is

---

295. Just as after Jacob's ladder dream, he exclaims, "Yнwн was present in this place, and I did not know it!" (Gen. 28:16), but in the very same breath he consecrates a tenth

the significance of this temporality if not to enable the nation and the *nefesh*, the soul that animates it, to make its way to redemption? Isn't this the purpose of concealment? The immediacy of presence would destroy an Israel unprepared to live it, so it would dissipate presence right away. Time is the space left to the soul to accomplish its *tikkun*, because the project of *tikkun* is lodged in the very constitution of the soul. Time is thus the germinative blossoming of repentance and consummation. "Why did you accomplish/pay evil in the place of good?" (Gen. 44:4). So royalty is founded in the shadow of Joseph's hidden augment (this is why Judah is the guarantor of Benjamin, who bears witness to the Josephic principle in absence), because royalty is the collectivity's endeavor to redeem itself and restore the one in the multiple. "We are twelve brothers, the son of one man..., and the youngster is with our father today, and the one is not" (42:13),[296] the brothers declare to Joseph, who they think is the viceroy of Egypt and not their brother. Or when the brothers ask Jacob for Benjamin to bring him back to Joseph, Jacob exclaims, "Why did you treat me ill by telling the man that you had one more (*od*) brother?" (Gen. 43:6).

The disappearance of the one amongst the brothers has a secret purpose. It is a secret treasure, the unknown foundation of multiplicity, because this disappearance calls for memory, surpassing, and passage on the part of the multiple, whose very existence derives from the passage of the one and is a fervent call to the one. Joseph is held back, preserved, not brought into effect. Because the sovereignty he carries was not actuated, it will exert its influence later.

In this light, we can see why Joseph was saved in his Egyptian prison by the cupbearer and not the baker (Gen. 40), by the principle of wine, which is preserved in darkness until it improves and yields its essence, and not by the principle of bread, which rises, gives everything it's got, and then goes stale. It is Joseph, whose story in Canaan, in exteriority, amongst his brothers, is over, who saves those who have fulfilled themselves immediately, who have not hidden, given, or set aside a portion, and so have failed to understand and imitate the divine gesture of creation and are unable to repair the created world. Joseph founds the possibility of *tikkun*, and, like the Maker of the Universe, he is the silent architect of this *tikkun*, forgotten, misunderstood, ignored, or disdained.

of what he has to God and calls the place "House of YHWH" and "gates of heaven."

296. This verse illustrates how Benjamin, the little one, bears witness to the one in its absence.

By keeping secret, by staying hidden, in retreat, Joseph enables the *tikkun* of the world. By withdrawing, he puts the world, and the nation in this case, in suspense and enables it to turn back and examine itself, to improve and redeem itself. This is the reason for the ongoing reiteration in Joseph's story: two dreams, two times Jacob calls on Joseph to find out how his brothers are doing (Gen. 37:13–14); two brothers intercede on his behalf (Judah and Reuben), and two brothers resent him (Levi and Simeon). He is twice in prison, Pharaoh has two dreams, his brothers travel twice to Egypt, and there are two stratagems involving concealed objects (4:25, 44:2). There are two hearings with Joseph, two brothers are accused of spying, and two brothers are invited to settle in Egypt. Joseph has two sons, he receives two places in the tribal count, and so forth. The story of Joseph is an invitation to look twice when it comes to Israel, for it is not revealed right away and all at once. It hides the seed of its own *tikkun*.

Thus, during the phase of absence of the Josephic logic, there is a principle of "remnant" at work. Joseph is sold, denied, and hidden; he is rejected by the totality of Israel. He is the castoff from the tribal count, from the sum total of tribes structured around the deadly hunger for the all and not on the invigorating passage of the one. But it is upon this leftover, this remnant outside the whole, that the future of the nation will be built. It is on the basis of this repressed memory that the nation of the all will begin its journey and passage toward the nation of the one. This remainder of the all, the concealed portion left intact, removed from consumption and offered to God, becomes the mainstay of Israel's future resurgence, its salvation from famine and inner consumption. Isn't this what Joseph says when he reveals himself to his brothers and, instead of taking revenge as they feared, tells them it was not their fault? "God sent me ahead of you to return to you a remainder (*she'erit*) on the earth and to bring life back to you by a great resource"[297] (Gen. 45:7).

The notion of "remnant" plays a decisive role in the definition of Israel and notably in the prophetic discourse where messianic Israel is supposed to emerge from the "remnant of the house of Israel" (Isa. 46:3), from the remainder that survives the trial of passage. The system of the remainder, implicit in the Josephic principle of absence, has other consequences. When this remnant, this cast-off portion, reappears, it creates an obstacle to the equal apportioning between brothers. Joseph's eleven brothers came together

---

297. The same terms are used when Jacob splits his camp in two; it is the one that makes the camp a remnant and a resource.

to cast him out and take for themselves a share of power worthy of interest, which his presence would have diminished. But with his reappearance, the "equal" sharing must be reworked. The problem is that the brothers endeavor to achieve rigorous equality (albeit an equality that could not be called just, since it was deadly!), and this is impossible. It is in fact the opposite of unity (and indeed "the one is gone," Gen. 42:13; Joseph has been removed from the count). Unity as the product of the sum of elements is an illusion. Josephic unity is a superaddition to the sum, greater than the sum of units whose reunification is structured by it. The nation's unity is based on what exceeds and underpins it.

Specificity and Substitution

We can now see why Joseph is the source, and not the effectuation, of sovereignty. Unity is testimony in the face of the sum of the multiple. It is alone and solitary, forgotten and hidden. It is not the crystallizing apotheosis of the sum of parts, equal to the whole. Such unity is monstrous; it is power and sameness, not testimony and calling. It turns the nation into a devouring Leviathan, fabricated from nothing like an idol whose mouth spews fire. In the perfect egalitarianism of the clan of brothers, the boundary of each share is adjacent to the boundary of the others. There is no vacant space, no room left over. Passage is impossible and forbidden. In the equality of sharing, the one is not possible.

So the one, the principle of mobility and of the counting process,[298] cannot embark on its journey. It does and undoes the count no doubt because sovereignty accommodates strangeness in its principle. It is in this way alone, Joseph's way, that the unity of Israel is present to the nation, to those born from the flesh of their parents, like a testimony and a perpetual appeal. Jacob will never be reincorporated in the tribal count, even if he gains an additional share through his sons. The one is beyond sharing; it is in giving. The multiple is not unified in the unique sum (for such unity would annul each one in particular); it is left as it is but gravitates in mobile configurations around the one that traverses it and of which it is a reminder. A concrete illustration of this system is that the Levite tribe is not reckoned in the tribal count, has no share in the land, and testifies, among all the tribes, to the unity of Israel.

298. As in arithmetic, it is by continually adding one that the numeration progresses.

Is this process of unity anti-egalitarian? Indeed, it fosters distinction and differentiation. *Yihud* denotes as much specification as unification. Therein lies the root of the principle of chosenness. Why Joseph and not his brothers? Isn't it unfair to Reuben? We have already seen that Genesis shows us repeatedly that the polity and order of human beings cannot be founded on natural law (the biological elder). The Other (and hence the lot of all human beings in the polity) is absent from natural law. The vocation of the polity is to repair nature (*tikkun*). Joseph's election undoes the natural order. It creates a vacuum in its selfish fullness; it is the agent of dissatisfaction, the absence of enough, of the satiation produced by the illusion of the all when the one is absent. It echoes the Other in the polity.

This register is beyond rigor (*din*), beyond the scale used to weigh equal shares. It is in the dimension of *rahamim*, of birth-giving mercy. But the one subtends the multiple—that is to say, it builds a very original structure of the multiple, based not on a principle of absolute interchangeability of parts and individuals but on their unique character, their specification. This is the lesson to be learned from the story of Joseph, and it is the lesson he teaches his brothers: the principle of an accomplished human relationship is based not on interchangeability and substitution but on the specificity of the one. The brothers are the ones who begin the cycle of substitutions when they simulate Joseph's death and replace him with a kid whose blood they spread over his shirt. In Egypt Joseph excels in unraveling the threads of substitution (Pharaoh's dreams of the lean and fat cows, and his courtiers' dreams). But it is on his brothers in Egypt that he tries out the negativity of this principle: with the escalation of gages proposed by his brothers, his demand that Benjamin be left as security, the substitution of the silver cup in Benjamin's bag, the money, and so on. A dialectic of gages unfolds in this story, until finally Joseph shows himself, Benjamin comes, and Judah is released from being held as a gage. But even afterward, there will be a semblance of substitution when Jacob chooses to treat Ephraim and Menasseh as sons "like Reuben and Simeon."

The status of each member of the nation is one of differentiation and particularization. Let us not forget that the project of being is to make visible the one, hidden, in the midst of the multiple. In the logic of such sovereignty, no part can be replaced by its counterpart. But if each one is singular, if each one is chosen, how can the members of such a nation unite and communicate with one another? Will this not lead to a world in which each one ignores the other, and no one ever meets? Can't such particularization produce immobility and hierarchization, precluding a relationship of equality?

To imagine that this can be true is to forget the role of the one, which is set apart from the projected uniqueness of each element of the multiple and stands in a relationship of testimony, appeal, and ferment with everyone. Here the one is the principle of mobility of the multiple. It is the one that unites each of the parts of the multiple, one by one: "take one wood and write on it, 'for Judah and the children of Israel, his companions,' and take one wood and write on it, 'for Joseph, Ephraim's stock, and all the house of Israel his associates'; bring them close (*karev*), one to one, for you, one wood, and they will be unified in your hand" (Ezek. 37:16–17).

The dimension of bearing witness to the one is very important from this standpoint. It is not to be identified with the state, which is an illusion of the all that remains bound up with the multiple, a mockery of the one. The one remains distinct from the power that characterizes the multiple: Joseph does not reign in Israel, and it is Judah from the clan of brothers who assumes this power but in the emanation of Joseph. It is, moreover, the logic of the all, which structures relations of equality on interchangeability, abstraction, and departicularization, that yields surreptitious hierarchies. No matter how hard one tries to achieve equality through the logic of the all, the unavoidable reality of the one of specification can never be eliminated. Repressed, it ends up being recreated in a warped way. In abstract relations of equality, hierarchies are recreated in practice,[299] although they masquerade as something else and are all the more uncontrollable as a result. On the other hand, in the logic of the one, the principle of unity is overtly assumed. Thus, the purpose of this complex system of nationality is to establish, on this basis of the one, relations of equality that, this time, would preserve the uniqueness of each element, starting from a privileged uniqueness that serves as testimony. Solomon's famous decision in the case between the two prostitutes is a judgment based on truth, because he gives priority to the one, to the specificity of the child in the dispute, in his relationship to his mother, over equality based on interchangeability ("cut the living child in two, and give half to one and half to the other," I Kings 3:25).

The Mobility of the One

In this regard, it is important to consider the mobility of the one. It is insofar as the one is not directly instituted in its effectiveness, as it is not

299. This is borne out by contemporary sociological analysis.

in a ruling position and does not constitute the summit of the edifice of
the multiple, insofar as it is a solitary, suffering witness in the midst of the
multiple (which is Joseph's lot), even if it is blessed in the one, that it does
not produce hierarchy. Such a process produces differentiation without hierarchization, thus escaping the totalizing impasse of abstract equality. The
nation thereby becomes a permanent effervescence, either in the memory in
the making or in the call of the one: it is never full and never at rest. The
nation never sleeps. Therefore, the conscience of the nation is embodied in
the voice of the prophet, alone and unique, "chosen," as it were (the suffering
Joseph), and certainly not in the self-contained positivism of the powerful
(Judah). The one runs through the multiple, makes it possible, allows it to
avoid depletion in the passage, stops it from falling into nondifferentiation,
sustains it, and helps it gather together, but it is not arrested there. This is
a fundamental principle.

A logic of nomadism, of emptiness, and of strangeness plays a decisive
role in the Josephic principle. It is a logic implicit in the advance of the one
through the multiple, because the one is hidden away, and it is in this concealment and passing that the multiple is deployed. Joseph leaves for Egypt, then
his brothers and mother join him; finally, his brothers come and go between
Canaan and Egypt. Then Joseph, in Egypt, imposes on the Egyptian people
an interior nomadism, an estrangement of sorts (on the basis of which he
logically establishes Pharaoh's power as well as his own): "and he transferred
the people to cities from one end of the country to the other" (Gen. 47:21),
so they recall that they have no portion in this country.[300]

This logic of nomadism, because it produces mobility and modifica-
tion, and counters the autochthony, nativity, and rootedness associated with
nature, informs the issue of nationhood. The nation by birth is recreated as
a nation by vocation and by *tikkun*. This is the truly messianic vocation of
Joseph in his family, a messianism of duration and silent humility. To be
sure, this experience is an ordeal, because it is so close to nothingness. The
Josephic problematic can lead to consumption, and mobility can comprise
empty moments. Similarly, exile, separation, and absence can be the nation's
structural state prior to a catastrophe—a potential state, inherent in its being as much as in its ingathering in the land of Israel. By opening up fields
of pasture for traveling flocks and removing the fences between individual
portions, the nation of Israel can accommodate a "pasture of wind" (Eccles.
2:11). By positioning the elements of the nation in incessant mobility, they

---

300. Joseph essentially removes the Egyptians (except the priests and his people) from
territorial possession.

may never find each other and may become unrecognizable. "Who are they?" (Gen. 48:8) Jacob asks when he sees Menasseh and Ephraim, who were born to Joseph in Egypt and whom he will adopt.

Later, "Joseph" will always refer to the kingdom of Israel, the ten tribes, in opposition to the kingdom of Judah, and, in this light, we can understand the exile of the ten tribes and their disappearance from the nation. Joseph is close to exile and disappearance. What can lead him to it is the effectuation of his principle and his sovereignty, which is Judah's function. When the house of Joseph pits itself as royalty against the royalty of Judah, it sets out on a journey of disappearance. Exile is the ineluctable product of the unwarranted effectuation of sovereignty by itself: effectuation of the one as actual power in the multiple, the one leaving its hiding place, Joseph taking Judah's place, when in fact he is the basis upon which Judah stands. It is as if the desire for immediacy in the nation (or in kingship) drove it out of itself, dislocated it, caused it to vanish, annulling the withholding of Israel in the promise and the concealment. Presence exposed immediately flees, because the world is annulled before God as a result. Forgiveness and repentance are denied it, and it collapses under the weight of too many defects.

If Israel's sovereignty is not hidden in itself, the world—and to begin with, Israel—cannot subsist. Exposed extemporaneously, Israel retreats into itself, and there is exile (*galut*). Exile comes from the lack of withdrawing the concealed portion; it comes from exposure. Thus, the first historical exile came when the house of Joseph set itself up as royalty, and the second exile occurred when the Hasmonean kings, who were also priests, didn't respect the Levitical separation from the people that should have kept them from assuming the kingship. Exile always comes from augment, from the failure of augment, from the additional one seeking effectuation by eliminating or covering up the very void to which its own placement in augment points (Joseph's absence, the estrangement in sovereignty, the Levites in the tribal count, and so on). Exile is a drama (that is to say, an action) of estrangement in Judaism, of the particular structure of particularity. It is a dramatic ordeal but by no means catastrophic, because it is there in potential in the nationality of Israel. Its experience also plays a part in the revelation of the logic of augment: then all Israel retreats from itself, as when all of Joseph's brothers go down to Egypt, and not only him and the Levites. All Israel gathers around Joseph in Egypt,[301] with the tribes around Levi, and this necessarily prepares the way for Israel's return to its spaces. Exile is a passage completely

---

301. For this reason, the messiahship of Joseph has been regarded as universal, oriented toward the nations, in opposition to David's, which is oriented toward Israel. This is at once

mastered by the nation and not its definitive breakup. In this conception of
nationality, the failure or rather the suspension of the national that is exile
is integrated with the nationality disappearing as a result. We can see, then,
how the nomadism inherent in the Josephic principle of augment underpins
the Levitical principle. What Joseph does to the Egyptian principle is put the
Egyptians through the Levites' future experience, depriving them of territorial
property and scattering them throughout the cities. This experience surfaces
in Jacob's vision of what will befall Simeon and Levi in the narrative that
brings Joseph's story in Genesis to an end: "[God] will divide them in Jacob
and scatter them in Israel" (Gen. 49:7).

A Process of Reversal

One paradox of the Josephic principle is that the position of augment immediately produces retreat, absence, emptiness in the tally of fullness. Joseph
is apparent in the nation only through Levi, and sovereignty (kingship of
Judah) only through that which is ineffective in sovereignty (the Levite tribe
assuming the priesthood).

A process of reversal is at work at the heart of the system of augment and
retreat. As we have seen from the narrative of Joseph, the more, the augment,
is manifested in the retreat (the absence of Joseph, thought to be dead), but
this retreat (subsequently embodied by the Levites) is a source of blessing.
We could say that Joseph's immediacy is Levi and that Levi's is Joseph: the
Levitical withdrawal attracting the surplus of blessing (the Levite priests are
the only ones to bestow the "priestly blessing" upon Israel). Joseph in himself
is augment, but his effect is Levitical (retreat). Levi in himself is withdrawal,
but his effect is Josephic (the blessing of augment). In sum, the augment is
perceived as retreat and absence, and the retreat as augment. Thus, Joseph
and the diasporic exile presage an ineluctable augment and blessing in the
form of a return. But beyond the destruction and reconstruction of the house,
retreat and strangeness are latent and inhabit the house in the positive being
of the "return." Nonetheless, the house, not Josephic nomadism and exile, is
the rule. Joseph cannot rise to power and authority in Israel.[302]

---

true (Joseph's dwelling of/in estrangement) and false: it is true that Israel gathers around
Joseph in Egypt, but the point of this gathering is Joseph's return amongst his own people.

302. But he does so in Egypt during his absence in Israel. It is astonishing indeed that
the principle of sovereignty in Israel founds the sovereignty of nations.

Exile is the intrinsic pull of the Josephic principle to which Israel is drawn when it loses control of its path and strays from the coupling of Joseph and Levi (the kingdom of Israel's big mistake was to set itself up as Israel's pole of effectuation). Augment is the source of power but is prohibited from wielding power. If augment exercised power, concealment would be dissipated, and concealment is necessary for power. And if concealment ceased, the world would involute and disappear. If Joseph stopped being hidden in Israel (that is, the creation of the kingdom of Israel) or if exile became the informing value, Israel would decompose in exile. Joseph's return to Israel (and first Israel comes to him with great difficulty) is immediately followed by Jacob's blessing, Joseph's death, and the instructions not to forget his remains. But Joseph as a person is never again counted as part of Israel; what returns to Canaan is his name and his mummy.

We have here the very structure of creation: God's withdrawal (*tzim-tzum*) creates the world/*olam* (the world is God's disappearance) by making a place for it. This retreat (which is so only for us, not for God, since God puts himself in augment to us because we are in augment to him) produces "more-being," an addition to divine being, which is the being of man. It is doubly understandable why Levi, the tribe without land, is consecrated to God: it bears witness to the divine retreat in the midst of the fullness of the people; it bears witness to the concealment and generates the benediction, the bounty for Israel. Levi is like God for man. Joseph is like God for God and for Levi.

Here we see the process of concealment at work. The augment, because it is over and above the count, is hidden from sight. This is why, unlike concealment, it is not in the realm of representation.[303] Augment can be hidden from sight only because sameness (the defensive, compensatory illusion that we devise in the void to ward off the fear it instills in us) leaves no room for the other within itself. It is the augment that posits the other, even if it does so in the silence of concealment, but it posits it in the more, not in the negative. It is augment, that additional life breathed into the soul of sameness, that enables the latter to leave its narcissistic identity and make room for the other, hidden in the augment. We see again that the ordeal of the void turns out to be a promise of bounty, from the standpoint of the augment,

---

303. Isn't this precisely the position of the attributes? Benjamin, whom Joseph leaves with his father, is a lovely metaphor for this when he is brought to Egypt. If Joseph embodies augment, hidden in Egypt, Benjamin, his brother, is the echo of this, the minor form of his brothers, a reminder of the missing Joseph. Benjamin has to be brought back to Joseph, in Egypt, for the benefit of augment to be felt.

rather than the tragic abandonment it seems to be from the standpoint of the retreat. Therefore the being of man, the being of Israel, is in suspense.

This reversal principle in the categories of Joseph and Levi is manifested in the story of Jacob's blessing. When Jacob sees Joseph's sons and blesses them, "Joseph took the two on them, Ephraim at his right, at Israel's [Jacob's] left, and Menasseh at his left, at Israel's [Jacob's] right" (Gen. 48:13). This is the first reversal, because Jacob and Joseph are face-to-face, so the position of the sons is reversed depending on the point of view, Joseph's or Jacob's right or left. The first reversal goes from the start of the augment to the initiating void. Then "Israel stretched out his right hand (opposite Menasseh) and placed it on the head of Ephraim, the younger (who is on his left: the movement going from Menasseh to Ephraim), and his left (opposite Ephraim) on Menasseh's head" (48:18). Now Jacob's arms are crossed in front of Joseph very uncomfortably; this crossing is compelled by the will and principle of Joseph, who has positioned Menasseh on Jacob's right so he will bless him with his right hand of blessing. Jacob, however, refuses to have his "hand forced" and switches hands despite Joseph's insistence: "This displeased Joseph... he took hold of his father's hand, to move it from Ephraim's head to Menasseh's. And Joseph said to his father, 'Not so, Father, for this is the firstborn; place your right hand on his head" (48:17–18). Jacob chooses, of course, Joseph's younger son. And thus the second reversal goes from the initiating void to augment, and Joseph receives two shares. Entropy is reversed into surplus and excess. The exile involutes into an even more bountiful and plentiful return.

The Levitical Principle

With the second thrust of the system of augment and retreat, the positive dimension of the Josephic principle is manifested, the true essence of the principle that we propose to restrictively term the "Josephic principle" while designating the dimension of retreat by the "Levitical principle."

The passage immediately generates retreat and absence, but ultimately it produces augment. It augments the being in its disappearance; the initial eclipse from the point of view of the other is, from the divine point of view and in terms of its own finality, multiplication and augmentation. Paradoxically, the nomadism of Levi is carried by a surplus of abundance and presence. From the standpoint of the tribes, Levi is subtracting, but from the divine standpoint, Levi is the more, the surplus of Joseph. Thus Israel's retreat from Egypt, the result of God's passage through Egypt (Exod. 11:4), produces a more: the gathering of the scattered people of Israel around Sinai. The absence to Egypt is presence to Sinai. Similarly, Jacob's crossing of the ford of the Jabbok produced two camps instead of only one: "I crossed this Jordan, and now I have become two camps" (Gen. 32:11). Likewise, Jacob sends over all his possessions and stays alone, alone in the more. "Jacob remained alone" (32:24–25) can be read "Jacob was alone more for him." This "more" (*yoter*) is like a remainder (*yevater*) of the whole, the aloneness of the one in the face of the all, the one that is not in a withdrawal from the whole but in the overplus to it. We can see from this that the remnant is in the more. This more is what escapes totalization, what rebels against and is irreducible to it because it does not yield to multiplicity even as it remains the principle of the multiple.

This experience of Jacob is exactly what Joseph lives through. He is the addition to his brother, the one "added" (*yosif*) to the others, and whose addition is so productive that it heralds the birth of another son, Benjamin (Gen. 30:24). This additional son who is Joseph, and in whose absence the forgetful totality of the tribes is formed, is like the witness for his brother; the overplus, the solitary abundance, is the principle of testimony. Announcing to their father that Joseph was still alive, the brothers "told him still/more (*od*) Joseph/the added one lives, and he rules over the land of Egypt... and Jacob's breath (*ruah*) was revived, and Israel said, 'Many (*rav*) still/more (*od*) Joseph/the added one, my son, live" (45:28). He who is in the more (*od*), which means that his disappearance, his extinction, his death is suspended when it seemed to be a fait accompli, is in the testimony (*eda*).[304]

In and despite his solitude, Joseph becomes the very principle of the *eda*, the community of testimony, betrayed by the clan of brothers. The more (*od*) is the other face of the promise. Both are in suspension, the latter in suspension of the projected accomplishment, the former in suspension of the apparent end. The latter is the initial point of view; the former, the terminal one. Solitude is by no means synonymous with poverty and death (Jacob says *rav*, "many," and *hai*, "alive"). Moreover, it is in power (*moshel*, "rule"). And indeed, testimony is that which subsists in the passage and is not destined for depletion. We can see why the community (*eda*) is founded on testimony, beyond the passing of generations. When all the brothers return to Joseph, who is in bounty and testimony to the truth, it is the entire *eda* that recovers its principle, transcending absence and manifesting itself in

304. *Od*, meaning "more" or "still," *ed*, "witness," and *eda*, "community of testimony," have close roots.

the more (*od*) of overplus and augment. All authority and sovereignty derive from this testimony of which Joseph is capable, Joseph who is doomed to die. For, if sovereignty contains strangeness and absence, it is itself founded in surplus. Its initial and immediate moment in the created world is absence and emptiness, but this is not its relationship to its own principle, a principle of bounty and presence.

In surplus, sovereignty follows augment. Let us consider the royal figure as an illustration of this. The royal figure is the positive relief manifested on the Levitical horizon of emptiness and absence. Whereas the tribe of Levi is absent from the possession of land and effective power, the king of Judah has the attributes of power and sovereignty. The figure of Judah echoes the figure of Joseph from all points of view, in terms of sovereignty, testimony, and position. It is Judah who suggests that the conspirators sell Joseph. He is the one who offers himself to take Benjamin's place and, by this demonstration of loyalty, compels Joseph to reveal himself. He is the one who defines Benjamin to Joseph in terms of surplus: "an old father and a small child from old age, and his brother is dead, and he is left/in addition, he alone to his mother, and his father loves him" (Gen. 44:20). Likewise, Judah is Leah's fourth son, and he is already additional. Leah knew Jacob would have twelve sons, and since he had four wives, each should have had three sons. This is why when Judah is born, Rachel insists that Jacob give her a child (30:1), since Leah has already had more than her share. Leah gives birth to Judah as an additional son: "she conceived again/more (*od*)" (29:35). And Judah, which means "praise Yhwh," is an unfolding of Levi. It is Levi's vocation to praise God, so by choosing to name this additional son Judah, Leah unfolds what is hidden in Levi. Judah is the surplus son, in augmentation of Leah's share, and this indicates already that the sharing is not "egalitarian," as will be borne out and established later by Jacob's preference and his blessings for Joseph. But Joseph is not wholly revealed in Judah, who is the local manifestation of sovereignty, and this indicates that he is also in Levi, in absence and withdrawal. Thus, Joseph as augment and surplus is the seat of sovereignty in its abundance and extreme positivity, the source of all authority and power, but his throne is hidden, veiled, and distant. The vision of this place is a vision both supreme and terrible, because few creatures can maintain themselves in the face of the most absolute. At the place where all is being, the void and passage where we are in the *olam* are dispelled like clouds by the wind. And so the glorious throne is hidden and veiled, preceded by the Levitical tribe, the tribal veil in the tribes, guardian of the sanctuary of the veiled Holy of Holies, before whose entrance stands the king, a feeble reflection of the full majesty of being. This is why the king, the embodiment of civil power, acts in the interior (*toch*) opened by the Levites. Similarly, Judah is the one who set in motion the rapprochement of the tribes to Joseph. This is also why all of Joseph's power is in dreams, an overplus of intellect, but he is also and especially a figure suspended from reality, the announcement of a not-yet-realized reality.

This suspension of augment appears to be the essential feature of this system of (non)totalization of the collective. The being is in suspense; this is the whole meaning of *olam* and creation. And this suspension preserves unity in the multiple and, through the multiple that it engenders by itself, it preserves the one despite its journey in the *olam*.

The journey of the Levites and of the ark amidst the tribes preserves the one, the divine unity, the unity of the people in their existential multiplicity. But the journey of the Levites, like Joseph's journey, is meaningful only because it has a sense and is not heading to perdition. Beyond the vicissitudes of his life, Joseph triumphs and grows in the world. The concealment and suspension are acts of ruse: a ruse with death, exposure, nondifferentiation, and extinction. They defer the accomplishment and thus give man the space to turn around, the arena for *teshuva*. They introduce time and passage in a world on the verge of disappearance and extinction, because God's foundational withdrawal harbors a danger, the danger of perdition for the creature that thereby appeared in the absence that is the world. This is, after all, the schema of the Hebraic day. Joseph sparkles with promising light but then quickly vanishes. This is evening (*erev*); then comes the night of absence, the exile in Egypt, the midnight of famine, and the slow coming of the eleven tribes to Joseph, who ultimately reveals who he is (thanks to Judah and also Benjamin), and at last the dawn, the hour of brightness and sovereignty. The light twinkles, disappears, and reappears.

III. THE PRINCIPLE OF NATIONALITY

This issue of augment and retreat structures the nation of Israel in the sense that it establishes a highly subtle system of affiliation with the collectivity and enjoyment of sovereignty. The perpetually mobile element in the total count of elements in the nation (whether it is hidden, replaced, or elsewhere) continually bypasses, postpones, and suspends the closing and totaling of the count. This architecture serves to avoid the nondifferentiated collective totality, the nation turned into a mass. The impossibility or multiplicity of the count makes it impossible for the nation to be truly counted as if it were an external object.

The prohibition again census taking[305] can thus be seen in a new light. The fluctuation in the count and in the elements of nationality taken into consideration makes census taking impossible, in any case, but the purpose of the prohibition is to prevent the nation from being grasped as a totality and abstraction, to prevent it from turning into a concept. Too much emptiness, diversity, and mobility in its intellectual and symbolic apprehension make this conceptualization impracticable. They are all stratagems whose purpose is to force the mind away from such a temptation. It is therefore with great difficulty that Jews manage to construe themselves as a collectivity. This constitutes a terrible ordeal of inner solitude, all the more so insofar as the presentification of the collectivity of Israel or its appearance in presence is the messianic goal of history—and this ordeal is so very rigorous that one can question the being-people of Israel and see in it only a metaphor of the people.[306] This difficult condition that is the predicament of the collectivity of Israel (that is, being a people and having difficulty perceiving itself as such) fulfills a positive role in light of the Hebraic problematic. This existence of the collective, subject to a prohibition of representation, basically aims at preserving multiplicity in the nation, evidence that alterity and strangeness inhabit it.

Safeguarding the one, as an interactive witness and not as an idol or a screen over the multiple, is in fact the deep-seated purpose of these complex mechanisms. The seemingly disorderly manifestation of the multiple (which, as we have seen, is systematically rigorous) prevents the crystallization of the one and safeguards it as it travels through the multiple (the nomadic tribe of Levites); in fact, its travels are what makes the unity of the multiple. Thus, the Levites form the cement of nationality, they themselves dispossessed of land to be "God's portion" and have God as their portion.

The system of nationality is embedded in a logic of *korban*, sacrifice/rapprochement, obtained from the cutting and separation as well as from the passage. Thus, it is in the Covenant between the Pieces that Abraham receives the announcement of offspring. Likewise, it is during the ladder dream, before going to take a wife and found a family, that Jacob vows to

---

305. See below, "All Israel and the Prohibition of Census Taking," pp. 367–390.

306. The people of Israel is metaphorical in the etymological sense: a being transported to an elsewhere, carried to a place beyond itself (see Trigano, "Langue du passage et principe métaphorique," in *Story of Disappeared Presence,* p. 318).

give God a tenth of his possessions and even of his sons in a thoroughly sacrificial intention (the sacrifice of the tithe).

What unites and founds the nation is thereby embedded in the logic of giving, separation, and cutting, of passage, divine presence, and suspense (oath and promise), and not (as is customary in the self-contained closure of a group identity) in a logic of hoarding, gathering, binding, immobilizing, of narcissistic consciousness and presentification. Such a national bond, based on that which precedes as an a priori the social level, clearly indicates that the biological is by no means outside the confines of the cultural, insofar as it does not suffice to be born to be Jewish (and in this regard, the systematic contesting of the biological firstborn son is highly revealing), and the distinction of Israel has a "sense," which is not the ideological rationalization of self-love and even less of a biological-ethnical cause. This destructuring of the national lodges meaning at the very heart of the biological.

Jacob's Camps

Jacob's division of his camp in two before crossing over to the land of Israel is the paradigm of this system. "He divided the *am* with him... into two camps, and said: 'If Esau comes to the camp of the one and strikes it, the camp of the remainder will be a resource'" (Gen. 32:8). This splitting and setting apart of the one in a camp that will henceforth be a remainder is meant as a propitiation. Jacob uses the term *kappara*; "with a staff, I crossed the Jordan, and now I have become two camps." "I will *kapper* his face with the camp that goes before me, and afterward I will see his face, maybe he will greet my face favorably" (32:21). The language is that of an encounter with God. Jacob even says to Esau, "I've seen your face like seeing the face of God" (33:10). Moreover, what is the camp that goes before him as a *kappara* if not the Levite tribe, the camp of the one, whose concealment will enable the camp of the remainder to subsist in the passage? And, in fact, it is in the camp of the remainder, in the place of the retreat, that Jacob will wrestle with the angel, with retreat,[307] precisely to make sure that the augment is posited at the same time as the retreat is taking place.

Jacob manages to resist the angel only because he sent the one over. At the same time, the one draws its potential from the fact that Jacob is fighting in the rear. This combat of augment is a combat in and against the passage

---

307. Israel's potential angel, if Israel became a nation like the others again, with its guardian angel, placed under the banner of cosmic determinism.

while the crossing is taking place. Israel needs the augment in order to resist the danger of abandonment and depletion.[308] The two positions are simultaneous: the position of the camp of the one is a separation; the position of the camp of the remainder is a combat. And, in fact, it is in the camp of the remainder that "Jacob is left/in addition (vayevater) alone" (Gen. 32:25), and so it is in the framework of augment that he undertakes his battle with the angel, out of which he will emerge with a more to himself, by becoming "Israel" overadded to Jacob. Therefore, there is no "national spirit" and no "national soul," no metaphysical, spiritual, or ideological collective entity. From Israel's standpoint, all Israel is not totalizable. What makes the collectivity of Israel is its relationship to the absence within it, the God of the covenant to whom the absent tribe of Levites bears witness.

The quadripartite division of Israel in the wilderness is symptomatic in this regard. There is a foretaste of this division in the meeting with Esau, when, after having split the camp in two, Jacob divides it in four, in respect to his four wives: Zilpah and her children, Bilhah and hers, Leah and hers, and finally, Rachel and Joseph. Actually, this quadripartition boils down to a splitting in two, since Zilpah and Bilhah belong to their mistresses, Leah and Rachel. But the most accomplished model of quadripartite division is that of the camp of Israel in Sinai, for which we have a complete description, with the arrangement of tribes, three by three, at the cardinal points,[309] around the Tent of Meeting, with each of the four secondary camps—the "standards" (Num. 10:1–3, 18–23)—in contact with it through the agency of one of the four patriarchal houses of the Levitical tribe, which take their place all around the Ark of the Covenant.[310]

From a global point of view, one can distinguish three camps: the camp of presence with the Tent, the Levitical camp around it, and then the camp

308. This is why the augment has to be preserved in the concealment, why it must not be effectuated and wasted in immediacy. Otherwise, the journey across could become terribly dangerous: the camp of the one is unequipped and weak, and the camp that remains exhausts itself and disappears, thereby endangering the camp of the one itself. Thus, the house of Joseph disappears when it becomes a kingdom, and, as a result, Judah is doomed to disappear, too. It is only when Judah finds within himself the concealment of Joseph, the fight with the angel, the accrual of the being of augment, that he leaves exile and reappears in the land of Israel.

309. Zebulun, Judah, and Issachar to the east; Benjamin, Ephraim, and Menasseh (and hence the house of Joseph) to the west; Gad, Reuben, and Simeon to the south; and Naphtali, Gad, and Asher to the north.

310. Moses and Aaron to the east, the Gershonites to the west, the Kohathites to the south, and the Merarites to the north.

of Israel, around the Levitical camp. If the two camps (Levi and Israel) are quadripartite, only the camp of the *Shechina* is one.

The quadripartition of the camp and the spatial centrality of the Tent of Meeting (or of the altar and later of the Temple) bring us to another dimension of the system of twelve that we haven't seen until now. And that is that in this system and its continual counts, it is God and His Name that are at issue. The four camps are clearly related to the four letters of the Tetragrammaton gathered around the unity of the divine Name. The impossibility of the total count would therefore go beyond the impossibility of representing and conceptualizing Israel and be related as well to the irrepresentability of God, the prohibition of representation, whose purpose of which, as we have seen, is to preserve the one in the multiple.

Indeed, all the successive configurations of Israel house the divine presence in their midst: the angel in Jacob's fight, the ark at Shechem,[311] the tent at Sinai, then the ark of the league of tribes at Beth El, and so on. Later, the Temple takes over in the heart of the land of Israel, and then, during the long exile of twenty centuries, it is the transportable Torah that assumes this role.

It would seem that what governs these sophisticated configurations and complex logics informing the tally is the need to house the divine presence. The tetragrammatic nature of the Name would thereby be decisive in this quadripartite structure (which can be brought down to a problematic of reduplication and bipolarity). Out of the four letters in the Name YHWH, two—YH—are, in fact, cardinal (moreover, they constitute a divine Name). Of the two remaining letters, one—the H—is a repetition. Only the W is added on; it is a coordinating conjunction that joins the first H to the second H.[312]

We can now see why the Levitical tribe stands apart from the other tribes in a differentiated place at the center around the altar, creating a place for God but also a connection between the two parts of Israel (the tribe of the *vav* of conjunction, *vav* meaning "and"). It is via the Levitical junction that the tribes, organized in groups of three, communicate with one another. So at the heart of Israel, there is a void, a tribal absence, that of the Levitical tribe, around a much greater absence, that of God, which, in fact, keeps an

311. To renew the covenant at Shechem before entering the Promised Land (Josh. 8:33), Joshua divided the people into two "halves," one near Mount Gerizim and the other near Mount Ebal, and in the middle stood the altar and the Ark of the Covenant surrounded by the Levites, the priests, and Joshua, and this to receive the "blessing first."

312. Leah has a *heh* in her name, which makes her fertile. Rachel, who does not have one, has difficulty conceiving; so she gives Bilhah, who has two *heh*s, to Jacob to conceive for her.

infinite presence hidden in the Temple. And the whole of this system, the architecture of the camp of Israel, is the Name of God in the world. Whoever looked upon Israel serving God in its midst, it was as if he or she had seen God! There is then no "national spirit" in Israel, because Israel houses the divine Name in its midst.

In the assembly of Israel, the particulars and elements appear distinctly in a privileged, particularized relationship to the hidden one, and all these relations taken together are what make the collectivity, in such a way that this system in continual motion cannot be represented. Tradition has represented this question according to the talmudic idea that "there is no star for Israel." Each of the seventy nations is under the guidance of an angel, but Israel is under the guidance of God alone. The collectivity of Israel escapes the determinism of archetypes; it cannot be charted on a star map. It is the star that crosses the sky and changes position evening and morning; it escapes natural determinism. But it also escapes celestial determinism. God does not delegate responsibility for Israel to one of his angelic servants.

Wrestling with the Angel

The relationship to the divine is a perpetually renewed relationship, a dialogue in the context of the covenant. In fact, this whole problematic implements the very logic of the covenant of God and Israel. Since Israel is continually positioning itself on the exacting level of the one, at no time can it expand massively to the point of becoming a self-sufficient, self-centered entity. But this does not mean it is the opposite. By rising, in the covenant and the dialogue, to the level of God, it raises itself to the level of the one, and this elevation makes it, despite all else, a collective being.

In this sense, one could say that Israel is one as God is one. This is the meaning of Jacob's fight with the angel before hearing the announcement of his offspring and making an oath to God to give him a tenth of his posses- sions and his children. And it is highly significant that this episode comes in this context. This fight is actually Israel's fight with its own angel, the fight with its metaphysical unification, with its own principle. And for this purpose, Jacob splits his camp in two. To found the nation of twelve tribes, Jacob has to force the very principle he carries inside himself. He thus be- comes "Israel" and changes his name. It is in the fight with himself, with his self as same, that the children of Israel become Israel. Israel is a project for Israel. The fight against the collective entity of Israel, against Israel as entity, is embedded in the collective being of Israel. Such a being, the being of the covenant, forces its limits—by accommodating the strangeness of the other in itself—and attains sovereignty and unity only by going beyond itself. In this sense, it fights with God, who has forced the fullness of his being to accommodate man and conceived in himself of the limit (the creation)—which is not his limitation but his illimitation: limit toward man, illimitability toward God himself. Israel's experience of the divine one is precisely what opens in humanity this experience of illimitability, thereby embedded in the very structure of its being, which, even when it defines itself and "identifies" itself, accommodates other than itself.

The system of nationality also pursues a second objective: it aims firstly to preserve the Josephic principle, the principle of fullness in a world marked by passing and unclenching, by decomposition. It aims at keeping the uneffectuated arena of the political intact at the very heart of the collectivity, the principle of power safeguarded from the vicissitudes of power. There is, then, in the assembly of Israel the perpetual resource of an entire power. The state can very well disappear, without power and sovereignty disappearing, for that matter. A tyrant can seize power, but there will always be a source of authority from which those who fight him can draw. This whirling system avoids identifying a holder of power with the power or "spirit of the nation." The "spirit of the nation" never settles on anyone or into anything. Neither idolatry nor dictatorship is possible on the basis of such a system. It is not totalizable. It remains, throughout time, an uneffectuation inside the being of Israel, an unaccomplished field, the guarantee of the nomadic movement of Israel within itself, the source of its perpetual life and permanence.

In a way, the state is secondary from the standpoint of nationality. It is less powerful than the nation and the "wilderness" that inhabits it and that it inhabits, because the state cannot fully effectuate sovereignty and power; it cannot synthesize, crystallize, and accomplish the field of the political. To the contrary, it is by way of the journey of Israel and its tribes through this field that the state can be born.[313] In the state, there will always be incompletion,

---

313. This state-generating journey through the state is accomplished by the Levitical tribe. We can see why the high priest wears a breastplate with twelve stones engraved with the names of the tribes for "remembrance before God, always" (Exod. 28:29). It is from the hollow space of these engravings that he can read the *Urim* and *Tummim*, the oracle concerning the destiny of Israel thus etched in the names of the twelve tribes carried by Levi. The passerby paradoxically bears the memory (before the great divine passerby). The one lives like a memory in the forgetful multiplicity of the people. The unity of Israel arises amid the tribes in the manner of a memory and an evocation. The *Urim* and *Tummim*, the "casting of lots," was used to assign each tribe its portion of land.

empty spaces, and absence. The only exceptions are the case of the golden calf erected in the wilderness, a case of idolatry in which a (bad) spirit of Israel is forged, and in the messianic promise of leaving the wilderness and entering the Promised Land when "the wilderness will blossom."[314]

The Josephic principle is preserved in a way through the agency of the Levitical principle. The nomadism of the Levite tribe, whose immediacy is dispossession and wandering, poverty and dependence, screens out Josephic positivity, to the potential bounty it carries. The setting apart that Leviticism effects in the people aims at pouring out torrents of its fullness over it, but by hiding the positivity, it safeguards and perpetuates it in the passage of the people. It is in the beyond of the transitivity of the *olam*, the access to the one, and the disclosure of the one, that the fullness of the Josephic principle is disclosed. Joseph thus asks the Hebrews not to forget his remains when they leave Egypt. In the passage and withdrawal, this injunction is a call to remember the positivity of Joseph, guide to the blessing of appearance in the land of Israel. It is a still diaphanous memory (because it is Joseph's mummy), but it presages the future plenitude: the Ark of the Covenant to which the ark transporting Joseph's remains leads.

After Sinai, the Hebrews head to the land of Israel carrying two arks, the Ark of the Covenant, carried by the Levites, and Joseph's sarcophagus. Death is carried by life, immersed in life. Such a strange convoy echoes the strategic ruse with death that the Josephic principle establishes: the concealment founds the abundance, and the life it impels and irradiates prevents the retreat in which the concealment is plunged from lapsing into extinction. "One [Joseph] accomplished what was written in the other [the ark of the Torah]" (Sota 13a–b). It is in the same spirit that once the twelve tribes were proclaimed ("these are the tribes of Israel," Gen. 49:28), Jacob instructs his children to bury him "in the cave" of his fathers (49:28), in the land of Israel and not in Egypt.

The nationality of Israel thus has a dual vocation of recollection and moving forward to life. It carries the ark of life over the passage and death of the generations that witnessed Sinai. In spite of death here below, it moves toward life. In spite of the lack, the absence, and the defeat, it continues to travel over the path and sweep absence into the rising tide of presence. Above all, it's a matter of staying on course, of keeping unfailingly on track. Such is the wisdom of the nation of Israel, what constitutes its creative and

314. This proximity shows why the golden calf is presented as a messianic apotheosis and why messianism often approaches the temptation of the calf.

enduring force. By its very dynamic and structure, it masters the continuity of the generation of Israel through fields and spaces, through defeats and victories. It is much more powerful in this than all the institutions it creates for itself, which serve its passage on earth but which, essentially, it could do without. It is not Israel that forges the nation but the nation that forges a state for itself. The nation is the great march of the people across lands and oceans, never stopping, overcoming its own failures, continually reactivating the people that has faded into oblivion, and awakening the dead seed buried in the sand.

The Josephic principle organizes the nation, not on the basis of a principle of lack and scarcity (from which strangeness would be expelled to preserve the possession of the heritage, and which is a principle of identity), but on the basis of a principle of alterity. In this symbolic, practical, and mental construct there is a universal of the nation that is structured not by negativity (the Levitical principle) but by positivity (the Josephic principle). This positivity is hidden, of course, in the sense that the nation of Israel is not so much that which is removed from the others as that which is added to the others to the nations, to the "*goyness*" that exists in Israel. "Who is like your people (*am*), like Israel, one *goy* in the land?" (II Sam. 7:33).

This is why the strangeness of the *ger*, of the nations, dwells in Israel, and they are not driven away, as is common practice in the constitution of nations outside Israel. Israel as a nation is added onto the "*goyness*" in it initially as a nation. It is in augment to itself and to the nations: a people in excess to the nations, in excess to itself, because Israel is the project of the children of Israel. This organization of the nation by bounty serves to establish the only possible figure of the universal for a people, if the function of the universal is invigorating and giving birth and not repressing the multiple and creating a mockery of unity. It serves to preserve the movement in the people, the nomadic state, the births and the birthing of generations, the breathing of the one in the multitude and in the mortal, the incessant return of life. Only overplus can do this, because it is beyond the reach of the erosion of the being in the passage. It is therefore not the boundary but the crossing, not the scarcity against which one protects oneself in jealously clinging to the national "treasure," but bounty and gift giving that form the foundation of the Hebraic nation and embed peace in its very structures, a peace that is disturbing because it is a living protest against the organization of the world's nations based on negativity and lack, a peace that is itself promised, because it is hidden and must be birthed.

CHAPTER 4

The Public of Israel:
The Levitical Principle in
the Fabric of the State[315]

THE SETTING ASIDE in augment that the Josephic principle implements is translated in its immediacy in the world into lack, absence, and penurious poverty (prior to the impending accomplishment and bounty it harbors). Herein (in the withdrawal, the gift, and the *korban*) lies the most spectacular manifestation of the Josephic principle, since what characterizes augment is that it is hidden, literally disappearing in the world. The passage, far from immediately manifesting itself as accomplishment, first appears in the world as a trial and a diminishment. This shadow cast in the *olam* by the Josephic principle is what we call the "Levitical principle."

The Levitical principle is the very process of the Josephic movement. Josephism is the overall prospect, promise, and superior logic of Leviticism, which is its architect in the world. The concealment is done for and in the *olam*. What is hidden is removed from the *olam*, but what "appears" in the *olam* is emptiness, absence, and withdrawal. Levi is something of a paradoxical manifestation of Joseph in the world (absent and sold but actually crowned and blessed). It is through Levi that we know of and experience Joseph's absence. Levi is the one who makes Joseph dwell among us and brings us back to him; Levi is the architect of sovereignty and builds a dwelling for Israel. It is through him that we will learn how the dwelling is really built, but the principle and plan are Joseph's. Through him we will learn how the interior of the house of Israel is *arranged* and inhabited, how one moves around in it, how Israel can be a people in such a dwelling and with such a sovereignty. In the overall system of "augret"—the movement of retreat coextensive with

315. The public is an assembly (*kahal*) united by a voice (*kol*). The Levites who sing on the steps of the Temple are united in a chorale (*makhela*). In its very form, the "public of Israel" is a chorale.

augment—the Levitical principle is the structuring principle, and the Josephic principle is the inner logic and finality. The Levitical principle is at work in the construction of the political arena and the state, of that which is structure in the shadow of sovereignty. But for the people that it lets pass (and that it hides) in the world, it also determines the area of its establishment in the land. This principle governs the Hebraic relationship to the land of Israel. Finally, Leviticism, by all its economic-type mechanisms, actuates an original economic problematic in the people.

I. THE POLITICAL FUNCTION OF LEVITICISM: HOLLOWING THE STATE

At the very heart of the nation of the children of Israel, the conditions imposed upon the Levitical tribe point to a void whose parameters are thoroughly concrete. The Levites do not participate in the tribal distribution of land shares. Not only do they not receive a portion of land in heritage, but they also find themselves scattered among the other tribes in a society in which tribes are circumscribed to their territorial space. They do not appear on the "face" of the Earth, except in cities that fall to their share, the houses they can acquire in cities and in the Temple, where they officiate. The distinction of the Levites, set aside from the total count of tribes, opens up a new problematic in collective existence. It benefits from an "interiority." The gap, the hiatus of differentiation it induces, hollows out the inner space in the nation: "You shall separate the Levites from the interior (*toch*) of the children of Israel, and the Levites will be mine" (Num. 8:14); "Take the Levites from the interior (*toch*) of the children of Israel, and purify them" (8:6).

The setting aside of the Levites is the other side in the exterior of their concealment (inside the dwelling); that is to say, an interiority might be seen in their absence. From the perspective of the exterior, their absence creates a void, and this place left empty by the Levites maps the place of the Temple in the people, in whose midst they are concealed. And through this place the people undertake their own concealment in the *olam*, in the world of passage.

There is absence and emptiness at the heart of the self, and this empty space is precisely what makes the inside, what makes interiority. What is the inside to empirical experience if not this place that is occupied in its fullness, from which all the places are taken, from which that which comes over and above the number already there and counted once and for all is rejected (outside)?[316] The interior the Levites construct is, to the contrary, a place of overplus and augment. By absenting themselves from the tribal count to be set aside in augment, they release a dynamic of void in the tribal mass that leads to mobility and the welcoming of the other. They open the count of the tribes upward and outward in the interior.

All interiors are built from setting apart and concealing. The sacrifice (*korban*) is the preeminent vehicle of this, insofar as it involves setting aside and giving to that which is not present (God) and which becomes present by this act. And the *korban*, as we have seen, is directly (in its etymology) an "approaching." The separation of the Levites from the rest of the tribes thereby produces an "inside" for them. The rapprochement of Levites before the Tent of Meeting[317]— "and you shall approach (*hikravta*) the Levites before the Tent of Meeting" (Num. 8:9)—induces a relationship of rapprochement in the nation that causes it to redeem the exteriority within it. Whereupon it can be said, "and you shall assemble (*kahal*) the whole *eda* of the children of Israel" (ibid.).

It is in this closeness, in the rapprochement that occurs in the midst of the tribes, that the whole nation is effectively constituted, forming a bonded, formalized, and instituted whole (building the state). Therein lies the entire field of effectuation of the Josephic principle. Without the Levitical conceal-ment, the tribes could not constitute a nation. The Levites help them become a *kahal*, that is to say, the space in which the voice (*kol*) of the people can resound and be heard, the pneumatic hollow in our internal organs that enables us to communicate beyond our narcissistic plenitude.

We have in the Levitical institution the very pivot of the existence of the collectivity of Israel in the world. The Levites open the way to the common ground where all parts of the nation, all the tribal specificities, can meet and cross the boundaries that separate them. But this place is not set up like a center, even though the Temple of Jerusalem, the one and only Temple of Israel (and previously the Ark of the Covenant in the time of their wander-ings), is its focal point, a specific point of attachment on Earth. Indeed, the Levites are scattered throughout the tribes, so the center of the nation is always everywhere close to everyone, to each of its members. We have here absolute and universal closeness.

316. From this standpoint, only outside is there a place for something added onto the total count.

317. A closeness that, according to the logic of the *korban*, could indicate the "sacrifice" of the Levites by the tribes, but also their capacity to service.

To be sure, the Temple is the preeminent place of the Levites, but it is so especially for a part of the Levitical tribe: the family of Moses' brother, Aaron, guardian of the priesthood: "and it will be for [Aaron] and for his offspring after him the covenant of an eternal priesthood" (Num. 25:13). This common ground that the Levites delineate (just as one incises metal or chisels stone) delimits the political field (or rather the political relationship) in Israel. In it, one can see the place of the state[318] in Hebraic society, which Leviticism etches *en creux* in the nation.

A Paradoxical Political Class

Immediately, the Levitical "tribe" in such a "state" looks like the "political class." From the outset, there is a temptation to view such a model disdainfully as purely and simply a theocratic state. This is not the case, since there is a dissociation in the Levitical tribe between the priests from Aaron's family and ordinary Levites.[319] Only the former are entitled to carry out sacrifices; the latter are responsible for other functions in the Temple, such as music, singing, and safeguarding. The priests are concentrated in the Temple of Jerusalem, insofar as there exists one altar only, while the Levites are scattered throughout the tribal lands. This means that the function of the Aaronite priesthood is elevated, but it does not extend beyond the bounds of the Temple.

On the other hand, Levitical existence is institutionally weaker, but it is more extensive in its reach as well as in the universality of its functionality. It is true that the Levites' distinction is directed toward the Temple. This is its purpose, since the purpose of concealment is the Temple, the abode of the absent one.[320] Thus is it said of the Levites that they are "given to Aaron and his children from within (*toch*) the children of Israel to serve their brothers in the Tent of Meeting" (Num. 8:17).

This does not mean they come under the authority of the Aaronite priesthood. They do so when it comes to operations of worship but not in terms of principles or essence, "for given, given to me they are from within the

318. Our purpose in this chapter is to examine the meaning and implications of the state's development in the nation, the (external) characteristics of the state in the nation, before turning in the next chapter to the characteristics and rules of its internal functioning.

319. Moses ruled as an ordinary Levite, not an Aaronite.

320. This must be kept in mind when speaking of the "state" in the Hebraic world; the sphere of the state stands in the shadow of the Temple, of the absent one.

children of Israel," God declares (Num. 8:17). [321] In a manner of speaking, the Aaronites are but a technical means for the Levites to fulfill their vocation in the nation. Concretely, Levitical functions consist in carrying the Ark of the Covenant, singing and playing music during the sacrifices, working in the Temple, guarding it, and atoning for the children of Israel so that the Levites will not be smitten as a result of the closeness of the holiness/separation induced by their vocation: "to atone (*kappara*) for the children of Israel, so that no harm will come to them when they approach the Holy" (8:19).

But beyond these functions, which serve to maintain a Levitical space as such among the tribes, the more important function is morphological. The Levites' modality of existence, this diffuse absence throughout the people that is their form of presence, leads to a certain type of morphology and structure for the people. This is what makes the Levites[322] a political "class." This is what we have to examine before turning to their more "positive" and substantial functions (responsibility for bearing the covenant, the written constitution of the assembly of Israel and testimony to the one, the music of the Temple, and the judicial function). It is as if the Levitical status in the morphology of the nation established a declivity, an incurvation that would gather all Israel within it.

The absence and the void firstly create a receptacle so that the collectivity crystallizes around the Levites as if mechanically. But its function becomes stronger with its spread through the people, which is what gives it a real universality. This constitutes an extremely original way for Hebraic society to build the universal. The Levitical political class is thus defined as cut off from rootedness, territorial identification, and worldly property. It is therefore posited in a relationship of overstepping and crossing boundaries of identity. Levi "will say that he did not see his father and mother, and that he did not recognize his brothers, and even that he did not know his own children. Because they [the Levites] will observe your word, and your covenant they will keep/hide; they will teach your laws to Jacob and your Torah to Israel" (Deut. 33:9–10). This incurvation in Levi's identity founds Israel's identity (which has nothing to do with self-sameness).

In the tribal world, the Levitical tribe does not have a self-contained identity that would assign it to a given territory, save perhaps the non-territory or the inhabited territory of a house or a city. Defined in relation to the nation

321. And the verse continues, "in place of the first issue of the womb, the firstborn of all the children of Israel, I have taken them for me."

322. The Levites, with the exclusion of the Aaronites, unless we see the latter as actors instrumental in a procedure.

and not in relation to the earth, its (one might say "theoretical") existence is based on giving. Its livelihood comes not from land revenues or from a direct economic process but from gifts, from the sacrifices made by the children of Israel. Moreover, the Levites do not receive these gifts because of their own specific identity and function; these are gifts addressed to God from which they benefit only indirectly, secondarily. Consequently, here is a tribe that lives freed (prohibited) from economic activities and that need not assume direct contact with the natural elements to ensure its existence. Because it lives outside the economic exchange circuit, it is available for another type of activity, which the tribes engaged in everyday activities and in "managing" nature are not free to take on. The Hebraic system thereby secures the guarantees of neutrality necessary for the efficiency of a political class.

Finally, Moses' prophecy regarding Levi draws a correspondence between its forgetting the relations of family kinship (*kirva*) and keeping the divine word, the concealment-preservation of the covenant—in sum, the assurance of God's closeness (*kirva*) to Israel. Would this be because the "kinship" of the divine takes the place of that of human beings (in this case, of the Levitical family)? Would this be because the Levites, who will henceforth be set apart from Israel, accompany[323] God and are in his *kirva*? It is at the cost of an unraveling of alliances and bonds in this world that God is known, and, in a certain way, this merely reflects the overall situation of Israel among the nations, when Israel, following Abraham's example, puts some distance between itself and the other nations, separating itself from them to accompany God.

The Levites in their relationship to the tribes are in the position of Israel in its relationship to the nations: "I gave you as the light of nations" (Isa. 49:6), "I gave you as a covenant of people (*am*), as a light for nations" (42:6). But the meaning of this distance (in the tribal kinship) that makes God dwell in the kinship of the people is deeper than a mere unraveling of family bonds. It has to do with the redemption of kinship through the agency of the gift and the *korban*, which serve to prevent kinship from becoming a self-contained, closed system: "For given, they are given to me from within the children of Israel, in the place of the first issue of the womb, of all firstborn of the children from Israel, I have attributed them to me. For all firstborn of the children from Israel, human or animal, belong to me. On the day I struck all the firstborn in the land of Egypt, I sanctified them for me. And I took the Levites in the place of all the firstborn of the children of Israel, and I gave them as assistants to Aaron and his children, from among

323. This is what the root of *levi* signifies.

the children of Israel, to perform the service of the children of Israel in the Tent of Meeting and to perform the redemption (*kappara*) of the children of Israel, lest a catastrophe befall the children of Israel if they approach holy things" (Num. 8:16–19).

Egypt, the preeminent world of totality, loses its firstborn when God passes through, because it ignores the *korban*. Israel survives in closeness to the presence, thanks to the gift of the Levites, but this gift also comes to redeem Israel for the death of the firstborn in Egypt, when God separated Israel from Egypt, "by taking a nation (*goy*) from the bosom (*kerev*) of another nation" (Deut. 34:4).

Scarcity and Bounty

But more than the guarantee of their neutrality, what the Hebraic system designates through the Levites is the dimension of gratuitousness and grace that exists in the world, the void at the core of human identity, the void of God. The deployment of the Levitical tribe in the people of Israel unfolds, nearly gesturally for all of Israel to see, the creating gesture of God, the creator of the world, the way of the divine Name through the *olam*: the passage. Thus, Leviticism embeds passage in the being of the nation of Israel. Israel is this passage in the illusory world of fixity, but what passes in Israel is the Levite, and the Levites enable the people to pass through them, following the example of the divine passage. And, as we have seen, this passage of the Levites forges the people by crystallizing the multiplicity of Israel on and around Levi, unique and alone, in the one that is in concealment, by gathering this multiplicity and separating/sanctifying it in the one.

The passage hides the one everywhere. We can see the political implications of the Levitical passage, and the Hebraic state is this experience. Through the system of Leviticism and Josephism, the system of augret, Levi is embedded in "negative" in Joseph, and the Levitical tribe itself in the children of Israel; the state is embedded in the nation in the manner of a setting apart in augment. In sum, unlike the Josephic logic of nationality based on bounty and absence of boundaries, the Levitical logic that subtends the state is based in its immediacy on absence and giving.

Is a logic of scarcity at work here? The concealment may give this mistaken impression, which is merely an optical illusion due to impatience. What is important to retain is that whereas the universality of the nation is organized in terms of "more,"[324] the universality of the state is organized in terms of "less." Does this serve to place the alien outside citizenship? There is no doubt a distinction of this type ("The citizen in the children of Israel and the alien who lives in their *toch*, one Torah will be yours," Num. 15:29), but this system would make citizenship pertain to the nation, not the state.[325] This system is to be reintroduced, however, into the finality of nationality, which is to preserve the mobility of the collectivity and of the destiny of Israel, not necessarily its "wandering," but its passage in an impatient world tempted by fixity, by arriving at the endpoint, by an untimely unity that is necessarily represented and not genuine.

The Josephic augment inspired a mobile void within the children of Israel, which is echoed in the moving count of tribes and exemplified by Levi's displacement, his removal from the count, and his condition of existence in the morphology of the tribes. Levi is the only one to live concretely (in anticipation of the Josephic accomplishment) the trial of the unaccomplished, the difficult, the striving, and this is the very arena of the Hebraic state. It is therefore also animated by Josephism, the arena of the striving toward the one, a striving that, if accomplished (Joseph's return), is equivalent to going beyond, to the passage of the "state." The logic of "less" is immersed, then, in the logic of "more."

The subtraction produces an addition. The state is deployed in this gnawing anxiety of the one in the world of the multiple: it is the supreme effort of the multiple to reach the one. But it does not reach it in the world of *olam*, of passage. If it did, there would be representation and nothing but a mockery of the one. It must, to the contrary, lead to concealment, in the shadow of the one. The state conceals the nation in the world; it keeps it hidden.

The passage of/in the nation is accompanied by a less, an absence, of which the state is the vehicle. It is in this reserving of/in the nation that its mobility in the passage is ensured, that the state finds its origins. This setting apart is meant, of course, to preserve at once the possibility of affluence and the multiple, but also and especially the one, which makes possible the

324. This is a way to make strangeness dwell in it, unlike the insular principle of identity, which is penurious and expels the stranger beyond its boundaries.

325. We will come back to this system, which presupposes that the citizen is in the national and the stranger in the interior (*toch*), that is to say, in the political place where the state stands. There would be a reversal of signs here. The nation, inhabited by strangeness, does not accommodate the citizenship of the foreigner, but the public sphere, founded on retreat, welcomes the alien; the nation organized in relation to strangeness leaves room for the stranger.

multiple. This means that the state hides the one; it does not embody it. What it manifests is the one's concealment and absence, not its accomplishment. Following the example of the absent one and of Leviticism, it "accompanies" the passage of the nation in the world and in itself.

This is the second figure of augret, the first being the nation of the children of Israel. This lessness of the nation that we see in the state is what we see in this world of concealment, the below-surface trace (*en creux*) of the overplus that exists in the nation, of that which in another sphere stands out fully (and in relief). The nation is inside and the lessness of the state outside, or rather, it is Levi or the state that maps in exteriority the interiority of this inside.

So the experience of the state is not that of flowering majesty, but that of the trials and sufferings of human beings in the passage and of their journey to the one. The belief that it already embodies the one, in this world of the *olam* and of passage, is the cardinal temptation of the state. This is why the arena of the state is one of the major stages of the drama of the one and of passage in the *olam*. The trial exists, of course, from the point of view of the one, not from the point of view of the world. It is Joseph who suffers in Levi, since Levi could benefit from the situation and take advantage of his power, which is, in fact, his greatest temptation. This is how we are to understand that in this world of waiting, "God opened Leah's womb, and Rachel is barren" (Gen. 29:31). Yet it is the Josephic finality ("Rachel") that should allow us to understand the Levitical logic ("Leah"), not the other way around. This is decisive (notably to avoid the illusion of the fulfillment of the one). The one is announced, like Joseph, and then vanishes. Thereafter Levi becomes Joseph's vehicle in the multiple. But at the end of Levi, Joseph reappears. Thus, the sacrifice of repentance ensures the blessing.

The sufferings and anxiety of the one are between two lights, twilight and dawn, both heralding the middle of the day. This explains a key phenomenon in the history of Israel: the episodic disappearance of the state in what could be described as a (perhaps overly) literal translation of lack and absence. But this disappearance, which, from the point of view of the illusion of the world, is a catastrophe, is plunged in perpetuity for Israel. It is Levi who confronts death and disappearance in Israel and Israel's death and disappearance, but Joseph is always in enduring life and bounty. It is even thanks to Levi, to the state that is Israel's (negative) vehicle in exteriority, that Joseph and the nation of the children of Israel in concealment must be preserved in the passage of the world. Levi receives the "blows"; he is the one who, through worship and sacrifice, takes on the sins and depravity of repentant Israel to redeem them. He can do so. He can "manage" the lack because he stands on plenitude, in the beneficial shadow of Joseph.

This suffering, which is the very substance of the world of the state, clearly evinces the fact that completion, advent, and embodiment are not in the nature of the state. The same can be seen in the Levitical system: the intercession of the Levites is needed for human beings to be able to secure, through the sacrificial offerings, their own redemption (*kappara*), the reparation of their soul and their condition; but, once the action is performed, within the Temple confines, the sole arena of Levitical sovereignty, the benefit of the action is felt outside, on the repentant people. No embodiment of the one is possible in the Hebraic state, because it is in concealment, as are the Levites, missing and gone from the geographic morphology of the tribes, hidden in the Temple, in passage with the being of passage. Presuming to attain oneness in this world would mean stepping out of the passage, leaving the Temple, which is a major wrongdoing for the Levites.[326] The state, within the nation, is poor, as are the Levites in the polity.

The Levites' status within the nation gives us an effective idea of the status of the state. If, as we have seen, they constitute the political class, this class is in "abasement" (at least in terms of the will to power). "You will set it down in your gates, and the Levite, for he has no portion or inheritance, and the foreigner, the widow, and the orphan who dwell with you [will come and hear]" (Deut. 14:18). As strangers, as the vehicles of strangeness in the people, the Levites find themselves in the company of the "fallen," the lowly, and the feeble, of all the outcasts who stand at the "gates of the city," at the very site of the seat of power and its bodies in the Hebraic polity.

This geosymbolic localization tells us about the Hebraic tradition of power: it stands by those on the fringes of power or who have fallen from it. Is this because power is associated with fallenness, or because it is thought not to possess strength? Is it a way of reminding power that its fundamental trial hinges on its relationship to such categories? Be that as it may, the Levites, and hence the state, are identified with the waiting for gift giving, with dependency on the other. They count among those who wait to be given in

326. It is interesting to take a look at Aaron and Miriam's sin (Num. 12). They spoke against their brother, Moses, in particular against Jethro's daughter, Zipporah, whom he'd married. Miriam was punished with leprosy. Having reduced Moses to exteriority and exhibition (by talking against him in his absence as if his *nefesh* were a lifeless object, as if absence rhymed with inexistence), she is herself reduced to exteriority, her skin infected with leprosy. For the Levite, to leave the Temple is like speaking against God.

order to live, in the (divine) waiting for human beings to recall that they were born (from God). Their income is not owed to them; it is a gift, not a salary or a tax.

Fundamentally, this gift is a compensation for the fact that they have no share in the land or the heritage; their portion is God! But this compensation is not imposed; the tribes give them a tenth part of the yield of their land of their own free will. What's more, the tithe is not theirs alone: "Speak to the Levites... when you will have received from the children of Israel the tithe that I have given to you from them as your heritage, you will take from it a tenth of the tenth as YHWH's tribute... and you will give YHWH's tribute to Aaron the priest; from all your donations you will set aside whole this portion for YHWH, taking from the best part what must be consecrated from it" (Num. 18:26–29). Likewise, their subsistence depends on chance events in human circumstances (sins or impure physical conditions), in sum, on nature and the sacrifices offered by individuals (see Josh. 13:14). If the tribes forget the terms of the covenant and neglect the tithe, the Levites, the political class of the Hebraic state, end up in utter scarcity and economic destitution.

The Universality of the Law

This is a political class whose destiny is intimately linked to the destiny of the law and the covenant without which there is no people of Israel. If the latter gives itself over to idolatry, the condition of the Levites worsens and the state collapses, not only symbolically, because the law is not observed, but very concretely: the political personnel flee in disarray. Thus, the Levites have a particular interest in the Hebrews' keeping of the law and in the perpetuation of the universal. The Levites poverty and dependence are absolute guarantees of the veracity of this paradoxical "identification" with the universal (which transcends identity). The Levitical class lives on a principle that opposes permanent civil-service employment. The uncertainty of life and of the future is the Levites' lot, not the lot of other citizens, as it is in the modern state.

Nonetheless the Levites can succumb to the temptation of forming a powerful cast and elite. Other mechanisms in the covenant work to counter this natural eventuality. Firstly, the class of priests, which would be most likely to undertake such an enterprise, is carefully differentiated from the Levitical tribe, so that the function of "mediation," the function of power, that could be expected from the Levites is limited and identified with the priests among them, which is in turn circumscribed in a restricted field, that of the

Temple, with a strictly ritual worship–related scope (the sacrifices). The rest of the Levitical tribe is assigned a function whose contours are extremely vague and informal. These Levites are "given" as assistants to the priests; they do not perform the sacrifices but carry out secondary services in the Temple. There seem to be two main aspects to their overall function: music in the Temple and pronouncing the law (Ezek. 44:24), plus a less clear-cut yet cardinal function related to their scattered presence in the Levitical cities throughout the country. The priestly class has no reason for being anywhere except in Jerusalem, at the site of the only Temple and the only altar in Israel.

The universality and dispersion of the Levitical tribe in each region of Israel points to the universality of the law, one and the same for all. The Levites' presence at the "gate of the city,"[327] alongside the poor, society's outcasts and foreigners, alongside the "have-nots," brings them closer to the people of Israel, who can approach them with no special formality. They benefit from none of the specific procedures of an elite class. The fact that they are seated among the feeble is significant. This guarantees the proximity of the state to those most likely to be cast out of it. The seat of the senate, which makes political decisions, is also at the "gate," so when the Levites provide instruction about the law, they remind the senate of the Torah and thus serve as a constitutional review body. "The Levites at the gate" may even designate a "Levitical council" parallel to the "council of elders"—that is, the senate.

This system evidences the symbolic status of the law in the people. It is there like a stranger, in the manner of Leviticism but also of sovereignty. Isn't the Torah the voice of the strangeness of God the creator, the memory of his creativity in the world? The law is at the gates of the wilderness. From the wilderness to the threshold of the polity, it speaks to settled, forgetful human beings. Fragile and appealing, it attests in the place where men exercise power, in a way that only those who are subjected to it and suffer from it can testify. Thus, the Levite bears witness to the laws like strangers in the nation. They pronounce laws on all the public squares but do not ensure their application. It is a cardinal principle that the Levites map the political arena but do not effectuate it. Civil power (the senate and the king) is responsible for deciding on the application and forms of application of laws. So the senate and the king enact the political field, but the commonwealth (*res publica*) does not pertain to them. It pertains to the Levitical class, which is, however, not entitled to implement it, since this is the sole prerogative of civil power.

---

327. The "gate" of Jerusalem is, of course, the Temple, the "gate of the heavens" (Gen. 28:17).

We could say that Leviticism maps the field of the political in which
the state of the nation is built up, but it is the latter that makes Leviticism
possible by actuating the augment. This, too, is a mechanism that wards off
the Levitical temptation to exercise power, but it is also one of the surest
devices against tyranny.[328] Political power is so mobile that it can hardly rest
on a single person or a single body for long. The political field is exercised
in negativity: the universal that it determines is held in suspense. It is not
inhabited in the sense of control, but traversed in the sense of nomadism.
It creates or reflects the void that exists in the people, a void that is not
nothingness, because one could say it has an assigned locus: the Levites. This
void corresponds not to the exposed nakedness of the agora in the heart of
the city-state, but to the midst (*toch*) opening in the heart of the people of
Israel, which makes presence absent in the polity while providing for a place
(*makom*) for it. The geographic and architectural place is primarily carried
by the physical, bodily presence of the Levitical tribe in the people. Now we
can better grasp the function of transporting the elements of the Tabernacle
in the wilderness, which is the role of the entire Levitical tribe, because the
Levites are the locus of the Temple, the interior, and concealment in the
body of the people.

This mobility of the political, its unseizability, can be read in the prohibition of census taking, counting the children of Israel without an act of
redemption (Exod. 30:12), for it is impossible to turn the Levitical void or
divine absence (which found presence and sovereignty) into an object of
census. Can God be reified and counted? And it is because there are Levites
among the people that the people cannot be counted, for the Levites are not
counted among them and are not countable. In addition, isn't census taking the preeminent act by which a power takes possession of all the people
and assigns each and every one to his place? In this way, the ruling power
renders the whole of society transparent, exposing it and taking it out of the
concealment that protects it, out of the passage.[329]

The Levites are the eternal obstacle to such an enterprise. And so they can
hardly be seen as a state bureaucracy. Their universality amongst the people
cannot lead to such a phenomenon; indeed, the Levitical principle is not a

328. The Josephic principle similarly protected against sameness in nationality.

329. This is a calamity, of course, because census taking exposes the people outside,
taking it out of concealment and dooming it to disintegration in the passage (see II Sam.
24:10–25, where David takes a census that causes much death among the people, and the
pestilence ceases only when he makes a sacrificial offering). Census taking is possible only
with the offering of a sacrifice that atones for it.

principle of rationalization[330] of collective existence, insofar as it is organized in relation to overplus, to the additional, hidden one, whereas the development of the rational is founded on the already acquired, its accumulation and hoarding. There is nothing of the sort in Leviticism, with its dispossession, concealment, voiding, and bearing witness. Here we are looking at an altogether different dialectic of the universal: the one is maintained in its uniqueness, and this is what makes the multiple and the assembly possible. The Levite is precisely the one too many, kept in hiding in the interior, and this concealment in the people is what makes the state possible in the nation.

Representation and Concealment

The logic of concealment is totally different from the logic of representation. Indeed, we could have expected the Levitical class to assume a function of mediation between the people and God (through the sacrificial services) and between the people and itself (the Levite dispersion serving as a guarantee of tribal unity). Everywhere this is the cardinal function of the political. But due to the concealment, an altogether different logic is established. It is not that Levites map the universal in Israel because they mediate the contradictory particularities of the people in a universal for which they are the vehicle. It is rather because they themselves stand out as singular by operating a concealment, because they stand apart as particular by following the one, that the universal of multiplicity is possible. This is why the concealment (the logic of augret), the setting apart of the one as overplus, is the opposite of representation, whose purpose is to cover up and mask the lack and the void. The Levites produce lack. They institute it. In this way, the institution of the Hebrew state differs entirely from the rational institution of the state.

There is no better proof than the narrative in Exodus that tells us how the Levitical function is established in the aftermath of the golden calf episode. This is in fact the supreme exemplification of the foundation of the collective through the mediation of a representation (here, the calf) intended to mask Moses' absence, to fill the void that exists in all collectivities as in the experience of each individual. Leviticism teaches something altogether different: in it, communication—the (universalizing) place of particulars—is instituted not via the object of collective veneration, the representation of the absent people (in the past or in the future, not in the *present*), but via

330. In the manner of Max Weber.

absence and the void, that is to say, by way of overplus, the one safeguarded in concealment and secrecy.

Overplus, unlike representation, creates a gap, a vacuum into which particular individuals come rushing. By throwing the hypnotic fascination of the self-contained, self-centered group out of whack, it surprises each individual's expectation of sameness and draws him toward the one. By situating the multiple on the plane of overplus and not scarcity or the additional sum (the representation), it affords a way to get around the impasse of mediation in the process of recognizing the other. It is a matter not of representing and simulating the other or the universal, but of giving the other the possibility of manifesting itself in a process of gratuitous affluence. The Josephic spacing of overplus founds the place of a collectivity in which the (universal) relationship between particulars no longer occurs through mediation or representation. It throws the original situation of the dilemma (how to go from the particular to the universal) entirely out of order.

The logic of Leviticism is diametrically opposed to the logic of the Leviathan, as described by Hobbes, who saw the modern representative state as a huge machine, an artificial monster, animated piece by piece, with all the elements of the particularity to compose a sufficiently universal representation so every person in particular can see him or herself in it. Levi does not substitute himself for the multiple and the people to represent them. It is out of his absence to himself (his concealment) and his absence from the sharing and the heritage that the people manage to communicate and gather together. Levi does not set himself up as a representation for the people to unite behind. To the contrary, he absents himself in the House of the Veil, the House of Concealment, the Temple, where all representation is forbidden! Leviticism takes the lack and the void inherent in the *olam* and in the collectivity and translates it into overplus, not representation, into the one sheltered inside and not an artificial semblance of the one. Thus, the Levite testifies to the memory of God, who withdrew, and he redeems the *kahal*.

Leviticism turns the political and the state into an accompaniment, a companion of the course of the living nation. The latter is no longer locked in by the immobilizing weightiness of representation, as it is in the "rational" state. Leviticism accompanies the passage, where it is the vehicle of the sole possible form of presence, because the one is the promise of passage, which is always passage of the one and hence an ordeal of absence, of unclenching in the passage. The Levitical absence is etched in Jacob's promise (Gen. 29:22) to give the tenth of his possessions and his children to God if God safeguards him on his trip to Laban's, and this immediately after Jacob has a vision of his twelve sons. Levi is this tenth son, given to God and removed from Jacob.

The birth of Jacob's children is embedded in this suspension of being, especially visible in the giving of Levi. Levi is thereby the security (from the same root as *lov*, to lend on security), the safeguarded portion on the basis of which the people of Israel is born, the being held in suspense that gathers all together in the suspense for which it is the vehicle in the people. It is from this standpoint that we are to understand that the Levites were given to God instead of the firstborn of Israel (Num. 8), who were safeguarded when the firstborn of Egypt were taken.

How can a particular "carry" the universal? How can it weave the weft of universality? How are we to account for the particularity of Levi, Israel's companion and escort in the passage? What is the status of companion, if he is what makes the universal a companion and not a paper figure, a drawing of a serene representation behind which the multitude would disappear? The companion, unlike the representation, can be called upon. What makes for the universality of the companion is his concealment, but he nonetheless holds on to his particular uniqueness, sheltered in the one. How could he abandon it when he is beside the one, the promise of each individual *nefesh*? His existential solitude is a guarantee of the universality, the solitude of the Levite's love for Israel, of God's love for Israel, of Israel's love for humanity, the solitude of the one that quenches the thirst of the multitude.

Herein resides the meaning of his singularity and particularity. The Levite is the vehicle of this specificity of Israel, and this is what immerses him in the universal. But due to the concealment that is at the very principle of this solitude, the distinction and particularity of the Levite in relation to the rest of Israel do not produce a hierarchical structure; they do not yield a dominant political class with a theological substrate, as part of a system of castes defined by how close they are to the Levitical source. Very much to the contrary, if there is a summit to a hierarchy, the concealment deprives the social ladder of its (Levitical) pinnacle. The problematic of the hidden one, insofar as it is founded on overplus and not on scarcity, does not engender hierarchy, which always presupposes a context of penurious conflictuality that compels classification.

The Hebraic political society is thus a society in which the hierarchical principle is defused, when it could have developed in it in a major way, precisely through the Levitical institution. The Levitical voiding produces a malleable context instead, whose very principle is mobility, and whose absent (yet real) center generates the multiplication of centers in the political field with which we are familiar and that have been illustrated in reality in Jewish history, from the chaotic anarchism of the era of Judges to the diasporic period.

Sacrifice and War

Consequently, far from founding a hierarchy, Leviticism is the vehicle of the *kahal*, Israel's public arena, where particular persons meet like stars gravitating in a nebula. The collectivity crystallizes around the spiral, drained by the void in the total tribal count and its absence: "and you shall approach (*hikravta*) the Levites before the Tent of Meeting, and you shall make a *kahal* of the *eda* of the children of Israel" (Num. 8:9). Through the proximity of *krav*, combat, and *korban*, sacrifice, in this rapprochement (*hakrava*), we can better grasp the violent past of the father of the Levitical tribe. From the outset, there is a hesitation between two forms of approach, and it is because Levi proved himself capable of violence that he must devote himself to sacrifice. The *korban* is the antithesis of *krav*. Levi needs the Torah in order to resist the drift away from his sacrificial vocation and toward his involvement in confrontational violence, wherein two aspirations to total fullness that do not leave room for each other clash.

The Hebraic *korban* is in this way the antithesis of the Greek *harmonia*,[331] whose root, *ar*, designates the close interlocking of the parts of a whole and hence a proximity in which there are no voids or spaces, no room for gifts. Harmony is the discourse of Ares, the god of war, and it underpins the Greek conception of social peace (via the *areopagus*, the tribunal that judges disputes). This harmony is an attempt to crystallize the whole by joining end to end separate pieces in a way that attenuates differences, smoothens the edges, and eliminates the gap that characterizes all things in the world and the relief that makes its depth. This is why night is its favorite moment, the darkness when there is no distinction, separation, or concealment (for daytime is the time of concealment). Daybreak is the time of the *korban*, the time when the relief rents things from darkness, separates them in the one, out of the jumble of the all, and distinguishes their differences. Rare indeed are the nocturnal sacrifices.

Two types of society here oppose one another in their founding principle (war or sacrifice), but the economies of existence developed by the two are

---

331. See Vernant, *Mythe et pensée*; and Nicole Loraux on stasis as "place of division."

surprisingly similar. There is a pronounced correspondence between the status of the Levites in the Hebraic society and that of warriors in Greek society, a correspondence in terms of structural function, of course. Hippodamus distinguishes three functional classes divided into three areas. The warrior class corresponds to the public sphere, where wars are conducted; the artisans to the sacred sphere, where the gods reside; and the farmers to the private sphere, the arena of individual action. It is noteworthy that the public sphere is that of the warriors, and indeed the agora was initially the place where the battalions gathered in prescribed order, the circle through which equals were "adjusted" in relation to one another and around which words were exchanged. The political arena is the arena of war, of combat (*krav*), and the class that oversees it is the warrior class.

Thus, with an aim that parallels the Hebraic intention, the Athenian city-state sought to isolate the military function from contact with economic life. The bearers of arms had no personal property; they were provided for by state spending on communal land. Assuming by their function responsibility for the communal or public sphere, they were entitled to no possessions *in particular* as individuals, and their public activity could have no private character. Thus, Greece constructed the universal through the mutual adjustment of particular individuals that enables war and fighting. This is a military universal in which the approach is that of combat and the officers are bearers of arms, not officiants. The political class is the class with the greatest power, the power of arms. The Greek city-state tried to build up its universal without including particular persons. Whence the status of this class was founded on a legal myth: that of the economic independence of warriors, as if the system that made it possible to provide for the warriors were independent of the economic sphere. On the contrary, the Levitical class, although it is removed from tribal property, receives the tithe and is thereby at the core of the economic system, to which it adds a very original dynamic.

In Greece, the political is founded on the symbolic (ideological) expulsion of the economic and professional, thus giving rise to an abstract sphere inhabited by men who are supposed not to really live, so that instead of running through all areas of life, citizenship is made into an illusory separate field, and political activity, into a profession all the more abstract in that it is detached from economic life. The state universality that Greece founds, despite its professed ambition of absolute autonomy, carries with it a whole, disjointed economic system and social classification, because they are not recognized as such or experienced or confronted for what they are. In the

Hebraic polity, such a trial is essential, and in this regard we can see the whole problematic of citizenship.

Rousseau develops a similar perspective when he describes the tribunate, in the manner of the tribunes in Rome, conceived in terms of the republic and the modern state as he imagines it prophetically. He basically sees the structure of the tribunate as we have described the Levitical function in Israel and the warrior function in Greece. "When an exact proportion cannot be established between the constituent parts of the state, or when causes that cannot be removed continually alter the relation of one part to another, there is recourse to the institution of a peculiar magistracy that enters into no corporate unity with the rest. This restores to each term its right relation to the others and provides a link or middle term between either prince and people or prince and sovereign, or, if necessary, both at once. This body, which I shall call the tribunate, is the preserver of the laws and of legislative power. It serves sometimes to protect the sovereign against the government, as the tribunes of the people did in Rome; sometimes to uphold the government against the people, as the Council of Ten now does in Venice; and sometimes to maintain the balance between the two, as the Ephors did in Sparta. The tribunate is not a constituent part of the city and should have no share in either legislative or executive power; but this very fact makes its own power the greater: for, while it can do nothing, it can prevent anything from being done. It is more sacred and more revered, as the defender of the laws, than the prince who executes them, or than the sovereign which ordains them."[332]

We have seen how this "link" or "middle term" is posited in an altogether different way in Leviticism insofar as it does not assume a role of mediation and representation that unites all the parts of the political body. The Levites enter into corporate unity with the others, unlike the tribunes or the military prytanes, even though they do so via the void. This is the gist of their structure in the people: they are an integral part of the people, but they are so based on their uniqueness and particularity, not on the artifice and illusion of some sort of universal neutrality. It is nonetheless certain that the Levitical dynamic institutes relations that are not exactly proportional between the parts of the state. It is more a moving procedure than a spatial model of division. It is through developing and traversing the nation that the state is constituted and formalized in a way more "Baroque" than "Cartesian." The Levites distinguish themselves not in *krav* and war, like the Athenian warriors, but in the *korban* and music.

332. Rousseau, *Social Contract*.

It is interesting to compare the elective activity of the "public" class in the Athenian city with that of the Hebraic public class. Through it, the vocation of the civilization as a whole emerges. What is found at the heart of Israel, at the very foundation of the state, is giving and music, not fighting and war.[333] The entire vocation of its existence is summed up in this. All activity (and notably economic activity by way of the tithe) is meaningful only to teach music to the Levites and the laws of sacrifice to the priests among the Levites. The tithe from the produce of the land finances the music of the Levites!

The finality of the art of governing, like that of offering sacrifices, is the gift and the passage, but to achieve this end they must first distinguish themselves in the realm of fixity. We can thus see why the Levite priests are responsible for sounding the horn "to summon the eda and set the camps in motion. And you will sound them, and all the eda will gather around you in council at the entrance to the Tent of Meeting" (Num. 10:2–3). They are both knowledgeable in sacrificial rigor and faithful to the eda.[334] They can sound the horn but not give voice to man. Only the Levites can do the latter when on the steps of the forecourt to the Temple they sing songs. To sing, to sound the horn, is to tear through the order of fullness, to introduce emptiness and movement, passage in the human. In sounding the horn, the priests go to the end of rigor and arouse the memory of the origin, of the withdrawal, of the gift. "On the day of your joy and your festivals, and for your ceremonies, you will sound the horns, over your burnt offerings and over your peace offerings, and they shall be a remembrance for you before your God; I am YHWH, your God" (10:10). This is why they can unite, in the echo of testimony, the community of testimony that stands in birth-giving mercy (rahamim). The Levites sing and make music; they are already in the passage. There are two complementary logics at work here: the one (priestly) is geometrical and spatial (examining the leper's lesions, knowing how to perform sacrifices, to cut the sacrificial animal); the other is mathematical and abstract (music and chords). Together they make the unity of the Levitical function, the only one apt to bring together the collectivity of Israel (8:9).

333. See below, Book IV, ch. 2, "Song of the Stars."

334. During the golden calf episode, the Levites alone remained faithful to the eda (Exod. 32:26).

II. THE OPENNESS OF LEVITICAL SPACE: THE LAND

As we have seen, the absence of the Levites in the apportioning of the land between the tribes is one of the more important characteristics of the Levitical system. This is where their removal from the final tribal count is most apparent, because it is manifested here in the very morphology of the people. But it would be a mistake to conclude that the Levites are removed from the spatial dimension in order to be integrated into a purely temporal one illustrated by their musical function. In fact, Leviticism involves not a renunciation of space but an altogether different relationship to it, one that obeys the logic of passing and crossing rather than settling.

From the Levitical standpoint, space is voided at its core, and it is in this void that the *makom* extends in space; this is the place of dwelling where strangeness lives. Leviticism also forges this *makom* in Israel through the agency of the Levite taking the place of the firstborn of Israel (Num. 8:17–18), and we can learn something of the nature of this place from the odd term used to designate the Levitical "replacement" or "exchange": "beneath (*tahat*)."[335] This is the place of another, someone else's stead, a place that is never totally self-identical. In the place there is other than myself.

The Levites are the place in the people where the other is most transparent and closest in the opacity of fullness and the occupation of land. This is why they are not granted the right to property. More than any other tribe, they know one can never really "own" land, can never appropriate as one's own the land "beneath" which divine gratuitousness stands, the land that is the very trace of divine effacement and withdrawal. "To possess," in actual fact as in spirit, is to forget God, to no longer recall his creational withdrawal, to believe in "nature." Obviously, such a vision of place carries with it an implicit conception of nature. Insofar as it sees place as a suspension of another place, as tension with another place, "nature" as a self-sufficient, objectified system facing man (presupposed in the relationship of ownership and property) does not exist. The Levites have a structural knowledge of the fact that nature does not exist and that there is nothing to possess in the world. This may explain their lack of direct contact with the agricultural world, for they live

335. It is said of the creation of Eve that God "took one of his [Adam's] sides and closed the flesh beneath (*tahat*)" (Gen. 2:21).

in "Levitical cities." Only through sacrifices do they come into contact with the land, and then only through the process of sanctification and separation.

The Firstborn

The Levite is more aware than others that he is in the place of the other, in the place left empty by the divine retreat. But how are we to understand this emergence of the self in the place of the other? Is it by way of substitution? Is a place necessarily a substitution for the original place? The Levites are "beneath/in the place of the opening of all wombs, of all firstborn from the children of Israel" (Num. 8:16). The Levite stands in the place of all openings, and there is opening because there is divine withdrawal. He stands in the place of him who withdrew to create place. The void is hidden in the secrecy of the place. It is because Levi stands in this void (which he echoes in the people) that he belongs to God, who removed himself and created this void so his creature could arise in it. "Because all firstborn are mine" can be read as "Because all emptiness, all opening, all beginning is mine."

The firstborn, inasmuch as they are the first to open the womb, the first to experience the opening and the void, are God's property. All that pertains to the *reshit* of the origin directly pertains to God. We are now in a better position to understand why it is always the younger sons in Jacob's family, not the firstborn, who inherit. We can also understand what Abraham did wrong when he questioned God about what he would inherit (Gen. 15:2), thereby situating his vocation in the context of heritage when it proceeds in fact from the wombing void. And his sin is logically punished by the announcement of four hundred years of exile (15:13), the experience of dispossession, void, and passage.

Why do the firstborn die in Egypt? Because God intervenes in his creation; he fills the void that is the *reshit* and, as a result, the creatures closest to the *reshit* die, because the void through which they pass can no longer sustain them. At that moment, the only possible strategy of survival is through giving and sacrificing—which Egypt ignores but Israel practices with the Passover lamb. Thus, the firstborn of Israel should have died. And because they were safeguarded, they doubly belong to God and must be kept in hiding.

They are consecrated to perform the *korban* for all of the families of Israel, because they alone know the meaning of the *korban*, which is precisely the experience of "making room for another." The *korban* is giving and offering, the consecration of all *reshit*, all beginnings; the sacrificial offering is "beneath/

in place of" the sinner (void). It does not take the place of the sinner. The sacrificer creates a vacuum in his possessions by his offering; he renews the place of the absent one. This sacrificial consecration is tantamount to a "death" of sorts for the firstborn of Israel; or rather, it is a strategy for getting and turning around their death, by and in life. Concealment harbors something of the appearance of death, because it is a way out of the ineluctability of death and exhaustion in the world of passage.

There is a natural tendency in this world to doubt him who vanished and made room for the other: "Is there Yhwh in our midst (*kerev*) or the void (*ayin*)?" (Exod. 17:7). The Levites are therefore understandably on the verge of nonexistence and dereliction. Therefore, we have Israel's political class counted alongside its widows and orphans.

But the golden calf episode challenged the concealment of the firstborn of Israel, who betrayed it precisely by renouncing their ability to "put themselves in the place of," by renouncing creational mercy and birth-giving virtue, by no longer being able to maintain themselves in the void, which is sanctification to God, by substituting an idol for themselves and filling the divine wombing void. The idol is, in a different way, "in place of/beneath" God. It fills his absence. The place of Israel collapses as a result, because the *reshit* has been given away, exposed, represented, taken out of hiding.

The Levitical institution actually dates to this moment, which is, no doubt, at the origin of all institutions in Israel, the Levites' taking the place and function of the elders of Israel and forming a tribe in their own right, a collectivity in the nation, with a function integrated into the plan of the collective structure and no longer dependent on what may or may not happen, in particular, with the eventual birth of the firstborn. From that time on, Israel became a formalized, constituted nation. Jacob's vow of giving a tenth of his possessions and children was materialized and formalized as a result of the golden calf that the Hebrews substituted for the wombing void, for the place (*makom*). The Levites are like the gift of all of Israel to the Temple, "Given, given are they to me" (Num. 8:16), and by their presence and the system that structures their existence, they reactualize the *reshit*, the void in the apparent "fullness" of the world. "Woe to you who join house to house and approach field to field to absorb the territory land and make yourselves alone the owners of the land" (Isa. 5:8). The Levitical function spreads emptiness, absence, and concealment throughout the people.

The Tithe

The question of whether the tithe is given to the Levites in compensation (as a substitution) for the land they did not receive is very important. The tithe actually represents the backward motion of the Levitical retreat. This is when the people manifests itself by the Levitical yardstick, and it becomes clear whether the educational thrust inherent in the Levitical structure has borne fruit.

It is the very meaning of the "function" that exists in Leviticism that is at issue here. If there is "compensation," then the Levitical voiding is annulled. The gap is filled in, a place holder is substituted for the void, a fetish that will be its vehicle, without having actually undergone the ordeal. The finality of the trial is not to find itself annulled but rather to enable the crossing over to a different state.

"Compensation" is a paraphrase for substitution, replacement, and ultimately erasure. It is one of the tactics of representation. It is in exchange for the services of their function that the Levites would receive the tithe, as a salary and compensation. But we are not employing the notion of function for Leviticism in this sense, which would be a theoretical look, after the fact. What is at work in the Levitical relationship is not an "exchange" or a substitution. The tithe, the backward motion of the Levitical withdrawal, is a gift. The tribes give it to the Levites in the Temple and at the gate, although no coercive law *obliges* them to do so. The Levitical retreat (like the creation of the world) is utterly gratuitous. It can yield no profit, because its purpose is to establish the responsibility of the one for whom the withdrawal made room. There is no guarantee from the start that the enterprise will succeed. In this sense, the Levite does not "socially" fulfill a "function." If that were the issue, we would still be in the realm of representation. There is a giving in the Levitical withdrawal; there is a giving in the tithe—that is to say, a reviviscence of the pure gratuitousness of the origin.

This is why the vocabulary of "redemption" and compensation is actually inadequate for all that pertains to Leviticism and sacrifice. It is a matter not of filling a void or rectifying a deviation but, to the contrary, of reopening to the void and the passage what was congealed in it. In this respect, the Levites stand at the edge of the universe's open womb, in whose vicinity man pursues his passage, his way to a birth that has not yet come to be. The gift of the tithe helps human beings in the world avoid or destroy the ever-lurking illusion that they are already born. It opens them to the void, takes them out of the petrifying illusion of fullness, and enables them to "pass on." In sum, it hides them.

Offering the tithe, the first fruits of the harvest, or delivering or freeing the firstborn[336] involves concealment, a concealment for the one who, by offering them, removes them from his own enjoyment, a true concealment in the Temple of an offering made to those who are "hidden" and absent in the nation. In this way, the divine Name is recalled, out of whose effacement the world was woven.

Isn't the sense of the term *kappara* related more to concealment than to redemption? Such a concealment is an antirepresentation, both literally and figuratively. Firstly, it does not give itself to be seen and does not expose itself; it turns objects into smoke. Moreover, it does not substitute one entity for another, but it allows the one that undergoes "passage" to continue to exist, because the passage is performed in veiling, in the "nonappearance" of concealment, in disappearance.

Thus, the Levites, the political class in Israel, are not "representatives" of the tribes and do not take the place of the tribes before God and men, because they efface themselves; they are the effacement in the nation that, through them, passes through a decisive step in its "identity," but does so without being effaced itself, without the Levites' standing in for it and representing it. In this concealment, the presence is never so hidden from view that it must be represented. The concealment is, to the contrary, what maintains the quicksilver motion of this presence. It is in this sense that we are to understand that the Levites are "beneath/in the place of the opening of all wombs of all firstborn." It is not that they take the place of or represent the firstborn, but they help them perform their concealment (*kappara*) in their passage through the world. The firstborn are more likely than younger siblings to surrender to the illusion of absolute self-sufficiency, an illusion bound up with the sortilege of forgetting inherent in the experience of passage in the *olam*, because younger sons know they are preceded by an elder who exerts a form of power over them. Consequently, they are more likely to remember the void of the world, to remember the Name of the creator. They are paradoxically closer to the womb's opening, which is why they need not be "redeemed/hidden," covered, delivered as the firstborn. The Levitical maieutics (bringing about passage in the world by removing from the threatening void) proves itself to be totally different from the philosophical maieutics, whose sole aim is to erase the memory of the world.

336. This is the meaning of *pidiyon ben*.

A Declivity in the People

Thus the Levitical principle helps the diversity of Israel move to a unity that, in its effects, is not representative and centralized at all, since it is hidden and held in suspense. It hovers but does not alight. The work of this principle in the nation builds a "hearth" (more than a "center," or a center without centralization) around which the nation unites beyond the passage. We can assess the whole scope of the Levitical construction in the national space.

The Levitical institution produces a "declivity" of sorts in the people that tends to spread out all over. It forces it to slope, to flow down to a "center," like "the streams that flow to the sea, and the sea is not full" (Eccles. 1:7), to a place that (literally and figuratively) is below the tribes, not above them, a place that is, moreover, the mouth and container of the waters of the people. This is why the Levite, who performs the *korban*, is also the one who effects the rapprochement (*hakrava*) of the social. The void he carries with him makes a place for all parts of the people. The people sink into the Levitical void, vanishing from the surface of the earth, to gather and unite in an interior (*toch*) that is the true center of the people, a center that curves inward rather than rising prominently.

The center is the place through which the world disappears, the place where one passes and where concealment is accomplished. The spatial system of its construction is complex. It is developed in all aspects of the Levitical logic to begin with, but also in the institution of the Levitical cities. By being removed from the sharing of land, the Levitical tribe becomes (through concealment, as we have seen) the tribe of all tribes. Each tribe in particular enjoys a portion of the Levitical share taken away from the Levites' global use. Thus, the territory of each tribe shadows forth a portion of the Levitical land, a similar portion in the variety of different landscapes of the tribal lands, so there is a similar referent throughout the diversity of lands, but a referent by mode of absence. A mute, absent territory rises in all the lands, which invests them with a presence that breaks the autochthony and forms a system of rapprochement of territorial singularities, overstepping the barriers between them.

Is this abstract and absent land, a land lost to the Levites for good, a way to make the "sphere" of the Temple visible and audible in every territory and property? Through each tribe's possession of the share of land that would have been bestowed on the Levites, a communication is established between all the separated and compartmentalized tribes. This possession of the Levitical portion by the tribes, at once in common (it is the portion of the whole Levitical tribe) and in particular (since each tribe possesses a portion of the total Levitical share), institutes the presence of the collectivity and unity in the very territory of property and intimacy. In the innermost depths of the most egocentric possession of land subsists a portion that memory assigns to the other and that opens the recesses of property to the other.

Thus, the principle of the collectivity is structurally embedded in the social system of occupation of space. Concealment is implemented in the land itself. In this sense, an overall and particularized system of balance in the relations between the members of the nation is set up through the Levites, which helps "compensate" (in the sense of counterbalance) for any morphological inequality between the tribes, any congealed particularization that would isolate a member from the whole. The dispersion of the Levites throughout the land ("the Levite who will be at your gates," Deut. 16:14) is the key procedure in this respect. The same particular Levitical tribe is found everywhere, alongside each (tribal) particularity. And it universalizes through this work, through this sharpening of the particular over the particular, this particularizing multiplication in the number of particulars. The particularization of the universal at work here is altogether astonishing.

The Levitical Cities

This multiplication undergoes an "institutionalization" in the form of the Levitical cities spread throughout the tribes, which spatially embody the Levitical share hidden in/beneath each tribe's land. Cities are abstract, wholly man-made forms of "territoriality" cut off from nature and topography. In a manner of speaking, they are an extraterritoriality within the tribal territoriality, and this is in fact their political status. "They shall give to the Levites from their share of property cities for dwelling, and the outskirts all around the cities you shall also give to the Levites" (Num. 35:2). The political class that carries the principle of sovereignty as dwelling, that makes of Israel a "house," could be manifested only in the weft of houses that constitute a city, which form the interiority in nature's exposed exteriority, the intimacy of the human in the rough adversity of the outside. The city turns anonymous geographical places into passageways (where things approach one another, where the walls of homes come close together), to make us pass inside it. In sum, the city is the preeminent place of concealment for the human. And where the Temple stands, there stands the city; it is even in relation to the

Temple of Jerusalem that the other cities are cities.[337] In this respect, the city is the basic vehicle of human history.

There is something paradoxical in seeing Leviticism, theoretically the vehicle of nomadism and desedentarization, produce urbanization—the sole urbanization in the tribal agricultural context. With nomadism invested in urbanization, the traditional categories of anthropology need to be reassessed when applied to the Hebraic case. A radical rupture with agriculture marks the Levitical cities. There are the cities but also plots of land around them to be used as pasture for the Levites' cattle. The Levites have a relationship only to beings with a spirit, a *nefesh*, human or animal, but not to minerals or plants.

Could the city be a mobile, nomadic element on earth? At any rate, it's clear that this is usually not the case, and we can see why Leviticism offers a countermodel, especially if we take into account the biblical tradition of cities. The city in the Bible can be the work of Cain's offspring, a place where concealment is used for misguided purposes (since Cain and Enoch build the city to escape responsibility for Abel's murder), or the site where the Tower of Babel is erected, a place where disclosure and representation are erected and opposed to the heavens, just as it can be the place where the Temple becomes the principle of representation.

Leviticism must prevail as much in the city as in exposed space. This means that it has within itself a propensity for misusing concealment. The city is therefore not a certainty for the Levite; it stands as a challenge not only in relation to agriculture but also in relation to itself. The Levitical city redeems the Cainic city in a way. This is why the total number of Levitical cities counts "six refuge cities." The notion of refuge[338] is interesting in relation to concealment, of course, but it is their purpose that is even more significant: they serve as asylums for accidental murderers seeking refuge to protect themselves against acts of vengeance while awaiting the pronouncement of their sentence.

By taking refuge in the Levitical cities, murderers escape banishment (*herem*), perhaps because vengeance and pursuit are forbidden in these cities that are themselves "banished" and extraterritorial, in their own way. It is nothing less than astonishing to realize that the Levites, the purest of the tribes of Israel, are living in their cities side by side with murderers! No

337. The Hebraic cities are Levitical cities because the Levites gather around the unique Temple.

338. *Miklat* also designates that which is taken in.

doubt, this has to do with their general hallowing function. The primordial importance of this function should not be lost from sight. Thus, the person who is the object of a *herem* is not subject to a prohibition of worship and sacrifice, or of participating in Temple ceremonies. Refuge cities stand beyond judgment. They are spaces of *rahamim*, just as the Levites stand on the verge of *rehem*, on the verge of the wombing void, and help the murderer escape the reversal of the womb's receptivity (*rehem*) that is the judgment of banishment (*herem*—the same letters in a different order).

The status of the six cities is fundamental to Leviticism. They underpin the possibility of the other Levitical cities, which are said to be founded on/ in addition to them: "and the cities you will give to the Levites, the six refuge cities you will give for the murderer to flee to, and on top of them you will give forty-two cities" (Num. 35:6–7). The number of Levitical cities, that is, forty-eight, is a multiple of six. This illustrates structurally the paradigmatic value of the principle of "refuge." The (Levitical) cities are modeled on the paradigm of refuge cities, and this is the weft with which the urban and spatial fabric of Eretz Yisrael is woven. The Talmud (Makot 9–12) tells us that "the roads always run from one refuge city to the other." The whole space of Israel is one of redemption and concealment. There can be no cities and consequently no roads (since roads run between designated places with names, and not between nameless, nondifferentiated sites) except through the prism of refuge cities. And it is this network of cities that creates the space of the land of Israel, formalizing and structuring it, taking it out of the adverse anonymity of passage through concealment. But their principle is one of redemption (*kappara*). These cities are reference points to the void in the fullness of space, and only "wombing paths" link them to one another. The city is a wombing abode that lends itself to passage in the heart of the fullness of the land.

City Outskirts

But aside from the meaning and import of the institution, and beyond the diversity and compartmentalization of the Levitical cities, their very number plays a role in promoting equality, harmony, and unity between the tribes. The Levites receive forty-eight cities in all (Josh. 21:41). In principle, this number can be divided by twelve. So even though each tribe gives according to its possibilities—"from those who have a lot you shall take a lot, and from those who have less you shall take less; each shall give of his cities to the

Levites according to the portion he inherited" (Num. 35:8)—the symbol of twelve tribes continues to be the principle governing the concession of cities.

Each tribe is supposed to give four cities, and by and large this is what actually happens (Josh. 21). The number four is significant in its own right, since it refers to the four letters of the divine Name of unity. Thus, there is at work a principle of coherence and "balance," of particularized universality, in a situation that is unequal and unbalanced by nature.

The concession made by all to the Levites, in their particularity, is the occasion of enacting a universal rule whose effectiveness produces the particularization of one and all. Thus, when they are put into a relationship with the Levites, the tribes find a principle of equality in the model of the twelve, a principle independent of their respective demographic or territorial strengths, which are necessary, not equal. It is the privileged relationship to a particular (the Levite) that creates a framework of universal reference. Thus it is said that the Levitical cities are taken from "the possession of the children of Israel" (Num. 35:8). This relationship is instituted through a procedure that involves giving, setting apart, and consecrating to the absent, needy Levites. And it is on the occasion of this gift and this setting apart (of the Levitical cities) that the condition of the tribes is harmonized according to a principle of equality.

The type of property that is given over to the Levites in the cities indicates the relationship to the land that emerges from the Levitical system. There is a paradoxical reversal in the expected terms of the relationship. The Levites possess the city not collectively, but rather one by one, through the houses each individual owns. On the other hand, the outskirts are owned collectively by the Levitical city as a whole. In this way, the houses are subject to the law of the Jubilee year, so if they are sold, they must be restored to their owners every fifty years, but the outskirts of the city cannot be sold and are not subject to Jubilee laws, since they are owned in common by the Levites. This means that this land on the outskirts of the city is the only place in the whole land of Israel that is not owned (which the cities are to a certain extent, inasmuch as their houses are owned). Setting their boundaries is problematical and necessitates an interpretation of the text. "The outskirts of the cities... that you shall give to the Levites from the wall of the city outward will have a thousand cubits all around. You shall measure from outside the city on the eastern side two thousand cubits; on the southern side, two thousand cubits; on the western side, two thousand cubits; and on the northern side two thousand cubits, and the city will be in the middle; this shall be for them the outskirts of the city" (Num. 35:4–5).

Israel's Interiority

The purpose of this complex, contradictory calculation[339] is to situate and position the city "in the middle" or "inside" (depending on whether the word is read *tavech* or *toch*). What makes the inside is what surrounds it (Num. 35:2); the outskirts of the city are the most critical part of the city. That is where the city that is their interior, their middle, takes shape.

An understanding of the principle underlying the calculation of the "outskirts of the city" provides insight into the principle of building a *toch*, an interior.[340] The city is in the space of the *toch* (interior), which is why it cannot be the object of possession. It is because it is given, because it is removed from "the possession of the children of Israel," that it is an "interior," a "middle," just as Abraham's sacrificial offerings in the Covenant between the Pieces gave him a *toch*, a middle through which to pass to conclude the covenant. This is what is meant by "and [Levi] shall not have a possession in the *kerev* of his brothers." Levi cannot have possessions in his brother's *kerev*, or proximity, because he is the one who makes the *kerev* possible. Here there is no property, only emptiness, gratuity, and passage. In this sense, the city that houses the Temple is the preeminent locus of concealment in the *olam*. Levi has no share in Israel, no part in the apportioning of the land of Israel, because he is the safeguarded portion removed from Israel. In Israel, Levi is the opening of the womb and the sphere of emergence, the very echo in the fullness of the nation of the pristine and primal void of the womb. His "presence" (on the mode of withdrawal) secures the perpetual renewal of Israel's upsurging, which is the principle of its long-lived permanence.

The setting "a*part*" of Levi, his elective *part*icularization within the nation, his concealment in the one, removes Israel from totality and from the main trap in the passage that is the world, thereby bringing the trial of passage to its elective culmination (the one). This "setting apart" in secrecy serves to ensure that Israel is not counted in parts that are destined to be totaled and hence set in a relationship of eventual interchange, infinite exchange, a relationship of anonymization, of "des-unicitation," of yielding to the flow of absolute passage, of anticoncealment and the sinking of the one into the multiple, which can lead only to petrifaction in the passage, to lapsing into

339. How it can be both two thousand and a thousand cubits is a question that gives rise to different commentaries by Rashi, Maimonides, and others.

340. The Levitical city, like the camp in the Sinai, is square-shaped (extending two thousand cubits from the city in the four cardinal directions).

nothingness instead of growing in the void. It is, as we have seen, because there are Levites in the nation that Israel cannot be the object of census taking; they are the uncountable part. Their irreducibility to a global count makes it impossible to establish a total count of the number of souls in Israel.

The Levitical setting apart thus engenders a void and an absence whose inner logic makes absolute division impossible (for the total division into parts presupposes the whole). There will always be a discrepancy, a "blurriness," a failure, a missing "part" in the division that will obstruct any pat arithmetical order. (Levi is the zero that is not counted but without which one cannot count from ten up, which echoes Jacob's tithe given in the form of his tenth son, Levi.) Levi is the hidden portion that attests to the apportioning, or, to be more precise, to its relativity, to the temporal nature of "property" in the world, a social, institutional echo of which is found in the Jubilee, when all acquired earthly property is restored to its legitimate owner at the end of every fifty-year cycle. A principle of estrangement at the heart of ownership weakens the entitlement to property and deprives it of the illusion of eternity and absoluteness that usually goes with it.

Human Geography

The division of land between tribes is implemented according to a very significant procedure. The land of Israel is "tackled" not conceptually and abstractly in immobility but through a course of travels. Before entering it, Moses sends "explorers" to scout the land. Likewise, to attribute the land to seven tribes that had not yet received their portion, Joshua appoints three men from each tribe to travel across the country so as to establish a map that will serve as a practical basis for apportioning it. The land is thereby something that is firstly to be scoured and traversed, and only thereafter settled. Beneath the roots, there is walking. Thus, the land is conceptualized via the thirty-six walkers[341] who travel all over the country. Could they be the ancestors of the "thirty-six" hidden righteous, on whose merit the world continues to stand before God?

There is an ethical significance to the number three. It tells us that the relationship to the land is one of bearing witness. The whole gamut of opinions will be possible when the three delegates deliver their report to the senate: one will say yes, the other no, and the third will bear witness for the

341. Based on the principle of three scouts per tribe multiplied by twelve.

other two. This is how the "census" of the land of Israel is established, in
the problematic of bearing witness. The land gains access to "existence" and
consideration through the men who traverse it. It does not exist "in itself."
The land registry obtained in this way (through the agency of witnesses) will
serve to establish a distribution plan. But the criterion of division is not the
external, physical reality; it is not an equal sharing of surface area according
to some inherent, absolute arithmetical principle. The distribution is based on
the demographic importance of each tribe, that is to say, on human beings.

The geography of the land of Israel is a human geography. Similarly,
the strictly spatial, external, and fixed criteria of distribution will be tempered by mobile aspects of the land: its fruitfulness, its capacity to yield, to
come out of itself, to "pass on," to become temporal through flowering and
germination: to move toward the one. Indeed, in the sharing, fertility will
compensate for size.

The ceremonial aspect of the apportioning is especially important. It
is by lottery that the land is attributed to the children of Israel. We have
here a principle of absolute gratuitousness, if not randomness, in any case,
a principle of antirootedness that presides over the tribal settlement of the
land. There is no possibility of romanticizing the relationship to the land
or raising it to the rank of absolute metaphysics. The land is destined for
all Israel, but only because the Levites are absent from it. And, indeed, the
lottery was cast "in Shiloh before God" (Josh. 18:10) through *Urim* and
Tummim, whose use was reserved for the Aaronite high priest. It is, then,
in the shadow of the traveling Temple, *ohel moed*, the Tent of Meeting, that
the lottery is cast. The Temple, locus of concealment and "center" of the nation," is precisely the site of this gratuitousness, this "occurrence," that is to
say, of "what happens" (like the *mikreh*, the "chance" happening in the book
of Ruth 2:3 or, more superficially, in Eccles. 9:2), in a passing and growing
world. Thus, Israel's settlement in the land is itinerant and mobile in a way
unlike the way of nations.[342] "For there is no share for the Levites in your
kerev, since God's priesthood is their property" (Josh. 18:7).

The Divine Portion

The portion in the midst (in the *kerev*) of the tribes that Levi does not have
is opposed to the divine portion (in terms of earthly property) that is granted

---

342. Aside from Benjamin, all the fathers of the tribes were born outside Israel.

to him, so there is reason to conclude that the removal of the Levites from their tribal share is the vehicle of their enjoyment of the divine "portion." In other words, the Levitical removal from land sharing, the Levites' absence from property, is the presence of God in Israel on the land. The Levitical system is the vehicle of this in the nation (we can see why the apportioning lottery is cast in the shadow of the Temple).

The prohibition of census taking thereby takes on new meaning, because counting Israel and hence the Levitical tribe is tantamount to counting God and undermining his unity, to disclosing the portion of the hidden God, his particularization in Israel, the passage of God in the being. In short, the Levites' lack of a "share" in the land imparts strangeness to Israel. Consequently, it is understandable that strangers are not refused a "share" among the tribes: "and you shall give their share to strangers who live in your midst like to your brothers, they shall be for you like those born among the children of Israel; allot them their portion from the tribe within which they live" (Ezek. 47:22). This is why we go from Levi defined as having God and his worship as his portion in the *kerev* of Israel to the idea of Levi's being "God's portion," the share consecrated to God by Israel, the hidden portion, set aside from Israel's possessions, in an offering to God, in a sacrifice of rapprochement to him.

"God's portion" can also be understood as the portion that God withdrew from himself, that he hid within himself to bring the world into being, his own retreat from himself that made room for man in him, in his *kerev*. This portion is what we call the particularization of God in the universal creation of the world. Particularization is another term for concealment; it is the removal that makes the totality and is the vehicle of the universal in the world. It is God with the particular name YHWH, God who manifests himself in a specific relationship to Israel, who creates the world: "YHWH said to Aaron, 'In their land you shall own no property in their *toch*; I am your share and your property in the *toch* of the children of Israel'" (Num. 18:20).

It is through Levi that Israel is Israel before God, and it is because Levi is cut off from the sharing that Israel gains access to the land of Israel. In a word, it is because the land is not entirely apportioned that it is granted to the children of Israel, to whom Levi bears witness as he bears witness to the land (that is why he receives the first fruits of the harvest). The children of Israel set aside a "portion" of the territory, which is not given to Levi, who is part of the children of Israel. It is because one of the sharing members receives nothing, because there is concealment in the division of the land, that the children of Israel can enter the land. Since, in this way, God's share is hidden, the presence of the absent one is safeguarded, and his memory is kept alive. The particularization of divine infinity—that is to say, the principle of creation of the *olam*—is not abolished. God passes into the being, and the world appears in his passage. Thanks to this, God always speaks to human beings, and the world maintains itself in the void.

The Temple Portion

There is a relationship between the Levitical concealment in the sharing of the land and the nature of the land of Israel, because this concealment of the land in the nation is what allows God to be present on earth.[343] This is true in terms of the Levitical system, but also from a very concrete standpoint. When the land of Israel was apportioned, a portion of it was set "apart" and not shared. This is Rashi's commentary on the verse "the good with which YHWH gratified us" (Num. 10:32): "they left it out of the sharing." This portion left intact in the otherwise apportioned land is intended to compensate the tribe that will have to give up a portion of its land to build the Temple. According to tradition, this concerns the territory of Jericho,[344] temporarily given to Jethro's children to hold until the construction of the Temple.

An undivided and unshared land subsists in the territory itself, one that resists sharing and attests to nonsharing, nonownership, and unity—all the more so insofar as a parallel is drawn to the Temple of the one. This land is held in suspense because its attribution is not definitive, and the whole point of this suspense is God's dwelling. It is set aside and hidden in view of an "exchange," a substitution, a gift in the place of the territory of the Temple. "Beneath" the Temple stands the land of Jericho. This means that that which will be removed from a tribe's land will not really be negativized, that it will always proceed from the unity of the unshared origin, whose oneness is maintained in hiding, the territory of Jericho, which is therefore much more than a cut-out piece of territory. The Temple is always in the one, in nonsharing, in concealment. In this way, from the outset, the one and the principle of the Temple inhabit the sharing of the land of Israel. The setting aside of Jericho is like a tithe of the land.

The "territory" of the Temple, removed from a tribe, is therefore "exchanged" for the territory of Jericho, to the benefit of the tribe that concedes

---

343. See II Kings 23:27: "YHWH said, 'Judah as well, I will remove from my presence, as I removed Israel; and I will reject this city I have chosen, Jerusalem, and this house about which I said, My Name will dwell there.'"

344. The first part of the land conquered by the Hebrews when they entered Canaan.

it. Yet it is not a true exchange, because Jericho, missing from the apportioning, cannot be an object of exchange; it cannot participate in a relationship of exchange. It is in essence a gratuitous gift, a nonproperty. The gift of the Temple land is regarded as a gift, not an exchange, yet the tribe giving it will not be made to suffer prejudice.

It is worth noting that the giving tribe is Benjamin and the traveling ark or the Temple is always found on land of the tribe of Benjamin, Joseph's brother, the one who was no longer expected, excess of excess, Jacob's favorite, Benjamin, who did not partake in the sale of Joseph, the only tribal father to be born in the land of Israel, the key stake in the relationship between Joseph and his brothers in Egypt, Benjamin, who is attributed four extra portions by Joseph at the banquet organized in the brothers' honor. And so it is Benjamin who is blessed with receiving on his land the divine presence. As far as Jericho is concerned, the way Joshua conquers the city is remarkable: he uses not swords but the "sound of horns" and the Holy Ark, voice and word, the basic attributes of the Levites and the Temple!

The Hidden Portion of the Land

This figure of the suspension of Jericho, a suspension prompted by the presence of the Temple on this land, indicates the character of the land of the nation of Israel. The epitome of a hidden land, neither revealing nor giving itself immediately or totally, the land of Israel comes to be and manifests itself by and in the waiting; heritage, promise, announcement, failure, and resurgence are all structures underpinned by delay, temporality, and patience. The land of Israel requires an approach, a journey ("go toward yourself," Gen. 12:1), a consideration from afar. It is a unique occurrence in history that the people are exterior to their land, to the point that they send "spies" (literally, "striders," "walkers") to take it in and apportion it globally before even settling in it. Before living in the country, Israel possesses the land registry! What demands centuries for other people is accomplished here from the start. This "abstract" and systematic relationship to the land is explained by the nature of the Eretz, which is the term used to designate it and which some commentators connect to ratzon, or will; the land of Israel is the will of Israel.

The overall problematic of passage can help us understand this. The land of Israel is the concealment of the universe, testimony in creation to the divine withdrawal, which in the illusion sphere of being-there and worldliness manifests absence and concealment, always slipping away from us while subsisting as a shore on which to land. The land of Israel bears witness to the void on earth; it is the land that eludes other lands and that other lands have always dreamed of absorbing but in vain. Every great empire in history tried to take hold of it, but it always escaped each one's grasp, because it is the hidden portion of the world, the particularizing world, the world as vehicle of divine particularization, of the presence of God to the world.

And so it is in Israel that the Lord of the Universe lives, becoming particularized in a particular place to talk to the world. The land of Israel is the portion of the world of nature kept in hiding in the one. "Who is like your people, like Israel, one nation on earth?" (II Sam. 7:23). For this reason it is allotted to Israel, for Israel is the concealment effected in the human to safeguard the one in and of the human; it is the kept portion of humanity. Thus, the land of Israel is the portion set aside in the same movement as Israel is chosen and set aside in humanity. "When the Supreme One set the nations by separating the children of Adam, he established the borders of the peoples (*amim*) according to the number of children of Israel, for his people are Yнwн's share, and Jacob the portion of his property" (Deut. 32:8–9).

The land of Israel is like a guarantee of the completion of the world in the grips of incompletion. This is why the preservation of concealment is the only way for the nation, and even for the whole of humanity, to maintain itself in the land that is a *kerev* in the midst of the *olam*. Those who uncover the concealment and yield to exposure and representation cut themselves off from the land of Israel and are spewed out by it, because they are governed by the logic of exteriority in the interior: "You shall keep my Law and my ordinances, and the country will not spew you out, and you will not follow the law of the nation that I expel from before you, for they did all this, and I was disgusted with them" (Lev. 20:22–23). Thus, "as long as the sin of the Amorites is not complete (*shalem*)" (Gen. 15:16), Israel will not gain access to the land. The stress on the accomplishment, on the integral totality of *shalem*,[345] is important here, because idolatry surrenders precisely to the mirage of totality and accomplishment, of gathering the being in representation. It knows nothing of gift giving, nothing of the portion kept in hiding for the one.

We are now in a better position to understand the Levitical mechanisms we have discussed. They underpin an economy capable of handling the reality of the land of concealment and of hiding even the path to it.

345. See above, "The Covenant between the Pieces," pp. 79–100.

Exile and Land

The land plays an important role in the great work of concealment, the covenant. The land of Israel is what is at stake in all the covenants, from Abraham to Jacob. It bears witness to faithfulness to the covenant, as much for God, if he gives it to the children of Israel, as for Israel, if it manages to stay in its bosom and not be "spewed out" by it. The land is permanent testimony to the state of the covenant,[346] and when the patriarchs seek to put God to the test, they question him about the fulfillment of this divine promise of the land. One could also say that Israel's exiles compel it, through the mouth of the prophets, to question its past faithfulness to the covenant and to see its lack of fidelity as the cause of exile.

The exile of Israel is a specific mechanism wholly bound up with the land of Israel. The children of Israel exist as a nation without necessarily being present in the land of Israel. They were a nation before even living there, and Abraham began his journey without knowing where he was going. But this existence is wholly informed by this journey to the land of Israel, by the fact that the country of Israel is the horizon, the pole, and the direction of the travels of the children of Israel. Exile designates a crisis in the relationship to concealment. The one, whose presence is "manifested" through concealment, slips away, and what the "people one" are doing on the land is eclipsed; the nation lapses into divisions, and Israel returns to the dereliction of the passage. What took Israel out of this dereliction of passage loses its effectiveness. It is once again overcome by the inertia of the *olam*. The void that is the world and that is the land of Israel becomes a "literal" reality. Israel is taken far away from the land; it is no longer inside (*toch*) and loses its closeness (*kirva*) to God. It has no interior anymore. Indeed, it loses the *toch* inasmuch as the latter is the political agency of Israel, as is the *korban* (*kirva*), not to mention the Levitical institution. But even though exile is a radical turning point for the nation, the state, and the Temple, it is not so for the being of Israel, insofar as this being is forged in the void and in peregrination, before settling on the land. The polarity is not between rootedness and rootlessness, since both are in the void and in passage.

Exile and presence in the country are modalities of the covenant, whether the covenant be a potentiality or a realization. If presence is accomplished through absence, then the absence of presence is not such a catastrophic turn

346. The blights that hit the land evince the betrayal of the covenant. For example, in I Kings 18, the land is struck by drought as a result of Israel's conversion to Baal.

of events. Israel comes out of it diminished but still alive. And because Israel does not forget the land of Israel, exile does not lead to extinction. Memory and waiting, announcement and promise are all strategies of concealment. The portion in concealment through which Israel was particularized becomes blurred, and Israel joins the chaotic multiplicity of the universe, scattered throughout the world because it is no longer governed by the principle of the one. It continues to be present around the world, but only because it continues to "dwell"—in strangeness and suspense—in Jerusalem.

This absolute fragmentation of Israel in the world (when it is numbered in the count of all the nations on earth!) is a sign of its relationship to the land-one, because no nation in the world is spread amongst all nations. Isn't this the modality of the Levitical tribe scattered throughout the other tribes? It is as if Israel disappeared and were kept in universal hiding everywhere in the world. And it is this concealment of Israel, when it reaches its greatest extension, that makes the land of Israel appear and surface in the nation. Israel's total giving to concealment generates the land.

It was the opposite in the times of Abraham. The land was hidden to the point that God did not mention it in his announcement. It was in such total concealment from the divine standpoint that it called for the emergence of Israel as a nation, for Israel would accomplish its concealment, whereas the Canaanites exposed it through idolatry. In exile, the people are so well hidden that it calls for the emergence of the land. And in exile, Israel no longer has to hide a portion, because it is itself wholly in hiding, a hidden portion. Israel is not abandoned by God; it is God's possession, God's property, God's portion. It is the immensity of the concealment, the absolute (and perilous) Levitization of Israel, that brings about the emergence of the land.

But the Abrahamic state and the exilic state are two extreme situations, and a middle way must be sought. Once the land has reappeared, the concealment must be implemented again—still in the opposite direction of the patriarchs—in order to stay in place.

The Sabbath Principle

This retreat of the land and concealment are altogether singular. The land is withdrawn from Israel's use, and Israel finds itself as if in the void, in the aridity of the desert. There is a process of "nomadization" and mobility in this, and, in fact, agriculture is then prohibited. Similarly, the Jubilee massively withdraws the nonoriginal properties from the hands of Israel. The underlying principle of these relatively rare, sporadic procedures (the *shemita*, or sabbatical year, when the fields lie fallow, presages, at a seven-year rhythm—seven times seven—the great Jubilee year) may very well be Sabbath, the occasion for Israel to withdraw from the world in total concealment, in the intimacy of absolute inwardness, a sort of exile from the *olam* of passage, to gather around the bright hearth of the one, a withdrawal that enables the world of profane days to reemerge, "repaired," in *tikkun*. The septenary rhythm is significant, because the Hebraic seven (*sheva*) is the language of satiety (*sheviut*). The satiety of this rhythm is evinced here paradoxically by the agency of concealment, of the kept portion, the offering, the cessation of the land's activity.

No doubt, the purpose of this political constitution of the land is to keep the void, strangeness, and passage in Israel in the very place where they would be most likely to be lacking: the quintessential place of sovereignty's hold, where the individual or the group can fence themselves into their own identity, to the point of forgetting the other and losing all memory. Thus, the principle of letting the land lie fallow is stated at the same time as respect for the stranger: "Do not oppress a stranger... you who were strangers in the land of Egypt. Six years shall you sow your land... and in the seventh you shall give it rest and leave the fruit, so the destitute of your people shall enjoy them, and what is left can be eaten by the animals of the fields.... Six days you shall be occupied with your work, but on the seventh you shall not work, so your ox and donkey may rest, and your maidservant's son and the stranger (*ger*) may renew their *nefesh*/be refreshed" (Exod. 23:9–12). Concealment is the very vehicle of the *nefesh*, of the human being's animated life. Exposed to exteriority, the *nefesh* experiences loss, because coming from God's concealment, from his inner unity, it seeks concealment at regular intervals to survive in the world. Indeed, the *nefesh* lives according to the principle of lack and absence; whenever it reaches the brink of satiation (the septenary thresholds) and complete plenitude, whenever it is on the verge of being petrified in the world of passage, forgetting itself and dying in the dereliction that is inherent in the world of passage, a concealment mechanism enables it to approach the one and find its way in the passage, to be at one again with its unique name, which makes the whole substance of its being in the world. And, having thereby enjoyed the twilight of presence, it can continue on its way to the land of the one. Every year, in any case, the land is called upon to contribute,[347] in the form of the first-fruit offering to the Temple for the festival of Shavuot, the Feast of (seven) Weeks, held seven times seven days

---

347. The land is summoned to concealment, since the first fruits of the earth are removed from consumption and hidden in the Temple.

after Passover. Seven always indicates the suspension of work needed for the concealment of the world, for taking it out of the passage of dereliction. On Sabbath, the thirty-nine categories of work needed for the construction of the Tabernacle are forbidden. This is why the sabbatical and Jubilee years are years of suspension of work. These mechanisms echo in the procedures of the land[348] the void that must not be forgotten or filled (see Isa. 5:8). "I gave you as a *kahal* of peoples, and I gave this land to your offspring after you as property of *olam*" (Gen. 48:4). It is in this manner that Israel possesses, that it is the owner, in the manner of the void. The land of Israel is said to have been bestowed upon Israel as an *ahuzat olam*,[349] in other words, a possession of disappearance, a property of the void.

III. THE SEPTENARY ECONOMY OF SATISFACTION

It is through the constitution of the land that we can best grasp the economic import of the Levitical system. There is no Hebraic conception of an "economic" body as such, just as there is none of the political body as such. We are here in a mindscape that is altogether different from the Greek's. It is through the Levitical prism that the economic and political levels are interconnected, that they stand in a brand-new relationship.

It would have been impossible to avoid the economic in the problematic of passage. Is it not the arena of passage? Is it not defined by the flow of objects and things? And it involves the flow of people, when people are assessed and measured in relation to things or to a privileged referent like money. In that case, the economic verges on the political, because, if the economic is the arena of regulating (and balancing) the flow of things, the political is the arena of regulating the flow of people. And if the Levitical principle brings all of its art to bear in the redemption (*tikkun*) of the political, through all the problematics of concealment that we have discussed, would it not do so equally, if not more, in the field of the economic? Herein the greatest dangers threatening human beings in passage hang in the balance every day.[350] These are contradictory dangers: that of debilitating passage, which makes

348. It is important to recall that the laws of sabbatical and Jubilee rest for the land apply only in the land of Israel.

349. This is usually translated as "eternal property," which may not be a mistranslation but is, nonetheless, a mistake.

350. Even if their finality is firstly political.

people anonymous and makes their faces "fall" by reducing them to mere interchangeable atoms in a depersonalizing economic game, as well as that of reification and petrifaction in the passage, in the illusion of escaping the perils and anguish of passage. If we were to characterize these two perils by the economic yardstick, we could say that proletarization and embourgeoisement are the two dangers that threaten us as we cross the world of passage.[351]

We tend to understand the economic in terms of exchange instead of framing it in terms of passage. In an exchange, there is indeed a passing between two separate agents who swap something, but the exchange, even though it is a relationship instituted in the passage, is not its sole modality and is not identified with the passage. "Exchange" is a matter of representation; it is a way of interpreting the passage in the sense of representation. The strongest characteristic of passage in economy is that it is an occasion for "payment," for evaluating in relation to a monetary index. In economy, one pays when one passes, the passage of objects becoming exchanged merchandise, the passage of merchandise across a variety of doors and thresholds[352] (customs, national taxes, when they pass from producer to distributor to consumer), the passage of human beings across certain places and thresholds (easements and taxes that sustain entire regions), and so on. It is a matter of fluidity in economic as in the political, where one cannot pass everywhere; those in power can pass through barriers and gateways, cross borders, and so forth. Power, like money, acts to ease the flow, and both can be a matter of representation. The same holds true for the laws that govern passage in politics as for the value that governs passage in economy. Exchange is only possible as a function of a mediating representation (money or merchandise).

Passage as Payment

One enigma of economy that is important to understand is how the passage gives rise to a payment, donation, or service in return. Would this be a manifestation of the principle of concealment? It all depends on the nature of this payment. Does it induce a relationship of obligation (*hov*) or redemption (*pidiyon*)?

351. Without, as a consequence, adopting the stand of the *petite bourgeoisie*, which, by its (regularly disappointed) craving to possess, is the antithesis of the Levitical figure. I understand by these two perils that of scarcity as much as that of property.

352. The "door" is a structuring concept in economy.

An exchange relationship is instituted between two people when each lacks what the other has. Each experiences an absence tempered by the nearness of its accomplishment (the other person possesses what I desire and need) and by the tension born of the nearness of presence and satisfaction. The experience of absence and strangeness presides over this relationship, which starts when the reverse expectations of both parties are satisfied by the transit of an object from the property of one to the property of the other, each party thereby inhabiting the other's place. Exchange is therefore an experience of the place of the other who inhabits all our own places (and hence of the masking of the other by a possible representation), but it is also and firstly an experience of absence within myself (the object that I lack and that the other possesses). Exchange is therefore necessarily an experience in the incompletion of the world, in the work that remains to be completed. In the exchange, one thing comes to live in the place of another. This is not really a substitution. It cannot be so, in any case, in terms of memory, although it can be in terms of representation. The principle that governs this relationship is not one of debt (*hova*) and obligation (*hov*), but one of release (*pidiyon*), if we understand it in the problematic of passage rather than representation, which is a perversion of passage.

The notion of *pidiyon* is enlightening in this regard. The term can refer to the sum of money a merchant receives for his merchandise, the payment of an obligation—in short, a reimbursement—but it also means ransom, delivery, liberation, release, and redemption: "Zion, through law, will be delivered" (Isa. 1:27). To pay in the form of *pidiyon* is to release something or someone in the grips of petrifaction and arrest[353] when the entire universe is in passage, so as to put it back into the flow of passage. In this sense, it is to accomplish its redemption (*geula*). In this sense also, the payment (*tashlum*, from the root *shalem*, complete) is an accomplishment (*shlemut*), an integration. To pay is to free a thing or a being from the restraint of its owner or creditor. To pay is therefore to pass.

We can see here the gap between the petrifying suspension that is debt and the suspension of advent that is concealment, one form of which is the *pidiyon*. *Pidiyon* and exchange are therefore instances in which the original place is revealed, the place of God's passage, of his creational retreat. We can thereby understand that in the economic, the passage gives rise to payment, to the loss of the one who passes (and to the profit of the one who enables the passage). Man draws his being and subsistence from the creational passage

353. In Jewish history, delivering captives ransomed by pirates is called *pidiyon*.

of God, who is himself divine "withholding" from himself, loss, "payment," dispossession. This is what makes the place of man. In all passage, the divine place for man is present. And this is where the essential trial of the human is played out; at this point the divine self-unclasping that is creation can lead to the illusion of man's exclusive property, to forgetting the origin, and to representation.

In this case, the exchange is founded not on *pidiyon* but on "debt." There is *pidiyon*, when God is present, and vice versa. And there is no "debt" in this case. When God commands sacrifices, it is not to reduce some debt that man would supposedly owe him eternally, but to release man through concealment. In this light, the system of the sabbatical year (*shemita*), when the land lies fallow and all debts are canceled, clearly illustrates the little significance that the debt relationship holds in the Levitical economy. In the passage, the relationship of God and Israel is governed by *pidiyon*. "From the house of bondage, I redeemed/freed you" (Mic. 6:4), which means, "I freed you from your reduction to a thing, and, literally, I put you back in the passage and flow, the crossing of the sea." "I will put a release/liberation between my people and your people" (Exod. 8:19). It is in this context that Israel accomplishes the *pidiyon* of the firstborn or offers sacrifices in the Temple. Israel is not caught in a relationship of debt and guilt, which is a relationship of forgetting, a degeneration of the *pidiyon* relationship that only the *pidiyon* can transcend and purify.[354]

The *pidiyon* involves transcending the exchange relationship construed as a cross-substitution, a replacement, or a filling in of the lack; *pidiyon* involves an advance without necessarily a return. Its purpose is to release things and beings (the firstborn, for example) from the prison of a specific relationship and return them to the passage. When one buys a piece of merchandise, one puts it into passage and circulation, but one also risks appropriating it

---

354. Credit is thereby one unexpected form of the world's suspension. The interest it produces for the creditor is a form of augment that arises from a withdrawal (from the creditor's property) to the profit of the being that emerges in this void (the debtor). But is it the benefit of passing time that increases the profit of the divine "creditor"? This is surely not the meaning of *olam*, whose augment is kept in hiding for the debtor until he "returns" what has been freely given to him, when he has reached the end of the logic of debt and *din*, when the scarcity reverts to bounty. Loans with interest are therefore a perverted form of passage. They stand in the passage but use it for "profit" when it is gratuitousness. Yet this gratuitousness is not the opposite of rigor (*din*). Otherwise put, the passage founds the order of rigor and scarcity (the first effect of the lack) that engenders relations of debt and payment, but opens onto abundance; the ritual debt (in the Temple) opens onto the remission of debts in the Jubilee year and not onto petrifaction and departure from the passage.

and removing it from passage. The *pidiyon* together with the whole Levitical system of giving serves to protect society from this peril.

The economic sphere is neither wholly good nor wholly bad. Like the political, it is an arena of trial. It fails most completely when it subsumes the political. It is the system that ensures the flow of things, that sets things into passage, but it must not govern the passage of human beings who govern the political, lest man be reified in turn. The Levitical system thus founds and limits the economic field by the political. All the mechanisms involved in the *pidiyon* aspire to this end.[355] The order of man must not be sucked into the order of things that threatens to take hold in the economic process. This potential threat becomes effective when the economic logic governs the political logic, when passage is "put to profit."[356]

Money is the focus of such ambivalence. Money makes things and objects flow and pass on; it returns things to passage, opens a place for them to pass through. As a result, it can save human beings from the reification involved in counting and measuring. Therefore a census can be taken only through the intermediary of the half-shekel given by everyone as a ransom for his person (as a *kofer*, a cover, for his *nefesh*, Exod. 30:11–16). But money also makes it possible to draw an equivalence between the value of a human being and the person's economic and financial weight,[357] mortgaging the "value to come" for an exchange value in this world and thereby taking the person out of the flow of passage. It also permits exchanging one thing for another on the mode of substitution. What takes place in the economic order proceeds, as we see, from the very nature of the world and of man. Indeed, the system of things and objects is elicited by the system of humans; in other words, the political elicits the economic. It is because human beings are beings of lack, need, and desire, because they echo their birth from a divine self-unclasping, that "objects"—which we tend to think we "find" in the world of exposure—exist and are called upon to enter the passage. Man is at all times on the verge of disappearing in the *olam* (his forces are ceaselessly and recurrently dwindling); to survive this breakdown, he tends to objectify the world, to absorb it, so as to hide it (savagely in this case) in

355. The *pidiyon* submerges the "debt," a mechanism of rigor, in the "redemption (*rachat*)" mechanism of grace.

356. In truth, it is "put into augment." This world, which ignores augment, or rather, which perceives it without grasping what it is, reads it as profit.

357. Weight becomes synonymous with heaviness, when God, in creating the world (which is his *kavod*, glory, from *koved*, heaviness), weighed himself down with a "weight" as light as grace.

a way that makes the world less opaque, lighter, more abstract, more fluid. The consumption of nature by man is the most global model of this tendency. And it is because objects are called to being by man's need that man risks becoming their prey and construing relationships in terms of debt rather than *pidiyon* (the latter being is the point of the *mitzvot*).

We can now see why the main part of the Levitical economic system undertakes to define and reduce property, lest it institutionalize the forgetting of God, "for the land is mine, for you are strangers residing with me" (Lev. 25:23). This economic mechanism is a mechanism of remembrance: "You shall take the money of the atonements (*kippurim*) of the children of Israel, and you shall give it for the work of the Tent of Meeting, and it shall be for the children of Israel a remembrance before YHWH to redeem (*kapper*) your *nefashot*" (Exod. 30:16).

Two Ways

To protect himself against the deliquescence that can develop in the economic passage, man faces a strategic dilemma: choosing property or concealment. Property is bound up with concealment, and all of humankind finds itself in concealment, be it in a perverted way or in an enlightened one. Property can establish the basis of the intimacy of the individual and the personality of the *nefesh* (which is why it is not renounced by Leviticism), but it also risks becoming a mockery of concealment, with the intimacy of the owner quickly turning into an avowed ignorance of and disregard for the other, and the walls of the house turning into a fortress rather than a shelter. In this case, the intimacy and accomplishment of the one involutes into the exposure and reification of the other. The excess of property deconstructs the passage. For this reason, property in the Levitical system is the object of restriction and depreciation for the sole purpose of promoting concealment. Concealment is the very principle of the Levitical economy. *Pidiyon*, which participates fully in this economy, has already given us some insight into the logic and institutions of the Levitical economy. In *pidiyon*, a being (or, in a wider sense, a thing) is freed by the concealment of a sum of money or a sacrifice. This concealment opens via the void onto a place, onto a passage for the being that is "redeemed" and accomplishes its *tikkun*.

This concealment has a directly economic sense, of course, since it corresponds immediately to a loss, to a removal from one's possession. Its gratuitousness, which escapes the reasoning of economic exchange, counters the logic of accumulation of wealth, weakens possession, and etches in the body of each fortune the mark of divine property, the sign of the strangeness of man in his own possessions. This concealment is not a joyful and vain squandering of a surplus of wealth.[358] It's a portion removed from the possessions of each person. The purpose of the concealment is to "manifest" in the world that the world is not finite. It materializes the infinite in the world of the finite and its illusions. The disappearance it engenders disarticulates the "integrity" and completeness, the totality of the whole. Such a withdrawal of fortune does not yield an accumulation, a provision of stocks and benefits for the future. This is not how the augment of this withdrawal is brought about. We are dealing here with a real gift to the tribe of Levi, which depends upon it to live, since it has no earthly possessions from which to draw its sustenance. What is concealed is intended to be eaten by the Levites, when it is not consumed by fire on the altar.

The setting aside in concealment (in finance and in products) is doubly materialized: first it disappears from the sight and possession of its original owners, then it converges onto the Temple, the central Levitical institution, where it is "hidden" and disappears. The Temple, not the marketplace—the agora, where everything takes place in the open, and where products, people, and animals are exchanged under conditions of exposure and nakedness, according to the principle of substitution rather than passage—is the site of this economy of concealment. Yet the Temple is but one of the poles of this economy of concealment that aims at "hiding" products, human beings, and animals. This economy is played out in two arenas, faithful in this respect to the bivalent principle of "augret": the economy of the Temple, centered on the institution of the Temple, and the Levitical economy, centered on the institution of the Levitical cities and the special economic mechanisms that concern them. The one is meant to oversee the passage of things, of products of the land, the other, to oversee the passage of human beings and work. One has the land and agriculture as its concrete base, the other, the cities, commerce, and industry. But each is in the other, and neither ignores the other. The sphere of the Temple economy is financial capital; that of the Levitical economy is real estate.

358. In the manner of Georges Bataille's "glorious consumption."

TEMPLE ECONOMY

The most immediate aspect of the Levitical economic system is the role played by the Temple. All gifts converge on it along with everything withheld in view of providing for the subsistence of the Levitical tribe. But actually, in terms of the coherence of the Levitical principle, the societal effects of the morphological situation of the Levite tribe (dispossessed of land) are more important than the need to find a remedy for an inconvenient situation (being deprived of a means of livelihood). To be sure, the gifts and withholdings sustain the Levites, but what is more significant in global terms is the economic system that this constitutes around the Temple as a result—namely, the establishment of a partially distributive economy.[359]

What does the economic movement in the direction of the Temple consist in? First, there is the cyclical and seasonal income in the form of the tithe, a tenth of the harvest given to the Levites, themselves descendants of the tenth son whom Jacob promised to God. "Any tithe of the land, from the seed of the ground or from the fruit of the tree, belongs to YHWH; it is consecrated to YHWH.... The tithe of cattle or of the flock... the tenth one shall be consecrated to YHWH" (Lev. 27:30, 32). Then, in addition to the tithe, the first fruits of the harvest go up to the Temple (on Shavuot) along with the firstborn animals. These offerings are partly compulsory (since they are set by imperatives in the Torah) and partly gratuitous (since they take the form of gifts).

In addition to these revenues, there are circumstantial and irregular everyday revenues: the sacrificial victims that the Hebrews offer in atonement for their impurities or simply as generous gifts, part of which represents income for the Levites (who are entitled to consume the meat of certain sacrifices and nearly always to keep the skins of sacrificial animals, Lev. 7:8). We are dealing here with something different from a market economy; the circulation of goods brought about by the Temple abides by another logic entirely. A whole series of withholdings are effected for a social category that enjoys a hereditary status that governs its economic position. These withholdings are in the form of gross products. They converge from everywhere in society upon the Temple, where they are burned, consumed, or commercialized by the Levites and thereby introduced into the market.

359. This means that what is withheld is then distributed in another economic sphere.

This movement up to the Temple is a procedure of sanctification/separation, the elevation of the products of the land and of production in general, as if all that pertains to the land were being taken out of raw inherence and moved into the passage, through separation and consecration—a passage of sublimation, since the Temple is the "gate of heaven" whence smoke from the sacrifice of animals and incense spirals upward. But the passage also introduces into the circuit of commercialization products that are not consumed by the Levites or by the altar fire. Nonetheless, the passage of sublimation remains the most significant aspect of the Temple economy. The share of products that revert to commercialization must have been restricted considering the size of the Levitical population that depended on them for their means of subsistence.

The central aim of this mechanism is to divest land and husbandry products of their mercantile value and signify the sole divine proprietorship of the land and the agricultural sphere. It is worth noting that divestment is manifested by the passage to and through the Temple of all potential merchandise, and that it is accomplished mainly on the basis of the gift and the offering; people are free to offer sacrifices if they want to avow an impurity or sin. The offering, be it compulsory or gratuitous, takes the relationship to products of the land (one cannot say economic products) out of the anonymity of the passage and the exchange.[360] Everyone brings the first fruit in his own name and accomplishes the votive "laying on" of hands on the consecrated sacrificial victim. In this way, the realities of the land and the animal world are humanized.

'Shemita'

The universe of the "Temple economy" is the universe of natural reality, of agricultural life, of all that belongs to the natural and physical order. Fundamental and pristine, it is thus immediately manifested most forcefully when we consider the economic problematic of the Levitical system. This is the way Leviticism confronts nature and assumes its management so as to bend its power to collective purposes. This is why the Levitical mechanism that characterizes the whole Temple economy is the institution of the sabbatical year (*shemita*).

---

360. In addition, the purpose of the relationship established through the offering is to "atone" for a sin or, depending on the temporal cycle, to accomplish the *tikkun* of the land. The sacrificial dimension is thereby embedded in the relationship to the world.

As the preeminent mechanism that englobes all the secondary mechanisms we have discussed (tithe, *pidiyon*, etc.), *shemita* evinces the very spirit of the Temple economy in the gift, in the setting aside of a portion of one's possessions, in the remembrance of divine proprietorship brought into the very heart of each person's individual enjoyment of property through the "sacrifice." *Shemita* is the principle that sees farmers abandon their farming activities to devote themselves to studying the Torah. All property becomes public property, and everyone is entitled to glean the fruits. For the Levites, the *shemita* also represents the loss of the tithe of harvests. It is actually as much (if not more) the land that is "exiled" from people as vice versa. Just as human beings withdraw from the land on Sabbath, so the land withdraws from human beings during the sabbatical year: "The land will satisfy the debt for its sabbatical years" (Lev. 26:34–35). The land has a "debt," and when it does not honor it, it "pays" with additional years of exile.

It is an old Hebraic idea that Israel's exile repays all the sabbatical years that were not respected when it was living there. To understand this, one must understand the status of the land of Israel: "the land will not be sold forever, since the land is mine, since you are strangers and residents with me" (Lev. 25:23–24). The land of Israel is bound to God; it is the portion removed from all the lands in the world and hidden away. It is the unfinished world's telltale sign of its future completion. This explains the strange laws and statutes, for it is the only land in the world that is "hidden"! Through it we have a glimpse of the future world.

Sabbath, *shemita*, and the Jubilee year have one purpose only, and that is to make the one appear, through a procedure of voiding. Thus it is said that the laws of *shemita* were taught at Mount Sinai and that allowing the land to rest concerns each and every person: "your field," it is written, because it brings the individual within reach of the one. Such laws deepen an approach to another world in this world and enable the land itself, not only men, to pass. The land escapes human grasp.

Shemita laws reverse the reification of the land and its products by banning their marketing or destruction. Instead they are declared public goods (*hefker*), and it is prohibited to make any use of them that exceeds the needs of each individual, which necessarily defuses the possibility of representation. This return to the void of the land, this negation of property by Israel, means not that the land belongs to "nobody," but rather that it pertains to the one and that, ultimately, it is indivisible. Consequently, the *ger* and the Levite benefit from it, since they have no share in the apportioning. Residence and ownership cannot be based on the expulsion of the stranger. The principle of *shemita* brings home through practical experience the extent to which, from the Levitical perspective, God and Israel are united in the same abode and rule of stewardship (etymologically, an "economy").

Nomadism and Remembrance

There is a surprising experience here in setting an entire society into "nomadism," a problematic of an extreme undermining of social establishment. And during the sabbatical year, all the people gather around the Levites (who have no tithe during this year precisely because the whole people is "Levitized"), who become, along with the Temple (but not the land), the sole locus of collective existence. Finally, it is during the Jubilee year (once every seven sabbaticals) that the whole system reaches its apotheosis. All land is returned to its legitimate owner, to the person (and his descendants) who received it as his portion upon entering Eretz Yisrael, when Joshua distributed the land. Thus, the origin is manifested in the usufruct of the land: divine property, sharing under the aegis of the covenant but also a reminder of the Levitical principle, of those who have no portion in the division (and who remain in the one). In this way, the passage is perpetually renewed for the sedentarized people. Every seven years and every fifty years, it is as if the people were once again crossing the Jordan.

This whole problematic lodges remembrance at the core of the very relations where it is most likely to dwindle and flag, the relations where the passage runs the greatest risk of becoming anonymous, because it is too close to the land and to human needs—namely, economic relations. Every fifty years, the land is restored to its original owners. In this way, each person's name does not disappear in the flow of the world, relations, and generations. There is, to be sure, a renunciation of the eternity of the land, but the land is central nonetheless, because it is the very basis of the existence of a name on the land. This is clearly evinced in Ruth's determination to fulfill the levirate commandment "to raise the name of the dead over his property" (Ruth 4:5). This is seen even in respect to the divine Name, because *shemita* and the Jubilee year serve as a reminder of God's ownership of the world and an echo of the Name of God in the land.

No doubt, there is an exceptional relationship between the Name of God and the land of Israel. This is where he must (and can) be recalled, because it is his portion in the world of disappearance, "because his people, Jacob, portion of his property, is Yhwh's portion" (Deut. 32:9). The problematic is paradoxical, because the Name is the passage of God and not being consigned to a place. But it is perhaps because he is passage that a fixed place in the passage, the land, was necessary to keep him in mind. It is, at any rate, a land in passage that serves as a reminder, the land of *shemita* and Jubilee, and not the land of entrenched proprietors. When the land escapes us, its Name is recalled. The essential spirit of the Temple economy is bound up with the problematics of memory, embedded in the very site of forgetting and erasure, in the most impenetrable site of the world's disappearance and of divine retreat: the natural cycles and the laws of nature, which can give man the illusion of the world's being-there.

The Shekel

However, the land is not the sole foundation of the Temple economy. Perhaps the paradox that puts the land at the center of a system that causes it to falter and lose its centrality is best expressed in the second component of the Temple economy, which, although minor or, in any case, more abstract than the mechanisms attached to the land, is no less important. This second component is the institution of the shekel. "When you will carry the head of the children of Israel in their census/records, each one will give the ransom (*kofer*) of his *nefesh* to YHWH on being numbered/recorded, and there will be no plague in their numbering/recording. This he shall give, he who passes before the census taker, half a shekel, of the holy/separated shekel,... everyone who passes before the census taker, from twenty years of age and up shall give an offering (*teruma*) to YHWH" (Exod. 30:11–16).

We have seen several times the deep-seated meaning and implications of the prohibition of census taking, of numbering the children of Israel.[361] And here we see that it becomes possible in this roundabout way: by counting the half-shekel and not "heads" or souls (*nefesh*)—that is to say, by counting objects and not people. So the soul is not taken out of its concealment—which amounts to death—and, what's more, it is counted by means of the shekel, in the interiority of concealment of the Temple, outside the sphere of the powers that be that usually exercise the prerogative of census taking. This shekel is presented to us as an offering (*teruma*) to the Tetragrammaton. This removal ransoms/redeems (*pidiyon*) the count thereby obtained and the

---

361. See below, "All Israel and the Prohibition of Census Taking," pp. 367–390.

indirect reification of the living that it produces. The very instrument of the counting becomes in this way the means of redemption.

For this reason, it is very important that the procedure take place in the concealment of the Temple. Ultimately, the shekel payment enables each person to accomplish his concealment in the Temple, to step out of the flow of the world and gather inside before God in unity. Hence the significance of the half-shekel: it takes two to make one. This is also why each person's contribution is the same whether he is wealthy or poor. It is the one in everyone that matters and not the compensated sum of all. We can understand, as a result, why the shekel is presented as a "ransom," as the *kappara* of the *nefesh*, the redemption, the covering, the hiding of the soul.

Two other Hebrew notions are involved in the mechanism of this paradoxical census taking: remembrance and passage. Indeed, the term used for the census taking is *pakad*, which also means remembering ("God remembered Sarah," Gen. 21:1), and being counted is described as a passage that logically gives rise to an offering. There is passage in the sense that this census taking involves concealment of the *nefesh*, not the exposure and revealment to which traditional census taking ineluctably leads. And, logically, this money, whose collection causes the collectivity of Israel to pass into concealment, testifies before God to the presence of Israel, to its memory, since the Temple is the very site of concealment, redeemed passage, and remembrance. "You shall take the money of the *kippurim* from the children of Israel, and you shall give it for the world of the Tent of Meeting, and it shall be a remembrance for the children of Israel before Yhwh to redeem (*kapper*) your souls" (Exod. 30:16). Removed from the labile flow of the *olam*, Israel is thus recalled to the memory of the Name. In this way, the collecting of the half-shekel participates in the same logic as the sabbatical and Jubilee years—a logic of remembrance of the Name, reminding Israel of the divine Name that it has forgotten, because it lives the life of the world, and recalling Israel and its name to God, who has withdrawn from the world of Israel to the secret of concealment that enables the world to unfold and exist.

The "management" of the souls of Israel and their names is subtler and more abstract than the sanctifying/separating "management" of the land and less characterized by the angularity and thickness of the latter. Here we leave the agricultural world and step into a monetary world, cut off from farming and breeding. This echoes the second aspect of the Levitical economic system, which oversees the more abstract areas of production and exchange on an altogether different basis (the cities), in a way that clearly shows the internal coherence of the whole system. With the collection of the shekel, the

"Temple economy" appears to be a financial, bank economy as well, inasmuch as the shekels acquired in the census taking—which serve the functioning of the Temple—constitute an important financial holding. Its management marks a shift from an economy based on gift giving and subsistence agriculture (because the creation of huge estates is impossible when every fifty years new ownership rights cease) to an economy based on investment and development. These sizable holdings promote the Levitical potential of intervention but also nonagricultural enterprises that overstep the constraints of the Jubilee and sabbatical system. The Temple's treasury thereby becomes a central economic institution while "sanctifying" the economic process by interiorizing it.

The secondary effect of the shekel collection is the production of a kind of national capital accumulation made possible by the agrarian system and making possible in turn all sorts of economic enterprises (notably financial) outside the confines of primary activities, inducing more abstract relations with the natural world. The potential accumulation is relative, however; any acquired sums cannot be hoarded, insofar as the subsistence needs of a landless tribe are such that the money is quickly reintroduced into the economic circuit. Nonetheless, the Levitical prism is the prism of fluidification and mobility. In this regard it is important that each person contributes a half-shekel: "the rich shall not pay more and the poor less than the half-shekel, to give the offering of Yhwh to atone for your souls" (Exod. 30:15). Rich or poor, everyone is presented alike and "remembered" before God in the Temple, but each also contributes equally to the Temple treasury, which is, in a way, the "national" treasury, and likewise has an equal share and hence an equal say in the collective use of it. This is something of the cooperative system on the national scale. We are not dealing here with a proportional income tax, of the type that kings would later levy, and for which there was no provision in the Sinaitic constitution. What we have here is a payment of equal shares that gives everyone equal rights and institutes a system of cooperative financing.

Other Economic Processes

In addition to the monetary mechanism of the shekel, there is a mechanism, commercial this time, attached to the Temple economy, and that is the marketing of "holy skins." In nearly all the sacrifices, the priests keep the animal skins, and their sale represents a significant source of income. Here, too, there is a strong symbolic thrust, because skin is the sign of exteriority,[362] but this exteriority is the product of interiorization. What characterizes the whole "Temple economy" is that it is informed by an initial, foundational problematic, not of profit but of sanctification, separation, gratuitousness, and memory, redemption and concealment of the soul, unity and personalization, passage and not assignation. Whatever this economy becomes thereafter, the spirit of its foundations is to free (*pidiyon*) man, to enable him to "pass" in the very places where there are the most obstacles, to conceal him where he is most exposed, and to safeguard his life where he is most reified. Indeed, the initial movement of the whole Hebraic economy derives very powerfully from the Temple economy, first because it concerns the primary sector, which is the fundamental sector of the economy, but also because it is the driving force behind a vital communication between farmers-proprietors in an agrarian system based on small plots of land.

Just think of the consequences of the Levitical institution. Deprived of income from land, the Levites are in need of all consumer goods, from crops to finished products. The Levites represent a strong demand force in the economy of the children of Israel and animate the entire economy by the incomes and products that pour into the Temple. They have the means of sustaining this demand by putting a sizable monetary mass into circulation. So we can see the effectiveness of a collective "division of labor" that might have been deemed inefficient at first sight because it throws a whole segment of society into a role of purification that appears economically unproductive and even noneconomic. Fundamentally, the Levites accomplish an austere sanctifying function, founded on withdrawal, but there is also an unexpected economic impetus to their role. This is the second phase of the sacrificial retreat, the phase of blessing. "You shall tithe... the produce of the field every year. And you shall eat it before YHWH, your God, in the place he will choose as a dwelling for his Name.... If the road is too long for you.... Then you may exchange it [the produce] for money, you shall gather the sum in your hand and go to the place YHWH, your God, will choose. You may spend the money on whatever your heart desires... and anything your taste

---

362. It is worth noting the extent to which malicious gossip is punished by leprosy and how the "leper" strikes all our envelopes (skin, clothes, house), envelopes of the *nefesh*. This is because gossip bares and exposes the other, and in so doing it negates interiority. It uses the absence of the other to denigrate him, as if he were reduced to powerlessness by his absence. There may be a share of truth in what is said by the gossiper, but it is isolated from the living spark of the target of gossip and turned into a caricatural trait. The gossiper chases the *nefesh* away.

wishes, and you shall eat it there in the presence of YHWH, your God, and you shall rejoice with your family. And you shall not neglect the Levite who is within your walls, for he has no portion or inheritance like you" (Deut. 14:22–27). We are here at the heart of the "augret" system.

The "religious" function of gratuitousness also fulfills an essential economic purpose. It is not by any means an illusory "pretext" with an economic end. To the contrary, the "detour" by way of the sanctification of the economic system is a cardinal and essential process: the separation from the weakening flow of the world, the hiding, at the basis of all things. In this sense one can speak of economy—as of the political—as a separate agency in the Bible. It is not altogether economy, but it is economic at any rate.

The "Temple economy" does not, however, fulfill only a directly economic function (creation of a demand that impels the economy and produces a market); it plays a socioeconomical role, sustaining the Levites and driving the economy, to be sure, but also redistributing income. And we are here in the strict logic of the Levitical spirit: sanctification, equality, concealment and de-reification, disanonymization, cooperation, and giving. "At the end of the third year, you shall take out the entire tithe of your crops in that year and set it down within your gates. So the Levite, who has no portion or inheritance like you, the stranger, the orphan, and the widow who are at your gates may come, eat, and be satisfied, in order that YHWH, your God, will bless you in all your handiwork" (Deut. 14:28–29).

All the underprivileged categories of society benefit from it, all those severed from continuous and autonomous relationships: the stranger cut off from a community, the orphan deprived of parents, and the widow deprived of a husband, all those whose unity is not complete, because they are missing a "helper against/facing" (Gen. 2:18) them. The Temple economy assumes the function of a "providential state"[363] ("state" is the appropriate term: "you shall set it down at your *gates*," Deut. 14:28) by sustaining those who have nothing and receive directly from the Temple, under the aegis of divine providence and from the Levite's hand, so they can extricate themselves from the dereliction into which they have sunk in the passage, from the reification to which their unsatisfied needs condemn them.[364] The Temple stands in for the missing "helper" and enables unity when it has been disarticulated. It thus harbors, at the heart of the Levitical system, the very ideal of community

363. *État providence* (welfare state): surprisingly, modernity had recourse to a theological category to describe the welfare state that it invented.

364. The needs of human beings must be met in order to accomplish the *tikkun* of the body.

when the latter fails and compensates for its deficiencies. We can now see why the Temple economy harbors the potential of assembling, of bringing together the community.

One important commandment in the sabbatical and Jubilee year is for all the people to gather in Jerusalem for the reading and study of the Torah. "Summon/make a *kahal* of the entire people, men, women, and children as well as the stranger who is at your gates, so they shall hear and learn and revere YHWH, your God... all the days you live on the land you are crossing the Jordan to possess" (Deut. 31:12–13). Every individual, while consecrating a tenth of his income to the Temple, is to put aside another tenth, a second tithe, to finance the three annual pilgrimages to Jerusalem. In this way, the Temple and the journey to Jerusalem, the pilgrimage and the passage, are embedded in each person's income. And the community is organized and takes shape through the figures of gift giving, concealment, and displacement, of journeying and traveling: the Temple and the Torah are its main poles.

It is only when these foundations are secure, when the community and the coherence of community and family relations have been equipped with the mechanisms that perpetuate them, regardless of market relations and the flow of the passage, that the second aspect of the Levitical system opens up: the Levitical economy.

LEVITICAL ECONOMY

The Levitical economy is distinct from the Temple economy in terms of its personnel and arena. The Temple only truly concerns one sector of the Levitical tribe, the priestly family that administers the Temple and related activities. The Levitical economy is staffed by the rest of the Levitical tribe, all those who are not part of the priesthood, who serve in the Temple episodically and cyclically (but not for sacrifices) but live mainly either scattered amongst the tribes or in the "Levitical cities."

This economy is not riveted to the land and the primary sector; it is fundamentally urban. It grows out of the economic order that results from the condition of the Levites, who are not part of the priesthood and reside in Levitical cities, which include the cities of refuge. This city-dweller condition relies for subsistence on a different economic order from one based on income from land. Broader and more abstract than the Temple economy, the Levitical economy is linked to real estate rather than landed estates. The laws of the sabbatical year, for example, do not apply to the city possessions of individuals who own land elsewhere. On the other hand, it applies to the Levites, who can have no other property. Whereas every fifty years their real estate in the city returns to its original owner, the realty originally belonging to a child of Israel is sold for good.[365]

If, in the final analysis, Jubilee laws and the Temple economy make land non-convertible and unsalable, urban properties are. The Temple economy, or the "priestly economy," is the facet of the system that opposes the anonymity and the flow, the facet where testimony to the origin takes place, whereas the Levitical economy is the facet that makes these relations possible: certain possessions can lose their name, the sole restriction being on the Levites, who, by the law that governs their realty testify themselves to the origin of the Name in the economy of anonymity.

The institution of cities of refuge also weighs heavily on the vocation of the city. These are cities of refuge, not jungles, offering refuge to (nonintentional) criminals awaiting judgment, a form of concealment that suspends the severity of the judgment. This vocation of the Levitical cities clearly manifests the hovering of the Name (the names of the criminal's victims) that is exercised in economic Leviticism. Thus, the unique Temple that governs the agricultural sector exists alongside multiple cities established under the aegis of Leviticism, freed from the agricultural basis, cities from which the Temple seems to require nothing, and whose activities are subject to fewer and less precise rules; this is conducive to greater, more flexible development of economic structures, dissociated from the land and to more abstract activities, such as crafts, industry, and commerce. There is, then, room in the Levitical economy as much for an economy founded on these sectors as for an economy founded on agriculture.

These two economic figures are to be seen as adjusting to one another within a global system. Each represents a different order and handles a different set of problems. The Temple economy aims to found an order of sharing, giving, helping, and enabling the Levitical organization of collective life, while the Levitical economy sets up a system of economic development that is more efficient but has no ethical validity if uninformed by the Temple's agricultural system. It is the higher stage thereof.

Even though the Levitical principle is omnipresent in this urban economy, there seems to be nothing in the Torah text directly related to it when there

---

365. This would presuppose a third "economy," neither Temple nor Levitical, in which tribe members can become proprietors in the real estate sector.

is a plethora of prescriptions concerning the land. The only way a name can disappear in Israel is through the sale of real estate! Does this mean that the hardest and most dehumanizing laws of economy are possible in the cities? It is hard to imagine where and how the principle of *shemita* could be applied in the urban Levitical economy. Where and how could the mechanisms of withholdings work in crafts, commerce, and industry?

This is an arena whose normativeness is less developed and less formal. Could it develop untrammeled, as long as the sphere of priestly economy is preserved? Would distributive justice coexist alongside the possibility of great injustice, with, on the one hand, the destructuring of value and the impossibility of assessing value, and, on the other, the ruthless reign of value above all?

In fact, the Levitical economy is interested in a different order of things. To be more precise, we are dealing here with an order not of "things" but of human beings, and its regulations differ radically. This is readily understandable, because, at such a level of abstraction in the economic circuit, human beings run the risk of anonymization and reification without violence. Consequently, the economic circuit is governed not by the principle of *shemita*—even though the "*shemita* of money," of debts, exists—but rather by another temporal and more abstract institution, equal to this level: the Sabbath.

Sabbath

In terms of principle, Sabbath belongs, like the sabbatical and Jubilee years, to the septenary family. It creates a status for human beings in an economic world. The suspension of production and work removes human beings from the absolute reign of economic efficiency. But most of all, it sets man up as a being of inwardness, irreducible to the reifying exteriority of production relations. The Sabbath puts the economy into suspension; it is a factor of disorganization in the order of things. It contributes in this way to positing human beings in interiority and concealment. The whole *halachic* problem of the Sabbath is that of delimiting its field, because it opens a reserved area in the heart of the city, a shelter for the living human being. The Sabbath reendows man with a name, a face, and privileged relationships. It restores him to himself, takes him out of the potential dereliction of passage, and makes him pass through concealment. It hides him in the world. Sabbath is thus the preeminent economic institution of the Levitical economy.

This is the basis of labor laws, complete with a status for employees and employers, economic power, and socioprofessional categories, the underlying aim and principle of which is bound up with the concealment of man and the preservation of the moving vivacity of his *nefesh* and name. The purpose is to prevent the reification and anonymization lurking in economic exchange. A whole complex of laws governing lending and borrowing, financial operations, labor relations,[366] and so on works toward this goal. Through this system, we can see that *homo economicus* cannot be reduced to the economic. He cannot in his essence be evaluated in monetary terms or reduced to his position in a professional structure. He cannot be treated as if he were totally exterior to us, in relations of lending, for example. He cannot be reified in a strictly economic logic, which can never have the last word.

From the perspective of the status of human beings, the question of social classes is crucial, because the system of production socially assigns individuals to their position in the mode of production. Stratification into classes is a fundamental process of reification, of petrifaction of passage. The economic system founded on the land protected by the Jubilee year works to prevent the unrestrained proletarization of an industrial economy. Farmers may sell their land and become proletarianized in cities, but after fifty years—to be sure, a long period in the life of a man—they recover their original property.

366. We can see in this light the question of biblical slavery, which is very real in the text, even though it is immensely humanized in comparison with Greco-Roman or Middle Eastern slavery. It is interesting to note that the category the term designates is ambiguous. The Hebraic slave is a worker (*eved*); Moses himself is described as "God's *eved*." And the Hebrews came from a "house of slaves." Hebraic "slavery" includes the case when "your brother, in your proximity, becomes impoverished and sells himself to you" (Lev. 25:39), and it limits the duration of his service to six years. That the septenary year is a year of liberation for him evidences the liberating thrust of the Levitical principle: "Like a laborer or a resident shall he be with you, until the Jubilee year shall he work with you" (25:39–40). The principle of septenary concealment also applies to the non-Hebrew slave, the "Canaanite slave," whose status is nonetheless inferior to the Hebrew slave. The statutes basically posit the slave as being the property of his master but not belonging to him in his own being. When the master seeks to dominate the slave's "body," which amounts to reifying him, then the slave must be freed. "If a man hurts the eye of his slave or his maidservant in a way that destroys the use of the eye, he is to set them free because of the eye; and if he makes the tooth of his slave or his maidservant fall, he must set them free because of the tooth" (Exod. 21:26–27). And a man who takes his slave's life risks the death penalty: "If a man strikes his male or female slave with the rod, and the slave dies under his hand, he shall be avenged" (21:20). Ownership of a slave is neither essential nor absolute, since it is suspended by the slave's flight! "You shall not turn over a slave to his master if he seeks refuge with you from his master. Let him dwell with you, in your land, in whatever place he will choose... you shall not molest him" (Deut. 23:16–17). Finally Job clearly evinces the idea of the unity of the human species: "Have I ever spurned justice for my slaves and maidservants when they contended with me? And what would I have done if God had intervened? What would I have answered, if he had asked for an explanation? He who prepared me in the belly womb of her who made me, did he not make him too, and did he not make both of us in one lone womb?" (Job 31:13–15).

This small "landowner" scheme seems to be the objective of the agrarian system and serves to attenuate the extremes of economic logic. Among the other safeguards that serve the same purpose are the social aid mechanisms of the sabbatical year and Sabbath.

Generally, the national division of social work is made to protect man. Its main pivot is the Levitical system, in which we see a tribe that has been taken out of the economic process implement a noneconomic rationality and become the driving force of the economy. The Levitical status is noneconomical insofar as it breaks with the immediate rationality of the economy and the logic of profit, not with the economy as such. It induces, to the contrary, a different process founded on bounty and gratuitousness (the "augment") rather than scarcity, even if, immediately, it takes scarcity to its highest pitch. The better to break through it.

Such an economy offers a considerable guarantee for the safeguard of man and his being in passage. "For the poor (*evyon*) will not disappear from the *kerev* of the land" (Deut. 15:11) is not to be understood as an apology and a perpetuation of poverty. Quite the opposite. It designates the very principle of the Hebraic division of social work, for the poor (*evyon*) at issue is said to be in the *kerev*, in the interior of the land, which is the Levite's place. This is why the Levitical principle centrally manages the land. It is noteworthy that poverty is said to concern the *kerev* of the land and not the children of Israel. This is Levitical-style poverty; the whole system is identified in this way, as confirmed by the verse "In truth, there must be no poor (*evyon*) in you, for YHWH will bless you in the land that YHWH, your God, gave you as property to inherit it, only if you hear the voice of YHWH, your God, to observe, to do this entire *mitzva* [the *shemita*] that I command you today" (Deut. 4–5). In sum, the Levitical model, which produces poverty in the short run, ultimately harbors bounty.

A Dual Economy

There is, then, a fully developed economy in the Levitical system, but it is less a model than a strategy to channel the flow of the passage by means of a whole series of light structures, safeguards in the form of splints rather than walls. It does not check the flow, since the goal is to preserve the passage while avoiding dispersal.

The main characteristic of this economy is its dual aspect. In fact, one could see it as two economies and even two societies: the society of the

Temple, with its poor classes, priests, and farmers, which is composed mainly of small property owners; and the society of the Levitical cities, with its Levites, industries, shops, and workers, which is composed mainly of realty owners, merchants, and Levites and enjoys greater wealth than the former. But the impression of a split between two societies and two economies is mistaken. What we actually have here is a two-level system, a fully integrated, two-step movement in which one figure (Levitical) is compensated for by another (priestly), and one figure (the priestly) founds the other and is exceeded by it.

Is this not another way of expressing the "augret" process? The procedure of retreats and withholdings, the concealment of the augment—the priestly economy—in sum, is compensated for by the system of collective solidarity and the well-being that the "Levitical economy" (more "gratifying" than the "priestly economy") procures for the economy as a whole.

The very purpose of the principle of withholding or of *shemita* is to delay enjoyment of bounty and fullness, not to deny its validity but to put it off to a more propitious place, a more accomplished time, somewhat in the manner of the oath and the promise, the time of concealment and *tikkun*. To be sure, in the present, the withholding is hard, but it bears fruit in the future.[367] If there can be withholding and setting aside, it is clearly because

367. Joseph put Egypt through the catastrophe of a non-Levitical economy: the drama of scarcity and bounty. The Egyptians experienced the cost of not giving, not withholding, not setting a portion aside. It is worth noting that Joseph established the new economy when Jacob and his brothers, seeking shelter from the famine, had come to settle there, bringing with them the divine presence ("I will go down with you to Egypt"), and after Jacob told Pharaoh about his *megurim*, his years of *gerut*, strangeness or sojourn: "Joseph fed/economized his father and his brothers, and the whole house of his father" (Gen. 47:12). Immediately thereafter begins the story of the famine that strikes Egypt and Canaan. Because of the grain Joseph has accumulated during the seven preceding years, the entire world comes to seek supplies from him. But once the food supply has been exhausted, the supply of money for commerce is depleted. So the Egyptians end up giving Joseph and Pharaoh their money, their cattle, their land, and finally their own bodies. Pharaoh thus becomes the master of the world. And the Egyptians, because they did not know how to give, end up losing everything, save themselves. Because they lived their lives in terms of exposure and ignored concealment, they dwelt in petrifying reification. There is reason to think it was the divine presence in Egypt that provoked this upheaval; since it inevitably calls for an altogether different mode of being, Egypt rapidly succumbed to it. The reform Joseph imposed is enlightening: "And he made the people pass on to the cities, from the end of the border to the other end, from city to city" (47:21). In a word, he made nomads out of all the Egyptian people (except its priests, who remained attached to their land); he made them experience the Levitical condition, for they had no portion of the land, like the Levites, and put remembrance (*zikaron*) at the center of a country oblivious to the Name. This was Joseph's only way of saving Egypt in its perilous proximity to the divine presence. "Joseph imposed it as a law [of the tithe] on the land of Egypt" (47:26) except for the land of the Egyptian priests (to which the adoptive family of his wife belonged!),

the starting point is one of fullness and bounty (*shefa*), not scarcity. It is an optical illusion that the "scarcity" consecutive to the withholding is manifest at first, because it is in fact borne by abundance. Doesn't the Levitical retreat (the fact that it is set aside in augment) directly increase the share of each original tribe? Is not the purpose of the scarcity contained in the bounty right from the outset to redeem bounty, to avoid dispersal in the flow of passage, its ruin in the present, and to unify it in the one?

During the course of the passage, the world of passage is pending its *tikkun*. This can be sensed in the septenary law (Sabbath, *shemita*, Jubilee) that seems to govern the economic sphere. In the seven, there is satisfaction, satiation, contentment (*sevia*). In the seven, there is also the oath (*shvua*)[368] that governs relations in a covenant, the promise to hold to a posture and keep an engagement regardless of the conditions of the moment. Concretely, Abraham's covenant with Abimelech is concluded with the sacrifice of seven ewes and the oath of "seven wells (*Beer-sheva*)." In an oath, man engages his future conduct in view of a time that is not yet. He commits himself even though he must traverse absence. In this way he is faithful to God, whose withdrawal left nothing but absence. Man must live without doubting presence for a moment. All this is implied by the septenary economy. The absence lasts six days and, on the seventh, the presence is announced: this presence harbored absence from the start, and it alone makes it possible to master absence.

The septenary rhythm is the rule of all creation in the passage, because creation is caught in a relationship of promise and oath, of waiting and movement in search of the one. "You shall fear YHWH, your God, and serve him, and in his Name you shall take oath/be satisfied" (Deut. 6:13). It is only logical that we feel its effects (abundance and eclipses of abundance or scarcity) in the economic relationship, in which we are summoned to enjoy and be satisfied (*sevia*) with the goods of the land and, first, to draw out of the land, through our efforts, what is hidden in it (fruits and products), thereby making it appear. Doesn't the earth itself obey this episodic eclipse

simply because the priests were already part of a system of retreat: "the priests received from Pharaoh a law (*hok*). They ate the law that Pharaoh gave them; therefore they did not sell their land" (47:22). This was when Joseph imposed the regular giving of a half-tithe to Pharaoh (not one-tenth of their production but a twentieth). Only after all of Egypt was "Levitized" in this way did "Israel settle in the land of Egypt" (47:27). Only on such foundations could the divine presence dwell in Egypt. Only then did Egypt become an abode! But what an ordeal to get there!

368. In Hebrew the term used for swearing or taking an oath literally means doing seven, or doing something seven times.

of presence? Doesn't it live through seasons[369] of scarcity and abundance of presence? In the forgetting that characterizes the passage, the rule of the seventh (day, year, year of years) is like a viaticum: it makes the memory of the future, the promise of Sabbath emerge from oblivion; and it is a guarantee and a means of consummation in the one, the promise of fullness, satisfaction, and accomplishment of the oath. "Keep the Sabbath day, and remember it to repair/sanctify it" (Sabbath prayer). The economy is paradoxically the preeminent field both of the oath and of the trial of its fulfillment (the contract is the common vehicle thereof), the field of waiting for the bounty that the oath brings into being to unfold. In this arena, one must learn to traverse absence, and it is in the framework of the Levitical logic of the rule of seven that Israel traverses it.

369. Thus, seven times seven seven-day weeks separate Passover and Shavuot (the Festival of Weeks), festival of harvest and bounty after the winter scarcity, when the first fruits are offered at the Temple in Jerusalem. This conjuration of seven (three times seven) takes us from scarcity and absence (the retreat from Egypt) to abundance and presence (the Sinaitic revelation).

CHAPTER 5

Abode of Testimony:
The Political Arena

IF THE HIGH PRIEST accomplishes sociality by "repairing" it (*tikkun*) in the concealment of sacrifice (*korban*) and constituting it as a relationship of *kirva*, he can do so only because this procedure is implicitly posited as part of something greater than itself. The proximity is effective only because it institutes an interiority, in which, hidden far from the outside, beings and objects can come close to one another. There is nearness (*kerev*) only within an interior (*toch*).[370] The very process of rapprochement founds an interior. This is the place we traverse to draw close to one another. In this interior, in a different place (a place that has become different), the rapprochement takes place on the social level. At bottom, the social unclenches itself in a place that is at once bigger and smaller and more restricted but that sustains it in all its extensiveness. However, this place, the vehicle of passage itself, is groundless in the sense that it barely constitutes an entity, since the law of passage is to yield, to give way continually. This is how it can sustain the whole of sociality, no matter how "small" it is.

The Political and the Social

The voiding that helps society establish relations of proximity, and in the shadow of which it always establishes them, constitutes the political arena, which is already present in the social but requires work, effort, and actuation to be instituted.[371] We have seen that it is in the voiding produced by the Levites that the king or other civil power is manifested and maintained. This inward movement, this concealment of the Levite, founds the site of

---

370. But we know this is what makes the Hebraic "outside."

371. In a word, the political sustains (is sustained by) the social, precedes it in its principle, but only the social can effectuate and constitute it as a dimension that exceeds it.

effectuation of the ruling power, from which the Levite is absent even though he constitutes the principle and condition thereof. If, in this concealment, the social takes shape, the concealment itself is the sphere of the fulfillment (and possibility) of the social, and on its level the political relationship is established.[372]

Even though this political relationship is in embryonic form (containing the seeds of the future) in the social, it is also its very framework. The interior where the area of the political is woven is at once accomplished (because without it society is not constituted) and pending (because society awaits *tikkun* and must find a way around the danger of exposure in passage). The political precedes the social while being its promise. The effort that commands the manifestation of the political area is the effort that the passage requires relentlessly: the interior of the social that is the political is the possibility offered to the social to continually "mend" itself, to ensure that the close relationships it induces are not perverted in the passage and the exteriority where they take place. The political thus appears to be a perpetual effort in the midst of an infinite tension. It hovers over the social like a bird over its nest. How could it be otherwise for an interior that must be "manifested," built in the exterior?

The preeminent institution of interiority and concealment in Hebraic society is the Temple, or rather the *ohel moed*, thanks to which God is said to "dwell in the interior (*toch*) of the children of Israel" (Exod. 29:45). This *toch* where God lives, which is found in the midst of the children of Israel, is the site of the political, hidden in the midst of the *kirva*, of Israel's sociality behind the veil (*parochet*) that covers the Holy of Holies. We can therefore understand why a formal model of the political is nowhere found in the Torah. The *toch* is not exposed. Therefore, the prohibition of census taking is only logical, insofar as any census would involve counting the Levites and hence delivering the interior that they produce over to exposure, to the power of the eye (the "evil eye"), reifying the interior.

The sole model we have of the political is that of the Tent of Meeting (*ohel moed*), which offers a model of the seat of power and its furnishings that is the only one that can enable the inside to "dwell" on earth. For this reason, the description of the Tent and its accessories comes prior to the prohibition of census taking (Exod. 30:11). The description of the making of the Tent is extremely detailed and provides insight into the Hebraic political arena. We are even told that the one is constituted from its assembly and

---

372. We can thus see that the vocation of the political is oneness in the individual.

the relationships of its parts: "to assemble (*haber*) the Tent to be one" (Exod. 36:18). The dwelling of testimony, *mishkan edut*, is what weaves even the *eda*. In this sense the political arena that brings Israel together is the arena of testimony. All the people assemble at "the gate of the Tent," where "Moses makes a *kahal* of the whole *eda* of the children of Israel."

The Tent is made of materials that come from the offerings of the people, and its construction is the result of "the labor of Levites" (38:21). The political is the building of a place in the void. However, because it is in the void, this place is mounted and dismounted, coming together and coming apart—that is to say, it is in passage. In its fullest manifestation, it is still out of sight and reach, for the Holy of Holies, hidden from view, is the vehicle of absence in the very place where, by a supreme effort, it manifests itself and speaks. By comprehending the nature and laws of this interior (*toch*), we can come to understand the nature of the political in Israel.

I. THE INTERIOR OF THE CHILDREN OF ISRAEL

The *toch* is to be understood not as a metaphor but as the actual site of the political. Admittedly, this is not an easy task. Perhaps it would help to look at a second meaning, or, more precisely, at a second lection[373] of the term: *tivuch*. *Tivuch* is the act of creating a link with the other, of interposing between two people, but not in the sense of a mediation, because *tivuch* creates a *tavech*, a middle or intermediary space/side/breadth (of an object). The connotation of interiority is, moreover, decisive insofar as this space—which is defined in relation not to itself, to its center, but to that which it unites—is said "inside (*toch*)."[374] Now, mediation is not inside, exterior to the terms it unites. It is, itself, indifferent to the other, valid for itself in the relationship it induces. Here, through the agency of interiority, the *tavech* unites, in its very field, the terms of the relationship that are no longer external to it, as in the relationship of mediation. The *toch* is thus at once a relationship and a place. It is interior in that it does not conquer a centrality of being external to all the terms. The *toch* is made from their union, and in their union it dwells. Thus, it is said, "I will dwell in the *toch* of the children of Israel"

373. Vocalized differently.

374. We find here the theme of the Covenant between the Pieces, when Abraham cuts the animals in their *tavech* and passes in the *toch* between the divided pieces.

(Exod. 29:45) and not outside the human, in naked space. It is because the *tavech* is human that it is immediately a *toch*. The Hebraic political field is hence diametrically opposed to an agora. Being in the Hebraic political area involves "entering." Yet this entry is read as a departure, because it involves leaving the outside in order to dwell; it is a going out leading to a *knesset/* assembly/entry. "I will dwell in the *toch* of the children of Israel. I will be their God. They will know that I am Yнwн, their God, them whom I took out of the land of Egypt to dwell in their *toch*. I am Yнwн, their God" (ibid.). In the assembly, the departure is brought about by the passage that constitutes it. God takes them out of Egypt by "passing" through the land of Egypt (12:12). Thus, Moses places the Tent of Meeting "outside the camp," so it is a departure from the camp as the political is a departure from the social (for its own *tikkun*). But because the *toch* is inside, and because the inside is not the residue of the outside, it draws its being from itself; it has an intrinsic reality that resembles the divine interiorizing of the origin in which the exterior emerged.

From the divine incurving into a *toch,* creation was born. Thus, the *toch* of Israel is founded on another *toch,* in the exterior of Egypt. God is said to have come to "take a people (*goy*) from the midst (*kerev*) of another people" (Deut. 4:34). Egypt has a *toch* only because Joseph forged it through an economic policy aimed at Levitical dispossession, a policy apt to hollow out a *toch* in the fullness of the world's totality. The political field can therefore originate only in interiority, in another *toch,* in this case, the *toch* of Egypt and the *toch* of God the creator. Unlike the naked space of the agora, the *toch* is a hidden space with ill-defined boundaries, because inwardness, even when contained within the four cubits of a place or a building, is infinite, in tune with infinity. Therefore, summed up in Israel's *toch* are all the *toch*s, all the political spaces of the nations (and this was the historical experience of the Jews), right down to and including formerly hospitable Egypt, now an enemy.

This is due to the fact that the *toch* echoes a fundamental reality, which has to do with the experience of creation. There is an analogy between this *toch* and the interior in which God the creator envelops himself and hides. The creational retreat manifests itself in this world, and in this retreat the faces are formed,[375] without which there can be no relationship. We can see why the faces of two cherubim are found above the Ark of the Covenant. The *toch* where the world is created arises from "God passing over his face"

---

375. On the meaning of *pinuy*, withdrawal, and *panim*, faces, see "Les Visages," in Trigano, *Story of Disappeared Presence*, p. 57.

(Exod. 34:6), from God's passing in himself. The *toch* shelters and hides the overplus in which the world was created.[376] It is for this purpose that it is found in the world, for this purpose that the *Shechina* is in the world: in order to catch up and accomplish the absence of that which set itself aside in overplus to let reality manifest itself. We have here the whole system of concealment. In the Tent of Meeting, the most important element is the curtain that sets apart the Holy of Holies.

Thus, the *toch*, while being "measured" (witness the measurements of the Temple) and "small," contains the infinite bounty of that which is in overplus, not scarcity. The presence held within it is limitless and infinite. Seeing infinity emerging in the finite presents a difficult paradox. How are we to understand the measurement? The measurement measures the finite, the edge of the finite next to the infinite. In face of the infinite, the finite is measured. Isn't this the very finality of the Temple? It is the empire of measure, of detail, of rigor (witness the detailed sacrificial regulations), but the whole system leads to the brink of infinity, to the suspension of measurement, to *rahamim* and compassion. The weight of measurement makes itself felt this strongly in the Temple because here it will implode and surpass itself. The Temple, which institutes the *toch* in the heart of the Hebraic *polis*, is like creation. The world of rigor and measure is inhabited by a pulsating nucleus, the hither side of rigor, *rahamim*—presage and promise compared to rigor, which is merely passing and which is applicable only for the apportioning but doesn't know it.

Power and Universality

So, like the *toch*, the Hebraic political arena is characterized by two fundamental traits. Presence is so bountiful in it that it overwhelms power, which, in its virulence, is established solely in scarcity and shortage. In the shadow of this presence, political power is put into perspective. It stands between the infinity that submerges it and from which it draws the strength and particularity that throw it back onto its destiny in this world, shattering the illusion of an experience in which it represents itself as infinite and usurps the cherubic throne behind the veil.

Power in the Hebraic polity can boast neither holiness nor secrecy. It belongs to the finite world. What's more, the *toch* lodges human freedom

---

376. This is why political power is so immensely desirable. It governs augment and presence.

in the political arena insofar as the divine retreat, the veil, leaves human beings to their own devices, their own destinies, their own paths. Thus, it is the task of human beings, not God, to build the Tabernacle, the *toch*, the political arena. The concealment and *kappara* that the created world requires to be accomplished in *tikkun* takes place through the building of the *toch*. Through the agency of passage, one thereby finds the temporal problematic of the political: this paradoxical institution that is the vehicle of passage impels the temporality and fluidity of the political field, one of whose key perversions is fixity, the sacralizing illusion of perpetual representation, in short, the perversion of time, which is growth, patience, and waiting. And so the Tent is intended for *moadim*—that is to say, for specific, defined, and passing times (the "festivals") and not for perpetual sojourning. One merely passes sporadically in and in front of the Tent.

The criterion of measurement is also significant here. The emergence of infinity in the finite throws the political arena back onto measurement. In this highly paradoxical structure, the infinite in its universality appears in the context of the particular and the finite, and the infinite is measured by the finite. It is in this way that the universal is manifested. This is a guarantee against its misuse by the political that sets itself up as its representative, not by assuming the details and the particularity but by covering them up and occulting them. A genuine dictatorship arises by covering the particular with the universal in the very place of their separation, in a way that annuls the possibility of accomplishing the *tikkun* of the world of creation, which must journey through this world of rigor to reach the perpetual rejuvenation of grace, its infinite presence renewed every instant!

By virtue of the veil, the *toch* in the midst of the polity enables strangeness to dwell among men, so the political arena is also the arena of strangeness. Its coherence is readily comprehensible when one knows the nature of sovereignty in Israel, and this demonstrates once again that the political arena is constituted not by the eviction of the other but, to the contrary, by the other's inclusion, behind the veil. The veil in the Temple is the greatest protection of the rights of the other in the Hebraic polity; it is before the veil that they stand.

Paradoxically, it is by drawing from this wellspring of strangeness that the *eda* is forged, in the crucible of the *moed*, the ritual meeting time. It is in the abode of the *toch* and its overplus that the *eda* stands. It is there only because it testifies to the absence, and, for this purpose, when it assembles and is manifested, it draws together "at the gates of the Tent," at the gates of the original void. It is through concealment in the Temple that the *eda* is constituted, inside. This strangeness is instituted in the same way as the *toch* is constituted. Contrary to many fusionist and essentialist conceptions of the interior of the home as a single, flawless block, united with the one it shelters, everything in the Hebraic Temple speaks of discontinuity, elementarization, and particularization. Instead of the magnificent symphonic architecture of cathedrals and temples of other religions, whose constituent parts cannot be discerned in the unity of the whole, the Hebraic Temple offers an assemblage, a montage of elements, described as such in great, seemingly insignificant detail; these are joined together not so much to produce a totality as to shelter the one, to house unity. "Assemble (*haver*) the tapestries each to the other/each woman to her sister... the dwelling shall be one" (Exod. 26:6).

The problematic of the totality, or rather, of the unity of the *mishkan*, the dwelling house, is extremely important, inasmuch as it gives rise to an original relationship between the element and the whole: the whole does not mask the particular and the singular by its universality. The one dwells in a relationship of one particular to another, but the singular finds itself valorized "in its place," insofar as it is from its place, in its elementarity, that it prevents the one from congealing in the all. It is important, therefore, that each element preserve its identity, that the Temple can be disassembled and reassembled[377] every time the camp picks up and moves somewhere else. In this way, the promise of the one, which each element as such harbors in its very principle, is preserved. The fact that unity is possible not by way of a transcendental cause but by virtue of an assembling serves perpetually to "dismantle" the "décor" of the political and keep it from its usual semblance and figuration.

Differentiation and Unity

In this way, the political arena is founded on the problematic not of representation and totality but of differentiation and reduction to the solitary uniqueness of each element, within the growth of unity, of course. The *toch* is woven through union with the other; this is why the relationship between the masculine and the feminine—which we have seen at work with the cherubim—is cardinal. Archetypically, the *toch* is made of the union of the two; this is the true (dual) figure of unity in the Hebraic mind. And in fact, the trial of the political is akin to that of sexuality. If the Greek *meson*,

---

377. Only the Levitical tribe can take part in this task, which is divided amongst all its families, so no Levite can control the totality of the process of (dis)assembling the tent.

or center, assumes the form of the goddess Hestia, as virgin and procreator, the arena of power is made of the exclusively male army of warriors (who constitute the *laos*, or people). The people are united in Greece in this warrior army, no doubt because the warriors fight to possess the forbidden virgin, like the Greeks' fighting over Helen in the Trojan War. But it is through the love relationship and its trials that the Hebraic *toch* is forged. "Its *toch* is paved/contiguous with the love of the daughters of Israel" (Song 3:10). It is contiguous as one can be when the contiguity is composed, by nature, of at least two elements, which goes to say that love, not war, is the skein of social fabric. And the *toch* so defined refers to the palanquin (*apiryon*) that King Solomon had made in the Song of Songs to house his convoy of love, the convoy of the *Shechina*, transhumance of the ark across the wildernesses of the world. This love is said to be "contiguous" to designate a relationship of bonding and fullness, linking two elements to one another in such a way that, whereas there are no gaps, they remain distinct. This love does not eliminate singularities; it unites them in the effort[378] and in the overplus of interiority and heart.

The relationship with sexual overtones that constitutes the *toch* is one of sanctification/separation (*keddusha*), not fusion. This is logically the role fulfilled by the Separate of Separates behind the Veil in the Temple. This relationship yields a concealment, that is to say, it covers up the nakedness, preventing the exposure outside the being that chases away all presence. This concealment is what makes the *toch* possible in the relationship. Thus, in the separation that the concealment of nudity produces, a voice emerges and rises from behind the curtain, from between the cherubim of propitiation. The *toch* is inhabited by the voice; in fact, it is born from its resonance, which curls up in concealment. This "voice" is not like the voices of people making themselves heard in the political arena through voting, interchangeable voices counted and tallied in exposure and nudity, mechanical elements taken in the totality. The voice manifested in the one cannot be totaled. The one that inhabits it rebels against such an attempt. It is a voice only in its perpetual movement back and forth between the cherubim.

The one is not the sum total of parts. It is indivisible, yet it arises from the reciprocal hovering of the one and the other. The Hebraic political arena comes from the multiple unity of the hidden voice rather than from the total

---

378. Just as three of the four species used in the festival of Sukkot are tied together in the *lulav* branch, while the fourth, the *etrog*, is held in the other hand and pressed against the branch for the *mitzva* to be accomplished, so the heart must come in addition to the elements of the whole for the whole to form a unity.

sum of voices that expose themselves to census taking. In this way, the living unity of each person, the singular uniqueness of the individual, is preserved instead of being objectified in a ballot that feeds representation, the imaginary Leviathanesque being of which is sustained by the self-effacement of human beings. It is in a *toch* where the voice rises up that the one inside, the Name, can dwell, the Name, that makes the whole substance of the social. "You shall not profane the name of my separation/holiness; I shall be separated/ sanctified in the *toch* of the children of Israel; I am Yʜwʜ, who separates/ sanctifies you" (Lev. 22:32).

The holiness of the divine Name has to do with the fact that it was separated/sanctified in the *toch* of Israel. In God's concealment, his Name became effective. And it is because Israel separated the Name that it is separated itself, taken out of the passage, the *halal* ("you shall not profane/*tehalelu*"), the yawning abyss of profanation and of the dangers inherent in passage. This is why the deepest reality of the Hebraic political arena is bound up with the fact that it shelters the Name. The Temple is an abode of the Name. Its most realistic and "magical" aspects can be understood only through the prism of the letters and Names[379] that sparkle in the supposed darkness behind the Veil, while the politics of exposure seeks to manifest presence in the demonstration of light and revealment. Any politics of exposure involves a dream of light and magical transparency, whose realization can only drive away the Name that sparkles in the shadows and in withdrawal, to replace it with the idol of God.[380]

The paradoxical quality of decomposition and elementarization of Israel's *toch* is clearly illustrated in Abraham's sacrifice of the pieces, which founds the *toch*, just as it forges the covenant. The decomposition breaks the wholeness of the world understood in terms of property and totalization, but it does not doom the *toch* to the dereliction of disjunction. The antithesis of "adjoining" is not dissociation, for although the *toch* can be decomposed, in secret it houses the one, indivisible and indifferent to assemblage. In Abraham's sacrifice, the vehicle of this is the bird, the only one of all the animals not to be cut. In the *toch*, in the milieu that it is and that makes the covenant, the one shines forth; and it is in relation to the one that the pieces are assembled rather than left in disorder. The one thereby appears to

---

379. This is the case for such supremely "magical" devices as the high priest's breastplate with its purported magical powers. Upon closer examination, it is clear that the power of the device lies in the interplay of the letters in the names of the twelve tribes with the letters of the Tetragrammaton and the names of the patriarchs.

380. Thus all politicians try to work magic to seduce and capture the souls in exposure.

be the essential lever in the subversive disarranging of the all, the intangible rock that opens the whole to passage.

The *toch* has therefore a paradoxical nature. It is simultaneously the locus of interiority and that of an unhinging, a disadjustment that becomes the very principle of the assembling. It is the site of interiority, of fusion and unity, because it is the four-letter Name that the creator left when he withdrew, the place whose name is *Peniel*, face of God, the place/name: "to bring you to the place that I have made ready, keep yourself from his face, and listen to his voice... for my Name is in his midst (*kerev*)" (Exod. 23:21). A marvelous, awesome place to stand by (*etzel*) God, "there is a place (*makom*) with me," a place that comes as an overplus to the places of this world, at once remote, set apart in infinity, and alien, but also close because, through it, the companionship (*hibbur*) with God is forged as well as the gathering of human beings in its political dimension.

This place that is veiled so as not to expose the nakedness of the *Shechina* is a vision of God and the universe, because it is a vision of the safeguarded portion, of the withdrawal from which the universe sprang, a vision of the most safeguarded secret in the world, revealment of the Name in the one. Here the distance is canceled in the *kerev*. But this is where the one is veiled and hides. "Keep yourself from his face, and listen to his voice." The whole Temple is here: the Veil and the prohibition against representation, on the one hand, and the listening to the voice, on the other hand, the voice in equal tension between vision and concealment. This is the only nakedness possible, a prudish and separated nakedness—such is the *Shechina* revealed in a separate place and in the midst of concealment! As if a nearness arose from the distantiation—such is the place (*makom*) that arises (*kom*) in the *toch* there. One is as close to the being as one can be, wherever one is (one is bound, united), and seized by the strangeness of *gerut* (one is separated, divided), of which the Veil of concealment is a reminder. The duality of the cherubim is a sign of this dual experience. The place manifested as an overplus, coextensive to a disappearance, originates in the interiority of concealment by which the all enters the one and the one is chosen outside the whole. If the place is indeed "real," it is as a twinkling, as light mixed with eclipse and matter with void.

The Law

This strange otherness that inhabits the place, from which one must "veil one's face," is the law etched on the tablets of the covenant in the ark hidden in the Holy of Holies. The place is bigger than itself. It contains an object in its incandescent, innermost core: the tablets of the Torah. This law is the exteriority, the strangeness in the *toch* that only the *toch* can contain. The Hebraic political arena is characterized by a hiatus, a nonadjustment that prevents the unity of the *toch* from slipping into totalization. Manifested in the form of an object, the law is the stranger in the *toch* and hence the principle of sovereignty. It is via the strangeness inherent in the law that the *toch* is *toch*. The elevated presence of the law in the *toch* is what makes the Hebraic political arena. Having come from Sinai, that law derives from somewhere else, from the other, and the *toch* is established around it. This is not the discourse of rationalization that would crystallize the configuration of the political arena after the fact. Neither the people nor the *eda* invents the law, even though they interpret and pronounce it for each passing moment.

There is a mighty otherness at the heart of the *toch* of Israel, the dwelling of the Name, a permanent reminder for human beings that they were created and born, that on the brink of infinity, they are measured and placed behind the Veil. The presence of the tablets of the law in the Tent of Meeting compels them to remember. It disarms the instinctive desire of human beings to be one, incestuously united, with the origin, infinity, the being, and the divine, to escape the trial of passage, a trial of concealment, and to recompose the whole.

Hence the significance of the prohibition of incest. Hiding the nakedness of those who are close checks the proclivity to fusion that risks engulfing the kin and negating the separation of birth. By such a catastrophic act, the creation of the world is annulled.[381] The prohibition of incest distances those who are closest to us and brings those who are distant closer. In sum, the law comes to tell us that there is exteriority at the heart of interiority and intimacy. The law assigns exteriority to its true place, that is, in the interiority, in the *toch*. In this sense, the law is structurally the word of God, because it resembles creation: exteriority emerges from the innermost interior, in the gathering of the divine into himself, which is also (altruistic being of the

---

381. It is interesting to compare this structure of *toch* with the Egyptian *toch* in which Pharaoh married his sister, committing incest to establish his power.

divine!) the conception of the other, for the divine self is infinite. Such is the paradox of creation.

Essentially, the question of the law leads us to discover that the operation of concealment involves exteriority. What is hidden and hence inside is so by means of an instrument of covering, and this instrument is exteriority. Figuratively, one could say that the veil that separates and hides the Holy of Holies crystallizes the exteriority of the world, and meditating upon the Veil, the *parochet*, the "fracturing" that separates the world inside from the outside, is meditating on the exteriority of the world.[382] The law governs actions in exteriority, as much to make the *toch* possible as to prevent its negation through fusion with the outside. It aims to preserve this portion set aside and hidden, this overplus in its own structuring, but also in relation to the outside and for the outside. The law is always the law of constituting and hiding the overplus. The gift and gratuitousness are paradoxically its beating core, its secret heart. The law is thus the middle way, subjected to contradictory tensions and aimed at preserving the path in the created world. Is this not the vocation and daily task of the political that occupies the interstice between the inside (God, man, the collectivity) and the outside (the actuation and realization of the latter)? The destiny of objectification is played out in the law. Through it, something is "found" in the world without being "found" in exposure. In other words, the law establishes an altogether different reality.

We can now see more clearly why the law is at the core of the political, just as strangeness is at the core of sovereignty, insofar as the greatest danger threatening sovereignty is to lapse into total adequation with itself, thereby reabsorbing the hiatus that is the world. The strangeness experienced by Israel in its own midst ultimately derives from the strangeness of the Torah in its midst, for the law comes from other than itself, yet it is of a piece with it, forming one body, a full body at the heart of the void and of retreat, a body steeped in writing! "...in the place that YHWH, your God, will choose to rest his Name. There you shall remember that you were a slave in Egypt, and you shall observe and do these laws" (Deut. 16:11–12).

Sovereignty in Israel is founded upon the fact that people are not the makers of the law. If the Torah departed from Israel, Israel would cease to exist, and sovereignty would escape it. The void that sustains it would turn to nothingness and engulf it. However, if the people do not make the law, they do pronounce laws through the Levitical tribe, the embodiment of the political class in the Hebraic *polis* ("they teach your laws to Jacob and your

382. Like the ten *sefirot*, ten veils drawn over the *toch*.

Torah to Israel,"[383] Deut. 33:10) and Sanhedrin. The *am* and its institution (civil power, in this case) can only adjudicate and apply the laws. The law logically resides in the *eda*, which is the overplus of the people/*am*, its concealment.

One can see the implications of this to a certain extent in the status of the Levites in citizenship. Everything points to the fact that the political body that sustains the Hebraic political community stands outside the confines of citizenship, as if to manifest the divide in which the political itself is born: the Levites are in overplus to the people, "hidden" in citizenship, because they are the very principle of that citizenship. Yet the Levites represent a hereditary status in the discourse of the law, one that is compensated, nonetheless, by the more open character (yet still dependent on knowledge of the law) of the Sanhedrin.

The law appears in the *eda*'s secret interior. It is never totally manifest. It is not "expressed." It must be drawn out of its hiding. And this act is precisely what makes the people/*am* and the laws. The law is in overplus, the hidden augment. It testifies to the bounty of *toch*, to the problematic of overplus for the world of lack, to the paradigm of perfection for that which lacks perfection, to the path of redemption for faulty conduct. This is why the thrust of the law in this world is mainly negative, for it is the agency of negative commandments for a world that sees itself in positive fullness.

We find here once again the system of "augret": retreat on one side, augment on the other. This is the model that structures the law of Israel. The law is written law before all else, etched in letters and hence set at a distance from the interior, outside the self in exteriority, in a relationship of otherness to the self.[384] That the reading of the law is not in adequation to its writing (defective consonantism) tells us about the *olam*/world/disappearance. Even though the law is placed within the *toch* in the Ark of the Covenant, it is placed "at the side," on the edge of the innermost interior within the most innermost interior. "Moses wrote this Torah and gave it to the *kohanim*, the sons of Levi, the bearers of the Ark of the Covenant of YHWH, and to all the elders [the senators[385]] of Israel... 'You shall read this Torah before/against all Israel, in their ears'" (Deut. 31:9–11); "You will take the book of the Torah, and you will place it at the side of the Ark of the Covenant of YHWH, your

383. This is not merely rhetorical redundancy: Jacob, the *am*, receives laws, and Israel, the *eda*, receives the Torah.

384. It is stone in the midst of the interior of flesh. It is in this sense that one must remember the slavery in Egypt, the pyramidal stone, in the place where the Name dwells (Deut. 16:12).

385. The members of the Sanhedrin.

God, and it shall remain there as a testimony against you" (31:26). There is, then, no aesthetics of symmetry in the *toch* where one would have thought the tablets would occupy a geographically central position. This "at the side" of the law evinces the strategies of getting around and avoiding centrality in the political that characterize the *toch*. One looks at the center and finds nothing. The Torah appears in a second look, once the central vision has been thwarted. In this sense, the Torah is "testimony," the founding testimony of a community of testimony (*eda*). In a way, Israel is a witness against Israel;[386] this is the founding retreat of the *eda* in the *am*. This testimony emanates from the Torah, which is external to it.

But the law is, in addition, written and placed in a relationship of silent exteriority to Israel. There before me, it says nothing. It lacks the voice; its interior is beneath the surface of the consonants that alone are engraved, to be read, to rise up in the interior. The law as writing does not, in this sense alone, house the political collectivity. It is a guarantee against the perversion of the political arena, but it is not, by itself, its totality. The dimension of overplus of interiority, of the *toch*, is required, the voice that rises in the *toch* to sing. If the collectivity is saved by the written word, writing alone cannot sustain it; it needs the overplus of *toch*, of the voice and the vocalization to say something. Man must "draw out" of this apparent exteriority the voice of the law for the law to be heard.

The primacy of the hidden voice, in overplus to the written law, is also evident in the lack of a specifically legal or constitutional style in the Torah. There is no distinction between narrative and legal discourse, and this has led some to conclude that there is no political constitution in the Torah. In fact, the recitative that characterizes the Hebraic legal register testifies to the interiority of laws that dwell within the *toch*, even if they are formally set down in writing. There is no distinction between the problematic of the law and that of being and existence. In addition, aside from the voice of vocalization, to read and understand this law requires a commentary, a readjustment of the written to the oral, a perpetual readjustment like the perpetual passage, the *tikkun* of the law's exteriority in the *toch*. The Levites are the agency of this commentary; the Sanhedrin is the agency of the law's formalization.[387] It

---

386. As Israel is Jacob's witness before the fight against the angel.

387. The law proceeds through three phases. First there is the Torah that belongs to the sphere of the Levites, in the *toch*, who comment on the divine word; then the laws (*mishpatim*) that emanate from the Sanhedrin, which belong to the sphere of the *eda*; and finally the regulations (*hukkim*) that are the prerogative of the *knesset* that is held in the *am*.

is around this very act of untethering the law that the *am* is forged and the sphere of the political is woven, as if this sphere were wound around this act.

From another standpoint, this means that the law is greater than the political or, to put it otherwise, that it is greater than the state or the people. Even though the *toch* is the ambient milieu of the state, there is a "stage" other than the state upon which something other than the gesture of the state is acted out. No doubt, there is an echo of this in the "at the side" of the law in the ark. The *toch* carries the whole stake of creation, all of being. It is only logical that Abraham hears his offspring announced in the Covenant between the Pieces. This is even the main motivation of Abraham's course of action. The principle of filiation that governs remembrance and passage, the economy of the Name of concealment in the world, is established in the *toch*. In this way, there is an order of law, independent and normative, that is superior to the order of the state. Families and human beings as such are governed by it in a higher way than by the civil order.[388] There is an order greater than citizenship.

This pristine order testifies "against" the political order. It bears witness to the preeminence of the law over power, of the *toch* over the political. Peoples, families, communities need a place of concealment; they need a name to live. This is what citizenship and the state try to uncover in order to ensure their inherent inclination to empire. This constitutes an attack on the *toch* in its innermost heart and the sign of the impending death of the political collectivity, because, without concealment, the *am* breaks down.[389]

We can see from this the extent to which the political arena concedes a very narrow register to politics. This system removes the state or the political from the realm of the essence and the absolute. Everything in it is relative. Placed under the control of the law, the state appears even more in the form of the court, where disagreements are judged and resolved. It is the organ of the *différance* that removes the individual from the magma of confusion and fusion. If it is in the unity of the *toch*, through the law that is in the *toch*, it is the vehicle of separation and particularization.

All law in the Hebraic political sphere is in the detail. This is what could be called the "style" of the Torah and *halacha*. They are not legal "codes" by any means; collective and patriarchal filiations and adventures are interwoven

388. For this purpose, the "management" of the civil state is subservient to the legislative body, not the state.

389. To compensate for this disclosure, in the era of the modern nation-state type of citizenship, when the state administrates civil status, collectivities have fallen back on charismatic authorities, on the principle of the leader, identified with the "father."

in a single narrative. The field of the law and the political (the state) is that of particularization. The "universality" and "generality" of this sphere are present or reached by the agency of the *toch* and totally marked by its qualities of interiority. But the universality is there by default and by withdrawal, because the *toch* itself is concealment, setting apart, the particularization of the universe, of God the creator withdrawing, putting himself in hiding to make room for the world. Human universality is marked by singularization. It could never be otherwise. The only possible universality is that of the face, the wombing mark of divine withdrawal and concealment. And there can only be *panim*, faces, in the plural, in a relationship between one and the other.

No doubt the written dimension of the law within the *toch* is to be understood in this sense, too. Writing is perhaps the only possible communication of this absence and withdrawal. It is an antirepresentation, the exteriority with which the *toch* covers itself for purposes of concealment. There is no image tacked onto the void, no image replacing it in an attempt to simulate presence. Just the opposite. The nonvocalized writing is there below the surface, withdrawn from itself. The veil that separates the Holy of Holies, the *toch*, from the outside is woven in letters from the sacred Scripture: the parchment of the Torah is the veil of concealment.

In sum, the whole thickness of the reality of this world (which hides the divine retreat inside) is made of the letters and words of the Torah. It is important that Scripture dwell in the *toch*. It is its strange presence in the innermost *toch* that enables the political to escape representation and the mock presence that begets idolatry. The letters of the Torah thus carry the secret of *tikkun*; they are redemptive elements scattered over the veil out of which matter is woven, its very woof and weft. From this standpoint, it is important for the Torah to be seen, in its consonants, so it differs from the way it is read with the addition, the augment of vowels. The *toch* is thereby in hiding and does not give itself over immediately, like representation. Thus, in the political sphere, man enjoys an indeterminate space—God's shadow over the earth—where he can make his way, setting out on his path to the one in a freedom paradoxically riveted to the very characters of the letters of the Torah. "The two tables of testimony were in his hand, on both sides, on this one and on that one, they were written; and the tablets are the doing of your God; and the writing, the writing of God, is engraved (*harut*) on the tablets" (Exod. 32:15); and the sages tell us, "Read not 'inscribed (*harut*)' but 'freedom (*herut*)'" (Eruvin 54a).

The Object Inside

The area that the *toch* opens is thereby characterized by a structural paradox: its interiority is founded entirely on positing exteriority in its very midst. The figure of the tablets of the law is significant in this regard. It gives exteriority the status of an object inside the *toch* (even if this object is made wholly of letters and transparency), since the tables are "written on both sides [literally, on both passages], on this side and on that side," an object in passage, but an object nonetheless, tablets of engraved stone. And yet the exteriority of the tablets is kept in hiding in the ark, behind the veil. The tablets are like a part of the world removed from the world and hidden: a stone part nearly "trans-substantiated" in letters but without the stone disappearing in the letter. This, then, is the Temple: placing the materiality of the world at the side of interiority, the proximity of which accentuates this materiality, almost to the verge of the "obscene,"[390] of that which exposes itself to the eye but is invisible. The Temple is the moment when exteriority is about to pass over to the interior.

We have seen the extent to which the presence of the object in the interior exorcised the irresistible inclination to fusion and totalization in the *toch*. The "tablets" as object (like the Torah as discourse) are like the stranger in the abode. Thanks to this object, the *toch* is not fusion but association. There is a whole conception of the objectification of/in the world that follows from this system, an objectification at once displayed and hidden. And isn't this a definition of the passage, of a world constituted from/in passing? It speaks of the irreducibility of exteriority in the world of creation, and it denounces the desire for fusional totality. But this exteriority is not to be left to itself. It has to be removed, withdrawn, placed inside the *toch* to be redeemed and "repaired." It would be a radical mistake to hold the object for what it is, for what it appears to be in its external manifestation. The object makes sense only as the veil concealing the interior. The veil—such is the status of matter. The mistake would be to stop at the veil. It is therefore only logical that the tablets of the law are a second object, replacing the first, broken tablets, which were, in fact, necessarily broken, because the object hidden in the *toch* is a "refined" object whose objectification acquires a higher level. Human assemblies always run the risk of organizing relations of exteriority alone, of being crystallized in a hierarchy and bureaucracy that thereupon become

390. See the seemingly "trivial" details of sacrifices and rites.

the exclusive support and face of presence and continuity. Such gatherings risk being reduced to a pattern or economy of exteriority. But the removed object that makes the *toch*, the tablets of the law in hiding, brings relations of interiority into human assemblies; it brings human beings together without diluting them in some magmatic fusion. The aim of the *toch* is precisely to preserve an overplus of being that prevents the gathering from destroying itself. It prepares a future while endowing itself with an interiority that keeps it from staying on the outside. The status of object[391] plays a primordial role in this creation of an overplus. It is from the objectivity of the world (the stone tablet) that it is taken, and it is because it is an object that it is in overplus, that there is overplus and, conversely, absence and empty space in the world from which it is taken. But implicit herein is a secondary statute of the object in the world, designated in its passage from outside to inside and taken out of its inherent reification. Anything that aims at reducing the object to itself is a negation of *toch*, a disclosure of the project of the *olam*. This is another name for idolatry, for the eschewal of concealment.

The object's purpose is thus to found the assembly of men without running the risk of identifying it with itself, of tallying the "sum total" of its individual components, which would thereby be objectified, reduced to what they are in the world, in the total exposure from which the *toch* is absent.[392] So in the gathering of Israel, in the heart of the *toch*, there is the *eda*, the community of testimony, which dwells by the tablets of the law, as "a testimony against you," hidden in the hearts of the *am*, which is its exteriority. The *eda* bears the Torah. It gathers inside near the *mishkan*, whereas the *am* stays outside. The tablets of the covenant are what enable the relationship between the two, because they are removed from the *am*, hidden within the *eda*, and it is by virtue of these tablets that authority is exercised in the *am*.[393] This is why the king is required to write a *sefer* Torah that is to go before him wherever he goes, as preceded by its authority—that is, by the very "figure" of the within, the antifigure under the surface of the stone, in letters. This procession of the *sefer Torah* serves as a "representation" of power, or rather an antirepresentation that accompanies the displays of power in the *am*, as testimony of the *toch* in exteriority. Here, the "object" functions as testimony/*edut* (from inside to outside) and not as a sign/*ot*, as exteriority. Testimony maintains a

391. Inevitably, it is also the status of the object offered as a gift.

392. See below the malediction attached to census taking in "All Israel and the Prohibition Against Census Taking," pp. 367–390.

393. When the tablets are late in coming, the *am* grows impatient with waiting, falls apart, and raises the golden calf.

tension with the inside: it is always (outside) looking inward. The sign, on the other hand, turns its back to the interior. It is mainly involved in *(dé) monstration*, pointing to not the object inside but the embroidery of the veil. This whole perspective of the *toch* is ultimately coherent with the idea of the *berit*, the rupture of the *olam*, of its passage, the shattering of objects and passage inside. This function is assumed by the object in the form of the tablets, to be sure, but even more so by what sustains the tablets—namely the law. The law is what takes us out of both reification and the violence perpetrated therein, out of autistic self-confinement, because it drives us to the exteriority of the other. No doubt this dual system is at the origin of the human *nefesh*, born within the *toch* and projected out into the *olam*.

The function of the tablets of the law as object and exteriority within the interior gives us a better grasp of the nature and movement that characterize the place woven in the *toch* that accommodates the political arena. It is a place of gathering and at the same time of separation, since the gathering therein is a separation, and all separation founds gathering. Separation is synonymous here with sanctification and concealment. The political is the sphere in which human beings are at once united as members of a single community and also separated from others; it is the meeting ground of the universal and the particular, but here the particular tends not to take the universal apart, nor does the universal disregard the particular.

The arena of the political thus appears to be the essential mechanism in the destiny of human beings in the *olam*. As they pass through the *olam*, they try to reconcile its permanence and its irresistible passing, the presence that unfolds in absence, the petrifying exteriority of the outside and the shelter of the inside. The *toch* is the preeminet political sphere, in that it posits the other in his alterity and exteriority, while pitilessly debunking the fusionist ideal. The veil that hides the Holy of Holies is the highest, most important instrument of politics. It provides society with a respiratory mechanism, a passageway where it can convene for a *moed*.[394] In this sense, the political assembly of human beings is freedom. It governs the contradictory relations of proximity and separation and provides an arena where all the experiences of the *olam* can come together in a coherent structure.[395] This coherence is derived from the strangeness that inhabits it and positions each individual in the collectivity according to a criterion exterior to this same collectivity. The

394. For this purpose the three annual festivals of pilgrimage *oblige* the people to gather in Jerusalem.

395. Cult ceremonies are ways of interrelating the universe and the soul on the threshold of the *toch*.

toch is the irruption in this world of a reference of another type altogether. But this strangeness that recomposes the landscape of the familiar, the overly familiar, derives this coherence more precisely from the law that harbors it, the genuine criterion of organization of the paradoxical movement that makes the *olam* and is enthroned, a stranger, in the heart of the innermost interior.

II. ALL ISRAEL AND THE PROHIBITION OF CENSUS TAKING

The tension that the *toch* organizes and that accounts for the fact that the political is inside without the other vanishing in it is manifested in an exemplary way in the prohibition of representation that governs living in the Abode of Testimony. Such a prohibition makes it impossible for the political to tend to the totalization it yearns for by nature (precisely because it is standing in the void and in passage); it makes it impossible for the state to become a supreme totality, crystallizing in a uniform representation all the asperities of reality and the details of individuals and objects. The one is structurally resistant to the sum of the parts. The state as totality is the ineluctable threat "lurking at the doorway" (Gen. 4:7) of the political sphere. Summoned to gather and unite, to make a community from and beyond the particular, politics risks turning the particular into an abstraction so as to achieve greater transparency and brightness. The dream of light, embedded in the very project of the state, will not tolerate particularity; it will only pulverize it in its radiance, because, unlike the one, particularity is an obstacle to it.

The Temple as Obstacle

With the Temple, we have the light of the *Shechina*, which dwells in the ark[396] but is hidden in the darkness of the interior of the Holy of Holies: an obstacle (the veil) manifests it rather than some form of grandiose, magnificent transparency, as one might have expected. The cardinal feature of the *toch* is to be "wobbly." There are plenty of obstacles in the layout of the Temple— objects, furnishings, a profusion of details and measurements—which make it impossible to draw a totalized or unique representation. There is a set of

396. Etymologically, the *aron*/ark is a device made of *or*/light.

strategies here that, while aspiring to the universal of divine presence, gets around and channels it by lodging the irreducible validity of the particular at the very heart of its structure. After all, isn't divine presence itself contained in a Name that can be called and invoked, and not in some neutral, abstract, universal category?

In the desire for exaltation that drives the impetus to the state, the Temple is an absolute handicap. The meticulous management of objects, spaces, and movements that it demands runs counter to this desire. The minor details seemingly devoid of meaning and the nitpicking obsession with procedure play a major role in reminding those who spend so much time near the heights (the presence), so close to nothingness (the dereliction of the passage), that they are but men, creatures who cannot eliminate reality, the opacity of the other, and the necessity of the world. The Temple gives the divine a dwelling among men, but it also reminds men that they are but men. To keep this in mind is the most important commandment human beings can be enjoined to respect in the political sphere. This is why the Temple is the most important site of power in the Hebraic polity. Aside from the clutter of objects in the Temple, the nature of the building itself, which gives shape to the political arena, bespeaks the inessentiality of the political as sphere and agency, the impossibility of attaining the essence of things thereby. The tent of the *moed*, the place of the collective, is put together and taken apart piece by piece, one by one, hook by hook; its junctions are visible. There is no attempt to give the impression of a smooth, shimmering surface, no attempt to make us forget its distinctive components. There is no "spirit" of political collectivity of Israel, no figure of Israel that could do without its particulars. That this is the case is dictated, to be sure, by the fact that the tent is itinerant. The political is in passage! So it cannot be monumentalized, congealed into a representation that would fool the desire for eternity by exposing what is in passing and hence removing it from the concealment that is the world/ *olam*. Representation is the greatest danger lurking in the passage. From the perspective of the political, it is the totality, the state form, that is the vehicle of such representation.

The Golden Calf

The golden calf episode was the experience of this temptation toward totality, where we see the making of *le grand-être*, of the being greater than the individuals, and this is the state as a representation, because it is in the face of the statue that the gathered and united individuals contemplate themselves as a unity, a collectivity. It is only logical that the golden calf was built when the coming of the tablets of the law was delayed. The calf takes the place of the tablets. It embodies the face of society looking for itself, necessarily theoretically united and synthesized, totalized in a single figure, exterior to each individual and reputedly shared by all but, at any rate, completely exposed outside.

Suggestive in this regard is one traditional commentary that says the Hebrews made thirteen calf effigies, one for each of the twelve tribes, as a tribal identity effigy of sorts, and one for all the tribes together, to crystallize the "soul" of Israel, the commonality of the twelve tribes. The state, the political society, which exceeds each individual in particular, assumes the traits of the Leviathan, an artificial, ideological entity built piece by piece from the labor of individuals gathered together. Commonality is thereby obtained by the addition of individuals and the substitution of an object to the assembled community, and this substitution, necessarily theoretical, inanimate, and reified (the sum of particular elements is inert, because it is anonymous), is what accompanies Israel in its travels. But the Leviathan state that "accompanies" the people is not the Levite tribe.[397] It is a caricature thereof.[398]

In the experience of the golden calf, the tribe of Levi stood apart and did not join in making the idol. No doubt this is because the Levitical strategies in escorting the collective that makes a collectivity differ completely from the state strategy that informs the figures of the Leviathan and the calf.

This is a sign that the golden calf hinders passing, obstructs the void, and removes from concealment. It is not bound by promise and testimony. It is born out of impatience and the desire for immediacy. Indeed, it is built when the people can no longer wait for Moses to return. The golden calf annuls the trial of passage. It does not overcome it. The sectaries of the calf are incapable of giving, retreating, and sacrificing (korban). They replace withdrawal and concealment with mediation. What Israel puts into hiding by way of the Levite, they immediately expose. Interestingly enough, only after the golden calf episode are the Levites instituted to carry out the sacrifice, on behalf of the firstborn, who have sinned and can no longer do so themselves.[399]

---

397. Etymologically, Levi means "he who accompanies."

398. "Leviathan" is a powerful Levi (eytan), as if Leviticism, which is synonymous with dispossession, had become a power and might.

399. In the fusional frenzy of the golden calf worship, they practiced human sacrifice.

What is at issue in the golden calf episode is Leviticism as a process in the making of the state and in the construction of the political arena. Thus, the golden calf appears as a perversion by the people in respect to Leviticism, or even perhaps Leviticism gone awry. The fact that the Hebrews turn to Aaron to take charge of the enterprise, and that he is the one who melts down the effigy, is very telling in this respect.

In the golden calf episode, *le grand-être* that is the collective is constructed outside, not in the *toch*, in exposure, not concealment. In this way, the collective is cut off from the world, removed from the retreat, from creation. It naturally leans in the direction of death, and this is precisely what strikes the worshippers of the golden calf.

Representation Versus Particularization

Contrary to the murderous exteriority of representation, in the *toch* the presence is inside without annulling recognition of the other. This is why representation—here the political representation (of the people) in the figure of the state—is a flight from passage, an arrest in fixity aspiring to iconic eternity. It is the antithesis of the concealment that redeems and delivers the passage. We can see how the procedure of *toch* is a suspension of reality, the instauration of a waiting, the oath of a promise, a testimony without which there can be no community. All these mechanisms arrange for the possibility of a presence that is not attained, not "embodied." The present is, in the *olam*, a fragile, fleeting time; it is a taste of divine presence that will never be total, because the world exists and, for this purpose, God withdrew. The presence of human beings is but a foretaste of divine presence, but it is the sole possible presence in the created world. Representation is tantamount to the annulment of presence; it aims at the full realization of presence already in this world, and it wipes out the withdrawal, the very basis of creation, since all presence derives in its very principle from divine presence. By taking God out of his withdrawal and embodying him in the world of creatures and creation, it suppresses the very spirit and breath of the *olam*.

Representation is therefore murderous in theory. It eradicates reality, the particularities of the world, particular persons—the only basis of the existence of the *olam*—crushed under the weight of the totality to which it ineluctably aspires, since the withdrawal of God in infinity is particularization, the upsurge of the particular in being, the appearance of faces and names. The particular exists where totality constricts itself to conceive the universe (the universal). God's Name is the name of his withdrawal, and this withdrawal, this absence, designates the person, the individual, the particular who must be awakened and redeemed (*tikkun*). In short, the *toch* is the "outcome" of a retreat in the being but also in man (gift giving, *korban*, consecration of a portion), another name for concealment. It is constituted from the entry of the all in the one, whose vehicle is a particularization (of the all and in the all, which ignores particulars), an election of a particular, the calling of a particular name distinguished from the all.[400] The God of Israel is thus known in the particularization of his infiniteness (witness the anthropomorphic attributes), which is also the particularization of his loved ones (the choice of Israel) and their redemption (*tikkun*) in the *olam*.

Toch, as the sphere of the political, thereby destroys the peril embedded in totality, and, for this reason, the status it confers upon particular persons differs from that of the democratic state,[401] in the sense that they are not called upon to lose themselves in the whole, to assume an anonymous function in the collectivity and become interchangeable voices in the total sum of individuals, independent of individuals, indifferent to their names, just as representation covers with its uniform screen the particulars it is supposed to represent. The drama of public being in the Greek world is its abstraction, that it is at once all and no one in particular. Here, with the procedure of *toch*, the community is forged, and at the same time the individual is "preserved," or rather constituted, individualized, particularized in his individuality, in his *yihud*. Thus it could be said that the lover of the community is solitary/singular (*yahid*), because it is as a function of this specificity (*yihud*) that the community stands in the shadow of the one. We can understand in the same way the strangeness that exists in the dwelling, in presence. This strangeness and solitude indicate that the principle of presence (and thus of the universal, of the transcendence of time and place) is particularization/*yihud*.

In the *toch*, however, there is, within the prohibition of representation, a *tzelem*; an (anti)representation remains in the form of the tablets of the law in the ark under the cherubic stand, and this is precisely why there is concealment! Hidden behind the veil is a "representation" made of letters (those of the Torah) and forms (the cherubim), over which the ineffable

---

400. The founding moment of the *olam* is thus necessarily the moment of the choice of an Israel principle.

401. Spinoza defines democracy as "a society which wields all its power as a whole." *A Theologico-Political Treatise*, in *The Chief Works of Benedict de Spinoza*, trans. R.H.M. Elwes (New York: Dover, 1951), p. 205.

divine presence hovers and which, by its very concealment, is the opposite of a "representation," because it is stolen away from "presence," enfolded in the hidden recesses of the ultimate presence of the divine. It is by virtue of this paradox that we can continue speaking of the collectivity of Israel, of the "totality" of Israel, *klal Yisrael*, or all Israel.

This "all Israel" exists by virtue of a "nonrepresentation," or a "representation" put into hiding. Isn't this whole system a definition of *tzelem*, of the paradoxical "image" of God in whose likeness man was created? This *tzelem* is kept hidden in the Holy of Holies; it is the text of the Torah. It is also the secret of masculine and feminine, of the two cherubim (one male, the other female) embracing over the ark. And, in a way, the Hebraic polity draws on the wellspring of this *tzelem* for man, the "unimaginable" image of God, God's retreat outside the picture. The veil creates a chasm between image and representation. This is why the text of the covenant, found in the Holy of Holies, seals the particularity of an elective name, Israel, the Tetragrammaton, but also the human species, because it is the human species that is at issue in the *tzelem*. The laws that preside over the secret arrangement of the Hebraic polity are, at bottom, the same that should govern humankind. There is some- "thing"[402] at the heart of Hebraic political power by which it escapes itself as specificity, and that is humanity. In this sense, the Temple, the center of the Hebraic polity, also contains and addresses the universal.[403]

The Temple is a wellspring that sustains *klal Yisrael*, which is what enables us to grasp this very notion that, as we have seen, is not easily conceivable. The *klal* here is an antiwhole, insofar as it is in nonvisibility and outside exposure. It is a superior entity that harbors the image of the accomplishment of Israel without necessarily coming to fruition in reality. It can be seen as belonging to the category of the promise, the untimely view of a reality that has not yet come to pass, and whose remoteness and distance are what enable what does come to pass in the meantime. The *klal* founds the arena of promise. It is the image *en creux* of what is missing, of what has withdrawn and is there, in fullness, but in suspension. It is already beyond the removed portion and the gift of the *korban*, hastily testifying in advance to the fulfill- ment of the promise. There in it is a twinkling of revealment in the manner of a flash of lightning. It carries in embryonic form the permanence of Israel,

402. The "tablets of the law," the invisible *tzelem*.

403. This is how all the nation's coming up to the Temple in messianic times (Zech. 14:16) is to be understood, not as submission to Israel as a specific state, but as a convergence unto the "image" of the human.

the scintillating presage of which transcends the failures and faults in the passage.[404] The *klal* is already nestled at the very heart of infinite presence.

This twinkling is not a consolation, and it does not encourage facility. To the contrary, it places Israel in an extremely demanding situation in order to keep itself up to the level of its accomplishment here and now in this world. It is an injunction to go beyond oneself, and this is the very nature of the promise and the hidden logic of concealment. This is why the people cannot "appear," reveal itself in exposure. It can never be manifested in its entirety unless it is the end of time. Consequently, if the people is in concealment, no representation can represent it. There is always an element of secrecy and concealment in it, an absence irreducible to representation. Otherwise put, Israel is always the "remnant of Israel" (Isa. 10:21). Any representation of it is partial, temporary, and eminently fragile. Irreducible to totalization, the essence of the people of Israel is in hiding. This can also be seen in the relationship between the *am* and the *eda*. No matter how hard the *am*/people may try to appear, the *eda* will always remain hidden and ultimately thwart any attempt at representation.

The Institution in Israel

We can therefore see why no institution can pretend to truly represent *klal Yisrael* (the state epitomizes such an attempt). Any institution in Israel is a fragile construction, inasmuch as it is the agency through which institutionalization is played out, the unfolding outside of the inner being of a nation. The institution is generally a substitute for interiority, a reification of the being of a nation. For this reason the institution in Israel always endangers the strangeness that resides there. It freezes man in the past by accumulating individuals as objective data. It takes over the collectivity only when this collectivity has already been deserted. The state, the supreme institution, is a substitute, a fetish of the community. Its bureaucracy is equal to the anonymity of the whole. This is paradoxical, because the institution is established to "manage" the reality of the other, to pose the other in the collectivity. Yet it is the most indifferent place in the world, because each individual is divested of responsibility for the other. It is an illusion of community. Here "its interior is not like its exterior";[405] the exterior is outside its interior, and the interior is not "inlaid with love" (Song 3:10). The other is positioned

---

404. The *klal* is never affected by the eventual, circumstantial mediocrity of Israel.

405. To use a talmudic expression, "*ein tocho kevaro.*"

outside, thanks to the state, and this is as it should be. But this is also a major impasse, because the other is rejected into the impersonal, outside any particularizing relationship.

In this way the institution in Israel can never embody the *tzelem* in Israel's hidden heart. The structures of power and state cannot "embody" the "spirit of Israel," *klal Yisrael*, even if this is the inexhaustible wellspring sustaining them. The only institution that the political can shelter—testimony *oblige*—is a court. The court of justice is the supreme institution of the Hebraic political sphere. The Hebraic polity is best embodied by its characteristics. The court's purpose and function is to settle differences, to manage the passage of particular persons in relation to one another under the aegis of the universal, and to do so case by case. The procedure is universalizing, but it preserves the particular. The court effectuates norms of passage, and, unlike the state, it does not embody an ideal or a mystical representation of totality. Individuals present themselves before the court[406] when they are suffering from a "disagreement," from a difference between them. The court hears testimonies and bases itself on the exercise of memory of the passage. It is convoked only to judge specific affairs in space and time. When the court comes together, it "gets the law going" (*halacha*) and accompanies the passage of human beings in the being, by providing them, whenever necessary, with the principle of concealment. Through the court, the universal norm is particularized.

The institution, as epitomized by the state, casts individuals out, drives them to exposure. It does not allow for *tikkun*, for the *tikkun* of their souls. This is doubly true because it includes them in a whole and perverts their march to unity and specificity, which admittedly needs a principle of concealment, a "state" or a community in this case, but not for the purposes of representation. The state is not diametrically opposed to Levitical concealment. It is the perversion and corruption thereof. The institution acts, in this respect, more as a screen that occults than as a structure of concealment. To be sure, there is concealment in the institution, but it is perverted by having an extraneous effect on individual human beings. The one does not inhabit it, because it has no interiority. The other emerges in it only as an effigy, not as a name. The institution "covers up," whereas the community "hides." After all, the entry into the community of Israel is governed by circumcision, the removal of an overplus of flesh, a paradoxical procedure of concealment

---

406. Consequently, the court's authority is not exercised by its own initiative. It is elicited and solicited by individuals for the sole purpose of arbitrating differences. In this sense, the court is passive.

wherein the withdrawal of the foreskin and the exposure of the glans penis express the deep-seated meaning of concealment. The withdrawal harbors the gift and the benediction.

From this standpoint, we can see that the significance of the political can be read in the significance of the relationship of masculine and feminine. The problematic of the *toch* is one of separation (*kiddush*) in the inside, of the advent of the other. The problematic of the state is one of covering up and retaining. One opens onto love, the other onto the homosexual or incestuous relationship (meaning a relationship in which the other is missing).[407] The *klal*, which in the *toch* is exigency and alertness, becomes here an instance of repression and suppression. The institution then becomes an instrument of oppression and enslavement, an instrument in the "normalization" of particular persons, whereby individual specificities are leveled to the norm of all. The passage in the being thereby brings about a status of reality that makes representation impossible. The *klal*, the very horizon of accomplishment, need not be simulated, "represented" from the outside. It opens the being of Israel in its very midst, beckoning it not to "settle down" and close up, but to take to the road in an ascesis of the oath and the promise, for even though representation is a perversion, the alternative is not to live in anticipation of the eternal return, spellbound by the origin, but rather to lead the passage beyond itself, by means of concealment. The promise of the being shimmers only in the future. This world here is not the shadow of a past world but the project of the world to come, daybreak dawning out of night and announcing the midday light.

The thrust of the prohibition of representation in the order of the state is best illustrated by the prohibition of census taking. "When you will take a census of the children of Israel, everyone shall pay YHWH the ransom for his soul when counting them,[408] so that there will be no catastrophes among them through the census. Thus, everyone who passes through the counting will give a half-shekel according to the sacred/separated shekel... half a shekel will be the offering reserved for YHWH... the contribution to God. The wealthy shall not give more and the poor shall not give less than the half.... *You* shall take the money of the ransoms (*kippurim*) of the children of Israel, and you

407. It is not surprising that the pharaonic kingship is forged from the royal incestuous relationship between brother and sister. The Davidic dynasty takes an incestuous path (Tamar and Judah, who beget Peretz; Ruth, who comes from Moab, born from the incest of Lot and his daughter), but its essential task consists in atoning for it. Ruth is the heroine of this *tikkun* of power.

408. The verb is hard to translate; it connotes counting, remembering, and ordering.

shall give it for the work of the Tent of Meeting, and it shall be for the children of Israel a remembrance before Yhwh to ransom/redeem (*kapper*) your *nefashot*" (Exod. 30:11–16). We have seen the significance of the proximity of this passage to a chapter that discusses the construction of the Tent of Meeting. It is also situated in the same biblical section (*Ki Tissa*) as the story of the golden calf. From this we can grasp one of the cardinal finalities of the Hebraic political relationship: the preservation of the *nefesh*, of the vivacity of life, a strategy of getting around the reification, the "thingification" of life through the concealment of the source of life, which is the Name of God, "a source sealed/signed, [such is] my beloved" (Song 4:12).

The rejection of census taking is the rejection of the totalization that would make the *klal* lapse into the destruction (*kelaia*) that is the all (*kol*). The aim of census taking is to draw a "picture" of the whole complex of elements of a population in a way that the heads, the *nefashot*, are calculated, "exposed," taken out of their interiority and concealment, and posited in a relation of objecthood. This would be the opposite of *zikaron*, remembrance (Exod. 30:16), and a mockery thereof. From this we learn that remembering does not involve building a votive monument or erecting a memorial stone; to the contrary, memory requires *tikkun* to become a *zikaron*. In the picture produced by the census taking, the *eda* would be transpierced and scattered. Indeed, the presence of the Levites, witnesses of the *eda* in the people/*am*, makes it impossible to count the people as a totality, because they are not counted or are counted apart: "you shall not take a census of the Levite tribe and tally it by counting them along with the other children of Israel" (Num. 1:49). Census taking is regarded as on the whole system of Leviticism, an attack on passage and on the accompaniment in the passage, but also on the principle of gift giving, dispossession, and the safeguarded portion. This is borne out by the necessity of offering a *korban* of expiation if, despite the prohibition, a census is indeed taken. After King David proceeded to count the people despite the danger (II Sam. 24:1), God sent a pestilence, and the people suffered severe losses. The king repented and offered a sacrifice, which put a stop to the calamities (25).

The Shekel

The mechanism of shekel collection (Exod. 30:13), an indirect form of counting, serves to "defuse" the danger lurking in census taking. Coins, not *nefashot*, are counted. From their sum, the number of donors and thus the population is deduced. But there is more. The procedure is doubly indirect, because there is no straightforward equivalence between the total sum of shekels and the total number of donors. The number of coins has to be divided in two, because each person gives a half-shekel. And so an operation of division, and thus of withdrawal, is required. This means that a "negative" is introduced into the "positive" tally of the population, which signifies in turn that concealment is maintained in the manifestation of the all. In addition, the collected shekels serve the building of the Tent of Meeting—that is, the construction of the collective whole. We have here a typically Levitical procedure for which we find counterparts in the fluctuating tally of tribes or the casting of lots, in the shadow of the Tent of Meeting, for apportioning land to all the tribes, except the Levites (Josh. 18:1–8). As we have seen, the purpose of the latter is to embed a principle of dispossession in property, manifestation, affirmation, or rootedness, so that, even in the process of settlement—and this is the absolute paradox of Jewish existence—passage does not cease, and concealment takes place. By the "accompaniment" that is Leviticism, a "totality" is produced on the mode of passage, a positivity on the mode of the negative, an affirmation on the mode of a removal. This is the paradoxical model of the Hebraic political that is the opposite of the model of representation. In short, Levi is not Leviathan, and the Levitical republic is radically different from the representative one. We have here a different problematic of presence, a different way of making "presence" in a collectivity, not by a totalizing representation but by a concealment in the passage.

It is because the political field is a *toch* that human beings cannot be counted. And census taking is a major political act of power. Counting people means pinpointing them, pigeonholing them, identifying them by making them identical to a norm, dominating them by acquiring a knowledge of them together that each person in particular does not and cannot acquire, thereby acquiring what is essentially God's point of view. But the power also appears to us from this perspective as the power of recollection, of recording the event in the book of chronicles. When King Ahasuerus is bored and cannot sleep, he reads the book of chronicles of his reign (Esther 6:1). This is why King Kohelet's thoughts lead him to question the writing of books (Eccles. 12:12). The people can and must never appear as an object (ex)posed in exteriority where I cannot enter because the people, equal to itself, becomes a self-sufficient entity from which the other is cast out. The principle of strangeness is banished. A counted people loses its sovereignty. The people in its essence is inside. Obviously, this refusal of "exposure" is to be understood in terms of passage and the portion set aside, because exposure is equivalent to a negation of withdrawal, of concealment, which undermines the very fundament of creation and the *olam*.

Protecting the 'Nefesh'

The very object of census taking (counting *nefashot*) gives us a deeper understanding of the principle of concealment. Concealment safeguards the *nefesh*, the animated power of the individual, hidden inside. Outside, the *nefesh* would wither; a total or overly long exposure would be fatal to the *nefesh*, because it derives from and is constituted in the interior.[409] Safeguarding it means preserving the living unity of the person, ensuring that no one is reified in a relationship of alienation, objectified in the external world of objects.[410]

This cardinal concern is illustrated throughout the Bible. No doubt, the Sinaitic law's sole ambition is to establish a mechanism that protects the *nefesh* from death and disappearance in the passage that is its very being. This undergirds the whole Torah and its commandments with respect to relations with one's neighbor. The Ten Commandments, for instance, safeguard the *nefesh* because theft, adultery, contempt for parents, and so on reify the other who is the victim. The sinner acts as if his victim has no *nefesh*, no interiority, as if the other were merely inert exteriority, deaf and dumb, and could therefore be ignored. I steal from my neighbor when I think he or she does not see me and will not realize what I am doing. I think I can steal from others because I think of them as absent when they are in fact there. I commit adultery when I think my spouse does not see me, and so forth. When they break the law, sinners mistake absence for nonexistence, emptiness for nothingness. They think they can shamelessly enjoy the world and draw power from it as if it were given over to arbitrariness and pleasure. Before God, sinners act as if God were not there, as if divine grace were an invitation to sin and power. The secret that is the first principle of the world is perverted and abused. To steal, the thief hides, but this hiding is a perversion of *tikkun*, because it reduces the other, the other's *nefesh*, and hence one's own, to an exposed corpse. There is here a misuse of testimony in the *kerev*. All the mechanisms of social and political order aim at preserving the nefesh, ensuring that it

---

409. See my forthcoming *La Naissance des fils*, on the path of the soul.

410. This is the spiritual perspective that informs the seemingly "magical" thinking of the Talmud about the "evil eye." The latter designates, in fact, a relationship in which the *nefesh* is exposed (through envy, jealousy, or ill will, in this case) and risks being reified and dying, because it is no longer kept safe in hiding. To see someone "totally" as if exterior to his or her *nefesh* is to expose the person to death. This is the meaning of the "evil eye."

is not measured and objectified. This is the case when the Torah prohibits exposing the corpse of a man who has been hanged on the gallows (Deut. 21:22), when it sets forth the laws governing work (24:14), and so on.[411]

The principle of concealment, of the "*nefesh*ization" of being, thus emerges as a major political principle whose implications are apparent in many areas. It innerves all the mechanisms that could reify human beings, annulling the particular in the interhuman relationship, be it political, economic, or ethical. We have here the cardinal principle of the political relationship in the Hebraic polity, and all the complex mechanisms we have examined have this as their ultimate purpose. A world can be built on this principle, the principle of creation, at any rate, the "soul (*nefesh*)" of the *olam*, the wellspring of all individual souls. This is the principle at work in the institution of chiefdom: "Moses spoke to Yhwh, saying, 'May Yhwh, God of the spirits of all flesh, institute[412] a chief [413] over this *eda* who will always walk at their head and direct them in all their movements so the community of Yhwh will not be like sheep without a shepherd'" (Num. 27:16). The chief appears here as a means of concealing the nakedness of flesh, the nudity of the collectivity, a means of "forming *eda*," of hiding. The act of appointing and instituting is expressed using the verb *pakad*, which refers to remembering, ordering, and counting. And it is the God of spirits who is concerned, because the *nefesh* is at stake! Is this not what is implied in the political relationship wherein the man of power, if his power is not informed by the principle of concealment, resembles Esau (Gen. 25:27), a "hunter of souls," a charmer who seeks only to increase his power, win over souls, and identify human beings in an object relationship?

At the very foundation of the political relationship in the *toch* lies a principle not of *habeas corpus*, for the *corpus*, the body, is not an agency in Hebraic anthropology, but rather of *esse animus* (which also involves the "body"). The flesh is held in the *nefesh*, and the *nefesh* is in hiding in the flesh. The *nefesh* is the active, meaningful unity of the human being. The vocation of the political arena is to permit and protect the passage of human beings, their access to unity and particularization, and not to obstruct

411. When Marx says the worker in the factory does not feel "at home," that is precisely what is involved—that is to say, a relationship where human beings are related to objects and quantifiable values. In this case, the *nefesh* escapes from that which is no longer but a corpse. From our perspective, the "home" is a very strong figure, by the problematics of concealment, interiority, and the secrecy it induces.

412. From the verb *pakad*.

413. See below, Book II, ch. 6, "Voice of the Prophetic Sign and Political Ethics."

or destroy it. Everything that stands in the way of concealment is banished from the Hebraic polity, in the shadow of the Temple. Conversely, anyone who transgresses the concealment and exposes himself, who displays his "soul" on the outside and breaks the law, puts himself in the sphere of objecthood, of the world of objects, and as such the collectivity punishes him, considering him the "object" that drives away the *nefesh* he has become by his own doing. The definition he has given himself through his acts is taken seriously. The aim of the punishment is to make the offender "pay," to force him into a significant dispossession that enables him to redeem and expiate his offense, to make him realize, through gift giving and the compulsory *korban*, that his is the sphere of the *nefesh* and concealment, not exteriority.

Prison plays this role in another way. It removes the offender from the outside world, where he was totally exteriorized. The purpose of prison is to compel the criminal, through caricature,[414] to rebuild his *nefesh*. There is also, of course, the next step up in terms of crime, and that is murder. One who has committed such an act can incur the death penalty and so be put on the level where he has put himself: that of a corpse. The spirit of the Torah itself prompts the collectivity to attempt a prison sentence before the death penalty, because the point is to make souls pass on, not pass away. But even so, passing away is not an end for the *nefesh*. It is a change of state, pending resurrection.

Equality

One of the most meaningful aspects of the prohibition of census taking is related to the status of the particular individual in the political arena. The impossibility of the tally is already significant. If the total number of individuals could be counted to yield the representation of Israel, if the sum of shekels could be divided by the unit value and not by two, the individual would be caught in a relationship of nondifferentiation vis-à-vis the all, of "equality" and hence anonymity, interchangeability, and elementarization. This, however, is not the case. This does not mean, of course, that equality is ignored in the Hebraic political sphere. We have seen, to the contrary, that the point of the principle of "*nefesh*ization" is to prevail against processes of reification and alienation, so individuals do not disappear in their appearance. If the person, a *nefesh*, is the object of a measurement (social, economic,

---

414. The concealment becomes a prison.

political, and so on) and, worse still, a negative measurement in relation to other measurements—and hence posited in a relationship of inequality—it is clear that this person is in a state of reification and sacrilegious exposure, treated as if his hidden being, his true interior Holy of Holies that shelters the veiled *tzelem* of God, could be reduced to this measurement and these dimensions in exteriority. Rather, the Hebraic polity conceives of equality as part of an altogether different relationship, patterned not on the geometrical model, or necessarily on the mathematical model, but on the model of retreat, the void, gift giving, the safeguarded portion, and accompaniment.[415] An entirely different procedure of positioning the particular in the all, not as an element but as a unity, induces equality as a function of the one, not the all. Thus, the tribes come together to form a collectivity based on the one and the particular, the Levitical accompaniment of this equality. This moment is pushed to caricatural extremes by means of a lottery. The fact that this total and dreadful equality depends on cast lots, hence on luck, throws the individual into a state of irrepressible anguish. The Levitical one emerges as a form of recourse, temperance, and solace against the backdrop of a harsh, adverse, and ruthless form of equality. It undertakes the *tikkun* of equality. In the Levitical process, equality between persons is achieved in the context of an interiority and concealment unknown in rational equality, where everything takes place in exposure and exteriority, and where the principle of equality throws each person back onto his *quant-à-soi* ("as for myself"), his elementarization and interchangeability in the whole, and turns this *quant-à-soi* into a prison. The one is impossible in rational equality; the number must be even, divisible. Rational equality does not know what to do with remainders, surpluses, the hidden, unlike the *toch*, which is wholly grounded in these mechanisms. The penumbra of the *toch* has an altogether different organization from the implacable solar order that reigns over the agora. In the *toch*, the order is accomplished below the surface, indirectly. In the agora, it is all above the surface in broad daylight. Thus, the *toch* is the preeminent dwelling of the one and makes unification (*yihud*) and particularization (*hityahdut*) the very vehicle of the political relationship, whereas the state aims at anonymization, at the effacement of the one in the universal of totality, and its main vehicles are abstract universalization and representation. In state equality, human beings lose the one, while Levitical

---

415. Indeed, equality remains a measurement, even if, by the equivalence of value that it introduces, it neutralizes all measurements. Nonetheless, measurement remains its rule, which is why it abolishes and anonymizes the particular and individuals.

equality invents the most complex and subtle procedure to make the one possible and to safeguard it.

The question of the one and the particular in this paradoxical universality of the *toch* is, of course, a fundamental question that determines the status of the individual in the political relationship. But it also has directly macroscopic implications in terms of the generality of the political arena. The same question comes up with regard to the meaning and implications of Leviticism in the Hebraic "state" as a whole. How can the generality and neutrality of the state be reconciled with the hereditary role and power that devolves on the Levites, particular persons at the very heart of the universal?

We have already analyzed the Levitical method of building the state as universal. Now we need to examine how Leviticism is possible and meaningful in the affirmation of the state universal that it contributes to building in the people. How can there be a "republic" and a "democracy" and, at the same time, the hereditary, essentialist power of Leviticism?

Korah's Revolt

Korah's revolt (Num. 16) provides us with a perfect occasion to answer this question. Significantly, Korah, a Levite himself, raises the question of the particular in the universal by contesting the differentiation within the separate Levite tribe itself. He rejects the particular as a vehicle of the universal in the name of a universal that corresponds to the totality. "The whole *eda*, all are holy, and in their *toch* is God, and why do you [Moses and Aaron] raise yourselves over YHWH's *kahal*?" (Num. 16:3). The protest against a sovereignty articulated by particular relationships is manifested at its very core—that is, in the Levitical Holy of Holies. Korah proceeds in typical democratic fashion. He gathers together a small Sanhedrin, where all tribes are represented except Levi (leaving aside Korah, of course), and criticizes the value given to the particular as an exorbitant privilege, thereby introducing dissension among the people: "there is too much for you [Aaron and Moses]!" (ibid.). Defiantly, he offers incense to God when this is the task of the priests.[416] The question is of primal symbolic import when we consider that Korah was not only a Levite; he was one of the highest-placed Levites, since he was a firstborn

---

416. Incense is the subtlest, most abstract and elevated form of sacrifice, and Korah therefore did not burden himself with the harder, weightier sacrifices, which harbor the particular and the temporal.

who would eventually have assumed the role of high priest.[417] He also had a sizable fortune from the wealth accumulated by Joseph.

Does Korah illustrate the Josephic tendency to seize power when he is merely the principle and foundation thereof? For a Levite, departing from his function and from the Temple's sphere of interiority is the greatest transgression of all! This is substantiated by his principal ally, Reuben, who is the real firstborn but was deprived of his birthright (in carrying out sacrifices, which is the criterion of its exercise), bestowed upon Joseph and then Levi. In short, Reuben and Korah are dissatisfied with the attribution of firstborn rights to the Levites, which establishes the basis of the priestly family with functions separate from the Levites but also superior to them. How can there be particularization if there is universality? How can there be universality without absolute, retroactive equality? Absolute universality exists since all the Hebrews witnessed the Sinaitic revelation, and all of them shared in the revelation, and heard the words "I am Yʜwʜ, your God."

Korah's accusation that Moses and Aaron have "too much (*rav*)" can be reread from this standpoint. *Rav* may refer to Moses and his family's possessions, but also to multiplicity in relation to unity and universality. What do you do with multiplicity, Korah asks Moses, you who have separated yourselves from the collectivity and deprived it of equal rights, when, in fact, all are holy? Korah defends the multiple against the one, against separation, although jealousy and desire for power motivate him. It is the eternal dilemma of the demand for democracy for the sake of an abstraction that ultimately knows no limits and tends to lose its direction when it goes from theory to practice.

There can be according to the Torah no hierarchy in power that would follow a hierarchy in revelation and knowledge. Aaron cannot claim this privilege. But one could go further and say that neither can the Levites. And that is precisely the paradox. This is the crux of the philosophical problem raised by Korah, champion of rational equality, even if his accusation rests on the suspicion that nepotism was at work in the appointment of Aaron by his brother, Moses. How, then, can the universality of the community of revelation sustain particularization? The theoretical problem Korah poses to Moses, according to traditional commentary, is enlightening. Does one need a blue thread at each corner of the *tallit* (Num. 15:38), if the entire *tallit* is made of blue wool? Is a *mezuza* (containing a verse from the Bible) neccessary in a house full of scriptural books? Why value a detail when the

---

417. The prophet Samuel is one of his descendants. His sons repented and were saved from destruction.

whole is of the same nature? Why maintain the validity of the detail and the particular in relation to the whole? And what is the validity of the particular in universality? Why is the separation that stands for the whole necessary when the whole is there? This is the fundamental "democratic" argument in its more theoretical form. But Korah does not realize the contradiction inherent in his argument. He defends an idea of democracy on the mode of the universal of totality, and in so doing he creates a faction in Israel.

The examples Korah uses in his argumentation are significant in themselves: the woven shawl covering the worshipper and the *mezuza* on the doorpost and threshold to the house. Does a garment need thread and a house need a sill? Does the universal need the particular? How can one enter the "universal" if not by way of the narrowing in the form of a threshold? How can one make a garment if not by intertwining individual threads? Even if it is Moses in particular that Korah's party denounces, doubting both his integrity and the exceptional character of his prophecy, it is in fact the whole edifice of the *toch* and the whole making of the people of Israel that are being questioned. The principle of concealment, of withdrawal, of particularization, is contested in the name of a universality on the mode of the all, in which particular individuals are supposed to vanish, in interchangeable relations, in the very downfall of the principle of Israel's chosenness. Korah is the advocate of a political arena designed for exposure, not concealment. His questioning contests the very principle of concealment. Why think about the abode? Why inhabit? He appeals to totality, disclosure, and exposure as part of the horizon of the universal, to the elimination of particularities and names, to filling in the emptiness.

We find in this the seeds of idolatry, an absolute rejection of *gerut* and the Levitical principle in the name of the universal and totality. Korah disputes the validity of the problematic of the safeguarded portion because he does not understand the principle of the world's creation and how God particularized himself, went into hiding, took leave of himself, so that man, a tiny particularity in the face of the divine being, could exist. It is extremely significant in this regard that Korah's sons, who repented and were saved, wrote Psalm 46 "on the *alamot*/worlds/disappearances."[418] Korah refuses to "lose" and seeks to possess.

Moses' response is also very powerful in this regard: "Is it little for you that the God of Israel distinguished you from the *eda* of Israel to draw you near to him?" (Num. 16:9). "In the morning YHWH will make known who is

---

418. *Alamot* is also a musical instrument.

his" (16:5). The distinction between Aaron and the other Levites is the same as that between morning and evening. To change this moving and germinative order is to overturn the order of the world and the path of being that is the passage of the one in the *olam*: it is to annul even the passage of the world. Moses suggests that the Levitical principle has a cosmic thrust (to give God his dwelling in the world as much as to give Israel its dwelling in God and in the world).

And, in fact, Korah vanishes in the place where he sinned. He criticizes the fact that the Levites were divided from the others, and he himself was divided from the earth, swallowed up, "lost" from the *toch* of the *kahal* (Num. 16:33). The gravity of the act was enormous, and the text uses the verb *bara* to describe it, the same verb that designates the original creation in Genesis. The foundation of the world is at issue in the status of the particular in the passage.

It is a crisis for the whole *eda* ("Korah gathered the entire community against them at the entrance of the Tent of Meeting, and the glory of YHWH appeared to the entire community," Num. 16:19), and its outcome tells us much about the vocation of the political arena. The fire pans of 250 men, the tribal representatives whom Korah had won over and whom tradition deems irresponsible (they thought Korah's complaint was honest), are melted and hammered into plates to *cover* the altar, as a covering for the very place of expiation and *tikkun*, the nerve center of the Temple and of the *toch* upon which everything social converges. Thus, Korah's ambition (to carry out the sacrifice of incense, the highest sacrifice, which only the high priest can offer in the Holy of Holies, and do away with the animal sacrifice on the outside altar in front of the Temple, where particular persons offer their *kappara*, atonement) is reduced to its proper proportions. Without the external sacrifice, without the Levitical procedure, one cannot reach the Holy of Holies. Yet, the fact that the material of these fire pans covers the altar is also an important sign. The negation of the particular in Korah's appeal to the universal contains a measure of truth about being that Korah did not know how to adequately "deal" with. And it is in the aftermath of this crisis that the structure of the *toch* is established with greater clarity, that the process of separation/sanctification is instituted, the process of successive dispossessions by which Israel gives the tithe to the Levites, who themselves remove a portion of this tithe to give to the priestly family (Num. 18:28).

Universal Suffrage

Such a conception of the particular is naturally accompanied by a grasp
of the collective distinct from that forged by the idea of universal suffrage.
Universal suffrage rests on the "fragmentation"[419] of the collectivity, on the
elementarization of the whole. These splintered voices are then brought back
together by universal suffrage, a numerical count of particular voices, as if
this second phase were the means to piece the whole back together. Majority
rule is then put into effect, perfectly illustrating the principle of counting,
addition, and exposure at work in the process: the democratic state "speaks"
as a totality on this basis. This is the infrastructure of its voice (*voix*); each
electoral vote (*voix*) is regarded as a fraction of the whole, and the will of
the whole is deduced from the addition of votes. Thus, every person votes
and voices an opinion, with the idea that he or she possesses the whole, that
the whole belongs to the individual. This is the stated intention of universal
suffrage. But ultimately, from the standpoint of the outcome, the reality does
not do justice to this intention, because it is not all the votes added up that
make the whole but the majority. Individual voices have therefore disappeared in the final whole. Voters in the minority find themselves outside
the confines of the whole. The democratic state escapes the minority and
ignores it. What's more, the representation for which it did not vote supposedly represents it nonetheless.

Democracy rests on this theoretical artifice, which raises a profound
philosophical problem. The phenomena of minorities and abstention point
to the hidden failure of universal suffrage as a representation of the all. How
can the idea of representation (and hence of equality) be upheld when absent
or opposing voices cannot recognize themselves in the representation? The
whole could hope to gain credibility only in a permanent, direct democracy,
and even so there would always be minorities! This internal contradiction is
the single most important feature of a conception of the political that sets
the state up as the democratic (and hence fragmented) representation of the
all. It is as if the emptiness of the *olam*, which is denied by the logic informing totality and representation, has nonetheless found a way of manifesting
itself (in the minority votes and abstentions in "universal" suffrage), albeit
in an unthought, repressed, and unconscious manner, at the place where
the system loses a handle on itself and reveals its nudity. An irreducible,

419. This is the etymological sense of the Latin word *suffragium*.

opaque area in representation negates the equality of the individual and the particular as well as the transparency it strives to embody. And what can it say about this except that, at the heart of its rational construction, there is the eventuality of the irrational and of chance, the "lottery" or an absolute "game" (as if democracy boiled down to "game rules")?

The Levitical polity is founded precisely on the "mapping" of this unthought dimension. Concealment, secrecy, absence, and the *eda* are at the heart of the exposed people, the *am*, and, in theory, this hidden element can never find expression in the exposure of the assembled *am*. This polity escapes the failure of representation; it develops on two levels, and this is precisely what explains the unity that inhabits it, a unity in dialogue. There is an understanding that the *eda* is not expressed in the expression of the *am*, an expression of the majority of voices, and therefore that the *am* is relative and partial, that it is neither total nor wholly representative, that lingering in it is the shadow of the *eda* that Leviticism builds. For this reason, the political relationship of the collectivity is forged not in universal suffrage (which is fragmentation, as we have seen etymologically, without the one) but through testimony, echoing back and forth between the *am* and the *eda*, the one for the other.

The hidden, obscure dimension that ineluctably exists in all collectivities (evidenced in such phenomena as minority votes and absenteeism, which rebel in practice against representation) is thought through and mapped out with centrality in Leviticism, at the very basis of the political relationship. The phenomena of minorities and of absence voice the principle of strangeness[420] that we have seen at the very heart of sovereignty in Israel and that representation sought to abolish through absolute positivization. This is the strangeness of the one. And its testimony sustains the *klal*, which we know can be neither totally fulfilled in the *am* nor realized in this world—a fortiori in an institution. The *am*'s vote—and there was voting (the kings of Israel were elected)—expresses relative and conjunctural truths. It needs the agreement of the *eda* to be valid, because only the community that bears the law—and is a concealed minority (the small number of Levites!)—may bear the *tzelem* of the people and testify for/before/against the *am* to the Sinaitic covenant and the application of the law in specific circumstances. Legality has its source in the *eda*.

---

420. The very existence of a minority tells the majority that it is not alone, no matter how strong it may be in numbers, and absenteeism is a reminder of the "absence" in the illusion of "presence."

The Testate

The Levitical system is a radical obstacle to the representation of sovereignty and to the pretension of the *am* to set itself up as the embodiment of the polity. The voice of the *am* can be expressed in an audible and meaningful way only through the Levitical megaphone and, therefore, in the context of Sinaitic law. What the Levitical polity does is rationally rethink the phenomenon of the hidden, secret dimension in the political relationship rather than leave it unthought and untamed (as universal democracy does with the self-satisfaction afforded by a veneer of peacefulness beneath which particular individuals cry out and struggle). The Levitical politics, while assuming the inevitability of the "lottery" in the *am* and its charge of irrationality, violence, and petrifaction of the individual succeeds in accommodating the one that liberates from the structural injustice of the *am*, in which a "minority" finds itself excluded from the *kahal*. It is the most imposing strategy yet conceived to compensate for the structural weaknesses of democracy and engage in *tikkun*, the *tikkun* of the *am*.

The image of the Hebraic political arena that emerges from all these mechanisms stands out against our familiar image of the state as the absolute, geometric representation of a nondifferentiated totality. Here instead it seems impossible to reach such a totality. There remain isles in the political arena that, in the manner of the *toch*, cannot be reduced to such an enterprise, shadowy areas that the state's desire for light and exposure cannot grasp.[421] Thus, universality as a form of totality is alien to the *toch*. This does not mean that there is no "universality" in the *toch*, that it can accommodate only archaic forms of power (monarchy, theocracy, regimes founded on an absolute personalization of power devoid of a "public" and a community of citizens). It is, of course, not in this sense that one should envisage the formalization of the Hebraic political field, whose designation requires a new word, a neologism that can translate the notion of *eda* or, more precisely, the relationship between *eda* and *am*. There would then be, pitted against the state, what could be termed a "testate," founded on testimony, not on social "states."

---

421. A misplaced desire for light, since it is driven by a desire for power, whereas in the *toch* an infinite secret light glows, concealed for the sole purpose of bringing the creature and creation into being.

The universality of the testate is structured, as we have seen, on the particular and on particularization, because it is the one (the promise of the one for particular persons and individuals) and not the all that is its founding principle, the one in the manner of the infinite, divine unity that is the universal foundation of the world. The universality derives from the fact that this unity is integrated into a greater unity, the infinite, divine unity at the (hidden) base of the universe. It is a hidden unity that manifests itself in, with, and through multiplicity. Likewise, this unity, this particularization, is no pretext for the imperialism of particularity and particularism—the opposite of the state—but is in concealment; and it is in the voiding of this concealment, which is always the concealment of someone, of a particular person, that the universal comes to be, because the absent one, the withdrawn one, makes room for all the others.

The testate grapples with a different problematic of the universal, where the universal is obtained no longer through the addition of particular individuals, but through the concealment of the one, through the particularization of and in the all, through the emergence of the particular that is a call to the one for all individuals. The state universal radically leaves the question of minorities and absentees unanswered. This is why it so needs the simulation of representation as totality and the recognition of each person. In the testate, the promise and oath that underlie the one create an emptiness at the heart of the assembly (by the separation for which the veil in the Holy of Holies is the absolute principle). And this emptiness, this abode of strangeness, becomes the most universal place possible, where each individual can dwell in his/her own name without, however, forgetting the common house, a place that—in its very principle—houses the other but without compelling each person *in particular* to be absent. In fact, the universal generated by rational equality and not by testimony unwittingly produces an oligarchy that is not even "ashamed" of its domination, because representation legitimates it in the exterior. This "unconscious" dimension is the "hidden" aspect of the collective that this representation suppresses in its desire for total exposure. It is because it suppresses the one, the Levitical elective principle that stands inside it, that it provokes a practice that contradicts its intention entirely. (But can we really speak of an ethical intention when, on principle, it drives out and persecutes the one and the hidden and drives away the other under the cover of its simulated apotheosis?) We have here the figure of the false messiah. The disclosure that occurs does not manifest presence. Only the one and its concealment make it possible to get around the consumption of the individual and the minority in the emptiness of the *am*, to avoid the constitution of castes and classes and avert petrifaction.

What establishes the testate is not the contract nurtured by relationships of "equality" and exposure, but the testimony that has to do with the oath and the promise, that is to say, with a relationship of suspension, delaying, withdrawing, and concealment. The testimony is not lacking in contractual aspects (as the Sinaitic *berit* clearly illustrates), but it transcends them. In every era, the renewal of testimony—that is, the "memory of the exodus from Egypt," itself a reminder of the "creation of the world," a reminder of the withdrawal, the concealment—is accompanied by the renewal of the consensus. The testimony in the testate is this system that associates, in creative tension, memory and consensus, freedom and dependence, the one and the multiple, scrupulous equality for everyone and the unique specificity of each and every person, the particular and the universal, presence and passage, inside and outside, giving and receiving, the *am* and the *eda*. In short, the testate opens the golden road to man, who is a being who is born, yet this birth does not cost him his freedom, even as freedom is the principle of this birth.

III. THE PUBLIC IS NOT A THING

The arena of the *toch* sparks relationships between human beings of a different nature from that of the state community. The community in the testate is not bound up with exteriority, things, and objects as it is in the state, where the "republic" (*res publica*, or public thing) makes it possible for each person to adhere to all. Particular persons gather together in a single assembly because of a common "thing," but this thing is supposed to be entirely exterior to them. This is, in fact, what makes it a thing. The adhesion of each person to all others is conceived in terms of participation, taking one's "share" (an equal share, in theory, of course), which is made possible by the fragmentation of one and the same thing. The state as the form of community can transcend the particularity of each person only in property terms, by magnifying the closed, self-contained particularity of each individual, and this is a negation of community. Indeed, the public "thing" is so external that not only can it not be shared, but it throws each person back onto his own self-contained singularity. Moreover, if it were actually shared, the community would lose all its foundations. The community in the state remains theoretical. The "republic" belongs to each person and to all at the same time, which means to no one in particular.

The testate is characterized by dispossession, not property, concealment, not division into parts, the suspension proper to testimony, not participation. How is commonality forged in the testate? The public sphere is not built on the practice of apportioning. Doing so requires something to share; it requires that a thing either preexist to be apportioned or arise from it. A thing is to be understood as an exteriority, ownerless and abandoned, that pertains to nothing and that one can appropriate.[422] This is not the case in the problematic of passage and concealment; the act of putting inside makes things emerge that are not merely lying there in absolute exteriority. If anything can be called a "thing" in the *toch,* it is the tablets of the law; this "object," put in the innermost recesses of interiority, cannot be fragmented. The only way to appropriate it is to read it. This form of appropriation involves a *mise en abîme* of the self to allow the voice of the other to resonate. The purpose of this "object" is to safeguard the other in his/her singularity against the danger of fusion.

The status of the Torah in the political sphere, the *toch,* is similar to the human being, in the divine retreat, inside. The created human being is not abandoned like a thing. This retreat is, to the contrary, God's mode of "possession," the creator's control of the world. God the creator is master of the world by way of giving and emptiness. In concealment, no "thing" would manifest itself (in exteriority). In absence, there is no abandonment; there is a form of presence. How would it be possible to "find" a thing to possess? In the retreat, everything belongs to God by the paradoxical agency of dispossession. The mechanisms of economy illustrate this, and, logically enough, it is on the occasion of the sabbatical year that the *hakhel* takes place, the gathering of all Israel to listen to the reading of the Torah. The common and the public are forged through this procedure, through this suspension of possessions in Israel. The testate is never more elevated than in these years of collective dispossession, suspension, and retreat.

---

422. As if the *olam*/disappearance carried "things," as if the absence of creation was utter abandonment.

The Common

For this reason, in the testate, it is the void and otherness that produce commonality. This voiding of each person's possessions maps a public dimension in the diversity of private conditions. In short, in the testate, the public is in hiding. If it manifested itself in exteriority, each person's *nefesh* would be exposed to a process of reification and removed from the migration of passage. The positivization of the public arena is a catastrophe in which the *nefesh* finds itself irremediably exposed. This is what happens with the demand for social transparency that emanates from the state. It is from this voiding, from this withdrawal, which is always the withdrawal of God in a movement of giving, that the common is forged, a common found in hiding, not in manifestation. In short, the community of human beings is "absent" or hidden in the world, and this hidden dimension makes it common to all human beings.

The state also "hides" the community, but in the misguided use of the absence inherent in the community. The state sets itself up as a manifestation but sees itself as a pragmatic absence. Declared a "thing," a *res publica*, and hence possessable, the state is so very abstract that no one can take hold of it, save by stealing, in the manner of dictators. Declared universal and hence the property of all, it ends up belonging to a few individuals at the summit of the state. Declared the "soul" of the nation, that is, its innermost, deepest being, the state reifies the being of the nation so intensely that it becomes alien to everyone. All are declared equal on the basis of a unique principle, an absolute center, but nowhere is there such a perfect center. We find here all the characteristics of representation as a simulated mockery of presence.

In the testate, it is the strangeness created by every person in his/her own abode that makes the community for everyone. Its universal center resides in each person's abode and is forged from the particularization of each person on the model of the *korban*. I am an individual only by virtue of the portion I consecrate, the share I give up. Individuation occurs through dispossession, not through narcissistic control. The one is attained only in passage and concealment.

This is why the public arena in the testate is not an external, reified representation of particular individuals as it is in the state, to the point that no individual could live in or even enter it. This sort of representation crystallizes all the power ("in the center, the power"),[423] whereas in the absent

---

423. See Vernant, *Mythe et pensée*.

community, birth-giving mercy reigns ("from his place, he takes on a face/ turns his face in his *rahamim* for his people," liturgy).[424] The "common" in the testate is not like the exalted image of a virgin mother (in the manner of Hestia, the Greek civil goddess who tends the collective hearth) whom everyone can possess without her ever losing her virginity, her specific quality for everyone. To belong to one and all (but to no person in particular), such is the feminine figure of the modern state, at once virgin and wife. The "king's daughter," on the other hand, whose "honor dwells within" (Ps. 45:14), is wedded, and the marriage/separation (*kiddushin*) is consummated: "He brought me into his chambers." This means that the bride is hidden, which is what sanctification, marriage, coupling, and love are about. What prevails in the world of exhibition is a relationship of uncovering and incest, of a return to the same rather than a separation. The "common" that is not shared in the testate is the *eda*, situated beyond relationships of more and less. Based on the principle of concealment, the testate has no need for "sharing" as a procedure of particularization in face of the common. Since the *toch* is not something in exteriority, and since the one dwells inside it, it can produce and sustain particularization without being endangered (which is impossible for the state, whose universality is in exposure), and the particularization need not take the form of spatial and topographical relationships of equality and sharing. In fact, the question does not even arise. Equality of condition and status is the result of the voiding produced by the retreat; through absence (gift and grace), the aggregate of particulars is positioned in relation to the principle of the one.

Citizenship

Citizenship could be defined as the passage through the *toch* born out of the break inherent in the covenant, the act by which one is dispossessed of a portion of one's possessions, creating the place of the other. Thus, the three pilgrimage festivals, which required the Hebrews to come to the Temple in Jerusalem with a sacrificial offering, were so many occasions to experience citizenship—to pass through the *toch* of the Temple. The Passover festival is

424. The verb we are translating as "turn," *lifnot*, is a radical of *pana*, to withdraw, from which *panim*, face, derives. *Lifnot*, to turn toward, therefore signifies "to make oneself a face" so as to present one's face to.... In this case, for God, who has no face, it is to enter into a personal relationship with man. To say, "you," to God is to address oneself to a face. Likewise, if God says, "you," to me, he makes himself a face (since in reality he has none). This face is the form of *rahamim* for his people (*le-amo*).

the cardinal figure of this passage, commemorating the foundational act of the people of Israel, the departure from Egypt. It is an obligation for every citizen of the *toch*: "the same law will govern you, as much the stranger (*ger*) as the citizen" (Num. 9:14), it is written with regard to the laws of Passover.

What rules of citizenship and circulation does the nature of the *toch* call for? We have seen that the question of rights and citizenship is posed in terms of not equality but strangeness. Citizenship is not determined on the basis of a center and an institution, in this case the state. One can say that it is greater than the state, in view of the great departure from Egypt, which illustrates the importance of the passage rather than the institution. Citizenship in the sense of passage precedes the constitution of the state. And whoever wants to participate in this citizenship is invited to start by taking part in the Passover lamb sacrifice, by making an offering. The state, from this perspective, is merely an annex to citizenship, not its underlying principle.

The Hebraic polity resembles more an itinerant camp, *mahane Yisrael*, than a citadel. Citizenship is therefore not distinguished from "humanity," from what makes the community a community, a dissociation imposed by the way the state and the exteriority of the political "reduce" humanity to an interiority that dismisses exteriority.[425] Here, the *toch* structures the political arena, and hence it is in "humanity" that citizenship stands, in an interiority vaster than the exteriority of the state and that sustains both.

In sum, citizenship has to do much more with concealment than with exposure. It drinks at the spring of the *tzelem* in hiding in the *toch*. This is why, in Israel's own place, where one would expect to find autochthonous laws, stands the stranger—an illustration of this exceptional case wherein the definition of the self does not require the exclusion of the other. The strangeness that is of a piece with citizenship is manifested not only in the principle of the origin of Israel but also in its contemporaneity, when Israel leaves Egypt with the "great multitude/the multiple mix" (Exod. 12:38) of slaves in Egypt who followed the Hebrews, freeing themselves from bondage. By the great multitude, the logic of nations continues inside Israel, as does the possibility of Israel's regressing into this logic. This inclusion of a contradictory principle in the collective project accounts for a good part of Israel's practical universality, in the sense that Israel, bearing other than itself, becomes a combat with itself, an inner struggle embedded in the very

---

425. Citizenship in this case refers to the impersonal and the abstract, and everything that pertains to history, embodiment in the world, individual names, is driven out of citizenship and assigned to the private sphere.

structure of its being. The "great mix," so far from the one, could cause Israel to transgress the Torah. Some commentators say that the "great multitude" incited the people to make the golden calf, but the whole stake of the exodus is as much to establish the basis of citizenship as to allow the "multitude" to attain *gerut*.

The Passover festival is instituted to serve as a *mishmeret*, a safekeeping, reserve, and conservation (Exod. 12:6).[426] Hidden in citizenship is the rest of the humanity of the nations. It institutes a separation in the humanity of the outside, a sanctification, a circumcision in which the nakedness, the skin of exposure, is covered up and hidden, so the *nefesh* can live and will not be reified. It is in this sense that whosoever desires to participate in the citizenship of Israel, let him come and "pass," notably by the sign of circumcision. Logically, "Pesach" (Passover) means passing over, crossing. This is why citizenship can never be totally revealed in the exterior.

Public and Private

Concealment leads to a sphere that could be likened to the "private" sphere, insofar as it escapes the visibility of exposure, where the particular shrinks back from the public. Concealment is the arena of the one, the realm of the unique. It is a place of unification,[427] where individuals attain the one, but this is where the exterior originates, where it is born. In the concealment, far from shrinking back, the one asserts itself and gathers the threads of the *olam*, which it weaves into a single veil, for the veil is the world, that is, disappearance. It is the field of freedom left for human beings to travel, the depth that allows man to go and to be going (*halacha*), because the place thus created is structurally passage. The place of concealment is thus the foundation of the world and its promise. If it can be likened to the "private" as opposed to the public, the world left in exposure, one could say that in the Hebraic *polis* the entire public is held in the hollow of the private, that the private is the fundamental place of the public rather than an enclave in the public sphere. The public awaits a *tikkun* that consists in immersing itself in the "private."

426. The term *mishmeret* denotes precisely the lamb intended for the paschal sacrifice, whose blood the Hebrews placed on their doorposts so their firstborn would be saved during the divine passage in the tenth plague.

427. The talmudic term for the private sphere is *reshut hayahid,* the singular in the sense of the unifier.

The difficult question of the borderline between private and public has to be addressed from the standpoint of presence. Where does presence reside, and what is its system? In the world of exposure, it is obvious that the public, for the particular individual, amounts to the extinction of presence, the eclipse of interiority. And it is in the private sphere that the particular individual recovers this presence, in the suspension and forgetting of the public and the other. The private sphere appears to shrink into a cranny in the public sphere, to be nothing but a consolation for the public, which, as we have seen, is irremediably in exteriority, where presence is supposedly attained for society. Presence and absence are thus divorced from one another, as are public and private. When I am present to myself, I forget the other. When I am with the other, I forget myself.

Conversely, the *toch* system is a differentiated organization of presence. The secret of the public, of the "universal," is in the private, in the "particular," as an instance not of aloofness and particularism but of the one and of unification. It is in the private sphere that the public is closest to presence, that its deep and desperately real emptiness becomes meaningful. The private sphere is not where I can appropriate the world. It is precisely where property is suspended, a sabbatical place where I find myself in the passage, as close to the one as possible. Returning to concealment after my exposure in the world, I return to the one, unifing myself. And it is in this sense that the private is the place of conjugal union, of the accomplishment of separation, whose purpose was hidden during the six days of exposure but whose secret was the very foundation. Sabbath, the locus of the one, is the place of marriage, not of solitude and virginity untainted by contact with the world. To the contrary, one exists only when two are united. In this sense, "his *toch* is lined with the love of the daughters of Jerusalem." In sum, the *toch*, where the private sphere is, is the concealment of nudity, of the public (*tzibbur*). It is the portion removed from the whole so the world can be set into passing. It is the "private" (the portion removed from the whole) that makes the public possible, that allows society to be the vehicle of the *tikkun* of the human that is its purpose. The public comes from the private and goes to it, and hence it is totally misguided for it to eliminate the particular so as to recompose the whole. The public is not the assumption of the particular and private. It is but a moment thereof. And this is the experience of the *nefesh*, which has the sense of going outside when it passes through the public sphere, and hence of leaving an interior before returning to it. We find here another expression of the idea that any gathering, any public assembly is a *knesset*, an entry, that is to say, in the position of a *toch*, a safeguarded portion. The experience of the exterior is an essential trial for human beings in the exterior, but it is not the end purpose.

The moment of unity in the private sphere that allows the multiple to exist outside does not produce the expected contradiction between the one and the many, and it delivers us from the search for unity in exteriority, an enterprise that, because of its aspiration to totality, always leads toward idolatry. As long as Sabbath is kept, the six days of the week can go any which way. The private is not a break, a contradiction, a rending, but a consummation, the satisfaction (sova) of the week (shavua).[428] The public is not a place of "savagery," because a portion—the private, the Sabbath—has been removed from it. When the toch is not removed, it turns into a place abandoned to the brutal forces of society (class, economy, power, and so forth), but this is not so in the testate. The private sphere is the place that orients the public, its place of insufflation, kavana, intention. This explains why the public is the realm of the Torah, and the private the field of the mitzvot. The latter are related not to the public sphere but to kavana, intention, and interiority. The law in the toch informs the main avenues of the public arena by the very fact that it resides in the toch. Its genuine application must necessarily call on intention, interiority, and the particularization of the nefesh. The testate thrives on human beings whose nefesh has been "redeemed" as it should be. This may be a criterion of separation between the private and the public, between the mitzvot that apply in the interiority of the nefesh and those that concern the collectivity.

The Hebraic polity ceases all public activities on the Sabbath, all the activities that concern the many, but the practice of the Sabbath in private is the sole responsibility and freedom of each nefesh. The one can clearly not be imposed by force; it is outside the confines of property and power, even though it is their source. However, it is "hidden," and that is its essential attribute. It is meaningless to impose it, because doing so would amount to taking it outside and idolizing the Torah. The one will not surrender unless it is desired and sought. The one involves an effort and overstepping oneself. Whenever it is imposed, its nefesh takes flight, and it becomes nothing but a ridiculous caricature, an idolatrous representation. For Sabbath, a time of passage, to exist requires the organization of collective and civil time that includes its possibility. And such an organization is Levitical.

428. The structure of the week (shavua) is the oath (shvua), and its aim is satisfaction (sevia).

People and Religion

From this perspective, a whole system of relations between the "secular" and the "religious" emerges, although the reader will have understood by now that these terms are inappropriate. Everything in the Hebraic polity is religious in the sense that the *toch* (which harbors the divine presence and the law) is its principle. But this ("religious") framework englobes a whole people, not a caste or a church. Leviticism is, above all, a system internal to the *people*. That the polity of the *toch* is not a "theocracy" proceeds from the nature of the covenant and the whole system of augment and retreat. The law concerns all the people ("You are present today, all of you," Deut. 29:9), and the people's consent is required to confirm it ("and they said, 'We are witnesses,'" Josh. 24:22). Leviticism has a precise function: it constitutes a mechanism for bringing the people into the *toch* but not for exercising within the *toch*. The *toch* is where the people moves about and act. We have here the problematic of the king and the high priest. If the framework of the polity and the ruling power is "religious," the exercise of power and of the polity is "secular." This means that the Levitical tribe has a mode of existence that structures the public arena, but it also has a precise, well-defined area from which it cannot depart without violating the very principle of its existence, namely, concealment. Thus, everything is as "religious" as it is "secular" in the Hebraic polity. This derives no doubt from the essential prohibition of representation, which immediately elevates the relationship (but in concealment) to the level of God and at the same time to the level of the people.

The principle of "a kingdom/state of priests, a holy/separate *goy*" (Exod. 19:6) perfectly illustrates such a paradigm with its underlying paradox. If the state is a state of priests, if every citizen of this state is therefore a priest, no clergy is needed to "represent" the people before God. If the *goy* is holy, the concealment and the Torah must not be foreign to him. We find here again the principle of the priesthood of each citizen. The priesthood is in the state, and the state is in the priesthood. The key to the relationship, however, is neither the priesthood nor the state, but the people, which is precisely the reason such an equation is possible. The "kingdom of priests" is not a clerical theocracy; it is a "holy people." Holiness is a kingdom of priests. In other words, there is on one side no clergy that would stand for the people before God and on the other no state that would stand for God (theocracy *oblige!*) before the people. There is no representation and no mediation in one direction or the other, and only the *toch* makes this possible.

It is in this enduring, unresolved tension that the Jewish polity is founded and maintained. This is the system of the "augret" in which any assertion, any position is offset by a concealment. The priest manages the retreat and the lack, but he abides in augment (this is a definition of the "private" sphere); the king, on the other hand, manages the augment but abides in the retreat (a definition of the "public" sphere). Private and public are figures of society like the *eda* and the *am*. But the public abides in the private.

The principle of presence means that any ruling authority is associated with it. Royalty or the power of the people harbors divine presence, that is to say, it is inhabited by strangeness and concealment. A kingship or other power from which presence has been driven would be a catastrophe. There are thus intersecting relationships between political institutions, which together form the *toch* of the Name, the dwelling, the *mishkan* (*melech*/king, *shofet*/judge, *kohen*/priest, *navi*/prophet). Each has its critical counterpart: the king is tempered and controlled by the priest, the judge by the prophet, the king by the judge, the priest by the prophet. The judge oversees the priest, but the priest preserves the law in the people and uses it structurally to this effect, and the king emanates from the people, while the judge pronounces the law, and the prophet divine will. These four functions can be paired: the priest and the king are in the sphere of the people; the judge and prophet, in that of God. And in the interweaving of these relationships, it is the *mishkan*, the dwelling of testimony, that is built in the *toch*, in the midst of which the prophetic voice resounds.

CHAPTER 6

The Voice of the Prophetic Sign[429]
and Political Ethics

THE NATURE OF the political arena governs a specific practice of communication. The environment created by the *toch*, with the relationship of
the particular to the universal and the absence of representation that results,
works to create a whole system of participation of particular individuals in the
collectivity. The notion of communication is synonymous with the constitutive process of particular individuals and the collectivity, even though it is
generally used to designate the act that induces such a constitution. Political
communication in the *toch* differs greatly from communication on the agora.
The status of language and of political actors and their actions is modified as
a result. On the agora, language is a form of mediation between individualities, thereby seen as mutually exclusive, self-contained entities that maintain
a relationship of exteriority to one another requiring an equally external form
of mediation in order to relate to each other. Posited in this way as absolute,
geometrical exteriority, language is instrumentalized. In contradistinction,
language in the Temple resides in the *toch*, with the tablets of the law.

If, on the agora, language signifies discourse, it makes signs; in the *toch*,
it is the very medium, the milieu of reality and existence. Sign making is
embedded in the inner logic of representation, whereas sign being is in the
shade of the veil of the Holy of Holies. In the *toch*, ontology is "of a piece"
with semiology. This means that the sign is in hiding, and its appearance
necessitates an effort of interpretation, separation, and sanctification. In the
political arena, the sign is the very vehicle of power, because power stands

---

429. *Kol ha'ot* (Exod. 4:8). Moses fears that to exercise power his voice will not suffice:
"they won't believe me, and they won't heed my voice" (4:1). God gives him a "sign" to
reinforce what Moses mistakenly thinks is his powerless voice, a sign in the form of a
staff that turns into a snake and the power to give and withdraw leprosy with his hand.
"And if they still do not believe after these two signs and do not heed your voice" (4:9),
then God gives Moses the power to turn water from the river into blood and finally sends
Aaron to speak for him, because Moses is afraid he will stutter.

over the void, as we have seen, and all its materiality is gathered into the sign, the garment of the void for which power is an echo, the void of the world's creation. How is communication produced in passage and interiority?

I. THERE IS NOTHING TO 'COMMUNICATE'

It is commonly thought that when we communicate, we are conveying and sharing "something." This conception of communication is based on exteriority and exposure. As a result, communication is regarded as a vehicle of light, the light supposedly garnered through exposure. It is seen as a way of removing people from their isolation, bringing them together but doing so in exteriority and exposure, by supposedly giving the self to the other. Such a relationship is an illusion and a misconception. Can binding *nefashot* be left to a "thing"? Experience shows that ultimately the *nefesh* remains secretly locked up inside itself,[430] hearing nothing but the resonance of its own inner logic, in such a way that the exteriority of the object of communication—namely, the sign—is susceptible to being instrumentalized and perverted in a variety of ways by people engaged in politics. Whereas, on the agora, the political relationship is exposed to the catastrophic influence of manipulations of signs and objects, in the *toch*, there is "no thing" to communicate, and communication does not take place in exposure.

The "augret" system is at work here. In the *toch*, communication is accomplished not through the agency of things, of signs as objects, but by way of withdrawal, passage, and voiding. Once again, we see that it is necessary to step out of the world, to withdraw from it in order to be present to it. In sum, it is by withdrawing from a relationship with a neighbor (from the exteriority of this relationship) that I communicate some-thing or that I communicate with the other.[431] By "transmitting" nothing, the other hears me, or rather the other hears nothing from me other than the resonance of no-thing. It is in despairing of all communication that I communicate. Thus there is a mark of flight in every face (*panim*), a trace of paradoxical absence at the very locus of the encounter with the other. It is the dimension of absence, the silence that exists in every face and enables communication. Solitude is the

---

430. Because it is born and survives in the *toch*, and nothing can change this.

431. The Torah generates thus a commentary by which one "withdraws" and through which communication takes place in the Levitical polity. Hermeneutics is the principle of public communication.

vehicle of communication. We can see here again the relationship between the particular (solitude) and the universal (communication).

The Hiatus of Reality

This absence that exists in any relationship of communication results not from the exclusion of the other, the *tertium non datur*, the "sacrificial victim" at the heart of all dialogues and all communication but, to the contrary, from testimony, the giving of the safeguarded portion, the interiorization of the self that makes it possible to welcome the other. My face is a face only for the face of the other. This means that my face is firstly the welcoming of the other, the other's abode. It is not through the mediation of the thing that we communicate, a "thingification" behind which the other can end up occulted or disappear, and the sign can take the place of the other. It is rather by concealment of the "thing" to be communicated, by setting it aside in augment, that we communicate. Indeed, how would it be possible to communicate if there weren't something more, an overplus to give? This is why concealment is such a decisive operation. Communication is the vehicle of darkness and strangeness in the place where it is least expected. In this way it harbors meaning. Communication takes place under the aegis of *tzelem*, from the setting aside in hiding of the divine (behind the Veil of the "Separate of Separates"), from its Tetragrammatic naming. It is in the framework of particularization, of the one, that communication is established.

Obviously, one always communicates with someone in particular. If there is "nothing to communicate," it is because each person is lodged in the one, and the one cannot be exchanged or "communicated." This is why the one God withdraws to make room for human beings, because the one cannot "communicate" (itself) to the other. Only through his removal can the other come to be. In this sense, when God speaks to human beings, "the voice speaks to itself" (Num. 7:89) in its unity. That is when it is heard by other "ones," when it takes them out of oblivion and nondifferentiation and toward the one. Paradoxically, it is this unity and this particularity that are the very vehicles of communication and collectivity. Communication occurs in the place of the divine retreat, where the divine "image," the *tzelem*, hides. This place of unclasping and dispossession is thus the place of a communication that needs this shadow to come to pass, because its main goal is the passage, and the passage would be ineluctably congealed by exposure.

This is why communication always takes place in the imminence of a hidden presence.[432] Likewise, it is judged by its respect for this immediate absence, by its ability to sustain this challenge to its credibility and its effectiveness beyond this absence, somewhat in the manner of the respect given to the bonds of an oath, a promise, a waiting. This irrepressible fact of the *olam*, of the world of disappearance, is what makes for the need to communicate, in other words, the adjournment (the temporality) that characterizes all presence in the world of passing. The hiatus experienced in this interval maps the place of communication, whose end purpose is reparation (*tikkun*), redeeming this break that is the world, the break of separation of this cosmic covenant of the world with God that is the creation of the world. At the outset, there is a nonadequation intrinsic in reality, because reality is created in the retreat. This hiatus is at the root of a basic misunderstanding that can develop in the world of passing, where representation can arise to mask the hiatus and not effect the *tikkun* of the world. To avoid this, it is essential to see in the hiatus the retreat of the safeguarded portion, the gift giving, and not chaos or a tragic gap that needs to be blocked and filled. One can see why the *korban* serves as a genuine pedagogy of this understanding.

Similarly, testimony is the royal road to communication because it stands in the hiatus of reality, in the gap between that which the world is in withdrawal and that which it is called upon to become through *tikkun*. The witness is a sort of visionary of the reality that has come to be already in this world, where it is in suspension. And already in this world of *olam*, his testimony works to dispel the illusions of adequation and guide human beings on the paths of *tikkun*. A full-blown conception of temporality is at work here. Understanding this adjournment along with the strength in waiting and respect that go with the oath are the essential tasks of passage in the *olam*; this is the essential trial that the *nefesh* faces in its journey through the world.

The story of Miriam's slander of Moses exemplifies this (Num. 12:1–16). Miriam criticized Moses to Aaron in Moses' absence, apparently speaking ill of his marriage to a black woman and questioning the loftiness and exclusivity of his prophecy. For this she was punished with leprosy. What is slander if not the misguided use of the other's absence, which turns absence to negation? Things are said in the other's absence that would not have been said if the person were present, as if his absence signified his eradication and absolute

---

432. In this light, one can see how and why the messianic phenomenon is the fundamental vehicle of communication with the people of Israel.

disappearance. But the fact is that in absence, the other's face is still present.[433] Slander runs counter to the waiting and asceticism that go with the oath and testimony. It is a betrayal of the promise. Speaking ill of someone amounts, in a way, to forgetting God, who is himself absent. Malicious gossip deems absence to be really "absent." Slander is an abuse of the birth-giving mercy (*rahamim*) of retreat (whose purpose is to give way to me), misused as an opportunity to assert power. For this reason, in betraying Moses, Miriam sins against God. She uses speech for improper purposes ("Miriam spoke... Was it only to Moses that God spoke," Num. 12:1). One can see why one term for leprosy, *dever*, comes from the same root as *davar*, speech. Miriam is stricken with leprosy, a punishment that affects her skin, the "skin" of the *nefesh*, whose concealment prevents incest.

Biblical Leprosy

Doesn't this punishment proceed from the same principle as the wrongdoing? To speak ill of the other is to consider only the exteriority of the other and reduce the person to his or her appearance ("skin"), as if the quintessence of the other's being were not in the dynamic of the *nefesh*. Whatever truth there may be in malicious gossip, it stops at a fixed aspect of the person, at the person's exteriority. It is a caricature from which the *nefesh* is dismissed. Slander reifies the being. And those who commit such a transgression are punished in kind: all their "envelopes" are struck with leprosy.

Biblical leprosy can also strike the walls of the house, the leather objects inside it, the person's clothes, and then the body. Some commentators see degrees of leprosy in this, starting with the outer envelope and moving inward until the slanderers themselves are struck, with each stage being an occasion to repent. Understandably, it is the priest who is in charge of "handling" the leper, since it is a disease of *kirva*, of social proximity.

The priest is the one who decides on the confinement (*hesger*) of lepers, on their "retreat" from society. Every case of leprosy involves a period of confinement for purposes as much of clinically observing the development of the illness as of making the slanderers understand that their sin is a perversion of absence, an end put to passage and the community, a moral reification, and that society is founded on the principle of absence that calls for responsibility beyond presence. The priest's examination of the sores is exemplary

---

433. This is the modality of God's presence.

in this respect. The criterion of interpretation is the status of the one and of the whole. The leper is declared pure if white patches spread over the entire body, even though signs of impurity persist. But if the wound diminishes, and the healthy color of the skin reappears on part of the body, the leper remains contaminated until the wound disappears. The *halachic* principle is the following: that which spreads out of impurity is pure; that which spreads out of purity is impure. To put it otherwise, if the leprosy spreads everywhere, the "leprous" individual, who removed himself from society through slander, thereby singling himself out through evil, is reintegrated into the collectivity. But if the evil singularity of the reifying relationship persists, then he cannot join the collectivity. Slander takes the *nefesh* out of the *olam*, out of passage. It is the opposite of concealment, insofar as it bends concealment away from its purpose, selfishly exploiting it, in the *din*, when retreat is gratuitous in nature. By betraying concealment, one lodges oneself in exposure, in the exteriority of the skin, in withering and death in the passage.

The Ambivalence of the Sign

Leprosy, as a sign of degeneration in the passage, shows us the ambivalence of the sign in the process of communication. The sign exists in reification and in that which participates in the *toch*. The sign is essentially a use, a management of the void. We have seen that representation exists as a possibility as much as retreat and the safeguarded portion. The sign exists because there is a void, and insofar as power stands over the void, we can see the importance of the sign in the logic of power. The ruling power will always be tempted to fill this void by signs, to cover itself in signs to make others believe in the reality of its being, rather than face the trial of passage and the covenant. There is also the possibility in the sign of using the object as a representation to screen the void. The sign always occupies the place of the other, of the original retreat. It can simulate it and deceive the beholder, because the sign of representation necessarily glorifies the other; in doing so, it reifies the passage rather than accompanying it.

The sign as representation plays a capital role in the social and political game. Through it society can be relieved of its presence to itself, which leads to a society outside itself, a mock community on a par with the theatricality of the social system of signs. But the sign can also stand for the removed and safeguarded portion, the pivot of the "augret" principle. In this case, the sign does not represent; it bears witness (to withdrawal and absence). It is a moment in the process of retreat and passage and is not there to cover them up. The sign is an actor and operator, not a passive instrument serving other purposes. Why the need for signs in the retreat? The sign serves as a boundary indicator: it delineates the dividing line between what withdraws and what remains, the rest, the remnant. The withdrawal is an "infinitization" for the being that retreats and hence, conversely, a demarcation of finiteness. "It is a sign between me and you" (Exod. 31:13), "a sign for the *olam*" (31:17). The sign is therefore the frontier formed in the infinitization of being. It designates the boundary of the finite, and in so doing it governs the contiguity of the infinite and the finite. There is finiteness in the sign; after all, it is arrested materiality. Now this materiality is derisive, to be sure, but it opens onto infinity, which is why the sign is the abode of meaning. There can be meaning, movement, and "passage" only in view of the infinite.

The sign is the agency by which the world of things adheres (*devekut*) to infinity, to meaning, to passage. The derisive materiality of signs therefore carries more than one might imagine, but what it carries is invisible in nature. From this standpoint, the sign founds the freedom of human beings in their relationship to God, by circumscribing the respective fields of man and his creator, by signaling divine infinity to human beings, but also by keeping man from the illusion of his own divinity, which is catastrophic in the management of social power, "in order to be a sign in your *kerev*" (Josh. 4:6).

This relationship of infinity and the finite, evinced by a witness, corresponds exactly to the relationship that the *berit* creates: "this is the sign of the *berit*" (Gen. 9:12–17). Every *berit* is accompanied by an object, the covenant of Sinai by the tablets.[434] The sign's object testifies to the break in interiority that creation and retreat represent, to the fact that the creature is at once separated, divided, and unified, in companionship with God, by the very fact of creation. But this sign is not an inert, self-contained object; it is not a "thing." The tablets are the quintessential sign, "written across/through two sides" (Exod. 32:15) as if one could see through one side to the other. In addition, the tablets are concealed behind the veil in the Holy of Holies. The sign testifies to presence in absence and passage. Thus, the burning bush burns and is not consumed, and "this is the sign I have sent for you" (Exod. 3:12).

---

434. Or, on another level, the stone seals the covenant between Jacob and Laban (Gen. 31:44).

The Ceremonial Sign

So the Temple cult and its ceremonies participate in the same logic, not of representing the absent but of testifying to and constituting it, in a process of bringing absence home to human beings, of reawakening the foundational retreat and renewing the concealment. Ceremonies reactivate the boundary of the finite and hence the proximity of the infinite.[435] Ceremonies and celebrations refer to themselves and reflect their own finiteness, and that is their vocation. But in so doing they put those who accomplish them in touch with infinity; the finite in touch with its finiteness is necessarily in touch with infinity. This is why the ceremonial signs in the Temple, which concern the *toch* and therefore the political, are of great importance to society and concern the entire collectivity. To distance oneself from them is to distance oneself from the world of passage, to set oneself up already in the one when the one is still in hiding. It is to undo the passing and therefore make *tikkun* impossible.[436] Indeed, through signs, what is at issue is the safeguarded portion (isn't the *korban* the summit of ceremonial acts in the Temple?), the access to the withdrawal, the act of concealment and sanctification that concerns each *nefesh* in particular, insofar as it is the one at stake in this procedure. To signify with signs is to bear witness to infinity in retreat, to testify for the absent, but also to define oneself in relation to the absent and therefore to put oneself into the passage, to effect concealment in one's own being. If I signify with signs, I go into hiding and place myself in the infinity and movement of meaning. Thus, the purpose of all ceremonial acts is passage. But we must consider the use of signs for improper purposes. Ceremonies

435. The archetypal ceremonial object is the high priest's vestment (Exod. 28:1–4), with each figurative attribute endowed with scriptural meaning (the breastplate bears the names of the children of Israel) and whose vocation is to evoke the remembrance (*zecher*) of Israel before God: "Aaron shall bear the names of the children of Israel... over his heart when he enters the Holy, as a reminder forever before YHWH" (28:29). The logic of the sign at work in the clothing and vestment is of highest importance. When Adam contravenes the divine will, he puts on clothing, which testifies to the fact that he is assigned to finiteness and separated from infinity. But this very separation of which the clothing is the sign testifies to the absent presence of infinity. The same can be said of Joseph's coat, a gift from Jacob to his favorite son and an object of envy for his brothers, who, after having sold Joseph, bring it back to their father stained with blood, as a sign of his certain death. Therefore, Joseph appears as a witness marker to infinity and separation (and hence to concealment and augment) in Jacob's family.

436. And it is, in fact, the intention that animates the interpretation of ceremoniality characteristic of Jewish philosophy (see Trigano, "Maïmonide," p. 141, and "Le hiéroglyphe et la *voix*," in *Forgotten Dwelling*, pp. 297–298).

can be drained of mobility. They can be turned into a mockery of the process
of the one and of passage, so they count among the most powerful tools of
the ruling power, as the all assumes the guise of the one.

The true sign is born of self-restraint and openness to the other, because
God's self-restraint and the restrained expansion of his potential is what gives
rise to creation in the world/in disappearance. The sign is an essential opera-
tive element in this self-restraint, carved in intaglio, full of absence but the
meaning of which harbors presence. By making the sign emerge in himself,
God created the world; the sign is the trait that describes and designates
his absence, his disappearance, his retreat, and hence the nearness of presence. The sign is the vehicle of remembrance, and remembrance is the very
core and principle of creation. This is why the "sign" has to be worn on the
male sexual organ by circumcision, which is a removal, a cut, at the very
locus of passage (the sexual relation, generation). Here, at the tip of the self,
the masculine must learn to remember God and the covenant. Here, at the
most powerful place of the exercise of desire and pleasure, he must learn
the self-restraint involved in withdrawal and welcoming the other. We can
see why the image of sexuality is omnipresent in the political relationship
and why there is an element of sexual and love seduction in the stratagem
of the political man.[437]

The Sign as Letter

The quintessential sign that engages self-restraint and openness to the other,
the sign we have seen concealed in the *toch*, is the letter. And the Hebrew
letters are the paradigm thereof, the very pattern of the world's creation, and
the sign of the world. The Hebrew letters are the shape itself of the sign of
God's creative self-restraint. The sign of the Torahic letter stands over the
void, espousing and cloaking it; it is "of a piece" with it, in its very structure.
God withdraws, and his withdrawal is his written word, the tablets engraved
on both sides. The letter bespeaks the finite, such that it is leaning against the
infinite. This is why human beings born in the sphere of letters and language
must do something to effect a concealment and redeem the letters of the
Torah. It is up to them to compose a commentary, which is the sanctification
and separation (*perush-kiddush*) of the text, the concealment of its letters. In
a universe marked by gaps and "woven" from the letters of the alphabet—and

---

437. Similarly, the sex life of the political man is one criterion of the nature of his power
and the strength of his personal ethics.

the *toch* itself is *toch* only because it houses the letters of the Torah engraved on the tablets[438]—the commentary contributes to the incessant readjustment of the broken parts of the world. The act of commentary is commensurate with the act of constituting the social, an act of *kirva* and *korban*. It is the same principle that is at work here.

Communication, as instituted in the *toch*, is held in scripture. Scripture is the vehicle of presence. Isn't the Torah kept in the Holy of Holies, in the place of hidden presence, and isn't it the vehicle of presence in the world of passage and exposure? This signifies that the existence of the collectivity in the exterior is in concealment, that it can hold in place only in concealment. Thus, the centrality of the text, of the narration of the Torah in the existence of the people, is to be explained by the hidden dimension of the *eda* in the midst of the *am*. The *eda* is in scripture, and scripture (the law) communicates the *eda* to the people/*am*. Its letters are signs to the people. Scripture is thereby a witness sign, through which the people is ascribed to its condition of exteriority (of people/*am*) but also summoned to open to its interiority, to concealment. We can see that the narration of the divine attributes, discourse of passage itself, its very essence (the attributes pass before Moses in their enunciation) is the preeminent vehicle of power. Moses asks that they be revealed to him in order to govern the people. "If I have found favor in your eyes, show me your ways, and I will know you, that I may find favor in your eyes and see your *am*, this *goy*" (Exod. 33:13).

The passing of the attributes is the passing of divine sovereignty in the world. There are two modalities of text, written and oral, which refer to two social modalities. Scripture as such sits there in the world like a stranger, as long as it has not been redeemed by commentary, by the hidden orality in its letters that human beings superadd to it, thereby discovering the experience of augment, of what is there in hiding in the letter and the text.

The full significance of the king's reading of the Torah in the sabbatical year becomes clear from the standpoint of political communication. At the end of the Sukkoth festival, the whole society gathers in the suspension of activity in the sabbatical year and the suspension of daily life in the booths, united in the king's reading, in the orality superadded to the Torah's text. The locus of retreat and of the safeguarded portion, the place of concealment, is reactivated and recalled to the community, which is thereupon assembled in truth. The text is the eternal beach on which the renewed wave of generations unfurls, bringing the origin close to them at every moment. This is also why

438. "Its interior, woven from love," is woven from the letters of the Torah.

the social has to keep "running" after the text in order to constitute itself. Language and scripture are the site of the hiatus and the nonadequation that exists in the world on the day of its birth, the very site where these are redeemed and the means of their redemption. What makes Jacob Israel is that he heard the voice of God: "after your having (*ekev asher*) heard my voice" (Gen. 22:18). *Ekev*, after, or in the wake, is also "trace/trail (*akev*),"[439] and this trace is the trail of the letter in the *olam* and the passage. Upon reading this letter and following its trail, one can hear the divine voice that speaks to itself in the Holy of Holies in resounding infinity.

II. SOUL HUNTING AND THE SHEPHERD

The ambivalence of the sign in the passage can give rise to two radically different types of political behavior. The sign is retreat and giving birth to *nefashot*, but it can be regarded as a thing and instrumentalized for selfish purposes. The sign, simply by being in the position of a sign, always harbors a very strong potential of infinity that can be misused by those in the politics of exposure on the agora to entice and "steal" the *nefashot* of human beings. This is the only way for them to appropriate *nefashot*, which belong, by their very essence, to the divine (retreat). They are born out of God's dispossessiveness, and this is what the politician of the agora exploits to establish his power. But there is also—and this is what characterizes the political man in the *toch*—a way of understanding the sign as a light and guide to souls, which serves to awaken souls, and not as an opaque mirror lending itself to enticement. On one side, there is enticement and unfettered soul hunting, in the manner of Esau's chosen activity; on the other, there is soul birthing (passage) and testimony.

The main question that arises in terms of communication in the *toch* is how to exercise power over people without ineluctably lapsing into a logic of reification. How can power be manifested without congealing the passage? And what reason is there for power at all if not because the concealment of the one within the multiple introduces such tension that the multiple aspires to rejoin the one?[440] The experience of power is necessarily in the *olam*, but

439. And also "heel," whence Yaakov, or Jacob, meaning "he will come on the heels of" (Esau).

440. The leader, the person in power, is always bound up with the power of the one, which is why his or her subordinates are always attached to him or her as a person, and

it must endeavor to avoid the pitfall of totality and impatience for the one that abolishes *nefashot*.

Power and 'Nefashot'

When the chiefdom of mediation takes the place of the people or the group and "represents" them, the passage may still exist, but it is a passage of occultation, not of advent. The chief stands at the head of the people, and the people fades into the background behind him. The leader "embodies" the people, feigns its presence and continuity, holds out the prospect of the one, but the one in question is a mockery; it is the glorification of a leader! The leader profits from the people, but in this relationship presence is eclipsed, because it is totally depleted and dispersed. In fact, there can be no possible concealment in this for the people, because no portion is set aside or preserved in this relationship, and no suspension is possible. Everything is fulfilled in immediacy. Here the gaze of the ruling power establishes a total visibility that fixes each being to the object. The concealment in the people is exploited to benefit the power.

The figure of the leader in Israel is totally different. Far from seeking to capture and abduct *nefashot* in order to feed the power of his own *nefesh*, to entrap their lights in the service of his own brightness, the leader in Israel is more of a shepherd who runs in "the tracks of the flock" (Song 1:8), behind his sheep, following their trail, running after the individual *nefashot* scattered in the central flow of the flock. The shepherd of Israel follows each one, each *nefesh* in particular, as he follows the whole flock. To put it otherwise, he follows the whole flock only by following the tracks of each animal, and he can do so only because he has an idea of the whole, an idea that derives not from all-encompassing presence but from the void and absence.

The shepherd is a *roeh*, a term close to *rea*, neighbor, and *re'ayah*, wife. The condition of the shepherd is related to the neighbor and the other in the context of conjugal love. This shepherdlike manner of leading the people and the *nefashot* is a leading of the spirit (*ruah*): "pasture of spirit (*reut ruah*)" (Eccles. 1:14). Grazing the spirit is very far from commanding. "No man commands the spirit" (8:8). This is the antipower in the power. This kind of power is based not on hunting but on hovering, birth giving, and

it is the *nefashot*, first and foremost, that are concerned by the relationship of power.

invigorating support. Its influence shadows forth in the withdrawal of the leader, in the gift giving at the core of power.

The shepherd knows how to accomplish concealment within himself. This is why the tale of presence that is the Song of Songs narrates the story of a shepherd and a shepherdess. The activities of both the shepherd and the hunter revolve around "animals," but their relationships to them are different. The leader (of spirits) hovers in the background over and around his flock, in the manner of God the creator, who stays in imminence, in the calling, behind his creatures. Hebraic leadership is first and foremost, then, a matter of acquiring knowledge of the trace, an exceptional form of knowledge, since it arises from consideration of the particular—a track is a necessary particular and composed of particular traits—but also of the whole based on and around this particular. What the power grasps of the flock are the tracks that its passage left on the ground in its wake. The shepherd knows how to pay attention to the *nefesh* of each one in particular, but, in doing so, he is once more attentive to the all. The all and its representation do not erase the particular trait, as chiefdoms are wont to do through massifying and totalizing particular individuals in a way that leads to the adoration of the chief's image. By so doing, the chief imitates the creator, that is to say, he puts his power in the place traced by God, where God exercises his power, in the gracious retreat and upsurging of human beings. We find here once again the importance of the determination of the divine act for the determination of power.

The Shepherd's Vocation

In this way we can understand Moses' wish: "And Moses spoke to Yhwh, saying, 'May Yhwh, God of the spirits of all flesh, institute a man over this *eda* who shall go out before them and come in before them, and the *eda* of Yhwh will not be like a flock without a shepherd'" (Num. 27:16). The Hebrew verb that denotes instituting (*pakad*) refers more specifically to remembrance. For God, appointing a leader means remembering his people, repeating the wombing act of creation, concealing and redeeming the real. For man, it means remembering God in this very site. And the reality of the people is oddly defined here by the name "God of the spirits of all flesh." The leader is himself described as "someone over the *eda*." The mention of the *eda* indicates that concealment is or ought to be at work in this leadership. The exercise of power should be based on the principle not of revealment but of concealment and *tikkun*. And the "subordinates" of the leader are defined here as "spirits of all flesh."

This description is important. It indicates that the purpose of leadership is not reification (the reduction of the living being to reified flesh [*basar*] in the relationship of command) but "*nefesh*ization," the spirit of all flesh and hence the spirit of each flesh in its particularity, for flesh cannot be anything but particular. And it is the vocation of the spirit to lead the world of disappearance to particularization, to the one.

The vocation of leadership is to "produce" and preserve the *nefesh* in the world of passage. Isn't this the vocation of divine withdrawal, of God's concealment? And, as such, leadership should assist the *ruah*, projected into the world, to effect its concealment, to be sanctified/separated—that is to say, to form a *nefesh* by enveloping itself/hiding in a *basar*, a "skin."[441] The purpose of the leader is to preserve the "skin" of *nefashot*, to shelter them in the world of passage, just as the shepherd builds a shelter to protect his flock at night. Indeed, these are the terms by which Moses defines the shepherd's vocation, depicted as busily tending to the smooth management of his flock. The flock of souls cast out into the world and wandering aimlessly needs a guide in the passage, a sign in the dispossession. In the multiplication that is the sphere of souls and the *olam*, some sort of echo (*hed*) of the one is needed to prevent the whirlwind of the multiple from destroying itself and sinking into nothingness.[442] So, after Moses makes his request, God chooses Joshua and tells Moses, "Have him stand before Eleazar the priest and before the whole *eda*, and order him in their sight... and give him some of your splendor (*hod*), so that the whole *eda* of the children of Israel hear him" (Deut. 27:19–20). This *hod*, splendor, is to be understood as *hed*, echo, the echo of the one that the shepherd bears for his flock. This is why he is "heard." Obedience is defined here as hearing.[443] And hearing is always bound up with the one.[444] Only the one (be it a mock one) can engender authority in the world of the multiple and of passage, because this is what all are seeking but cannot "find" by themselves. "Hear, Israel, YHWH, our God, YHWH [is] one"

441. But "skin" exists as a separate entity only in the corruption of the *basar* that comes from the *nefesh*'s leaving it.

442. The leader enables this echo to be heard, and around him the nebula of human beings crystallizes for a time in a specific configuration.

443. *Mishmaat*, discipline, comes from *shama*, hear.

444. See below, "The Face in the Voice," pp. 500–515.

(Deut. 6:4). In the written form of the text, the final letter *ayin* of the verbal form "hear (*shema*)" is enlarged, as is the final *dalet* of the last word, "one (*ehad*)." Joined together they spell the word *ed*, witness. Hearing is firstly a question of testimony, and it associates the plural ("our God") and the one.

This is the charter of leadership in Israel. The magnificence of the leader derives not from power but from interiority and heeding. And it is as an *eda* that the children of Israel hear this echo (*hed*) overflowing with splendor and majesty (*hod*), the echo of divine unity, of the one promised to human beings cast into separation and passage. The relationship of authority takes hold in interiority, in the shadow of concealment, not in revealment. This unity is that of the *tzelem*, the divine image, and it is the prophet who conveys it. From this unity, the leader in Israel draws his "majesty," or rather his "echo" of the one. The ambivalence shows how readily the leader can yield to the illusion of power, to believing in his own majesty, in the sense of the will to power, when in fact he is merely passing on the echo of the one, in the sense of the discreet and contained hovering of birth-giving mercy. The trial is rending because, even though the leader bears the luminescence of the divine *tzelem*, he "possesses" leadership not in his own name but through his own withdrawal, his absence as such. The leader is effectively the vehicle of concealment of a collectivity, by way of which the collectivity "hides." The spatial remoteness of the holder of power manifests this. In this way, the shepherd is in "the tracks of the flock," behind the flock. It is on the basis of this very concealment that passing human beings make their way through the world of disappearance and absence, governed by the principle of the one. Israel's shepherd is like a ray of light in the darkness of concealment that plots a path for the people; like the flame of the Ark of the Covenant behind the darkness of the curtain, "its traits are the traits of fire, flame of YH" (Song 8:6). The accession to power is always prey to absolute perversion: the substitution of man for God, of representation for being, of discourse for speaking, the exercise of the one in terms of *din*, not *rahamim*. Perverted power hasn't the strength of the oath and the promise, and it is akin to incest's exposure of hidden nudities. Only the leader's concealment—in other words, his capacity to offer a *korban* in the Temple—enables him to escape the irresistible and inevitable temptation that always brings him close to the petrifying idol, to the death of reification. The proximity of power is proximity to God (flame of YH) but without *korban* this proximity can be deadly, "powerful like love and death" (ibid.).[445]

---

445. Love is synonymous with the one. Both terms have the numerical value of thirteen.

In sum, the leader, in and of himself, is nothing in the assumption of power. The act by which he is put in the position of power is demanded of him in turn, so all is returned to God, and God remains sheltered behind the curtain of the Holy of Holies, despite the twinkling manifestation of his *tzelem*. For the ruling power, it is always a matter of abiding in the tension and suspension of *tzelem*, in the promise of the one, so as not to fall under the spell of its fulfillment.

Moses' Leadership

Moses is the archetype of "Israel's shepherd," as much by his attributes as by his experience of power. He opens the way for Israel to leave Egypt, but he also benefits from the divine revelation, and he is the one who institutes the safeguarded portion in the midst of the collectivity of Israel, through mechanisms of divine service. The centerpiece of Mosaic leadership resides in Moses' ability to establish a relationship of power that is not a relationship of mediation, one that functions, to the contrary, on the model of the "augret." When the Hebrews say to Moses, "Speak to us and we will hear, but let not God speak to us, or we will die" (Exod. 20:16), it is a matter not of mediation but of concealment. The Hebrews are not looking for Moses to mediate between them and God, to embody in both directions a representation of the two partners. They want him to effect the "retreat" within them, to set aside the portion in them and be the vehicle of that which they put into concealment. In this way, a leader figure surfaces whose appearance as leader effects concealment in the people. The leader is what the group hides within itself.

The leader's eminent position is to be understood less as the rational summit of a hierarchy than as that portion of the collectivity that is set aside as an overplus in the one, in the particularization, and that corresponds to the concealment of the whole. "The man Moses is very humble" (Num. 12:3); he stood facing God in a *mise en abîme* as God "passed over his face" (Exod. 34:6), at once over the face of Moses and over the face of God, when God disclosed his attributes, because the relationship between man and God is governed by the *korban*, by mutual retreat and giving. Moses possesses the virtue of retreat, and it is this excessive humility, which seems to negate power, that causes his people to rebel as much as they do against him (and hence against the divine authority). The people regard the restraint Moses expresses with regard to power as a power vacuum. This trait is what Miriam criticizes in Moses as well. He is too withdrawn, too much in the overplus of the one, too much inside the tent.

This trait can turn out to be a defect, as seen in Moses' speech difficulty. The voice withdrawn into the self has difficulty coming out, so Moses stammers. The movement of retreat cannot be easily reversed into augment. This is why Aaron is assigned to assist him. "Aaron, your brother, the Levite, I knew that he would speak... and I will be with your mouth and with his mouth to speak, he for you, to the *am*. He will be for you as the mouth, and you will be for him in God" (Exod. 4:14–16). The relationship of Moses and Aaron takes place in the mode of the "augret." Moses is withdrawn and "absent," and Aaron fills his absence and steps in for him as his presence. In truth, however, Aaron is the one who is in the retreat of the *am*, who stays there, while Moses is in the augment of the tent, near the one.

We can grasp here the very gist of the process of power as related in the narration of the personal revelation to Moses on Sinai in the same chapter as the golden calf. "You say to me, 'Take this people up,' without telling me whom you will send with me.... Let me know your way... see that your people is this *goy*" (Exod. 33:12–13)—these expressions all describe the function of power over the people. This power is shown to us in action as the passage of God, the Tetragrammatic naming: "'Show me your glory.' And he [God] said, 'I will make all my goodness pass over your face, and I will call by the Name YHWH before you and I will grant grace and I will womb (*rihamti*) the one whom I will womb (*arahem*)'" (33:19–20). Its process espouses the process of the world's creation. So, if there is "a place with me" (33:21), Moses is placed in the cleft of the rock, "shielded with the [divine] hands" as long as God is "passing by" (33:22). Only then does he "see" God, from behind, not facing him.

Thus, the manifestation of power is accomplished in suspension and retreat, in the most concrete concealment of the holder of power. On this condition only, power does not foster representation. Just before this revelation, God considered never walking in the midst (*kerev*) of the people because of the golden calf episode. And he said, "My face will go before you, and I will protect you" (33:14), to which Moses replied, "If Your face does not guide us, don't take us out of here... how shall it be known that I have found favor in your eyes, your people and I, unless you walk with us? Your people and I will be distinguished from every people on the face of the earth" (33:15–16). Genuine power fosters real presence in the collectivity, the sole presence possible in the *olam*, the presence that characterizes the *kerev*, the opposite of the illusory presence of the idolized fetish.

III. THE PROPHET: WITNESS TO THE ONE

The figure of the prophet is, in many respects, central in political communication, but he is equally paradoxical. The prophet can take on the traits of a leader, but if he does so he is denying the very sources of his power and authority. The prophet is not a shepherd. His role is not to track the many footprints of the flock, to follow the trail in its particularization and multiplicity, because he has an idea of the all. The prophet bears witness to the one already in this world of passage and disappearance. His is a preeminently untimely, premature testimony. In this way, everything unites and everything separates the prophet and the shepherd, the prophet and the political leader. The prophet opens the passage by the radiance of the one that he produces, while the shepherd runs after his scattered flock to guide it, but it is because he has a vision of the one that he can do so, a vision that allows him to take into account at the same time each particular one in his flock and the flock as a whole. It is in the prophetic light, however, that the shepherd manages to read the tracks of his *nefashot*, so he can find them and bring them back to the transhumant flock. In sum, the shepherd faces the passage (in the sense of the one), while the prophet opens it (by positing the one).

The abruptness, the suddenness that governs the prophetic manifestation is a sign of the untimeliness of the one in the passage. We have here an anti-institution that does not seem to have a social infrastructure or tradition, or an established process of transmission of authority, even though we know there were elements of all this in antiquity.[446] The prophet appears out of the blue, springing up from a social nonplace, as much in terms of social marking—since prophecy can take hold of anyone—as in terms of his astounding irruption in the public debate. How could the prophetic interpellation arise otherwise? After all, the one that has withdrawn from the passage to set itself aside as augment, as a promise for human beings, manifests itself only from outside the passage. It does not emerge from the multiple, neither is it constructed in the multiple, since this would be the all. It is not the rational and consecutive product of the multiple. Its absence makes room for the multiple, and it is manifested to the multiple from elsewhere. In the

---

446. The expression "the children of prophets" (I Kings 20:37) leads us to suppose there were prophetic brotherhoods.

multiple, the particular is its vehicle, because particularization heralds the one in the multiple.

Prophetic solitude and peculiarity perfectly evince this strangeness close to the one whose echo can nonetheless shake up the established order of the multiple and of society. The prophet manifests the echo of the void, of the original break in the edifice of society. This is why he always embodies the memory of the covenant for those who have forgotten it, because the *berit* is this rupture, this original break reactualizing the foundational hiatus of the world, the retreat of God. The prophet comes, Levitically, to create a vacuum in the fullness of collective existence, and he points to the trying truth of the world. The void sustains our steps, and we move forward in a strange world, we, the *nefashot* that have been thrown into the passage and wrapped in a protective concealment. The prophet shakes our preestablished convictions. To the illusion of establishment[447] and accomplishment that threatens any civil power and collectivity in this world of passage, he responds that the path is not yet accomplished, that we have to get back on the road, that there is still a way to go and that the flock has not yet reached the haven of the one, that any such idea is but a mirage of the all, as long as we are still in the passage.

The prophetic irruption makes the *toch* a testate. It situates the political sphere not in the order of the natural but in the order of *rahamim*, not in the framework of an anonymizing all but in that of the particularizing and nominative one. This is what makes prophetic speech anticommunication. The demand of the one is too exacting; the spectral vision of reality projected in it is unbearable. As it gives voice to the emptiness in the fullness, it can also be seen as a vision of death, when in fact it evinces the impulse of life.

The prophet opens an arena for perpetually rewriting social forms. This is a critical mechanism commensurate with passage. The perpetual rewriting testifies, of course, to the incompletion of the world, but it also manifests presence in this world of forgetting and disappearance. The prophet, more than the leader, harbors the divine *tzelem* insofar as his testimony is utterly particularized and singularized and insofar as he has no direct political responsibility, save the unity of Israel. And so, already in this world, the prophet gives voice to the echo of the *klal*, of the community on the bank of the one. His words are like a hovering of the one over the world of the multiple.

The manifestation is disconcerting. On the one hand, it brings Israel's future horizon closer and makes the culmination of the path glimmer in a

447. The term "state" says precisely this.

way that reinstills deep-seated coherence in Israel's disorderly existence in this world of passage and reforges the thickness of its social fabric. On the other hand, it is inaudible. No one can really understand it. After all, it is the highly particularized speech of a single individual, the speech of the one. The bearing of the *tzelem* by the prophet (the *navi* in Hebrew, or the one who brings) is a living challenge to the state's pretension that it is the bearer of the *tzelem*. A *tzelem* that would emerge in the passage could only be a figure of the all, a recomposition of the origin, an abolition of the passage and of its trial, a cardinal trial for *nefashot* and the *olam* in their process of coming to be. In every prophetic statement there is a suspension of the state and of the ruling power that forces them into concealment: and then the one dominates the all, in the manner of a cavalier steering the horses of his carriage in a possible direction. It is the singularized and particularized manifestation of the void in the all. It thereby invalidates the theatrical comedy of power whereby state dignitaries fall for the illusion of embodying the *tzelem* in their own name (for any power draws its legitimacy from this *tzelem*) and carry its effigy with great pomp through the people like some sort of magical icon. The state always verges on idolatry. This is also true of the experience of human beings in the passage, but it is so even more of the state, because it is the crystallization of the experience of the passage.

The prophet speaks from within the *eda*, but he is essentially speaking for and in the *am*. He is the manifestation of interiority, of the *toch*, in the world of political exteriority, and he pushes the people of exposure and nudity to concealment, sanctification, and circumcision. In sum, the prophet is the architect of the safeguarded portion. One could say this of the priest and the king, but the position of the prophet is totally different. The priest is at the behest of the *am* to forge the *eda*: he organizes the continuity of the *eda*, but his role is passive. The king is a sort of emissary of the *am* to the *eda*, the bringing together of the *am* to forge the *eda*. The prophet is the active emissary of the *eda* in the *am*. This is no doubt the reason for his solitude. He has to be alone (and fragile). Otherwise, the *eda* risks turning into a caricature of itself and assuming the traits of a totalitarianism seeking to impose itself on the *am* that is totally in exteriority. Testimony cannot be imposed, just as interiority cannot be generated by a power. It is voluntarily that one listens to or gives testimony, because it involves an engagement of the being in suspension and promise that can arise only from within. "Who will make prophets of Yнwн's whole *am*?" (Num. 11:29) is to be understood from the perspective of summoning the people to draw together and interiorize in the *eda*. The prophet incites the *am* to come together as an *eda*, to open up in the *toch*, inside, to conceive emptiness in its illusion of plenitude.

It is easy to see what could be strange and frightening about the prophetic figure and why he is the object of persecution. But the prophet also always meets the king and the priest on his path. The priest risks being sucked into the interiority where he stands and mistaking his passiveness in relation to the people for an end unto itself and his calling for a finality, when in fact they are meaningful only for the *am*, on the horizon of the divine, of course. Priests run the risk of forming a selfish caste, drawing from their wombing function a self-serving argument of power. Leviticism, turned into a doctrine of power in the *olam*, is a caricature of the *eda*. It is an absolute failure when the driving force of itinerancy settles into establishment. The prophet also meets the king on his path; they meet going in opposite directions. The king goes from the *am* to the *eda*, and the prophet from the *eda* to the *am*. The king can be the vehicle of the *am*'s temptation to be instituted for its own sake: exalting the nation, its representative, and the state. The king may forget that he occupies a place only in the movement of the *am* to the *eda*, in the intention of the safeguarded portion and the *korban*, in the act of concealment. In the immediate vicinity of the *eda*'s concealment, the king can interpose his own image, invest himself with its potential in order to mask the *eda*, to mask God, and this negation of withdrawal leads to the domination of the *am*, to tyranny.

We can see why any tyrannical enterprise on the part of royalty is always associated with idolatry, with the iconization of the *tzelem*, its perversion in the *am*. It implies a betrayal of the freedom of which human beings are made, a betrayal of the testimony. Hence the initial opposition to kingship of the prophet Samuel: "YHWH said to Samuel... It is not you whom they have rejected; it is me they have rejected as their king" (I Sam. 8:7). "This will be the practice of the king.... He will take your sons.... He will exploit your daughters... your fields... your slaves, the elite of your youth, he will take" (I Sam. 10–17). Knowing that the book of Ruth was written, according to tradition, by Samuel sheds further light on the prophetic conception of kingship. The subject of the book of Ruth is the "mother of royalty," Ruth, and the Davidic genealogy. Ruth's path outlines the desirable profile of the king, whose acts are governed by *hesed*, grace, and *devekut*, fidelity, despite the unclasping of the self, the trial of dispossession, gift giving, and *korban*.

There is therefore greater conflictuality between the prophet and the king than between the prophet and the priest. At issue in the relationship between king and prophet is the articulation between the *eda* and the *am*. But there is strife only when the king fails. It is the king's failure (when the shepherd forgets the one) that awakens the echo which emerges from the *eda* in the form of the prophet. The priest can also assume the role of an administrator of the state. This spells the failure of the *eda*, which is entirely dispersed in manifestation and exposed in the *am*. The priest then forgets the secret of the *korban*, of gift giving, and reverses it into a dialectic of power and exposure, thereby annulling concealment. The occasionally recurring criticism leveled against sacrifices is to be understood in this sense only. It is not so much a condemnation of the principle of concealment at the heart of sociality as a reminder of its meaning against the logic of exposure, for the *korban* loses all meaning when used in a logic of exposure, when reduced to its formal, external appearance.

The prophet is the touchstone of the testate, since the testate is a paradoxical "state," and it is thanks to the prophet, the vehicle of the *eda* in the *am*, that the Hebraic state is a testate. The prophet posits the foundations of the state paradoxically and *a contrario*. He is not the figure representing the testate, nor is he its leader. He is rather its architect, its mobile element, and its memory. He is the vehicle of the testate principle without standing at its summit, a summit that is, moreover, incurved, not pointed.[448]

To say that the prophet bears the divine *tzelem* is to say he bears the discourse of God's attributes, the very keys to power in the world, the power of God the creator. In this sense, he reveals the divine Name to the people of the *am* and makes its attributes pass through the people, just as God made them pass before Moses "in the cleft of the rock" at Sinai. In the shadow of the secrecy of the *eda*, the prophet discloses them to the *am* of the exterior, which must, like Moses, cover its face to hear them. This grants a particular status to the signs that accompany the prophetic disclosure. They are signs in exteriority and even manifested as miracles, but there is a secrecy to them. They are signs only by their interpretation, the vehicle, by their very formality of secrecy, summing up the strangeness of passage and the paradox of communication.

One communicates with the other only in the saying of oneself, in one's own particularization, in the solitude and echo of strangeness. Only then does the other hear us. Otherwise, the will to communicate, that is to say, the will to open oneself to the other through disclosure, ineluctably engenders mediation and almost irresistibly leads to idolatry. There can be no communication

---

448. This definition of the prophet's role disputes the Maimonidean doctrine identifying the prophet with the king in the Platonic tradition of the philosopher king.

in exteriority. There can be no communication in disclosure. There can be no communication without a *korban* and a covenant. Such communication would run counter to the testimony exemplified by prophetic discourse: a voice emerging from strangeness, as if speaking to itself in solitude, finding its strength within itself, a manifested voice, impelled by the one, splitting across the abundance of the multiple, and whose existence does not depend on its reception or acceptance. Those who can will hear it! Voiced in the middle of the desert or centuries ago, it will end up reaching the ear that will hear. It draws on the wellspring of eternal youth and the living promise of the one.

CHAPTER 7

The Journey Across the Nations: Israel's Messianic Politics

ISRAEL'S SOLITUDE and concealment forge a strange, paradoxical presence for it in the world. Its being continually eludes apprehension, yet it is not bereft of presence. And in its apparent absence from the concert of nations, there is something like a gentle but powerful hovering over the domains of civilization. How is this presence intrinsically manifested, and, especially, is there a way to manifest it? Is there a possible "deed" for the one who is the vehicle of the stranger in the abode of being and hence in the abode of nations? Can the earthly sign of God's estrangement in his world, of alterity, and consequently of the world's estrangement to itself (since it emerges from God) be something "more" than a sign? Because the sign, as we have seen, is in the "more" and the overplus. How could it be manifested other than by the reality of its very being, preceding action? The overplus is already in the "world" of accomplished deeds, beyond the *olam*, where "man will not be able to find the deed" (Eccles. 8:17). A sign, it manifests—is it not written the "sign's voice"? (Exod. 4:8). But its manifestation is not the result of an intention or a deed, and it does not emerge from nothingness and stillness. The sign may twinkle only in scarcity but it is already in bounty. For Israel, being "Jacob's voice" (Gen. 27:22) would be its only deed. This is, no doubt, a (foundational) level of Israel's manifestation, and, as we have seen, it translates what is in fact an action, namely, that of concealment and separation/sanctification.

Israel's being in the world is not a divine diktat. The withdrawal of God the creator calls for Israel's appearance as part of the plan of creation. But this appearance arises from a deed, out of Abraham's course of action when he answers the call of the place. The aim of such an act is to institute being, to anchor a shore to the sea of infinity. It is a cosmic act that requires human centuries to be instituted. This founding moment is the initial stage of Israel's way through the *olam*. It calls for a second moment, a stage of unfolding, when the being turns around to the other in whose shade it is born. The voice has to cut words to become manifest in the world and be heard.

Here the question of messianic politics arises: in its relationship with the world, what can and must Israel do to enable humanity to "pass," to effect concealment in the human? In a way, the emergence of the testate among nations is already a decisive act, and this is why the whole aim of the Torah is to build a society and a polity that allow the voice to be heard in Israel, without which no calling or word could emerge. This second phase could be described as messianic, for this would be the time when the testamentary particularization, making its way through the world, would make the one appear in it. Since the sign is constituted in concealment, its manifestation is inevitably "messianic," characteristic of revealment. But how would "she who comes up from the desert" (Song 8:5) appear? Such a development depends on Israel's completion and accomplishment but also on the maturation of the nations, on the exhaustion of the void in being.

I. HUMANITY OF THE ONE, HUMANITY OF THE ALL

The constitutive act of Israel—in sum, Israel as sign—makes a voice emerge in the world of disappearance, a voice that, although singular, calls the world passing through multiplicity to the one. In the gesture of the world's creation, there is necessarily particularization, insofar as creation is the breaking of the all (and hence the "breaking" of the covenant), rupture in the self-contemplation inhering in the being, the irruption of another in the being, the naming of names. Israel's election resembles this gesture, meaning that there is the echo and remembrance of the world's creation in Israel. Its presence amongst the nations continually manifests the "origin" to a forgetful humanity caught in the passing. That is the significance of Israel's "particularity" amongst the nations and its particularization in being. The particular arises from the safeguarded portion, set aside from the totality and hidden away. The concealment is what breaks the universal of totality (which is but a particularity raised to the universal and ego-centered) and, what, by the particularization it brings about (the secret, dark area at the core of the domination of the universal), irradiates multiplicity and multiplication. In secrecy, it shelters the one, the generator of bounty and multiplicity, the occulted reason of the all that the all corrupts but that is its absolute hope.

In a creation altogether in need of *tikkun*, created humanity is also in need of *tikkun*. The separation of Israel from the nations is to be understood as a portion withheld from the being of humanity, a concealment of a part of humanity, for the sake of the *tikkun* of humanity, and as having the effect of founding and enabling the multiplicity of the (seventy) nations but also sheltering and announcing the one, moving it forward in humanity. There is no multiplicity of nations without the one, without Israel. In the being of the human, Israel is thus gift and rapprochement (*korban*), offering to God, "God's portion." It founds in the human the gap necessary for the gaze and for the echo of the voice. It is the space of remembrance and of the covenant that opens the way for passage and birth in the full places of civilization. In this way, in immediacy, it is particularity, obscurity, and incomprehension for the universal of the nations. Its love for humanity makes it a loner. But it testifies to the one in this multiple that its offering of retreat founds and silently makes possible. And it has a name forged through the trial of the void and giving.

It is in the place of Israel's retreat that the nations are deployed and inhabit the passage that is the *olam*. This aspect is cardinal, for the election of Israel is the opposite of a totalization that would set it up as the representation and synthesis of humanity, as a substitute and mediation for humanity, in the manner of a paradigmatic "astral" body. To think so is to misunderstand the sense of its particularity and the decisive criterion of its restrictive bounds. Israel is the element of the human gesture, but it is not the human gesture as a whole, and it fulfills its vocation all the better inasmuch as it is content to be itself. This is an absolute condition. The particular unseals the all and enables the many to spring out. However, the particular does not replace the one. To the contrary, it breaks up the all, which was just a simulacrum and a mockery of the one, and keeps the one hidden away, held as a promise to the multiple that has forgotten it owes its being to the one. Such a perspective lends itself to all sorts of misunderstandings from the standpoint of the all, which is imbued with its narcissistic universality and regards anything distinctive, differentiated, particularized, and bearing a name (which is, consequently, the vehicle of emptiness and passing) as a source of darkening and hatred.[449] Haven't Israel's enemies presented it as the "enemy of humanity"?

---

449. Make no mistake about Israel's particularity: it enables the multiplication of particularities in the void, but it is not equivalent to them, because it is bound up with the one, although, admittedly, it, too, can lapse into particularity as a modality of the multiple.

Two Versions of Humanity

Two versions of humanity here encounter the question Israel poses to the world's consciousness (and there is consciousness only because there is Israel, retreat, and unsealing): humanity of the one and humanity of the all. The latter is a mockery of and substitute for the former. The particularity that is the vehicle of the former is beyond the antinomy between the universal and the particular. Here the universal is animated by something other than the maelstrom of the all. The breath of hovering animates it. The all is so close to the one, yet it is nothing but a representation and perversion thereof.[450] Its universal glimmers with flames stolen from the one, but it is false and misleading.

In the experience of the all, however, there is still a chance for *tikkun*, and Israel is the vehicle of this chance. In the order of the world, Israel recurrently faces a succession of figures of the all[451] that episodically over-power the nations (and more rarely itself), figures to which Israel always appears as a disturbing element, a conflictual and odious particularity that incites them to destroy it. After all, Israel is witness to and memory of the true one, a factor of multiplicity that the empire of the all always seeks to eliminate through totalization. Inevitably, Israel will be there to stand in the way of empire builders. And in any case, the latter will know how to find it and set out against it. In a way, Israel bears witness for and against the na-tions, to their own lost freedom engulfed by the all. It constitutes a factor of particularization and nomination of nations for themselves, even if they have forgotten their own names. In Israel the memory of the name and spirit of each nation is kept alive. Its role is to remind each nation of what it should be in essence rather than to invite other nations to join the people of Israel.

According to tradition, Israel gathers within it the principle of the seventy nations of the earth (ten times seven).[452] The children of Israel who went down to Egypt numbered seventy souls (Gen. 46:26).[453] Israel, the principle

450. See above, the "unity" of Babel, "Kinship of the Name," pp. 104–144.

451. According to tradition, Israel will confront four empires (see Dan. 7:2–7) before the coming of the messianic days. Are they not the four letters of the Name, which hold court in the void and which each empire dreams of appropriating by filling in the void and blocking the passage?

452. The ten of the tithe, the portion set aside, combined with the seven of the septenary economy of satisfaction.

453. Likewise, the Sanhedrin is composed of seventy members, each a "specialist" in the language and civilization of one of the seventy nations!

of particularization, potentially carries all forms of particularization in the world, but since concealed in its particularization is the one, the promise of the one, it is not itself subject to the principle of particularization, and hence it is not counted among the seventy nations. It is in overplus, in concealment, under the principle of the one. This means that it transcends the particular, which breaks the all.

There are two ways for the seventy nations of the world to come together and be unified. They can unite in a universal of addition, that of the all, and thereby lose their names, by filling any gaps in the passage (this is Babel); or they can unite around the testimony of Israel and follow it in the passage, the withdrawal, the gap, the void, in remembering their names and inhabiting them fully. The "total figure" of the one is a mockery of peace/accomplishment. In fact, it is war that wells up in it, the war that will be fought against Israel at the end of time, when the nations gather together against Jerusalem (Zech. 12:2–3) in the name of peace. The "particularizing figure" is, on the other hand, promise and yearning, the opening of the voice that enables words to arise and lift off the palate.

Election as Concealment

The most remarkable character of the separation—of the "election"—of Israel is related to its concealment, which is what confers upon its condition a dimension of action. Separation/sanctification must be undertaken and maintained in order to be. The path is mapped out, but those called to travel upon it must set out on it and follow it. Because Israel is summoned to do and be an actor in its own right, it is something more than a mediation for humanity. If it were merely the latter, we would have not passage but representation, a tensing of the project of the one in the all. Israel's action and being are accomplished, to the contrary, in the retreat and the setting aside in overplus, in the surplus of concealment. Israel is removed from the total count of nations but concealed in augment. What is withdrawal and lack for the nations is augment and benediction for Israel. The main thing, of course, is the transubstantiation of lack into augment, the experience of the situation from the standpoint of augment rather than lack. For this reason the system of election/separation comprises an economy of the remnant. Israel in the *olam* is always the "remnant of Israel" (Isa. 46:3), remnant for the world, in the sense of loss, but also, because of the founding gift, the founding retreat, whereby everything "left" is necessarily a "remnant." But the remnant of Israel addresses the absolute gift that constitutes it, and that is in hiding in secrecy. The idea of the "remnant" makes Israel's presence in the world a failing and paradoxical presence. A portion of Israel is always absent and hidden, even when Israel is manifested in presence. There is darkness in the glowing of its light, the darkness of the sky that is the backdrop of the nebula of stars. This is why the appearance of "she who comes up from the desert" is vague and uncertain, like a mirage out of the blue.

The structural void and absence for which Israel is the vehicle among nations are manifested in different ways. The land of Israel serves as the vector and indicator. When Israel draws on the wellsprings of bounty, invests concealment, and takes its place in the land of Israel, the empires confront it and struggle to cast it into nothingness and exile. When Israel stands on the side of lack, that is to say, in the orbit of the nations, the land eludes it, and there is exile. But, even then, it holds the potential of its reversal into return, provided it effects concealment, giving, and separation, in order to extricate itself from exile and the domination of exteriority, over and within it. Exile is the most drastic testimony to the void and passage, to which the Levitical relationship to the land has already testified, on a first level. It is a unique phenomenon in the world, and it touches on the universal, because Israel in exile is scattered, in terms of its unique attachment to the land of Israel, throughout the nations of the world. However, exile is the augment, as it is read in the penurious terms of the nations and not in the true terms of bounty. To be sure, it is not altogether radiant with the one, but there is in it a hidden radiance of the one without which it would sink into nothingness. It is for this reason, for this potential, that exile is exile, that is to say, emptiness, an emptiness that persists and is not swallowed up. That the exile lasts testifies to the fact that the one inhabits it, albeit buried. And it is paradoxically the sign that the exile does not open onto nothingness, that it harbors its end, its resolution, provided that the light of the one that sustains it shines forth and melts the dross that surrounds it, so that concealment, the passage to augment—that is, the return to the land of Israel—is possible again. Israel's power to return depends on its ability to turn scarcity into bounty, to open itself to the reading of the real from the viewpoint of overplus, not retreat. This internal revolution triumphs over exile.

II. PEOPLES OF THE EARTH, PEOPLE OF THE VOID, AND ABRAHAM'S SONS

In the void of the *olam* inhabited by the nations, Israel develops specific relations with each collective entity—that is to say, with each assembly of scattered human beings—in an endeavor to bring out a light, a memory of the origin, a warming ember along the way, a concealment in the infinite passage.[454] The nations that are formed, one by one, in this way try to bring out the light in the passage, but they do so with the aim of immediate revealment and enjoyment, unable to sustain the torment and suspense of anticipation and promise. This is why the constitution of a nation is congenitally the setting up of a representation, an explosion of power and strength (each and every time it is a matter of arresting the course of the world, of stopping all movement in the hopes of attaining the one). In this enterprise there seem to be some shimmering intimations of the one, but they are a sham, and in truth what is really manifested in it is the all. This is why, in the cult of the one (of its unity, oneness, and specificity), which each nation is and around which each nation unites, one can see the empire, the extreme figure of the all, the opposite of the universal, when the "universal" is achieved by means of the exponential expansion of the particular, in lying and deceit.

The positioning of nations (and of Israel) in the gesture of passage will govern, each time, a certain type of relationship. The area of passage is the site of the four-letter Name, and we can discern in the passage of Israel four modes of relationship with the inhabitants of the disappearance that is the world. One could say, on a deeper level, that each of the four modes of establishment (assemblies) of human beings in the *olam* has a privileged relationship with one of the four letters, but that Israel, architect and surveyor of the passage, knows how to bring them together in the perfect oneness of the one Name, as it can be pronounced and sung. When Israel is united, when it draws the forces of union from within, it is the universe of passage that is united.

---

454. The number seventy is significant in this respect. The nations are formed around the seventy lights born from the divine retreat at the origin. A nation is constituted when it discovers and draws on such a light.

The Inhabitants of the Land

The relationship with the "peoples of the earth" (*am-ha'aretz*) is the most antithetical and conflictual of all Israel's relations with the world. Herein are opposed those who accomplish the passage (into which all beings of creation are projected by their very existence), who sanctify and separate it in concealment (the prohibition of incest), and those who leave and ignore the passage in their desire for immutability and eternity. The latter worship, without restraint and with immediacy, the earth and its cycles and the forces of nature. They prohibit concealment, uncover everything, and commit acts of incest. They hold the earth and its manifestations as the only reality, and they see the world not as passage but as the sole, implacable truth. The classical figures of the *am-ha'aretz* are the peoples of Canaan that Israel immediately encounters in its foundational passage, the exodus from Egypt and the journey through the wilderness to Canaan. It is no accident that the most power-ful expression of the moral state of these peoples is that they show "*ervat ha'aretz*," the nudity of the land, in an incestuous sense, through their acts, their being, and their beliefs (where incest and prostitution figure as sacred procedures). The Torah tells us, in this way, that their civilization is one of revealment and nudity, not concealment and hiddenness. It is the opposite of gift giving and the sacrifice of rapprochement, the opposite of the break of the covenant, the opposite of passage.

This mode of establishment in the *olam* is governed by a figure of the divine that, though misdirected and perverted, reflects an echo of the four-letter Name. Firstly, there appears a misguided consonance with the masculine *yod* of the Tetragrammaton, the powerful and violent figure of Baal and his female double (a feminized masculine),[455] Anat, or Astarte, divinities of lust-ful worship and sacred nudity, divinities demanding human sacrifices. The masculine is perverted into a figure of power and violence instead of mastery (*gever*, male, and *gevura*, heroism) and acts of concealment.

The exact signification of the term *goy*, which we have translated as "na-tion" or "people," is revealing in this respect. Originally, the *goy* is a figure of this masculinity. The *goy* derives from the *gvia*, the phallus/penis/glans, which exposes itself in exteriority, so much so that it verges on death (*gvia* also means corpse), and which must be circumcised to escape the agony of the world. Thus, Israel is described as a *goy kadosh*, a holy people, meaning

---

455. Often represented in statues of phallic-shaped orants.

a nation of exteriority that has undertaken the "separation" of circumcision, having practiced concealment and hence redeemed the exteriority. It is in the sense of this noncircumcision that the seven (!) peoples of Canaan are *goyim*. They expose their *erva* and consequently that of the land. There were ceremonies (of fecundity) in Canaanite religious practice during which representations of the phallus were paraded through the streets.

Populations riveted to the earth erect representations that crystallize power and domination. This is why the Bible designates them with the word *nechar*, which indicates the alienation in them.[456] Isn't their supreme god Baal, the "Master" in his undifferentiated and undifferentiating power, subsuming all particulars in the mass of orgiastic practices in which each individual loses his name and even his/her sexual difference in the entanglement of bodies outside? Similarly, doesn't Molech, another Canaanite god who required child sacrifices, bring in his bloody, terrible shadow the kingship (*malchut*, from the same root as Molech)? In Molech, we have a preeminent figure of the peoples of the earth. Its idol is hollow, divided into seven cavities, one of which is used for the throwing of young boys into the flames. This is not a void for the conception of the other and the advent of the child. It is an all-consuming and all-devouring void that must be quickly blocked lest it engulf the earth. All the plenitude of the peoples of the earth is asserted in this profoundly deadly obsession. Yet with the peoples of the earth, we are still at the dawn of representation, with an idol so crude that, unlike the marker testifying to a passing being (see the *matzeva*, the consecrated stone in biblical covenants), it does not point to an elsewhere, but gathers in itself its whole being. Worshipping divine effigies is, from Israel's point of view, tantamount to worshipping stone.

With respect to the earth, which becomes an agency and an autonomous being, the relationship between Israel and the peoples that live on it is necessarily conflictual. The resurgence of the rejected and forgotten passage in the land that was deemed the end of the world causes a windstorm ("Who is she who comes up from the desert?" Song 8:5) and destruction. Confronted with its own principle, the earth can no longer stand steadily on its foundations and collapses like a sand castle. This is where the whirlwind of passage takes hold of it, the passage of divine attributes that judges it. It is too weak in

---

456. *Nechar* is close to *ger*. These two categories of stranger differ profoundly, because the former is a category of alienation, not oath. When Israel yields to the temptation of the land, it estranges itself (*nechar*), and the idol is similarly a form of estrangement. The *nechar* is a perversion of the strangeness (*ger*) of human beings on earth, because being a stranger in the abode is not a matter of alienation (see Deut. 8:2–6).

its mad dream of power to resist, because it has forgotten the very principle of the world. It betrayed what founds it and gives it life. It did not separate from/sanctify itself in the knowledge of God, whom it replaced with stone and, in so doing, condemned itself to this selfsame stone. In this situation, two opposing principles clash. The earth seeks the death and engulfment of Israel, of the passage that submerges it, and erects stone walls in opposition to this frail nomad, whose kingdom is within. Egypt, for instance, wants the death of Israel, thinking it will derive life from this. Hence the dying Pharaoh ("the king of Egypt died," Exod. 2:23), despite his dream of eternity in stone (the pyramid sheltering his eternal life), bathed in the blood of the children of Israel, who were murdered to restore his skin (exteriority), when he was struck with leprosy.[457] The secret and the weakness of the peoples of the earth is that they owe everything to passage and will not admit it.

In Israel's confrontation with these peoples of the earth,[458] the relationship is governed by a principle: the choice of exteriority confines those who make it to exteriority, and it deprives them of the effusion of the grace of giving and interiority. The Canaanites are punished in direct relationship to their sin, that is, through the earth. The shelter generated by concealment is removed even more because they did not remove it themselves. Thus, Israel is enjoined not to give the Canaanites an earthly residence: "Do not give them a settlement on the earth" (Deut. 7:2), which can also mean "Do not show them favor." There is a dimension of trial in this that aims at exhausting the meaning and gravity of the choice of the earth. Israel does, however, create a place for them to reside, giving them a status of foreignness, not metaphysical (like Israel's by its very nature) but political and social. This political condition is actually an initiation into the accession to the metaphysical condition: the peoples of the earth experience in exteriority everything they rejected, banished, and repressed in themselves. In a way, the emergence of Israel among them makes them strangers on their own land and in their own homes. It is the permanent condition of Israel, the deep-seated, specific condition of human beings, the condition of God the creator, which the peoples of the earth ignore. Their condition as zar, as strangers, is therefore a state of experience of strangeness. The zar is a nechar, an "alien" who lives in the abode of Israel, but the "alien" ("other" in Latin) is doubly remote and

457. According to the story in the Midrash.

458. These people are of no present-day relevance, save when humanity falls into the grips of the demon of nation idolatry, in which case, yes, they still stand on the path of passage.

strange, because he remains rooted in the earth, whereas the *zar* in Israel is ultimately called upon to become a *ger*, to enter into the passage of Israel.

This principle underpins the practical morality of Israel in its relationship with the peoples of the earth, which means that conflict and war are not inevitable. If the peoples in question allow Israel safe passage, if they let passage pass through them, they are to be left in peace. If they refuse, war is inevitable. We are speaking here of Israel's passage after going out from Egypt[459] but also of the principle of passage itself. If the land accepts the passage, it is rescued. Its redemption is always a possibility, and the act of redeeming always brings with it contrition, a reduction of being, and retreat in the immediate. By withdrawing into themselves, the peoples of Canaan would be putting Israel into augment, into concealment in the world, thereby reproducing Abraham's gesture. In sum, they are enjoined in their confrontation with Israel to do one thing only: to enter the passage.

This is why, before declaring war, Israel always proposes peace. "When you approach (*tikrav*) a town to fight it, you will call for peace. If it responds with peace and opens to you, the whole *am* present there will pay tribute to you and serve you" (Deut. 20:10–11). It is this moral provision with regard to all the peoples of the earth that gave rise to a great universal idea, that of the seven laws of Noah, which apply to all humankind. Those who do not abide by them exclude themselves from humanity. The laws of Noah are a paradigm for the peoples of the world. They encourage them to join in the *tikkun* of Israel, in an intermediary stage, enabling them to undertake concealment, to leave idolatry and gradually become a *zar*, then a *ger*, and join the *toch* of Israel. What inspires these seven laws is the principle of "*nefesh*ization," the injunction not to treat the other—shelter of the lifebreath—as an object, a corpse, a naked exteriority, but, to the contrary, to practice withdrawal, concealment, gift giving, so as to make room for the other.

Idolatry and blasphemy are prohibited so God will not be reified or cast outside. Incest or adultery, murder, theft, and deception are prohibited so human beings will not be reified, so fellow men will not be treated as if they were not there, as if they cannot see, as if they were not in hiding and can be present entirely in exteriority. It is forbidden to eat the flesh of a living animal in order to preserve the *nefesh* of all living beings and not reify a being animated with the breath of life. The *nefesh* principle is a principle of

459. Israel had to ask the peoples on its way to Canaan for the right to pass through their countries, eventually paying for the use of water or pastures (see, for example, Num. 21:22). The refusal led to war. The issue of "passage" is the criterion that governs Israel's relationship to the peoples of the earth.

life, similar to the movement of divine withdrawal that spans God's life and hence the life of the world. Finally, the only positive principle of the seven laws of Noah, that of enacting justice and establishing courts of justice, is something of a synthesis of the other six imperatives, since the situations in which reification is possible occur when two *nefashot* are in a dispute and one can be led to reify the other. Justice is the act of separating them from one another, specifying and particularizing them, so the life of the one does not destroy or trample on that of the other. Justice thus appears as the vehicle of particularization, whose pivot is the universal, which makes the Name inhabit the world of passage.

The prohibition of idolatry forbids Noah's offspring to "associate the divine Name with something else,"[460] and this means to "add" to God's being, which is structurally for us as creatures, and because he is the Name, a retreat, a concealment that harbors the augment of withdrawal—that is, infinite divine bounty. This foible could describe the peoples of the land in their relationship to concealment and the safeguarded portion. Having confronted the numbing, silent void of the world, they conclude that it has to be covered up and filled by a representation. They thereby add to the immediate void of God the fullness of the idea and of stone. In doing so, they annul the principle of the world (withdrawal) from which their very being springs; they put themselves to death and tear the divine Name in the *olam*. They make the mistake of "adding," in the *olam* of disappearance, when the augment is in hiding. Instead of gift giving, they opt for immediate gratification. They think they are already partaking in revealment and in the one, but, because they are still in the *olam*, they are actually dooming themselves to exposure and nudity, to the dereliction of passage. This outlook bespeaks an utter misinterpretation of the project of creation.

Oriental Religions

Establishment on the earth perverts the *yod*, the first letter of the divine Name, but another type of "establishment" tore away from the earth, joined the movement of passage, and yet remained at the stage of disappearance and the void, adoring the passage for its own sake, without bearing the one and enabling it to shine forth. This form of establishment is linked to the *heh*, the second letter of the Tetragrammaton, which welcomes by spiritual

---

460. Tosafot, Sanhedrin 63b.

virtue and pictorial structure the whole void, the whole wombing gift that welcomes the child (the *heh* has a feminine value; it is the feminine grammatical ending: Saray becomes Sarah, and Abram crosses the Jordan and become Abraham, surveyor of the wombing void).

The epitome of this form of establishment on earth is the Asian world, notably the religions of India. While being polytheist and idolatrous, it sets the sacredness of nothingness at the summit of its interiority. In a way, the portion is removed and safeguarded, but instead of being set aside in augment, it is scattered in the passage of the world. Hindu spirituality is fascinated with nothingness, with renunciation, retreat, and absence. The Hindu form of establishment in the *olam* is the opposite of that of the peoples of the earth. It involves contrition, negation, self-sacrifice, and self-annihilation in the void, a perpetually animated void, that of a passage wherein the *nefesh* is caught in the cycle of reincarnations. There is no will to power or celebration of force here. Renunciation is the way of the faithful. There is not the slightest doubt that the religions of India harbor an experience of the passage. But this passage is tragic, because it does not open onto the one. It does not harbor the force of specification, of particularization that presages the one. It opens onto deperdition, which, in its spirituality, is a very elevated value. But because it does not aspire to the one, this passage is caught up in worldly forms. For this reason, even though it is a vehicle of passage, it is polytheist and idolatrous, like the peoples of the earth, like the corrupted *yod*. And because it does not bear the project of the one (even as it unwittingly heralds it through passage), it is prey to a dualistic view of this world and the world to come that makes it renounce the worldly, physical order in a way more akin to Greek tragedy than to the Levites. How could it be otherwise, since it has renounced specification and particularity?

There are no real or discursive contacts between Israel and this world. Is this due to the happenstance of history or to deep-seated realities? With one losing itself in passage and the other surveying the passage to the one, it would have been hard for them to meet but not impossible, because the one can come to the passage, and the passage can see its subtly glowing light in the depths of its turmoil. What matters most is the inclination to passage, without which no relationship or symbiosis with Israel is possible. Hidden in withdrawal, the world of India has yet to meet Israel, but this eventuality is present potentially in the passage and ever ready to manifest itself.

Christianity

We face a whole different world with Abraham's family, as embodied by Esau, Jacob's twin brother, traditionally considered the archetype of the West (and hence of Christianity), and by Ishmael, Isaac's brother, archetype of the East (and hence of Islam). In this case, the relationship of Israel with the nations is governed by a family conflictuality that hinges on the problematic of the safeguarded portion and the system of "augret." With Esau (the West), the conflictuality is sharper and more direct. The theme is clearly stated in Genesis. Esau and Jacob are twins, so the question of birthright, preeminence, and holding a single place is cardinal in their relationship. Esau is the first to emerge from his mother's womb (Gen. 25:24), and he seems destined to inherit his father, but in the end, Jacob becomes the heir, thanks to his mother's subterfuge.[461] Esau is therefore the preeminent surrogate, who, by his very identity and by congenital necessity, holds the place of Jacob, who is in retreat and in hiding (he takes time to be born). Jacob is so hard to discern in the real world that, from the standpoint of exteriority, he seems to have robbed Esau of his rightful place as firstborn. When the blind Isaac is about to bless Jacob disguised as Esau, he refers to him in a way that indicates a parallel between Esau and negativity. Issac's, "I will touch you, my son, if you are my son Esau or not" (27:21). Esau is positioned in the negative of the place where Jacob stands. He is the one who sees in the gift giving and withdrawal of Jacob, "who sits in the tent" (25:27), an occasion to assert his own power in exteriority when he is out hunting.

To Esau, concealment is weakness and nonexistence. He cannot endure the trial of promise and waiting, and he seeks to achieve the promise in the very place where it was announced and sustained.[462] In this way, Esau occupies the place of the retreat that created Israel-Jacob, taking its place, sacrificing it in a misguided attempt at rapprochement. He exploits the weakness of Israel to drive it definitively, he thinks, into the nothingness of passage and take his place, turning his particularization—a process of the one, a process of struggling with difficulty through the passage to the one—into

461. Covering Jacob with animal skins to imitate Esau's hairiness and trick the blind Isaac into mistaking him for Esau.

462. Isn't this what is at work in the Christian conception of God? It is as if it holds for "dead" God the creator, who has withdrawn, and hence overadds to him in this world the manifestation of Christ, God "fulfilled," hominized in this world. This is a reversal of the original problematic: the withdrawal is interpreted as a lack, when it is overplus from the divine standpoint, and the void is regarded as the site of plenitude, when it is passage.

a particularism against which he pits his declared universality.[463] There is
something of a resurgence of the all in the establishment of Esau and the
West, but in a way that assumes the appearance of the one, a circumstantial and artificial one behind which the game of the all is being played out.
The ambition of the "catholic," meaning the universal, is embedded in such
an identity, but inevitably it comes up against the obtuse "particularity" of
Israel, as all empires do. Faced with the empire, Israel always plays the role
of rupture and caesura, that is to say, of the covenant, the *berit*, and hence
of particularization, alterity, and the evocation of the one.

The West sets itself up in exteriority and manifestation (redemption is
already here),[464] like the peoples of the earth, but in this case the earth is
supposed to have undergone a process of atonement, of the hidden portion,
of sacrifice. These are indeed recognized but as a onetime occurrence in the
past, having happened once and for all, as if we were already in the one.
And, in fact, Esau leaves Israel, the concealment, separation, and gift giving, for "he went to a land, outside his brother Jacob's face" (Gen. 36:6). He
leaves his brother's face to go to undifferentiated, anonymous lands, posited
precisely to hide departure, dialectically, behind a universal. But we are not
yet in the one, and Israel basically bears witness for humanity that human
beings are not born yet, that the being is awaiting the one, and that this
promise sustains and founds the being in the passage. Christianity (unlike
the Covenant between the Pieces, in which the one, the bird, is not divided)
glorifies the sacrifice of the one (God's particularized hominization and his
human death on the cross) and thus renounces (despite this glorification)
the actuality of the gift giving, the waiting, and the promise. It excludes
itself from the promise, even though its aim is to fulfill it, but it impatiently
believes it is actually fulfilling it in immediacy. It disregards the necessity for
separation/sanctification insofar as it reveals the concealment in its desire to
demonstrate and exteriorize the advent, when we are still in concealment.
Isn't this what characterizes Israel's untimely messianisms, when mercy is
denied and reversed into rigor (*din*) out of an excessive desire for accomplishment? Mercy is in suspension in the world of *din*. This is what makes
for its artistic and monumental genius, but its palaces do not shelter the
one, and they extinguish the echo of Israel's testimony, the memory of the

463. "There is neither Jew nor Greek, there is neither slave nor free... for you are all
one in Christ," says Paul (Gal. 3:28), discounting the possible particularization of Israel
and investing its cosmic concealment with a sense oriented to the whole, not the one.

464. This is as true of Christianity as of modernity, both of which set themselves up
as messianic comings.

promise and the waiting, the projection of the shadow of concealment that opens for humankind the path of its fulfillment. The persistence of Israel's existence, even hidden, is a reminder that the one has not yet come to be.

This representation of the one in the all, which short-circuits the history of being, expresses itself in the extreme (and creative) tension that inhabits the being of the West. This takes the form of an intrinsic dualism (body and spirit), a unity expressed through the multiple (the Trinity), a need for icons and representations to support the face of the one (in a way akin to the peoples of India, the peoples of Saint Nothingness), an unexpected dualization of the advent (the overadded idea of the parish), and a capacity to shift from an apologia of the one to an affirmation of the all (modernity), always in this bizarre synthesis. With India, representation left its infancy, became fluid and in close touch with the passage. With the West, it reaches its highest stage via dialectization. But we are still in the world of representation, so close to the one and at the same time so far removed from it.

This deep-seated paradox that constitutes the being of the West (inhabiting the being of Israel but not being Israel) underpins its persistence over twenty centuries—a unique adventure in the history of civilization—but also its tragic inclination toward incomplete consummation. There are intimations of this in Esau's powerful, bitter, and utterly sincere cry when he learns that Jacob has "taken" his birthright from him. The tragedy lies in his perception of primogeniture solely in terms of property and power, when what it institutes in fact is dispossession, not a reproduction of the *same* via heritage but the invention of the new. The West lives in overplus without having undertaken the retreat. It would like to reap the fruits of withdrawal, gift giving, and sacrifice while sparing itself the efforts that produced them.[465] How can one take part in a "new covenant" when one hasn't taken part in the "old covenant"? As a result, the gift giving to which the West would like to devote its being is so obsessed with sacrifice and contrition that it makes a virtue of ascetic self-negation. The giving is rendered impossible, because it has turned its back on *din* and glorifies itself all the more for having done so. The gift giving opens onto the void, which is nothing other than nothingness and destruction if it is not accompanied by *din*. This is because it neglects the virtue of *kirva*, of sacrificial approaching,[466] having opted instead

465. Hence, Christianity logically abandons the *mitzvot*, the "law."

466. The *kirva* is totally absorbed by the sacrifice in the figure of Christ, of God's sacrificing himself to approach human beings and save them. The Hebrew *kirva* saves human beings, and God the creator's retreat is not his "sacrifice" in this sense. The *kirva* draws its

for exteriority, whose shortcomings and chaotic incompleteness have been demonstrated throughout (its) history.

In the void where the four-letter Name resounds, the Western establishment is attached to the third letter, the *vav*, the letter of conjunction (*hibbur*, the conjunction of coordination). *Vav* equals six, and it is the key letter that opens the seventh day of consummation, the coming of the one into the world. This is the letter symbolic of Israel. Israel possesses the secret of the *vav*, the secret of the conjunction of the Tetragrammaton letters, of the resolution of the void in the one. But this knowledge, founded on the *vav*, requires the knowledge of all the letters of the Tetragrammaton. Because the *vav* is between one *heh* and another, because it links two *hehs*, the *vav* as the figure of the West is filled with an immense nostalgia for the *heh*, the void, Saint Nothingness, femininity. It is close to India and approaches Islam, the second and final *heh*, but it does not link them, because, not having traveled through the void of passage, it lacks the force of the *vav*.

This unexpected figure that arose in the passage considerably upsets the relationship of Israel to the nations of the *olam*, because here is a being that claims to be Israel but is not. Everything in it stands in the way of Israel's appearance and its path to the true one, which demands the particularization of Israel, its separation, its detachment. In its eyes, concealment is imprisonment, gift giving is weakness, and testimony is the mark of sin. If Israel indeed arose, if it were not condemned to the sedimentation of the past, the very nexus of the West would fall apart. This clever and subtle system works to make Israel's journey through the West its most trying, terrible experience, because the conflictuality with the nations takes place in the secrecy of its being and not in the open, even though it is in exteriority. The conflict is not fought on equal terms, because Israel's own weapons are turned against it. The concealment is turned into imprisonment. For this reason, the experience is ambivalent. It creates confusion in the world and delays the advent of the one. Everything becomes more obscure in its wake. On the other hand, it eradicates as surely as can be the establishment of the peoples of the earth and fights to include them in the space of Israel that it itself occupies, in its oblivion to Israel. And it is not Israel's message that reaches humanity through its intermediary. The idea that does in fact reach humanity contributes to making it impossible to hear Israel and to masking the newness of its message. Israel's trial in the West is not in the form of a

positive dimension from the structure inherent in the promise and the oath. The Hebraic sacrifice saves the partners of a rapprochement from death.

war, as it was with the peoples of the earth. From Israel's standpoint, it is
hand-to-hand combat in secrecy, but from Esau's point of view, it is a war
against an enemy without weapons. "Esau took to hating Jacob... and Esau
said to himself... 'I will kill my brother Jacob'" (Gen. 27:41).

The murderous persecution of Israel is a constant feature of Western history, and it is as if Israel could not respond violently. This combat between
Israel and Esau is Jacob's combat against the angel the night before he goes
to meet Esau before entering the land of Israel. In this struggle Jacob has one
purpose, and that is to hold out, not to give way, to persevere until daybreak,
the hour of the one, when the angel is thrust back into the night (Athena's
owl), its kingdom, where it will have to experience the concealment and
withdrawal that Israel lived through in humility during Esau's preponderance.
For Israel's concealment reaches its consummation, the manifestation of the
one, only with the maturation of the light, when the one can arise, when the
waiting has been accomplished. And the auroral one can arise only when
the darkness of concealment has reached its darkest pitch, when the separa-
tion/sanctification is thoroughly consummate, when Israel has found in its
innermost depths the necessary forces—the forces from the one of particularization and its emergence that shatter the totality of Esau's establishment.
That is when day breaks and the angel departs (32:25). Now Israel-Jacob
can continue on his way and find the strength to call on his twin brother to
practice concealment, to sanctify himself, and join him in Abraham's blessing, because he has heard his brother's cry and is profoundly shaken by it.

Islam

Lastly, a fourth figure appears in the void and the echo of the Tetragrammaton,
another member of the Abrahamic family: Ishmael. This figure is as strange
as that of Esau, for it, too, is unexpected in the passage. Whereas the figure
of Esau takes refuge in augment without retreat, and hence in mercy without
rigor, that of Ishmael takes refuge in retreat without augment, in *din* without
rahamim. But in the real world the relationships crisscross: The figure of Esau,
who sings the coming of the Messiah, lives in the glorification of mortifica-
tion and suffering, while the figure of Ishmael, who stands in the harshness
of the desert and nomadism, lives in the invocation of the wombing God
(*Rahman*). This intimate crisscrossing of the two figures imparts a tragic
dimension to the experiences they govern. The figure of Ishmael entered
the final *heh* and represents something of a counterpart to the first *heh*, the

world of Hindu Saint Nothingness.[467] Indeed, Ishmael knows the passage and is in the passage (and, it is written, "Ishmael, I have heard you," Gen. 17:20), which is not the case for Esau. The figure of Ishmael is even more in the passage than India, because before it and between it and India comes the moment of the *vav*, even in the simulated form of the West. The most immediate proof thereof is the absence of representation, polytheism, icons, or idols, and the absolute affirmation of unity. This makes the establishment of Islam the closest to Israel's.

Ishmael is in the passage. After all, hasn't his lot been one of nomadism and wandering? Ishmael is the only one in Abraham's family, besides Jacob and Isaac, to have undertaken a migration, a passage. He did so to Moriah with Isaac (according to tradition, he is one of the two "young men" who accompanied Abraham and Isaac) and then with his mother, Hagar, when Sarah chased them away (Hagar, from *heger*, to emigrate, to become a foreigner, or, literally, to "make dwell"). Later, the *hegira*, emigration, would be the foundational act of Islam. Esau is rooted. He does not move, except to run from his brother (Gen. 36:6), to forget. There is passage in the being of Ishmael, but this passage remains incomplete. Having left for Moriah, the place of the giving of the *korban*, Ishmael is left on the way, because he does not see the light of Moriah in the distance (Midrash Rabba on Gen. 56). Ishmael's passage, even if he is the vehicle of the one, does not seem to harbor its culmination. Ishmael enters the passage, where he perceives the one but does not leave it. As long as Abraham is alive, it is said of Ishmael, "and on the face of/before all his brothers, he will dwell/be present" (Gen. 16:12). After Abraham's death, "he fell on the face of/before all his brothers" (25:18). The abode where he was dwelling became a fall into undifferentiated nothingness for him.

Aspiring to the one, and not the land, like the Saint Nothingness of India, Ishmael's particularization does not succeed, perhaps because there is no gift giving and retreat. And yet, driven away with his mother, he disappears for a while, into concealment, to reappear thereafter. Ishmael is thus closer to the one than Esau, even if he does not attain it.[468] If Esau can make

---

467. This relationship is manifested in the agreement between Sufiism and Hinduism.

468. Whereas unity in Islam is affirmed in a movement from retreat to augment, in Christianity it is affirmed in a movement from augment to retreat (from the overadded son to the father), which is why it is not as "pure" as Islam (as the dogma of the Trinity illustrates). But in Islam, unity remains theoretical, proclaimed without the assumption of *din* (Ishmael could not go as far as Moriah), while the passage is incomplete and does not see its culmination. Ishmael does not know he must leave the passage, where he dwells.

use of representation because he occupies the place of the *vav*, the place of Israel, Ishmael cannot. Ishmael is more authentically in the passage than India, more truly in the passage than Esau, but he cannot leave. (When Esau leaves—Gen. 36:6—it is to go not to the land of the one, as he thinks, but to an undifferentiated land.)

It is as if Ishmael were unable to step out and take shape on earth, wholly gathered into the erring in an unending passage, where the one glimmers nonetheless. Just as Ishmael left with Isaac for Moriah but didn't reach it, Islam has difficulty appearing, emerging from its concealment (it was, of course, the last monotheism to be formed, six centuries after Christianity). No doubt its concealment is incomplete, or else it has not gotten to the end of it. Thus, the one to which Ishmael aspires can produce forms of the all. In parallel to the Catholic universal is the idea of *Dar el Islam*, whereby the "peoples of the book" are tolerated but reduced to an inferior status, in opposition to *Dar el Harb*, "the Abode of the Sword," where Islam wages war to extend its empire. No doubt this is because the one God of Islam does not retreat, hide, set aside a portion, is not truly God the creator. "God is God," proclaims the Muslim profession of faith. This means that he is as he is in himself and not in the other, as is the case with Esau, for whom, however, the other is a simulation: position/negation of Israel. The son is posited in relation to the father in the crucifixion, that is, in his negation. That is the sign of his mediating representativeness. "No one knows the father except the son and those to whom the son chooses to reveal him" (Matt. 11:27).

In its movement to the one, Islam has forgotten the other; it has forgotten Israel. This is one consequence of the being of Ishmael, more autonomous than that of Esau, who always has his eyes set on Israel... only to negate Israel. Thus, Islam thinks of itself as the summit of the lower levels of successive truths (Israel, Esau, Ishmael). This oblivion of Israel is a cardinal factor in Ishmael's being. It is perhaps the origin of his less violent relationship to Israel than Esau's. Esau fights Jacob to occupy the place of the one; his being depends on Jacob's. Ishmael left, driven away well before the coming of Jacob and his nomination in Israel, like an Abraham who would not have brought Jacob into this world, an Abraham who would have left his home without ever coming to the land of Israel, an Abraham covered in blessings and "gifts" ("God was with the boy," Gen. 21:20), provided with twelve symbolic descendants (25:16), but who cannot endure the waiting, the retreat, and the sacrifice (the binding of Isaac) that the promise required of Israel. In this sense, Ishmael is the being of desire and immediacy. He does not wait. From the perspective of the "augret," Ishmael behaves like Esau to

Israel. Israel's withdrawal and concealment is translated by him in terms of his power. Esau occupies Israel's place and adds a "testament." Ishmael does not occupy Israel's place or add a "testament," but, much more radically, he replaces the Torah with the Koran.[469] Israel's concealment, its positioning in augment, in the one, is read by both as a nonexistence that needs to be occupied, appropriated, filled in by adding a text that covers up and masks the divine text and even the very existence of Israel. And this text is underpinned by forgetting, by the refusal to wait, by an obliteration of the promise and the Name in the passage. Islam, like Christianity, structurally *lodges itself* as a challenge to the validity of the safeguarded portion.

Conflictuality

We can see that the object of conflictuality in this triangle is the land of Israel, in other words, the "concrete" testimony (in the worldly order) and the vehicle of Israel's particularization and differentiation, a memory marker of the origin and the safeguarded portion. Both the empire of Esau and the empire of Ishmael try to appropriate it (the Crusades, the Muslim conquest, the wars between Israel and the Arabs). The universal of the one, even when mixed with the representation of the one (the West) or its memory (the East), cannot tolerate what it sees as a protrusion. Israel curbs its heady narcissism and frenzied drive for power. It is against that which withstands all empires that it will direct its vague desire, which is crystallized here into a desire for the place of Israel. Whereas Islam and Christianity conceived of the empire (the totalization), Israel never conceived of anything more than a delimitation, the separation/sanctification of a land, *Eretz hakodesh*, to appear in the world. And this is the telltale sign that it is truly in unity, because the universal of domination to which Islam and Christianity aspire arose only because they both aspired to the particularization of Israel. The universal is an inflated compensation for their difficulty in gaining access to the being and to the place of Israel. This is why they have systematically endeavored to

469. Paradoxically, Islam is at once closer to Israel, because it conceives of itself in terms of withdrawal, and infinitely remote, too, because it effaces the Torah. This shows the theoretical nature of the unity it proclaims on the basis of withdrawal. It gives itself a substitute text, the text of the one, of the coming, as if it were not yet in retreat. Christianity knows that it is speaking from the standpoint of augment and that the retreat persists (and Christianity, which is secretly aware that it is maintained in it). It thus adds a text (the Gospels) on top of the Torah it condemns to withdrawal and lack for all eternity. It fills in the retreat that is the law. Ishmael does not want to recognize the retreat, even though its own withdrawal is more genuine than Esau's.

blur the boundaries of separation, to erase the mark of this particularization that they were unable to achieve in itself or in its authenticity.

The question of the land is more critical for Ishmael, whose place is formless, than for Esau, who is eminently formalized, since Esau occupies Israel's place (and aspires to speak from the height of the universal). This is why Islam opposes the particularization of the land of Israel with all its might, striving to keep it within itself as an anonymous, abandoned place. Unless, to the contrary, it elicits and produces a dual and contradictory particularization that will logically become, even in the farthest, most removed places in the Islamic world, the vehicle of formalization, particularization, and unity. We have here the pattern of contemporary conflicts. The main thing for Esau and Ishmael is to oppose Israel's return, Israel's departure from the original concealment, which they turned into an imprisonment by exploiting Israel's consequent weakness, and so condemn Israel to wandering in the exteriority of the world and of passage and prevent it from manifesting the one with force and intensity in the world of the void—a manifestation that is a process of particularization.

The relationship Israel can establish with a partner like Ishmael is very different from the one with Esau. The negation of and violence toward Israel in Islam is not as strong as in Christianity, but it harbors a more secretive and complex animosity. The name Ishmael, about whom God said to Abraham: "*Leyismael* (for Ishmael/God will hear/he will hear God) *shamaticha* (I have heard you)," thereby designates his most precious treasure, the Koran, which itself derives from the name with which God announces Isaac to Abraham, "for in Isaac a seed will be named/read/*yikarei* for you" (Gen. 21:12): from *kara*, reading/calling/naming. The desire to benefit from Israel's blessing and birthright is deeply embedded in Ishmael, who does not completely assume the spiritual independence of his being, which is much more complex than Esau's, and who is removed in the same text from the rights of the firstborn, because "in Isaac" indicates that not all of Isaac (Esau and Jacob) will be called to the particularization of the one. "In Isaac" signifies neither Ishmael nor Esau, but Jacob, who stands in Isaac's incomplete interiority.

The system informing Esau's relationships to Israel is very subtle. The question is how to occupy Israel's abode while chasing him away and denying him. Everything in Esau is bent on occulting Jacob, even when greeting him with great pomp (Gen. 33). Ishmael's intentions are less manifest but equally determined. Both Esau and Ishmael feel that the very existence of Israel violates their identity and being. But instead of responding with patience and endurance, as Israel must with Esau, the appropriate response to Ishmael is untimely ardor, because here the confrontation is situated in the tense arena of particularization, not under the massive blanket of the all. The relationship with Ishmael in the particularization of Israel is one of armed peace. The untimely is necessary, because only action can tear Israel from the pull of wandering into which Ishmael wants to drag it to prevent its particularization. The moment of confrontation with Ishmael is daybreak, when Israel is summoned to arise and manifest itself, to depart from its own exile and, doubly, from Ishmael's wandering. The only possible relations Islam can conceive of having with Israel are in its formless wandering, but this opening ceases when the particularization of Israel reminds it of its failure in the particularity, in the one.

Ishmael needs the particularity of Israel to have access to the world. It was because Isaac undertook to go up to Moriah that Ishmael entered the passage. Indeed, when Israel manages to be particularized, Ishmael can then find a way out, a vehicle out of the passage, where he has lost his way. So Islam tends paradoxically to seek and encourage Israel's particularization. In fact, throughout history it has permitted Israel's particularization, unlike Catholicism (both classic and modern), which occupies Israel's place and resorts to the universal of totality to make Israel impossible. Unlike Christianity, which never ceases to extend its empire so as to more firmly establish its domination over Israel's place, it is particularity much more than the empire that is Ishmael's impossible dream.

As a result, when Israel seeks to particularize himself on his road to the one, he goes toward Ishmael, because he can do so in his midst. And thus, Israel springs up again in the heart of the Arab Orient, the only place where this is possible.[470] But if he finds his place of particularization in the place that was held longest by Ishmael during its exile, he can attain it only by making use of Esau's and Ishmael's contradictions. He can do so in the midst of Ishmael, because Esau would oppose it in his own place, which is Israel's (Ishmael has no place, at least no formal place). But he can do so only with the help of Esau's universality, by playing on Esau's desire. Otherwise, in a movement of attraction/repulsion, Ishmael would prevent Israel from successfully particularizing himself, fearing that this would thwart Ishmael's ambitions. We have here the key to the last century of Jewish history and to the birth of the State of Israel.

---

470. In the Emancipation, democratic citizenship welcomed individuals and not the people of Israel, which was formally rendered impossible. On the basis of this observation, early Zionists spoke of "autoemancipation" for a historic and democratic collectivity.

Indeed, wholly bent on the contemplation of the all, Esau pays attention to the rise of Israel's particularity only within his confines.[471] In the universality of Esau, Israel could not arise, but neither could he arise in the grips of Ishmael's incomplete particularization. It is under the combined impact of Ishmael and Esau, when the two move toward one another, when they meet even conflictually (colonial empires), that Israel manages to particularize himself, which is the key moment in the process of the one.[472] At that point, the most diametrically opposed principles,[473] the least susceptible to meeting, because they are not situated in Israel's trajectory, encounter one another and, canceling their effects of enmity to Israel, further reinforce the rise of the one. Beyond the anguish of the respective inborn pull to power and wandering, Esau and Ishmael can then see the good that comes from Israel's particularity, the chance for them to embody their own being and occupy their proper place in Abraham's family, in the particularization toward the one.

III. SURVEYING THE PARTICULARITY OF THE ONE

It is the gesture of the safeguarded portion that enables us to understand Israel's behavior amongst the nations, but if its unfolding is governed by the temporality of the promise and the waiting, what it involves in actual experience is effort and action and the purposeful surveying of the void in the direction of the one. Let us not forget that *tikkun* is the project given to human deeds in the *olam*, actions woven out of the skein of waiting and illuminated by the promise. The concealment of separation is far from a passion or a passiveness. It lasts only for a while, the time of its accomplishment in the one. Hence, all its time is filled with action that seeks to surpass it, because it is also necessary to undertake the *tikkun* of the concealment of retreat by making it give birth to the one. Thus, Israel's patience in the process of the safeguarded portion opens onto action, the true departure from concealment. In sum, it is perpetually inhabited by the breath of the

471. The experience is always in fact dual. Esau contemplates the all but is obsessed with the particularity. Israel turned toward Ishmael at the time of modernity, when the nations and national particularisms asserted themselves in Europe—that is, when Europe, too, was approaching the principle of Ishmael.

472. It is due to the support of Europe, which controlled the Middle East at the time, that Israel as an entity managed to be established in the land of Israel.

473. See Trigano, *Mythe et pensée*, p. 141.

messianic spirit and will, vehicles for the sudden reversal of all situations, accelerators of the climb up through the void. At every moment, historical time can blossom into the flower of oneness.

The politics of Israel, that is to say, the government and displacement of all the people of Israel in the arena of the void and disappearance, must firstly reckon with a primordial fact: Israel's passage and withdrawal are taken in the "world" for a weakness bordering on nonexistence. Israel's shepherd must acquire this deep knowledge of the laws of passage and evanescence of worldly forms; his skill consists in ensuring that Israel does not let itself be swept into the external drift of the passage, the disappearance in the void. The mechanism of concealment alone can provide Israel with a saving viaticum, insofar as it leads to turning retreat into augment, to working the retreat together with the augment, to making it produce the opposite of what it seems to give. In this way, what looks like a process of weakening in the eyes of the nations turns to an advantage for Israel.

Israel's solitude and apartness in the concert of nations do not risk turning into a tragic impasse in this case. It carries instead the potential of oneness; it becomes the vehicle of oneness. There is an inevitable austerity in Israel's condition among the nations, but its solitude is with God. It is the solitude of love, as we have said, and this becomes the secret pivot of the community of nations. Everything in the nations risks obstructing Israel's passage, and especially its particularization and emergence, and contributing to casting it into the catastrophe of exteriority: "They divide my clothes among themselves, casting lots from my garments" (Ps. 22:19). But Israel's shepherd knows how to widen the straits. On its journey, Israel must not deviate from the viaticum that concealment, separation/sanctification, provides for it, and from which it learns to transform situations of retreat and lack into situations of bounty. Israel exists for the sole purpose of concealment. If it moves away from this and gives itself over to exposure and exteriority, it exposes itself to consumption and disappearance in the void.

Depending on whether Israel is in a phase of prevailing retreat or augment, its behavior changes. But who decides whether reality is shining in the hidden light of augment or in the exterior light of the world of withdrawal? (For we know from the logic of "augret" that what is in retreat is simultaneously set into augment.) In the *olam*, all things and all times are always possible and actualizable for those who know how to be in the *toch*, and for Israel when it really dwells in its abode. This is not true, however, from the standpoint of the nations, devoured by the illusion of retreat and driven to cover it up or fill it in instead of practicing withdrawal, concealment, and gift giving. The void, experienced as a lack, must be exhausted. It must be "scoured" every which way, so that the logic of augment will become manifest in it. Scarcity must be exhausted.

The Movement of History

The farther the reaches of the empire of the nations extend, and the greater its appropriation of the disappearance that is the world—even in material terms—the more "actualized" and exhausted is the void; and thereupon the moment when scarcity is reverted into abundance (*shefa*) draws nigh. Israel is the being, the link, one of whose segments is in retreat, the other in augment. When it measures up to the standards of its inwardness, it harbors the potential of turning retreat into augment, in a reversal that directly governs its destiny in the world of nations. But when this is not the case—that is to say, when it loses its concealment and is in the exteriority of exile—then its own course of action follows the movement of the nations and depends on it. Scarcity governs it. Its condition changes from freedom to destiny. But even then, Israel's course of action is not naturally sustained by the logic of the depletion of the void.

It is the effect of Israel's very existence in the world—no matter how passive and incomplete—that, by its presence alone, plots a path for the void that Israel cannot fail to take in its erring and that amounts to an action. However, in this case, the particularization in the Babelian universe of nations involutes into a strict, confined particularism. Israel is reduced, even forced, into a provincial impasse of the universal. Withdrawing from its vocation, Israel departs from the sphere of graciousness that underpins it, and, too fragile to withstand the flood of passage, its destruction draws near. In this catastrophic figure of Israel's condition in the *olam*, the question of Israel's messianic politics does not really come up, insofar as this situation rhymes with Israel's abandonment of all politics—its abandonment, in other words, of its condition of freedom, its role as a free agent in its own history and in world history. It all depends on its ability to leave the empire of retreat, to escape its informing power and the domination of nations (*shi'abud mal-chuyot*) and turn its destiny into freedom. The only means of doing so is, of course, concealment, a practice of *tikkun* of both the world and itself. We are speaking, in other words, of Israel's conduct befitting its vocation.

We have a telling example of this when Jacob goes to meet Esau, his rival brother (Gen. 33). To be sure, his diplomatic conduct is governed by fear and abstention. When he enters Esau's spiritual area, his territory, he deploys the family of Israel (33:2) so as to safeguard the most important portion in case of aggression. In this way, active diplomacy obeys the balance of forces in reality. Jacob has to use cunning and cajoling to deflect Esau's violence. But the crux of this apparent diplomacy of submission or subterfuge is the operation of concealment—concealment, not cowardice. Before taking his family across, Jacob set aside the safeguarded portion; he practiced concealment.[474] He knew how to draw the necessary power from its true source in order to confront the world of retreat and the void, and invert the logic of withdrawal into a logic of augment. And, indeed, in the diplomacy of retreat, he advances preceded by the numerous gifts he offers to his brother (32:14–22). We have here the embodiment of Israel's messianic politics in the withdrawal, where the nations are. The main thing is safeguarding Israel as well as its passage. But the journey through the nations can be accomplished only by virtue of concealment. The imperative for Israel in the era of passage is to keep itself from perdition and pursue its way to the particularization that heralds oneness in the anonymousness of the passage. And what is Israel's particularization in the passage if not its heroic effort to maintain the potential of unity of its many centers, scattered by exile, to maintain oneness despite exile and exposure—in other words, to undertake concealment and *tikkun*?[475] It must find its way in a universe that seeks to engulf it, to prevent it from emerging, no doubt because it is, first and foremost, the universe of disappearance. This is why the stratagem is the archetypal tactic for this being in hiding.[476] Israel can manifest itself in the world of nations only in an abrupt and surprising manner, springing up suddenly where it is no longer expected, thereby manifesting the hidden "subterranean" life that the world of the void forces upon it. And necessarily it "will be scattered to the west and to the east" (Gen. 28:14); after all, it is in the secrecy of augment! In theory, every moment Israel has the choice, the resource of augment, if it knows how to actuate it in scarcity. There is always an exit for Israel if it knows firstly how to open a way to it within itself.

474. See passages above on the "camp of the one" and the "camp of the rest," pp. 201, 221.

475. A paradigm of this situation can be found in the book of Esther, where Israel is defined by Haman, its die-hard enemy, as "a one-*am*, scattered and divided among the *ams* in all the states [of the empire], whose laws diverge from any *am* and [who] do not abide by the king's laws; for the king, it is not equivalent/advisable to let them subsist" (Esther 3:8).

476. Israel's stratagem is not deception. It is an untimely truth that can be neither heard nor voiced in this world of absence and needs to hide, to cover itself in order to induce the nations to undertake an action whose meaning they cannot understand.

Thus, Israel's politics in the world of emptiness works toward its particularization, meaning that its own destiny is the aim of its politics. But
this destiny opens a way to the universe by opening the ways of the one for
the nations. Working on its own destiny, it works toward the redemption of
humankind. It cannot be otherwise in this world, wholly structured by lack,
scarcity, and representation. In the world of nations, there is no universal,
aside from Babel's. Genuine universality comes shining through the opening
of the one, the narrow passageway for this world, the recognition of God,
who made himself one in creating his world.

Messianic Policy

The question of Israel's messianic politics does not really arise until Israel
has conceived enough interiority within itself to enter its *toch* and reverse
its "destiny." This moment can depend exclusively on its own spiritual clarity
(*zachut*) and merit (*zechut*), or it can come about "naturally," through the
exhaustion of the emptiness in the condition of the nations. It is this moment in the passage from retreat to augment that is the "messianic" moment,
because as soon as augment comes back to work in the being, the *olam* that
is disappearance disappears. A transubstantiation of creation and of the being
is summoned to take place. This is the retreat that produces its fruit in the
one. "When Israel came out of Egypt... the sea saw it and fled, the Jordan ran
backward, mountains leaped like rams, hills like sheep.... Tremble, O earth,
at the appearance of the God of Jacob, who turns rock into a pool of water,
granite into bursting springs" (Ps. 114).

One of the clearest signs of this reversal, of Israel's successful concealment, is the end of exile, the departure from the realm of the adverse nudity
and exteriority of the nations, and this reaches its fullest expression in the
ingathering of exiles in the land of Israel. Then the question of what to do
and what to say arises. These are the questions that characterize the era of
augment, when Israel is no longer abiding by the principle of retreat, and
Jacob's policy in confronting Esau becomes outdated and useless. It is a
matter no longer of Jacob but of Israel, henceforth the name of overplus.
Israel must now abide by the principle of the bounty of the being, change
the economy of its being, even leave behind all economy, and make sure
to distribute this blessing throughout the world of the nations. This is a
terribly trying moment, because the change of being is a radical upheaval.
Israel can be swept away by the torrent of being and disappear. The wisdom

of concealment must guide it more than ever. From this point on, it must combine its particularization with the one that is close to it, while conducting a policy of self-maintenance (which means positioning itself as such, as Israel, among the nations), assuming its nominative interest, and heralding the one, giving voice to the one in the resonance of nations.

The enterprise is difficult, since it involves combining the politics of the state, which necessarily faces conflict and war, with the politics of surpassing the state, by opening the paths of the one for the nations. This explains why prophetic discourse voices this threshold moment in figures of wars at the end of time. Indeed, the world of the nations (to the extent that it is the illusion of an autonomous worldliness, separated from the divine project of creation) is heading to its disappearance, for the nations are summoned to their particularization in the one. "Whoever will have survived amongst all the peoples that came up against Jerusalem will have to come each year to bow before the king YHWH-of-armies (*Tzevaot*) and to celebrate the Feast of Booths"; "On that day... YHWH will be king over all the earth; on that day YHWH will be one, and one will be his Name" (Zech. 14:16; 8–9). The nations will gather in Jerusalem as Israel does for *hakhel*, during the septenary year.

Hence, Israel, living in the land of Israel, is led to conduct a politics of state governed by the criterion of the safety of its passage as well as by the imperative of fully assuming the fragile new positivity of its being in augment (otherwise it would be swallowed up by the void again), and the whole point is to keep this tension alive so as not to recreate the all precisely at the time when the one is taking shape in the world. In the passage from Levitical withdrawal to Josephic bounty, the true sense of the new positivity can be the object of illusions and perversions. Leviticism cannot bring about the petrifying recreation of the all (it does not rebuild Babel on the far side of the passage). But this does not imply that it implements the politics of the undifferentiated, of a fake withdrawal and a mockery of peace.[477] It is in the tension between these two extremes that the testate can take shape in the *toch*.

Israel's messianic politics, therefore, is not a politics of renunciation or of mediation in the salvation of nations. This would make of Israel the "representative" of the nations. One can hear the echo of renunciation in prophetic discourse, but the prophets were speaking about both the time of exile and the time of return—in the manner of the relationship between retreat and augment, with one secretly nestled in the other—and firmly asserting Israel's return to a transfigured positivity. It is in this sense, in terms of a discourse

477. "Neutrality" is another word for this.

of augment hiding in a discourse of retreat and arising out of it, that the prophetic text speaks of a messianic time when the nearness of the one will bring shame to those who call themselves prophets, and when the voice of the one will not use the name of prophecy: "On that day, prophets will be ashamed of the visions they have when they prophesy... and each will say, 'I am not a prophet'" (Zech. 13:4–5). The prophet who announces the era of augment during the period of retreat is immersed in his own announcement. It is, to the contrary, by fully assuming its particularization (but a particularization in the vicinity of the one) that Israel draws the one nigh in the being and unifies the divine Name among the nations.

Thus, to accomplish its universal vocation, the *tikkun* of humanity, Israel does not stay in the background, as it would in the case of a mediation. It appears, it comes forward, and manifests itself. And in this there is humility, for while announcing to the nations the community and the one, it helps them become what they are, without imperially projecting its being onto them, for its aim is to bring *them* to life, to awaken them to their particularization, from the perspective of the one in its seventy reflections of light. Proselytism has nearly always been alien to Israel. The point is for the nations not to resemble Israel but to come alive to themselves. Israel calls them to concealment, as their coming to Jerusalem for Sukkot illustrates.[478] Thus, for the nations, Israel is the welcoming place, the Temple, the abode, the priest of nations. By its nature, Israel is the active agent in the destruction of totalities. Its existence is the sign of liberation and of trust in the being, inasmuch as it triumphs over the project of empires to drive it out of the world, and it calls the deep-seated being of each people to leave the reification of the exterior and rediscover the profound breath of its *nefesh*.

---

478. They are invited to hide there, under the cover of tents (*sukkot*), in the shade of the Temple.

BOOK III

FOUNDATION

CHAPTER 1

The Theory of
the Safeguarded Portion

IN ALL OF the developments of Israel's prophetic politics, we have shown the effectiveness of a unique problematic governed by the system of "augret," by the process of the "safeguarded portion," which is at work recurrently and on all levels. We have seen in this way that the social arena is structured by the *korban*, sovereignty by the suspension coming from strangeness, politics by the prohibition against representation and reification, the state by the Levitical principle, nationality by the Josephic augment, communication by the prophetic sign, and messianic politics by the election of Israel.

The theory of the safeguarded portion[479] carries sufficient hermeneutical power to cover not only all Hebraic and biblical fields but also, no doubt, all spheres of existence. It deals with the fundamental human experience of having to face the rending trial of the more and the less, the full and the empty, surplus and lack, accumulation and dispossession, eternity and passage—in sum, the finiteness and infinity that subtends all experience for the created being that is man. All the methods of existence imagined by humankind have to deal with this empirical contradiction that determines the possibility and nature of temporality. It is as if humankind were confronted explosively at

---

479. I am employing here a term and perspective already developed in *L'Intention d'amour, Désir et sexualité dans Les Maîtres de l'âme de R. Abraham ben David de Posquières* (Paris and Tel Aviv: Éditions de l'éclat, 2007). The term *part gardée*, translated variously as removed, preserved, or safeguarded portion, part, or share (pitted against Georges Bataille's *part maudite*, or "accursed share"), seems to me to correspond to the Hebrew *mishmeret*, which denotes guarding, keeping watch, the time of the watching as much as the preservation of something for a given time. "That a full *omer* [of manna] be safeguarded for your generations" (Exod. 16:32). The text specifies that the "*omer* is a tenth of an *efa*" (16:36). "All that remains, put aside to be safeguarded until morning" (16:23). The term also designates the guarded object. "The Levites safeguard the safeguard of the Abode of Testimony" (Num. 1:53). "Abraham heeded my voice, and he safeguarded the safeguard of my *mitzvot*" (Gen. 26:5). The term *shimurim* is also close. It is used to describe the night of Passover as "a night of watching."

the very root of its being[480] with the requirement of totality and, at the same
time, with the impossibility of this totality's finding expression all at once, in
full presence to itself. It is as if this powerful discharge[481] of the being (the
void), which unfurls in the world and which it constitutes by so doing, were
lashing out against the narrowness of a bottleneck, an imperious narrowness,
because it would be the sole way out, the sole problematic of manifestation
(and, effectively, it is the finiteness of the world that is at issue). In fact, it is
precisely because there is such narrowness that the discharge of being that
produces the void occurs. The world's finiteness is governed by the nature of
retreat, because retreat is necessarily creative. The creature is the emergence
of the finite in the infinite. In other words, it is as if the very essence of
omnipresence were affected by a strong coefficient of absence and unclasping.

The Drama of Absence

How can we manage this absence in presence, narrowness in magnitude, and
din in *rahamim*? How can we bear the fact that God's only possible presence
to us is in absence? How can we endure the withholding and waiting in the
process of being, tolerate the multiple when the one is at stake, and bear the
other when our soul is being born? What is at stake at this moment is the
advent of the particular, the particularization of the one out of the whole, but
through all the multiplicity to which the all gives way when it is transpierced
and dismantled by the germination of the one. The human being, arising in
a place of abruptly deserted omnipresence, is intrinsically marked, worked,
and filled by absence in presence, by narrowness imbued with the memory
of presence, and by the voiding at the core of plenitude. It is because he
then creates a place, a *makom*, that this tension, this contradiction, occurs.
The whole reality of the place is the product of a relationship in the form
of a hiatus and a difference in level. Withdrawal is at once the reversion of
infinity and the emergence of the finite. The place stretches to the very brink,
in the contiguity of the finite and the infinite. It is the edge of the reversive
movement of being. This is why it becomes the site of a very strong tension,
drawn to the call of infinity and yet thrown back to the finite, to the horizon
line. The horizon is the principle of the place. In the very midst of fullness,

---

480. Defined as omnipresence.
481. In the sense of an explosion of power, an unloading, an emptying.

there is a tugging lack and absence.[482] And this lack echoes and attests to the emptiness that exists in the apparent fullness of the world. It is a sign that the world is in passage, that it is still in incompleteness. In a word, it attests to the one that is pending in the *olam* and beyond the world, and it notifies us that the one cannot yet dwell in this world (which would thereby recede into the all), that completeness can only be forthcoming.

Thus, the drama and anxiety of emptiness and lack bear the trace of hope and satisfaction. Emptiness calls not for fullness but for completion. Its relationship to the latter is one of testimony (*edut*), of activating an overplus (*od*) in the world of *olam*. The *olam* by its nature arouses this need. The lack, or rather the disappearance that is the world, is an overplus for God's being, a setting aside into augment. There are two points of view here. For creatures, the world is removal (of God but also in itself). For the creator, it is an addition (after all, there can be no removal from God).[483] We have here a classic paradigm of the system of the safeguarded portion (the removal amounts to an addition; the emptiness is in fact overplus).

Contrary to what Naomi says in her ignorance of the safeguarded portion, "I went away full, and YHWH brought me back empty" (Ruth 1:21), human beings actually start out empty (ignoring the fact that they come from fullness) and return full. We have a beautiful illustration of this subtracting addition in the way Eve is added to Adam by subtraction (the removal of his side). The subtraction makes the appearance of the other possible and harbors not lack but fullness, the other as overplus. There is something of a fullness that subsists in this lack, and its tip even emerges from the void. This is the remnant, the remainder, the *yeter*, or overplus, in the manner of the eternal witness: "The children of Israel have abandoned your covenant and have destroyed your altars; they have killed your prophet with swords, and I have remained (*yivater*) by myself" (I Kings 19:14). Israel is witness to absence and presence.

This paradox invites us to query the notions of full and empty and rethink their meaning. The existence of testimony indicates that the void is not hopelessly empty, that the secret "more" is fermenting in its depths and spreading bounty (*shefa*). But testimony must exist to sustain the possibility of "fullness" in times of emptiness and in spite of it, and the testimony must

482. Note that accumulation and concentration are irresistibly drawn to dispersion and disintegration. In any rise of the being, the fall is forthcoming. Appearance has difficulty maintaining itself for long in the passage.

483. But neither can there be an addition, which is why the overplus is always simultaneously a removal.

be recognized and assumed as such. This is the vocation of human beings upon which the reality of emptiness and fullness depends. There is also an "economy" of being that characterizes the safeguarded portion in all the strategies of temporality (testimony, oath, promise, and so forth) implemented in the Hebraic *polis* to sustain presence. This economy reverses the principle of scarcity, the structuring principle of all aggregates, into a principle of bounty, albeit withheld, impending, promised. "I am dark and beautiful, daughters of Jerusalem" (Song 1:5). The suspension is like a means of taking charge of the manifestation of overabundance, destined in the passage to sink into nothingness.

The cardinal task of the biblical character consists precisely in finding the key to testimony. Job bemoaning the annihilation of his possessions, Kohelet proclaiming the emptiness of possessions, and Joseph disappearing are so many figures of human beings striving to find the key that controls the preservation of bounty and presence in the passing time that ineluctably erodes it. If man is the criterion of effectuation of emptiness and fullness, there can be neither emptiness in itself nor fullness in itself. They are the movement constitutive of man. Emptiness can be grasped best through lack, which is the immediate experience thereof. This brings us to reconsider the void and the frightening experience of it that is lack. Lack (*hisaron*) is also a subtraction.[484] It is interesting to note that subtraction yields a "remainder" and addition a "total." But this lack is also a defect, a deficiency. And *hisaron* is close to *hisachon*, the profit that results from reducing expenditures, what is saved by a condensation (*tzimtzum*) of the "outflow" of money. This is a principle of interiority and suspension. Abstention bears differed fruit. In the additional meal benedictions,[485] God is blessed as the "creator of many souls (*nefashot*) and their lacks." This lack is understood as being that of *nefashot* that have not yet been created and that are opportunities of resurrection for *nefashot* that have died. The creation of the multiple and of lack is thereby described as a blessing. The lack is presented as a chance for life, beyond death, a promise of presence beyond the dereliction inherent in the lack. Lack exists only because the multiplicity that exists cannot be totally embraced, since we are no longer in the all. The lack harbors nothingness, but it also carries the potentiality of *tikkun*. That is the purpose of testimony, which grasps the

484. In Hebrew, one "lacks," for example, six out of nine, which leaves three. The *mehasser* is the number that is subtracted, taken away.

485. Tosefta Berachot 4:14 and Mishna Avot 6.

lack in the fabric of fullness. *Tikkun* adds, but this addition does not fill in; instead, it creates emptiness, which enables the lack to depart from itself.

Emptiness is not destined to be filled, for filling it would amount to recreating the all. Being is passage, so the one is impending in emptiness. That "all the streams flow to the sea, and the sea is not full" (Eccles. 1:7) indicates that filling and accumulation can never be absolute. For the streams to keep flowing, there has to be a release and a letting go. Repairing the world is to be understood not in terms of "production," that is to say, of a process of rendering visible and apparent what is hidden and absent, but rather in terms of concealment. The concealment may seem to involve a removal, and, indeed, from the point of view of subtraction, there seems to be a lack. But concealment, in fact, safeguards that which has seemingly been taken away. This means that it actually produces overplus. This augment is hidden. That it is hidden is exactly what makes it an augment; otherwise, it would be caught in the deactivation and erosion of passage, where there is no surplus. The surplus is a "secretion" of concealment. It is not canceled by concealment, as one might think; concealment constitutes it. Immediate consciousness (prey to the illusion of primal fullness), then, sees loss and gift giving when, in truth, there is augment and wealth, but solely in the order of concealment and secrecy.

We have here another figure of the overlapping of finite and infinite. Concealment is a factor of infinitization in the finite world, where, everything being identical to itself (which is a mistaken, perverted perception of emptiness), there can be no surplus. For rational thought, it is truly remarkable that this process of infinitization is accomplished by way of an apportioning of the world/*olam*, a giving of a part, and a particularization in the possession. We see that infinity is the opposite of the all (the latter consists in gathering together that which, in the absence of the one, it illusorily takes to be its parts under the artificial unity of representation).[486] Hence, the concealment is logically the locus of bounty and plenitude, because it is a process of infinitization, and infinity is limitless. The portion hidden in concealment is the ultimate limit experience, that of finiteness, which, as we see, belongs to the visible world. It is the portion removed from the visible world, set aside in hiding where darkness and silence are factors of infinitization, of

486. In the paradigm of the safeguarded portion we have the very pattern of the origin of the world. There is no anteriority and preexistence of the world for us, as we are of concealment and disappearance. To the contrary, the concealment is what makes the world. In other words, the safeguarded portion is the vector of the world. This is why it is meaningless to debate the anteriority of the world.

erasing limits and boundaries. Indeed, isn't the place where the portion is offered in the Temple near the infinite, hidden divine presence? The giving of the portion paradoxically materializes infinity in the finite world. And as such, it is not easy.

The safeguarded portion is a real, withheld portion, removed from the *nefesh*'s vital power, and not a consecration of useless, superfluous elements. The giving of the portion is not a gratuitous luxury. It empties an absence in the *nefesh*. This ordeal is what is most important. There is no swapping, no saving, and no capitalizing. The safeguarded portion reverses the apparent order of the world, the derelict order of passage, by switching it from a principle of scarcity to one of bounty. Isn't this precisely the definition of blessing? Isn't this the *tikkun* of the passage? The safeguarded portion thwarts the lack that spontaneously invades emptiness. How paradoxical! It fights against the lack by a giving, that is, by another lack, and not by a fullness, like representation. In sum, it restores the truth and former dignity of emptiness prior to its inherent decline; it recovers the emptiness before it breaks down into nothingness. In its midst (*kerev*), the indwelling of the Name takes place: "My Name is in its *kerev*" (Exod. 23:30), and in its midst, "there is a place with me" (33:17) in secrecy. Concealment is that which in our innermost selves escapes our grasp, the portion of ourselves that we do not own, that is not our property, but, contrary to what one might think, is a place of abundance, not deprivation, because this is where something greater than ourselves arises.[487]

Liberation

The concealment of separation (which differs completely from the concealment of magic) is the prerogative of human beings, the culmination of the safeguarded portion. It is the supreme act of *tikkun*: not so much sacralizing and spiritualizing the object as freeing the obstructed passage, releasing the *nefesh*. In concealment, human beings "remake their *nefesh*" (they do *kappara*

---

487. Anthropological studies refer to the notion of the potential of estrangement hidden in the core of human beings (variously called "mana," "numen," the "sacred," and so on). Psychoanalysis sees it as the "unconscious." This "potential" that harbors concealment results, to be sure, from human deeds when the concealment is brought about truthfully, but it can also be manifested in savagery, for there is concealment in the being since the world was created. In principle, concealment does not pertain to the imaginary or the symbolic. It is at the very foundation of reality that is reality, of emptiness, the middle of all things, gathering inside as modalities at once materiality and nothingness.

for their *nefesh*, Exod. 30:15–16) by amending the absence that constitutes them. They remove it from the exteriority where it was doomed to petrifaction. This is the meaning of *kappara*, which designates the act of redeeming or expiating a sin but which actually denotes more precisely "covering." The relationship is understandable because the sin uncovers the concealment and disrupts it. It exposes the *nefesh* in exteriority and dooms it to nothingness.

Kappara is always nominal, confirmation of the name of each individual *nefesh* (which is why the individual sacrificer must lay his hands on the *korban*), particularization in the midst of oblivion, and hence memory (for there can be no memory without names in particular).[488] And the act of *kappara* is the *korban*, the setting aside of a portion of the whole. Concealment always involves separation/sanctification. *Pidiyon*, redemption, is akin to *pedut*, which also designates separation,[489] in the sense of differentiation: "I will put a separation between my people and your people" (8:19). Its purpose is to enable the world of disappearance to continue on its way to accomplishment. It is a repetition on the human level of the divine creational gesture. This repetition is not a substitution, for passage is not a never-ending exchange. The aim of concealment is, to the contrary, to enable singularity, particularization, and oneness to dawn. It is precisely in the passage that interpersonal relationships develop (economic exchange, sexual intercourse, power rivalry, relationship to the divine), and that is where there is an eternal temptation to forget names, and where names must be transmitted, not for selfish purposes but because they are vehicles of the one.

---

488. Witness the institution of *kappara* in Israel: "I will take the Levites instead of/under every firstborn among the children of Israel. I will give the Levites given to Aaron and his sons from the interior (*toch*) of the children of Israel… to make *kappara* for the children of Israel, and there will be no plague among the children of Israel when they approach the holy/separation" (Num. 8:18–19).

489. Cf. supra. The term is used in a financial context for exchanging cash for an object, a debt, or a prisoner. The payment in this case is an act of liberating something arrested and petrified. Another term for payment, *shalem*, also means completion (in the sense of passage) more than exchange. Payment is therefore a matter not so much of dependence as of freedom, of putting into passage, of *olamization*. The question that arises is why things and beings are petrified and objectified. Sin takes the *nefesh* out of itself, as we have seen. There is also a situation, inherent in the relationship of economic production, which has to do with the production of objects and hence the status of objects we "find" in the world. Take a look at the relationships between economic production and morality. Here we are dealing with the same universe. The status of the object in the relation of production must be examined, the object as prism of visibility, exposure, and exteriority, since the "object" is not a self-explanatory entity. Why are there objects in the *olam*? This question is the starting point of this study.

This is why the giving of a safeguarded portion is not comparable to paying a debt, because the debt is bound up with the past. The debt haunts the flight of presence and shackles it to the past. The debt puts the present into the framework of the all and ineluctably produces representation, because it undertakes to perpetuate the all in the passage. The safeguarded portion, on the other hand, is in the realm of remembrance, because it is the remembrance of the all that is dismembered in the procession of the one, the unfolding of the world. Oath and waiting and promise, not debt, sustain remembrance. Remembrance is the actor of the one; debt reactivates the all. Remembrance is the effectuation of the gratuitous (*rahamim*). "I remembered you, the youthful compassion (*hesed*), your betrothal love" (Jer. 2:3). Debt is an obligation. Whereas remembrance is the path of becoming, debt rivets human beings to their origin. In debt, the origin is manifest and exerts its power. Remembrance exists only insofar as the origin has receded. Remembrance can manifest itself only in the *olam*. The debt is a mockery of it in the will to power. Thus, disappearance is the context of remembrance, the manifestation of bounty, of overplus in withdrawal. Memory is governed by abundance, while debt is modeled on scarcity. The bounty (*shefa*) that emerges from this problematic is greater than the filling of a lack, for it carries with it both the retreat and the overplus. "Scarcity" is a misinterpretation of bounty, an optical illusion. Bounty is animated by emptiness. This is what makes it mobile and infinite. The more it gives, the less it loses. The wellspring of a limitless bounty is hidden in the world, and from it human beings can always draw sustenance. This explains why passage does not engender undifferentiated exchange ad infinitum but can carry, without disintegrating, the multiplicity of ones and particular individuals on their way to the one.

Three Movements

If we endeavor to systematically summarize the process of the safeguarded portion, we can distinguish three main movements. Its starting point is clearly a revolution in consciousness that leads to a loss of illusions about fullness, about the origin as plenitude, and a discovery of the pertinence of withdrawal, of what makes it overplus at bottom and not lack. The practice of retreat, in its modality of the safeguarded portion, thus emerges as a pedagogy in understanding the *olam*. Its aim runs counter to the aim of illusory plenitude. Its purpose is not to produce lack, but rather to lead to "fullness." It is because there is no fullness at the start that there can be lack.

This withdrawal is a concealing that manifests absence but houses overplus, a lesson about an emptiness that would harbor augment, not lack. This is the second movement in the process. The emptiness is revealed and assumed. It is no longer the occasion of a devouring and engulfing that has to be continually filled to repletion, but rather a process of journeying across the *olam*, that is to say, of reversing retreat into augment, so as to clarify reality no longer by retreat (through which it is grasped immediately) but by augment.

Finally, the third movement attains completeness, the apotheosis of and in emptiness. This process gathers together a great many perspectives and crystallizes the wisdom of the world that teaches human beings the way to live in the *olam*. The Five Scrolls[490] provide this wisdom with its most secret lights. That is why we can see in it the prospective of Marcel Mauss' conception of a "total social fact," an organizing principle of a society's institutions and sphere, including its political and economic aspects.[491] This is what we have already shown with regard to the basic institutions of Hebraic society. We have here a different explanatory problematic of the sacred and of holiness in its authentic modality. It is apparent, in this respect, that the augment in concealment is the mobile principle underlying what ethnologists call the "sacred." This is why the process of the safeguarded portion has direct implications for the analysis of the life of the *nefesh* and temporality.

A Hermeneutic

Lastly, the theory of the safeguarded portion offers a hermeneutic theory of the biblical text. We have shown in principle how the Torah is the divine withdrawal, the locus of human beings. This gives us, in practice, a mode of investigation and analysis of the Bible. We can see it at work as much in the content of the text as in its structure. Insofar as content is concerned, we have shown the extent to which this is the case in the Five Scrolls, but we could do as much for any other biblical text, narrative or legal. Concerning legal aspects, we have seen the pertinence of the prism of the safeguarded portion in the analysis of the *korban*, which is the principle of all rituality and all *mitzvot*, and in the analysis of ritual and festival temporality (the cycle

490. See above, Book I, ch. 2, "Passage."

491. In fact, a whole approach to living organisms emerges in the theory of the safeguarded portion. Its processes structure it, and everything in it tends toward concealment, an essential condition for continuity in an *olam* overcome by objectification, a concealment that sometimes finds expression in brutal, uncontrolled forms: property, for example, is a misguided form of concealment.

of the year). Concerning the narrative aspects, if we consider the degree to which the biblical narrative is the story of a peregrination, an individual or collective passage, of a trial that involves dispossession and recognizing the truth, we can see the effectiveness of the prism of the safeguarded portion, which is this very journey in the *olam*. The stories of the binding of Isaac, Abraham's migration, and the exodus from Egypt are all major manifestations of this. But on an even deeper level, we can decipher the effect of the safeguarded portion in the structure of the biblical text itself, each sequence of which takes the form of a chiasmus, a form of opposition, with two parallel movements' opposing one another by the summit, whereby the second picks up, "repeats," and accomplishes the first.

This is the idea of the *Mishneh Torah*, the "repetition of the Torah" that is the act of studying, and this "repetition," as we have seen, is the very meaning of *tikkun*: dispossession, revelation—trial and reprise. The median movement is obviously that of remembrance and oath, the moment of reversal of the retreat, of the passage of the *olam*. The consummate paradigm is no doubt the binding of Isaac (Gen. 22). The moment in verse 7 of "Here I am" is the summit, not only of the literary text but also of its signification, because Abraham in this trial has to bear witness to presence even though it seems to have irremediably vanished with the injunction to sacrifice his son ordered by the compassionate God of Abraham.[492] The Babel narrative (11) provides another significant paradigm in this regard. The summit of the reversal is found in verses 5–7 ("Yhwh went down to see the city and the

---

492. If we examine the literary structure itself of the "binding of Isaac" narrative, we can see the paradigm of the safeguarded portion at work again. "Here I am" (verses 1, 7, and 11) and "together" (verses 6, 8, and 19) appear as leitmotifs. These thematic devices are related to presence, because the purpose of the trial on Moriah is to reveal the son to the father, to make the relationship between the two possible, in terms not of Oedipal murder but of presence. The *korban* gesture that begins to emerge enables the *kerev* between father and son. Two inverted stories structure the text: the problematical rise to the sacrifice and its preparation, and the "descent," the avoidance of sacrifice and the "substitution" of the ram for the son, as an initial step toward the future *korban*, to be accomplished by human beings. Between Abraham's "Here I am" in verse 1 and "[they stood up and departed] together" in verse 19, the whole journey of the *korban* takes place, which is structurally the vehicle of the story's unfolding. This movement of withdrawal and that of augment are inverted into one another by the dialogue at the summit of Moriah, where the "Here I am" in verse 7, the presence to the self and to the other, confronts the "together" in verses 6 and 8, in Hebrew, *yahdav*, literally "the unity to him."

tower... 'Let us go down'), and immediately the work of Babel described in the first part finds itself reversed.[493]

There is a logic of novel significance at work with the safeguarded portion, in which the unfolding of the subject goes down untrodden paths. The fact that the origin of the being's unfolding is in the retreat calls for a movement in which "going beyond" is irrelevant, because there can be a beyond only when there is primordially a limit, a set count, a subject of affirmation. But the subject is not at the origin, and what is at the culmination is greater than the subject. To start from emptiness is to bypass the phase of objectification and alienation. Contrary to dialectical logic, in the safeguarded portion, it is concealment that causes objectification. Hegelian logic situates the articulation of the relationship between master and slave in concealment, when in fact there is freedom in it, not bondage. Thus, it is clear why all the Hebraic political and economic strategies are related to the moment of concealment (*shemita*, the sabbatical year). The removal of the object from visibility radically alters the relationship of subjects. The "augret" system is not dialectical, because the retreat does not eliminate. It garners positivity. There is negativity solely from the standpoint of lack, and it is a mistaken impression. The principle of effectuation here is the separation (*keddusha*), a separation that ultimately governs overplus, not loss. In this way, the giving of the *korban* is not a negation of the subject's self, an objectification in exteriority, a fulfilling of a debt. To the contrary, it is a reversion of the original emptiness which does not fall into the trap of a fullness that can never be filled, because one is in the passage. The passage moves not toward the eradication of the one and the particular via their negativization but rather toward the one via particularization. Consequently, concealment is nomination and particularization, completeness in the one. Then the subject is announced, but the concealment and unclasping that subtends it institutes the subject, not in the sovereignty of a will to power and the universal of domination but in the kinship of the Name, whose concealment is the great act of creation.

---

493. Applying the theory of the safeguarded portion to the areas we are analyzing here requires support from more detailed demonstrations, which we hope to undertake in the future.

CHAPTER 2

God's Concealment: The Passage of the One in His Attributes

ALL OF THE PROBLEMATICS of the safeguarded portion have a single paradigm, and that is the great gesture of creation. *Tikkun* itself is but an imitation of the act of divine concealment from which the world emerges, its replication in creation, which elevates the world to the level of divine freedom by replacing it in the procession of the one.

In creation,[494] the appearance of the world is divine withdrawal, the outpouring of emptiness in being, but what the creator withdraws from being, what he gives of himself, is set aside in augment, in secrecy in the *olam*. From the divine perspective, this movement corresponds to a different configuration. What, for the world, is divine withdrawal (the place of origin from which everything emerges) corresponds, in God, to divine plenitude. In withdrawing, God does not become "smaller." His withdrawal is infinitization in relation to the finite, which is delimited in its emergence in the midst of the void. God puts himself in augment to the world, in secrecy, in concealment. Isn't this the very purpose of the problematic of "augret"? Corresponding to the retreat, at the same time and for the same being, is an augment.

We can thus discern two levels in the great act of creational retreat: the immediate, human level and the deeper, divine level. That we can move, in reversal, from one level to the other draws our attention to the fact that

---

494. Our perspective gives us new insight into the debate about the eternity of the world or creation *ex nihilo*. From God's standpoint, the world is created *ex nihilo*, but because this creation results from the concealment of part of the being, man in the world, one could think that the void of the *olam* is preceded by something, namely, the safeguarded portion. There is then an element of truth in the idea of the world's eternity, but it is only an optical illusion. The real issue is altogether different. And it is so in the terms themselves, because if the world is disappearance/*olam*, the question of the anteriority of the world, the anteriority of a disappearance, the anteriority of an absence, does not arise. This absence is the very locus of time! On the other hand, if the world is disappearance, and God prefigures the world, God is in presence. The safeguarded portion enables us to rethink the question of origin in other terms.

one element of the relationship plays a dual role. This element is the human being, who is at once in the void of divine retreat that founds creation and in the augment where divine infinity outpours in the bounty of the one by withdrawing and voiding itself. If man is born from the withdrawal, he is also called upon to seek the one and undertake concealment. God's withdrawal is also by the same token the setting aside in augment that man is called upon to undertake in order to escape the dereliction of the passage with which he is ineluctably threatened. In sum, the setting aside in concealment of man must strive to join up with God's concealment.[495] Thus, God is taken out of his retreat, the world of his absence, and the one is known and implemented by the human. It is at the intersection of these two movements (divine and human) of the safeguarded portion that the vocation of *tikkun* is situated, which appears thereby as inhering in man, as the central architect of the *tikkun* of the divine Name, of God the creator, architect of his unification, of the passage of the one across the void.[496]

This intersecting movement of *tikkun* rests entirely on the fact that the human being is simultaneously in retreat and in augment. So we can see why the divine attributes, the outpouring of divine powers shining forth from the *toch*, are basically anthropomorphic in nature and could not be otherwise. Human beings are at the core of the safeguarded portion. In the project of creation, the human being is set aside in hiding, in the one. It is in this sense that human beings are created in God's *tzelem*. Humankind is constituted by withdrawal, but by vocation it is in concealment.

495. It is the human being who joins up with God, not vice versa. An illustration of this conceptual model can be found in the story of Joseph. As we have seen, whereas Joseph exemplifies augment and the positive, Levi represents withdrawal and the negative. In hiding, Joseph/augment leaves a secondary positivity in retreat (negativity), an echo of augment that must be brought back to him in Egypt (that is, in the negative), reunited with Joseph-in-the negative to bring the story and peregrinations of his *nefesh* to completion. The human being is in Benjamin's situation, and Joseph is in God's. In withdrawing, God leaves human beings who must then turn to him, provided they know how to give (Benjamin to Joseph). After all, isn't God's dwelling on Benjamin's territory? In this way, the attribute has to be brought back to and reunited with its augment, and God's presence brought back to the one to be "repaired."

496. The terms of the daily liturgy are significant: "his weightiness/honor fills the void (*olam*). 'Where is the place of his weightiness to praise him?' his servants say." The place where God becomes weightier, where he gathers the augment of the being, is hidden, so it cannot be "found." This is why the blessing can be accomplished only from this place: "Blessed be God's weightiness from his place," "from this place [where] he makes himself face [and hence absence, spark of presence] by wombing mercy for his people, who unify his separated Name, evening and morning," that is to say, in absence and in presence.

The Signification of the Attributes

Setting aside the one in concealment is what makes the passage and, as we have seen, what gives rise to multiplicity. But the hidden one continues to shine forth, which makes the passing ceaseless. The one shines in the void and makes the many increase. What shines in the passage, and is the passage, are the divine attributes, by which we describe the countless powers of the creator in his sovereignty. The one seems to communicate to those in the void via terms of multiplicity.[497] How could it be otherwise, since the one is in concealment? The attribute exists only because God withdrew into concealment. And the attributes are necessarily anthropomorphic, because the human being is God's withholding, his safeguarded portion, his gift: the human being is the way of his unity. Indeed, the one can emerge and be announced only because the all was shattered in the creation of humankind. The portion removed forever from the all opens the way to the one. God is one, not for himself but for human beings, because he created man, outside the all. Nevertheless, this unity is what comes closest to the innermost truth of the divine being, outside its relationship to the being of man—the divine being that we, as creatures riveted to the process of creation, cannot know. The attributes are like the procession of the one traversing the passage, and, like the passage itself, they have no substance save by and for the one.

The principle of attributes is therefore a principle of particularization of the divine to the extent that the safeguarded portion is the choosing of a portion of the one out of the all. If God is inside, as is the principle of humankind, then this divine particularization—that is, the creation of human beings—is also a *part*-icipation of the divine in the attributes that designate human beings (anthropomorphisms). However, this particularization of God in the form of an attribute is to be understood in terms of *tikkun* and concealment, as pertaining to the hidden augment behind the withdrawal (of/ in God) that it represents. This *tikkun* of attributes to which human beings are called is similar to the *tikkun* of the passage. The part(icularization) is withdrawn, in concealment. And this concealment is what makes the universal. The *hityahud*, the making-oneself-one[498] of the all, is not a disregarding of the rest; it is not a form of insularity. It is, to the contrary, the very path of

497. Whence the misguided understanding of human beings contemplating the passage and mistaking this multiplicity for the epiphany of God and, in this case, gods. This is the polytheistic stage.

498. See Trigano, *Forgotten Dwelling*, p. 384.

the universal. We have seen that the one engenders multiplicity by preserving and isolating itself in concealment. The problematic of the "augret" does not open onto a Maimonidean type of theology of negative attributes.[499] Retreat yields an entirely different relationship from negation. In it, the negative is harbored in the positive. It is neither agency nor mediator. Ultimately, it is the passiveness in creation, and the whole purpose of *tikkun* is to make the logic of the augment emerge from the retreat and, in this case, the logic of the one from the attributes.

How is the concealment of attributes effected? It is not a matter of "adding" to God, of adding in the withdrawal. It is not a matter of removing from an existing fullness. It is certainly not a matter of having recourse to the intercession of a representation or an icon. That would be a way of fleeing passage, of escaping the trial of the world, the trial of the undifferentiated on the path of the nomination of the one. If God is invisible, it is, of course, because he is in retreat but also in overplus to us, insofar as we are for him in a relationship of augment.

The discourse of attributes is of a piece with the reality of creation and the passage of the creator. It is bound up with their reality as with the reality of the world. The attribute is the name of creation, the measure of the inside with the outside. Contesting their validity or rejecting their trial amounts to denying the world's passage. As every presence in the world is presence for the body and for existence, divine presence in the world takes place in an attributive mode. Attributing to God qualities that are necessarily drawn from the field of creation, and hence pertain to the sphere of the human, does not "add" to his being, to infinity. It is rather this attributivity that pertains to infinity, inasmuch as infinity is this augment hidden in bounty, the reversion of an arena that is, by this very fact, the arena of the finite. Thus, in the setting aside of a safeguarded portion, the one is always preserved as testimony to the unity to come, which is why in Abraham's Covenant between the Pieces, the bird is not cut, it is concealed. Infinity can be measured against the finite without being diminished by it in any way. Infinity is close to it, as it is to "my dove in the cranny of a rock" (Song 2:14) or to Moses before God "in the cleft of the rock" (Exod. 33:22). Like a cave on the seacoast, which fills with water when the tide rises, yet the sea remains undiminished,[500] the Tent of Meeting is filled with the glory of God

499. Maimonides seeks the negation of absence (*shelilat haheʾader*) when it is a matter of voiding the illusion of presence, of concealment. To be sure, the augment is at work in both strategies, but this changes everything.

500. See Midrash Rabba, 46–47.

without the world's being diminished. But infinity exists for the finite only. Infinity stands on the finite just as the attributes stand on the one. To try to remove the anthropomorphisms from the attributes, as Jewish philosophy[501] does, is to try to remove God from presence, for it is the creation of human beings that makes presence for God and in the world.[502] It would be more to the point to work on their sanctification and passage, as is the case for everything that is of this world.

The "augret" in the divine is the very figure of creation. "There is no more (or empty of more: *ayin od*) if not him alone" (Deut. 4:35). The *ayin*, emptiness, and the *od*, overplus, characterize the one who is alone in his concealment. And this movement of being is powerfully evinced in the shimmering of the divine Names: "I will be who I will be." God says moreover (*od*) to Moses: "Thus shall you say to the children of Israel: the God of your fathers, the God of Abraham, the God of Isaac, and the God of Jacob, has sent me to you. This is my Name for the *olam*, and this is my memory from generation to generation" (Exod. 3:14–16).

From the outset, the divine Name is expressed in terms of *od*, surplus, and, logically, the Tetragrammaton is set forth as unpronounceable: "This is my Name for the world/disappearance," to the point that "my Name" is "my remembrance," which means that the revealment of his Name corresponds to his concealment, "from generation to generation," for this world of incessantly passing generations. This memory that God is for human beings also has an ambivalent role. The Tetragrammaton is like a sign for human beings to remember God, but it also reminds God of human beings. The Tetragrammaton exists only for man and creation. "I will meet with you there" can also be read as "I will make you an *eda/od* in name." We find here the crisscrossing movement of the two levels of the safeguarded portion, whose intersection is man. Thus, the revelation of this Name of a one God that is said in the future is followed by the mention of the remembrance of God for human beings: "Go and assemble (*asafta*) the elders of Israel, tell them... Yнwн, the God of Israel, has appeared to me to say, 'I have remembered (*pakod*) you'" (ibid.).

The name of overplus is for the void. In a way, the Tetragrammaton is like the sign of the "augret." The augment is in the four consonants, the

---

501. I am using this expression in the strict sense defined in *Forgotten Dwelling*.

502. Not in the Christian sense of incarnation, but in the sense of all humankind. We can see in this Christian dogma how the idea of the one, of augment and particularization, can drift far from its original logic.

withdrawal in the concealment of their vocalization.[503] Hence, there must also be a *tikkun* of the Tetragrammaton to release the forgotten voice in the consonants and turn the retreat into fullness. But there is also a whole problematic of divine Names: if YHWH is the hidden Name of God, Elohim is the manifested Name, the Name in retreat; the Tetragrammaton is the Name in the concealed augment, and hence it was pronounced only once a year, by the high priest in the Holy of Holies on Yom Kippur.

How this augment is communicated and what relationship it induces are central issues in the Hebraic perspective, as we have seen, especially through the prism of the problem raised by the attributes. Adding to God in withdrawal is idolatry, because doing so is a matter of representation. But adding in augment, in concealment, and hence, simultaneously, retreating in this world that, in the immediate, is taken for fullness, revealing the withdrawal to oneself, and revealing its reality to the world by putting it back in the passage—this is a matter of *tikkun*.

The Torah as the Attributes of Passage

When we speak of attributes, as when we speak of the world, we are referring to one and the same thing: the Torah. Indeed, the hiatus, the discrepancy in level, or the concealment that makes the world is the emergence of the Torah in God. "YHWH passed over his face, and he called/read (*vayikra*)" (Exod. 34:6). This reading (*mikra*) or spelling of words that is the creation of the world is the passing of the Torah in God. The Torah is the vehicle of passage (of the enunciation of the attributes, which is another name for the creation of the world). It is the safeguarded portion concealed in the creation of the world, the absence harboring infinite bounty that was revealed at Sinai to Abraham's family, because they managed to effect concealment: "my house with God is none other than the covenant of *olam* that he put for me" (II Sam. 23:5). The covenant of *olam* is the dwelling of man with God. It is "prepared for all things and kept" (ibid.), like what is kept with the safeguarded portion.

In a way, the Torah is "YHWH's house" (Gen. 23:17). God enunciates the Torah when he creates the world—that is to say, he sets it in augment, in

---

503. This is from a divine perspective, since for man the vowels are hidden and manifest themselves as a lack, while the consonants seem to appear.

concealment.[504] To formulate the Torah, God does not lose anything of his being. He puts it into augment, into profusion, but for the being thus created it seems that there is a loss for God or that the Torah comes before him. The Torah is in fact an internalization of God in the intention of creation. It is at once the very foundation of the world and the principle of its government. We could also say, from another viewpoint, that it is the Torah that is presence in God and constitutes his presence. The "tracks of the flock" that the Song of Songs enjoins the shepherd to follow are the letters of the Torah. They contain the very principle of the functioning of the universe and, a fortiori, of the collectivity. "For ever/*olam*, Yʜwʜ, your word subsists in heaven" (Ps. 119:89). This perpetual existence of the word in the void of heaven is the existence of the world in the void. God's word is for the passage (*le'olam*): "The word of our God will stand forever (*le'olam*)" (Isa. 40:8).

In sum, God's presence is not "perpetual" or essential insofar as God's being is concerned. If God's presence arises from concealment and augment, "presence" exists only for and in the world. In the unknowable divine being-for-itself, there is no presence, because there is no absence. This would explain why presence in this world is ungraspable, withheld, hidden. It has a specificity in an exclusive relationship to this world of creation, this world of emptiness, concealment, and disappearance. God is present only for our world, not for himself.

The notion of the safeguarded portion, the moment in the being that it represents, excludes any idea of mediation in the relationship of God and the world. The "safeguarded portion" is not a *logos* that would actuate the world. Its internalization opens other ways for this relationship. Already, it puts it in the framework and principle of interiority, whereas *logos* externalizes it. Already, it makes it a being of God-for-the-world and not an entity exterior to God, a "second God," Philo of Alexandria's *deuteros theos*. Already, it identifies it with the world itself, the *olam*, passage and disappearance, instead of making it the instrument in the formation of the world. God's attributes, or the Torah, are the world itself, the very "material" of the world that is passage and concealment. In absolute terms, there is no perfect paradigm of the world for which the world would be but the cast shadow. If there is a paradigm (the "augret"), the world is but an aspect thereof, as is the Torah, the word of God, which is for the world only, not for God. Understanding the intention of creation is, therefore, of fundamental import.

---

504. The midrashic idea that God created the Torah before the world is to be understood in this sense.

Oneness

This whole problematic, as we have seen, revolves around the principle of one-ness, the procession of the one in the passage that puts it in hiding. The only thing to be read in the Torah or in the attributes is the one in concealment.

Just as Joseph (removed and put into augment in what was to become for him Egyptian bounty) ultimately resurfaces different from himself for his brothers, the hidden portion undertakes for the all, which has been dismembered thereby, its movement toward the one. It is potential oneness. The Torah, or the attributes, or God in concealment are potentially one but not yet one.

This is why "unifying" the Name has meaning for Israel. The safeguarded portion potentializes the one in the passage. Remembering is remembering the one that, like the stranger, dwells in passage. For this reason any return, any re-pentance (*teshuva*), is a return to the one in oneself, a return because the one, even though it is at the heart of the self, is alien to it: the passage is a way to the new, a waiting for revelation. Everything in the passage, if put into hiding, moves to oneness: "everything goes to the place of the one" (Eccles. 3:20); "All the streams flow to the sea, and the sea is not full" (1:7), for the one is an infinite sea beyond the tally that bounty never inhabits. Indivisible, the one is infinite. It is always present, beyond relationships of equivalence and apportioning, which are measures of the finite. This bounty, which escapes exclusive localization, is the divine dwelling, the sign of divine presence, always in the one, although in all places at once and separately. God says to Moses, "I will be with you, and this is the sign for you that I sent you" (Exod. 3:12). Wherever Moses goes, YHWH will be with him. The one never departs from itself, and yet it gives rise to multiplicity. "See, this I found, said Koheleth, one by one to find the tally" (Eccles. 7:27). "Like a rose among thorns, so is my beloved among the girls" (Song 2:2). By the one, multiplicity is produced, and it is so one by one. There is never a mass merging under the one. "In the place where they will be told, 'You are not my people,' they will be told, 'Children of the Living God'" (Hos. 2:1). Access to oneness is access to a place that alters the very being of the one who enters it. One by one, the patriarchs mounted the path to the one, taking the first steps on the path to oneness, so their offspring benefit from a course in the passage that is already mapped out. This is what is called *zechut avot*, the merit of the fathers.[505]

505. It is written of Abraham, "to the place where he stood" (Gen. 19:27), of Isaac, "to go out in the field" (24:63), and of Jacob, "he 'banged' into the place" (28:11).

The announcement of the one is important for the passage, since it is because the one is in concealment that the concealment takes the passage out of it-(as-)self, out of weightiness. By the shimmering and radiance of the one, passage is redeemed from endless exile. By the power of the one, there is a return in the being and the world. If the passage and the withdrawal establish the foundation of the other and of creation, this does not mean that the latter are abandoned to eternal absence. The one is the promise lodged in the withdrawal. The return makes the other and creation as much as the retreat, exile, and the one. It is critical to always consider the one at the same time as withdrawal.

Thus, *nidda*, the "exile" of women's blood, is the safeguarded portion in the human being, the withdrawal, like the exile of the *nefesh*. But this exile that creates emptiness in the *nefesh* is drawn and governed by the one. This is why the woman is unapproachable at this time, and this retreat is inhabited by the potential of generation. This withdrawal, a setting aside in overplus of the one, is truly an overplus, since it opens onto the potential of the child.[506] "One is my dove, my perfect one, one is she for her mother, pure is she to the one who bore her" (Song 6:9).

Sanctification and Completion

The one, nonetheless, is separated from the passage, but it is firstly separated from the all. This is why access to it is governed by a process of sanctification/separation (*keddusha*). Paradoxically, this separation is not a dismembering or decomposition, as one might have thought, but to the contrary fulfillment and integration. By this we see that *shlemut*, or completeness, is a particularization, not a totalization. This astonishing quality of the one safeguards the other. It is love. Attempting to achieve completeness without particularization and without the one is a criminal endeavor. In this way, after Cain killed Abel and attained peace in his own world by eradicating the other, he "withdrew far from God's face." He withdrew far from the one, to be swallowed up once again by the anonymity of passage: "His face fell." In this sense, Israel establishes, as we see in the story of Jacob's crossing the Jordan, the "camp of the one," which, by passing before, becomes the main impetus of the "remaining camp" (Gen. 32:9). And it is with this camp of the

---

506. It will be up to the male to plot the path to *tikkun* in the tide of the "augret" carried by the female. This is why the sexual act is a *tikkun* of the woman but also of the child, for it is concealment, as we have explained.

one that Jacob hopes to practice concealment before his rival and brother, Esau. "I crossed this Jordan, and now I have become two camps" (32:11); "I will redeem (make *kappara*) his face by the camp that goes in front" (32:21). And it is there, in the "remaining camp" where he is, that Jacob will fight until "daybreak," until the moment when the night recedes, and his eyes can see the camp of the one on the other side of the river. The one is the locus of *yitron*, of *yeter*, of overplus. It is hence the place for the other: "if they fall, the one will raise his companion" (Eccles. 4:10). The one is always in companionship: "seated in the gardens, companions listen to your voice; let me hear!" (Song 8:13). It is love: "you have driven to my heart, my sister, my fiancée, you have driven to my heart with the one from your eyes" (4:9).

This is why the one is in perpetual motion, even though it has withdrawn from the passage, even though it arises from a distantiation in the being. In the one, being is hardly at rest. It concentrates, to the contrary, on an infinite action that draws the passage to its completion. It is therefore the very principle of all relationships in the passage. This is what makes the relationship between man and woman the perfect paradigm thereof, as the Song of Songs shows us so well. The "lovesickness" of the beloved woman is a yearning for the one by which she pursues her beloved while fleeing him, but this does not mean she does not meet him. "Come back, come back, O Shulammite, the complete one; come back, come back, and we will see you in vision, what will you see of the Shulammite, like the dances of two camps" (7:1). One necessarily stands in relation to the other. So the "two camps" (*mahanayim*) is a dual term, two in one.

The Name in the Passage

The concealment of the one in the passage establishes the name. We have seen that God has a name for human beings only and that his Name is pronounced only in the inwardness of the safeguarded portion. If the one opens a place, the sole place in the world in passage, this is because the one is the name. "I send you an angel before you to keep you on the path, to bring you to the place that I have made ready. Keep yourself from his face, and listen to his voice... for my Name is in his *kerev*" (Exod. 23:20–21). This angel is the guard and the face on the path of passage, and this safeguarded portion of God corresponds to the *makom* about which it is said that the name of God is in its *kerev*.

The ability to safeguard this place depends on the preservation of the safeguarded portion (covering the face and listening to the voice). This place is the Name of God, the Name in unity. As far as proximity (*kerev*) is concerned, the patriarchs gave a name to the place where they had successfully withstood a trial, where there was a consecration or a *korban*. Obviously, the name designated a relationship more than a locality, a relationship that is carried by the locality and that, for this reason, earns it a name. This procedure is preeminently manifested in the story of the fight with the angel that earns Jacob his name Israel. "Send me away, for dawn is breaking.... Jacob called the place Peniel, because 'I have seen God face to face (*panim*) and my soul has survived....' The sun shone on him when he passed Penuel" (Gen. 32:27–32). Peniel becomes Penuel, the *yod* (numerically ten)[507] becomes a *vav*, six, because six is the vehicle of passage, a day in the world's creation, the eve of Sabbath.

It is because the place is name that remembrance evokes and creates the place and that the place is its very throne of remembrance. In this sense, we can see why the patriarchs name the place where God revealed himself to them, insofar as this revives the remembrance of the creation of the world, of the concealment. The place of withdrawal is thereby inhabited by presence.

Remembrance is sanctification/separation in the undifferentiated. It is always an evocation of God and of the place that this induces, but because it crosses the passage and attends to the emergence of the one, it is the key to time and direction. Through the name, the place, and the one, human beings step out of lack, nothingness, and division, and enter *hibbur*, conjunction, association, companionship, because the one is dialogal. The quality of the place is to unite. Reaching this place is finding what was lost, healing the wounds of suffering, being at the heart of being, inside the one. The place is at the core of time's soul. The vision of place is freed from distance, time, corruption, from the bad separation of lack and violence but not from the separation of sanctification and the one. It opens an infinite expanse flowing with bounty, like a "land flowing with milk and honey." It is Moriah, the place where the Covenant between the Pieces and the binding of Isaac take place, a place that the Midrash describes according to the paradigm of the safeguarded portion: a "mountain in the shape of a valley," in the manner of "the anguish of the dawn on the mount of the valley" (Josh. 13:19). The *makom* is a wombing place where all the directions in the world are gathered together, which is why it cannot be counted. It is the place of the more and

507. Or the value of the tithe for Jacob's sons.

dazzlement of the crown jewels, a powerful echo of the one. There can be no promise for the future save in the place "given in heritage," the place of the fight to death against lack and semblance. Jacob is scared only at the place of completeness, where divine presence self-discloses, the very place of the land that is promised to him but from which he distances himself and on whose threshold he pronounces the oath of the tithe, of the safeguarded portion, at a time when he is in lack. In fact, this is the place where the lack is accomplished, where what was waiting in heritage is at last given. Only that which takes responsibility for the lack can one day enjoy completeness and bounty, provided that the poverty does not give rise to filling up, to the impatience of completion, embodied in representation. It is the one that prevails over scarcity by the strength of its unity. "There will be no poor in you, for YHWH will bless you in the place that YHWH, your God, gave you" (Deut. 15:4), and this is so because of the safeguarded portion, because of the concealment, "for the poor will not disappear from the *kerev* of the land, which is why I command you, saying: open up your hand to your brother, to the poor, to the destitute in your land" (15:11).

Awesome and frightening is the place of the one, because manifested in it is the womb of the powers of the world, whose bountiful torrent is nonetheless retained and withheld. This withholding is the retreat, and it is in the withholding of creational power that the world appears. The power is exercised there only in a sort of slow, majestic hovering of might. In this place, divine infinity and the world's finiteness intersect and adjoin each other. This is where they are close and converse. Here lack meets infinite bounty, and therein lies the terror for one and the other, each in its world. There is terror because each one awaits its inversion and discovers that it carries the other in its innermost core. The terror points to this limit experience, when one concentrates all one's might on surpassing oneself. But the terror can be read as a waiting, a promise that is as yet unaware that it is a promise and that will not be aware of this as long as the oath has not transsubstantiated it and the gesture of the being has not yet become a drama rather than a tragedy for those who have undertaken to set aside the safeguarded portion. Here is the door of the being that opens to the top and the bottom. Everything converges on this one place, the "balance" point of the safeguarded portion's double movement.

This is the place Jacob discovers upon awakening from his ladder dream: "YHWH was in this place, and I did not know!" (Gen. 28:16). The process of "augret" awakens this place, ever present in the creation of the world but in the creator's silent retreat, because it is through the "augret" that what is given and

removed is put into augment and into the profusion of the one. The passage of
the world has to be repaired and redeemed by concealment and by setting aside
the safeguarded portion, so in this place augment and blessing will shine forth.
Then, beyond the withholding and the night, the "gazelle of the dawn" springs
forth, leaping out of the lunar star, the first morning star, consummation of
the forgotten light from before the night, simultaneously remembrance of twilight and harbinger of noon, bringing together, pacified, the light in the one.

> In the asceticism of divesting and the narrowness of withdrawal
> In the passing of self and access to the face
> These words have come, stroke by stroke, to be added and hidden
> Under the wing of the one and its wise love
> May this gift make presence in absence
> May this dream regain Jerusalem.
> Blow the horn of its rebuilding!
> Come back, YHWH,[511] to its midst
> The world goes by, and I am waiting

17 Tammuz 5739

---

511. Pronounced *Hashem*, the Name.

BOOK IV

❧

SPLENDOR

CHAPTER 1

The Gazelle of the Dawn[512]

BEYOND THE FORMLESS ocean of night replete with exile, the whole of Israel's being comes together in the morning at the moment when dawn breaks in a twinkling, still uncertain thread of blue that beams the lights that had vanished with the dusk back into the being and attributes to each its place. Only in the morning, in the light of day, does the *makom* become manifest, the place where the one can unfold in each one, the particularization beyond the undifferentiated passage of night. This is why "Abraham awoke early in the morning" (Gen. 19:27) and Jacob woke from his dream at dawn (23:18). Similarly, Jacob wrestles with the angel until the moment at the "break of dawn" when he is called "Israel."

Now, what is dawn if not the first flickering of light piercing the kingdom of the night, an undreamed-of potential of the being that suddenly surges up and irremediably drives away the night by the strength of its unique light? The intensity of this light's brightness is equaled only by its particularization, its singularization in the ocean of the sky. However, particularized in the nocturnal universal, it heralds the diurnal universal. "Who is she who is viewed like the dawn?" (Song 6:10). To express this sight, the text uses the same term that describes the Temple windows as "*shakuf*," transparent-opaque (I Kings 6:4), narrow on the outside (singular, particularized) and wide on the inside (universal).[513] Such is the dawn: narrow outside by the faintness of its light in the sky, and wide inside by the power of all the light in the world, heralding the midday light.

Amid adversity and despair, the dawn is the principle of hope and blessing, embodying the power to turn a situation into another. To the hopeful, it is the main axis of the night, the fundamental intuition that governs the

---

512. *Ayelet Hashahar*, the title of Psalm 22. The psalm is attributed to Esther, the hidden one, who, according to tradition, wrote it before she presented herself uninvited before King Ahasuerus.

513. Like a reversed cellar window, built as if to allow the greater light inside to shine out.

nocturnal concealment and inspires those who are etiolating as night draws to an end to know that "God's appearance is as sure as daybreak" (Hos. 6:3). Dawn is the link in the chain of day and night, withdrawal and augment. Through it, night receives day and unites with it. It is the engagement ring, the wedding canopy of this union under the banner of the one. But once the union has been sealed, the dawn—avant-garde and keeper of the light of presence—fades into the day that rises from the bosom of the night.

I. MORNING STAR

This illuminating power of the one that defines Israel was conceptualized in Hebraic tradition in the figure of the "gazelle of the dawn," a figure both stellar and animal. This is the name that tradition gives to Venus, the morning star, the first to herald daybreak, in whose light Jacob, having vanquished the angel, became "Israel," a name created with the beginning of time that could join Jacob only at dawn, a name of augment for a person about whom Scripture says "a star will rise from" him (Num. 24:17). What other star could have better carried the migration of Israel in the constellation of the universe? It is not only the moment of light that it represents that gives it this vocation, but also its physical nature. Venus is a planet, so it shines not by its own light but because it is illuminated by the sun. It is the morning star but also the evening star, shining most brightly either at dawn or at dusk, in the twilight hours, as if it were the relay between the light of the sun and that of the moon, escorting the light through darkness from midday to midday. Moreover, Venus does not always appear in the same spot. When it appears at dusk, it is in the western sky, as if following the solar majesty. At dawn, it appears in the eastern sky, as an unexpected and surprising harbinger of the solar kingdom. Its being is characterized by the humbleness of dusk and the creative boldness of dawn (retreat and augment). Choosing the sun, at a time when it is setting and seems to be disappearing forever, forges the strength (*ayelet*, gazelle, is from a root that denotes strength) of the one (the dawn) that can herald the sun to the night as it chases the night away.

We can see the model of "augret" at work here again. Venus, the "gazelle of the dawn," is not self-illuminating, as we have noted. She receives light from one greater than herself, places herself under the aegis of presence, is not her own end. The one comes from elsewhere and is illuminated not by what comes before but by what comes "after" (the ram, *ayil*, in the thicket, hidden in augment,[514] which saved Isaac, is found "*ahar*," meaning after or behind), which discloses itself to the one, who, in withdrawal, makes the greatest effort to reach it. This is one reason for the strangeness (as for the paradoxical particularity) of the one. Dawn, the ram, and Israel are governed in the manner of Venus by the one and not by retreat. The retreat as such has no intrinsic purpose. It is predicated on the one (concealment). Dawn—like the ram—heralds the one that comes at noon, in the future. And its vocation is to pass on. Dawn lasts only a short while. It does not die, of course, but it vanishes when it rejoins one greater than itself, which it heralded through its strength and shining solitude. It unites with its deep-seated nature, from which it has been exiled by creational will. The ram "passes" into the sacrifice. It brings about Isaac's passing and the rapprochement of Abraham and Jacob, via Isaac. Note that the term for "ram" is the masculine *ayil*, which is close to *ayala*, gazelle (the male of which is *ayal*), and that all these terms derive from the root *ayal*, meaning strength.

The story of the binding of Isaac tells of the secret of dawn and its conception. It is because in the morning Abraham, whose being is in the morning, agreed to bind his future (Isaac), to withhold it, to let it pass (like the passing flicker of dawn giving way to the sun), that Jacob becomes possible and Israel's noon is set in motion. As soon as the binding is accomplished, night comes to an end, the ram appears in the light of day, and history moves on. Because the dawn agreed to be bound, its light appears. The dawn heralds the midday sun because it retains its being, sets aside a safeguarded portion, withholds its natural inclination to spread throughout the universe and set the sky ablaze. This is how it pierces the night. Only Isaac could have accepted this, not Esau, who knew nothing of withdrawal and who endeavored to colonize the sky. "'You who live in clefts of the rocks, who have settled on lofty heights... even if you established your aerie as high as the eagle's, even if you set it amidst the stars, I will cast you down from there,' said Yʜwʜ" (Obadiah 3–4).

Just as night (dusk is the suspension of light, the withdrawal of the light like a hidden portion in the dawn) was the necessary passage and condition for creation to take place, dawn is necessary for *tikkun* to take place. At both times, the gazelle/Venus is present in the sky. She is the very principle of the safeguarded portion, in its dark side as much as its bright side. Tradition has often seen the ram, the substitute for Isaac, as figuring *knesset Yisrael*, whose worthiness derives from the binding of Isaac. We find

514. What will save Isaac, trapped in a situation of scarcity, is the profusion of augment.

thus the typical ambivalence of "augret" in the morning star, here described as the very structure of the sky. "I sleep, my heart waketh" (Song 5:2). Its absence is a wakeful waiting, and it turns the blackness (*shahor*) of the night into dawn (*shahar*) and freedom (*shirur*), in the manner of the dark-haired one (*sheharhoret*) in the Song of Songs (1:5) who nevertheless shines with a great light of presence. The darkness of the night participates in the dawn, which is precisely a transubstantiation of darkness into light and in which, consequently, light is not yet steady.

It is significant that Israel is invested in the figure of the gazelle of the dawn and in Venus understood in these terms, while Greece is manifested in the night owl. The animal figure[515] of the gazelle is in fact a figure derived from the gazelle of the dawn, like the animal correspondence of the stellar principle: "its horns are spread here and there, like the dawn spreading here and there" (*Yalkut Shimoni* on Psalm 22). *Keren*, the horn (of the gazelle), also signifies the ray (of light). The *Zohar* describes the gazelle as the most compassionate (*rahmana*) of all animals.[516] Ever yearning to receive the waters of benediction—"like a ram yearning for streams of water, so my soul yearns for you, God" (Ps. 42:2)—she quenches the thirst of all the animals in the forest.

In accordance with the logic of "augret," this symbol of bounty and fullness (the augment) is underpinned by restraint and abstention. When it is morning, the gazelle retains the temptation within her to pour out all the lights she contains. While she feeds the animals, she also saves the midday light, puts it into hiding, and lets it come to be little by little. She nurtures others while restraining herself, and she feels satisfied by what she has fed them. "While it is still *night*,[517] she gets up to give food to her household and daily fare to her servants" (Prov. 31:15). Augment is therefore subtended by retreat. If there is still darkness in the dawn (though it heralds the light), it is because there is retreat in it, the extreme of retreat at the very moment when it vanishes into bounty. It is in this retreat that light rises (as it is written, she gets up in the still-night); it rises in the *od*, the surplus of the night, the withdrawal. This ambivalence of the gazelle is what makes her the herald and the architect of *tikkun*: this strength to make light rise in darkness, to

515. There is an ambivalence in this animality, because the term for animal, *haya*, also means "living." This is the term used by Ezekiel to describe the beings that carry the celestial chariot (ch.1), so the gazelle of the dawn also refers to an aeon in being, built on the logic of "augret" (in kabbalistic terms, this is the tree of the *sefirot*).

516. *Zohar* III, Pinhas 249a–b.

517. The emphasis is ours.

awaken the *od*, the "more" in the lack. Thus, all the animals in the forest gather (*kanes*) around her—in other words, they are interiorized through her when they moan for food and water. Then she leaves them to seek sustenance in very distant regions (a carrier of light, she braves the night), but she never forgets to return to where she started.[518] Faithfulness and memory are the cardinal attributes of this behavior. The gazelle's withdrawal, her departure into the distance, when all are gathered around her in her presence, speaks not of abandonment but of promise and memory. Having left during the famine in search of abundance, the gazelle will come back to stand amid the hungry and thirsty, to distribute portions to them, before and even without partaking herself. She is nurtured by nurturing others, thereby illustrating that the safeguarded portion, retreat, and withholding are not deprivations but rather the structure of satisfaction itself.

Pressed by the famished animals, the gazelle also implores God, moaning again and again in the hopes that God will hear her and redeem the world. Her voice moves God, and her leaping over the hills in search of food arouses his compassion. In addition to the stellar and animal aspects, there is an aquatic thrust to the "economy" of the gazelle. The animal yearns for streams of water, and the morning star appears at the same time as the morning dew, moisture from elsewhere that appears out of the blue and waters the plants. "From the womb, from the dawn, yours is the dawn of true birth" (Ps. 110:3). And let us not forget the connection between the movements of the ocean and the rotation of the moon, heralded at dusk and driven away at dawn by the gazelle of the dawn, the planet Venus. It is at the very depths of retreat and of the night, at the farthest point of its absence (at midnight), that the morning star, herald of light, the light from elsewhere and from the one (from the sun and from the moon), reaches the wellspring of blessings and resumes its ascent in the sky. Thus, it emerges from the night and approaches the sun to garner enough light to drive the night away at last. Having descended to the pit of being, it reemerges from its peaks. This is the moment of *tikkun*. Once the animals have had enough to eat, a voice, the voice of the one, calls out in the middle of the sky and assigns each and every one to its place. In the bright lights of the morning, the souls wandering in the night without shape or direction rediscover their place, the place where they were standing, without knowing it, in oblivion. "YHWH was in this place, and I did not know" (Gen. 28:16). And this voice

---

518. Quite the opposite of the extravagant, lascivious Greek and Roman Venus.

cries out: "Those who are near, gather to your places. Those who are far,[519] leave. Let each be added to the other in the place that is appropriate for it."[520] The gazelle is also portrayed as a parturient, in the manner of the dawn (Ps. 110:3), helping a woman who is about to give birth but cannot.[521] She writhes in pain, the "labor pains of the Messiah" that are associated with the pain of exile and absence. The baby is very near at hand but remains in its mother's womb. She has yet to give birth. In this way, the experience of gestation is an experience in "augret." The child is here but absent, within. Similarly, Israel carries the redemption of the world in its womb, but, cast into the world of passage and drifting, it has difficulty giving birth, spawning and manifesting the redeemed world. "As a pregnant woman about to give birth writhes and cries out in her agonies, so we have been because of you!" (Isa. 26:17). Herein lies the suffering of Israel, so close to presence and yet still dwelling in absence! This painful "delay" proceeds, of course, from the very nature of this conception, but also from the fact that the passage has deviated off course. The greater the deviation, the more it blocks the birth of this world. Suffering from this withheld abundance, from this bounty that is prevented from appearing, the gazelle moans and raises her voice, cry after cry, up to seventy cries (like the number of letters in "May YHWH answer you on the day of trouble," Ps. 20:2). In the state of suspension in which Israel "stands," the seventy nations are formed and manifested, as if born from Israel's exile, as the world was from God's exile.

When the gazelle comes to the end of the seventy cries,[522] God hears, remembers her, and helps her give birth. "The king will visit the gazelles by which he will be glorified and called the king of kings."[523] "God's voice causes gazelles to give birth" (Ps. 29:9). This voice pierces the membrane of the amnion holding the baby whose birth was delayed. From this birth, hastened by God,[524] a stream of fluid spreads all over the world, which then draws from this wellspring of blessing. That is when all creation cries out,

519. The term is *klipot*, literally, husks.

520. *Zohar* 3:249.

521. Her womb is "closed up (*nistam*)," the *Zohar* says, using a verb that also denotes hiding.

522. When all the nations have been constituted.

523. *Zohar* 1:114a–b.

524. That, according to the rabbis, may or may not be hastened, depending on whether Israel is worthy or not. Commenting on the verse "I, the Lord, will hasten it in its time" (Isa. 60:22), the rabbis say, "If they are worthy, [God] will hasten it; if not, [he will come] at the due time." Babylonian Talmud, Sanhedrin 98a.

"Blessed is YHWH in his place!" (Ezek. 3:12). The gazelle as parturient, as the "begetter" of the world, is not, however, summoned to disappear in the birth of the redeemed world. In fact, the absence and withdrawal lead not to nothingness but rather to the particularization of the one. As the light of the sun spreads, the gazelle, its steadfast architect, remains standing. Thus, it is said that even after having given birth, the gazelle's "womb remains narrow," giving her husband as much pleasure as on the occasion of their first union.[525] This tightening and narrowing bespeak to begin with the anxiety of retreat but also the particularity in the universal of retreat, the singularity of the inside in the outside, the paradoxical conjunction of the (narrow) particular and the universal (the matrix) in the creation of the world. The identification of Esther with the gazelle of the dawn[526] elucidates the gazelle's trajectory in her birth labors. Esther, the hidden one, saves her people (augment), who are doomed to sink into nothingness (the dereliction of the passage), sets aside her own destiny (withdrawal), and finds within the strength to venture into the innermost recesses of the forbidden palace so as to arouse the mercy of the king, which will ultimately save Israel. For this, Esther is likened to the dawn in the history of Israel. However, just as dawn marks the end of the night, Esther's story marks the end of all miracles, small flickerings of stars in the dark expanse of the night.

Once again, we can see the problematic of the "augret" at work in the book of Esther. Esther finds herself "cut off" from the Jewish people in a time of distress, lack, and impending disaster. She is hidden in the palace of the king, where, one by one, young women come before the throne, before the one, and where she musters the strength necessary to reach deep inside, helped by the retreat effected by all Israel through fasting, so as to establish the augment. Esther's withdrawal ensures the survival of all Israel, without causing her, the gazelle of the dawn, to disappear. After reaching, as a particular, the one, she comes back to bring redemption to all of Israel in exile, by giving birth to the future emperor Cyrus, who will grant the Jews the right to rebuild the Temple and return to the land of Israel.

It is interesting to follow in the book of Esther the meandering path of the gazelle of the dawn in the arena of concealment and to see the function of Haman, paradigm of evil, and, to a lesser degree, that of Mordechai.

---

525. Midrash *Yalkut Shimoni* on Psalm 22.

526. The feminine figure stands at dawn. Esther said three times, "My God, my God, why have you forsaken me?" because she had fulfilled the three feminine *mitzvot* (*nidda, halla,* and candles), and yet God had abandoned her.

It is Haman, in a way, who drives Esther into a corner; he is the power of evil that pushes the gazelle of the dawn to manifest herself, to reach deep down in order to come outside and appear in the celestial constellation of Israel. In the core of the palace, Esther garners the strength she needs to confront the king by composing Psalm 22. The psalm is structured on the problematic of "augret" and depicts the situations and states of mind that characterize withdrawal and absence. "Why have you abandoned me?" "Far from my salvation," "and you are holy/separated." We find in this psalm several expressions of reversal: "Do not go far from me, for trouble is near." In the abandonment and in the pain of absence inherent in the passage, the gazelle steps out of concealment and is exposed to view and divided under the eye of her enemies: "I will count all my bones, while they look at me... they will divide my clothes among themselves, casting lots for my garments." And here is one whose destiny is inside, in the vivifying unity of the *nefesh*. "Save my *nefesh* from the sword and my oneness from the dog's clutches." This invocation of the one reverses the passage, which shifts from suffering to a rise in the power of salvation. Such is Esther's capacity of reversal: "the opposite happened" (Esther 9:1). There is a swing between counting (*asaper*) her bones and recounting the divine Name, "proclaiming (*asapera*)" it "in the *toch* of the *kahal*." And this *tikkun* of the passage in the name of the one shows the "gazelle" that the concealment was not abandonment or oblivion: "for he did not scorn, he did not spurn, the plight of the poor; he did not hide his face from him, neither did he fail to hear him, when he beseeched him" (Ps. 22:25).

The vow is destined to be fulfilled, the promise to be kept. "My vows I will fulfill before those who fear him." And this conviction yields bounty and satiation. "The poor will eat and be satisfied, those who seek YHWH will praise him, their hearts will live for ever/for testimony" (Ps. 22:27).

This strength of credibility of the promise and the bounty that is born from the suspension underpin memory. In the passage, all is not destined to disappear, to "the noughts of the earth." From all ends of the world, scattered to the four winds, the lights of creation will come back to the foot of the divine throne and not sink into oblivion: "all the noughts of the earth will remember and return to YHWH" (Ps. 22:28). This return of presence is the promise made to the collectivity of Israel: "Of you, I will offer praise in a large *kahal* (Ps. 22:27). "For kingship is God's and he governs the nations" (22:29); "in the *toch* of the *kahal*, I will praise You" (22:27).

Thus, at the end of the dispersion and oblivion of exile, Israel will gather together, and, like the gazelle of the dawn, it will leave the night and herald the day, the return of power to Jacob, the resurrection of royal presence in its midst.

II. STAR OF JACOB

To apprehend Israel as the gazelle of the dawn, the cardinal morning star and evening shepherd, one must apprehend the sky in its scattered immensity filled with raining stars! "Count the stars if you can" (Gen. 15:5), says God to Abraham, who is trying to envision his offspring. He might as well try to take hold of a multitude of sheaves that he cannot get his arms around, or a nebula of planets, or a cosmos where everything is spinning like trails of stars! One rises, "a star rises from Jacob, looking for its way" (Num. 24:17), the other descends, whole patches of Israel's sky vanish into the darkness, new constellations take shape. Everything is in perpetual motion, in incessant evolution, swept into a changing, inextinguishable current where fixed points nonetheless appear now and again, like a peak emerging briefly out of a raging storm, or the crystal flicker of a planet appearing no sooner to be engulfed by the night, only to reappear to great amazement.[527] In Israel's passage, there is the passing of the world. The people of Israel resembles the cosmos. "Thus spoke YHWH, who created the sun for light by day, gave the moon and stars the mission to light the night, who stirs up the sea and makes the waves roar, he whose name is YHWH *Tzevaot*: 'If these laws cease being immutable before me... only then will the offspring of Israel cease to form a nation before me for all time" (Jer. 31:34–35).

The stellar symbols of Israel are echoed throughout the biblical text. From the outset, Israel is born not as a mass but as a stellar pattern of individuals having come together from the horizons of the sky to unite into a single system: Abraham, Isaac, and Jacob, like three stars, sure of their particularity and their unity in the same sky, which is suddenly given shape by their synergy. "All the horizons of the earth will remember and return to YHWH, and all the families of the nations will prostrate themselves before you" (Ps. 22:28). As soon as Jacob receives the name Israel, "the sun shone on him when he passed Penuel" (Gen. 32:32). Joseph himself has a star dream, a

---

527. This is what we learn from looking at the historic course of Israel, made up of the incessant rise and fall of centers all over the world, in the diaspora from Jerusalem. When one goes out, another lights up, and the history continues, migrating to another place on earth.

vision of his future relationship with his family: "I saw the sun, the moon, and eleven stars bowing down to me" (37:9). This is the dream that triggers the hatred of his brothers, who, unlike Joseph, do not understand the solar energy that empowers them.

Jacob's twelve sons, similarly, reproduce the pattern of the twelve zodiac signs, and the shifting total count, discussed above, only designates a problematical planet (one more? one less?): Venus, the gazelle of the dawn, the one founding the multiple but outside the confines of the multiple and not reckoned in any count. And doesn't David find himself granted a cosmic kingdom? "His line shall continue forever. His throne shall be before me as the sun, as the moon, he shall last eternally. The witness in the sky (shahak) is faithful" (Ps. 89:38).

An Israel compared to the stars is innumerable, as much by its unending number as by its individuality maintained while belonging to a constellation. Only the figure of the gazelle enables us to grasp the ungraspable and comprehend the coherence of the dense cloud of Israel.[528] Likewise, the sky is filled with stars but also with darkness, which is their setting, the figure of the void, emptiness, disappearance, and oblivion, which also exists in the being of Israel. Throughout its history, in each generation, there has been a hidden portion in Israel, an absent part of the Jewish world, potentially forthcoming, with stars shooting out of it from time to time, glowing brightly and then vanishing into the dark.[529] This hidden side of Israel is present in it from the start in the form of the erev rav, the great mixture or the great evening, which leaves with it from Egypt. Is this darkness a weakness on the brink of the cosmic abyss, or is it the very condition of the stars' luminescence?

So there are two modalities of being for Israel, diurnal and nocturnal, bright and hidden, eda and am. Light does not necessarily appear first in the world. The people of light, the eda, rises from behind the people of the evening, the am, whole sections of which disappear into the night. But it is the people of the evening that exposes itself to the light of the world, whereas the eda hides. It is out of this union of light and night at dawn that

528. We can see why Moses, too, is called "the gazelle of the dawn." It is on Moses that the swirling movement converges in which the people is formed. That "Moses penetrated the middle of the cloud" (Exod. 24:18) tells us something about Israel's nature, its gathering, and the meaning of leadership in Israel. The leader is like the center of the cloud, drawing down the lightning and thunder upon himself.

529. The "remainder of Israel," manifested Israel, aspires to join this part. This aspiration is exemplified by the ten lost tribes—lost at the time of the destruction of the kingdom of Israel (descended from Joseph) and its deportation to Babylonia. Ever since, all messianic hope in Israel aspires to rediscover these tribes, this hidden part.

the community of Israel is constituted in daylight by "his people, who unify his Name evening and morning" (liturgy). "You are all summoned today/for the day" (Deut. 4:26). From this assembly, Israel is constituted in the world when "dawn rises" (Gen. 32:27). "The Jews had light and joy" (Esther 8:16), when, in answer to Esther's summons, they gathered together in a *kahal*, "when the morning stars sang together, and all the children of God shouted for joy" (Job 38:7).

The contemplation of Israel thus involves a trial. Israel is the figure of passage, the face of unclasping, an absence that is not nonexistence but whose fleeting presence is continually being announced and fading. The trial consists in contemplating death on the basis of life, baring the thread of life in the fabric of death and oblivion, catching a glimpse of the light in concealment. Fully confronting passage, the passage of Israel enables us to see beyond the passage, to make the thread of the one shine "like the splendor of the firmament" (Dan. 12:3). Contemplation is more powerful than thought, because an expanse cannot be apprehended conceptually or reduced to an image or scheme. And yet it does not look like much, seen from the Earth, just some microscopic fragments of dim and distant lights, intermittent and far apart. How can we believe the "sky" exists beyond these particular, radiant individualities? It is the very image of the one, animated by the multiple and greater than the unit, that is manifested in this filled with stars, sky, which can gather only around the morning star gazelle, its shepherd.[530]

The logic of the safeguarded portion is also at work in the contemplation of Israel's stellar being, for only the principle of concealment maps an order in the formless, raging uproar of its being and discloses the hidden pivot around which the light of the nebula spins like a boundless vault. The safeguarded portion can be seen as the principle of the sky's star architecture. What would this safeguarded portion of the stars be? There is a concealment in the sky, a black hole from which light springs, the gazelle that lights up the day against the obscure, dark backdrop of the night.

We can see why light is a metaphor for being and especially for the one. Through the cycle of the stars, it relentlessly undergoes periods of eclipse, suspension, and return. Before our very eyes, each and every day that God makes, the entire gesture of the world's creation and of Israel is played out again and again. Firstly, it is the infinite gratuitousness of light and the world and the mercifulness of the return that are made visible. The seeming indifference of stars to human realities, their imperturbable cycle, their

---

530. [Venus is known in French as the *étoile du berger*, the shepherd's star. Trans. note.]

implacably cold dimension may simply be the most controlled figure of mercy and suspension of judgment. Being far from human beings, they are far from judging them! The sky has a king, the sun, but not really a center, for its infiniteness shatters it in a multitude of lights in all directions. The "rivalry" of the moon that presses forward behind the sun, receiving everything from it yet disappearing when it appears, shows the sun's grace in giving its light to beings unrestrainedly and ad infinitum.[531] And this giving is what makes its splendor and radiance, and yet within it is an obscurity of sorts, the shadow of self-concealment that makes the gift giving. This radiance, as we have seen, is the very principle of passage. Without light, the world is fixed, locked onto the Earth and motionless. It does not exist, if existence means rising out of the undifferentiated. Light is the vehicle of its passage. In the brightness of the sun, it is as if terrestrial bodies were being drawn upward, sucked up by the blue, pierced through and through by light. And doesn't the sun's motion make their profile, their abstract being, and their shadow move over the face of the Earth? Light is the medium of the world's passage, and night is one of its moments, the reason for its splendor, its glory (*kavod*), and its weightiness (*koved*), but also its brightness. Conceiving being in terms of light rather than mass or energies alters our understanding of the world. We find ourselves in a different mindscape, where things are conceived in terms not of obstacles, structures, immobilization and retention, narrowness and lack, but of passage. It is through this prism that we can understand the idea, for instance, that "his glory fills the world/his weight fills disappearance."

All the problematics in politics,[532] economics, linguistics, and so on can be formulated in these terms. The essence and basis of terrestrial reality is light. The different aspects of terrestrial reality—vegetal, mineral, water, animal, and human[533]—are the many, varied reflections of divine splendor. Born from the retreat, the very being of terrestrial reality is reflection, ray, release of light. When Moses found in his relationship to God the place (*makom*)

---

531. The sun seems intangible—"he named the sun and made light shine" (liturgy). On the other hand, the moon's shape changes, as if to show that the sun is greater and that the moon can wane. This is why it is written immediately afterward, "he saw and repaired (*hitkin*) the form of the moon." The moon therefore needs a *tikkun*. In this sense, we can see why it symbolizes Israel.

532. It's not land that is the founding principle of power, but light. Or, if land is so, this is solely because the light that gives shape to all things is there first! In the *Kuzari*, Yehuda Halevi defines the uniqueness of the land of Israel as the land "where the first light was created and then the sun."

533. The contours of the land that "stand in the way" of the light can be seen as the suspension, the retreat, the safeguarded portion of creational light.

reserved for human beings, "the skin on his face shone" (Exod. 34:35). In their completion and fulfillment, humans are beings of light and transparency, not opacity. Before eating the fruit in Eden, Adam and Eve had no skin, or they were covered in a sort of translucent skin like the flesh under our fingernails. Then "they knew they were naked. They sewed together fig leaves and made themselves loincloths" (Gen. 3:7). This clothing was the sign that human beings had become "opaque."

What are words themselves if not solidified rays of light? God says, "Let there be light," and there was light. Light is of a piece with the divine speech pronouncing the light. "The heavens shall be rolled up like a scroll" (Isa. 34:4); "The heavens recount the glory of God." This is why the whole Torah is like a wellspring of light, streaming with rays of creation. It is the formula and structure of the world. This is why, due to the gap of retreat and concealment, it contains a sort of echo, once removed, of creation. It manifests itself in the form of a narrative and not the spectacle of creation, which may make it seem that it is but a narrative amongst others. But there is here an imperative of creation itself, commanded by the withdrawal. Since there is a withdrawal in the being, the all will no longer appear, save in language and in words. Creation will be manifested only in the Torah, the very locus of language and voice. Isn't it because God pronounced the words of creation, making a voice arise within him—that is to say, a retreat—that the world was created?

CHAPTER 2

Song of the Stars

LEAPING LIKE A GAZELLE, dawning like daybreak, spinning in interstellar space, present but hidden, what makes up Israel's appearance? What makes up its paradoxical manifestation? At Sinai, during the revelation of divine passage, "all the people saw the voices" (Exod. 20:15). This offers a perspective that assists us in thinking about the profound question of the nature of Israel's presence in being and existence. Isn't seeing voices impossible in an order of things wherein vision is bound up with masses, surfaces, and exteriority, while the voice seems to belong to the realm of the immaterial, of breath, sound waves, and interiority? Sight pertains to the gaze, to eyes, the voice to speech and language. One sees what is given to view, outside; one listens to what one endeavors to hear, in immateriality, inside. This is the nexus of the question, as we have seen in the relationship between interior and exterior as it is manifested in the problematics of the safeguarded portion and Israel's presence. And, as we have seen, the reality of the relationship (between interior and exterior) in Israel's being stands out against the manifestation of appearances.

Israel's interiorization does not contradict its living in exteriority. We could say that Israel's outward existence embodies a different modality of exteriority, entirely drawn inward, entered/assembled (*kanes*) inside, an exteriority dependent on the interior, hidden, without being removed from exteriority. The problematic of light can help us understand this mechanism, provided we understand that light can be words, can be Torah, and that Torah can be the landscape of reality; provided we understand that the world is not cast out or offered in exposure and reduced to radical outwardness. Rather, it is animated by the wave of light and voice. In the depths of exteriority, a voice is nestled, and a light secretly shines forth that transcends the opaqueness of things; and Israel knows how to evoke it, to make it glimmer, to let it be heard. It is in the withdrawal that is *panim*, the face, in the concealment that it undergoes in itself, in the gift that it gives as a *korban*, that the voice rises and cries out. And it is because there is a voice that a face, as a figure of exteriority, abides in the exterior and offers itself to the light, that it appears in the exterior and lets the song of the stars, the Levitical music, be heard. When light is heard in the voice, exteriority is redeemed!

I. ABSENCE IN THE FACE

The face bears the stamp of absence. When we contemplate it insistently, an impression of absence emerges in the very features of its incarnation. It speaks, it occupies the present moment, and yet it seems to be absently "functioning" and nothing more. Isn't there something of this same impression that arises in the most intimate moments of the individual, in the sexual act, when human beings, thinking they are attaining the height of their selves (and admittedly attaining its limit), seem to be merely performing an act dictated by the anonymous law of the species? The bright, glowing flesh of which the face is made reflects absence and shines with vanished radiance. Where is the being? It is this feeling of absence that gives a taste of the harshness of the world and its infinite rigor. Where is the presence that is so close to us?

We can thus assess in each human being, in each face, the state of absence that strikes it. The *alef* is missing in the face as in creation. The "features" of the face suggest chaos, *tohu-bohu* (*tohu*, read *tav hu*, means "it is a feature"), and yet what is hidden (*bohu*, read *bo hu*, "it is within") must be sought— unless, that is, true features are inside. After all, doesn't face, *panim*, mean inside, *penim*? It is in the *penim* (of concealment) that the *panim* appears, in the *tikkun* of absence. Thus, it is said of the sages that they are *sagi nahor*, blind seers. They see a light that the eye does not see.

It is, paradoxically, the gaze that conveys the most self-absence of the being who is gazing. It comes down to something resembling a retreat of the whole being, an unconsciousness. The face does not extend in space or occupy it, as one might think; it is the agency through which the being escapes itself and the other. *Panim* is related to *pana*, meaning remove, evacuate.[534] Thus, in the being of the human, the face is like the stranger in the abode, the place where I can feel a stranger to myself, where I feel that

---

534. This is why the question of anthropomorphism in the biblical text is not a real problem. The forms of the body, far from bespeaking an embodiment, an incarnation, a presence *in carne*, in fact bespeak self-absence. When Philo tells us that Cain cannot flee the face of God, because God is everywhere, he does not understand that God's face is already absence and flight.

I am other than myself. Such is the dwelling of the face, by way of which presence eludes localization and representation. And this self-estrangement at the core of the Holy of Holies of personality and individuality is the security, the safeguarded portion, the concealment in the being that makes the other possible, that enables the voice (which begets the other).

Now the face must be aroused from its spontaneous absence to presence. A *tikkun* of the face is required every morning. Presence is a human endeavor to be wrested from this immediate absence. It aims to bring out what is hidden and veiled, to force the being to inhabit the face that one does not constantly inhabit (but how could one in the world of passage without dying as a result?). The migrations of the biblical characters from Abraham to Ruth constitute training in ways of lifting their faces from absence to presence. This is why the face (*partzuf*) revealed to itself is a breaking forth (*peritza*); it is a breach in the uniformity and in fullness. A face taken out of its absence by another, by the voice, is sudden appearance. This is how Peretz ("What a breach—*peretz*—you have made for yourself!") was born to Tamar from Judah (Gen. 38:29). Thus, Israel is an outburst in the world of nations. Concerning Jacob's offspring, he is told, "you will burst out to the west and to the east, to the north and to the south" (28:14). There is something womblike in the face that opens up to the other's reach and in which the frailty of the flesh is manifested.[535] The lips are perhaps what remains most of the womb, its strongest memory. And indeed it is with lips that we address the other. If our eyes and ears receive what comes from the world, only our mouth expresses the will of the voice, by the articulation of the double curtain of lips that close it. It is at dawn that the face is manifested. This is when Jacob sees his opponent's face (in a place he will call Peniel, meaning God's face, Gen. 32:21) and receives the name of Israel, the reception of the other in one's own identity.

In its movement to and fro between absence and presence, the face is the process of the other. What is most properly mine (no two faces are the same) is hence fundamentally posited in the relationship to the other. My face is mine and the other's (*panim* is twofold). But what it bears must first be freed, taken from fear and closure (*pen* in the singular means stepping back out of fear) to the radiance of dualization (*panim*).

There cannot therefore be such a thing as faceless human beings. No one has a face in Egypt, because everywhere there is rejection of the other,

---

535. Makeup is, for this reason, a travesty of the womb. It aims at concealing the frailty, to put on a frozen, arrested expression devoid of passage. If it remains sheer artifice, it is a perversion of *tikkun*.

death masks, petrifaction, and mock living. A single living gaze would topple everything! And so, in the interiority (*penim*) of the face emerges the exteriority of the other, just as in the Separate of Separates (or Holy of Holies), hidden behind a veil, dwells the divine presence. In the face, conceived in this way, there is sacrifice and offering. It is not by accident that one category of sacrifice bears the sign of the face. One of the highest offerings was *lehem hapanim*, bread of the face, presented "before you [God]," on the "table of the face" inside (*penim*) the Holy of Holies, which was not the case for the blood sacrifices. These loaves were shaped like faces or, according to Rashi, "in the shape of a box split open" (Lev. 24:5–9), in that they had "one face here and one face there." Whence the extraordinary temptation of imperial Rome to introduce its images, its frozen death masks, into the Holy of Holies to take the place of the *panim*.

This question of sacrifice present in the face is forcefully evinced in the story of Cain and Abel, where what is at issue is God's approval of sacrifices. "Yhwh looked upon Abel and his offering favorably, but upon Cain and his offering, he did not" (Gen. 4:4–5). There is a close relationship with the face here. When Cain is judged, his "face falls" (4:5); he runs far from "God's face" (4:16) and bears a mark on his face, the sign of the absent other, because he did not bring the figure of the other to life within him. This is why he settles in the land of *nod*, of wandering.

We can see that passage is of central importance with regard to the face. It is a matter of bringing the light and radiance of the face out of undifferentiated passage but also, and as a result, of enabling the advent of the other to pass over it. It is the essential act of creation by God, about whom Scripture states, "He passed over his face" (Exod. 34:6). "His face" designates God hidden in his face of absence, from which he emerges to reveal himself. But "his face" can also be Moses, for God's passing over his own face would pass over Moses' to reveal himself to him, in a relationship of alterity, "*panim el panim*," face to face (33:11).

Passing over his face, God created man. Thus, every human face bears the memory of God the creator. The splendor of the divine being shows through in the contemplation of the immense diversity of human faces. The idea of the universal rises out of this astonishing experience of a multitude irreducible to additions and sums, a multitude riveted to its particularities, reflecting a shimmering multiplicity. In the passing of human faces, God passes. It is the sign that it is in the shadow of one greater than us that we exist, and that everything in us is a reminder thereof. This is why the beheld object escapes our hold, just as unity, whose concealment is what makes reality, escapes our grasp. Here we rediscover the meaning of the interiorization that puts the one into hiding and nevertheless underlies the plurality of faces.

Now we can better understand the reason for the initial, immediate absence that infuses every face. Its contemplation is a trial, the trial of facing the void, but the journey through it clears the way for the voice, for the words by way of which the face takes shape and comes to life, a face that lights up only insofar as there is concealment in it. Its contemplation is exhausting, but it is equally nourishing, as it was for Moses on the mountain and for the Hebrews at Sinai, who "saw the God of Israel and under his feet... and he did not strike the children of Israel; they beheld (*hazon*) God, they ate and drank" (Exod. 24:9).

II. THE FACE IN THE VOICE

There is a deepening void in the absence and withdrawal that characterize the face, a space that surges up and spreads in the midst of the fullness of organs. "Keep yourself (*shamor*) from his face, and hear his voice... because my Name is in his *kerev*, for if hear you will hear in his voice..." (Exod. 23:21–22). This void is the voice, the *kol* into which the flesh of the face's true being is woven, its interior image, the word (*dibbur*) that expresses it. The voice is the withdrawal in the being, the safeguarded portion in which the world is manifested. Thus, every voice is a reminder of the world's creation, of the void in the being that was the creational voice calling the world into existence, spelling out the creational words that are the very essence and nature of the world. Every voice is an experience similar to that of birthing. It is the womb that opens up to a new being in the physical fullness of the body. In Peniel, which is the retreat of the divine face (the angel with whom Jacob wrestles goes away), Jacob receives his name and becomes Israel. This retreat of the face is the true face of the divine. This is why God is not representable, for representing him would be negating the reality of the world. And this is why words that speak of God and his attributes bear in their essence the trace of this absence, the absence that is the voice. Such words are not a mediation, a representation between two beings of fullness and completion.

The Covering of the Voice

The voice can also be held for the safeguarded portion in the *nefesh*, for the retreat and giving that open up to the other. Without the voice's openness, the other could not stand before me, the other to whom I am linked through the voice, through the void. The voice intrinsically harbors the other. Witness the phenomenon of echoes. In a place of solitude and absence of the other, the voice doubles when it is sent out, as if to signify that the *nefesh*, even isolated, is not alone, that it carries the other, that it carries God. The space of withdrawal, the moment of the void that the voice creates in the *nefesh*, the concealment it creates there, is the true place (*makom*) of the other, what makes for the fact that I am not entirely involved in myself and can open up to someone other than myself. The moment of self-unclasping, when I step out of myself, is the voice. The voice is already in actuality the *tikkun* of the face, the secret of the face, that which is hidden in the face's veiling and withdrawal, like presence and unity in hiding. It harbors the *tikkun* of the *nefesh* and calls for its own *tikkun*, for the completion of the *nefesh*'s *tikkun* in concealment. Indeed, in this withdrawal of the face that yields the voice, there is freedom and hence the possibility for the voice to be perverted. The voice is deployed as much to the music of Cain's children (Gen. 4:21) as to the Davidic psalms. This deployment is that of the arena of action in the world, with its potential for the best and worst in the context of creational concealment. The mouth of human beings is theirs; that is where the *nefesh* resides, and they can sully or sanctify it.

A voice is not manifested in its nudity. As it says, "a woman's voice is *erva* (nudity)."[536] It must be covered in words. "You saw no image, for there were only voices" (Deut. 4:12). However, this absence of images is not nought: "and all the people saw the voices" (Exod. 20:15), and "he beholds the image of YHWH" (Num. 12:8). The sanctification-separation, the *tikkun* of the voice, is *dibbur*, the spoken word, in the rhythm and flow of which the face takes on its true features. The one, who is hidden inside in the voice and is to be announced to the *olam*, must appear in speech.

Thus, in the gigantic passage that is the being in the *olam*, the face as outwardness (*partzuf*)—what makes me me—exists only for and in the world (and, indeed, death will destroy it). But it is borne by its hidden principle and essence, the voice, which must shine forth in the face and is the *tikkun*

536. Berachot 24b.

of the face. *Dibbur*, speech, is what manifests the voice in the face. Thus, the voice speaks through the lips, the part of the face that cuts up the words. The voice issues, and the lips cut. That is when the *panim* take on shape and differentiation and become *partzuf.* Without the passage through the lips, all that is meditation in the human being has no existence. Therefore, it is important in *tikkun* to know how to cut, that is, to know the art of circumcision, of the covenant.

Nothing resembles the voice's manifested and differentiated power to dispel darkness. Similarly, the sound of the *shofar* contains a peerless power of clarification, the power to dispel a guilty conscience and sin, to purify the *nefesh* of its dross. It carries the memory of the voice of creation, of the bountiful light of the world. "God rises in the *terua*,[537] YHWH in the voice of the *shofar*" (Ps. 47:6). We can see that Israel has this gift of the mouth. What does "worm Jacob," signify if not a being whose whole body is a mouth, an extension of the mouth, a tiny, insignificant being whose mouth uproots trees? Thus is Israel small and weak, but its voice, its prayer, can uproot mountains. In voice and mouth, Israel is very close to God. But because it echoes absence, secrecy, and passage in the inhabited places of civilization, its own absence can be regarded by the nations of the world as an unbearable nudity, which exposes their own nudity masked by representation, and which is transferred onto Israel, who is accused of their own failing. In this sense, the nudity is that of the voice that hides like one "hides nakedness" to avoid incest. Israel's voice is capable of concealment, because the voice has to keep silent so speech can arise, at whose core thus resides an absence and a silence, a testimony to the foundational retreat: "For you, silence is praise" (65:2). "And lo, YHWH passed by, and a great and mighty breath parted mountains and split rocks before YHWH, not by the breath of YHWH, and behind the breath a great noise, not by the noise of YHWH, and behind the great noise, a fire, not by the fire of YHWH, and after the fire, the subtle voice of silence" (I Kings 19:10–12).

From this devastating passage in which there is nothing but "not" emerges the only "positive," namely the sharp, high-pitched voice of silence. The voice is like the instance of passage in the *nefesh*. It brings it from one state to the other. It thus carries exile, departure, and anxiety. Adam and Eve "heard the voice going away in the garden" (Gen. 3:8). And Israel's exile is likened to the exile of the voice in the *nefesh* of all Israel. "For Zion, I will not keep

537. A tone of the *shofar*.

silent" (Isa. 62:1), that is to say, I will do everything to bring the voice out of its exile and accomplish its *tikkun*.

Likewise we can see the Torah is and has a voice, "the voice of the Torah," that requires a *tikkun*. The *tikkun* of the Torah takes the form of commentaries that bring words out of the voice, that draw them from the voice like water from a well. The commentary is, in this sense, a *perush*, a separation or tearing away. And so the exile of the voice, the exile in the voice, is not everlasting. The voice bears the embryo of its return. "YHWH's voice causes gazelles to give birth" (Ps. 29:9). Thus, the world of *olam* is full of voices looking to be born and to which words have to be given. There is a procession of voices in the world awaiting *tikkun*. Who will hear this immense, silent roar that rises from the barren expanses of the world, this mute voice looking for a passage and suffering from not being pronounced, like the gazelle that cannot give birth? The prophet is the one who can assist the gazelle in giving birth, who can take the dead out of oblivion through resurrection. The power of the prophet's words is great; he turns the wilderness into luxuriance, and his melodious speech releases the voice from its exile. The Hebraic prophetic discourse may announce the exile, but it draws the return from the exile. And it is Jerusalem, through its Temple, that becomes the vestibule of the path of voices in this world.

The Face as Temple

We have seen in the face something of the House of the Temple. The voice would be the essential moment of approaching, *hakrava*, the moment when the *korban* is offered up. Thus, the Temple has an "image" (Exod. 25:9), a structure or blueprint, communicated to Bezalel, so he can build it. The *korban* is harbored and embedded in its very structure, just as the voice and absence are harbored and embedded in the face through all its openings and transparencies, which manifest absence. But in it is the voice that makes the *korban*, the approaching of the *korban*. The voice is the moment when the whole *nefesh* binds itself like Isaac on Moriah, to offer itself up on the summit of the mouth.[538] Isn't it at this very moment that Abraham hears the voice say to him, "Abraham, Abraham, do not raise your hand against the boy!" (Gen. 22:12), words by which Isaac will be saved from sacrifice and

---

538. Thus, several organs participate in the manifestation of the voice in words (for the *Zohar* there are seven: heart, lungs, windpipe, tongue, teeth, lips, and flesh). A similar thing takes place in the sexual act, which is why "the woman's voice" can be "nakedness."

death and will stand, the son facing the father? It is in this intimate *korban* that one sees God: "and after my flesh falls, from the midst of my flesh, I will envision the divinity" (Job 19:26). The voice is sacrifice, sacrifice of the face, but of the face that opens up, not of the hard, impenetrable face, like the mask of representation that human beings don in the world of passage and exteriority.

By this process of the voice, in addition to that of the sacrifice, the Temple is the preeminent instrument for eliminating the misunderstanding that inheres in the social. The voice of human beings is redeemed in it. After all, the voice is an integral part of the ritual, on all levels of the sacrifice. To offer, to give, to divest oneself is to emit a voice. So the voice, which houses the strength of the other at the heart of each individual's specificity, is the preeminent pathway to divine presence. What comes out of the hidden Holy of Holies if not the voice? The face, the place where the being is most transparent, where the skin hints at something, at a presence behind it, is an invitation, as is the Temple, to draw near to God. In the final analysis, God's face is the veil in the Holy of Holies. It is through the face that I meet the other, who is another face to me.[539] But it is through the voice that I establish a true relationship with the other. What is at work in the relationship to the other is at work in the relationship to God. It is the voice more than the face that manifests God's paradoxical presence. In it the whole act of creation can be gathered. If God is the voice, this is so for us, his creatures. What manifests itself for us from God is his voice. "When you hear this voice come out from the midst of darkness, whilst the mountain was on fire.... Lo, YHWH, our God, has revealed to us his glory and greatness, and we have heard his voice from the midst of fire" (Deut. 5:20–21). In the Temple, what reaches the people from God is the divine voice, which "speaks to itself" from above the cherubim; it is the voice (*kol*) of the bells on the bottom hem of the high priest's clothing, which transmit every one of his movements to the people, who do not see him.

Psalm 29 portrays the strength, the power of stupefaction of the divine voice over the waters, its power to break trees and strip forests, its power to cause gazelles to give birth. The psalmist lists seven (*sheva*) voices in the divine voice to indicate the extent to which the void and absence are filled to satiation (*seviut*). The voice appears in God the Creator as in an intimate

---

539. Obviously, the intercession of a representation—as in idolatry—would be a mockery and a perversion of meeting and presence. In the one, the face carries the voice, bringing the other to be. In the other, it carries the gaze, reducing the other to an object.

process of gift giving and sacrifice that finds infinity approaching the human being. This is what the protocol of the divine voice in the Holy of Holies suggests to us. The voice speaks from above the Ark of the Covenant and, more precisely, from above an element of its covering, the *kapporet*, the propitiatory seat (Exod. 25:22). The term is telling, because it immediately brings to mind the *kappara*, the redemption, the ransoming of a sin through the sacrificial offering. Giving and hiding are present in the very essence of the voice. Speech is born from it in the manner of a *kappara*, a *tikkun* of absence and exile. And even in its paradoxical manifestation, the divine voice testifies to the retreat and the hiatus. Indeed, when the divine voice speaks to human beings, it speaks to them and is heard by them only by speaking to itself (Num. 7:89). This withdrawal of the voice into itself is surprising. Doesn't it run counter to communication? Does God communicate with human beings only by ignoring them? In fact, herein may lie the very principle of communication and passage. There are two cherubim over the *kapporet*, one male, one female, and the voice emanates from between them as if the cherubim were talking to one another. The voice and speech are always between two, in the void of dialogue, which illustrates how the being itself of every voice is caught in a relationship to the other. But we can also read several levels of meaning in the significance of alterity and unity. A voice is never one's own alone; it is always the echo of another voice, a testimony and memory of the voice of creation. The voice carries the echo of the absent creator within it. This is why it is dualized in the wilderness, indicating to the *nefesh* that it can never be alone and that it has within it another voice that speaks. The voice always speaks to itself as if there were a dialogue within, as a sign that God is always with the other, but also as a sign of solitude, insofar as talking to oneself can imply that one is alone. It is in this solitude of love, of God's separating from himself, hiding, and receding in his unity to make room for the world, that creation takes place, that the voice arises in the *nefesh*. It is in making himself one, in separating himself from the rest of the world, that God founds the community of human beings and the divine relationship to them in what is ultimately a paradoxical solitude, filled with love. This is how it is for the solitude of the divine voice that speaks to itself, in a dialogue, and the silence does not absorb everything, for, after all, there is voice and speech: "there was silence, and I heard a voice" (Job 4:16).

Hearing

The internal dualization of the divine voice that enables human beings to hear it shows us the dual character of the voice. A voice does not exist in itself and for itself. It exists as a "voice" only insofar as it is heard, even and especially by those who push it away. One could even go so far as to say that it is the hearing that makes the voice, that without hearing the voice is nothing and, consequently, that without human beings, creation is nothing, nothing but an endless, anonymous passing. What makes God's Name, the purpose for which God needs a name, is man. "He took the book of the covenant and read it in the ears of the people" (Exod. 24:7), and "all the people answered with one voice" (24:3). Finally, let us not forget the term that names Jacob, "following/in the wake of (*ekev*) that which you heard in my voice" (Gen. 22:18). "My voice," God's voice, is preceded by and predicated on hearing. However, the voice reaches hearing through the agency of words: "you heard the voice of words" (Deut. 4:12), but the hearing in this relationship is by no means pure passivity. The ear has to arrive at hearing words, discerning them, cutting them, making a covenant. "If you hear in my voice, you will keep my covenant" (Exod. 19:5).

The ear has to conquer an interiority (King David's "hollowed ear," Ps. 40:7) that enables it to undertake its own *tikkun* and that of the voice. Hearing is the most secret principle of the voice. The voice can spring forth only in the hearing, which means that in the voice there is always already someone listening. This is another expression of the dialogue where one speaks and the other listens. This dimension of *tikkun* that hearing has to accomplish is expressed in Israel's main "profession of faith": "Hear, Israel, YHWH, our God, YHWH is one." It is illustrated by the work of the *nefesh* on itself, a work of testimony. Indeed, in the biblical text the last letter of "*shema* (hear)," the *ayin*, and the last letter of "*ehad* (one)," the *dalet*, are written in capital letters, thereby uniting hearing and unity in *ed*, testimony. In this way, hearing, if it activates *tikkun*, always includes a doing: "We shall do, and we shall hear" (Exod. 24:7). The "we shall hear" is situated on the level of the voice, and the doing on the level of the hearing, because hearing is always preceded by a voice, but a voice exists only to be heard. To the divine exhortation ("hear!"), humans reply by doing, that is, by the journey through and the sanctification/separation of the passage, after which comes the supreme hearing, the entry into the one.[540] Thus, the "we shall do, and we shall hear" is preceded by a voice that cries, "Hear, Israel!" We can see, therefore, that the voice cannot be heard and maintained save by the strength of testimony, a strength drawn from the memory of hearing, for a voice comes, goes, and passes on. Who will recall, if not for that which has remained in the ear? This is why we can see the dwelling of testimony (*mishkan edut*) as the dwelling of the voice, the palace that houses the echo of the divine voice in the world. It is by going through the trial of testimony that the initial hearing is redeemed, that the glimmering of the one that departs, withdrawing in the safeguarded portion, is redeemed and accomplished.

The voice is feeble, because it passes by and depends on the testimony of the ear, but its might is infinite, because it traverses all elements of creation and communicates through them. Are they not in themselves the materialization, the crystallization of the voice (the creational voice)? This is why, despite its evident materiality, the world is held in the breath of the voice whose secret (the specific frequency and wave of its emission) is known to God the Creator. If he reiterated the specific tone of this voice, the Creator could shake the foundations of the world, annihilating or transubstantiating it.[541] Thus, the voice runs through wind, water, rock, and beings. It is the active component of light. It is the void and the retreat in the light that causes it to travel across vast expanses of the universe and gives it its reverberation (which is why we can "see voices"). It is the place of the world/*olam*, but, as we have seen, this place is hidden, so it does not reach us immediately. The world resounds with its echo, and human beings must be able to hear it. Isn't this the role of the prophet (*navi*), who can bring to pass (*havi*) the "dialect (*niv*) of the lips," giving words to the voice that shoots through the world and seeks to speak? Scripture writes that Moses "stood between YHWH and you at that time to convey the words of YHWH" (Deut. 5:5). The prophet does not "act"; he calls, transmits the voice and modulates it. His power is at once mighty and feeble, but if he becomes an actor, he loses the

540. The *Zohar* tells us that seven (*sheva*) organs come together to produce *dibbur*. Satisfaction (*sheviut*) and satiety are convened in the accomplishment in the one of what was in retreat or suspension in the voice.

541. When Moses struck the rock, his mistake was that he did not have enough faith in the power of the voice. "You will speak to the rock before their eyes" (Num. 20:8), he had been told, yet Moses struck it not once but twice. It was important that the rock "give of its waters," bring forth waters from its minerality by itself, become water, so the "miracle" would be complete. Instead, Moses undertook to "take" water out of the rock (20:10), as if it were found underneath, and to do so using his rod. Some commentators consider that this is why he was not allowed to enter Canaan.

prophecy! He is preeminently the being of suspension and of the safeguarded portion. Admittedly, there is a danger in this, because the prophet can clothe the emptiness of the world's voice in lies of his own making, betray it by covering it with representations. We are faced then with "false prophecy," or, more precisely, with the "prophecy of lies."[542] This demonstrates the political stakes of the voice. Control of the voice is as important to people in power as controlling light. Doesn't discipline (*mishmaat*) derive from hearing (*shemia*)?

Israel's Voice

When it was a question of taking responsibility for Israel's destiny and hence influencing those in power, Esther was summoned to speak up, to let her voice be heard ("if you keep silent at such a time," Esther 4:14). Israel's mission is hidden, and the nations do not hear it, no more than they would hear the sand moving in the wind of the dunes. She has to let her voice out, to let her words be heard, so the Name of the one will be heard. It is the essential challenge of Israel to measure up to its voice, that is, to let its voice out in the world of absence and deafness. This is why its being is defined by the voice and even by a doubling of it: "the voice, voice of Jacob" (Gen. 27:22).[543] There is a process involved in this doubling,[544] because the first voice (*kol*) is without the *vav*, whereas the second has one and thereby benefits from greater clarity. When Joshua comes down from the mountain where he has accompanied Moses, what comes to him first from the people, which tells him about its moral state, is the voice. "Joshua heard the voice of the *am* in evil and said to Moses, 'A voice of war in the camp.' He said, 'There is no answer of a voice of heroism and no answer of a voice of weakness; a voice of answer I hear.' And when he approached (*karav*) the camp..." (Exod. 32:17–19).

The voice is Israel's identity, and when Israel is in exile, words retreat into the voice, which remains sheer potential, unfulfilled and awaiting its appearance. There is a whole logic of the political in the process of the voice in the world, and this political logic of the *kol* is unlike the logic of *logos*. It is significant in this respect to observe that democracy is built on the notion of

542. Which is a degree of prophecy nonetheless, since it perceives the original void.

543. See the talmudic notion of *bat kol*, literally, "daughter of the voice," which reaches human beings only indirectly. It is the vehicle of revelation after the disappearance of prophecy, when we see the light as if reflected by a mirror, and we hear the voice as if echoing the wilderness.

544. No doubt the entire path from *am* to *eda* is implicated in these two voices.

voices, in the form of "the electoral voice," the votes by which the *vox populi*, the will and identity of the citizens, is expressed. The model of a politics of the *kol* would stand in opposition to the use of visual criteria (localization, territorialization, differentiation, discrimination, substitution, and so on) , which presides over customary political practice, based on setting up obstacles. Its vocation would be to facilitate the circulation of the voice—the passage of the *nefesh*—through the collectivity. This means essentially preventing images and representations from taking shape that could be seen as crystallizing the voice. In sum, it is as if representations were being brought to the surface and at the same time blocked and held in suspense. We have here the definition of "words" in relation to the voice. This objective is attained by setting up hiatuses, differences in levels, discrepancies at each step in the process of the voice, to prevent it from congealing.

Thus, standing between the kingship-state and the people is the sage-prophet of the voice, the epitome of an anti-institution, whose calling is to shatter representations through the sole exercise of the word, to restore to a blocked voice the power of its release into the world. Representations that aspire to the total adequation of the people and the state cannot take hold because of the prophet. For this reason, the political collectivity of Israel was established from the moment "they saw voices." This is the charter of Israel's existence as a power and political institution. Indeed, Israel is described as a *kahal*, a "community of the voice (*kol*)," and as a "*kahal-goyim*," community of the voice/chorus of nations" (Gen. 32:11)? The *kahal* is also a septenary institution whereby the Jews gather in the shadow of the precariousness of booths on Sukkot to study the voice of the Torah after the Jubilee year of withdrawal, gift giving, and suspension. That is when they are called a *kahal*, a collectivity in which the voice circulates. The *kahal* is the supreme being of the collectivity of Israel. The gathering of men is the circulation of the voice among them. It is because this gathering retrieves the voice within, because it manages to make a voice emerge from within,[545] that it creates a place, and specifically a political place, the *toch*, whose whole substance is the voice. Indeed, the voice alone forges unity: "I call them, and they stand together (*yahdav*)" (Isa. 48:13).

The destiny of the voice is cardinal, because it is essential in ensuring that unity is not falsified, that it not give rise to totality. The voice has manifold

545. And it gathers for this purpose around a specific voice, the voice of the one: "they formed a *kahal* around Moses and Aaron" (Num. 16:3). (Don't forget that the one is an internal relationship of two.)

registers. As we have seen, it is at the core of the condition and existence of beings in nature: "the morning stars sang together" (Job 38:7). The "high-pitched voice of silence" passes through the world in this way. Nature is filled with the voices of animals and elements (water, sky, plants). There are a variety of registers to the voice of human beings, too—their cries, their prayers, their lies, their downfalls.... If Israel is not true to the covenant, "write down this song for you, teach it to the children of Israel, and put it in their mouths, so this song will be a testimony to me among the children of Israel" (Deut. 31:19).

Music

The multiplicity of the voice's registers reflects the multiplicity of human deeds, which finds expression when it comes to conjoining and articulating voice and speech. But one supreme register stands above all others, one in which the very gist of the voice and its consummation in the one is expressed. That register is music and all the singing, poetry, and psalmed prayers that accompany it. The essence of music is embedded in the process of *tikkun* of the voice and the world. It builds an architecture in the emptiness of passage, bringing about relationships in the void as if it were full. The musical movement is the constant deployment of a subtraction of tonalities that are perpetually returning and resurfacing in the fullness of the musical phrase, which is continually being suspended and resumed to produce rhythm. The leitmotif inherent in music illustrates this interplay of manifestation and disappearance that weaves the fabric of the musical text. Music is the preeminent discipline of "augret" and passage. Doesn't it cause the *nefesh* to pass from one state (a state of debasement) to another, from anguish to fullness and exaltation, from one thing to its opposite?[546] Music makes the people pass from absence to presence. The text says, "you will sound the horns, and you shall be remembered before Yhwh your God and delivered from your enemies" (Num. 10:9). Thus, the Levites, through the intermediary of the priests, blow the horn to convoke the gathering of all Israel "for an institution of *olam*, for your generations" (10:8). "Make for yourself two silver horns, you will fashion them from a single piece,[547] to call the *eda* and

546. This was David's power as a musician.

547. Silver is associated with the dimension of *rahamim*. That two horns are wrought from a single piece is an expression of unity in dialogue, the dialogue of the *eda* and the *am* in the *kahal*.

set the camps moving. You will sound them, and the whole *eda* will gather around you in council, at the entrance to the Tent of Meeting" (10:2–3).

There is even an instrument called the *edut* (Ps. 60:1), which refers to the testimony (*edut*) underpinning the *eda*, and another instrument called the "gazelle of the dawn" (22). That music is used to summon and unite the people is very significant; the immaterial and sublime void "crystallizes" the movement of the people. Is music an art of government? Music testifies to the safeguarded portion in the universe. In the worlds of fullness, it echoes the void and accomplishes a *korban*. This is why it brings together human beings with greater ease than any other procedure. Music bears the one in the voice, because it manages the feat of hiding it and at the same time making its melody heard. "All the people answered in one voice" (Exod. 4:3). The *nefesh* shuts its eye upon listening to music. It takes refuge deep within. Music is not, as has been maintained, a science of "equal ratios." It is bound up with the asymmetric ratios of the safeguarded portion, because its fundamental structure is not a division into equal parts but a retreat, a concealment, and especially the formidable release of a withholding that attempts to reach completion but is continuously held back and suspended. The discharge that results is what makes music so appealing to the *nefesh*. In listening to music, it is taken on a journey that pushes it to accomplish its *tikkun*, to make the one emerge in it, that gives it a glimpse, already in this world, of the heady lure of the one, in the universal concert of souls united beyond time. This is why music acts as testimony and is a powerful weapon against oblivion.[548] It works on the soul like a burin on metal, taking it out of the gangue that has opacified and eroded it over time.

Consequently, if music is the supreme science of the safeguarded portion, it is not based on the principle of harmony. Harmony, from the Greek root for jointing, for tightly fitting together the parts of a whole, flattens unevenness and smoothes the edges. This is the state of things at night, when nothing stands out. But the music played on the gazelle of the dawn bursts through the parts of the whole, introducing a gap into the beautiful harmony, a void, a separation, a disjunction that makes the one shine forth and dawn pierce the night.

There is a fundamental difference between the music played on the gazelle of the dawn and that of Cain's children. One of these children, Jubal, "was the father of those who played the lyre and the piper" (Gen. 4:21) and devoted himself to witchcraft and idolatry. His brother invented the instruments of

---

548. The Bible tells us that the prophets used music to help themselves prophesy.

war and death, and his sister Naama invented prostitution. The music played
on the gazelle of the dawn makes the dawn shine forth; the music played by
Cain's children spreads the reign of the sleep-filled night. The former echoes
compassion and mercy; the latter spreads death and war or a peace and quiet
forged through war and negation. Therefore, the Greek root *ar*, from which
harmony derives, also yields Ares, the god of war, who unites human beings
in warfare.[549] Music, like all of creation, is prey to perversion and can be used
for depraved purposes, for murder, lust, and idolatry. The joining in auroral
music is achieved not by totalizing but by particularizing and naming.

Yet it is true that music passes through the trial of violence.[550] Isn't this
the function of sons of the violent Levi (cursed by Jacob), who killed Dinah's
lover? And doesn't it accompany the sacrifice? Herein lies its challenge: to
transcend and transubstantiate the perversion of the passage, to carry it to
its *tikkun*.

There is much to be learned about the nature and use of a musical instrument from the *shofar*. It is the instrument of the gazelle of the dawn, for the
plaintive sound of the ram's horn calls to mind the ascension of Isaac in the
akeda, the giving of the safeguarded portion, accomplished in access to the
one, a reminder of withdrawal and presence. And, in fact, the *shofar* is the
instrument that, alongside the lyre, comes closest to the voice. In tradition,
this instrument has a special function of redemption and atonement. The
power of the "voice of the *shofar*" is such that it has the capacity to shake
up and wake up. It liberates the voice from its crystallization in objects,
thereby undermining representations and disrupting false consciousness.
God is manifested in the disruptions of its blast: "God rises in the *terua*"
(Ps. 47:6); "They saw his face in the *terua*" (Job 33:26).

To know God is to know the blast of his *shofar*. "Happy is the *am* who
knows the *terua* of YHWH. In the light of your face, they will go" (Ps. 89:16).
To hear the *shofar* is, effectively, to hear the sounds of the world's creation.
The sound as such is significant. Its blast is not monotonous but modulated,
comprising three sounds: the *terua*, a short blast; the *tekia*, a long blast;
and *shevarim*, broken, staccato blasts.[551] The fact that God "rises" out of the

549. See note 181, p. 176.

550. The Muslim tradition ascribes the invention of music to Moses' striking the rock.
The term "music" would come from "*ya moussa ski*/O Moses, make drink!" And from this
derive the seven original modes of the musical phrase (paralleling the seven patriarchs).

551. In the Kabbala's symbolism, each tonality is the vehicle of an aspect of being.
Tekia is related to *rahamim*, *shevarim* to *din*, or rigor, and *terua* to the power of the
kingdom. Abraham and Jacob are manifested in the double *tekia* (initial and final), Isaac

shofar's powerful voice designates the modulations of this blast and their symbolic value in the alternation between forbearance and impatience. The variation in the *shofar*'s sound lends itself to hollowing out fullness, to voiding the void within, to breaking the unity of totality. That God appears in this breach heralds the unity in God and reminds those who have forgotten of the break/conclusion of the covenant.

The importance of the voice and of vocal technique, of the music of the gazelle of the dawn, is so deeply embedded in the heart of Israel's being that it has been instituted in collective living and in the very edifice of civilization. The Levitical function institutes music at the core of the social being. In addition to their dispersion throughout Israel and their function of pronouncing the law, the Levites perform ritual songs in the Temple at the moment of the rapprochement of sacrifice.[552]

Let us consider what this strange musical accompaniment to sacrifices may signify. It is not (as Maimonides would say) to cover up the racket occasioned by the sacrifice. The sacrificial music is not there to counter the aesthetic absence of the sacrifice; it has intrinsic meaning. In fact, the gist of the sacrificial process passes through the Levites' exercise of the voice (accompanied by instruments), and it does so in a major, accomplished way. From the sacrifice accomplished on the altar, only the Levites' voice and the perfumed scents reach God. "The voice is good with the perfumes" (daily liturgy), because the voice united in the melody of the song crystallizes and completes the sacrificial process. Perhaps this is because, as we have said, there is an assumption and a transubstantiation in the music of the voice, a completion of the violence of rending and separation in passage. That is why this function falls to Levi, who vented violent gestures in the past. Only he can take it on, because he has the force to "handle" the sacrifice—and perfect it—without being overwhelmed by it. Let us not forget that the voice and music harbor the potential violence of Cain's sons. But just as the Levitical sacrifice is a transubstantiation of war and murder, a redeeming of sin, music can make the *nefesh* pass from one state to another, from sadness to joy.

in *shevarim*, and David, the kingdom, in *terua*. Thus, the whole procession of God the creator is manifested, as is the lineage of Israel, in the ritual of the *shofar* sounding (*tekia, shevarim, terua, tekia*).

552. The Levites have an auditory and declamatory role that the Aaronites from the same tribe of Levi lack. The latter's role in performing the sacrifices, and hence in the deed and not in the voice, goes hand in hand with their role in judging lepers, a function based on sight and intellect.

There is a kinship between the practice of music and that of sacrifice. Both require rigorous training and knowledge. Both require skill in using instruments (the knife and the musical instrument) and a relationship to exteriority. Both necessitate an effort and the taking on of norms (whence the contradictory proximity of music to war). Music and sacrifice modify and restore the state of the being. Music traverses *din*, knowing how to tame its forces and bring them into mercy, which is itself the apotheosis of rigor, rigor's journey through itself.

Levitical music, lodged in the complex of foundational functions of Leviticism in the politics of Israel, appears from this perspective as the supreme art of prophetic politics.[553] Those responsible for forging Israel's unity through their dispersion and their withdrawal from amongst the tribes, and for building a different type of harmony, are the ones who devote themselves to music as the ultimate expression of their art of government. In song and music, *nefashot* are in the one. Levitical music undertakes to implement particularization, to make the one appear in the separation, which is an act of concealment, not revealment, and to find thereby fulfillment and order in a seemingly chaotic instability.

The Levitical art of instituting society and the land in terms of the one, not the all, is expressed in the melody of a different form of music. Here concealment and setting aside in overplus underpin the development of the song of the voice, which is itself the very being of withdrawal. The political condition of the Levites expresses the common subtraction that "nurtures" the musical being. It is as much, if not more, by singing and making music as by their territorial condition that the Levites build the marvelous, changing architecture of passage and the advent of the one. The peaceful music that emanates from Israel's being is like the music of stars, the interstellar music

---

553. Indeed, in lodging the Temple plot in the constitutive act of the people of Israel (the apportioning of the territory among the tribes), music was also being lodged in the Levitical domain. As we have seen, the territory of Jericho was removed from all the apportioned lands and entrusted temporarily to Jethro's sons to compensate the tribe (Benjamin's) that would have to give up a piece of its land for the Temple (and that therefore receives Jericho in compensation). It is interesting that Jericho, the first city reached after entering the country, was not conquered by weapons. Likewise, blunt iron or bronze instruments that could cause blood to flow could not be used in the building of the Temple, because the Temple is the locus of *rahamim*. Therefore, to hollow the Levitical place out of Israel's territory, Jericho was conquered at dawn (Josh. 6:15) by trumpets, which were blown for seven days, like the seven musical tones. And therefore, through music, the Levitical arena, the locus of the voice that is the Temple in the core of the people and the land of Israel, is vicariously "cut out," pending a future exchange, substitution, or displacement.

that accompanies the passage of God the Creator in the morning (Job 38:7), a passage that can be manifested only in song and voices.

That music—which is effort, giving, and painful separation—is accomplished in mercy, and that Levi redeems Cain in this sacrificial offering[554] is illustrated by the Levitical place in the collectivity of Israel, whereby the tithe set aside by the whole society introduces the void into the land, enabling a part of itself to find the leisure to devote itself to music. The economy is transubstantiated in music. This is, no doubt, because music is important for politics. Here, the earth becomes music, and terrestrial nature rises up into the stars. The gazelle of the dawn draws a whole nebula of stars into her musical wake, a nebula formed and constituted in the whirl of sounds of cymbals, trumpets, and singing into which it is swept.

554. According to certain commentators, Moses is a descendant of Cain through his mother, Jochebed, a Kenite, and this heritage comes to the fore when he kills the Egyptian foreman (although other commentators see him as a resurrection of Abel, avenging his murder). Right after the murder, Moses flees to the Midianites, who are Kenites ("the descendants of the Kenit, the father-in-law of Moses," Judg. 1:16). There he works like Abel as a shepherd and marries Zipporah, who releases him, by the circumcision of their son, from the cycle of Cain. In this regard let us also recall the assignment of the Levites to cities, when Cain is regarded as the founder of cities, and the institution of cities of refuge to provide shelter to murderers! Isn't this a form of redemption of a Cainite sign?

CHAPTER 3

The Vision of Israel's Voices

THE BREAK OF DAWN is a moment of great hope but also of uncertainty and despondency, because one compass of time has come to an end, but the light of the era on the horizon is not yet shining. Dawn is the suspension of the being at the gateway to the one. Everything is tinged with the radiance of the one, yet the one has not yet taken shape in these moments of what is called the darkness of dawn (*kadrot hashahar*). At this point in time, all of creation awaits the manifestation of a God who will transcend absence and the void, offering a voice and face for contemplation that untether established attitudes.

I. PROCESSION OF BREATH

God the Creator is then called upon to return from exile, from his retreat beyond the depths of the abyss. Infinity, in whose shadow creation has been projected, experiences a start and a stirring, untimely forerunners of its projection in the concealed one. The retreat contracts to the point of reversal, expressing the one it has sheltered as if behind a veil, the dark veil of the absence it harbors. At that point, the void is on the verge of knowing the fullness of being, a fullness that, instead of filling or annulling it, will infuse it with its light in an intense gleam. The break of dawn is the moment when light is about to come back into the dark void of passage. The imminence is extreme, and it seems so long in coming. Time stretches. Joy is convoked, but anguish grips the heart. It is a time when the end and the beginning are side by side, when a second revealment emerges, which is different from the original. We can see an illustration of this situation in the story of Joseph, when he reappears in the lives of his brothers, who have forgotten him. It is a moment filled with dread and trials for them. That is when God moves away from his own "image" as Creator. The being is shaken up. After all, wasn't it constituted precisely by enveloping itself in the concealment of the one? Didn't the brothers come together in their oblivion to Joseph? And now here is the one appearing out of its concealment, "as the dawn is ready— imminent is the discovery of Yhwh" (Hos. 6:3)—a certainty resembling the assurance that the concealment will bear its fruit, the one. "I will rescue my people from the lands of the east and from the lands of the west" (Zech. 8:7). Yes, Joseph, the forgotten one, will be brought back to his father, because nothing is really forgotten in the void of passage, and the humbleness of the foundational one will be compensated. This hope is what animates the prayer for the coming of the divine kingdom over the *olam* in its totality and in the altruistic weightiness of God. "Our God and the God of our fathers, reign over the entire *olam* in your glory/weight (*kavod*)... and each creature will know you created it" (*mussaf* prayer on Rosh Hashana). The kingdom stands in God when the void of the world receives divine judgment. Having successively disappeared behind the four worlds, governed by the four letters of his Name, God the Creator reinvests the unity of his Name; and this inner return shakes up the order of creation, because his Name for the void ("this is my Name for the *olam*") now blazes with new light, on fire to consume itself, burning with all aspects of the multiplicity without touching the one.

This moment is a trial for witnesses of the light. They have faithfully fol-lowed God in his retreat and departure, but they are waiting for him where he will no longer appear. They wait for him at the gates of the west, for "divine glory is in the west,"[555] when he manifests himself at the gates of the east. They wait for him in anxious retreat, when he answers them from the midst of the palace of clemency. They wait for him in withdrawal, when he manifests himself in overplus and bounty. Isn't this the preeminent Josephic moment, when Joseph reveals himself to his brothers? They think they are in the grips of adversity, having to face Egypt's vizier due to the famine in Canaan, when in fact their brother Joseph will amazingly reveal himself to them as a blessing. Joseph appears where he is no longer expected. The faithful awaited him at dusk, when he arose at dawn. The God whom the witnesses await is subverted by a voice they did not expect. Thus, the remembrance subtending the way to the one is transfixed with surprise, because only those capable of wonderment and even impudence can hear the song of the dawn rising. The God of retreat is transfigured in the one God who has returned.

555. Baba Batra 25a.

There is something like a secret of the divine that takes the whole dawn to be revealed.

In the order of the world, a sort of inversion of places occurs. The returning light restores each to its proper place after the confusion and darkness that prevailed at night. Dawn is like the coming of a new world. In the Temple, a voice surges up from behind the retreat of the veil, a very strange voice, full of a presence all too harshly retained and delivering itself at last. This is why the Temple leads the high priest to the far west, where the light disappears and the Holy of Holies is situated, but opens up onto the east, whence the presence of the one returns on a path strewn with glimmering stars, and where the prophet stands. The high priest, master of remembrance (he wears the "breastplate of judgment," "in remembrance" of the tribes of Israel before God), is surprised by the prophet, master of wonderment. In this way the procession in the Temple is paradoxical. It leads to a place in the direction opposite that of his steps.[556] Isn't this the very meaning of Israel's birth and adventure, of the experience of *olam*? The retreat subverts through bounty. "From within the narrowing, I called YH, and he answered me in the largesse of YH" (Ps. 118:5).

In the straits of passage, there is a place for a voice, a calling out/recitation, a remembrance of the creational word, and this remembrance opens up to the largesse of God. Thus, the dawn of the being, beyond the night, brings a blue sky over Israel. But this is a disturbing moment, when the light leads Israel to strike camp, to break away from the security of well-trodden paths and set out on the road to as yet unprobed lands. The moment is permeated by astonishing clarity, by keen and acute insight that casts new light on accomplished history, but also by anxiety and even poignant erring. The moment when the entire void is summed up is close to a derealization, an awareness that nothing has been accomplished, that the trial of crossing the void, of testimony, and of waiting may have meant nothing.

The intense gratuitousness of the impending clemency is dizzying. This is the time for Israel to understand its road, to arise and continue its march to the one in the beauty of its emblems, the pennants that announce the presence. "Who is she who appears like a dawn, beautiful as the moon, pure as the sun, and awesome as a banner?" (Song 6:10). "Do not be downhearted! Do not be afraid of the noise that will ring out over the land!" (Jer. 51:46),

556. See Trigano, *New Jewish Question*, annex 2.

for "a star will rise from Jacob" (Num. 24:17), a light will dawn out of the darkness of the early morning sky, which will lead you with its unique radiance.

This vision aims at grasping the procession of Israel's voices as a story of breath in the resonance of the void. It is this vision that illuminates the matinal moment of daybreak, this vision that is made possible by the unfolding present time of the being, this vision that Israel needs to pursue its course. "Without vision, the *am* breaks down" (Prov. 29:18).

In the imminence of the dawn and the last darkness of the night, Israel is summoned to marshal its forces, to retrieve the deep-seated lifebreath of its being so as to awaken the powers of renewal and calling that it secretly harbors. In its *nefesh*, there is a point of observation that it must reach to embrace its whole course through the star-studded sky in a single, prophetic vision and to hold the many, scattered stars in a single sheaf. In the passage of the *olam*, Israel followed the memory of the one and systematically confronted the trial of the all in all its manifestations, the trial of concealment and the safeguarded portion, the trial of setting aside in augment within retreat. This path, this arduous journey through the being, not unlike the massive movement of Israel's camp through the desert by way of a series of "stations," has brought it to the steps of dawn.

The trial of nocturnal darkness, of the void of the passage, is the main trial of this progression. Sheltered in the innermost recesses of the secret of concealment, while the world/*olam* unfolds in exteriority and consecrates itself to the outside, the remembrance of Israel in the exterior, in the gaze of the nations, seems to weaken and totter. The trial is in the ascetic experience of concealment, wherein Israel withdraws deep into presence but also finds itself brutally exposed and naked in the exterior world. To be sure, the flame of the Torah sustains it through the adversity of exile, but it must fight on three fronts. It has to create enough interiority to make the light shine from within (though it is invisible to the outside), but also to brace itself against the outside lest its interiority disconnect it from reality and exteriority, and at the same time to continually strive to effect the *tikkun* of its concealment, which is itself the *tikkun* of its degraded exteriority; for the light must reemerge in exteriority and pierce its concealment, and the passage must resume in the élan of the one.

The heroism to which Israel is summoned is not uniquely an internal combat, a matter of wrestling with and overcoming the self. Intrinsically and by the very nature of things, it is the vehicle of a radical rebellion in the being and the world. Its gesture is wholly a retreat from the all, a dissidence, a fissiparity in the all. If there is concealment, it is to break out of the all, shatter its totality, and anchor the floating frigate of the one in the sea of the all.

Israel's Journey

The great moments in the history of Israel are part and parcel of this process and this problematic. It is significant that the collective history of Israel is preceded and heralded by the history of a few individuals, the patriarchs. This indicates that what is at stake in history is the one, the process of singularization called upon to grasp the undifferentiated, anonymous human mass so as to bring each person to his or her name. All these founding fathers leave their native lands, lands of the all, figures of the empire; and they leave it not when they have been defeated, not because they are poor, broken wretches, but precisely when their social fame is at its pinnacle.[557] All undertake a march, a movement in space, a migration. In sum, they experience passage but always focused on the land of the one, because without the guidance of the one, the passage becomes loss and catastrophe. The one is Israel's sole viaticum in the passage. All the most extravagant movements of Israel's stars in the night sky are meaningful only with regard to their pivot in the morning star: the gazelle of dawn, harbinger of the one.

The departure from Egypt was precisely a concealment in relation to Egypt. It was as if Israel had vanished from the international stage. After all, wasn't Israel in the wilderness? And this gathering inward in the one, which climaxes in the moment of hearing the Sinaitic voice (the Torah), engenders its emergence in a redeemed exterior, its sudden appearance in the land of Israel. This exterior in the process of being perfected that the community of Israel forges in the land is like a concealment, a *tikkun* for the world, the safeguarded portion of the *olam*. At this point, Israel is close to the one, in the *toch* of concealment. For Israel, this is the experience of a removal and an absence. It is when Israel moves away from the viaticum of the one in its land that the land rejects it, and it is plunged into exile. Its concealment in the one becomes disappearance.

The nature of the exile from the land of Israel is different from the exodus from Egypt. It is not a concealment and a *tikkun*, but an exposure in

557. Terah, Abraham's father, provides the court with idols, and Moses is an Egyptian prince. Similarly, the great Zionist migration in the modern era originates at the height of the Emancipation.

exteriority, a loss of inwardness and a destruction, for presence in the land of Israel is interiorization and accomplishment. In exile, Israel is naked, delivered to the domination of the world and the all. It must then effect the *tikkun* of this exteriority, retrieve the one inside it, and garner its forces to undertake concealment in exile and exteriority. In sum, it must help the *toch*, that is, the community of Israel and the land of Israel, to arise again and spread within it, thanks to the safeguarded portion, until it has taken hold of its whole being to the point that what was inside the soul of Israel becomes its base in exteriority. Exile, strictly speaking, is, from the standpoint of the one, a setting aside in exteriority, a loss of concealment, a decline in the passage and in the particularization of Israel that was unable to maintain itself in concealment. When the passage of Israel is successful, Israel is in concealment, as the safeguarded portion—that is to say, Israel keeps itself in the interior of the land of Israel.

There are two modalities of passage. When it is successful, it is the concealment, the dwelling in the land of Israel. When it fails, it is the disappearance in exile and the exiles of exiles, the endless wanderings of Israel. The exodus from Egypt is not, strictly speaking, an exile, because the presence in Egypt was a sojourn in nakedness and exteriority. In Egypt, Israel was in exile.

The exodus from Egypt is a successful process of concealment, a return to the land of Israel. In leaving Egypt, Israel rejoins the interiority of the one. Understandably, this is not Egypt's point of view (or the nations'). For Egypt, Israel is going into exile when it leaves Egypt, and when it stays, it is amongst the Egyptians, in their own presence.

The failed modality of passage, namely, exile, is at once a catastrophe (a breach of the *toch*) and a new opportunity for redemption. There is always a foretaste of return, of coming back to live in the land of Israel. Having surrendered to the appeal of the world's positivity and immediacy, Israel loses the interiority, and its exile brings home the deep reality of the *olam* that it had forgotten. Set back to zero in the experience of the *olam* in passage, the exile enables Israel to undertake *tikkun* and retrieve the meaning of concealment, which alone can make it come back to the one in hiding.

Thus, the whole of Israel's history—all the movements of the soul and mind as well as its demography—is part of the fight against the angel that is the process of concealment. The redemption of passage that the exodus from Egypt constituted brings Israel into the concealment of the *toch*, which the patriarchs only sensed in their singularization. In the land of Israel, Israel dwells in the *toch*, and it is obvious that at that point it is near the one, wholly centered on the unity that inhabits the Temple. What enables it to remain hidden in the *toch* are all the traditional mechanisms of the safeguarded portion: the sacrifice and, on a global level, the sabbatical year and the existence of the Levitical class. As long as the concealment is maintained and reactualized by these procedures, Israel remains in the land, but when they lose their hold, Israel is driven out. This is precisely what is at issue when traditional commentators equate the number of years that the Jubilee was neglected in the land of Israel and the number of years in exile, seeing the latter as an atonement for the former.

Because of the failure of the *toch*, first with the destruction of the Temple of David and then with the destruction of the Hasmonean state, Israel was driven into exile. The *tikkun* of the first exile was quick. The presence of the prophet Ezekiel in Babylon no doubt played a role in this, but it was especially the time of Esther, mistress of secrecy, who enacted the *tikkun* of the one and heralded the *toch*, the return to the land of Israel led by Ezra and Nehemia, with the help of Cyrus, the "messiah" son of herself and Ahasuerus. The continuity of Israel in the passage also depended on a remnant, a safeguarded portion. Not only did the ten tribes disappear, but only a part of Israel came back.

Once again, there were weaknesses in the dwelling of the Second Temple, due to the triumph of Hellenism and the cult of exteriority in the land. Israel was again thrown into exile, the longest in the history of the being. The first exile was just a trial, but the failure of the redemption therefrom could only lead to an even greater trial. Everyone had to be driven away, and a total vacuum created in Israel, for it to retrieve the power of the one and of concealment from its innermost being. During this twenty-century exile, Israel went through the worst adversity and the greatest dereliction of passage. As with Moses, Esther, and Ezekiel, it was the strength of interiority that helped it undertake concealment. The Talmud is another moment in the heralding of the one and the inside, at a time when they could come to be. This is what kept Israel from breaking down in the passage of exile. It kept Israel in interiority and interiority in Israel. And Israel set aside the safeguarded portion and went into concealment—despite the adverse conditions of exile—in its study and in the study of the Torah in general. But the Talmud, like all things in the world, was but a moment of light in the rising light of day. It was mainly the kabbalistic interiorization, notably the Lurianic moment, that attained by some of its aspects a clear awareness of this process, taking interiority to the pitch of the conception, deep inside, of the one. And wasn't this produced at the core of exile in the land of Israel, in the *toch*? So, having touched the one, Israel embarks upon a process of return; the land assumes increasing importance and gains ground until it shelters a very sizable portion of the Jewish people with the creation of the State of Israel.

But this process of the land's upsurge in the withdrawal of the exiled people and of the people's absence in the land is dialectical in nature and generates irrepressible phenomena. Between this moment of interiority waiting for the one and the moment of access to the *toch*, all kinds of perversions and errings can occur. Swept along by the upsurge, Israel is shaken and thinks that, while staying in the *toch*, it attains exteriority. In much the same way, the children of Israel recovered Joseph and their salvation but thought they were standing before Pharaoh's vizier.

Modernity was essentially this illusion of appearance (outside), illusion (from the outside) yet also appearance (manifestation inside), envelopment of the *toch* but also Israel's lack of awareness that it abides in the *toch*, in a continuous process of constitution. The Marranic experience was the emblem of such behavior, with the troubled awareness of being at once completely inside and totally outside,[558] prefiguring the Jew in modernity. Thus, the paradox is that, if modernity led us to the *toch*, it also witnessed the disappearance of the Jew and of Jewish history in the history of the Jews, and the out-and-out disappearance of entire segments of the Jewish people through violent destruction, self-elimination, and abandonment of Israel's march in the world.

In this ultimate access to concealment at the heart of exile, in nudity, the condition of Israel is shaken up and overturned in its process of particularization. This explains the paradox of disappearance: an immediate disappearance out of the appearances of the world, and a process of resurgence whose core cannot be perceived but whose external manifestations are legible in this world. Jewish modernity presents higgledy-piggledy a show of rubble and deterioration with scenes of resurgence and construction. It is the site of a profound disturbance and structural confusion. It is the confusion that takes hold of the passage when it is about to be accomplished, when the one is about to detach from it and hasten its fall into nothingness, because then it ceases to be. The prophetic tradition has always described this period as one of "labor pains" in giving birth to the Messiah. We could legitimately see

558. See Trigano, *New Jewish Question*; and *La Demeure oubliée*.

in it the figure of the Messiah, son of Joseph, because it is exactly Joseph's experience that it conveys in the condition of the people, how the project of benediction and advents is spun from adversity and disappearance—and there dangers, suffering, and famine exist.

Joseph is the one who was singled out and separated from his people and who, once gone, devoted himself to the one and learned how to effect *tikkun* in order to turn dereliction into hope. In this way, he was the vehicle of the safeguarded portion for the whole of Israel. But in the meantime, his brothers found themselves plunged into famine and anxiety. And their *tikkun* consisted in going beyond themselves and reaching the one, setting out albeit unwittingly in search of Joseph. So it is with modernity: the one is kept for Israel, at its disposal, but Israel has to set out in search of its goodness and bounty. From the start of modernity, which dates back to the sixteenth century for Israel,[559] presence hovers in imminence, and this extreme nearness makes Israel's self-absence even worse. The closer the one, the more catastrophic the condition of those far from it, as they are gripped by the rending torment in the wake of the one that separates itself in the waters of passage. An act needs to be accomplished; the passage, the concealment of nakedness, stepping outside exile, recognizing the one, awakening, waking the dawn, and shaking off the sleep of the night. "What are you doing sleeping? Get up and call your God!" (Jon. 1:6).

Now, the greater part of Israel pursues its night. In the gradual dawning of the one and the upheaval caused by the apparent reversal in the direction of the world, it is in a state of confusion and stays riveted to exteriority, to the multiple gone mad and senseless, when the one is dawning in the singularity of the *olam*, moving toward its universalization in the completion of the Name.

We could formulate this experience otherwise. In modernity, when the one is breaking loose and Israel is called upon to come out of the nations, the *eda* is infinitely hidden, having disappeared nearly totally, leaving the *am* in the nakedness of the outside, to grapple with the exterior. It is as if the *eda* were hit, so to say, by the nearness of the one, lost in its contemplation, and the contiguity of the one detaches it from exteriority, but also everything in the world of the all ostracizes it, because its unity becomes greater and greater. It is as if the *am* were lost and bewildered. It finds itself reduced to exteriority without the help of the *eda*, and the tie loosens and comes

559. Its origins go back to the eleventh century (see Trigano, *Forgotten Dwelling*).

undone. Inevitably it surrenders to the attractions of the outside, mistaking it for the sole possible reality, the fulfillment of the promise, the impact in the real world of the coming of the one.[560]

For the *am*, modernity is a time of poignant solitude. Delivered to its own devices, threatened by dissolution, lacking in a spirit of unification, of a binding inwardness, the *am* is driven to assume responsibility for itself, as if the outside had to find within itself the forces of its *tikkun*, its recovery. Thus, in the paradoxical and eminently poignant occultation of the *eda*, we witnessed the *am* organize itself on its own foundations and set out on its march to Zion. The experience of political Zionism seemed to take place in a totally adverse context and without the help of the *eda* or having forgotten the *eda*, but finding the strength to go up to the land of Israel. However, if this was possible in terms of exteriority, it was no doubt because the *eda* was already in the one and in concealment, albeit forgotten.

Thrown into solitude, benefiting from the power of the *eda*, of concealment (all the more so in that it shelters the one), the *am* sees an immense arena of action open up before it and profits from its fruits without realizing what it owes them to. The *am* is thereby naturally given to excessive pride and self-sufficiency. Its illusion of solitude leads it to acts of desacralization whose implications it does not measure. The time of the *am* is a time of adversity and of rough, brutal, and abrupt relations. This is where the pain of giving birth to the Messiah is felt more sharply and where the suffering and effort are the greatest. In this arena, the world of nations unites to destroy Israel, and Israel regularly gets back on its feet, benefiting from the distant protection of the *eda*, which has withdrawn to be close to the one. The effect of this protection seems miraculous in the eyes of the nations, for the *am* appears so weak and easily buffeted, when it is but the tip of the iceberg.

The closer Israel gets to the one, the greater the fury of the nations of the all. Auschwitz was a paroxysm thereof. The *eda* had reached its lowest point in the *am*, having curled up deep inside the one while the *am* was lying outside decomposing, and all the while it remained an *am* in the eyes of the nations, even if it was no longer one in its own eyes. This divide is what made its existence so dangerous at every moment. The gap is of being referred to the one in the multiple, even as it gets farther and farther from

560. This was the case for modern Jewish consciousness, which saw modernity as the messianic fulfillment (see Trigano, *La République et les Juifs* and *The Democratic Ideal and the Shoah: The Unthought in Political Modernity* [New York: SUNY, 2009]).

the one, and into this gap destruction rushes. But the tragedy of the *am* was the limit experience of its solitude. It was as if the impact of such dereliction had drawn the *eda* out of the inner recesses of the *am*: then, the *am* was in fact on the threshold of death and extinction. Its *nefesh* could only seek the *eda* in its depths and call it. This is why, in a certain way, the *eda* was already present in the camps. Wasn't this the first time the individual citizens whom the Jews had become in modernity found themselves united as a collectivity? Alas, a tragic collectivity, a mass of suffering.[561] So the six million victims, as if assembled before a demonic anti-Sinai, can be counted in the eternity of Israel and the resurrection of the New Jerusalem. The strongest evidence is that the *am* recovered some of its lost unity afterward and physically pulled itself together. The creation of the State of Israel is supreme testimony to the fact that the *am*, secretly retrieving the *eda* in adversity, has begun its climb to redemption, to the moment when the *eda* will join it, not in tragedy and death but in light and freedom. This time is still to come.

The constitution of the state appears like the emergence of the particularization of Israel in the world of nations. This singularization of the *am*, reduced in appearance to the singularity of nations ("a people like others"), is in fact subtended by the one, which is there in hiding in the *eda*, although no one clearly perceives it. Through the state, the *am* becomes the vehicle of the particularization of Israel, breaking the totality in the nations and establishing a hiatus in the world of nations.[562] It traces the wake in the water, so the waters of the one can pour forth. In this respect, the state that the *am* gives itself while occulting the *eda* bespeaks Jacob's experience in the fight with the angel, the Josephic effort to escape the passage, the experience of *tikkun*, by confronting the elements and dreams of power. Its enterprise is taking place in the light of the one, but it is itself withdrawn from this light. The state of the *am* is the effort of combat at the end of which emerges the promise of the dawn, the radiant name of Israel, the rise of the star of Jacob. Enormous effort, tremendous frailty. But it is possible only in and for the armed combat of Jacob.[563] It is the field of combat of the singularization

561. See "Les Juifs comme peuple à l'épreuve de la Shoa," in S. Trigano, ed., *Penser Auschwitz* (*Pardès* 9:10, Paris: Cerf, 1989).

562. One of the strongest manifestations of this break can be seen in the rupture of the mythic unity of the Arab world that the State of Israel brings into its geographic midst.

563. According to some commentators, against Esau's angel. It is true that, in order to be born, the state had to confront the West's modern universality. We have seen that it was through a set of circumstances, a "historical ruse," that it succeeded. But now it is

versus the all. The one is not yet manifested in it, which is why it is, at once, immense strength and stirring deception, why it yields a sensation of lack and absence. The one does not yet dwell in Jerusalem.

II. RETURN OF TESTIMONY

In the hollow of the imminence of the one, presence is called upon to manifest itself. In this there is imminence, and the sense of despair and senselessness must be driven out of Israel's soul. The danger of resorting to representation, of short-circuiting the presence, also exists. This is a time of false messianisms, which bear witness, in their own way, to the advent of a new era. This is the time of the dawn watchers.

It is important at this point to undertake the *tikkun* of this moment of light, to bring the hidden seed that gave birth to it to its term, freeing it from the eschatological sentiment that takes hold of it. The end is there, to be sure, and it must be materialized, but the moment especially marks the beginning of a new time on earth. All meaning has always been in relation to this time.

This is what is at stake today: the *am*, which has made the heroic effort of bringing itself up to the steps of the one, is falling apart and ruining itself, so close to the one and yet unable to reach it.

It is time for the *eda*, so deeply hidden near the one, to return and make the presence of testimony shine forth in the confusion of the *am* outside. The *am* has gathered at the entrance to the Temple, around the one, around the Holy of Holies, where it cannot enter. It is waiting to hear the words to recover its lost direction and restore meaning to the gathering.

The main spiritual and historic drama of our generation is this collective gathering in search of presence standing on the brink of the void and nothingness. The *am* is a gaping vacuity desperately waiting for the *eda*, which is late in coming. The fight with the angel has to cease, but the coming of the dawn is delayed. At the foot of Moriah, we stumble over the rock and lose all perspective, unable to climb to the summit. The stars have gathered, but the beam of light that would tie them together to make a sky hasn't come

with Ishmael that the combat is taking place, because Ishmael envies and covets Israel's particularization.

forth. We are in a time of accomplishment and despair. The people lags behind itself. The land is ahead of the people.

The *eda* must rise out of oblivion and decline at dawn, to bathe the *am* in its light, remove it from its self-abandonment, from its negation of its own historicity, from the exteriority of its sociality. This is the task of our times; to ring out the burning topicality of Israel's eternal testimony that, infusing darkness with light, will make Israel shine forth in the being and send the fragrances of the one to the ends of the earth.

In Israel's inner recesses, in the depths of the *am* exhausted by so many trials, there is immense historical strength and a creative force ceaselessly outpouring in the being, but all the wells have been covered up and obstructed, and this generation must locate them and open them up. Under the hardened crust of the planet, in contact with the coldness and the outside, an infinitely generous magma bubbles, ready to gush forth when it has been totally forgotten and sweep away the vestiges of absence. Under the gray garb of the *olam*, Israel wears a robe of light. In the darkness shines a tiny light more radiant than the sun. In the silence of the desert, one hears in the windy distance the murmur of presence approaching in the subterranean roar of its manifold procession. Israel is new this morning, and the vein of its creation has not run dry.

This hidden power of the *eda* is the heart and principle of Israel's historic continuity; in it resides all the historicity lost in the *am*. It is as if Israel today does not inhabit its name, as if it has stepped outside itself. The return of its presence, to itself and the world, depends on its boldness in clearing the path of the *eda*, in dwelling once again in the sphere of testimony, in reopening the dwelling of the *toch*. The voice must be heard in the light for the song of the dawn to begin.

The *eda*'s return transubstantiates the reality of the *am*, modifies its being from the inside. It is a new collective undertaking unfolding in the order of history and the mind. The coming generations of Israel will not be able to avoid this task, because the very physical survival of Israel depends on it, not to speak of its interiority, the breath of its being. It is a matter of releasing the fragrances of testimony in Israel's being. Just as at the threshold of every new era, the testimony of the covenant that makes the community of Israel has to be renewed, so on the verge of the land of Canaan, the tribes renewed the covenant under the guidance of Joshua. Before leaving the desert and entering the land, this covenant had to be renewed. This renewal is not merely a solemn declaration, a ceremony, and a monument ("On that day,

Joshua sealed a covenant with the people and imposed a law and rules upon them in Shechem. Then he recorded these things in the book of the Torah of God; and he took a great stone and set it up there....'This stone shall serve as an *eda*,'" Josh. 24:25–27). It is the new foundation of a political community, a new instituted power, a new interpretation of the book of the covenant, and a new outlook.

Today the era of testimony inaugurated by the Talmud is fading, an era of the greatest exile in history and that represented the pact of all Israel, the renewal of the covenant in an unparalleled situation. During the talmudic period, this contract underwent crises, breaks, and ineluctable erosion, but a new testimony never replaced it. To be sure, the kabbalistic moment was a great one, but it remained at the stage of an announcement and a call, at the midnight of exile, unable to become the vehicle of a new convention of the community of Israel, of *kahal Yisrael*. Today, this *kahal* has lost its voice. Its resurgence and reviviscence depend on the manifestation of this voice. The time has come when such a rebirth of the *eda* in the *am* has become an imperative. "I called, you did not answer" (Isa. 65:12); "Before they call, I will answer" (65:24); "I said, 'Here I am! Here I am!' to a people who no longer called my Name" (65:1); "As a pregnant woman about to give birth writhes and screams in pain, so we were because of you, YHWH" (26:17–18).

The unforeseen gathering of so many stars in the constellation of the land of Israel makes this rebirth possible and credible, and this situation is without antecedents. This miraculous gathering of Israel brings out the potential of a new historical prospect, the constitution of a new social bond, the renewal of the testimony that harbors the project of a new polity, the New Jerusalem, the project of the "testate" that we have endeavored to outline in this book.[564] The *eda* can arise at any moment, because it is its nature to be sudden and surprising. The *eda* is already in presence, and when it manifests itself in the past that is the world, it is as if it shines with the future and the still to come. The resurgence of the *eda* can forge a new social bond among the people. The *eda* is greater than the nation (*uma*) that the *am* in political Zionism tried to use to give the *eda* a symbolic, external representation. The union of the evening gathering that is the *am* and the dawn gathering that is the *eda* is not forged through ideology and representation, both unavoidable in the nation (*uma*). In the powerful force of the *eda*, she who has disappeared resurfaces, the Name inhabits remembrance, and presence beams its

---

564. And that we hope to examine more fully at a future date.

rays among the people. The community is bathed in the light of *tikkun*. The resurgence of the *eda* in the return to Zion may very well be the greatest historic experience of modern Judaism, the impetus of a reviviscence. It may transfigure the nature of the social bond, revive Israel's long-lost historic breath, and launch a new era of creativity for the Jewish people, at last at peace with itself.

The new creation brewing for the being of Israel must illustrate itself above all by a transformation of hearts, a reawakening of soul and conscious-ness, a whole new era of intellectual creativity, and the dawn of a new way of thinking. Indeed, if the era of nakedness and destruction is over, the modality of testimony that went with it and was adapted to it, and all the thoughts that ensued (along with all forms of society and authority), lose something of their present-day relevance. It is not that they lose all validity in the order of truth, because everything that pertains to this modality of testimony is forever true. But like the silvery light of the moon, which at night joins the emerging light of dawn and dissolves into it in the end, so it is with the various historic modalities of testimony.

The mechanisms that applied to the *eda* in the most total exile, when the *am* nearly disappeared in adversity, while the *eda* drew more and more inward to find the one that would rescue both it and the *am* from nothing-ness—these mechanisms are no longer valid when the *am* is being reconstituted in the exterior, which is the cataclysmic sign of the *eda*'s greater proximity. The contradiction spontaneously carried by the *am* on the outside only bears this out. As far as the historical moment of the *eda* is concerned, the testi-mony and social bond instituted by the Talmud[565] are less and less adapted to what the new situation requires of Israel. We cannot now live according to the principles of light on the basis of an economy devised to deal with the absence of light. To live at dawn as if it were the middle of the night would be a spiritual and historical catastrophe ("a time for each thing under the sun"). Didn't the Talmud replace the Bible for twenty centuries, sometimes to the point of thrusting it into near oblivion? To a certain extent, the Talmud could be said to have taken form when the Bible was forgotten, when other texts (the Gospels and the Koran) were being established in its place. And only the Talmud kept the memory of the disappeared Torah alive.[566] But when

565. See "Le Temps retrouvé," p. 244.

566. Unlike the Gospels, which add to the text of the Torah, or the Koran, which replaces it, the Talmud wraps around it.

the day is about to return, the Sinaitic word is in potential emergence. Its gradual dawning erases all the texts deposited over it. From this point on, the commentary is conjoined with the text it interprets. Biblical times are returning in the spirit of Israel.

The twenty-first century will be the age of the biblical word. This does not mean the Talmud will be less true, just as in the times of the Talmud the Torah was not less true. To the contrary, the new hour of light only confirms it supremely, but its light will reach its apotheosis when it unites with that which is greater than itself. Everything in the revolution of light is true. Every hour of the day is true. Aren't dusk, midnight, dawn, and midday made of the same infinite light? But time traverses light, and the light passes through itself, for we are in a created world. The new covenant (Jer. 31:31) is not an annulment of the first covenant but rather its reversion, renewal, and transubstantiation. The covenant that illumined the passage turns back onto itself, just as the light of dusk pours back into dawn. The parallel between the covenant and Israel is cosmic ("YHWH established the sun... the moon... the stars.... 'If these laws should ever cease... then the offspring of Israel would cease to form a nation before me,'" 31:35–36), and this parallel is drawn following the announcement of a new covenant. This shows how the covenant, which is eternal, a covenant of *olam* ("And I made a covenant of *olam* with them"; "a covenant of *olam* will never be forgotten," Jer. 32:40), is to be understood and lived according to the modalities of the *yom*, of the day's unity with its diverse moments: dusk, midnight, dawn, noon.

It is by drawing from the dawn that we can clear the path toward a new burst of Israel's creativity in thought, law, society, and politics. All the strategies of the night fade with the dawning of the day and the imminence of the one. Maybe one has to be in love with the one to understand that faithfulness follows the different hours of the light, the different ages of life. To try to keep someone in his adolescence is to doom him to misery. And Israel has not yet been born. Its constitutive process has not been completed, just as the day continues. Israel is still alive today because it understood this. There are collective beings whose authenticity and legitimacy are bound up with a period in history. Israel, because its covenant was made in terms of the day, traverses all periods. The people of Israel will draw its future greatness from its capacity to invent the society and world of the dawn. The floodgates of creation, the boldness of invention and of pursuing what has already been done, must be opened in Israel's soul. This is the boldness of sap transubstantiating earth into sky.

Israel's reinvestment in its historical role is predicated on this prophetic boldness, which, alone, can help us face the present moment and find the shepherds to lead a lost people up craggy slopes. The Talmud opened with the collapse of history, the breakup of the state and society, dispersion and dependency, with the night. And in that hour it made the moon shine, so Israel could pursue its path. Now the state has been reestablished, and the exile is over. The talmudic system plainly does not have the spiritual strength and intellectual resources to face the new hour of creation. Indeed, until now, any renewal of Israel has come from outside the Talmud, from farther away, because it necessarily aimed at leaving the exile, to which the Talmud is structurally linked.

Any messianism that has stimulated history has come from elsewhere, notably from the kabbalistic ethos, the only one (aside from modernity) to have attempted to add to the talmudic system. The Jewish condition today shows us that this phenomenon has not only generated immediate catastrophes (the example of Sabbatianism is the most memorable case in point). It is clear today that political Zionism, which is divorced from the Torah,[567] provided the Jewish people after the Holocaust with the sole symbolic and existential framework for its survival.

In sum, the Talmud forged the *eda* in times of adversity, but it neglected the *am*. The *eda* retreated deep inside and grew weaker, for it is meaningful only in relation to the *am*. The Talmud kept Leviticism alive, but so radically that it was at the expense of the rest, at the expense of the *am*. And the rest is what is essential, what gives the *eda* its validity.

This is why, in the era of the dawn, there is something of a revival of biblical time, the time of the manifestation of the Sinaitic word in its translucent splendor. This word returns with the end of the exile and the resurgence of the land and the prophetic voice. But the return of biblical times is not a return to the past. Biblical times return like a twinkling of light that helps us detect the course of an imperious creation and march. The present-day relevance of the biblical and of the land of the biblical invites this generation to "augment" the text, to set it in "augment" and not in retreat, to make it grow in the concealment of the hidden portion, to interpret it, to accomplish its *tikkun*. This unparalleled way of thinking carries a different destiny for humankind. It has to succeed where Jewish philosophy has failed,[568] unable

---

567. See the thesis in Trigano, *New Jewish Question*.
568. See Trigano, *Forgotten Dwelling*.

as it is to conceive of the particular in the one; where Kabbala failed, unable as it was to give body and existence to its dream of the one; and where the Talmud left off without harboring in its being the power of the dawn. If the prophetic returns, it is not to reiterate the prophetic discourse that gazed on the spreading night and foresaw the distant dawn. This time it is the other way around. The standpoint is from the dawn, not the dusk.

The lighting of a new flame in the thinking of Israel, like the building of the New Jerusalem in the collective being, can be predicated only on *knesset Yisrael*. Individuals and groups can embody it, herald it, and mark the way, but they can never found it by themselves, because it is all Israel that gathers before the tablets of testimony and concludes a new covenant for the time to come. If a new voice arises to proclaim and call for a new *kahal*, only the procedure of the covenant can give it life and validity, in the manner of the reaffirmation of the covenant by Joshua on Mount Ebal and Mount Gerizim (Josh. 8:30–35). For the pact of the one to have meaning, the multiple must be summoned before the one, for this is the constitutive act of a society, of a place for the voice to echo. This convention has taken on different names in the past: *adat bnei Yisrael*, the Sanhedrin, and so forth. It can and must enter a new age today with a new name and get down to the task of communicating the Torah to an Israel that stands in the light of dawn and is opening the gates of the City of David. Recovering the legal and constitutional creativity of Israel is essential to the historic continuity and life of the Jewish people.

It is no longer by appraising itself in comparison to the past or mainstream thinking that Israel will forge its presence in the world. It is by founding all upon its auroral strength, relying wholly on the one, and opening up for humanity the way of the universal via the one. Humanity is in fact called upon to undertake a similar reversion. It has journeyed across all the fields of being to the Far West,[569] following the fading light, but it has reached the limit, because the light has disappeared to reappear in a place where it was not expected,[570] where Israel has always stood. Israel's rise at dawn restores the crucial thrust of its vocation. Its footsteps echo once again in the world, heralding the time of judgment and solace, because the return of the dwelling of the one changes the face of the earth. In its presence, malice and falsehood

569. This is the whole process of the history of civilization, traveling across the being from East to West. Modernity brought us to the boundaries of the West. After all, didn't Christopher Columbus think he had reached the Eastern Indies when he came to the Americas? See Trigano, *Story of Disappeared Presence*.

570. According to the process of "augret," by which a face always harbors another face.

cannot abide for long. In its presence, empires are like wisps of straw. In its presence, truth is intimated to every being. Here is Israel, back to retrieve its testimony in the world, to bring fulfillment to Ishmael, to give Esau his place, to open up paths to the sons of the Orient who have never heard its voice, to bear witness in humanity to the eternal youth and quicksilver quality of the Sinaitic voice. The resurgence of the bond and testimony of Israel calls for the conclusion of a covenant between peoples, not in the shadow of the stone of Babel but under the foliage of the booths of Sukkot (Zech. 14:16). And just as the Sanhedrin embodies the assembly of all Israel, the assembly of all Israel calls for a Sanhedrin of the peoples, in the shadow of the one, hidden in Jerusalem. The time has come "to gather all the nations and languages, and they will come and see my glory" (Isa. 66:18)."[571]

571. *Zohar* III, Pinhas 249a–b.

INDEX